Milton W. Hamilton

June, 23, 1976

SIR WILLIAM JOHNSON
Colonial American, 1715–1763

1. *William Johnson.* Portrait painted by John Wollaston Jr., c. 1751.
Courtesy of the Albany Institute of History and Art.

MILTON W. HAMILTON

SIR WILLIAM JOHNSON

Colonial American, 1715–1763

National University Publications
KENNIKAT PRESS   //   1976
Port Washington, N. Y.   //   London

Kennikat Press

National University Publications

Series in American Studies

General Editor

James P. Shenton

Professor of History, Columbia University

Manufactured in the United States of America

Published by
Kennikat Press Corp.
Port Washington, N.Y./London

Library of Congress Cataloging in Publication Data
Hamilton, Milton Wheaton, 1901-
   Sir William Johnson, Colonial American, 1715-1763.
   (National University publications: Series in American studies)
   Includes bibliographical references and index.
   1. Johnson, William, Bart., Sir, 1715-1774.
   2. United States—History—French and Indian War, 1755-1763.
   3. Indians of North America—Government relations—To 1789.
   I. Title.
E195.J664   973.2'6'0924 [B]   76-10657
ISBN 0-8046-9134-7

TO THE MEMORY OF
MARGARET

ACKNOWLEDGMENTS

Publication Sponsored by
**The Albany Institute
of History and Art**

The author is indebted to many persons: scholars, fellow researchers, colleagues, and many librarians for indispensable aid. It is quite impossible to mention all who have so helped, but to all I am grateful. A few deserve special mention: the New York State Library, repository of the Johnson Manuscripts, research librarians Mason Tolman and Mrs. Mildred Ledden; the Historical Society of Pennsylvania, Dr. Nicholas B. Wainwright, biographer of George Croghan, director; the late Paul A. W. Wallace, and his successor in the Pennsylvania Historical Commission, William A. Hunter, experts on Indian names; the late Col. Edward P. Hamilton, Fort Ticonderoga, expert on military history; Dr. Isabel T. Kelsay, authority on Joseph Brant; and Col. Charles B. Briggs, of Johnson Hall.

Other collections most used were: the Public Archives of Canada, repository of the Indian Records and Claus Papers; the William L. Clements Library, Howard H. Peckham, director; the New-York Historical Society; the New York Public Library; the American Antiquarian Society, Marcus A. McCorison, director; the Massachusetts Historical Society, Stephen T. Riley, director; the Buffalo Historical Society; the Schenectady County Historical Society; and the Albany Institute of History and Art, Norman S. Rice, director.

While the author alone is responsible for content and interpretation, and any errors, I wish to thank the publisher, Cornell Jaray, and his editor, Donald K. Moore, for their collaboration. For encouragement and support, and for help in proof reading, I am indebted to my wife, Anita G. Hamilton.

Publication of this biography of Sir William Johnson has been made possible by the generous cooperation of James W. Johnson of Spokane, Washington. Mr. Johnson is a direct descendant of Sir William, his son Sir John, and the latter's son, Col. John Johnson of Point Olivier, Canada.

CONTENTS

ILLUSTRATIONS

PREFACE

There has been no lack of commentary upon the noteworthy career and character of Sir William Johnson. He has had no fewer than six formal biographies, and he has been delineated in folklore and fiction. For some time, too, his letters and his official papers have been in print. It would seem that he has been well presented to the public and that there is no great need for a new biography. On the contrary, a fresh, critical, and well-documented biography is sorely needed, and the true historic importance of Sir William has yet to be fully appreciated.

Perhaps the reputation of no important colonial figure has suffered so much unjust representation over the passage of time as that of Sir William. At the time of his death his fame and honorable standing among his contemporaries were high. He died in 1774, however, on the eve of the American Revolution, after which all historic personalities were judged by Americans on their relation to that struggle. His son and nephew, the heirs of his property and official position, were arch Tories, and historians of the early nineteenth century painted them in blackest hues. The family of Sir William was disgraced, and if he was made an exception to this judgment, it was a grudging concession. Would not he have been a Tory, too, had he lived?

The hostile feelings of the Mohawk Valley residents were generated by patriotic writers of the school of George Bancroft and Benson J. Lossing, who played up the role of the patriots and pictured the Johnsons, Butlers, and other Tories as beasts. In this climate the diligent antiquarian and folklorist Jeptha R. Simms recorded in print the thrice-told tales of old residents and gossips. Succeeding generations frequently accepted these as sober history. Next came writers of fiction from James K. Paulding (*The Dutchman's Fireside*) to Harold Frederic (*In the Valley*) and Robert W. Chambers (*Cardigan, et cetera*). By 1900, much that was nothing but legend and folklore had been woven into historical writing, so that the novelists believed that they had a solid historical foundation for their tales. Their readers found them convincing, and a whole generation took its concept of the Johnsons from this fare.

Objective historical study of Sir William Johnson began with the elder William L. Stone (1792-1844). A journalist by profession, but a historian by avocation, he made the border wars of America, and especially the Indians, his field (*Life of Joseph Brant, Thayendanega*, 1838). He embarked on a study of Sir William and assembled a collection of Johnson manuscripts from the family in England. By 1801 there had been deposited in the office of the Secretary of State of New York seven bundles of Johnson papers; and in 1850 an additional lot, which had been acquired by John Tayler from the sale of confiscated property, was presented by John Tayler Cooper. The last group of papers was acquired by the state from Henry Stevens of London in 1866.[1] Not all of this, however, was available to the biographer.

At the time of his death the elder Stone had written seven chapters on his *Life*. The work was taken up by his son, William L. Stone (1835-1908), who in 1865 published *The Life and Times of Sir William Johnson, Bart.* (J. Munsell, Albany, 1865) in two volumes. Conceived in the nineteenth-century pattern of historical biography, this was an admirable work. The younger Stone had little idea of the role of the biographer when he took up the task from his father, but he developed into a fair and discerning writer. Printing much from the manuscripts in full, Stone eschewed the questionable folklore which was current. (Some of it already had been printed in Simms's *History of Schoharie County and Border Wars of New York*, Albany, 1845; and in his *Trappers of New York*, (Albany, 1850). He took a sympathetic view of the Johnsons and noted that it was his purpose to correct the exaggerated view of the character of Sir William given by earlier writers (Charles Johnston in *Chrysal, or the Adventures of a Guinea*, 4 vols. 1760-65 volume 3, chapters 1, 2, and 3; James K. Paulding in the *Dutchman's Fireside*, 1831; and G. P.R. James, *The Gipsy*, 1847). He displayed a restraint in judgment which was lacking in the volumes to follow.

Perhaps because the Stone volumes suited so well the needs of their time, no new biographies appeared until the end of the century. In the meantime, the manuscripts in the State Library had been calendared, and were available for study. But the new biographies were disappointing. *Sir William Johnson and the Six Nations*, by William Elliot Griffis (Dodd, Mead and Company, New York, 1891) in a series devoted to "Makers of America," added little and leaned heavily on Stone. The writer, a Reformed Church minister and missionary, noted Sir William's tolerance in matters of religion. He deprecated the gossip of Simms but repeated a number of his tales, thus giving greater currency to dubious legends. He relied on Parkman for the military events and thus reflected the New England viewpoint. Because it slighted much that was significant, the volume lacked balance.

Of the next volume, *Sir William Johnson*, by Augustus C. Buell (D. Appleton and Company, New York, 1903) a good deal has to be said, and an appendix is devoted to it. Buell was a facile writer, but unscrupulous, and his work is filled with forgeries and lies that have become so widely accepted that it must be the task of any scholarly biographer to detect and expose them. It is a principal reason for the present work. Although the writer has already pointed out a number of these falsehoods,[2] they are so imbedded in much that has been written about Johnson that they should be pilloried for all time.

Another biography awaited the appearance in print of the early volumes of *The Papers of Sir William Johnson*. Editing of the manuscripts in the New York State Library was begun by the first State Historian, Hugh Hastings, and at the time of his retirement in 1907, some three volumes were in type. The work was stopped by his successor, Dr. Victor Hugo Paltsits, who found fault with the editing and suspended publication. Then in 1911 came the disastrous Capitol fire, which destroyed or seriously damaged a large part of the manuscripts. The salvaging of the manuscripts by archivist A. J. F. Van Laer, and careful editing by the compiler of the *Calendar of Sir William Johnson Manuscripts* (1909), Dr. Richard E. Day. made a resumption of the work possible. The first tree volumes of the set known as the *Sir William Johnson Papers* were published in 1921-22. By 1930 three more volumes were in print, and in that year two biographies appeared.

Johnson of the Mohawks, A Biography of Sir William Johnson, Irish Immigrant, Mohawk War Chief, American Soldier, Empire Builder by Arthur Pound in collaboration with Richard E. Day (Macmillan Company, New York 1930), has long been regarded as the standard life. Dr. Day, the meticulous scholar, bibliographer, and editor of the published papers, was fully grounded in documentary research. His knowledge of the sources was exploited by Mr. Pound, a felicitous writer with literary experience. Correcting many errors in previous works and bringing to bear a critical study of the documents, this was a distinct advance over all previous efforts. It is not surprising, however, that some thirty years later one can amend and correct and even expand this coverage. Seven more volumes of the published papers are now available, and much research has added to our knowledge. In the biographical mode of his time, Pound spiced up his narrative and sometimes resorted to flights of fancy. Yet this was in many ways sound, and still is a useful book.

In the same year appeared *Lords of the Valley, Sir William Johnson and his Mohawk Brothers* by Flora Warren Seymour (Longmans, Green & Co., New York, 1930). Undocumented, but with a critical bibliographical note, it had the same limitations without the advantages of the Pound volume, which it unwittingly challenged and by which it was eclipsed. It is not so well known as Buell's; it deserved a better fate, for at least it was an honest effort.

Nearly thirty years later, with the advantage of six more published volumes of the *Johnson Papers* and considerable published research, came *Mohawk Baronet, Sir William Johnson of New York*, by James Thomas Flexner (Harper & Brothers, New York, 1959). Now seemed the time for a definitive biography, since most of the sources were in print. Mr. Flexner, like Pound an able writer with books to his credit in several fields, did not choose to do a "life and times" or to confine himself too strictly to the sources. He conceived a romantic, oversexed Johnson, more in keeping with the tales of folklore than with the sober record of the documents. He sought to write a popular book, with more regard for the market than for historical accuracy. Numerous errors and dubious interpretations in this volume are painful to the historian.[3]

The present work shows the background and character of Sir William in a different light. Instead of finding that poverty and distress were motivations for his coming to the New World (as postulated by several biographers, including the last), one who studies his Irish origins finds him to have been of the gentry, in comfortable surroundings, with ambition and good prospects behind his venture. The term *immigrant*, used by Pound and others, is inappropriate for one who collected tenants in Ireland for his uncle's lands and led them to America. The folklore about his marriage and liaisons is now replaced by new material about his wife and family. His relations with the Indians, so vital to his career, can only be explained by the narrative of his gradual development from small storekeeper to trader, supplier of the frontier garrison, confidant of chiefs, and acceptance as a sachem. Speculation about his being a "blood brother," fathering innumerable half-breeds, and his life as a "squaw man," is supplanted by the record of his Indian diplomacy, which is one of honesty, trust, and respect. Anyone who has immersed himself in the Johnson documents can see the inconsistency of the popular picture.

Since Sir William's career was to a great extent built upon his success in the colonial wars, his campaigns and battles have been given fuller treatment than in any previous biography. His victory at Lake George, which appeared to rest upon luck and good fortune (as do so many of the issues of war), showed in the overall campaign his qualities of intelligence, good judgment and leadership, which were to emerge time and again. The victory at Niagara was due not only to his initial advocacy and to his control of the Indians, but to his ability to take advantage of circumstances.

Through all his campaigns and overlapping all his ventures was the formulation of a farsighted and humanitarian policy in Indian relations. This conformed to his interests and to those of his neighbors on the frontier, who longed for an era of peace and safety, but it rested quite as surely upon the British colonial and imperial interest. He struggled in the making of the peace of 1760–63 against the economy-minded ministry at home and the shortsighted military leaders in America. He had a clearer view than most had of the dangers from the Indians on the frontier, and it was unfortunate that his policies were not followed. They could have changed the course of history.

This volume, and this phase of Sir William's career, closes with his building of the frontier mansion, Johnson Hall. The author has uncovered new material on the site and on the building of the Hall. He shows that it was the center of a farm which had been cultivated for two years. It was intended to usher in for Sir William a period of bucolic ease and land development—the erection of a manor and town. This was interrupted and delayed by the Indian uprising.

The final years of Sir William's life, which will be treated in another volume, were still dominated by his management of Indian affairs, though he was often frustrated by imperial policy. His rising importance in the life of the colony, in imperial politics, and his varied interests and pursuits provide a valuable insight and commentary upon colonial life and culture.

---

1. *Johnson Papers*, 1:xiii-xvi. "History of the Manuscripts," by W. R. Leech.

2. Milton W. Hamilton, "Augustus C. Buell, Fraudulent Historian," *Pennsylvania Magazine of History and Biography*, 80 (October 1956): 478–92. *Idem.*, "Myths and Legends of Sir William Johnson," *New York History*, 34 (January 1953): 3-26. *Idem.*, "Sir William Johnson's Wives," *New York History*, 38 (January 1957): 18-28.

3. The writer here repeats criticism which he made in a published review. See *New York History*, January 1960.

A NOTE ON SOURCES

Any biography of Sir William Johnson must depend principally upon the Johnson manuscripts, practically all of which are in print. *The Papers of Sir William Johnson*, fourteen volumes (Albany, 1921-65), generally cited as *Johnson Papers*, and in notes abbreviated *JP*, are supplemented by two earlier publications: *The Documentary History of the State of New York*, four volumes (Albany, 1849-50), and a quarto edition with different pagination (1850-51), abbreviated *DH*; and *Documents Relative to the Colonial History of the State of New York*, fifteen volumes (Albany 1853 - 87), abbreviated *DR*. Volumes 6, 7, and 8 contain documents from the Johnson manuscripts as well as from the Colonial Office, London, and Volume 10, Paris Documents, has translations of important French documents. Both sets were edited by E. B. O'Callaghan. By editorial policy the *Johnson Papers* did not reprint documents which had appeared in these earlier State publications.

Major manuscript collections in libraries were drawn upon for inclusion in later volumes of the *Johnson Papers*, and these have been utilized by the author. Chief among these are the Indian Records and Claus Papers in the Public Archives of Canada, Ottawa; the Johnson, Warren, and Banyar papers, and the Fort Hunter Registry of the Reverend Henry Barclay in the New-York Historical Society; the Croghan, Peters, and Penn papers, and the Gratz Collection of the Historical Society of Pennsylvania; the Gage and Clinton papers of the William L. Clements Library, Ann Arbor, Mich.; the Loudoun and Abercromby papers in the Henry E. Huntington Library, San Marino, Calif.; the Shirley Manuscripts and the Parkman Collection in the Massachusetts Historical Society; the Johnson and Schuyler manuscripts, the Indian Affairs Collection, Emmett Collection, Chalmers Collection, and William Smith Diary in the New York Public Library; the Draper Collection (on microfilm) of the Wisconsin Historical Society; the Samuel Fuller Journal and the Daniel Campbell Letter Books and Account Books in the Schenectady County Historical Society; the Yates Diary and the Severance Collection of the Buffalo Historical Society; and the Peltz, Sage, and Tayler-Cooper collections of the Albany Institute of History and Art.

The New York State Library not only has the Johnson manuscripts—the originals for the published *Papers*, many of which were damaged or destroyed by the Capitol fire of 1911—but a great many other related documents. Among the more important for this study are the Warren Johnson Diary, the Ogilvie Diary, the Colonial Land Papers, Colonial Council Minutes, the Papers of the Commissioners of Forfeiture, the Van Rensselaer Papers, Butler Accounts, and several orderly books and accounts. The Loyalist Claims Papers were used in the Public Record Office, London. The Papers of the Society for the Propagation of the Gospel in Foreign Parts, London, are on photocopy at the Library of Congress.

Printed sources and important scholarly studies are cited in the Notes and Appendices. Of special importance are: *Calender of the Sir William Johnson Manuscripts in the New York State Library*, compiled by Richard E. Day (Albany, 1909), cited as *Johnson Calendar*, which is the only source of information of the contents of documents lost in the fire of 1911. *Wraxall's Abridgment of the New York Indian Records* (cover title), edited by Charles Howard McIlwain (Cambridge, 1915), cited as *WA*, is an important source. The manuscript was destroyed in the Capitol fire, and so McIlwain's transcription and editing are valuable. *Daniel Claus' Narrative of His Relations with Sir William Johnson and Experiences in the Lake George Fight*, Society of Colonial Wars of the State of New York (1904) is useful but must be checked against the manuscript in the Canadian Archives.

Cadwallader Colden was not only several times acting governor, a major participant in colonial affairs, and Sir William's correspondent, but also a leading scholar. His *History of the Five Indian Nations Depending upon the Province of New York in North America* (New York, 1727) was reissued in London in 1747 with the title *The History of the Five Indian Nations of Canada, Which are Dependent upon the Province of New York in North America*. This edition, while badly abridged, contained additional material bringing the history up to 1746, including events in which Colden and Johnson were participants. Colden's voluminous letters and papers have been published in the New-York Historical Society *Collections* I (1868), and in subsequent series of the *Collections* (1917-23), *Colden Papers*, vols 1-7; and (1934-35), vols 8-9.

Contemporary newspapers, especially those of Boston, New York, and Philadelphia, have been used in the library of the American Antiquarian Society. Significant contemporary articles and illustrations appeared in the annual volumes of the *Gentleman's Magazine, London Magazine,* and *Royal Magazine*, all of London.

SIR WILLIAM JOHNSON
Colonial American, 1715-1736

I

IRISH BACKGROUND

> The harp that once through Tara's halls
>> The soul of music shed,
> Now hangs as mute on Tara's walls
>> As if that soul were fled.
> So sleeps the pride of former days,
>> So glory's thrill is o'er,
> An hearts, that once beat high for praise,
>> Now feel that pulse no more.
>> —Thomas Moore (1779–1852)

No one raised in rural Ireland in the early eighteenth century could escape the spell of "former days," especially if he, like young Billy Johnson, grew up at Smithstown, County Meath, in the very shadow of Tara Hall. After roaming over the lush green fields of the Manor of Killeen or trudging but a few miles down the road past Dunsany Castle, he could climb the Hill of Tara, where the ancient kings of Ireland were crowned.[1]

No longer do the strains of the harp echo through Tara's halls. But if memories of them could stir the poet Moore years later, perhaps Billy Johnson, who one day would import an Irish harper to play in the wilds of America, did indeed feel there the pulse that "beat high for praise." For was he not descended, as the Johnson family later claimed, from the "Royal family of O'Niel of Dunganon, and Tyrone, Princes of Ulster and Monarchs of Ireland"?[2] And did not the Warrens of Warrenstown come from the Norman Warynes who were with Strongbow (Earl Clare of Pembroke), who at the behest of Henry II came to the relief of one of the Irish kings and thus conquered Ireland? The Hill of Tara was truly historic and sacred ground for the Johnsons of Smithstown and their neighbors, the Warrens of Warrenstown.

William Johnson was the son of Christopher Johnson of Smithstown, County Meath, "a gentleman of great credit and repute," and his mother was "Anne Warren, daughter of Michael Warren of Warrenstown Said County Esq."[3] Several generations of the Warrens had resided here. Michael Warren had married Catherine Aylmer. Both Peter Warren, the son of Michael, and Matthew Aylmer, brother of Catherine, became rear admirals—Peter was to be Knight of the Bath, and Michael, Lord Aylmer of Balreath.

The Johnsons of Smithstown had not long held that name, for William Johnson's grandfather, of the same name, was alias Mac Shane (or McSean); before the enactment of the penal laws both the Warrens and Johnsons may have been Roman Catholic. After 1703, according to the earl of Charlemont, the "greater part of the Catholic gentry, had, either from conviction or convenience, conformed to the established and ruling religion."[4] Michael Warren was a Catholic, but after his early death, his son Peter was raised by his uncle, Rear Admiral Lord Aylmer, as a Protestant.[5] The uncle soon put Peter in the navy, where his subsequent career made him the most distinguished of his clan.

The country gentry of Ireland were of two sorts; the absentee landlords, many of them English, who lived in England on the income from their estates, and who thereby drained off the wealth of Ireland; and the "improving landlords," who lived on their estates and thus had an interest in their proper care. Frequently this did not mean that the latter were successful, that their farms were well managed, or even that they might not be facing bankruptcy. They could enjoy some prosperity in the early part of the century before economic conditions became so bad, and generally they had "an agreeable existence."[6]

The country gentry were not of the highest class, but they held land on which tenants and laborers slaved for a pittance. They owned horses and cattle, but if the estates were not well managed, their cash income would be small. This condition aroused some public-spirited persons to urge improvement for the good of the country. The Reverend Samuel Madden in 1738 denounced absenteeism, as well as the tendency of landlords to allow their buildings to fall into disrepair. He deplored the tendency of the gentry to make new purchases rather than to improve the land they had. The failure to make improvements had caused tenants to be more wretched, and had led some to emigrate. Why should not the landlords follow the good example of Colonel Newburgh, in the county of Cavan? They should plant forests and orchards, enclose with hedgerows, build sheepwalks, and encourage the manufacture of woolens and linens.[7]

But many of the gentry, according to Madden, were content with their social customs, often to the detriment of the country. The landlord "for the glory of the king senselessly hospitable feeds an idle crowd of eaters and drinkers at his table, and swills their guts with French wine, that is, with the blood of his country."[8] One of the first customs to be abolished would be "that of giving large quantities of liquor, and especially *aquavitae* at funerals," marriages, and christenings, at great expense. For this contributed to the laziness and indolence of the people.[9]

It was to the shame of the gentry, too, that the masses were so miserable. For "we must confess that in Ireland our tenants (I speak of the poorest and greatest part of them) have rather huts than houses, and those of our cotters are built like birds nests, of dirt wrought together and a few sticks and some straw, and like them are generally removed once a year. . . . Numbers of them have no chimney, either for want of wood, or skill to build one, but vent the smoke, like those of the Hottentots. . . ."[10]

Christopher Johnson belonged to the class of gentry who lived on the land. His estate of about two hundred acres was leased from the Earl of Fingall in 1728 (he was then occupying the land) for the sum of £208.19s and a yearly rent of £63.13.6 for the period of thirty-one years. By the customary terms of such a lease, he was required to do "suite and service att the said Earls Mannor Court att Killeen and to grind all [his] corn at the mill of Killeen."[11]

The thirty-one year lease was required of Catholics, and so Smithstown may have been in possession of the Johnsons before they became Protestants. The text of the deed refers to "Christopher Johnson of Warrenstown," so he may have been a resident with the Warrens before the deed was drawn. According to Arthur Young, who wrote of conditions in Ireland in 1776–78, such estates were sublet in smaller plots to laborers or farmers on a few acres. A farm of two hundred acres might have from eight to twenty-five houses, and up to forty laborers.[12]

Thus the proprietor of Smithstown, while leasing his land from the lord of the manor, was himself an employer. He belonged neither to the "people of considerable fortune" nor to the mob. He was of the class of small fortune—country gentlemen and renters of land. "This class enjoyed conditions not commonly found in England: large tracts of land, but few markets; plenty with inconsiderable taxes, and with prices much lower than in England; and a great many horses and servants."[13]

The Johnson residence was probably comfortable but modest. Both Madden and Young found Irish homes quite inferior to those of England. Said the latter "there are men of five thousand a Year in Ireland, who live in habitations that a man of several hundred a year in London would disdain." Both observers scored the failure to keep up the grounds and to care for the buildings. But Young found many new and excellent houses being built, and it is quite evident from Madden's criticism that many persons saw the need of improvement.[14]

Smithstown House[15] still stands in the midst of the two-hundred acre estate. Although it is an eighteenth-century dwelling, it may not have been the residence of Christopher Johnson in 1738. (The Adam decoration indicates later improvement, perhaps when Sir John Johnson, Sir William's son, took the deed.) Of whatever date of ownership, its setting and surroundings convey much of the atmosphere which must have prevailed in the early eighteenth century and imply that the family of Christopher Johnson belonged to that "class of small fortune," the country gentry.

The family of Christopher Johnson at Smithstown in 1738, when his son William left the ancestral lands, was composed of three sons and five daughters. William, born in 1715, when his father was thirty-six and his mother, Anne Warren, nineteen, may well have been the eldest. Peter Warren, usually called Warren, born in 1732, was a much younger brother, and John was nearer to William's age. Probably all of the girls were at home. It was a closely knit family. Only six years after William went forth to make his fortune, Anne Warren Johnson died.[16] Christopher was comforted in his old age by the presence of his daughters, and his son John was in nearby Warrenstown. Even so, he fretted that he heard infrequently from his son William, of whom, however, he was both fond and proud.[17]

With a growing family, the Johnsons had been faced with the problem of proper careers for the boys and perhaps husbands and homes for the girls. For the former, there was the army, the navy, the church, or the land; to be properly launched one had to purchase a commission, or a place, or have an estate to manage. It was the natural thing, then, to look to the relative whose wealth and achievement made him the logical source for such aid.

Uncle Peter Warren was still a young man. Born in 1703, he entered the navy at the age of fourteen and quickly went through the ranks to become a captain at twenty-four. After three years in European waters, he sailed to the West Indies and North America. There he captured rich Spanish and French prizes, some of which he took to the port of New York, where their conversion into cash enriched both the mariner and the local merchants. One of the merchants was Stephen De Lancey, who recognized the up-and-coming captain as an eligible son-in-law. In July 1731, while his ship the *Launceton* was refitting, Peter Warren married Susannah De Lancey and thus laid the foundation for his career in America. She brought him "a pretty fortune," and through her mother, née Anne Van Cortlandt, was connected with the landed aristocracy of the Hudson Valley.

Persuaded no doubt by the prospect held forth by his wife's relative, he seemed about to settle down in the New World. He purchased a farm of three hundred acres on which he built a residence, "Greenwich house."[18] This farm, now Greenwich Village, provided him with firm roots in Manhattan, and a home for his bride when he again returned to the sea. Soon he was enticed by another opportunity to purchase land, for this was an era of wild speculation. The scramble for lands was becoming intense. It was necessary, however, to have friends in the government. Indian purchases were quickly made but had to be confirmed in the province. James De Lancey, Peter Warren's brother-in-law, had been named chief justice by Governor William Cosby, who had arbitrarily tried to crush his opposition. Making use of his position, Cosby had acquired for himself a vast tract of land along the Mohawk River, which he left to his widow. No doubt it was James De Lancey who put Captain Warren in touch with Mrs. Cosby. In July 1736, Cadwallader Colden was informed by a shocked correspondent:

Captain Warren has made a very Great purchase of Mrs. Cosby at Boston 13,000 a (cres) of the Govrs. Land at Trohenonder Hill for 110£ how she became so infatuated I know not, Sure it could be so Trifling a Sum ready money that Bewitched her . . . .[19]

The captain, probably with ready prize money at the port of Boston, knew little of Mohawk lands, but he was quick to make a deal. Colden's informant was disturbed that this removed Warren from the market for other lands. Great ideas were afloat for settlement of Mohawk lands with immigrants from Europe, and Warren no doubt had visions of his own manor in the New World. George Clarke, the new lieutenant-governor, had just outlined proposals for settling five hundred Protestant families with two hundred acres each on the Mohawk, through advertisements to be sent to England, Ireland, Holland, and Germany.[20] And with these prospects Peter Warren returned to Warrenstown and County Meath. Herein lay promise for the future of William Johnson.

As to William Johnson's motives in leaving Ireland for America,[21] there has been much speculation—as though a young man seeking to improve himself and make a career would not jump at the prospect which was offered him by Uncle Peter. It was outlined "by the many letters he wrote me when yet In Ireland" and by subsequent letters "that He would give me a certain tract of Land in Warrensborough, and Supply me with all things necessary to carry on my Work."[22] In 1737, at the instance of Peter Warren, William began in Ireland the recruiting of families to populate the tract in the Mohawk Valley. According to his later account for expenses, he procured twelve families and brought them to America.[23]

II

TO THE MOHAWK VALLEY

The project for the settlement of Uncle Peter's lands must have been vigorously carried out, for William procured twelve families in the vicinity of County Meath. The group, which also included his cousin Michael Tyrrell, met the captain in Boston in the spring of 1738 and purchased supplies and equipment there.[1] A party of this size, and there may have been others of whom we have no details, was indeed a test of the abilities of the young Irishman, and his success in this venture was a token of his capacity for great things to come.

That there were blunders and mistakes in assembling the outfit is not surprising. Neither William nor the captain knew anything of frontier conditions or needs, and they had collected some articles which would be of no use.[2] Other articles were intended for the journey overland, or for the hazards they were led to expect—a smith's vise (the smith came later); a beam and scale and some weights (for his trading operations); padlocks, keys, staples, and hasps; six muskets, a bullet gun, two broadswords, two powder horns, a pair of leather saddlebags, a saddlecloth; dishes, plates, candlesticks, and snuffers; a case of bottles; and handcuffs for Negroes.[3] Doubtless there were many other things, either not rendered in his account or paid for out of other funds.

We must assume from available evidence that the journey was made overland from Boston to Albany. If the party had gone first to New York, where certainly Peter Warren had the best of contacts, the supplies would have been purchased there. But the captain had made Boston his home port since he brought Mrs. Cosby, widow of the governor, there in June 1736, on her way to England. There he had made the deal for his Mohawk lands. In 1738 he made several voyages between Boston and London, so that William and his party might well have come to the New World aboard the *Squirrel*.[4]

There were two possible routes westward from Boston for horsemen and wagons. One went northward to Deerfield, Northfield, and North Adams, Massachusetts, then by the Hoosic River to Hudson and Albany.[5] The other went via Springfield, Hartford, Norfolk, and Canaan, Connecticut, to Great Barrington, Massachusetts, then to the Hudson via Claverack, to Kinderhook, or Greenbush, and then across the river to Albany.[6] Horses and wagons had to be hired for stages along the way; some stretches on the route through the highlands—the Berkshire Hills—may not have been passable by wagon, and packhorses might have been used.

This journey into the wilds of America must have been a trying one for William Johnson and his party. By the time he reached Albany his temper was frayed, for he wrote his complaints to his uncle who, still at Boston, admonished him: "Don't say anything about the Badness of the Patrones Horses, for it may be taken Amiss, he is a near relation of my wifes, and may have it in his power very much to Serve you."[7]

Approaching Albany from the east, travellers probably stopped at Claverack, and again at the Van Rensselaer residence at Greenbush, Fort Crailo, across the river.[8] Ferrying across, William Johnson probably visited the patroon, to whom he had been commended by Peter Warren. Important visitors generally were received in one of the great houses, of the patroon or of the Schuylers, and then went forth to view the town.

Having seen Boston, and some British towns, on this journey or before, William may have reacted as did his brother Warren some twenty years later. To him it was "a fine River, And but a Nasty dirty Town"; "the Streets of Albany the Dirtiest I ever Saw, & worse than Edinburgh in Scotland for litle houses."[9] But Peter Kalm has left perhaps the best description of early Albany by a contemporary visitor.

The houses in this town are very neat, and partly built of stones covered with shingles of white pine. Some are slated (roofed) with tile from Holland, because the clay of this neighborhood is not considered fit for tiles. A great number of houses are built . . . with the gable end toward the street being of bricks and all the other walls of boards. . . . The eaves on the roofs [the rainspouts] reach almost to the middle of the street. This preserves the walls from being damaged by the rain, but it is extremely disagreeable in rainy weather for the people in the streets, there being hardly any means of avoiding the water from the eaves. The front doors are generally in the middle of the houses, and on both side are porches with seats on which during the fair weather the people spend almost the whole day, especially on those porches which are in the shade . . . .[10]

A few years before Kalm's visit, Dr. Alexander Hamilton came to Albany and commented upon the public buildings. He was a guest of the Anglican clergyman, had tea at the Van Rensselaers' and supped at the Widow Schuyler's.

I went before dinner with M—s. and saw the inside of the Townhouse (Stadt House, or Court House). The great hall where the court sits is about forty feet long and thirty broad. This is a clumsy heavy building, both without and within. We went next and viewed the workmen putting up a new palisading or stockadoes to fortify the town.[11]

A newcomer from Ireland, however, would be more interested in the people who lived in this frontier town. Brother Warren displayed an intense dislike for the Dutch, and with the same Irish background William may have soon developed such an aversion to the inhabitants who were to be his future neighbors and associates. Peter Kalm found Albany undeniably Dutch:

The inhabitants of Albany and its environs are almost all Dutchmen. They speake Dutch, have Dutch preachers and the divine service is performed in that language. Their manners are likewise quite Dutch. . . .

In their homes the inhabitants of Albany are much more sparing than the English, and are stingier with their food. Generally what they serve is just enough for the meal and sometimes hardly that. The punch bowl is much more rarely seen than among the English. The women are perfectly well acquainted with economy; they rise early, go to sleep late, and are most superstitiously clean in respect to the floor, which is frequently scoured several times in the week. Inside the homes the women are neatly but not lavishly dressed. The children are taught both English and Dutch. The servants in the town are chiefly negroes.[12]

Warren Johnson was less objective: "The Dutch are an odd & very bad Sort of People, & there is noe Confidence to be put in them."[13]

Albany was indeed the gate to the new life in the Mohawk Valley, and there one saw other evidences of the strange new world. There were sloops and bateaux in the river, and fur traders and Indians on the streets. They were unlike anything seen in Ireland or England. One had to make adjustments to both the land and the people.

Leaving Albany through the gates in the palisades, one climbed the hills beyond and found himself in an unfertile land of clay and sand with numerous pine trees. It was an uninteresting landscape. Reaching Schenectady after travelling some sixteen miles overland, he found, in the words of Brother Warren, "a litle dirty village."[14] A better tempered traveller, Lord Adam Gordon, somewhat later wrote that "after traveling so far over a waste . . . the first view you have of Schenectady, the Mohawk river, and the country on its Banks is remarkably pleasing. The Streets of Schenectady are Spacious, the River there very beautiful, and the Soil excellent."[15]

Here it was necessary to transfer to bateaux for the trip up the Mohawk. An introduction from Peter Warren to Major Jacob Glen enabled Johnson to make proper arrangements. Uncle Peter later thanked Glen for his "great civility to my nephew Mr. Johnson whose welfare I have much at heart."[16] Down by the river was a public landing, and nearby the bateaux (commonly called "battoes") were made.[17] If a sufficient number were not readily at hand, there may have been some delay until all were obtained and equipped. While individual travellers might go up the river in bark canoes, Johnson's party needed a fleet of bateaux to carry all the baggage and equipment brought over from Boston. Peter Kalm has left a good description of these boats:

They are made of boards of white pine; the bottom is flat, that they may row the better in shallow water. They are sharp at both ends, and somewhat higher towards the end than in the middle. They have seats in them, and are rowed as common boats. They are long, yet are not all alike. Usually they are three and sometimes four fathoms [eighteen to twenty-four feet] long. The height from the bottom to the top of the board (for the sides stand almost perpendicular) is from twenty inches to two feet, and the breadth in the middle about a yard and six inches. . . . The boats made of the bark of trees break easily by knocking against a stone, and the canoes cannot carry a great cargo, and are easily upset; the battoes are therefore preferable to them both.[18]

Somewhat larger bateaux were used on the lakes, and in wartime for transporting troops and supplies. These were poled by three or more men, and were sometimes fitted with a mast and sail. But if they were too large and heavy, they might be too cumbersome to handle over the portage or carrying place.

Finally, embarking on the last stage of the journey, the Irish immigrants observed the country in which they were to live. The Mohawk River in its lower reaches is still a beautiful sight and then in its pristine verdure in the summer of 1738 may well have seemed the promised land. No one in this group described his first impressions, but Lord Adam Gordon years later went over this same part of the valley and wrote: "It is a narrow vale or Strath of excellent Soil, hemm'd in on both sides with high grounds, uncultivated, and covered with a variety of Timber, but exceedingly pleasant to the Eye, and cut by a thousand little Brooks, descending rapidly from above. It much resembles Westmoreland, or the Banks of Tay, above Perth."[19]

As the bateaux slowly ascended the river, poled through the current at times, at others drifting into protected pools, sometimes near the wooded shore, the immigrants had time to speculate upon the lands they would inhabit. Less travelled, no doubt, than Lord Adam, they may have found it strangely unlike the lands of Ireland. Where in this wilderness would their habitation be? How much labor and back-breaking struggle would be needed to clear the land for farming? Who would be their neighbors, if any, and what of the "savages," of whom they knew so little? Would there be fish and game to sustain them until their farms produced?

Many there were whose fondest hopes were centered in these forests. Would here begin for them a new life of independence and freedom? The possession of land, the lure of all settlers, meant security and wealth, which as Old World laborers they could never hope to attain. Fear and trepidation for the unknown were mixed with optimism and promise. The young Irishman, their leader, was a spirited and resourceful person whose "diligence and application" did much to ensure the success of the venture.

Warrensburgh (also written Warrensborough and probably so pronounced)[20] was situated along the south bank of the Mohawk River at the mouth of Schoharie Creek. Known as the Chuctenunda tract, it extended three and a half miles along the Mohawk and, because of the stream's meandering, some five miles along the Schoharie. It was hilly or rolling country, with little of the flat bottomlands so much desired. Heavily forested, it did have good loam over clay, if the land could first be cleared. That it had to be cleared was a distinct disadvantage, however, and Johnson later wrote of "Clearing a Farm out of the thickest timbered Woods I ever saw."[21]

There were small streams, the Chuctenunda and the Willigee, providing some waters for cultivation. But resources in springs and woods, in wildlife and natural foods, were to them yet unknown.

Although the tract was of considerable size, not all was equally good, and there were neighboring holdings, some of which were better. Boundaries had to be fixed, and there were complications. The year before, William Corry, another Irishman, at the behest and backing of Governor George Clarke, had begun a settlement west of the Schoharie. Already it was running into difficulties, and Corry later became involved and was sued by young William Johnson.[22]

Adjacent also was a farm taken up by Joseph Cowley, from Huff's patent of 1736, and this too was in difficulties, for Johnson told his uncle of the possibility of getting it. Uncle Peter advised him to take "Care not to be within Cowley's Masering in your improvement, yt. wou'd be Bad indeed." But, "As to takeing Cowly's farm I can say nothing to it but if you shou'd it wou'd not be proper to Improve it for yt. wou'd be a Means of raiseing the price on Me and I make no doubt of haveing it one time or other."[23] Then on another corner of the grant was the lot by the Willigee Creek where some Negroes were located and had cleared land; "as to the land ye. Negroes possess ask Mr. Collins about it . . . and the other Clear land you Mention."[24] He did not get this, however, for the next year it was being surveyed and threatened to encroach upon Johnson's clearing.[25] There was indeed a wild scramble for plots not yet taken, or on which claims had not been fully registered.

As to that land between yu. & Jn. Wemp, I had formerly a letter from the Cheif Justice Abt. it desireing I would Look into, and Enquire abt. it wh. I did of Jn. Wemp, and Severall others who tell me that Captn. Butler has an Indn. Deed for it, wh. I asked one of the Cheif Indns. who tells me the Same; people here are mad Everry day purchaseing land & Surveying, so that land must be verry dear in a Short time.[26]

To the original twelve families which Johnson brought from Ireland, others were added, so that by 1742 he had drawn up twenty-six leases.[27] Some of these came from up the valley where the Palatine Germans had migrated in the fifteen years since their trek from the ill-fated tar camps on the Hudson. The captain encouraged this source of settlement.

I wou'd have you by all means incourage setlers for yt. is all yts. wanting. and Especialy those Germans yt. one of the Tenants are gone for, I don't Mean you should bee at any Expence in doing it only give them Countenance, and the smaller their farms ye. more the Land will hould, and ye. better the Improvements will bee.[28]

In the spring of 1739, urging Uncle Peter to visit Warrensburgh, he told of

Severall others who are Inclined to Come and Settle on the land, but wait yr. comeing. . . . They are all people in Good Circumstance and would like being near me in hopes of haveing a good Neighbourhood Soon here.[29]

In the fall of that year he reported that some families sought to settle on Warren's land who were obliged to "quit the Improvement they have Made, By Reason of the lands not being laid out in Lotts." In fact he had three families now in his own house waiting for the land to be laid out for them.[30]

The captain was free with advice as to how these lands should be cultivated and developed. He envisioned a countryside like that of England, or Ireland, with orderly plots divided by hedgerows. William smiled, no doubt, at some ideas, but he kept his own counsel and did what was feasible.

As you have great help now you will Girdle Many Acres, in doing which I woud be regular, and to it in Square feilds, and leave Hedge rows at each Side which will keep the land warm, bee very Butiful, and no more Expence then doing it in a slovenly Iregular Manner. . . . I will send you ye. vine and other things you Mention in the Spring. . . .

I hope you will plant a large Orchard in the Spring. it wont hinder your Indian Corn nor Grass, as you will plant your trees at a great distance. I shou'd think it would be worth your while to inquier strictly if ye. Medow you Mention is on My land, for it wou'd help you with hay and twoud be a good place to plant Corn in, I think were I you I woud do that at a venture . . . get ye. best kind of fruit trees for the Orcherd if they cost something More, and a good Nursery would not be Amiss.[31]

It would be a year or so before the yield would more than cover the outlay, but in 1740-42, produce and timber were being shipped to the Warrens in New York: "15 Bushls. of Indian Corn 40/ and 10 do. of Peas 4/6 per"; "20 Bushls. Peace £8–30 do. Indian Corn." In 1743, there were "225 Bushls. Pease @ 5/ per £56.5" and four hundredweight of flour, in casks. The gristmill was working, as was also the sawmill. "200 Inch boards 9d. per £7 . . 10 . . 140 Inch & ½ do.15d. per £8 . . 15. . . . 66 pitch pine do.14d. per £3 . . 16." There was also charged at £18 . . 16, "A parcel of Timber cut down & Squared by Order & design'd for Building a House at Greenwich."[32]

Thus indeed was Peter Warren's tract yielding produce and building material for his home in New York.

Peter Warren realized, however, that it was not on the farm alone that the success of the venture would depend. The De Lanceys, merchants of New York, could brief him on the profits to be realized in the fur trade, and in barter with Indians and settlers. William should set up a store; when his produce came down from Albany the captain would send up remittances in goods, which then could be sold. The sailor's idea of the time and availability of the produce, as well as the kind of goods wanted in exchange, however, left much to be desired.

. . . It will Answer to send wheat, Corn, Pease, or any of the produce of that Country to this place, and early in the Spring, if you Can Ingage ye. first sloop from Albany to take in what you May have, and order it to be sent Me I will send ye. returns in such goods as you May desire and as for what Skins you Can procure I will send them to London, and ye. produce of them Shall be sent you in proper goods. I have wrote to Dublin for £200 ster: in Linnen from 8d. to 20 pence pr. yard, and to Scotland for £50 ster. in Check linnen, all which I hope you will have early in the Spring, besides about £200 worth of goods from London. The difficulty will be in Makeing remittances, when you receive your goods if you can get a good profit for them in any of the towns and ready Mony, I wou'd Sell as Many of them as I did not Imediatly want for the Suply of my Constant Customers, and remit ye. mony as I shall hereafter direct. . . . you ought to be carefull to who you give Credit as you are a Stranger. . . .

You see you will have a pretty good Cargo, the whole produce of it Must be remitted as soon As possible, to be Laid out again till you with your increase Can have a very large Store of goods of all kinds proper for that Country.

pray lett Me know what Rum and all things sells for there such as Axes and other wrought Iron, them I coud send from hence, if I found ye. profit great I wou'd soon have a thousand pounds worth of goods there, what wou'd them leather Caps sell for, and what profit had you on the linnen and any of your goods.

how can I Judge what is best for you when you dont perticularly tell me the prices only say at large this and yt. sels well you ought to be more Circumspect and particular. . . .

There are some people gone up and Many things an acct of them you will receive, with them. I Box Containing Ribands lett me know how they Answer.

You shoud always tell Me you receive everything Agreeable to ye. inventorys I send you, or how do I know they get safe to you, write by all Oppertunitys. in the winter there is a Post from Albany to New york by which you May write to me. . . .

I will send for Books for you to keep yr. Accts. which You Must do very regular.[33]

William's letter in the spring acknowledged the help and advice, but his reactions were mixed.

I must Acknowledge Dr. Uncle that wt. great favours yu. Were pleased to do me, was a Sufficient Beginning And am wth. all the Gratitude Imaginable Contented wth it, and for the future shall be no way Expensive, nor troublesome to yu. No farther than perhaps I may want Some goods or Necessarys wth. the procureing of wh. I may perhaps make bold to trouble yu., but not wth. out the Money for it. as for the goods wh. yu. and Mr. Middleton Sent here they will not Answer. for When I over Looked them I found all the Stockings Mostly Moth Eaten, and I fear the Rest will be so to, if not Already, I have Aired them all verry well wh. is the best thing Can be done wth. them. I long to hear from yu. wt. yu. will have done wth. them. were they proper goods for this Country it would be much better

Yu. Mention in yr. last of Sending More large Casks here, and Iron bound Barrells wh. if yu. have not as yet Sent, I would be glad yu. Would keep them, because the one large Cask yu. were pleased to Send me is Sufficient together wth. what Small ones I have Already.[34]

Peter Warren had great confidence in his young nephew, for he had written Glen, "if I am not Much Mistaken in him his diligence and Application will put him Soon in a good way."[35] His cousin, Michael Tyrrell, and other friends and neighbors, now settlers and tenants, were in his care. In this new country there were to be many tests of his tact and character. The captain surely knew a great deal about men and of how to get on in the world, and he knew also the weaknesses of his countrymen. "Keep well with all Mankind," he advised. "Act with honour & honesty both of you [and] dont be Notional as some of our Country men are often foolishly. . . . My love to Mick live like Brothers, and I will be an Affecte unkle to you Both."[36]

The next spring William could reply, "as to my keeping in well wth. all people yu. may Assure yr. Self of it Dr. Uncle, for I daresay I have the good will of all people wt.soever, and much respected, Verry much on yr. Acct. and my Own Behaviour, wh. I trust in God I shall always Continue."[37]

III

WILLIAM JOHNSON, MERCHANT

Speculators in New World lands like Peter Warren were not able to make an immediate profit. Resale of land brought some returns, but clearing and establishing settlers was slow, and some without plenty of capital were soon discouraged. Hence, it was wise on the part of the captain to set up his nephew in trade. Fort Hunter and the Chuctenunda lands were not far from Albany, which was a mecca for traders. From the days of Fort Orange, the Albany Dutch were *handlers*, middlemen in commerce. They were well situated to engross furs brought in by the Indians as well as to transport trade goods by water. Their shrewdness, greed, and even rapacity gave them an unenviable reputation with their neighbors, which was reflected in the opinions of travellers. Peter Kalm had no love for the Albany Dutch, but his observations are valuable for their explicit detail.

All the boats which ply between Albany and New York belong to Albany. They go up and down the Hudson River as long as it is open and free from ice. They bring from Albany boards or planks, and all sorts of timber, flour, peas, and furs, which they get from the Indians, or which are smuggled from the French. They come home almost empty and only bring a few kinds of merchandise with them, the chief of which is rum. They are absolutely necessary to the inhabitants of Albany. They cheat the Indians in fur trade with it; for when the Indians are drunk they are practically blind and will leave it to the Albany whites to fix the price of furs. The boats are quite large, and have a good cabin, in which the passenger can be very commodiously lodged.

. . . . .

Many people at Albany make wampum for the Indians, which is their ornament and money, by grinding and finishing certain kinds of shells and mussels. This is of considerable profit to the inhabitants.[1]

It was this business into which young Johnson was catapulted. He learned soon what Uncle Peter could not realize; all trade was in barter or credit—hence prices were fluctuating, and he could not tell what "all things sells for." Neither could he be sure of the market, and what items were salable, or what they would bring in New York. One thing he learned was that one had to tap the commerce which passed up and down the river. So when his uncle chided him about purchasing land north of the river, he countered that "it would be the properest place on the Whole River for a Store house and Shop in Winter, by reason of all the High Germans passing by that way in the Winter, and all the upper Nations of Indians, whose trade is pritty valuable."[2]

Uncle Peter was a little miffed by Johnson's purchase of this land on the north bank in his own name, lest he set himself up as a rival developer. Yet it was all in keeping with the Albany pattern of a merchant.

Which [land] in Everry Bodys Opinion is a good Bargain, and Can any time I please Sell it for the Money And More So that I hope Dr. Uncle yl. not continue yr. Opinion when yu. See it and know My Design (wh. is this) to have a Carefull Honest Man there Who will Manage the farm, wh. will at least Clear I am Sure £30 per Annum, Moreover the Chief thing is a fine Creek to build a Saw Mill on, haveing Loggs Enough att hand, half of wh. Creek belongs to Me, so that I intend after a little time, please God, to build a Mill there, wh. May Clear £40 per Annum, and that wthout Much trouble, so that the Income of that May Enable me to go on in the World.[3]

Timber, planks, and boards were in great demand and were even supplied for Peter Warren's own building operations. Other goods were packaged in casks or hogsheads, placed on bateaux and poled down the Mohawk, and then carried to Albany, where they could be be placed on the sloop of Peter Van Alen for New York. There the factor for a while was Edward Holland, who shipped aboard the *Antelope* for Jamaica or Curaçao.[4] These several handlings often entailed loss and misunderstanding. Letters are replete with advice, complaints, suggestions, and price revisions. William was not established two years before he was contracting to supply Philip Livingston in Albany, who wrote on February 25, 1740/41:

I am very much pleas'd you have not agreed for more wheat @ 3/3d. which price I Suppose will not be maintaind. 3/ would have been enough and at that your wheat from ye. westward will not do for boatting pease I Conjecture will be in demand because of ye. hard winter and bad Crop but what price they will be I cant Say I am in want of Some I wish you would Spare me abt. 50 or 100 Skiple at a Reasonable price.[5]

Cured meat and dairy products, too, were shipped to New York, but commodities of this kind were not properly packaged for the market. Anthony Duane in New York, May 16, 1746, even returned part of a shipment.

Have received the Two Hhds. of Gammons and Four Bbls of Butter, the former of which are so very large they will neither doe for this Markett nor to ship off wherefore desire youd. send orders for my sending them up again, as I apprehend they may either doe for your Familys use or to send to Oswegoe. With regard to the Butter shoud. have been able to sell it at a very Good Price if it had a been Packd in Firkins, however have sold Two Bbls: and am to have whatever I can gett for the Others. . . . P.S. The Hhds. are a Mixture of Large Gammons, Shoulders and Bacon and not well dryd. whereas for this Markett they ought to be all Sizeable Gammons and well Smoakd.[6]

Neither were the packs of furs sent down always acceptable. The occasional lots brought to him by barter could not compare with the vast quantities brought in by the fur traders. This was a field which Johnson, too, was to enter. Edward Holland, his New York agent, retorted to a complaint about the price for Johnson's furs:

You Say you are Sorry I Sold your Skins as they are rising & that Mr. Duane sold some of the same sort for 4/3 if they were of the same sort, he has not let the People that bought them see them, for I do ashure you those I had were Exceeding bad. Mr. Duane was present when I sold them & not for money, neither.[7]

The fur trade was one of the oldest in the New World, a commerce which had changed the habits and modes of Europe, had won fortunes, made some nations prosperous at the expense of others, had conditioned much of the settlement, changed the course of history on this continent, and most serious of all had transformed the culture of the American Indian.

Hides, which were commonplace to the Indians of North America, proved to be real wealth to the North American conquerors. Failing to find the gold and silver which so enhanced the possession of Spanish America, the explorers from Holland, France, and England would have had little reward indeed without the fur trade. Henry Hudson, ascending the river in the *Half Moon*, turned back, disappointed in not finding a route to the South Sea. Even the land with its rocky shores seemed inhospitable, and reception by the natives was mixed. Some outcroppings gave indication of mineral resources—copper perhaps—but no ready wealth. Later voyagers engaged in trade and soon found furs the most negotiable product. The Dutch West India Company decreed a monopoly on the trade in their efforts to bring home profits to their directors. Although in 1629 the inauguration of the "patroon system" emphasized settlement of the land, the profit motive directed most of the capital into trade. Fort Orange, the site of Albany, was settled in 1624 and received its preeminence as an outpost of trade with the Indians.

Of all the pelts brought there by the Indians, that of the beaver proved most acceptable and seemed in generous supply. To the Indian, who hunted and trapped for food, clothing, and shelter (never purely for sport or so much as to diminish unduly the supply), the white man's preference was incomprehensible. Yet, tempted and plied with rum, he complied with the demand as far as he was able until the supply of beaver began to run low. By 1640, it was said that there were no more beaver to be had in the bounds of present-day New York. But the trade was now well established at Albany, and the Indians, who had earlier trafficked in pelts of their own catch, became middlemen for the supplies brought from the interior. The entire economy of many Indians became dependent upon intertribal commerce which focused upon Albany.

When the English acquired New Netherland in 1664, the colony became New York and Fort Orange was named Albany, but there was no change in the economic structure of the province. The Dutch in Albany continued their rôle as traders in furs, with routes of trade radiating North and West. Their preoccupation with this business gave them a reputation for avarice with such travellers as Peter Kalm. Latecomers of other nationalities, like the Irish or Scots, found them jealous of this monopoly and resentful of interference.

Into this well-established traffic William Johnson was to force his way. He was an interloper, one who should have been satisfied with lands on the Mohawk and his store with its local commodity exchange. But the young man was enterprising and had resolved "to go on in the world." He was adaptable and followed even the questionable tactics of his shrewd rivals.

By the middle of the eighteenth century the Albany merchants controlled the fur trade through two channels. "Most of the merchants in this town," wrote Kalm, "send a clerk or agent to Oswego, an English trading town on Lake Ontario, to which the Indians come with their furs." There the traders spent the summer exchanging rum and other commodities with the visiting tribes and freely cheating them when they were drunk. At the close of the season they returned to Albany with their loaded bateaux to ship and exchange their packs of pelts.[8]

On the other hand, "a number of Indians come to Albany from several places, especially from Canada; but from this latter place, they hardly bring anything but beaver skins."[9] This trade with Montreal, early begun by the Dutch, became illicit when the intercolonial wars began in 1689, and it was a principal cause of discontent and friction with the Iroquois. In years to come, William Johnson was to have much to do with both channels of trade. But now his concern was how to enlarge the field of his own operations.

In his May 10, 1739 letter to Uncle Peter, William indicated both the extent of the Oswego trade and his disinclination, or fear, of breaking into it. In asking for goods to be sent him in exchange, he mentioned:

Indian truck, and fitt to trade wth. to a place Called Oquago to the Southward from this on Suscahannah River, towards Philidelphia, where I intend if yu. think proper to Make a tryall this fall wth. abt. £200 worth of Goods wh. I am Credibly Informed by those that Came from thence that I Can to advantage dispose of them to the Indians there, better than at Oswego because there are to many traders go there, and all a parcell of Meer Bites, But here att Aquago there are but verry few go there, So yt. I Conceit I Could Make a good hand there, haveing a fellow here who I would take wth. me that Understands their tongue and way of dealing So that if it hitts well wth. me I may be a great deal the better of it, If not I Dont fear Selling the goods Elsewhere, Indian truck being the best that goes of here. I would Willingly have yr. Advice abt. it, by the first opertunity. By Reason I would be provideing one little thing or another again the time wh. is in August the best time to go.[10]

Whether Uncle Peter provided the Indian truck and approved of this stepping out into Indian trade is not recorded. The plan, like so many projects, may have encountered difficulties, or the trade may have been begun without Johnson and his interpreter going. Like the Albany merchants, he may have sent an agent. At least, by 1753, his bateaux were going to the Indians at Oquaga, and carrying them rum.[11] Indeed, Johnson had found that there was no trade without rum; and that if the Anglican missionary, the Reverend Henry Barclay, was to succeed in banning the traffic in rum, it would injure trade. The Indians informed him that this was the missionary's doing; rum was the commodity most in demand.

The Oswego trade began with the establishment of a post there in 1727 by Governor William Burnet. This wise and far-reaching step had been taken to counter the pressure of the French traders engrossing the furs traded by the Iroquois. For the French were not content to sit at Montreal or Quebec, like the Dutch at Albany, waiting for business to pass through their hands. The famed *coureurs de bois* lived among the Indians of Canada, went into Huronia to the westward, and brought the furs annually in fleets of canoes over the waters to market. Niagara, Lake Ontario, and the St. Lawrence River became the highway over which the furs were floated down to Montreal and Quebec. If this tendency to monopoly were not broken, New York province would lose much of its valuable trade.

Oswego was strategically located to break into this route. As the fur-laden boats from the west hugged the southern shore of the lake, they put into the coves and bays for shelter and supplies. A post at the mouth of the Oswego (Onondaga) River would attract all passersby. Furthermore there was a natural water route to the Onondaga country, Oneida Lake, and thence by portage to the Mohawk River and Albany.

At the time William Johnson sought to break into this traffic, the situation was aptly described as extremely favorable for the New York traders:

> Governor *Burnet* through his earnest Application, and at first chiefly with his money Credit, and Risque, erected a Trading-House and Fortifications at the mouth of the *Onondagues* [Oswego] River, called Osneigo [Oswego], where the province of *New-York* supports a Garrison of Soldiers, consisting of a Lieutenat and twenty Men, which are yearly relieved.
>
> At this Place, a very great Trade is carried on with the remote *Indians*, who formerly used to go down to the *French* at *Monreal*, and there buy our *English* Goods at second Hand, at above twice the Price they now pay for them at *Osneigo* [12]

A few years later Cadwallader Colden, that astute New York observer, could report

> that Mr. *Burnet's* Scheme has had its desired Effect: The *English* have gained the Trade which the French, before that, had with the *Indians*, to the Westward of *New-York*; and whereas, before that Time, a very inconsiderable Number of Men were employed in the *Indian* Trade Abroad, now above three hundred Men are employed at the Trading House at *Oswego* alone; and the *Indian* Trade has since that Time increased so far, that several *Indian* Nations come now every Summer to trade there, whose names were not so much as known to the English before.[13]

These traders, the English counterpart of the French *coureurs de bois* and the Dutch *boschlopers*, were in a different class from the merchants, like Johnson, who stayed on the Mohawk or in Albany. Of whatever nationality, they were much alike. According to Witham Marsh, in 1744, those in Pennsylvania were

> as wild as some of the most savage Indians, amongst whom they trade for skins, furs, &c for sundry other kinds of European goods and strong liquors. They go back in the country, above 300 miles from the white inhabitants; here they live with the Indian hunters till they have disposed of their cargoes; and then, on horses, carry their skins, &c to Philadelphia.[14]

When Colden spoke of three hundred at Oswego, he did not mean that all were resident there, but that from this point they went among the tribes. Johnson entered the Oswego trade by sending bateaux loaded with trade goods to these adventurers, receiving their furs in return, and shipping them on to New York. In spite of disadvantages in the arrangements and his expressed preference for Oquaga, he continued to deal with the traders. One of them, Hyde Clark, wrote him, May 19, 1743:

I have safely rec'd ye. things you sent me but can't promiss as yet to let you have any of my peltry till I have settled Accts with Mr. Holland.... As a stranger to ye. place according to your desire have spoke to ye best of my ffriends for advice for your intrest in this place which is Mr. Peters he says if you send a batoe up you'll be ye. looser for ye. Trade decays much especially this year. I have wrote to Mr. Holland to send me 3 or 4 hogsheads of Rum up for I have disbursted many Barrells of ye. Handlers to ye. Soldiers & Indians. . . .[15]

Later that year Johnson was given a summons to appear before the commissioners in Albany "To make oath of the full Quantity of Strowds or other Cloaths Rum or other distilled Liquors you have Sent Carried or transported for Sale to the Indians or french since the first day of November Last," since this trade was contrary to an act of the General Assembly for supporting the garrison at Oswego and regulating fur trade.[16] Evidently he was doing enough business to embarrass the Albany interest, and his ventures there were resented.

Later Thomas Butler and J.B. Van Eps, at Oswego, wrote Johnson for boatloads of goods, seeking to pay him in furs.[17] Thus he began the transport of trade goods by the water route, which was to be the highroad of all his ventures. Built and outfitted at Schenectady, these sturdy boats carried a substantial cargo and had a crew of at least three men. Fortified with rum, which was their principal wage, the "battoe-men" made a hardy and resourceful crew. As they proceeded up the Mohawk, these craft encountered a series of rifts, or rapids, over which they were forced by poles and ropes, sometimes hauled by men on shore. As they reached the Little Falls, "a descent in the river of forty feet in half a mile, boats could not be forced up the current, and it became a carrying place for them, and merchandise, which were transported around the rapids on wagons with small, wide-rimmed wheels, the water craft launched and reloaded to proceed onward."[18]

Having ascended the Mohawk, the bateaumen made the principal portage, to Wood Creek, on which they then floated their craft to Oneida Lake. At this "Great Carrying Place" they commonly found some of the German settlers ready with horses to carry goods and boats to the other stream. In 1754 there was a protest by some of the "Traders (or Handlers to Oswego)" that the Indians along the route fell upon them with knives and axes and forced a kind of toll in rum from each, even compelling them to employ Oneida Indians at a high price at the Carrying Place.[19]

The portage from the Mohawk to Wood Creek, about a mile over a small ridge, which required only an hour's time for an Indian with a birchbark canoe, took considerably longer for bateaux and their gear and larger cargo.[20] That horses and wagons were used suggests the size of the boats, which carried perhaps four or five tons in weight. Having reached Wood Creek and relaunched their boats, traders found a tortuous stream with rifts and obstructions. Some years later military engineers built a dam and sluice gate to provide sufficient water to float laden boats over the rapids. Yet a traveller then reported that so winding was the route, that "from Canada Creek to Oneida Lake is 10 miles, but by the Windings of the Creek is 30 miles."[21] Once the lake was reached, however, there was good navigation, albeit close to the shore lest one encounter the squalls for which that body of water is well known. The outlet of Oneida Lake, the Oneida River, soon joined the outlets of the other lakes, the Cayuga, Seneca, and Onondaga, in the stream known as the Onondaga (later the Oswego) River. Here the combined waters provided fresh currents and rippling rifts which bore canoes and bateaux swiftly along toward their destination. But one major obstruction lay ahead.

It was on this stage of the route that the naturalist John Bartram, on a canoe trip with geographer Lewis Evans, recorded the nature of the river:

At three o'clock we came to the last mentioned river [the Oneida] down which the Albany traders come to Oswego, half a mile further we came to a rippling, which carried us with prodigious swiftness down the stream, soon after we encountered a second, and a mile further a third, very rough.

In about an hour by the sun, after many other ripplings, we found ourselves at the great fall, the whole breadth of the river which is above 100 yards wide and is eight or ten feet perpendicular; here we hauled our canoe ashore, took out all our baggage, and carried it on our back a mile to a little town, of about four or five cabins; they chiefly subsist by catching fish and assisting the *Albany* people to haul their *Bateaus,* and carry their goods around the falls; which may be about ten or twelve poles, then they launch again into the river, and down the foaming stream that furiously on all sides dashes one half against the rocks near a mile before they come to still water, and indeed it runs pretty swift all the way to Oswego.[22]

The bateaux, especially when heavily laden with trade goods, encountered more difficulty, but the later traveller, cited above, found adequate facilities had been provided at the portage:

The batteaus at this place [Oswego Falls] are carried 30 yards on rollers into the river below the fall, which for about a mile is full of rifts which make the navigation dangerous and often exposes the goods in the batteaus to damage by water. We were informed that in coming up the river the batteaus must be unloaded at this place. Here there is a small fort and saw mill, both of which are abandoned. The Fall is 16 feet high, and makes a fine appearance. The river at this place is 250 yards wide. Twelve miles below this is Lake Ontario, Oswego, and Fort Ontario. In this river are two or three dangerous rifts, but so well known to the batteau men that seldom any accidents happen.[23]

Whether Johnson travelled this route during his first venture in Oswego trade is not evident in the few references in his papers. But in spite of his earlier hesitancy in breaking into this traffic and over the opposition from the Albany traders, he soon became deeply involved. In a few short years his reputation as a trader grew, and he became the official supplier of the Oswego garrison. This was a route with which he later became extremely familiar and would journey over time after time.

The rapacity and greed of Indian traders, the Albany traders in particular, have been emphasized by many observers. Kalm especially told how the Indians at Oswego were frequently cheated and got but a tenth of the value of their goods, and that they were plied with brandy until they sold all for mere trifles. The traders, too, gloried in these tricks.[24]   Robert Rogers, the ranger, in his play *Ponteach*, characterized the trader Ogden as one who

> like an honest Man bought all by Weight,
> And made the ign'rant Savages believe
> That his Right Foot exactly weighed a Pound.[25]

And the Indian Records are replete with accounts of unscrupulous traders. These rough and often ignorant men were playing for the "fast buck," with no thought for the future. It soon became apparent to wiser heads that these tactics only bred trouble. Contempt for the Indian, the easy dupe, left no room for realization that the worm might turn, that the savage some day would resent his treatment. A wiser trader, indeed, would look to the future, and cultivate and win favor with his customers.

Perhaps Johnson at first fell in with the traders' ways; he sold rum, and even complained that the Reverend Barclay's measure to stop the liquor traffic would hurt business. But he was far-sighted—he wanted not just today's trade, but a continuing business. He consulted the Indian chiefs,[26] and he learned what the habits of the tribes were. He watched for his opportunities and therefore cultivated not only the goodwill of his neighbors, but of the Indians as well. Perhaps this made him unpopular with the older hands at the game.

Thus it came about that in eight years after his arrival, by 1746, while trade declined, and with it the interest of the English colony among the natives, the business of the young merchant had made him a man of affairs, and his trade with the Indians had won him their friendship.

IV

THE IROQUOIS

Whoever would treat with the Indian nations must learn not only what the Indian is like as a hunter and trader, but something of his social and political life, his traditions, his customs, and his vast heritage. Though the Iroquois had no written language, their tribal memory was prodigious, and they revered the deeds and customs of their forebears. They had developed patterns of conduct by which their policies were governed and which gave their group life continuity and stability. Yet the impassivity of the individual Indian belied the influence of this culture. The white man regarded him as a "savage" with primitive urges such as lust and greed, common to all mankind, but without the "refinements" of the European. In his way, however, he too had his finely woven web of cultural behavior which was expressed too often in acts which the white man thought "curious." Many observers developed a respect for Indian virtues, which they thought remarkable because unexpected in a savage. When whites became friendly with Indians they often found them loyal, courteous, dignified, honest, or courageous to a degree which put their more civilized brothers to shame. At the same time the misunderstandings of the clash of two cultures frequently brought out the vicious and brutal sides of both. Where understanding was lacking, there could be no real basis for friendship and mutual respect. Hence on the frontier both white man and Indian tended to degenerate.

It was to the eternal credit of William Johnson that, although surrounded by greedy traders and Indian haters, he developed respect for the Indian and learned to appeal to his better nature.[1] He did not despise the Indians' customs or way of life, and he could live, work, and dress with them as brothers. He learned their language, discovered their forms of social conduct and their government, and hence learned to work and speak in their terms. This sympathetic understanding of another people is the real basis of diplomacy. Thus Johnson rose above the rôle of merchant to that of diplomat and statesman.

The Algonkins of New England and of lower New York and Long Island made the first friendly contacts with Europeans and hence shaped the white man's concept of "Indians." After Champlain had made friends and allies of Algonkin tribes along the St. Lawrence, he was induced to fight his famous skirmish with their enemies, the Iroquois. Henry Hudson and the Dutch had friendly and hostile contact with the River Indians (Wappingers and Mahicans) and from them learned of their mortal enemies, the Mohawks. From these contacts arose the concept of the warlike, hostile Iroquois, and the traditional deadly fear of the Mohawk. It was not the Iroquois, but the white man who originated this idea. The contacts of the Dutch of the Hudson Valley, when they finally accommodated themselves to Indian trade and gave up the belligerent wars of Governor Kieft, were limited largely to Algonkin tribes. It remained for their successors, the English, to conciliate the Iroquois. And they naturally first met the Mohawks, the easternmost members of the Five Nations.

The French, on the other hand, after Champlain's initial sortie against the Mohawks, made further expeditions into Iroquois country as allies of the Iroquois' enemies. Hence there grew up the myth of an inveterate hatred between Frenchmen and the Iroquois. These early contacts undoubtedly shaped and directed later ventures into the backcountry, but they did not preclude friendly relations between Frenchmen and Iroquois, nor did they insure friendship for the English.[2]

About the year 1300, western and central New York were occupied by the Iroquois nations, who later formed a confederacy. A beautiful legend describes the founding of the league by Deganawidah the lawgiver and Hiawatha the diplomat, who persuaded the warring nations to come together and plant the great tree of peace. They sought out the wicked and vindictive Ododarha, the cause of tribal dissension, and "combed the snakes out of his hair." The great white pine tree, with its spreading branches and roots, was the symbol of their peace, and the longhouse, the council of sachems (chiefs), was their governing body. The confederacy was known as the Five Nations, or Iroquois Confederacy, and considerable autonomy was enjoyed by its members. These nations were the Mohawks, or "Keepers of the Eastern Door"; the Oneidas, or "People of the Standing Stone"; the Onondagas, or "Hill People"; the Cayugas, or "Swamp People"; and the Senecas, the "Keepers of the Western Door."[3] Within the nations, society was divided into clans (called Wolf, Turtle, and Bear, etc.). These governed the Indian's social relations, marriage, inheritance, and parental authority on a matrilineal basis. They indicate the importance of family councils and of the women in making important decisions.

Each nation had its *longhouse* or governing council, and there was the central longhouse at Onondaga for the Five (later Six, with the coming of the Tuscaroras) Nations, in which fifty sachems sat as representatives. These civil sachems who governed in council and kept the Great Peace were distinguished from the warrior chiefs, who were originally of lesser importance.[4] It is significant that Sir William Johnson was taken in as a Mohawk sachem, since his chief work was in government and negotiation in keeping the peace. Decisions of the longhouse were unanimous, the result of long consideration and much oratory. Yet on many questions the nations could not agree, and there were many instances of nations making war and peace independently.

The Iroquois Confederacy as a strong governmental organization has been hailed by some as responsible for the great power of the Six Nations. Others have pointed out its lack of unanimity and therefore have looked for other causes. It is quite evident that by the eighteenth century, Indians had been greatly influenced by contact with white men.[5] They no longer relied solely on skins for clothing, and they were fast losing their primitive ways of hunting and fighting. Guns and powder were taking the place of the bow and arrow, the spear, and the tomahawk. Their economy was changing. Many of the Iroquois had become agricultural people, with settled villages and tilled fields. The white man, however, urged them to hunt in order to provide skins for traders and for the European market. Their tribal wars, which often started with murders and affronts to individuals or families, now became conflicts over hunting grounds, not for subsistence, but to obtain the pelts for trade with the whites. And to other urges was added the appetite for liquor and the consequent degradation of the Indian.

From the time of the Dutch rule in New York, the Indians were forced into the fur trade. The principal market was for beaver skins, and when these could not be supplied by neighboring Mohawk tribes, these Indians acted as middlemen to bring furs from the Indians to the westward. By 1640 beaver were scarce in central New York, but the Dutch traders at Albany were engrossing the fur trade from distant areas.[6] The Iroquois nations developed routes of trade which brought furs from their principal suppliers, the Hurons. When sources of supply were cut off or interrupted, the Iroquois fought to control the trade. A series of Beaver Wars (1647-75) enabled them to dominate their neighbors and to establish a kind of hegemony or "empire" over subject tribes. Successively they defeated their ancient enemies the Adirondacks and Mahicans. The Senecas drove the Neutral Nation (so called by the French because they were between them and the Hurons) from western New York, extended their sway over Huronia (north and west of Lake Ontario and Lake Erie), and the tribes of the Ohio Valley and the Susquehanna. In these exploits they developed a power and tradition of warfare which helped them to rule and dominate their neighbors for a number of years.[7]

In reaching out for the supplies of furs in Huronia, the Iroquois encountered the French *coureurs de bois*, who ranged far inland through the lakes and up the Ottawa River, channeling the supply of peltries to Montreal and Quebec. Soon the Iroquois fell to raiding the canoe fleets which carried the year's furs to the French posts. The French in turn cultivated the supply tribes—the Hurons, Neutrals, Tobacco Nation—and sought to turn them against the Iroquois. The French now took the aggressive part against the Iroquois tribes, and through the latter seventeenth century conducted a series of raids into the Iroquois country. Thus the French tended to drive the Six Nations into the arms of the English. It was this situation which confronted the provincial government when it sought by negotiation to improve its relations with the Indian tribes.[8]

Dutch relations with the Indians had not been harmonious. In 1622 a Dutch official at Fort Orange was persuaded to join a force of the Mahicans against their enemies, the Mohawks, and was badly defeated. He and three of his men were killed by the Mohawks; one of them "they devoured, after having well roasted him."

Governor Kieft seemed bent on a war of extermination of the Indians of the lower Hudson, which proved so disastrous as to occasion his recall. And Peter Stuyvesant, plagued with other troubles, was forced into a punitive war, but finally made a treaty of peace at Esopus in 1658.[9]

One exception among the Dutch was Arent Van Curler, a connection of the Van Rensselaer family, who came over as a minor official. Near the end of the Dutch period he made contacts with the Mohawks, who recognized his honesty and sincerity and chose to deal with him in preference to Dutch officials. Because of this success he continued his role of intermediary after the English took over in 1664, but was accidentally drowned in Lake Champlain in 1667. The Indians called him "Corlaer" and later applied this name to successive governors of New York.[10]

Dealing effectively with the Iroquois Nations, as distinguished from trade and barter with small groups or single Indians, was an art learned by few. It meant placing the good of the community above the immediate profit of the individual, and it had to recognize the nature of Iroquois society and the springs of interest which governed. One had to live near, or among the Indians; he had to learn something of their tongue, or at least their figures of speech; and he had to observe their forms, particularly the condolence ceremony, and to acquire some of their patience in overcoming divided counsels. Misunderstanding might result from poor and misleading translation of the Indian tongues. Few traders, who often served as interpreters, acquired more than a rudimentary knowledge of one dialect, and might not be aware of the variants, even among the six nations of the Iroquois Confederacy. Furthermore these interpreters were often crude, unlettered men themselves, quite incapable of the responsible diplomatic tasks thrust upon them.[11]

As the consequences of Indian relations became evident to the governor and councillors in New York, delegation of the actual conduct of affairs was given to officials in Albany. The mayor and the magistrates there, being near the tribes, as was Van Curler of Schenectady, were felt to have a particular interest and more insight. At the same time, however, they were all fur traders who saw in these affairs no conflict of interest. Hence it was fortunate that the first mayor of Albany, after its grant of a charter from James II in 1686, was Peter Schuyler (1657-1724), and that the town clerk was his brother-in-law, Robert Livingston (1654-1728). On these two men fell the responsibility for Indian affairs for some forty important years. Schuyler was a man of character who was able to win the trusting confidence of the Indians. Even after his term as mayor expired, he was employed by the English governors to negotiate with Indians; he managed to win their confidence and to keep them friendly. They returned the good faith of the man whom they called "Quider."[12]

In 1710, in order to solicit more aid and concern for Indian affairs, Peter Schuyler and Colonel Francis Nicholson visited London with four sachems, commonly called "Four Kings," who were presented at the court of Queen Anne. They were lionized, fêted, and their portraits were painted in colorful costumes, arousing much interest. One named Hendrick, became more famous in later years as a leader of the Mohawks and a friend of the English. Another, surnamed Brant, was supposed to have been the grandfather of Joseph Brant of the American Revolution.[13]

Their visit so impressed Queen Anne that she resolved to promote Anglican missions among the Iroquois. She sent over Bibles, prayer books, and communion plates for her "Chapel of the Mohawks" and "Chapel of the Onondagas."[14]

Robert Livingston (1654–1728), an ambitious young Scot who had been driven to the Netherlands due to the political views of his Calvinist father and who had come to New York in 1675, was the next most important figure in dealing with the Indians.[15] With his knowledge of the Dutch language he was a useful person in the early days of English rule. First secretary of the Colony (or Manor) of Rensselaerswyck, he also became town clerk of Albany and *ex officio* secretary of Indian affairs. From Governor Dongan he received two grants of land, which he maneuvered into an enlarged claim, later known as Livingston Manor. Through these offices he became a key figure in government, and through his accumulation of wealth as a merchant he was able to lend money to the governors for public measures. Finding it difficult to collect these advances, however, he sailed to England in 1696, and there persuaded the ministry to make the Indian secretary of the province a permanent official with a salary of £100. Continuing in the office until his retirement in 1721, Livingston had a hand in all Indian affairs of his time. He assisted at Indian conferences, translated speeches (in Dutch, English, or Indian language), and kept the records which became the basis for Indian claims and for the formulation of Indian policy. Had he been less ambitious and avaricious in the promotion of his own great estate, Livingston might have become a great diplomat in dealing with the natives.

The first governor to show real appreciation of the power of the Iroquois was Thomas Dongan, sent over by the Duke of York in 1683. An Irish Catholic of good family, he enjoyed the confidence of the Duke and was better fitted by training and experience than most such appointees. He was given few instructions, save an injunction not to become embroiled with the French governor of Canada.[16] In spite of this, he took a strong hand vis-à-vis his opposite number and challenged French domination of the Iroquois. Jesuit missionaries had made converts and established a foothold among the Onondagas and Senecas, and this bolstered the claim of the French governor, who called them his children and sought to control their trade. Dongan also noted that the new charter of William Penn for Pennsylvania threatened encroachment upon the territory of the Iroquois. Hence he decided to cultivate the Five Nations and to make them the wards of the English. He journeyed to Albany, held council with the sachems of the Nations, and spoke in the name of the Duke and the King of England. When the Iroquois and the French were engaged in hostilities, he took the side of the Confederacy and advised them how to strengthen their position. By treaty he brought them under his protection and gave them the arms of the Duke of York to set up in their castles. Most noteworthy in his policy was the treaty of 1684, when Lord Howard Effingham of Virginia met the chiefs of the Five Nations in Albany and made peace with the Iroquois, who thereby endeavored to restrain their subject peoples in Pennsylvania and Virginia. They buried the hatchet in the corner of the courtyard in Albany and thanked Governor Dongan for his mediation.[17]

French Jesuit missionaries had made early advances in their attempts to convert the Iroquois. The saintly Father Jogues and others had labored in spite of hostility and torture. In 1646 Jogues was endeavoring to make peace between the Indians and the French when the Beaver Wars broke out with fury, and he suffered martyrdom. Father LeMoine and others briefly (1654–58) held a mission on Onondaga Lake, Ste. Marie de Gannentaha, but fled in anticipation of a fresh outbreak.[18] The savagery of the Iroquois raids upon the canoe fleets going to French Canada, their success in defeating and subjugating the Hurons, Petuns, Neutrals, and Eries led the French governors to seek reprisals. Courcelles and de Tracy in 1667 raided the Mohawk villages and destroyed their corn. Denonville in 1687 invaded the Seneca country and struck a crippling blow. In retaliation two years later the Iroquois surprised the French on the St. Lawrence in the massacre of Lachine. Now the counterblows seemed to parallel the war in Europe, and French and Indians in 1690, in retaliation for Lachine, burned Schenectady and killed or carried off its inhabitants.[19]

The enmity which these attacks seemed to indicate was mitigated on both sides by efforts toward peaceful exchange. Since 1669 French Jesuits had drawn Iroquois converts to a colony on the south bank of the St. Lawrence, and by 1680 two villages of transplanted Iroquois here each had a population of two hundred. One, largely Mohawks, was named Caghnawaga after their old village of that name. These Iroquois allies of the French were reluctant to fight against their relatives of the Five Nations.[20]

Likewise the Dutch *handlers* of Albany, middlemen in the Indian trade, kept up their intercourse with Montreal merchants. They could sell trade goods to Canada cheaper than the French could get them elsewhere, and in return Canadian pelts flowed to Albany. In the eyes of the New York governor—who was cultivating the Iroquois—as well as in the view of the New York Indians—who wanted to handle the fur trade to Albany—this was an illicit arrangement.[21]

Now the French governors sought to counteract the Iroquois hostility, abetted by the English, by appealing to the English king. They also appealed to Governor, Dongan as a Catholic not to oppose the French missionaries. The astute governor, however, realizing that the Jesuits were being utilized to further political aims, countered by offering to bring English Jesuits to the Iroquois and by proposing that the "praying Indians," the Mohawks at Caghnawaga, should be brought home to New York.[22]

Thus Dongan laid the foundation for the later Indian policy of New York. The Treaty of Utrecht (1713) was to confirm his protectorate over the Five Nations, by which New York gained an enduring claim to their territories. As the historian Edward Channing wrote: "To him [Dongan] must be given the credit for first seeing the importance of the position of New York and the Iroquois in the international politics of North America."[23]

The English colonies were convinced not only of the seriousness of the French threat, but of the necessity of the Iroquois alliance. As Dongan had wisely said, "These Five Nations . . . are a better defence to us, than if they were so many Christians." And the secretary of Pennsylvania, James Logan, wrote, "If we lose the Iroquois, we are gone."[24]

Now came the first of the intercolonial wars in which hostilities in America reflected the wars in Europe. The Iroquois, however, were more interested in peaceful trade than in being a buffer between English and French. They preferred peace with both sides and neutrality in wars which did not concern them. By 1701 the Five Nations made peace with the French at Montreal; they did not agree to fight against the English, but rather to remain neutral. The French agreed not to wage war upon them.[25] This came as bad news to the English governors, for it made possible in the years to come the steady encroachment of French traders on the territory of New York, with or without Iroquois approval. But to the Dutch traders of Albany it made easier their clandestine trade with Montreal. Thus was the policy of the province of New York doubly compromised; first by the neutrality of the Iroquois and their friendship with the French, and second by the commercial interests of Dutch traders in Albany. Some of these same traders were the colony's commissioners for Indian affairs.

Hence for years the Indian policy of New York was devoted to checking the French influence. It was with great alarm that the commissioners reported increasing inroads of French traders in central and western New York. French agents came down from Lake Ontario to the Onondaga Indians for their trade and sought to wean them from the English. Lawrence Claessen, the interpreter sent out by the Albany commissioners in 1707, told how five French priests gave presents to the Onondagas; that the French supplied smiths to repair their arms gratis; that traders set up their houses for barter; and that they planned posts at Niagara and at Onondaga, where they built a blockhouse.[26]

The governor tried to win over the sachems, who met him in Albany, but without success. Finally Peter Schuyler was sent to Onondaga to exhort them, but he found it difficult to equal the French in gifts and services. He destroyed the blockhouse of the French, but the Indians demanded ammunition and smiths to work among them. "You have destroyed the Fort which was just now built, but if Pouder & Lead keeps so dear with you how shall we defend ourselves if Attacked, with Bows & Arrows we cannot. Let us not want Pouder & Lead."[27]

The visits of the English agents were countered by the longer residence among the Indians of the Frenchman "Jean Coeur," as he was called—really the elder Joncaire.[28] He was, indeed, a formidable foe, whose intrigue and stratagems were the more effective in that he, like the coureurs de bois, really became one with the natives. Joncaire came to America as an officer of marine and may have accompanied Frontenac. On an early expedition he was captured by the Senecas, was adopted by them, and married a Seneca squaw. He learned their language and customs and thus acquired great influence among them. About 1700 he was sent by the governor of Canada on a mission to the Senecas to obtain the return of prisoners. From this time forth he spent much time in the Indian country, sometimes as agent and negotiator bearing presents for the Indians, sometimes as a trader, always promoting the French interest and undermining the efforts of the English. When a French Indian named Montour became an English agent, Joncaire on orders murdered him. His missions took him to Detroit and the Illinois country. To control the trade of the "far Indians" the French desired posts in the west and particularly had designs on Niagara, a key point on the trade route. Joncaire early made efforts to gain this and other strategic points for the French.

But his conduct was equivocal. He was a braggart and so assured of his own position that he seemed absolutely fearless. The French suspected him of double-dealing, of making huge profits in trade with the Indians, and of diverting government funds or presents to his own use. Yet he was invaluable to them and a constant threat to the English.[29]

During Queen Anne's War, strenuous efforts were made by both French and English to keep the Iroquois as their friends. Joncaire dwelt among the Senecas, and Longueuil was said to have an equal place among the Onondagas. In 1711, however, the English planned an expedition against Canada, and Schuyler enlisted some eight hundred Indians to fight against the French. Some were River Indians and from other tribes, but they were mostly from the Five Nations. They marched as far as Wood Creek, inlet of Lake Champlain, when the commanders learned of the British fleet's destruction in the St. Lawrence and had the expedition turn back. This was a great blow to British prestige with the Indians. They spoke frankly: "Bretheren we have now tried twice with you to go to Canada in order to reduce it to her Majesties Obedience, We are therefore now so ashamed that we must cover our Faces." [30]

The Treaty of Utrecht confirmed the British protectorate over the Five Nations, but the struggle for the Indians' trade went on. Longueuil and Joncaire, the latter bringing his little son, came up the river to Onondaga with canoes loaded with goods, and threatened to build a fort which this time Schuyler could not tear down.[31] The French, to control the western trade, planned to build forts or trading houses at Irondequoit on Lake Ontario and at Niagara. The English protested all these steps, but the Indians argued that it was in the power of the New York governor to stop the French. When Governor Hunter in 1717 met ten sachems of the Five Nations at Albany, one put it this way:

That the French have built no fort at Irondequat belonging to the Sennekas, but that they have built a Trading House there & supply the 5 Nations & other Indians with Pouder & Lead to fight against their Enemies the Flat heads, & that thay are also furnished with other Goods wch prevents a great deal of Bever & Furrs coming to Albany, but says Dekannissore, the French are supplied with all their Goods from the People here at Albany wch goes first to Canada & from thence up Montreal River & so to Irondequat where the French Trading house is built upon Ground belonging to the Sennekas; if you stop the Trade of Goods being carried hence to Canada that other Trade will fall of Course.[32]

The Indians seemed willing to take the advice of the English; they suspected that Joncaire was a spy, and they reiterated that French buildings were made without their consent. But the French continued their expeditions across Lake Ontario to Niagara. They intercepted furs intended for Albany and sought to forestall that trade. In 1720 the much discussed trading house was built at the Niagara Falls portage and was occupied by Joncaire. Known for years as the *Magazin Royal* it was an effective outpost for French trade.[33]

Immediately the English sought to have the building removed. Myndert Schuyler and Robert Livingston, Jr., went to the Seneca country, and Lawrence Claessen bearded the French traders and told them that since the Iroquois chiefs did not sanction this building it should be torn down. The French refused; Claessen told the Senecas in council that the governor of New York would get this building demolished. But these threats could not be carried out, and instead rumors came that this was to be the base of future building.[34]

The Albany commissioners had not succeeded in thwarting Joncaire, and now the task fell to the new governor, William Burnet (appointed in 1720). He sought to recapture the trade of the western Indians, which Joncaire's store was designed to intercept. First he got a law passed to stop the trade in Indian goods to the French to the northward. Then he proposed to build a blockhouse at the mouth of the Onondaga River (Oswego) where traders could meet the Indians from the west. It would be "a Beaver Trap," which would catch the pelts otherwise destined for Montreal. The Onondagas eagerly approved, though they suggested a post on Oneida Lake, which quite obviously would not do. Oswego was established in 1727.[35]

Now Joncaire again entered the picture, advising that with the English at Oswego it would be necessary to fortify Niagara. But how could this be done without arousing the suspicions of the Iroquois? The Senecas and Onondagas were persuaded to give their consent to a new trading house, being told that the old one was inadequate. While these negotiations were still in progress the French were making preparations for building a stone fort. Two barques loaded with workmen and materials came in 1726; and in 1727 the "Castle," which still stands today, was erected on the strategic point formed by the Niagara River and Lake Ontario. The Indians knew they had been tricked and protested, but the French were obdurate.[36] Governor Burnet charged violation of the Treaty of Utrecht and asserted that the French were encroaching on the lands of the Senecas, the wards of the English. But the French contended that the English never held Niagara; and were not the English seizing land at Oswego? Burnet now resolved to strengthen and fortify the post at Oswego. He sent workmen to build a stone house, or fort, with consent of the Six Nations, and a detachment of sixty soldiers to protect the building. This the French governor protested, and he even sent a detachment to warn the English and to demand that it be demolished. So each side took an aggressive diplomatic stand; both sought by show of force to intimidate the other and to influence the Indians in their favor.[37]

It was not long before the English could report that Burnet's policy was bringing results. A good trade with the western "far" Indians passed through Oswego, where as many as one hundred traders went yearly. In fact, the fur trade of the province by 1740 had grown to five times its former size.[38]

The wily Joncaire now tried a stratagem. He appeared among the Senecas as a fugitive from Canada seeking asylum, for they had protected him before and he was one of them. He asked only that he be permitted to earn his livelihood by building a trading post at Irondequoit, on Lake Ontario one hundred miles west of Oswego, midway to Niagara. This was a little too obvious, and Lawrence Claessen, the interpreter, promptly asked why, if he was a fugitive, he was accompanied by French soldiers. Did the Iroquois need more proof of French deceit? Had they not always asked for simple trading houses, which they later converted to forts?[39]

But try as they would, the emissaries of the commissioners seemed unable to thwart the French agents. "French Men ... resided amongst the Sennecas, that they give 'em presents, drink with them, Dance with them & make use of every possible Artifice to engage their Affections, wch they have so far effected that the French have built a House among them at ye. side of a Creek between Two of their Castles."[40]

French priests were active, and Joncaire was inducing sachems to visit Canada and trying in every way to win approval for his house at Irondequoit. To check this influence one Myndertse was sent from Albany as a permanent resident among the Senecas.[41]

Finally in 1739 Joncaire died; but even in death he was a menace, for the sachems proposed to go to Canada to condole for one who had lived so long among them. The interpreter Claessen went among them, called them to a meeting at Albany, and informed them that the governor "would take it extreamly ill to have them absent in Canada condoling the Death of a Man who had ever been an inveterate Enemy to this Colony."[42] They decided not to go.

It was but a brief calm before another gathering storm. Anglo-French rivalry was to erupt in King George's War; another Joncaire was to carry on the pattern of intrigue begun by his father; and the Indians of the Six Nations were to be equally displeased with the English and the French. Into this struggle—for trade, for Indian friendship, and for land—there came a new force in the person of William Johnson. Conforming to the needs of a new country, he in turn shaped the course of its history.

V

DOMESTIC AFFAIRS

As a settler and trader living in a new house built on the north side of the Mohawk River, William Johnson needed a wife, a helpmate and consort, to provide the household and family so necessary on the frontier. A bit of folklore had him acquiring his mate by forcing a neighbor to sell him an indentured servant.[1] There was but little truth in the yarn, but it was often retold and elaborated until it gained some acceptance. It is now possible to fill out the story with some detail.

Catherine Weisenberg was indeed an indentured servant, but she was a runaway from New York who probably joined her friends or relatives among the Palatines in the Mohawk Valley, and she was found there by William Johnson in the summer of 1739. In Zenger's *New York Weekly Journal*, January 22, 1738/9, there appeared the following advertisement (printed a second time in the issue of February 5);

RUN away from Capt. Langden of the City of New-York a Servant Maid, named *Catherine Weissenburg*, about 17 Years of Age, Middle stature, Slender, black ey'd, brown Complexion, speaks good English, altho a Palatine born; had on when she went away, a homespun striped wastcoat and Peticoat, blew-stockings and new Shoes, and with her a Calico Wraper, and a striped Calamanco Wraper, besides other Cloaths:

Whoever take her up and brings her home, or secures her so that she may be had again, shall have *Twenty Shillings* Reward, and all resonable Charge; and all Person are forewarned not to entertain the said Servant at their Peril.[2]

Captain Richard Langdon, mariner of New York, made several voyages between that port and London in his ship *Oswego* in 1738. It is quite likely that he had as passengers indentured servants, Palatines who had come to England earlier and thus had acquired a command of English. Bound for their passage, these Palatines could have their indentures either sold by the captain or—most likely in the case of a household servant—retained. Thus did Captain Langdon keep Catherine Weisenberg, until she made a break and ran away to join relatives, friends, or at any rate, other Palatines in the Mohawk Valley.[3] What could be more likely for an attractive and high spirited young woman? She next appeared in the neighborhood at Fort Hunter.

William Johnson, now 24, saw something he wanted in this slight, dark-eyed German girl of 17 and lost no time in taking her to wife. She could speak "good English" and no doubt had other attributes which had commended her to Captain Langdon. If William knew she was a fugitive, if perchance she had found employment on the Mohawk, or if she merely found refuge with friends or relatives, it did not matter. She had placed many miles between her and her former master. But it could be a reason for not formalizing a marriage. There was no union by marriage with William Johnson in the register of the Reverend Henry Barclay at Fort Hunter, and when her first child was born in 1740, as well as when her two other children were baptized later, she was plain Catherine "Wysenbergh" (later spelled "Wysen Bergh" and "Wysenberk").[4] Sir William Johnson later referred to her as his wife, and she so served him with honor until her death. That he held her in affection and honor was testified to many years later by the references in his will. If, as has sometimes been asserted, there was a later ceremony, no record of it has been found.

Catty kept the house, possibly assisted in the store, and soon provided William with his first child. Ann, or Nancy as she was generally known, was probably born on May 26, 1740. She was baptized "Ann Daughter of Catherine Wysenbergh," on June 8, 1740, at Fort Hunter. In an affidavit made in 1800, when she was the widow of Daniel Claus, she averred that she "hath alway understood and doth believe" that she was born on May 15, 1739.[5] She no doubt erred about the year, for her mother appears not to have come to the Mohawk Valley until 1739; and the date of baptism favors the year 1740. May 26 would be the same as May 15, Old Style.

In about a year a son, John, the future heir, was born and duly baptized at Fort Hunter, "Febry. ye. 7, 1741/2." On January 27, 1819, Sir John gave his birthdate as November 5, but his age as 76, which would make the year of his birth 1742. On the day of his death, January 15, 1830, his age was given as 88. This would give the date of birth as 1742. Since he was probably correct on the day of his birth, though confused as to the years of his age, we conclude that he was born November 5, 1741, and was baptized the following February.[6]

Mary, later known as "Polly," was baptized October 14, 1744, and hence was Catty's third child.[7]

So in a few years there was a little family of five residing at Mount Johnson, the house north of the Mohawk which Johnson had built in 1739. The growing trade on the river, the shipments to Albany and New York, the barter with the Indians, and the dispatch of traders to Oswego or the Susquehanna occupied so much of William's time, however, that he gave little attention to mother and babies. Others did not forget her. In 1741 after he went to sea, Michael Tyrrell, who had made the initial trip up the Mohawk, sent his "Best Respects . . . to Catty and all that Inquire for me."[8]

An eighteenth-century husband was content with a wife who was seldom seen or heard, especially if he was a man of affairs and she beneath his station. Her interests were in the household, so Catty made little impression on the records of the time. Perhaps she was regarded by her husband as a social inferior and was not known to share in his interests and entertainment. This, too, may account for the ambiguity of her marital status.

Lack of notice in Sir William's papers led to a mistake about the date of her death. An earlier biographer, William L. Stone, thought she died in 1745, because in that year Johnson was invited by James Willson to occupy "a room" in Albany, with no mention of his wife or family. Yet family tradition had it that Catherine died in 1759, and this is supported by several facts. On May 23, 1759, Peter Wraxall, writing from New York, commiserated with Sir William on his loss. "When I left you I thought there appeared little hopes of Mss. Katy's Life. I condole with you thereupon & I hope Miss Nancys management of your House will supply the Loss you have Sustained." That her death and funeral occurred in April is attested by Sir William's purchase of crepe from Daniel Campbell in that month, and reference in Campbell's letter "concerning preparations for a funeral." Shortly after this Molly Brant, the Indian housekeeper, is noted at Fort Johnson.[9]

The question of the legitimacy of his first-born children was of little concern to the frontier merchant and landholder. In this rugged world the facts of life counted for more than literal observance of legal formalities. William could not foresee his title, nor was he at this time ambitious for social recognition. He was making something of himself, as well as a profitable trade, and as he became known as a public figure, domestic affairs receded, or were turned over to others.[10]

While the children were small, Catty was assisted in their upbringing by her mother. This was the grandmother, or "Granny," so affectionately referred to at her passing by John, then a young man abroad.[11] Occasional references to the "old woman" by Johnson and his correspondents show that she was a constant member of the household.[12] A frequently cited description of the strict and secluded upbringing of the two girls, Ann and Mary, by a governess, "the widow of an officer who had fallen in battle,"related by the garrulous Mrs. Anne Grant, has no confirmation in the documents.[13]

Kith and kin were constant associates of Johnson at his Mohawk settlement. Among the first families who accompanied him were Irish neighbors and relations, some of whom soon left for other ventures. Michael Tyrrell, his cousin, went to sea with Captain Warren on the *Squirrel* and wrote enthusiastically of his experience, though somewhat nostalgically of those left behind. With him were also Jack Pain (?), Pat Flood, and Messrs. Hall and Tattan, who were probably among the initial group of immigrants.[14] Six years later his brother John wrote to William asking "what became of Patt Flood & James Rogers."[15] But Patrick Flood turned up later in New York and sought Johnson's certificate of character; as given it was none too enthusiastic: "I have known the Man these Sixteen Years past [since 1739] and cant Say I ever knew him guilty of any Villany."[16] Thomas Flood, perhaps a brother of Pat, was to serve Johnson as overseer for some time, not always soberly and with satisfaction.

When word of Johnson's success and prosperity reached Ireland, relatives and friends sought his help, and others planned to migrate. Brother Warren, likewise a favorite with Uncle Peter Warren, was encouraged by the latter to enter the army. He anticipated seeing his brother when he arrived in America but went first to

Boston, where Uncle Peter sent him to recruit a company for service in Canada. He hoped it would be all Irishmen. One Irish friend, James Rogers, he made "a serjeant," but the ranks filled up slowly and he asked his brother for "ten or twelve able bodied Men" to be sent to Boston for him. Finally in October 1746 he reported his company of a hundred men complete; but in midwinter he was in New York, and the expedition to Louisbourg was deferred. He found time to see his brother, probably in Albany, without getting to Mount Johnson.[17] But in all this he asked few favors from brother William, for whom he expressed the greatest affection. He then returned to Ireland, family, and friends, and was closely associated with Uncle Peter until the latter's death in 1752. Brother John wrote to William, while Warren was with his company at Wexford, that "Sr. Peter takes notice in his letters that he hopes Warry will prove a good man."[18]

Sister Catherine had married Matthew Ferrall, and this worthy in 1750 "was obliged to give up Buissness & advised by our Friends in the County Meath to go to you for your protection & hope you'll shew him some Countenance upon her Account. She's now Settled with my Father & Sir Peter Allowe's her 20£ a year."[19] Matthew made out all right, became engaged in the Indian trade, and by 1754 was joined by his wife. But Catherine was sickly and died the next year, after her husband had lost his life in the Lake George campaign. Yet Catty was the means of mollifying the family back home for William's oft-chided neglect in correspondence.[20]

Far less acceptable was Silvester Ferrall, who left Ireland under a cloud to mend "his tattered fortunes by your means." He had run up debts of more than a thousand pounds, before he skipped his bonds and left Christopher Johnson to face a suit for £200. But he was a rolling stone who did not stay.[21]

More stable was Robert Adems, a merchant's clerk from Dublin, who acted for years as Johnson's bookkeeper. It was his young wife who was entrusted with Johnson's letter and gifts to his father in 1754, while Robert and Matthew Ferrall were trading with the Indians. With Robert, too, came his brother William, who in later years was known as a doctor.[22]

These Irish friends and relatives were clannish and gossipy. They longed to have a little transplanted County Meath on the Mohawk. Before his affairs became so complex, William Johnson delighted in their company, was indulgent with their failings and impositions, and proved a rallying point for all his countrymen.[23]

He was not adverse to a convivial evening, and once apologized for his failure to make a call on Jacob Glen by saying that he was forced by "the Company who were with me, to Stay so long with them that we all gott Merry."[24]

To care for the growing needs of his family and for the expansive entertainment which friends, relatives, and visitors to his establishment were constantly demanding, Johnson needed a small retinue of servants. Negro slaves he had from the first, some having been brought from Boston.[25] From time to time he traded for slaves, and even ordered some when a shipment arrived in New York.[26] These were generally employed as household servants or specially trained for specific tasks. Aunt Susan Warren desired a Negro for a coachman, and William promised to train two for this service.[27] Others might qualify as helpers for a blacksmith or to care for horses.

White indentured servants also could be bought, and there were other servants who were hired for their skills or ability. The Irish girl, Jane Watson, having been a servant for Johnson, went on to New York to work in the household of Governor Clinton.[28]

Soon the one-and-a-half story house which he built north of the Mohawk in 1739 and which was named "Mount Johnson" was too small for the growing household. Across the river on Warrensburgh were the tenants of Peter Warren, with their servants and slaves, and as new settlers came along and took up land, houses were scattered along the north bank.[29] It seemed time for William Johnson to branch out. His Oswego trade, his dealings with the province, and his mounting influence demanded a new establishment commensurate with his needs. His acquisition of adjacent land had not lagged, and he could select an excellent site for his new house.[30] Farther up the river, it is the location since known as Fort Johnson.

Like his first house, it had the advantage of facing the river with a narrow strip of bottomland suitable for cultivation. In later years there were said to be thirty acres of cultivable land. The ground rose abruptly in the rear, as it did behind his other house, and this may have been his reason for retaining the name "Mount Johnson." It was not very accurate, but in those days any bit of rising ground could be dignified as "mount."[31]

In the midst of many duties in the winter of 1748, he laid plans for his new home. Urged by the governor's secretary to pay a visit to the city of New York, he declined giving this as his excuse.

"Now I am busy prepareing all Materials to build me a good House next Spring. which must deprive me of that Happiness, as I am oblidged to be present to forward the Work."[32] At the same time he wrote to the Bakers, London agents, for certain "trifles . . . and of a good Sort, as they are for a House which I am building for my self & that thy may the better know what Sort, & Size I shall give you the dimensions of the House, which is 60 foot long, by 32 Wide two Story High, all Stone."[33]

Only the best materials were to go into this substantial stone structure. The roof was to be of either slate or lead, and he asked for estimates for the cost, including freight from England. But much of the material could be assembled during the winter, especially stone and timber. No doubt his experience in this construction supplied the details written down by brother Warren ten years later. "My Brother gets Lime Stones carried, ten Miles, upon Sleas [sleighs] , at Nine Shillings currency per Load."[34] He already had his mills nearby, and "A good Saw-Mill saws, in 24 hours, 16 Logs of 13 Boards each, at 1s. per Board"[35]

Next summer he was hiring the craftsmen; "A Carpenter has here 8s. per Day with Meat & Drink & Common Men [laborers] 4s. Current." "Brick burners have 5s. English per Day."[36] And then he reported to Uncle Peter, "I Am busy to build me a good Strong Dwelling House in the Mohawks by my Mills, all of Stone."[37] Later, during the period of warfare, it was to be equipped with wings, fortified with barracks, and renamed "Fort Johnson." Work progressed until Johnson was able to move into the house in January 1749.[38]

His mills were in operation before the house was begun, and—judging from the usual practice—other outbuildings, houses for servants and slaves, were constructed at the same time, so that soon the new Mount Johnson was a bustling community, and its appearance much as described by a French observer in 1757:

Col. Johnson's mansion is situate on the border of the left bank of the River Mohawk; it is three stories high; built of stone with port holes (*creneleès*) and a parapet and flanked with four bastions on which are some small guns. In the same yard, on both sides of the Mansion, there are two small houses; that on the right of the entrance is a Store, and that on the left is designed for workmen, negroes and other domestics. The yard gate is a heavy swing gate well ironed; it is on the Mohawk River side; from this gate to the river there is about 200 paces of level ground. The high road passes there. A small rivulet coming from the north empties itself into the Mohawk river, about 200 paces below the enclosure of the yard. On this stream there is a Mill about 50 paces distance from the house; below the Mill is the miller's house where grain and flour are stored, and on the other side of the creek 100 paces above the mill, is a barn in which cattle and fodder are kept.[39]

This description comports well with the drawing by Guy Johnson, engraved and printed in the *Royal Magazine* of 1759. There were two blockhouses which Sir William built late in 1758, when the enemy threatened to attack the nearby settlement. In these he could house a garrison of forty men. The outbuildings included a cooper's house; a bakehouse; a pigeon house; a mill with a millrace running from the mill dam to the mill; a sheephouse; and a very large barn with stables. In the formalized drawing, Mount Johnson rose abruptly, "very high and steep," across the stream from the house. At the foot of the mount was the Indian council house, a single gabled barn with lean-to sheds on either end; small tents were indicated for visiting Indians. The fields included were a garden between the house and the river, cornfields, and a pasture. Several islands in the river were a part of the property. In the distance, at the bend of the river, were shown his former home and its barn.[40]

The management of such an estate required constant attention, so that during Johnson's frequent and sometimes protracted absences on public business he delegated the work to others. Eventually he was to have an overseer, or bowmaster. During one such absence, in January 1754, he left detailed instructions:

Memorandum of Such things as I would have done Untill I come Home again—
. . . What Grain You receive [in payment of debts owed him] to Store it Safe in the bake House wh. keep locked always, and let Wolfe put Some Boards for lineing in ye. Inside They may Store Wheat in ye. Mill at the North End thereof.
To let the Negroes take Good Care of all the Cattle & feed them well also to ride Home all the Hay from the Old Farm, the Oats of the Island & the Wheat [*as fast as possible.*] Rest of the Negroes to keep Cutting & Clearing the Side of the Road at the End of the Stone Wall quite to the next Bridge. When it is good rideing after they have done bringing home the Hay, Wheat, & Oats, then let them ride Home the Stones from below round the Wall here, and also the Stones out of the feild, beyond the Bridge for a fence, to be laid Streight—. . . as soon as the Skow is finished let the Hands fall abt. rideing Home ye. Wheat as fast as possible, and feed all the Creatures plentifully with ye. Straw of it. and to bring home all the Turnips. very good care to be taken of the Breeding Mares, & the Colts, & Calves &ca.
A Shed of Boards to be made for ye. big Mare in ye. Barrack Yard, & to have her taken Good Care of.— . . .
If there should be good rideing you can get up ye. Cyder from Albany and the Slays to bring down Pease, & Store it at Bentheusens.— . . .
To send the ps of Chains that are here to ye. Smiths to get them putt together and fastened to the Skow and keep her locked on the Island only When they want

to use her, by no means to allow any body to use her but Just for carrying of ye.
Grain from the Isleand—
    If there should be much rideing yet, you can Store pease on ye loft of the New
House, gett ye. trap Door neiled down, and Hinges & a Lock on ye. Door at ye.
Gable End—done Shingleing ye. top of ye. New House which will be done in a Day
or two.—
    To have some Loggs laid under the Bak House
    To secure the Store House in Case of Need.[41]

Midwinter chores, of course, depended much upon the condition of the roads
for sleighing, for "rideing," for lack of snow and periods of thaw would hamper
travel. The river, too, would be frozen over during cold weather. The "skow"
could be used when the ice broke up.

Warren Johnson, visiting during the winter of 1760-61, left many comments in
his journal of the effects of the excessive cold, so unused was he to this climate.

It freezes there soe hard in One Night as to shut up the Rivers, on which One
may walk the next morning. . . . Decemr. 28th, it was soe cold as to freeze almost
any thing even by the fire's side: The frost is soe intense, that if you walk in
Leather Shoes & Gloves, you are frost bitten.[42]

That indeed was a winter of excessive cold; rum and Madeira froze in the cellars;
houses could not be kept warm, and bread froze so it could not be eaten. Troops
marching two miles were frostbitten and lost toes and fingers; in bed people were
cold even with ten blankets on. "This is as Severe a Winter as hath been for some
years." But he learned too the advantages as told him by the residents.

tho always cold they would chuse in winter to have a hard frost & snow on the
Ground, 'tis Wholesomer; & they can the more Easily ride down their Corn on the
Ice to Albany, and bring their Fireing [firewood] home.[43]

A thaw, and rains, however, could change the picture and make the roads
"scarcely passable." Snowshoes were necessary in the woods until late in spring;
horses then could be ridden, though one was careful of the river ice—still capable
of bearing the weight of men and horses. On the Mohawk, life was often conditioned by the weather, which made life interesting, if hazardous. "March the 23d.
A Thaw, about 9 'Clock this Morning the Mowhawk River broke up at Fort Johnson, the Ice carried every thing before it, & really appeared dreadful."[44]

The household was quite as busy as the farm, and during his absence a set of
instructions, perhaps for a new housekeeper and maids, was drawn up. Although
only a fragment of the paper remains, it gives a picture of the care bestowed and
the standards maintained in this fine residence, not only for the family but for the
guests:

    [   ] be done at Supper [   ] always clean, with Candles fitted [   ]
Chamber maid to make all the beds [   ] lighted up in the Bedchambers at
Supper time [   ] with Water & a Towel be placed in each lodging [   ]
Slippers & a Chamber utensil—

The H. to be washed Twice a Week beginning at Daylight [   ] parlours, & proceedg to the Bed Chamrs after the Family [   ] The Laundry Maid beside the Family Linnen is to see that [   ] in readiness, a proper set of Table Linnen, Towels [   ] &ca.[45]

Warren Johnson was amazed. "More Custom at fort Johnson than any Inn in England from the Number of Regular & Provincial officers passing by every Day, as the River Mohawk is within 40 yards of the Door."[46]

It was not only the officers, although they were special guests in view of Johnson's military rank, but all kinds of travellers stopped and found a generous hospitality. The missionary Gideon Hawley, accompanied by Deacon Timothy Woodbridge, seeking help for his work among the Indians, came in 1753. "At sun set we were politely received at Colonel Johnsons gate by himself in person. Here we lodged. His mansion was stately and situate a little distance from the river on rising ground, and adjacent to a stream which turned his Mill. . . . Mr. Woodbridge and I took our leave of him in the Morning. . . ."[47]

Not only lodging for the night, but sports, music, and polite society of the ladies were mentioned in letters of appreciation. "The Company with whom I was so agreably entertained at Your house, often talk of it, Drink Your health, and join with me in present thanks and acknowledgments, and we make boast of the Pidgeon Shooting Match all the Day long."[48]

Entertainment varied from the convivial drinking bouts of Irish compatriots to the more polite gatherings attended by ladies.. After one of the latter Johnson wrote reprovingly: "If Paddy is at York pray give my Service to him . . . the young Indian Ladies [and] the Albany Ladies here upon hearing he was an Irishman, are ever Since quite out of Conceit with my Countrymen for they say he is An out of the way Animal Wherefore I could wish he would improve a little before he comes again among so polite a Sett of Ladies."[49] Some visitors, indeed, were smitten with the feminine society. Joseph Chew wrote, "I hope the young Ladys at the Castle are well my Compliments to little Miss Michael at the Mohaws & madam Curl'd locks at Conejesharry."[50]

A group of Irishmen far from the Emerald Isle could not fail to celebrate their patron saint, and St. Patrick's day was never overlooked at Johnson's. In 1747 they drank to the health of Governor Clinton "& all freinds in Albany wth so many other Healths, that I Can Scarce write."[51] Warren Johnson recorded that for 1761. "March the 17th. cold frosty Weather, A great Meeting at my Brother's House to drink St. Patrick, & most got vastly Drunk."[52]

Such bacchanals as the Mount afforded sent some of these devotees of the Liquid God on their journey with a standard hard to equal. Thus Samuel Cramer in April 1750 recorded in hilarious fashion the exploits of his party at other stops along the route to New York. There was much to read between the lines in the account of their conduct, but he apologized for "a Long detail of Nonsense which must Grate your [ears] , " and concluded with their compliments. And he left behind a "ruffled Shirt in the Room."[53]

Indeed, William Johnson appeared to love the role of country squire, genial host, and proprietor of a growing estate. His boast to Uncle Peter in 1749 showed his eagerness to acquire property: "I have purchased one of the best Houses in Albany last Winter, and another in Schenectady, also a very good, low land Clear Farm adjoining to the one I live on. I thank God my Estate begins to increase."[54] The Albany house in High Street was a two-story brick house, with good yard and stables, and could be used by him or his family as they journeyed eastward, or to New York. For a while his sister, Catherine Ferrall, with her husband Matthew, occupied it; after her death, he established a housekeeper in charge.[55] In addition he acquired a "Water Lot" with a frame house, and subsequently more land in Albany. The Schenectady house, too, was a convenient stopping place, and a base from which he could carry on his business there.

VI

MILITARY ADVENTURES

William Johnson's success in trade and his growing stake in the Mohawk Valley were soon reflected in other activities, the beginning of his public career. It was but natural that the merchant on the river should so expand his enterprise that even military expeditions could not pass him by. His contact with traders soon introduced him to government, and his trade with Indians gave him insight and *entrée* among these omnipresent wards of the state. An English writer, commenting on his career, noted that

he, till lately, traded largely as a merchant with his *Indian* neighbours, and more especially with our *Indian* traders, who go every spring from *Albany*, and other parts, to *Oswego*; where multitudes of Indians from distant regions assemble and barter skins for European commodities. These the principal traders used to take from Sir Wms. store; on credit, as they passed by his door in their boats on the Mohawk River in their way to Oswego; and pay for them on their return, the ensuing fall, in the goods they got in exchange.

Few merchants had faith like him, to trust large effects in the hands of young raw and unexperienced men, whom he chose to encourage for their industry; indeed few could, none having such a capital, nor any in the country so large an assortment; add to this, that his house, very properly called Fort Johnson, is situated 30 miles back from Albany by land, a great way farther by water; which considerably lessened the expence, trouble and time of traders and consequently enabled them to deal to better advantage. But what rendered him of more utility in this respect, was, that in all his transactions he ever acted with so much openness and integrity, that those who once dealt with him thought themselves happy in improving the correspondence.[1]

This Oswego trade, which Johnson at first thought too competitive for him to enter, had burgeoned after the establishment of the fort there by Governor Burnet. Colden wrote:

At this Place, a very great Trade is carried on with the remote Indians, who formerly used to go down to the *French* at *Montreal*, and there buy our English goods at second Hand, at above twice the Price they now pay for them at Oswego.[2]

Furthermore the Six Nations Indians found that when many traders (some three hundred in one summer) were at Oswego the "Goods are sold Cheap, but when there is but a Trader or two, they are cheated, . . . & instead of pure Rum they receive half Water."[3]

This competition and thriving trade caused the French to renew their efforts among the Six Nations and to threaten to destroy the post at Oswego. So it was reported by a delegation of Onondaga sachems who returned from Canada in 1740, and the English sent the interpreter Claessen to get their disavowal. Reassured, they could only get the Indians' statement that they wished to be neutral. Now the Indian commissioners demanded that the governor "enlarge & Strengthen the House at Oswego by some Fortifications."[4] The Indians gave their consent, and a small garrison of one officer and twenty men joined the commissary stationed there. Still the French traders and a smith resided among the Onondagas and managed to keep the Oswego River route open.[5]

In June 1744 war was declared between the French and English, and both sides sought to keep the Indians neutral. The Caghnawagas of Canada invoked their neutrality treaty. Governor Clinton of New York at a conference in Albany called upon the Six Nations to keep their warriors at home and to stay in their compact castles. On the other hand, he said, it was now necessary for more cannon and soldiers to be sent to Oswego, which was a bulwark of strength for their protection.[6]

The war did not immediately impair the Oswego trade; in fact warlike preparations and reinforcements meant an increase in river traffic as supplies and troops moved to the fort. In September Thomas Butler wrote Johnson, "I gave you some Small acct. of the French being on their way hithr. but find since it hath been a false Alarm. I dont now in the least suspeckt that this place will be atacked, as the Five Nations Seem to have it at Heart."[7]

Governor George Clinton, however, had no such feeling of security. Oswego was not only a prime trading post; it was also of strategic consequence, and Clinton had sufficient military experience to know it. Other points were to be fortified, but Oswego should be held at all cost.[8]

From the beginning of his administration he had urged that reinforcements and adequate supplies should be sent to Oswego and that a suitable person be employed to do this. The Indian commissioners demurred that no one would incur the expense at his own risk, and that the Assembly had not been willing to vote funds.[9] In this extremity, Clinton now found the man for the task in the young trader, his fellow countryman, William Johnson, who also had a considerable stake in the Oswego trade. They had much in common and were each to gain by the association.

George Clinton had come to the governorship in September 1743, with no experience in administration or knowledge of his duties. He had spent his whole life in the navy and was better suited to command than to negotiate. Thus he turned for advice to one who was well acquainted with provincial politics, Chief Justice James De Lancey.[10]

Clinton was described as "easy, good natured, unambitious, and somewhat given to high living."[11] De Lancey, according to Colden, not only had the advantage of his high office to recommend him to the governor, but "his disposition to good fellowship, which suited the Governors humour." Clinton dismissed the Assembly and immediately made several appointments to the Council, who turned out to be relatives or cronies of De Lancey. Among these were Captain Peter Warren, the uncle of William Johnson, and Jeremiah Van Rensselaer, "the patroon."[12] Thus it may be seen that the governor would not be unaware of the young trader on the Mohawk and may even have seen or heard of him on his first trip toward the frontier.

In April 1745, Johnson was appointed justice of the peace, his first public office and a recognition of his importance in the community. When Clinton had his second Indian conference at Albany in October 1745, he may have seen the young "squire." However, next spring the governor and Assembly "agreed that I shall Supply the troops at Oswego"; but he remarked of "the little notice I have had."[13] He stated that it would be well done and with expedition. He set about it at once and soon had his agents scouring the countryside for cattle. Thomas Butler reported:

That day I came from home got to Mr Fetterleys bo't two Kattle of Van Alstine yesterday. Yesterday I was al over Stone Robie and bought all the Kattle that was good to be found. last night left at Wormwood's where I bought three. I have now in all bought thirty Seven. I think very good oxen. Excepting two cows which are about six years old and good. I am now going over the River to one Countreymans where I hear is two large oxen. The remainder I proposed to buy at the Flatts. . . . I shall send you from the great Flatts an Acctt. of all the Kattle bought. I have ordered the people to drive up the Kattle next fryday to Herkemans and think to sett them of ye. Next day for Oswego.[14]

Wagons were rolling over the roads from Schenectady, and bateaux poled slowly up the river toward the Little Falls portage. Jacob Glen of Schenectady helped supply the boats, and others along the route cooperated with men and supplies. The energy and resourcefulness displayed by the young Irishman on his first task for the government commended him to those in authority, who did not hesitate to employ him further.[15]

The sequel to all of this was the difficulty of reimbursement, which had plagued others. Frontiersmen often kept poor records and had to be reminded. Johnson wrote John Lindesay at Oswego, "You would Send me down Receipts. . . . They must always mention the Quantitys of provision as Allowed by Act of Assembly. otherwise they will not pass."[16] The next month he wrote Clinton: "I have agreable to your Excellcys orders Sent the Provisions, and Releif to Oswego, which as it was Unexpected, put me to a good deal of Difficulty and needless Expence. yet should not so much mind that, could I but get my money regularly payed, which the Province is Justly indebted to me."[17]

In the meantime Johnson was assigned a new duty by Clinton, the management of relations with the Indians, which was to open a new career to the young trader.

How was it that this newcomer to America, this greenhorn of a frontiersman, who should have been more at home among clodhoppers and bogtrotters, became so soon a friend and confidant of the "savages" of the forest? Could it be his Irish openhanded generosity, his freedom from cant, or from restraints of military life?

Was it the contrast between his friendliness and the somewhat crabbed and grasping commercialism of the Dutch traders of the area? He had a rugged and straightforward way which belied all suspicion of deceit. He liked to deal man-to-man, and he showed a genuine respect for the other fellow, whether of high or low estate. He could be frank and demanding; he could tell off his opponent with rough candor, while at the same time he required respect. His success with the band of Irish settlers showed qualities of leadership. But above all his was a warm heart with an honest love for his fellow man.

The American Indian, for all his cruel savagery, his lust and greed that frequently led to his corruption and degeneracy, was as ingenuous as a child. There was a childlike wonder and simplicity about him which craved affection and understanding. At his best he was honest, truthful and generous. Hospitality and brotherliness, loyalty and respect for friends and family had been inculcated for generations. And he appreciated these qualities in others. While he often appeared stupid to the white man and was taken for a dupe, he frequently sensed the true nature of the white man and saw through his pretense. He quite as easily recognized worth according to his own standards. He had no prejudice based on color or race, and he readily adopted the white man for his brother.

So William Johnson, who never recorded his first impression of the Indians, was proud of the fact that these natives accepted and trusted him. In his first letter to Peter Warren he twice mentioned his consulting with Indian chiefs, and he stressed the value of their trade.[18] (Other traders talked only of the value of the pelts to be gathered.)

The Indians in turn were wont to show their goodwill for the white man by giving him a descriptive name. Thus the governor had become "Corlaer" after Van Curler, Peter Schuyler was "Quider," and William Penn and his successors "Onas" (a quill). Johnson's Indian name, "Warraghiyagey" (variously translated as "doer of great things," "much business," "Chief big business") was really given to him as a trader. Daniel Claus, who knew the Indians and their tongue and, as a contemporary, well knew the Johnson story, related that the Indians were amazed at his rapid clearing of the forest and development of a settlement so that they "took Notice and gave Sr. Wm a Name in their Language applicable or signifying a great & toilsome undertaking." As his enterprises expanded the name was taken to signify much more. Brother Warren wrote in 1760 that "Warraghigagey signifies A man who undertakes great Things."[19]

The title of *sachem*, often honorary and conferred with little éclat, may well have been given at this time. In the Six Nations government, a sachem was an administrative chief, not a warrior, and was distinguished for his wise counsel. This then was in keeping with the growing respect and confidence of the Indians which Johnson enjoyed.[20] This rapport was not known only among the immediate parties, but was widely known and commented upon. When war broke out, his influence was known to the French and their Indian allies, and a reward was offered for his head. James Willson heard that "the french have told our Indians that they will have you Dead or alive."[21]

It was natural that Johnson should become associated, first of all, with his neighbors the Mohawks. "Keepers of the Eastern Door," they had traded with the Dutch in Albany, become allies of the English, and sold land to the Palatines who settled in their valley. Young Conrad Weiser, from a Palatine settlement in the Schoharie Valley, spent the winter of 1712–13 living with the "Maquas," learning their language and thus qualifying as an interpreter.[22] The Albany Indian commissioners found the Mohawks on their doorstep and so more numerous at the various conferences held in Albany. Yet it was clear even then that the council fire of the Six Nations burned at Onondaga, and many journeys were made there by such agents and interpreters as Lawrence Claessen, Peter Schuyler, and Robert Livingston. It was natural that the first missionaries from the east found the Mohawks among their early converts. The Jesuits in the seventeenth century had worked among them, and had induced numbers to migrate and settle under their protection on the St. Lawrence. Now the English missionaries in the eighteenth century made Albany a mission center and later under royal patronage established Queen Anne's Chapel at Fort Hunter.[23]

The reputation of the Mohawks for ferocity and warlike temper dated from their early history, but it persisted for many years. They had conquered and subdued the Mahicans and had intimidated the New England tribes. Colden wrote that the very name *Mohawk* was enough to strike terror among the Indians of New England.[24]

But if the Mohawks appeared the most savage of the nations, they were among the first to admit civilizing influences. Of the four sachems selected to go to England with Peter Schuyler in 1710, three were Mohawks, and on their return, with the blessing and aid of Queen Anne, they did not lose their influence but continued in the councils of the longhouse.

Of these none was more famous or influential than Hendrick, Tiyanoga (c.1680–1755), who with his brother Abraham received the surname Peters. From the term applied while in England in 1709–10, he was often called "King Hendrick" by the English, although such a term bore no relation to his place of distinction as a sachem. Fêted, clothed with elaborate costume and presents, and having their portraits painted and widely published, these Indians might easily have had their heads turned. Hendrick visited England a second time in 1740, when his portrait was again made, showing him in laced coat and cocked hat, with upraised tomahawk. In it something of the ferocious Mohawk was conveyed in his scarified countenance.[25] But Hendrick had become a convert to Christianity, showed talent as a preacher, and dwelt at Canajoharie, the Upper Castle of the Mohawks. From here he was to participate in numerous conferences, to journey to New England and to Pennsylvania, and to serve as a principal spokesman for his people. Already aged and a veteran of many adventures, he was a vigorous orator and a redoubtable opponent.[26] That Johnson won him as a friend and loyal champion was to prove a keystone of English strength among the Iroquois. He was one of the greatest Indians of American history.

As an orator Hendrick had few peers among his people, and his powers of persuasion were well known. This was observed by Dr. Alexander Hamilton in 1744, when the Massachusetts government brought some of the Mohawk chiefs to Boston.

We were called to the windows in the Auction Room by a noise in the Street, which was occasioned by a parade of Indian Chiefs marching up the street with Colonel Wendal. The fellows all had laced hats, and some of them Laced Matchcoats and Ruffled Shirts, and a multitude of the plebs of their own Complexion followed them. This [sic] was one Henrique [Hendrick], and some other Chiefs of the Mohocks, who had been deputed to treat with the Eastern Indians bordering upon New England. This Henrique is a bold, Intrepid fellow. When he first arrived at the place of Rendezvous, none of the Eastern Chiefs were Come, however, he Expressed himself to the Commons to this purpose: "We the Mohocks (said he,) are your fathers, and you, our Children. if you are dutifull and obedient, if you brighten the Chain with the English our Friends, and take up the Hatchet against the French our Enemies, we will defend and protect you, but otherwise, if you are disobedient and Rebell, you Shall dye, every man, woman, and Child of you, and that by our hands, We will Cut you off from the Earth, as an ox licketh up the grass."

To this some of the Indians made answer that what he said was Just, as for their parts they would do their best to keep their end of the house in order.

"It is true you are our fathers, and our Lives depend upon you, we will always be dutifull, as we have hitherto been, for we have Cleared a Road, all the way to Albany betwixt us and you, having cut away every tree and bush, that there might be no obstruction. You, our fathers, are like a porcupine full of prickles, to wound such as offend you; we, your children, are like little babes, whom you put in cradles and rocked asleep."

While they delivered this answer they appeared very much frightened. and in the meantime one Lewis, an eastern chief, came upon the field, who seemed to reprove Henrique for delivering his embassy to the common people while none of the chiefs were by, telling him it was like speaking to cattle; but Henrique with a frown told him that he was not obliged to wait his conveniency and time, adding that what was said was said, and was not again to be repeated, but do you or your people at your peril act contrary to our will. At that the other Indian was silent and durst not speak.[27]

With the outbreak of war the Six Nations held a kind of balance of power between the English colonies and the French. Their location in New York, as Dongan had shown, made them a buffer and defense if they could be kept friendly or neutral. Their tributary tribes in Pennsylvania, the South and the Ohio country, were also a source of danger, either from their own hostility or from the intrigues of the French among them. Strenuous efforts were therefore made to influence these Indians through the Six Nations.

Conrad Weiser had proved himself invaluable to Pennsylvania as an interpreter and intermediary with the Indians of New York. His good friend was Shickellamy, who resided at Shamokin on the Susquehanna and there served as a kind of viceroy (or half king) of the longhouse over the Delawares. Through him the Six Nations delegates had come to Pennsylvania to treat in the settlement of the colony's land claims. Then Conrad had made two perilous journeys to Onondaga on diplomatic missions, thus keeping the good will of the Iroquois which William Penn (Onas) had advocated but which his successors had so often violated.[28]

Now in June 1744, Conrad Weiser was the mediator, diplomat, and interpreter at the treaty formed at Lancaster, between the representatives of Maryland, Virginia, and Pennsylvania and the Six Nations. Sachems of the Onondagas, Oneidas, Tuscaroras, Cayugas, and Senecas journeyed into the Pennsylvania town and met the commissioners of the three colonies. The purpose was to remove Indian claims to some of the provincial territory, and also to insure that further outbreaks would not occur along the frontiers. For the Indians, in following the foothills of the mountains as they journeyed southward along the Tuscarora path, often fell in with westward-pushing settlers. Hence it was promised that the road would be kept open for the Indians, and the Six Nations, in receipt of presents, gave assurance that they would restrain their people and allies. But it was not possible to end the long war which raged between the Six Nations and the Catawbas to the south, which had occasioned the passage of war parties through Pennsylvania. Nor was it possible at this time to treat with the Shawnees of Ohio, who did not come to the meeting.[29]

The Indians, informed that war had been declared and that the English had already won an important battle, were asked to assist the English against the French. They promised to help the English; and they even hoped to influence the "Praying Indians" of Canada, who lived near the French governor, not to assist the French.[30] Like all such treaties, this was duly sanctioned by gifts—a hundred pounds of gold, rum, and laced coats for the sachems.

It will be noted that New York was not a party to the Lancaster meeting, nor were there any Mohawk sachems among the delegates. And because all problems had not been solved nor all tribes conciliated, there were to be other missions and treaties. Peace with the Indians was a continuing negotiation. The governor of Virginia wanted Weiser to go to Onondaga again in order to settle the matter of the Catawbas. He hoped that the Indians might be induced to send delegates to Williamsburg. This Weiser doubted, but he was willing to make the journey on behalf of Virginia and Pennsylvania. Then, due to the difficulty of the overland route to Onondaga, and also by his own inclination, he now resolved to visit the Mohawks, where he had not been since 1729.[31]

Both Pennsylvania and New York desired the services of Weiser. The former, because there had been a fresh outbreak of the Shawnees in Ohio; and Governor Clinton of New York sought his help to mollify the Mohawks, among whom there had spread an unfounded rumor that the French and English were about to destroy them. Weiser, his two sons, and several Moravian missionaries were warmly received at Onondaga; they visited Oswego, then went eastward to the other nations. At the Upper Castle Weiser conferred with Hendrick, Abraham, and Aaron (Arughiadekka)—the three most important chiefs. He told of his mission on behalf of the governor of New York, and they retorted warmly about their dissatisfaction with "the Albany People." They confirmed the story of the alarm spread among them but said they were convinced that it was false, and wished to forget about it. But the English governor continued to bring it up and to seek for the person who had spread the rumor. They did not care to punish any among them who may have been responsible. Weiser reported all these things to Clinton.[32]

Governor Clinton, who wished to be a strong governor and sought a vigorous prosecution of the war against the French, now found himself checked and frustrated. The Assembly in the first instance had heeded his requests for funds, and important support and supplies had been sent to Governor Shirley of Massachusetts for the attack on Cape Breton; and Captain Peter Warren's naval exploits had been warmly backed. Now, however, the Assembly became recalcitrant, the councillors were divided and failed to cooperate, and De Lancey, his confidant, was developing a faction.[33] Indian affairs, which he thought he had handled successfully the year before in conference with the Six Nations, were in a bad way. The confederacy was teeming with resentment against the greedy land grabbing of speculators, and the Albany traders were condemned for their high prices and their illicit trade with the French. Weiser's report of his visit to the Mohawk castles was disagreeable, nor was his advice heeded.[34]

There seemed but one alternative, to call a new Indian congress at Albany with representatives from New England and Pennsylvania to concert a vigorous prosecution of the war, and a rapprochement with the tribes. So in October 1745 the conference was held at Albany. The Six Nations, save the Senecas (who were at home condoling the loss of their leaders), with their leading sachems (Hendrick, Abraham, and Aaron from the Mohawk castles; and Canassatego, the Onondaga orator of the Lancaster treaty), 464 in all, met with Clinton and his councillors and the delegations from Massachusetts, Connecticut, and Pennsylvania. Jacobus Bleecker and Conrad Weiser were interpreters. The provincial delegates conferred and agreed that Clinton should speak for them.[35]

Disregarding the advice of Weiser, the governor brought up the matter of the rumor among the Indians that the English intended to destroy them. Who had spread the rumor, he asked, and why; was it merely an excuse of the Indians to exact concessions? Aaron as speaker replied that it was one Van Patten who had told them; but the English doubted the story. The Indians disliked this approach; they admitted they were misinformed, but now they wished to forget it, and why did Corlaer persist on this line? There were other causes for their discontent.

Hendrick, who conceded that he had believed the rumors, said there had been reports of such a plan from "Jean Coeur" (Joncaire), but that when the Indians sought an explanation from Wemp, the smith, they got no reply. He spoke for more than an hour, and the interpreters (said the official report) could make "Neither head nor tail" of the harangue. Since he resisted their investigation, the English felt he may have invented the story for a purpose.[36]

The Pennsylvania commissioners were uncooperative. Two were Quakers and insisted on wearing their hats at the meetings, or else they would walk out. They didn't want Weiser to interpret for the others, unless they gave their permission. They were afraid that the others sought to enlist the Indians in the war, which they opposed, and demanded that they treat with the Indians separately. Weiser did not agree with their pacifism.[37]

The Massachusetts delegates wanted the Six Nations to take an active part against the French. They had received a report of an attack by French and Indians on the fort at Great Meadow and wanted Governor Clinton to demand that the Nations take up the hatchet immediately. Governor Clinton realized that New York would have to supply the war parties and was not so eager for immediate action. Moreover, the Indians wanted time to ask their brethren the Caghnawagas, the French Indians, if they would remain neutral. Yet it was quite obvious that they were engaged in the hostilities for the French. Finally, Clinton had to be content with a conditional promise of the Indians' support; and as for the help Massachusetts desired, he would have to consult the Assembly.[38]

No one was really satisfied with the meeting. Indian affairs were in a far from happy state. Weiser, veteran of many conferences, and at this one in a detached position as interpreter, vented his feelings in a private journal. Clinton he viewed as a coarse, profane "Monster of a Man." And from his description James Logan of Pennsylvania wrote of the "Weakness, Sottishness & Dishonesty of the G—— of Y." Weiser and the Pennsylvanians disliked both the governor and his policy.

Pictures such as these stand out from its pages [Weiser's journal summarized by his biographer] : Governor Clinton damning the Indians to their faces; Governor Clinton disputing with Conrad Weiser and damning him also (by proxy; the Governor damned his secretary for letting him know that Conrad Weiser was right and the Governor wrong); Governor Clinton nagging the Indians about the "late alarm among the Mohawks;" Chief Hendrick interrupting him and speaking "very bold and rude" until Conrad Weiser took the Governor's wampum belt into his own hand and told Hendrick to "forbear and hold his tongue;" Governor Clinton declaring war "in the name of God" against the French, and throwing down a belt of black wampum with a war hatchet inworked; the old Chiefs restraining their young men (who wanted to dance the war dance at once;) and telling the Governor they would hide his hatchet in their bosom until the ways of peace had been tried further; Governor Clinton giving the Indians a present that had somehow dwindled in value from the £1,000 set aside for it by the assembly to what Weiser estimated to be a mere £300 worth of goods; a party of Mohicans waiting on the Governor with a present of venison and being damned by his secretary and dismissed without seeing him.

"Everything was by this time in confusion" writes Weiser. ". . . The Governor began to hurry away & the Indians asked him for a Barrel of Beer to drink, he damn'd them and sayd he gave them some the other day and order'd them a Barrel of Beer."[39]

The overt act which would bring the Six Nations into the war was not long in coming. The next month, on November 19, 1745, the governor received an express from Albany informing him that the French and their Indians "had cut off a settlement in this province called Saraghtoge about fifty miles from Albany, and that twenty houses with a Fort . . . were burnt to ashes, about thirty persons killed and scalped and about sixty taken prisoners."[40] The governor called for the Six Nations to honor their agreement and to end their neutrality, and he proposed to send the fusiliers to Albany. The Mohawk sachems in January came to Albany, renewed the Covenant Chain, and offered to send some of their warriors "to Lye this Winter at the rebuilt Fort at Seragtogha & to go on the outscout." Then the interpreter, Arent Stevens, was sent through all the Six Nations telling them that "the Hostilities committed at Seragtoga by the French & their Indians has put an End to all our hopes of Neutrality & that our Govr therefore has taken up the Hatchet against the French & their Indians & expects the 6 Nations as our Bretheren & fellow Subjects will join in the War & for their Encouragment the Govt have appointed £20–to be paid for every Male Prisoner taken from the French & £10–for every Scalp."[41]

Yet Stevens at Onondaga received a flat refusal from the Six Nations sachems to take up the hatchet against their relatives, the Caghnawagas. They said the Covenant Chain (their ancient alliance) was not broken, but they would remain neutral. The commissioners suspected that a French Belt (a message of wampum) was still among them, and that the same rumors as before were being spread. The Indians somewhat justifiably felt that the English were not prosecuting the war with vigor; they wanted to know why forts were not built at Cayuga and at the Carrying Place to protect them and their children. Why were they not consulted by the English as to their plans?[42]

At this juncture in the spring of 1746, Governor Clinton found himself almost completely thwarted. Granting his ineptitude, lack of tact, and personal faults, his was an unenviable position. Cadwallader Colden, a friendly critic, summarized his predicament:

His Excellency Governor Clinton, had perhaps more Difficulties to struggle with on this Occasion, than any Governor of New York had at any Time; The Six Nations had on several Occasions given Grounds of Mistrust; the Governor of Canada was attempting all the Means in his Power to divert their Affections from us; the People of the County of Albany had for some Time past, entertained a Dissatisfaction in the Conduct of the Commissioners for Indian Affairs; the Commissioners themselves were divided in their Sentiments, and Several of them refused to attend their Meetings; and they confessed to his Excellency that they had lost all Influence on the Indians.[43]

Raids by Indians along the frontiers increased, and panic seized the inhabitants of the frontier settlements. In April there occurred "the Barbarous Murder & Scalping of a principal Farmer at Schaahkook by the French Indians"; and in May came "several other Attacks Murthers & Scalpings." The farmers along the eastern side of the Hudson deserted their farms and came to Albany with their families for protection. At Albany too the "Inhabitants are kept in such constant Alarms & so wore out with Watching & going on the out Scout & as the Indians sit still & will remain Neuter unless a considerable Force be sent up from the Lower Counties to the relief of Albany the whole County will speedily be abandoned & the Inhabitants must leave it."[44]

The commissioners, finding that the governor had employed others to deal with Indians without consulting them, now wished to be dismissed.[45] This was no doubt desirable, but it meant that the governor had to go to Albany; and this he had little stomach for. Disease was rampant there, and he himself was sick.[46] Nor did Clinton have the backing of the Council when he went to Albany in July; only Philip Livingston and Cadwallader Colden, who replaced the intriguing De Lancey as his adviser, went with him. Because of the smallpox, which he had never had, and a malignant fever then prevalent, he remained on the sloop one night before daring to remove to the fort.[47]

The Albany conference of 1746 was a failure in every respect but one. It brought to the fore William Johnson as an Indian negotiator and thus marked the beginning of a new era in New York's Indian relations. Out of Clinton's frustrations and despair, his search for new and dependable counsel, and his real desire to press for an attack on Canada, came his recognition of this new figure who was to play such a large rôle in the future of the province. His liking for Johnson is not hard to understand. A fellow Irishman, who had no more love for the Albany Dutch than did the governor, Johnson was also a man of action. With no military or naval training, he had the very qualities which appealed to the naval commander. Furthermore, as they learned later, they both enjoyed a convivial cup, and Johnson was to toast the governor on the anniversary of St. Patrick.

The Oswego supply had shown Johnson's capacity and resourcefulness on the frontier. He knew how to find cattle for the garrison, how to barter with farmers and to dicker with traders, trappers, and Indians. With the latter he gradually won confidence and acceptance. He knew better than to tell them bluntly what he wanted of them, or what they ought to do. One rather helped them to make up their own minds. Becoming at home in their castles, learning to know the chief men, and probing their thoughts and feelings, one adapted himself to their train of thought. Then when some hostile influence was manifest among them, it was possible to turn their thoughts in the other direction. As Johnson wrote of his efforts, "I shall endeavour all in my power to keep them steadfast as possible and give them but little rest, ... till thy do some thing that will sett [them &] the French & their Indians by the Ears."[48]

Dismissing the commissioners and distrusting Philip Livingston, the secretary for Indian affairs, Clinton sent Johnson among the Mohawks, while Stevens the interpreter went to the other nations to bring them to the English interest. On June 23, Johnson wrote Clinton of his success:

I am heartily glad I can send you so good an account of our Indians at the Mohawk Castle, yesterday I went there and called them all together and told them how forward the expedition was at Cape Briton and would be so here likewise in a short time wherefore told them I hoped they would be as ready as well wh. would be the only way of recommending themselves to the favors of ye. Government & all their Brothers here and a great deal more too tedious to mention. Their answer to me was that they would all as one man join heart and hand to fight with us against the french our Common Enemy whenever called upon which I returned them my hearty thanks and gave them a fine large Bull of 5 years old Bread and Liquor equivalent wh. I think they deserved I never saw them behave so chearful before on any occasion they are to meet & receive the interpreter all painted feathered & dressed.[49]

When Clinton arrived at Albany, he learned of French plans for an invasion from Canada, as told by an Indian scout sent out by Johnson. Having travelled day and night to the Mohawks, and then from there to Mount Johnson, the messenger was sent to Albany with one of Johnson's men.[50] Sixteen Mohawks sent by Johnson to spy on Crown Point, to get prisoners, and to learn of the French strength, were so impressed with the forces there, and by what other Indians told them, that they returned empty-handed. Clinton replied to Johnson that these reports must have been "Artifices of the French to intimidate the Indians or to amuse them, with Design to frustrate the Treaty."[51] Yet reports of French influence were persistent.

The publick Interpreter, whom the Governor had sent with others, to invite the Six Nation to meet him at Albany, wrote to the Commissioner of Indian Affairs, That they met with great Difficulties and Obstructions from the Sachems, who had lately been at Canada; That the Oneydoes refused to give any Answer, tho' they had staid there thirteen Days endeavouring to persuade them; and that the Cayugas had absolutely refused to meet the governor. On which his Excellency desired to be informed by the Commissioners of Indian Affairs, whether they knew of any Person of Influence or Interest with the Indians, and fit to be sent among them on this Occasion. They answered, that they knew of none; and that the Indians were in a very bad Disposition and much under the Influence of the French.[52]

The commissioners were indeed at the end of their rope. Clinton wanted to send some of the troops to live near the castles to keep them loyal, but the rangers had not been provided with pay by the Assembly and would not go out unless Clinton gave them his personal bond. When they did go out they were so alarmed by newly discovered tracks that they fired their guns, thus giving warning to all French Indians in earshot.[53] There was only one bright spot in the picture.

While the Interpreter was at the more distant *Indian* Castles, *Mr. William Johnson* was undefatigable among the *Mohawks*; he dressed himself after the *Indian* Manner, made frequent Dances, according to their Custom when they excite to War, and used all the Means he could think of, at a considerable Expence, (which his Excellency has promised to repay him) in order to engage them heartily in the War against *Canada*.[54]

Thus Johnson "succeeded beyond what any Man in Albany thought could be done." Still, some of the sachems of the Upper Castle wanted to remain neutral. This was the French game; they had no hopes of winning all the sachems (though they had gained some), so they tried to prevent their helping the English. The best the interpreter could do was to persuade these sachems that they should come to Albany to hear what the governor of New York had to say. Even so, several stayed behind.[55] The story was graphically related by Colden, an eyewitness to much that happened, and a participant in some of these events.

When they of the more distant Nations came along with the Interpreter to the lower *Mohawk* Castle, and found that Mr. *Johnson* had already engaged many of the young Men there to join the Army against *Canada*, the others blamed the *Mohawks*; telling them with some Warmth, That they had been very rash in engaging so far. They ought, *the others said*, to have considered that they, the *Mohawks*, were the smallest in Number of any of the *Six Nations*, and ought not to have proceeded to so great a Length, without the previous Consent of the others.

To this the *Mohawks* answered, *It is true, we are less considerable as to Number, than any of the other Nations; but our Hearts are truly* English, *and all of us are Men; so that if our force be put to Trial, perhaps it will be found greater than you imagine.* These Disputes, however, continued so far, that the *Mohawks*, and the other *Five Nations*, would not go in Company to *Albany*; the *Mohawks* marched on one side of the River, while the other Nations went on the other side. [*There are two Roads from the* Mohawks *Castle to* Schenectada, *one on each side of the* Mohawks *River*.]

When the *Indians* came near the Town of *Albany*, on the 8th of *August*, Mr. *Johnson* put himself at the Head of the *Mohawks*, dressed and painted after the Manner of an *Indian* War-Captain; and the *Indians* who followed him, were likewise dressed and painted, as is usual with them when they set out in War. The *Indians* saluted the Governor as they passed the Fort, by a running Fire; which his Excellency ordered to be answered by a Discharge of some Cannon from the

Fort; he afterwards received the Sachems in the Fort Hall, bid them Welcome, and treated them to a Glass of Wine.[56]

Another witness of this dramatic advance of the Indians on Albany was Peter Wraxall, later to be Johnson's aide. Already, said he, Johnson "had the Honour of a Sachem conferred on him," and was "habited & painted after their manner."[57]

I was at Albany at this Meeting & it was then said that his personal Influence over the Indians was the great means of bringing them into the above Declaration of War, wch the Commissrs had vainly tried their utmost Interest to do.[58]

Colden, however, who was there as the governor's agent and member of the Council, and who delivered the governor's speech, took some credit. Two of the sachems of the Upper Castle (Canajoharie) could not be persuaded by Johnson. They were of the Tortoise tribe, not as numerous as the Bear; but some twenty years ago Colden had been received in that castle as a sachem, and now with the Reverend Henry Barclay as interpreter, he was able to bring these to be "as hearty as any of the others."[59]

That Johnson deigned to identify himself with the Indians as brothers, to don their dress and war paints, and to march with them to Albany was widely noted. If he demeaned himself in the eyes of the whites, he won great credit with the leaders of the Six Nations. Here was a man who did not take lightly his honor as a sachem. Others had exhorted them to take up the hatchet, as did the governor in his speech. But Johnson showed them that he meant to join them in the war by the acts which were most significant in their eyes. It registered the honesty and sincerity which were to be his strength in all their councils.[60]

The conference thus so successfully begun, however, was to prove a failure. Despite pledges of loyalty sealed by the Great War Belt and presents, and followed by the war dance, no general Indian campaign was possible. Some seven hundred Indians had congregated near Albany: now at least twenty got the smallpox, and many others were taken sick. It was thought necessary to send them home as soon as possible, for by circulating in town they spread the disease. A few were sent out as scouts to spy on the French and to bring in information. Embassies were sent to enlist the River Indians and the Oquagas on the Susquehanna. But even these became sick while in the woods a few days; others died on their way home, and fear of the sickness spread among the rest.[61]

An order was given to Johnson to enlist warriors to go out in bands and to harass the French. But as some of their ablest young men died and their numbers diminished, one of the chiefs who had promised to go out turned to him and said: "You seem to think that we are Brutes, that we have no sense of the Loss of our dearest Relations, and some of them the bravest men we had in our nation. You must allow us time to bewail our Misfortune."[62]

At the close of the congress, Governor Clinton laid upon Johnson the responsibility for translating the Indians' resolutions into action. He was empowered to equip whatever Indians would go forth against Canada with "Arms, Ammunition, Clothing & Provisions," with the assurance that upon rendering an account he would be reimbursed.[63] But leadership was also needed, so Johnson was made a colonel and given explicit instructions August 28, 1746. He was empowered to enlist "all such Christians & Indians" who would volunteer to go under his command, to pay the Christians two shillings a day, to issue commissions to men to serve under his command to lead the Indians, and to have power to discipline the latter. He was ordered to

send out as many Party's of the said Indians as you possibly can against the French & their Indians in Canada to harrass and Alarm their Quarters in all Parts and to take Prisoners for Intelligence as soon as may be, likewise Scalps, and for every such Prisoner or Scalp so taken of the Enemy, the Person producing the same shall Receive the Reward allowed by an Act of the General Assembly of this Province.[64]

Yet Johnson was to be more the organizer and diplomat than the leader. Wrote Clinton,

I am of Opinion that your residence among the Mohawks, will rather promote his Majestys Service, than if you was to go out with any Command Your self, You are therefore hereby required to reside near the Indian Castles in order to send out the Several Partys as aforesaid, and receive them, at their Return, And to give me Intelligence from time to time of what they have done & of what further Encouragement You shall think necessary for the Service.[65]

One party of seventy Indians and whites struck a French settlement north of the St. Lawrence, about ten leagues from Montreal, and brought in eight prisoners and four scalps. Another group of nine Indians openly used their friendship with the Caghnawagas to enter Montreal as though to negotiate, but to return with intelligence for the English.[66]

The English troops arrived in Albany in September, "Five Hundred Troops from the Jerseys & Four hundred from Philadelphia," which with those from New York amounted to two thousand. The four Independent Companies of New York, the only regular establishment in the colonies, were now formed into two battalions under the command of Lieutenant Colonel John Roberts, "formerly an Exon in the Horse Guards."[67] But the lack of a regular support for these companies, and the failure of the Assembly, in its hostility to Clinton, to appropriate money for their payment, jeopardized the command. When the new levies saw the Jersey troops being paid, but that no pay for them was forthcoming, they became mutinous.[68] Johnson was ready to bring up auxiliaries from the Mohawk country, but as he said he had "fixed on no certain time, fearing a Disappointmt." In fact, there was a great uneasiness among the Indians whom he had brought to such a willingness to join the expedition, "for they are almost in Dispair, or out of Patience so long waiting."[69] But they were limited to scouting and scalping and the bringing in of prisoners for intelligence. Thus the Crown Point expedition waited upon success in other fields of warfare.

VII

INDIAN DIPLOMACY

Winter came on, the smallpox epidemic subsided, and the Indians, having condoled their losses, were ready to go out. Saratoga, somewhat rebuilt, was an outpost of the frontier north of Albany, and there were hopes it could be fortified. In mid-March 1747 a party of thirty-two "Christians and Indians" was sent out by Johnson to intercept the French near Saratoga but found none. When Clinton wanted Indians stationed there Johnson told him it was not to their liking—"they never like to keep in a Garrison among So Many Christians." But they were "ready to go against Canada where they Say thy can do more Execution."[1]

Hence the principal activity of the "Colonel of Indians" was sending out scalping parties of the Mohawks against the French and their Indians. Bounties for scalps were offered both by the New York Assembly and the government of Massachusetts. Agents were sent to the other castles, up the river, to recruit warriors. All that was needed in addition to the promise of payment for scalps was to outfit the parties. This went on apace at Mount Johnson, where "Blankets, linnen, paint, Guns, Cutlashes &ca." were almost exhausted.[2]

These small parties were soon back again, claiming their rewards, which they expected immediately. Johnson had all of his houses full of Indians, some coming in, some waiting to go out; all were eager, and the aims which he had earlier expressed seemed well justified. In March he wrote "I am of opinion We shall make the french Smart this Spring by taking Sculping, & burning them, & their Settlements." He exulted that "My Peoples success is now the talk of the whole Country."[3]

This was well enough, but the Indians expected the governor to proceed with the promised reduction of Canada. To do so would require not only Indian parties but whites to serve as their officers. "Indian Shoes" were needed for them "with out which they cannot go through the Woods." Other supplies were lacking and the men themselves were slow to appear. They expected extra pay for this service, and it was really necessary for this exceptionally hard duty. Yet no provision was made, and Johnson suffered one disappointment after another.[4] As Indians flocked about him, expenses mounted:

There is one thing I Wish yr Excellcy would please to Consider of, wh is my Extraordinary Expence of keeping severall hands imployed to attend the Numbers of Indians I daily have at my house, these 12 Months past as also a Clerk who with Myself &ca, have more work than Man Can well bear.[5]

He called upon Colonel Roberts at Albany to detach a number of men of the regular companies for the expedition. Roberts reported that a council of war of the six companies' officers revealed that the camp was "very sickly," that the men at Fort Clinton (Saratoga) were mutinous, and it would not be safe to reduce his forces. He added weakly, "I have given some leave to go as Voluntiers. I heartily wish you Success and a pleasant March."[6]

Governor Clinton gave no encouragement. Earlier he had explained that it was well known that many of the richest men in Albany had engaged in trade with Canada in the past, did not want such an expedition, and would work to thwart it. Finally, hearing of Johnson's plans and resolution, of which he highly approved, he hoped that his previous letters had not been discouraging.[7]

The Colonel of Indians saw his opportunity. He and his men were eager, champing at the bit; the Indians were ready and demanding action. Let the faint hearts and the backbiters stay behind. He was going.

Here was the situation. A party of scouts sent to Crown Point found there "few French and but about 40 Indians." At Lake Saint Sacrament (later Lake George) they found "five or six hundred men encamped upon an Island." These were the source of raids against the English which had been doing much damage and eventually might "entirely ruin us."

"I am determined," wrote Johnson, "(with the general approbation of all the Indians) to march against them with about 300 Indians, and as many Christians most of whom are Volunteers; if I can but have the opportunity of meeting them, dont doubt giving Your Excellcy a good account of them, for the people are all in high spirits and the Indians quite eager for action." Even if he had no success, the effort would satisfy the restless Indians, terrify the French, and give the Six Nations a better opinion of the English. About twenty Senecas and Ottawas had come to his house and reported that their people were eager to destroy Niagara.[8]

On August 28, the expedition to Lake St. Sacrament was under way, now with "400 Christians mostly Volunteers and about as many Indians here present, besides vast numbers by the Road." So popular was the call for Indians to join, that more were expected, even Conestogas and Susquehannas, and a few men had to be left at Mount Johnson to fit them out. Twelve days at the most was to be the duration of the journey, and Johnson was probably home by September 10. No great success was reported. Now the problem was to keep these Indians in their present happy mood of service, for there were few supplies for them. It would be bad to "let such a parcel of fine stout Fellows go back again without employing them further."[9]

But the aggressive mood of the frontier was not reflected by those in command. Their eyes were on Nova Scotia, where all regulars were to be concentrated. In August Governor Shirley informed Clinton that the Canadian expedition was to be laid aside; efforts against Crown Point must be carried on by soldiers in the pay of the colonies without assistance from home.[10] To the Mohawk Valley this change in plans was shocking. Johnson resolved to present the Indian situation to the Council directly. On September 19, he set out for New York accompanied by ten sachems of the Six Nations.[11] On October 3, 1747, he was examined before the Council.

Perhaps this was the colonel's first visit to New York. He had applied himself so diligently in his own area that he had little time for such travel. Yet he came now not just as a frontier settler, but as a personality who had gained recognition. Governor Clinton relied heavily upon him for Indian relations. Cadwallader Colden, somewhat condescending at first, was beginning to credit Johnson's superior skill in handling the natives. Governor Shirley of Massachusetts began to rate him first in that field. And if these were not enough, the testimony of the Indians was to be conjured with. Flanked by the Christian sachems, among whom may well have been the redoubtable Hendrick, he commanded attention.

Somewhat impersonally he began by asking "that Some Person who has Influence over the Indians, Should be sent to Oswego, and entrusted with presents to be distributed among some of the Six Nations, and the Far Indians, In Order to preserve their present good Disposition."[12] He was well aware of the importance of this, for in his supply of the Oswego garrison he was compelled to pay double for transportation, due to recent hazards on the way.[13] Since he had taken over the management of Indian affairs a little over a year before, their sachems had been brought over from a reliance on the French to being "hearty" for the expedition against Canada. But they were now disappointed that it was not carried out; and since they had been kept from hunting during the summer, they wanted many necessaries for themselves and families. It would greatly encourage them "if two Fortresses were erected as Speedily as may be, One in the Senecas Country, and the other in the Country of the Oneidas."[14]

The frontier settlements were in a critical state. If the Six Nations could not be kept friendly, and the French and their Indians prevented from encroaching, by means of the supplies which Johnson requested, he would be obliged to leave his settlement in the Mohawk country. And that, he was told, would oblige the other inhabitants to abandon their settlements.[15] The French had put a price upon his head, and were doing their utmost to counteract his influence.

Without the kind of help which he then sought, and with practically no aid from the militia, Johnson could only resort again to small scalping parties with two or three whites and the same number of Indians. None of these parties exceeded twenty, and they could easily fall a prey to larger groups of the French and Caghnawagas. One incident in March 1748 dramatized for all the risks involved.

A small party of scouts led by the Mohawk Gingego, "the Chief Warriour of all the Nations," was surrounded by an enemy group of about thirty. It was two o'clock in the morning when Gingego heard them approaching on snowshoes. He awakened the others and told them to stand and fight like men. But in the face of greater numbers they fled, the Caghnawagas in hot pursuit, crying that they would have them. Gingego with another Mohawk jumped behind a tree, and hearing the taunts of the enemy cried out: "I am Gingego a Mohawk a Man who will never fly from you or Mankind." Giving three Indian yells he fired upom them, but immediately was riddled by their volley. Now Gingego and the others were scalped, their heads cut off, their bodies dismembered, roasted, and displayed. One young Indian escaped to relate the story of the brave Gingego. Other parties brought in the bodies. Turning to Johnson, they blamed the English for not supporting them with troops. Here indeed was opportunity to join the Indians to the English cause. But after this they were determined not to go as "outscouts," but only with parties of forty or fifty soldiers. Yet if nothing were done, said Johnson, "there will be no Staying in those parts for Any of Our People longer. As this Cruel Affair portends a Bloody Summer."[16]

French emissaries were now making strong efforts to sway the Onondagas. One agent sent by the governor of Canada arrived with seven Caghnawagas to condole the deaths by smallpox in the last year, "but chiefly to enquire & find out who had bruised (as he called it) his childrens heads last fall with the ax; in order to make it up with them. Upon that he threw a large Belt of Wampum 6 inches broad & 7 foot long, as the Indians described it." But he was answered sharply that their action was "taking up their Brother the Governour's Ax, last fall, at Albany." Whereupon the Frenchman hung his head and marched off.[17]

Other wampum belts were sent to all of the Six Nations asking them to come and speak at Montreal, "a verry kind Invitation to old Hendrick to go & See the Governour." This, said Johnson, must be stopped at all costs. If the governor would send him with a guard to Onondaga, he would attempt to persuade the Onondagas. But since there was now "an open Rupture between the Indians, it will be verry dangerous for me to go out without a Strong Guard." And the French, if they learned of the mission, could be expected to try to interrupt him.[18]

It was indeed hazardous, so he planned it with care:

Intend to Sett of next thursday from my House wth. a guard of 50 Men Captn Thomas Butler, & Liut. Laury officers. We Shall have a fatigueing Journey of it And I reckon pritty Dangerous, for I am informed Last Night by Hendricks Son that the French at Cadaraghque haveing heard of it by Jean Cuer [Joncaire] were quite Uneasy att the News and Said they would prevent it wh. is very likely they will attempt it for It would be a thing of great Consequence to them the worst of it is we must march thorough a thick woods for above 100 miles on foot to go thorough all the Castles by the Way In order to talk to some of the most obstinate of them privately.... I reckon I shall have a great deal of Difficulty to prevent their going, or Overset all that the French have been doing Since last Fall, However I shall leave no Stone Unturned yu. may depend upon it, to Accomplish wt. I go abt. Either by fair or foul Means, for if they are obstinate, I mean the Onondagas, I shall Certainly talk verry harsh to them & try wht. that will do. I hope to return (if nothing extraordinary happens) in abt. 3 weeks.[19]

His reception at Onondaga on this mission was evidence of his growing stature as the representative of Corlaer, the governor. The formality and ceremony, the solemn observance of Indian custom, and the careful following of Indian protocol showed that both parties respected each other. This first great council held by William Johnson may be taken as the prototype of scores of meetings to follow.

At my first entering Onondaga I was received by all the Sachims & Warriours who stood in order with rested arms and fired a Volley, after which my party returned the Compliment, then I was Conducted by Some of the principal Sachems to my Quarters which was a large Indian House cleaned out, with new Matts laid on the Cabbins to lie in, They had another large house clean for to lodge the Indians whom I had with me and two Houses more for my Party all in very pretty neat Order.

Every Castle I passed through did the same Hoisted English Colours such as they had everywhere and beat their drums realy beyond Expectation.[20]

Indian diplomacy was never hurried. A welcome from all the sachems assembled an hour after his arrival was the formal opening. It recognized the occasion, the call, and their regard for his message despite the inconvenience of being kept home from their hunting. Johnson replied with assurance of "Brothership," of the traditional meeting place, and the way of their "Forefathers, whose Steps I have now traced here in order to keep the Road clean and open." Nor was he to be hurried; he was fatigued by his journey, so he would meet them tomorrow to tell them the news and deliver the message from the governor. They were kept in anticipation, but he took no chances of their being in a good mood. "And I will this Night provide a Feast for your Sachems and another for the Warriours & dancers who I hope will be merry which is my greatest pleasure to make & see them so."[21]

His speech the next day recalled the ancient origin of their brothership, which they may have forgotten. He, though a "foreigner," had learned of this in an old and valuable record which was thought to be lost. This told of "the first great Canoe or Vessel at Albany.": how they in their desire to care for that vessel had tied it with a rope to the largest nut tree on the shore. But fearing that this would not be secure, that the wind might blow down that tree, they made a longer rope to tie it fast at Onondaga, "and the Rope put under your feet." Then they offered the governor to enter into "a Band of Friendship with him and his People which he was so pleased at that he told you he would find a strong Silver Chain which would never break slip or Rust to bind you and him forever in Brothership together and that your Warriours and Ours should be as one Heart, one Head, one Blood, &ca."

Now the French, their common enemy, were trying to blindfold them, to get them to slip that chain. With a belt of wampum he conjured them not to listen to the deceitful French but stick fast to the old agreement. The governors of New York and Massachusetts had sent him to stop them from going to Canada, as they had planned, for that would be contrary to the agreement. But this did not mean that other roads should be stopped—only the road to Canada. Last year they had been given permission to go to Canada to bring back their "flesh and blood," the captives held by the French; but instead they had stayed there the whole summer, which was wrong. In fact their going had caused us to lose scalps to the French, while our hands were tied. But if they stay home, the governor will endeavour to bring back their "flesh and blood."

"Now Brethren you see we have got the Frenchman's Ax sticking fast in our Heads Day after Day"; and the Five Nations people too are murdered in their own fields. They have the power to strike and destroy the Caghnawagas, and if they will do so the King has sent orders to the governor to take care of their castles, their families while the men are at war, and to erect forts to protect them. He, Johnson, had been looking for proper places for such forts, and will see they are built. And the King had sent them goods in token of his love.[22]

These promises had their effect, but the next day the Five Nations speaker reiterated some grievances. It was hard for them to have their flesh and blood rotting in jail in Canada, and if the English had gotten them out, they would not have gone to Canada. True, they only had succeeded in getting two of their people. Indeed, they were ready to use the ax against the French, but where was the promised English expedition against Canada? They had only gone in small parties, and there was no sign of an army now. They were glad for the presents given, and that the English would erect forts for their protection. They would be glad to meet the governor at Albany this summer.[23]

The mission was successful; the Onondagas would not go to Canada; they recognized the chain of friendship and would be true to their obligations. It now remained for the government to fulfill its promises. Thus the nations and their allies were called to Albany in July to meet Governor Clinton and Governor Shirley of Massachusetts, and to receive the promised present. This was urgent because by staying home the Indians had lost their hunting season, and the supply of corn was low. Then foremost in their minds was the recovery of their people held prisoners in Canada.

As an earnest of their intention Shirley had brought with him to Albany fourteen French prisoners who were to be exchanged for the Indian captives. But the exhortations to the sachems to keep the French from their castles and to have no dealings with them were somewhat weakened by the news that the English and French had signed preliminaries for a general peace. It was not possible to keep this from the Indians, although no reference to it appears in the official record of the meeting. The Mohawks, especially, had lost numbers of their best men and were bent on revenge. Yet they did agree to expel the French from their country, to send no agents to Canada, and to deliver up their prisoners for exchange.[24]

It now remained for Johnson to effect the exchange of prisoners, and this was no easy task. It was intended to send off a delegation via Oswego without delay, but the completion of arrangements and effectual exchange took about two years. In the meantime the Indians chafed at the delay. Johnson was indeed sympathetic. He wrote Clinton in January 1749 (six months after the Albany meeting) seeking "Speedy recovery of our People there [Canada] , & particularly the 4 Inds. who are now two years & Eight Months there, an Age indeed, for such people who were never used to any Confinement, & as nothing but their Steadfastness to the Brittish Interest, could have caused the French to detain them so long."[25] He also had trouble with the English traders who had gotten Indian children "as pawns or pledges" and were reluctant to give them up in exchange.[26] The next summer the Mohawks were again stirring themselves to go to Canada to get the captives. They had received appeals from the captives, especially from "Nichus the Sachim in Goal." But Johnson knew this would overset all plans, play into the hands of the French (who would be able to get a better deal from the Indians), and prevent any proper exchange. Thus he succeeded in getting the Mohawks to deliver to him all their French prisoners, nineteen in all.[27] He now made a trip to New York to complete arrangements only to find on his return that sixty Oneidas and Canajoharies had been waiting at his house for eighteen days, before setting out for Canada to redeem their people on invitations from the French. Now Robert Saunders and Major Vanderheyden with five others set out for Canada with six French prisoners.[28] In spite of these efforts it was not until 1750 that the exchanges were "happily effected." It was a sort of diplomatic triumph, for Johnson noted that "at the Conclusion of all former Warrs between the English and French the Indians depending on this Province were suffered to go to Canada to make Peace separately and to exchange prisoners there to the great weakening of their dependance on this Province."[29]

It was in the pursuit of these objectives that Johnson found it increasingly necessary to have some control over his neighbors of the valley. If left to follow their own devices, traders could very well blot out all his gains with the Indians. In no area was this more apparent than in the liquor traffic. Upon first coming to the valley he had asserted that this was a necessary commodity. Now he realized that its sale must be controlled, and he wrote Clinton May 7, 1747, for an Act

to prevent selling any kind of liquor to any Indians in the Mohawk country or at Conojoharie; for it is impossible to do anything with them while there is such a plenty of liquor to be had all round the neighbourhood, being for ever drunk. The worst of all is, one Joseph Clement who sell liquor within 20 yards of my house, & as soon as they get their bounty money, & that for guns, hangers, &c. they immediately go to his house & spend all there, which leaves them as poor as ratts, notwithstanding all they get of me. I have forbid him several times but in vain.[30]

This became a problem for government, in that Johnson then had to support these very Indians on his funds.

There is another grand villain George Clock lives by Canajoharie Castle, who robs the Indians of all their Cloaths &c which they get of me. I had several complaints of Hendrick &c about his behaviour, upon which I wrote him twice to give over that custom of selling liquor to the Indians, the answer was he gave the bearer, I might hang myself. If these two were made examples of by employing the King's attorney against them, it would put a stop to the rest, & be of vast service.[31]

There was also the pernicious practice of some unscrupulous persons buying the arms and clothing which were supplied the Indians. Clinton insisted that they were in fact the "King's Soldiers," and the laws against their selling equipment would be the same as for the whites.[32]

Johnson had been made "colonel of Indians" for this service, but since nearly all groups sent out were both Indians and whites, Clinton decided to give him command of the militia, in place of Colonel Philip Schuyler, who had shown little disposition to cooperate. His appointment as "Colonel of the Fourteen Companys of Foot rais'd for His Majesty's service in the Pay of this Province," February 29, 1748, was indeed late; his commission was dated May 1, and in the interim he was concerned lest the Assembly "be so Unconscionable as to Expect I should take

Command of these 14 Companys without a Sallary." He was given the power to hold courts-martial, and he quickly gave proper orders to the guards stationed in Albany, Schenectady, and Kinderhook.[33]

Another encroachment upon his authority appeared in the person of John Henry Lydius, who was being employed as Indian agent by Massachusetts. This chameleon-like individual appeared on the surface, and in their letters, to be friendly to Johnson, but as early as 1746 the Council warned of his being in secret correspondence with the French.[34] The son of a well-known Dutch dominie in Albany, he had a house for trade at the bend of the Hudson north of the city, the future Fort Edward. There he was in a position to contact the Indians on their journeys northward to the lakes and to play along with the Dutch in their clandestine traffic with Montreal. He spent several years in Canada, married a Frenchwoman, and turned Catholic. This raised a suspicion in some quarters that he was associated with "Popish emissaries," and therefore that he sympathized with French efforts to subvert the Iroquois. In 1745 his house was burned, and he moved to Albany. Now Johnson made known his displeasure at his activities among the New York Indians on behalf of Massachusetts.[35] Governor Shirley expressed extreme surprise that "Coll: Johnson should take umbrage at Lydius's being concerned with him in what has been done by this Governt. . . ." He made an effort to smooth over any implication of impropriety; but in view of the man's later history this early suspicion is significant.[36]

His success in several endeavours worked to Johnson's misfortune. His favor with the Indians and the vigor of his management were in sharp contrast with the qualities of his predecessors, the Albany commissioners, and they were bitter in criticism. Whatever he did backed by Clinton was resented by the governor's enemies in the Assembly. And the extent of his supply of Oswego, the troops, and the Indians was looked upon as a part of a profitable business venture on his part. Others were unwilling to take the risks, but they begrudged him the business. During the crisis some of these jealousies were forgotten, but the Assembly repeatedly failed to appropriate money for Johnson's reimbursement. To keep him going, for he was drawing on his own store, Clinton made him a loan.[37] Finally the Assembly voted him reimbursement from a fund which was already exhausted.[38] As Johnson became more perturbed over this treatment, Clinton carried his accounts to the Board of Trade, where he did his best to extol Johnson's services, his influence with the Indians, and his connection with Sir Peter Warren.

Johnson's accounts were indeed extensive, and in the view of the tight-fisted Assembly, or of the distant, economy-minded Board of Trade, they may have appeared extravagant. It was only by action, full supply, and generous gifts that his ends were achieved. This naturally cost more than the crabbed, ineffectual efforts of the commissioners. But his accounts were detailed. From December 1746 to November 1747, a bill of £3,064 was rendered, and this was paid in July 1748.[39] Yet in 1750, there was a balance due him of £1,971.8.6, for which he and Clinton appealed over the head of the Assembly.[40]

Johnson was not one to let his grievances go unheard, as he threatened to give up his offices. Colden wrote Shirley, July 27, 1749:

I am told that Sr Peter Waren has advised Coll Johnson who is his Nephew no longer to assist Govr Clinton in the Indian affairs & to decline all publick business & to attend only his own private affairs. It is so much Coll Johnson's interest to please his Uncle that it is expected he will submit to his Desire which the ingratitude of the Assembly might make him likewise incline to do.[41]

In 1750 Johnson put it up to Clinton that since nothing was being done in Indian affairs, except what he had done, "I should therefore choose with Your Excellenceys Consent, to give it up entirely, as Continuing it longer on such a footing, must hurt both my fortune & character."[42] The next year, March 1751, he repeated his desire, but now seemed petulant at Clinton's somewhat apologetic attitude toward the ministry. "By Your Excellency's laying so much weight, on the payment of my Acctts. wth. out objection, it seems as if you Suspected me, which I should be glad to know!" And why should he now be asked to influence the Albany people with regard to the Indians? "I must Say, I dont think it is my business at Present, as I have nothing further to do with them."[43]

Finally, taking the issue in his own hands, Johnson resigned and sent a belt of wampum among the Indian tribes to inform them that he no longer would manage their affairs. This was a shock to Clinton; Colden referred to it as an "odd step, such as nothing of the kind had ever been done before."[44] Clinton hurried to Albany with three of his Council to hold a meeting with the Indians. The Indians were aroused, and Hendrick, as speaker, made an eloquent plea.

We were very much shocked when Coll. Johnson sent a Belt of Wampum through the Six Nations, to Inform us that he declined acting any more with us, and it was the more Terrible, because he was well acquainted with our publick Affairs.... In War time when he was Like a Tree, that grew for our use, which now seems to be falling down, tho it has many roots; his knowledge of our affairs made us think him one of us (an Indian) and we are greatly afraid, as he has declined, your Excellency will appoint some person, a stranger both to us and our Affairs; and we give your Excellency this Belt of Wampum in order to raise up the falling Tree.

We desire to have an answer to what we have said and that Coll. Johnson may be reinstated, for he has large Ears and heareth a great deal, and what he hears he tells to us; he also has Large Eyes and sees a great way, and conceals nothing from us.

A String of Wampum

Our fire is kindled at Coll. Johnson's, which fire is now a going out, and here they gave a string of Wampum to have the fire renewed.

We desire his Excellency will be pleased to reinstate Coll. Johnson or else we expect to be ruined.[45]

The next day Clinton did his best to assuage the injured feelings of the Indians. Johnson's refusal to continue was unexpected and against his inclination; he could not help it, but he would try to appoint a good man; he would kindle a new fire in another place. This did not satisfy. Since Colonel Johnson belonged half to the governor, and the other half to them, if His Excellency could not persuade him, they would send a messenger for him with a string of wampum and try what they could do. Meeting him near Schenectady, the messenger came with Johnson to Albany, and he appeared before the Council on July 5.[46]

Before the Council and the chiefs, Governor Clinton requested Colonel Johnson to continue, since the Indians were uneasy at his refusal. The latter answered at length, giving his reasons and reviewing his expenses and his losses, as much for the governor and Council as for the Indians. It could not have been unfamiliar to either. Out of £7,177.3.2 ¾ advanced for the management of Indian affairs and the supply of Oswego, the Assembly had provided for payment of £5,801.7 . . , leaving without provision and still owed him £1,375.15.10 ¾. Yet there was never any objection made to his accounts. Of the amount for which the Assembly had voted payment, £2,404 was yet unpaid. And since November 1748, he had expended, at request of the governor, in the management of Indian affairs £595 . .12 . .8; of this he had received no part, and knew of no provision for its payment. Hence it was impossible for him to serve, since the arrears and expenditures would only continue.[47]

No urgings of the Council or promises from the governor would budge Johnson from his determination. He would assist them in the present meeting, but "he declined being sworn of the Council, as sitting as a Councillor, . . . as the Indians would thereby imagine that he was continued in the Management of the Indian Affairs."[48]

VIII

PROVINCIAL POLITICS

Political preferment was of no immediate concern to William Johnson. He came to the New World to settle land, to engage in trade, and, as he put it, to make something of himself. His location on the frontier was far from the center of government, so it was not his doing that he became involved. The historian William Smith, not a friendly critic, said he "aspired to no higher than the life of a genteel farmer in the vicinity of Fort Hunter, surrounded by the Mohawks."[1] Yet if one looks at New York provincial politics, and not merely at the immediate causes of involvement, it is apparent that a political role for Johnson was inevitable.

Three factors seemed to dominate the politicians of the province: land, trade, and family connection. From the time of the Dutch patroons, the holding of vast tracts by a few individuals projected them into public concern. The ambitious thus saw their way to wealth and preferment through the possession of real estate, however acquired; and some, like the redoubtable Robert Livingston, coupled land hunger with fortunate marriage. Thus by a combination of land and family one climbed to the top, insured one's position and that of one's children and posterity. The pattern was repeated over and over.

Compared with the great landholder, so much respected in Europe, the merchant was an upstart with little claim to political recognition. Yet the advantages possessed by the shrewd trader in the New World, his accumulation of considerable wealth, sometimes by questionable means (there were fine lines between importers and smugglers, between privateers and pirates, and between legal booty and stolen goods), soon gained for him social and political recognition. Moreover, his wealth could be converted to real property by speculation. The new aristocracy of land did not hesitate to engage in trade and to ally with the merchants through marriage. Hence there came about that interlocking of interests of the great families which was to be the hallmark of New York politics, the marvel and the despair of royal governors and of others outside the magic circle.

Within ten years of his arrival, William Johnson met the three qualifications for entry into politics. From a small landholder near his uncle's grant, which he managed, he had acquired such an estate as befitted a country gentleman. From his store on the Mohawk River his trade expanded, and he held a contract to supply the Oswego garrison. And when his uncle, Peter Warren, now an admiral and the hero of Louisbourg, was knighted and became a power both at home and in the colonies, the third condition for a political role was met. The young Irishman, however, far from recognizing his destiny, or the talent so natural to many of his countrymen, was actually reluctant to mix in politics. His own concerns and self-interest thrust him forward. And even when he had the opportunity, he subordinated politics to his larger aims.

Little did Johnson know the import of that line in the captain's first letter to him in the Mohawk country: "and dont say anything about the Badness of the Patrones Horses, for it may be taken Amiss, he is a near relation of my wifes, and may have it in his power very much to Serve you."[2] Coming to New York by way of Boston, he could not have seen his Aunt Susan and her husband, the chief justice for several years. But he was to learn where power lay.

The big name in New York politics for decades was De Lancey. Stephen De Lancey (as Etienne de Lanci, a Huguenot refugee from Caen by way of Rotterdam) had enriched himself as a merchant in New York. In 1700 he had married Ann, the daughter of Stephanus Van Cortlandt and Gertrude Schuyler, thus allying himself with two important Dutch families. Their children also made significant connections by marriage: Susannah married Captain Peter Warren; Ann married John Watts, an enterprising merchant; Peter married Elizabeth, the daughter of Cadwallader Colden, savant and later lieutenant governor; and James married Anne, the daughter of Caleb Heathcote, a wealthy merchant and office holder.[3]

James De Lancey received an exceptional education for his day. After the best schools in New York, he attended Cambridge University as a Fellow Commoner of Corpus Christi College, where his tutor was Dr. Thomas Herring, later Archbishop of Canterbury. Returning from England, he began the study of law and soon rose to eminence in that field. He became a member of the governor's Council in 1729, and in 1733, during the controversy of Governor Cosby with the Assembly, he replaced Lewis Morris as chief justice. As such he presided over the famous Zenger trial. He and his family were beneficiaries of the Cosby land policy, and he thereupon possessed one of the richest estates in New York.[4]

The rise of James De Lancey, however, was due as much to his personal charm and traits of character as to his inheritance and the accidents of politics. With wealth, which alone would have set him apart, he had the classical and legal education to sustain a reputation for erudition. His ready wit and affability gave him an unusual capacity for swaying men in public speech as well as in counsel. In fact, his opponents regarded him as a demagogue.[5] He had a commanding presence which made him stand out among his peers, and his wealth and the ostentation of his public appearances did not detract from his his popular appeal.

His snow-white horses and gilded chariot with outriders in handsome livery excited no envy; his grand mansion on Broadway and his still more elegant country seat were objects of pride to the inhabitants of the city. The latter was on the Bowery above Grand Street. The house stood in the rear of the block between Rivington and De Lancey Streets. It was a broad stately brick building, three stories high, expensively furnished, and contained a generous and well-chosen library; the Walls of the apartments were embellished with Choice works of art, and it was otherwise invested with the refined taste of him who built and beautified it. An avenue shaded on either side by handsome trees, which in summer time formed a leafy arch overhead, led from the mansion to the Bowery Road. The estate spread over an incredible Number of acres.[6]

De Lancey's political influence under Cosby placed him on the side of the governor and his prerogative. Under Governor George Clarke, who had administrative experience, he was less influential, but the arrival of George Clinton in 1743 gave him his opportunity. Clinton's inexperience made him turn to the man who seemed best able to advise him, who was both chief justice and member of the Council. He later confessed his implicit confidence, and his failure to "entertain the least suspicion of his designs, . . . even after they were apparent to others and till after he had compleated his faction as he desired, having introduced into the Council and Assembly by his influence with me, such men as he knew would serve his purposes."[7]

The first conflict came when Clinton sought a vigorous prosecution of the war, both in support of the New England forces against Louisbourg, and in a New York campaign against Canada. The Albany Dutch merchants, who were trading with Canada and of course had their men in the Assembly, were charged by the New England commissioners with impeding the effort. Philip Livingston, a member of the Council and commissioner of Indian affairs strongly entrenched through his great possessions and his inheritance, was suspected by Clinton. "It is a vile family," he wrote.[8]

When in 1746 Clinton travelled to meet the Indians in Albany, only two members of the Council would go with him. It was then that he turned to Cadwallader Colden as adviser to replace De Lancey. There is a story that the break with De Lancey came while they were dining in a tavern. Clinton objected when De Lancey in his usual manner made a decision. The chief justice, finding he could not budge the governor, arose and left, "declaring with an oath, he would make his administration uneasy for the future: His Excellency replied, he Might do his worst."[9]

Clinton fought back, sought the removal of some of the councillors who opposed him, and called for the backing of the ministry, in that he was upholding the prerogative of the crown and carrying out his instructions.[10]

In his perplexity Clinton found a sympathizer in Governor Shirley of Massachusetts. Returning from Albany to New York on a sloop together in 1748, they talked over the pretensions of the Assembly, and Shirley promised to draw up a report for the ministry on the conditions in New York. His concerns at home, however, diverted him from the plan and he contented himself with friendly advice to his fellow governor.[11]

De Lancey, with the backing of most of the Assembly, became its champion in a constitutional struggle. Reflecting the issues of Cosby's time, the Assembly curbed the governor by withholding support, by making salary appropriations annual, and by attaching its own measures to wartime supply bills. Among these was the appointment of Robert Charles, Sir Peter Warren's secretary, to be the agent of the colony in London.[12]   The Assembly turned upon Cadwallader Colden, senior member of the Council, for his support of the governor in Indian negotiations, whereupon the governor tried to have Colden named as lieutenant governor, a post then vacant.[13] The upshot of this was that De Lancey obtained the commission for lieutenant governor, while remaining as chief justice; but Clinton refused to deliver the commission. The strategy was obvious. Clinton had believed that Sir Peter Warren was anxious to succeed him; but when other honors were showered upon the admiral, De Lancey's ambition became clear.[14]   The end of the war lessened the demand for money bills; Clinton, for some time in bad health, now planned to retire and go home to England. Yet the old warrior hated to back down; he thought of a method to make the executive independent by assigning quitrents to pay salaries, but De Lancey's grip upon the Assembly was complete.[15]

Clinton's appointment of Johnson to handle Indian affairs was a kind of affront to both the commissioners, whom he succeeded, and to Philip Livingston, who was removed as Indian secretary. These had been in the favor of De Lancey, and thus Johnson was regarded as Clinton's man. When his accounts, as well as the Indian expenses, came before the Assembly they were loath to act. Anything done for him might be taken as a minor success for the governor. Hence, through no fault of his own, Johnson was a victim of the faction.[16]

Protesting his efforts in Johnson's behalf, Clinton was finally glad to have Johnson come down to New York to make his own appeal. In July 1749, therefore, he made his appearance as lobbyist. He would attempt to see the chief justice, brother-in-law of Uncle Peter. It was customary for De Lancey to hold forth with his cronies in a tavern, or coffeehouse, where plans were formulated for political measures. It was at one of these that the famous break with Clinton had occurred.

After a week in town, while the Assembly was sitting, Johnson wrote that he had not seen the chief justice, "tho I constantly frequent the Coffee House he uses Morning & Night." Finally, after twelve days, he was able to see De Lancey, "but Could not find him Inclined to do me any Service, or even take much notice of me, wh. Surprises me much as I never disobliged him, or any of the family. I am sorry to say he is the Primum Mobile of the Opposition."[17]

This could have been no great surprise to the admiral, who had many irons in the fire, and who had turned from any possible venture into colonial politics. Nor did he offer his nephew any opportunity to forsake America in this period of distress; he had written to De Lancey, he would use his good offices with the governor, and that appeared as far as he would go. William felt that some sort of recognition was due him.

I am Sorry to hear there is no prospect of any thing being done for me at home, having all along flattered my Self that my hearty endeavours for his Majesties Service when represented by my freinds, would have been taken Some Notice of, but as there is no further Expectation of it I shall observe yr. advice as most wholesome by following my own business which I shall make the Cheif object of my Attention.[18]

In spite of being "as Cautious in my Conduct with the discontented as I possibly Could," William saw that "they are realy the Majority in our Assembly, & I believe are so in all Assemblys upon the Continent, and naturally aerse as I find to any thing their Governours do."[19] Now he was learning what the real issues were. Leaving out personalities, the popular branch was endeavoring to emulate the House of Commons, to hold the purse-strings and by that means to control the government. The governor, reading his instructions and citing the needs for defense, denied complete legislative power to the Assembly. When they published a remonstrance which Clinton refused to let them read to him in person, he denied the right of the printer James Parker to print it. This, the Assembly asserted, was a "violation of the rights and liberties of the people."[20]

Yet the governor had undoubted power; he could dissolve the Assembly, and he could remake the Council. By late 1747 he had singled out his enemies thereon: "Danl Horsmanden (suspended) their [the faction's] Secretary, and Writer, Joseph Murry their Councellor and Sollicitor, Stephen Bayard (suspended) their Common Cryer, Phillip Livingston formerly a Trader with the enemy at Albany. . . ."[21] As some of these were suspended, or otherwise removed (Philip Livingston died 1749), Clinton formed his own group. Sir Peter now gave his assent to his nephew's appointment to the Council, and in April 1750 Johnson was named for the place vacated by Livingston. The governor's secretary in notifying him hoped that he would use his place to press for payment of his accounts, as well as continue his support for the governor.[22] Along with the honors went an invitation to become "a Member of Your Excellencys. Club wh. I find is Composed of all those whom I most esteem, & toast Constantly."[23] In the future, at least, when he went down he would not have to drift about the coffeehouses in search of his confreres.

But, now he was in no mood to cooperate; he was threatening to give up his Indian post, and he was in no hurry to assume his new duties. After his resignation from the management of Indian affairs he reluctantly attended the Albany meeting, and on July 5, 1751, refused to be sworn in as councillor, lest the Indians misunderstand his role; on the 10th, however, he was recorded as meeting with the Council.[24]

In holding aloof from the Council after his appointment, Johnson was not unusual. Members living at a distance from New York City, where most meetings were held, frequently did not attend; with a total of twelve councillors, only three were necessary for a quorum. Too much abstention, however, might be a cause for suspension. Members were not paid, but received honors and perquisites which were much coveted. Also they were entitled to be addressed as "Honorable." Not least important in the councillor's influence were his local functions. In his own county he was justice of the peace; he advised on all appointments, and had something to say about land grants.[25] When it came to elections, he could generally sway a number of votes, partly because of his leadership of his tenants, but also because of his political patronage.

As early as 1745 Johnson had been asked to support candidates for the Assembly. Albany was remote from Mount Johnson, and perhaps he could round up votes in his area.[26] But until 1750, he was not aroused. Then he became concerned as he found politicians pushing to control the votes of his area, and he expressed a mild disapproval.

I must tell Your Excellency that this place has been full this time past of Yorkers, who I find came on purpose to Make Interest against a New Election. they have been busy all along the way from York to this [place], Working up the People to their tune. . . . the Cheifs that were here, was robt. Livingston of the Mannor, James Livingston, John Livingston, Nichks. Bayard, Collo. Gosbeek from Esopus, Collo. Matthews from the High Lands &ca. I heartily Wish they may be disappointed in their Expectations.[27]

By July reports reached him from Albany of unusual activity, but the leaders there were secretive of their intentions, and the names of candidates were not revealed.

Yet It may bee Easeley Seen throe that the Intention of the heads here In gennerall are for puting In Collo. Schuyler and Peter Winne whoo with thier party here work. Very hard from morning till night and Mr. Collins Sends Letters to all parts of the Country. Mr. Depoister is very Deligint and I Cant find out whether for him Self or for others. . . .

Your frinds . . . long to See You here and Say if You appeared it would mache a great allteration as they Confes it is In your power to Turn the Skeals. If you take it in hands.[28]

His friends were scattered in the country and inactive, which gave "oppertunity to the other party I am affeared to goe a great way In ganing the freeholders to thier Interest."[29]   But Johnson was not ready to stir his followers to political opposition. He preferred diplomacy and negotiation, so he issues a statement, "To all the Messrs. [Voters] of Canajoharie," which made his position clear.

Considering how troublesome & Inconvenient it would be to all the Farmers to have an Election att this time of the year [July], I went Imediately to Albany to See to make it up Easy now without any trouble. Phillip Schyler & Hanse Hansen[30] were Sett up by the people of Albany, so I sent for them, & told them if they would do their best for the good of the Country We would not Sett up any body against them now but if thy would not do good now for the Country, We would Sett up others next time. Whereupon thy promised me thy would do what they could, which I wish thy may for the Country never wanted it more.

Now Gentlemen, & freinds I thank you all heartily for your good will for me, as well as if you voted everry bitt, and hope whenever there is another election, you will be all as one Body to Stand by me, and putt in other good men, if those wont do good for Us Now, which I am afraid thy wont. for my part I am resolved as I live, here to stand by you all, for the good of the whole River. so hope we will always be true to one another. I am with hearty thanks for all your good Will.
         Your true friend, & Welwisher
                                                    W.J.[31]

As he suspected, Johnson found he could not trust the Albany politicians, and he reported to the governor in September.

I understand the Mayor of Albany [Jacob Coenraedtt Ten Eyck] is of the other Side, and Says he will not be major longer if he can help it—this I thought proper to let Yr. Excellcy. know lest you be deceived in the Man, as I realy have been. . . . In Case You have an Inclination to make a Change. Mr. Saunders is the fittest Man in Albany for Mayor, as is Mr. Vanscoike for Recorder. Pardon my freedom in giveing Yr. Excellcy. my Sentiments.[32]

Perhaps as a result of this advice, Robert Sanders was appointed mayor of Albany October 15, 1750, and served until 1754. Clinton was grateful for Johnson's support and his sending information, and he now began to press him for a more active part.[33] As time for the election of a new Assembly approached, it was evident that he was deeply involved. In December 1751, Clinton sent him a "Commission as Surveyor of the Woods . . . which I congratulate you on, and make not the least Question, but you will make proper use of for the Good of the Cause." Clinton conveyed his "gratefull Sentiments, and Approbation of your indefatiguable trouble & pains in Dutchess & Albany Counties, when you went up, and make no doubt, but Fortune will favour the Brave that you may carry your point in both your Nominations for Albany."[34]

It was difficult indeed to counteract "the Albany Grandees, whose Soul and Blood are money," in their "villainous designs of tampering & Corrupting the Electors."[35] But Johnson had his agents at work in the valley. Arent Stevens, the interpreter, wrote of his efforts in Schenectady, and Hendrick Frey from Canajoharie asked that "you'll Keep the pole opened Till Monday in the Afternoon," until he rounded up some stragglers.[36]

But the opposition was too much for him; he did not carry the election of January 1752, and the sheriff quickly sent in the returns before the more remote ballots could be counted. His candidates, Beekman and Fisher, now claimed "an undue election" and demanded a "scrutiny." This entailed their presence in New York, however, which was difficult for them, and their protests seemed of no avail.[37]

When things went against him, the governor could always prorogue the Assembly, which he did March 14, 1752, until the end of April, citing as his reason the prevalence of the smallpox. He was indeed planning to retire and had ordered a ship to carry him and his family to England.[38] Now he felt unsure of his allies—he turned from Cadwallader Colden to Lewis Morris—and he knew that De Lancey, whose commission as lieutenant governor he was holding up, must take his place until a new appointment was made.

Johnson too had cooled. His resignation must mean a loss of some influence although he was still in the Council. Knowing of Clinton's forthcoming retirement, he had no incentive to continue his political efforts. But he had gained valuable experience; he knew now where he stood, and he was in a position to bargain with the next governor. His brief excursion into local politics was useful training for many encounters to come.

IX

FAMILY PROBLEMS

Preoccupation with public affairs, his business projects, land deals, politics, and the ever present Indians may account for William Johnson's neglect of his family in Ireland. It is hard to condone his failure to write his father for years on end; brother John noted in 1747, "We have not had a letter from you [for] more than two years."[1] Three years later he further complained of William's neglect; there had been news of him from other sources and the old man was piqued. He wanted to hear of his son's successes directly. Had material success turned his head; or had America wrought a change? "We are all greatly rejoyced at the plenty full fortune your Unckle has placed you in. I must now also acquaint you what great concerns my poor father is under for not hearing from you often he is like one reaving at your remissnes in Corresponding with him he seems realy to be doteing on you above all his Children for in all his discourses about you the[y] usually end in tears . . . and hopes it is not afflunce of your fortune makes you forget him. . . ."[2]

Brothers John and Warren kept William informed of conditions at home, as did some friends of the family. But the welfare of the Irish family seemed tied to the rising fortunes of Peter Warren. His namesake, (Peter) Warren Johnson, had been encouraged to go to America and to raise a company for the Louisbourg expedition. He returned to Ireland after the war, however, somewhat disappointed that Uncle Peter had not purchased him a commission.[3] Cousins Michael and Richard Tyrrell were both in the British navy, where they could bask in the reflected glory of Captain Warren. After Louisbourg, Cape Breton Island, in 1745, the latter became Sir Peter, and was promoted to Rear Admiral of the Blue. In 1747 as second in command he was a hero of the victory over the French squadron off Cape Finisterre, and was further honored and promoted, by the Cross of the Bath, and the ranks of Commander in Chief of the Western Squadron, and Vice Admiral.[4]

His nephew Warren gloated over his success and prospects. "He now must be one of the Richest men in England & not one has done his Country so much Service; he must be worth three or four Hundred Thousand Pounds Sterling."[5]

Peter Warren's interests in the New World were all too apparent. Lady Warren's family in New York, his estate in Greenwich, his lands on the Mohawk all beckoned to him. William was urging him to come and to reside at Warrensburgh. Nor was he entirely removed from the political intrigues of the faction. Governor Clinton, who deferred to him at first, and in 1745 made him a member of the Council, now feared that he was ambitious for his seat. Earlier Warren had written Captain Anson that he might take the government of Jersey when it became vacant, for it would be "an introduction to that of New York, where I would be at the pinnacle of my ambition and happiness."[6]

These places not being available, he turned to London, where he settled in a residence on Cavendish Square. He was generally recognized as one of the richest commoners in the kingdom, and he was a member of Parliament for Westminster; he was elected on July 1, 1747 and sat until his death. The freedom of the city had been conferred on him after the victory off Cape Finisterre, and in June 1752 he was elected alderman of the Billingsgate Ward.[7]

In the meantime he kept an eye on Ireland. By purchase he now rounded out and enlarged the family estate of Warrenstown, though he had no intention of living there and used it to care for his relations. In January 1750, John Johnson explained:

Sr Peter Warren has purchased that part of Warrens town that Rowley had and is now in possession of it and hath lately purchased two very fine town lands from the Barron of Galtrum for which he is to give £6000 and odd pounds for he has been pleased to appoint me his received not only for what he has already purchased but for what he may hereafter purchased in which station I shall endeavor to make it my Cheifest studdy to keep up to the great duty we all owe to so good an Unckle in which station I expect . . . an improvement in my fortune.[8]

Brother Warren revealed that "My bro: Jack is Removing to Warrenstown with his little Family to Settle by Sir Peter's desire . . .he's return'd from London but two Months where he has been about Sir Peter's Affairs . . . Jack is to hold all Warrenstown at 280£ a year in Lieu of my Father's part of it he gives a 100£ yearly which is better for him."[9]

"Warry" was very attentive to Sir Peter, "the Best of friends & I am for ever bound to him for his Goodness to me." When Sir Peter went to Dublin to receive an honorary LL.D. from the university, he was on hand, and thus was in attendance when Sir Peter was taken with a fever and died. Although his health was poor, his sudden demise was unexpected and a profound shock to the Johnson family. Warren wrote the details to his brother William.

It's with the utmost Sorrow I give you the most Dismal Acct. of the Death of our most Dear Dear Uncle who died in Dublin last wednesday night 29th. July of a most Violent Fever which Carried him of in four Days. I was up day & night with him & wd to God I cd have died in his stead Oh my Dr Bro. such Grief as our poor Family are in is unexpressible for we have lost our all & all. And you I am sure will be as much Shocked as mortal Living, but Let [me] beg of you to Muster up all your Resolution to bear this most Dismal Acct. I arriv'd here [London] in two days from Dublin with the Melancholy news to Lady Warren, whom from my very heart I pity & hope God will preserve her Life for her poor Family's sake. he made his will two days before he died & how he has Settled his affairs no one as yet knows, nor 'till I return with her Directions to have it Opened. I Set out in two hours & expect to be in Dublin the 7th he's to be intered at Nock Mark, in a Private manner

his Executors are, Lady Warren, Capt. Tyrrell, & the Chief Justice DeLancey, & be Assur'd of a faithful Acct. of every thing as soon as his will is open'd.

I hope in God my Dr Brother will endeavour to bear this Shock with patience our Loss is very very Great & what to do now with myself I know not[10]

The shock to William Johnson, who apparently had had few dealings with Uncle Peter after his retirement to London, was nothing compared to his surprise on learning the contents of the will. He had been treated as the favorite of Uncle Peter; his success and achievements, in spite of some disagreement, he conceived must have been watched by the admiral with pleasure. Now by an unusual provision of which he first learned in November he was cut off from any part of the wealthy man's estate, and even made to contribute to bequests for his brothers and sisters.

How much the other Johnsons knew of the will is problematical. Peter Warren had made an earlier will in 1746; then, two days before his death, he made a revised version, in which he changed his bequest to William. Since he suffered from "a Most violent fever" for four days, he was, as the will states "Sick in Body" when this will was drawn. It is hard to conceive that Warren, who was attending him, did not know some of the contents of the will; he did know who the executors were to be. These circumstances may well be considered in connection with the later controversy.[11]

There is no way of telling the size of the estate, for a large part of the wealth was in land and was not enumerated. Although James De Lancey was named an executor, his brother Oliver was charged with the actual settlement of the estate and went to London to take up the task for his sister, Lady Warren. It was from Oliver De Lancey on his return to America that William Johnson learned the terms of the will. He immediately expressed his chagrin and his determination to resist what he considered unjust treatment.[12]

Peter Warren was not forgetful of his nephews and nieces when he drew his will. After first providing for his wife and children, a possible heir unborn, and the contingencies of their marriage or death, he turned to his other relatives. Of these Captain Richard Tyrrell seemed a favorite; if all the Warren children failed to inherit, Tyrrell was to receive one third of his personal estate. Of whatever sum was due him from Richard Tyrrell, Warren left one-third to Tyrrell's two sisters, and the other two-thirds divided among "My Nephews and Neices the Children of Christopher Johnson Excepting my Nephew William Johnson for whom I have a great esteem but consider him as not wanting a share."

Then came the controversial provision as related to William Johnson: "My Will also is that whatever Sum shall appear to be due to me from my said Nephew Mr. William Johnson one third part thereof he shall retain to his own Use, the two Thirds shall be Equally divided between his Brothers and Sisters."[13]

The difficulty in this peculiar kind of bequest was that no one could tell, and Peter Warren evidently did not know, how much was due him, and therefore what if anything was being bequeathed. In his earlier will of 1746, which this superseded, Sir Peter mentioned the amount of William's debt—four thousand pounds sterling.[14] Subsequent to this William had given his bonds, which it was understood were for part of this debt. This the will did not make clear, and William was called upon to settle the account. His attitude and the basis for his countervailing charges he set forth in his letter to Oliver De Lancey.

As to what dealings (if I may properly call them so) was between my Dr. Uncle & me, I never kept any acct of. takeing it for grant. by the many letters he wrote me when yet In Ireland, by what he told me when he sent me from Boston to Settle here, & by Several subsequent letters, that He would give me a certain Tract of Land in Warrensborough, and Supply me with all things necessary to carry on my Work. He did accordingly Send me many things out of his own good Will severall of which realy were useless to me. these things I used, in Clearing a Farm out of the thickest timbered Woods I ever saw where I laboured sorely the best of my Days, not doubting in the least it was for myself. I being at York He desired I would give him Bonds for them Sums, which I did, but never made any entry of them, so easy I was about it. . . . .[15]

Incredible as this lax accounting seems, there was apparently some justification for William's thinking his benevolent uncle would treat him generously; the wills even indicate that bonds were designed principally to make the young men diligent. Turning to Chief Justice De Lancey, who referred him to Mr. Nichols, William learned that he had given "three different Bonds, at different times to the amount of £1025 Sterlg." Now much perturbed, he asked to have his accounts settled. "I doubt not but You Sr. and the other Gentlemen concerned will think it reasonable (If I am not to have the land I Improved on Warrensborough,) that then I should be allowed the Expenses I have been at, which was verry considerable."[16]

In spite of his lack of records (he submitted no vouchers), William rendered a detailed accounting of his expenditures in the settling of Warrensburgh, including labor expended and articles delivered to Sir Peter and Lady Warren, and laid this before the attorneys for the estate. A balance was then struck which showed a credit in Johnson's favor of £933.7.11½. In addition he listed "Some Articles Kept by Lady Warren out of a Cargo of Goods reced Anno 1742 Amot. to £966.2.7 which I kept no Acct. of but believe her Ladyship knows what it was to whom I refer it"; and the "Expence I was unavoidably put to, by the Six Nations coming to Condole the Death of Sir Peter Warren at my house . . . £132.13.4." Thus there was a considerable amount due him, for which he did not intend to press, and hence nothing to be distributed to his brothers and sisters.[17]

John Chambers and Richard Nichols of New York, who examined the accounts for the De Lanceys, certified to the correctness of Johnson's accounts, and his interpretation of his obligation. They noted that he had objected to no charges in Warren's accounts, nor to the bonds, and that they believed him "a Man of Honour & Integrity and worthy of good faith and Credit."[18]

This statement was far from satisfactory to Lady Warren, as executor, and to some of the beneficiaries. She wrote an irate letter to brother Oliver, denouncing

Johnson, and complaining that she was threatened with suit on the part of the others.

I am extreamly surprized at it, I should be glad to know what he has done with the produce of all the Labour he Charges for, as he had the profits I think he has no right to make such unreasonable Charges, & I hope it wont be in any bodys power to make me pay so unjust a demand. Mr. Chambers & Nichols were no strangers to Sr. Peter Warren & therefore they must if they consider his character know that he would not have left such a Legacy to Mr. Johnson & his Brothers and sisters unless he had been very sure that Mr. Johnson was in his debt.[19]

Was William Johnson guilty of sharp practice in thus turning the tables on his uncle's estate, and so depriving his brothers and sisters of a bequest? It would seem that Chief Justice De Lancey and his brother would have sided with their sister Lady Warren, if she had a case. Perhaps they felt it was a dispute only of interest to the Johnsons, for the estate lost nothing thereby, unless William Johnson sought to collect his balance. At any rate, the arbitrators Chambers and Nichols, friends of Sir Peter, had given their decision.[20]

Johnson's account against Warren's estate had some merit. For the three or four years covered by his account, he appears to have been in partnership with Sir Peter for his trading operations. If the debt of £4,000 represented trade goods, then his three bonds for about half that amount were his share, and so should have been balanced against the charge, as was done in the accounting. Presumably each of the partners should have received half the profits, but there is no record of these.

If Johnson felt that in time he was to be the proprietor of Warren's lands, he may have rendered no accounting for the produce and other chattels (slaves for Lady Warren and timber for building the Greenwich home of the Warrens), but when he moved across the river he must have concluded that he had to provide for himself, or that Warren might come to live on his lands. Certainly, he should have had credit for these advances, if not in Warren's books, then in the general accounting. It is hard to determine whether charges for labor by him and others were justified by the earlier arrangement. Undoubtedly, his successful settlement and management of Warrensburgh had been profitable to Warren. Portions of the land had been sold, and there were a number of tenants (William charged for drawing twenty-six leases). Now William was hurt that his reasonable expectation to profit from his wealthy uncle's estate had been blasted.

The arbitrators noted that

Sir Peter from time to time wrote to Mr. Johnson several most kind and Affectionate Letters greatly pressing and Encouraging him to Carry on the Settlement of his Lands and Real Estates in the County of Albany of which he the Said William had the Care and Superintendency for him to Said Sir Peter, and also that from thence he the Said William might reasonably Expect to be generously Considered and rewarded by his Said Uncle who often Declared in his Said Letters for to have his the Said Williams Interest and preferment greatly at heart And it also Appears from Sundry Letters from the Said William Johnson to Sir Peter that he Expresses himself to be greatly Obliged to him for all his favours and kindness to him.[21]

Lady Warren's protest reflected the chagrin of the other Johnsons in being thus bereft of their inheritance. Brothers Warren and John Johnson, by the terms of the will, had their bonds to Sir Peter cancelled. John, who had been managing the estates at Warrenstown, was to continue to occupy these lands at a favorable rental. But the sisters had little, except for a similar share in the obligation of Captain Richard Tyrrell to Sir Peter. It was indeed a peculiar kind of left-handed bequest that Sir Peter had hit upon. Threats or rumors of his family's discontent reached William Johnson, so that he made a gesture of reconciliation—not without a veiled warning. He wrote a letter to his father Christopher Johnson, October 31, 1754, which was delivered, along with gifts, by Mrs. Robert Adems, wife of his book-keeper. He was endeavoring to repair his record as a poor correspondent.

Since my last to you of the 26th of May, I have had no acctt. from you, so that I am anxious to know whether you receive mine duely. if not, I should Deem myself very Unhappy as it must undoubtedly give you an Ill Opinion of me, which I should by all means possible endeavour to avoid.

I am Sorely troubled to hear that some of my nearest Freinds, entertain so bad an opinion of my principalls, as to Imagine I would wrong them of Anything might be their Due. they Imagine, as I understand, Nothwithstanding the acctt. was Settled here, & Sent Home, that I am indebted to the Estate of Sr. Peter Warren Deceased. Had He fulfilled his promises and Engagements to me, which was that I should have such a parcell of his Land, whereon I lived, & laboured hard many Years. then Indeed, I should have fallen Something in his Debt, but as that was not Settled, as promised, I was obligded to Charge for my Improvements, wh. tho Short of what I expended thereon, makes the Ballance in my favour above Nine Hundred Pounds this Currcy. the thought of paying which, is what gives Lady Warren Uneasiness, about the Acctt. not for my Brothers or Sisters Interest, I am Convinced. I hope My Brothers & Sisters may never be prevailed upon to do so rash a thing as to Commence a Law Suit with me who have Suffered too much already in this distant part of the World, by means of those, whom I inclined to belive my best freinds, untill deceived.[22]

Here indeed he put his case strongly. The implied promise of Sir Peter is now asserted as a fact. Lady Warren is worried for her own obligation, not by thought of the Johnsons. And a lawsuit against him would be considered rash and inspired by those he had believed his friends.

Sister Catty (Ferrall) now living near him and the object of his patronage, "desires her Duty to you, and begs you will excuse her not writeing to you, as her Eyes are verry weak after a fitt of Illness She had Comeing from Sea." She would not contest the settlement—she was to die the following year.

Christopher must have been a bit mellowed by the gifts and remembrances. Or were they a peace offering?

I send you by her [Mrs. Adems] an Indian Pipe to smoak with, as it may be a Curiosity there, it is Cutt out of the solid stone by them, only with a Knife. My Sister Catty tells me you take Snuff, wherefore I send you my Box, which tho trifleing ye. present beg you may think them worth acceptance, as Comeing from Him who is Ever Yours &ca.[23]

Finally, he sent the old man a fine oil painting of himself, a fitting reminder of the boy—now quite a man—who had left Ireland sixteen years ago to become an important personage in the new world.

Honord Sr
As I cannot wait of you myself yet a while, I send you my Picture, wh. I had drawn four years ago, the Drapery I would have altered, but there is no Painter now can do it, the greatest fault in it is, the narrow hanging Shoulders, wh. I beg you may get altered as Mine are verry broad and square.[24]

With a "lively sense of favors to come," the brothers and sisters did not further press the matter, and William showed a greater attention to his family. Soon he was to rise to greater eminence, and his family and friends rushed to do him honor. Brother Warren became closer than ever, visited the Mohawk Valley for a season, and the rift in the family was well on the way to be mended.

Then fifteen years later, in 1769, Abraham Sterling, husband of Bridget Johnson, youngest daughter of Christopher, revived the claim to a portion of Sir Peter's bequest and obtained a subpoena against Lady Warren. She repeated her former arguments in a letter to Oliver De Lancey, who relayed them to Sir William Johnson. This raised the hackles of the latter, who not only asserted his former position, but protested his own restraint and generosity in regard to what was owed him. He was sure that none of the others of his relations were concerned, and that Sterling's own circumstances, or his character, were responsible for the issue.[25]

Johnson's brothers and sisters were generally favored and well treated by him in the years that followed.[26] He seemed much inclined to favor them when he could, and they benefited greatly and in turn were devoted followers. Brother John's son Guy became his trusted aide and son-in-law. Sister Anne's son, John Dease, came to live with Johnson and was his personal physician. They were all to be well remembered in Sir William's will. But that will, too, was to benefit them little.

X

WIDENING INFLUENCE

It was a period of frustration for William Johnson. His services for the crown and province, which had been privately acclaimed, failed to bring any reward from home, and his accounts had not been paid by the Assembly. Because he could not get sufficient funds, or reimbursement for his advances, he had resigned the management of Indian affairs and had seen them returned to the inept hands of the commissioners. The Indians, chagrined by his action, were going back on their good intentions and friendly attitude, and all his gains seemed about to be lost once more. As a principal resident and merchant in the valley, he was concerned over this trend, and yet there seemed little he could do. He could not continue without full support of the government.

Added to this was his disappointment in being cut out from the will of Sir Peter Warren, and the consequent controversy with the family over the terms of the will. If his accounts against the estate of Sir Peter are taken as valid, he was even the loser by a considerable amount. That he had his way, both in resigning, and in getting his accounts accepted, did not give much solace.

In politics he saw Governor Clinton, his ally, defeated and retiring in 1753. The chief justice was in power, and soon succeeded to the governorship. And Johnson's efforts to win local elections for his men were doomed to failure.

In spite of all this William Johnson's star was rising. His business prospered, his lands increased, and he seemed even more powerful and influential. This paradox needs to be explained. The Indian sachems of the Mohawks who had adopted William Johnson reacted strongly when he resigned from his office in charge of their affairs. It was necessary for him to continue at the last conference to save it from complete failure. This rendered the task of the newly appointed commissioners more difficult. They were to serve in conjunction with the governor and Council, and Johnson was a member of the Council. The commissioners included some of the old group and represented the same interests. Johnson, perhaps with tongue in cheek, had suggested the name of John Henry Lydius, often his arch rival, a neighbor who knew the Indians but was a slippery person. The suggestion was not taken.[1]

There now appeared on the scene a man whose service and devotion to Johnson in the ensuing years was so great that his merely coming to America may have been a turning point. Captain Peter Wraxall had raised a regiment for the abortive expedition to Canada in 1746. The next year he returned to England with Governor Clinton's blessing, presenting the case against the faction.[2] Now in 1752, he returned to New York with a commission as clerk of the city and county of Albany, together with that for Secretary of Indian Affairs in succession to Philip Livingston. Unfortunately for him, Clinton had already appointed Harme Gansevoort of Albany to the post, and the latter refused to make way for Wraxall. The appeal to the Lords of Trade was decided in Wraxall's favor, for it was a royal appointment, and the governor's power was limited.[3]

This initial obstruction by an Albany Dutchman was the beginning of Wraxall's intense dislike for the Dutch and for the Indian Commissioners in particular. He became convinced that Indian affairs would never be properly handled until a single commissary was again put in charge. The office of secretary, which may have looked like a sinecure from England, proved disappointing. The salary of £100 was not appropriated by the Assembly; he had to pay expenses of journeys to Albany to Indian conferences, and the hire of a deputy, out of his own pocket, or from his £65 fee as a receiver of quitrents. And he was denied fees as county and city clerk by Gansevoort, who forced him into an expensive suit.[4]

To explain the situation, the industrious Wraxall compiled an abridgement of the four volumes of Indian Affairs, for the years 1678 to 1751, which he addressed to Lord Halifax. Completed in 1754, this was the most eloquent testimony for the reform of the management of Indian affairs. It spread abroad the knowledge of Johnson's role and his exceptional qualifications for Indian diplomacy. Wraxall's future association with Johnson was to be intimate, and profitable to both.[5]

Other influential men were reflecting the views which Johnson often expressed, in Indian conferences and in company with his fellow councillors. One of the latter was Archibald Kennedy, the receiver general, who had attended the Indian conference at Albany in 1748. An effective writer, he published in 1751 a pamphlet entitled *The Importance of Gaining the Friendship of the Indians to the British Interest Considered*. This, opined Dr. Richard Shuckburgh, was "but a Repetition of yr. Letters, if I remember, of the Present State of the Indians wrote to the Govr. & lay'd by him before the Council of this Province & sent home." Nevertheless, Schuckburgh was so convinced of the future that he proposed himself as secretary and said that if endorsed by Governor Clinton, he would go home to promote the plan.[6]

The already venerable councillor, physician, and savant, Cadwallader Colden, who first put Johnson in print in his revised *History of the Five Nations* in 1747, now turned to him as a friend to whom he could entrust his son John, appointed in 1749 to a clerkship in Albany.[7] Later that year, he sent a letter with Peter Kalm, "a Swedish Gent'n a Professor in the Academy of Sciences there . . . now travilling in order to make discoveries in Botany & Astronomy . . . He comes strongly recommended to me by the King of Sweeden's Physicean & other friends in Europe & therefore what civility you shew him will lay an obligation on me."[8] Not only

did Kalm visit Mount Johnson, but he was so hospitably entertained and generously assisted in his tour that he protested his inability to express his thanks. Perhaps anticipating the publication of his findings, he promised

if God spare my life, I shall an other time have a better opportunity to let the
world know your great qualities, and when I have only said the half of them and of
your kindness, every body shall find, that they greatly do surpass all others and put
the mankind in admiration.[9]

He had been provided an excellent guide and interpreter, William Printup, to accompany him, and at Oswego John Lindesay and his wife at the instance of Johnson had been generous in their help.[10] Upon leaving this country Kalm again wrote
of his great appreciation, and when he later published findings, the world of culture and science were told of Colonel Johnson as an authority on the Indians of
New York.[11]

Even more closely connected with Johnson's future than Wraxall was a young
German who now made his appearance at Mount Johnson in company with the
Indian diplomat Conrad Weiser. This was Daniel Claus, an ambitious and talented
young man, who, like so many other Europeans, had been induced to come to the
New World to make his fortune. Born in 1727 in Bönnigheim, near the free city of
Heilbronn, he was descended from a good family, as he related it, who as Protestants had suffered in the religious wars. His father was prefect of his city and was
entitled to arms with the imperial insignia. But so great were the disturbances and
uncertainties of the time that Daniel hoped to better himself in the New World.
A smooth-talking neighbor, the son of a clergyman, had returned from Virginia
with a glowing tale of mercantile success—

of being concerned with a respectable House in Virginia who wanted to establish a
House upon the Rhine & in Holland for the Silk & Tobacco Trade, having these
Commodities brought from Am[erica]and manufactured in that part of Germany
on accnt of the Cheapness of Labour; and in short convinced people unacquainted
with those Matters of the most plausible prospect of Success and Advantage,
offering Mr. Claus a share; & at the same time buying up Quantities of Hock and
Rhinish wines and agreeing for the Building of Silk Manufactories enticing even a
rich German Nobleman to carry on said Buildings to whom he engaged the Chief
management of carrying on the work in Germany and Mr. Claus was to go with him
to America as being of proper Age to acquire the English Language & get acquainted with that Trade.[12]

Embarking for America with these high prospects, Claus soon suspected, even
while still on the voyage, that he was the victim of a deception. Arriving in Philadelphia in 1749, he contrived to get enough money for his return in 1750 but was
unable to get passage until fall. Accidentally meeting Conrad Weiser, who no doubt
pitied the plight of the unfortunate Württemberger, he was given the chance to
accompany a mission to New York and the Iroquois Indians. He accepted and set
out in May 1750. With Weiser there went also Henrich Melchior Mühlenberg, the
leader of the Lutherans of Pennsylvania. They travelled to Bethlehem, thence
across the Delaware and via the Rondout-Neversink Road to Kingston (Esopus),

thence to Rhinebeck, the old East Camp of the Palatines, where they were joined by Pastor John Christopher Hartwick. They stopped at Livingston Manor and then on to Albany.[13]

Weiser now led them to his old haunts in Schoharie, where he had lived with his father before migrating to Pennsylvania, and where he had learned the "6 Natn. Language." They stopped briefly at Johnson's new home, and then proceeded to Stonearabia, Canajoharie, and German Flats. Weiser's familiarity with the Indians and their way of life was a revelation to the young German. They carried gifts to the tribesmen and shared food with them. Later they had to eat the Indian concoctions, a "Diet of Indn. Corn Squashes, Entrails of Deer &c. which altho no Hardship for Mr. Weiser who experienced the likes before, was a great one for Mr. Claus, who never saw such eatables made use of before by Mankind, and was pretty well pinched with Hunger before he could persuade himself to taste them."[14]

Returning to Philadelphia, Claus was disappointed in again being too late to sail for Europe. Now Weiser introduced him to Governor James Hamilton, who saw a possibility of using the bright young man as an Indian interpreter. While staying three weeks at Onondaga, Claus had collected a vocabulary of Indian words which he methodically recorded in his journal. By the spring of 1751 the governor had prevailed upon Claus to go again among the Indians of New York, along with Weiser's son, Sammy, who it was thought might follow in the footsteps of his father.[15]

Whether as tutor of Sammy Weiser, as Conrad called him, or as prospective interpreter for Pennsylvania, Claus in the spring of 1751 again found himself in the Mohawk Valley. As he related it, he was

to take a Tour of the Mohawk Town at Fort Hunter & endeavour to improve in & acquire the Iroquois Language as Much as he could; [the governor] offering every Encouragement & Advantage in behalf of his Province & his Interest with the neighboring Provinces; One of Colo. Weisers Sons was also sent to accompany Mr. Claus, and a Credit was given him from the provce. to Mr. James Stevenson Mercht. at Alby. to answer any Sums of Cash Mr. Claus might draw upon him for, towards fixing themselves at one Brant's an old friend of Colo. Weisers and Chief of the Mohawks of Fort Hunter.[16]

Actually this was the mission of Conrad Weiser to endeavor to settle the war with the Catawbas. They went via New York, where Weiser visited Governor Clinton, and then on to Albany. Since Johnson was commissioned to settle the Catawbas' affair, old Conrad left his son and Claus in Albany and returned.[17] The arrangements did not turn out as expected.

Young Weiser did not like his Situation & without acquainting his parents returned to pennsylvania, and Mr. Claus continued his Studies; about that time an Alteration happened in Sir William's Family and one Mr. Robert Adams his Store Bookkeeper being dismissed and one Mr. James Wilson from Albany employed, who was an entire stranger to the Indians and their Language, Sir Wm. proposed to Mr. Claus to stay at his house where he could improve as much in the Indn Language as at Brants there being always 6 Natn. Indians about the house to which Mr. Claus consented and made himself as usefull as his Capacity would allow, but it coming to the ears of the Govr. of Pennsylvia. that Mr. Claus resided at Sr. Wms. then

Colo. Johnsons it created a Jealousy & Dissatisfaction and he was directed to put himself under the tuition of King Henry at Canajoharee with which Mr. Claus complied and fixed at that Chiefs house who was very proud of it and did everything in the world to make his Situation agreeable to him, instructing & entertaining him with the Traditions of his Ancestors, their Customs, Wars with their Indn. Enemies & Mr. Claus took Memorandums of it & then began to improve in writing the Indn. Language by getting his Indn. Tutor to dictate him Speeches, Messages, and other Forms and Customs used by the Inds. in Councils, Ceremonies of Condolence & &c.[18]

Weiser was worried and disappointed in Sammy and irked that he and Claus used up their money and asked for more. Finally April 24, 1753, he wrote; "I have ordered Sammy to come home and bring me an Account Mr. Clause may Chuse for himself, either to stay or come."[19] Claus stayed, and later reported to Governor Hamilton the many advantages he enjoyed at Johnson's. There was more opportunity to use his new knowledge there.

Doubtless your Honour will have been informed of my Living at Present with the Honble. William Johnson, that since the time my Indian Landlord ruined himself by marriage, & was forced to leave his place & move 20 miles higher, when above sd. Gentleman generously offered me his Lodging, & in Order not to be Looser of the Indn. Language, confided the Keys of his Store in me, to see the way of Indn. Trade, & in short, introduces me to all affairs necessary & advantageous to my Employ, . . .[20]

Peter Wraxall had a keen appreciation for the talents of young Claus, for as Indian Secretary he had learned the deficiencies of those who acted as interpreters. Not only where many corrupt, as traders and parties in the treaties, but so ignorant as to understand well neither the Dutch nor English language. "The Interpreter ought," he wrote, "in my opinion to have a handsome Salary & be a Man of Substance, & Character to be upon Oath neither to be concerned directly nor Indirectly in any Indian Trade, & if possible Not to reside within the Area of Albany."[21] On his first appearance as interpreter for a major Indian treaty, Claus was given an accolade by Wraxall. Although there were three older and seasoned interpreters present (Stevens, Clement, and Printup), Wraxall wrote

N.B. This speech was translated and wrote in the Indian language by Mr. Daniel Clause, a German Gentleman of education who hath lived for sometime amongst the Indians of the upper Mohawk Castle in order to make himself master of their language, herein he was assisted by the other Interpreters under the inspection of Coll: Johnson. Before it was delivered in public it was read in Indian to two chief Sachims and Eminent speakers of the Onondaga and Onejda Nations, and was afterwards spoken to the whole Body of Indians with their consent and approbation, by the Onondaga Sachem called Red Head who was prompted by the Onejda Sachem to whom Mr. Clause read the speech with a low voice paragraph by paragraph, Colonel Johnson having first read it aloud to all present in English.[22]

It was at this time, too, that Johnson began his active support of Anglican missions. Like other traders, he at first felt that the men of the cloth in trying to control the rum trade were interlopers. He had so mentioned the Reverend Henry Barclay, whose early zeal and gains at Fort Hunter had been followed by a period of frustration and reaction. Johnson never seemed to like him.

Son of the Reverend Thomas B. Barclay, first minister to St. Peter's Church in Albany, where he was born in 1714, Barclay was graduated from Yale in 1734, and began his work among the Mohawks as a catechist in 1736. The following year he went to England for holy orders, which he received in January 1738. Returning as missionary at Albany he displayed considerable energy and rebuilt the chapel at Fort Hunter. He preached in Dutch, and at a treaty in Albany he addressed the Indians in their own tongue. He baptized most of the adults at the two castles and had Indian lay readers to serve in his absence.[23]

Then with the outbreak of war in 1744, his work was undermined and all but collapsed. French agents spread the rumor that the English intended "to Cut them all in pieces," and that, in Barclay's words, "I was the Chief contriver of the Destruction intended against them, That Notwithstanding My Seeming Affection for Them, I was a very Bad Man in League with the Devil Who was the Author of All the Books I had given them."[24]

While the Lower Castle did not believe the rumors, the Upper was all aflame. Although Hendrick had laid the rumor to Joncaire, and other French agents, the evil persisted, and attendance at the mission fell off. As noted above, no one was quite sure of the status of the Indians when William Johnson was first called to serve the provincial government. In October 1746, Barclay was offered the rectorship of Trinity Church, New York, and accepted. In leaving, he promised to seek help for the Indian missions from the Society for the Propagation of the Gospel and to look for a successor. "The State of My Parish at Albany when I left It was Truly Deplorable, Several of the Inhabitants having been Oblidg'd to Seek New Habitations, And another Such Year as the last will I fear Reduce It to a Garrison Town."[25]

The Mohawks of the Upper Castle also complained that after he left them, Barclay still claimed as his possession the land they gave him for a house "as his particular property," whereas they understood that it should go to the next minister, his successor.[26]

Barclay did not forget the Indian mission and at the return of peace in 1748 he recommended to the Society for the Propagation of the Gospel a young Scot, John Ogilvie, who was just graduated from Yale. Since he was then serving as a lay reader in Connecticut, it was arranged to have him go to London for holy orders. He returned to New York in 1749, but in such bad health that he was compelled to wait until the following spring before going to Albany. In the meantime he prepared himself, studying the Mohawk language under the tutelage of the Reverend Mr. Barclay.[27]

The young Reverend Mr. Ogilvie, then but twenty-six years old, was well suited to the task before him. He was able to preach in Dutch as well as English, a prime requirement for the church in Albany, and he displayed considerable tact and adaptability. He soon was preaching in Mohawk and making regular visits to the two castles. In fact, his ministry was threefold: he was rector of St. Peter's Church, Albany; chaplain to the military garrison at Fort Frederick there; and missionary to the Mohawks at Fort Hunter. He had to make strenuous efforts to recover the lost ground caused by the war and the relapse of the work for four years, but by 1752 he could report considerable progress. In spite of the ravages of the rum traffic, which took a heavy toll in murders and other deaths, the mission was actively carried on among the Mohawks. He was assisted by the Reverend John Jacob Oel, who lived near the Upper Castle, and also by Chief Abraham, who acted as an Indian lay reader. In Albany, the church was rebuilt and refurnished with a new bell. Yet the work was slow and often very discouraging. Nevertheless, he had no stronger ally than William Johnson.[28]

It is difficult to draw the line between the religious and secular functions of such a pioneer cleric. As a chaplain he had to bolster the morale and correct the morals of the military—no mean task. In winning the Indians for the Anglican church he was confronted by the French Catholics who were attempting to loosen the English hold upon the natives. It was a contest with both political and religious goals. If the French used their Jesuits to wean away the Iroquois from the English interest, it was necessary for the English to counteract this work with their own missionaries. Johnson appreciated Ogilvie's work, gave him every assistance, and eventually asked the Board of Trade to supplement his salary.[29]

Ogilvie in return became Johnson's agent in Albany, served to relay messages and funds from New York, and even put up the Catawba Indian peace mission in his house. He accompanied Johnson upon journeys into the Indian country and participated in treaties. It was an arrangement of mutual advantage. For ten years Ogilvie was in Albany and the Mohawk area and a constant participant in public affairs.[30]

Relieved of his Indian responsibility for a time, Johnson tried to recoup his losses by commercial activity. An opportunity offered in the gathering and sale of ginseng, a root then found in the wooded valleys and swamps which made up so much of the unsettled area. Interest in the traffic may have been stirred by the visit of Peter Kalm, who described the plant in the record of his visit to Canada in 1750. Even then it was known principally as valued in China, the culture first having been begun there. American Indians seem not to have valued it, but "Chinese ascribe it power to cure several diseases and of power of restoring new strength to the body lost through exertion of mental and physical faculties." French Canadians had begun to gather the roots early in the eighteenth century, shipping them to France, whence they were sent to China. The dried roots brought six francs a pound in Quebec, but in Peking might be worth seven or eight times their weight in silver. (The odd-shaped root often resembled a human form, and this to the Chinese symbolized magical power.) According to Kalm, the French exploitation had caused the price to fall in China, and consequently in this country.[31]

Johnson in 1751 heard that the French were getting a good price for the roots and had the Indians gather them for him. After three months they were able to get enough for three casks which he shipped to his factor, Samuel & William Baker, in London. He did not know how much he should pay, but figured if they sold for less than twelve shillings, he would lose out. The next year he made another shipment, this time to George Liebenrood in London, and reported that some of his sold for thirty-two shillings a pound; others were reported to have obtained forty shillings.[32]

This apparently made a good profit, for Johnson was eager to cash in before others began to flood the market. I "expect as there is not any quantity shipped from these parts yet, that Mine will fetch the highest price being verry clean & well dryed."[33]   Then a little later, "I hope you may dispose of them all at a good price before there comes Many to market. There are severall buying them up here, but as they are quite strangers to the management of them, know not how to Cure them Soon. So that I have got the start of 'em, which I hope you will improve to my advantage & your own."[34]   For a while the rush for quick profits in ginseng, stimulated by Johnson's enterprise, was the chief activity of the valley. Claus wrote to Weiser in Pennsylvania, August 23, 1752,

I cannot adequately describe what Furore there is round here over the famous Roots. Coll. Johnson has already bought over 1600 Bushels, and for 3 weeks has been paying 40/ for the green and £4 for the dried, most of the good people of Albany are laying out money and goods in speculation in the stuff and many of them dont know where to send it; as I hear Coll. Johnson sends his to London and from there it is sent to China where it is bought as the greatest rarity; In Canada this Root Business is said to be much bigger because the french Indians in Oswego give 1 lb of beaver for every Pound of green Roots. The Indians call it Ochdéra. I wonder if the same is to be found in Pennsylvania. Samy and I were out with brand [Brant] helping him look for the stuff he is at it all day long, it makes the Mohawk river quite Rich since a child can earn 10/ a Day, Coll. Johnson has sent Belts of Wampum to the United 5 Nations to collect the stuff for him, and he is the originator of this trade, which makes him very popular. . . .[35]

Aside from his popularity and the widespread employment which he gave, there is little indication of the effects of the speculative flurry. Johnson built up a good credit with his London merchants and was able to order furnishings and books to adorn his new home. But the excitement soon wore off as rumors of wars and frontier aggression filtered in from north and west. The ginseng trade as an extractive exploitation of the natural growth diminished with the supply. Indians continued to bring in small quantities as an item of trade, along with their pelts. But future references are mainly inquiries as to the state of the market.[36] There was little interest in the aromatic root as a medicinal herb, although Dr. Richard Shuckburgh had written Johnson for a pound or two which he hoped to introduce in his practice "both as a Pectoral & Stomachick."[37]

If there was activity of any kind in the valley, William Johnson was likely to be a party, and now in a period of relative calm there was a resurgence of land speculation. He had taken advantage of opportunities to get adjacent land and to pick up property here and there. But the great speculations in land could not be hid; government and officials were involved, and if one were a councillor, he was well aware of what went on, for the Council had to give its approval. Governors were not immune to the fever, and just as Cosby and George Clarke had feathered their nests, George Clinton could be expected to do likewise. Had he no inclination for such a venture he would find himself beset by those needing his influence and pressing on him a share in their schemes.

Johnson's feelings about land were always somewhat mixed. As a merchant, a settler, and a young man on the make, he desired land and seized upon it when he could. Yet he early deplored the unseemly scramble of speculators, the frenzy to get all one could regardless of the means. He was a reasonable man, and he liked to see things kept within bounds. He also had respect for law and orderly procedure. If one acquired land he should follow the rules. Then there was the problem of the Indians' claims and title. With his responsibility for Indian affairs he was well aware of the evil consequences of defrauding the natives. He had spent some years keeping them mollified, in the British interest in wartime, and satisfied with their trade and gifts. One could not do this and at the same time be an unabashed grabber of Indian lands. There were plenty of such land-grabbers about, and Johnson became their natural enemy. Such fellows held the Indians in contempt, drugged them with rum to get their marks on deeds, and stopped at nothing to satisfy their greed. Frequently these land-grabbers had no interest in settlement or use of the lands; they held on for a profit, for resale, and were adept at litigation and legal skulduggery. They were an incessant problem for the authorities and provincial officials.

It was hard to avoid trouble if one bought land of Indians, for it was not always clear who owned their land. Indians generally were agreeable to the prospect of sale and could be persuaded. They well knew that their assent was not enough, and that sale could be reviewed by the Nation. So Johnson moved warily. Arent Stevens wrote him May 8, 1751:

According to your disire I stopt Hendrick the Indian yesterday morning and keept him here, and examined him who was the Owners of that Land which you have an Inclination to Buy, And Beg'd he would tell me the truth as you would not have any disputes after you had Bought it. . .[38]

In this instance Hendrick assured him the Canajoharies owned the land, not the Oneidas, and that the principal sachems would be called to Johnson's home to seal the bargain and to sign the deed.[39]

Such a move was only the first step, however, and after an Indian claim was established and bought, a petition must be drawn describing the Indian purchase and presented to governor and Council. Since there was a limit of two thousand acres to a purchaser, the petition had to include enough names to meet this require-ment, for most petitions were for many thousands of acres. These were dummy names, as everyone knew, of persons who would sign away their claims later. There were other obstacles and details, and Johnson was fortunate in having good friends in New York to aid him. The provincial secretary, Goldsbrow Banyar, explained the process.

And if you were to follow the Custon in such a Case, your 2d. pet'n. should be in the Names of some Friends in Trust for you and in whom you can confide to re-convey the Lands when patented. It is also necessary (perhaps not absolutely so) to incert the Names of all the parties to be concerned, the Contrary has been practised sometimes but after the purchase made it is without doubt necessary to incert their Names when you Petition for a Patent . . .The Lands you purchase must be surveyed by the Surveyor General or his Deputy in the presence of the Indians and the Boundaries incerted in the deed in their presence. An Interpreter must be Sworn, by a Justice of the Peace to be also present, & the purchase Money or other Consideration must be paid in the presence of the Surveyor or his Deputy & the Justice And Certificates of all this endorsed and signed on the Back of the Deed.[40]

This was for a large grant of 130,000 acres, two miles wide on both banks of the Susquehanna River down to the Pennsylvania border. There were certain flaws in the description, which Banyar pointed out, and he urged Johnson to come down to New York to straighten them out. This he did not do, and the petition was denied, at least for a time. Johnson was to get a grant there many years later.[41]

One difficulty was that Johnson had presented two petitions on the same day. The first, for land surrounding Lake Canunda (Onondaga), had been pressed upon him by the Indians, who feared the advances of the French. They wanted to forestall these claims and to get the protection of the English. This was quickly granted by the Council, for it had political implications.[42]

Apparently as consolation for the failure of his larger petition, Banyar threw in Johnson's way Governor Clinton's share in the Stevens Patent on the Mohawk. Since Clinton was leaving in 1753, Banyar persuaded him "that his landed Interest here was too inconsiderable to employ much of his Thoughts in England, I told him I would venture in your behalf to pay him the same as you paid me for mine." This was £213, and Banyar opined it was better than if he had gotten the Susquehanna purchase, which would have cost him so much more. This sixth part of the Stevens Patent was no mean acquisition.[43]

Thus began a correspondence and a friendship with the deputy secretary which was to be of the greatest significance in the career of William Johnson. Born in London in 1724 (thus nine years the junior of Johnson), Banyar came to New York in 1737, and in 1746 he began his long career in the provincial service. Successively he became deputy secretary, deputy clerk of the Council, and deputy clerk of the supreme court. Later he was register of the court of chancery, judge of probate, and examiner in the prerogative court. The right-hand man of governors and councillors, he proved to be eyes and ears for Johnson in New York, as his letters show.[44]   His good turn for Johnson was many times reciprocated, and both profited by the connection. In all land purchases he handled the legal details; Johnson was the indispensable man in dealing with the Indians. They had other interests in common, although their personalities were vastly different. Banyar was one more friend in Johnson's widening circle of acquaintance and a vital influence in his career.

XI

IMPERIAL PROBLEMS

When Johnson surrendered the responsibility for Indian affairs in 1751, he was not able to detach himself from their problems. As merchant, landholder, and councillor, he had an immediate interest in the safety of the frontier and peaceful relations with the natives. He could not sit idly by and see the commissioners bungle through. The Indians themselves turned to him, and, from the contacts he had established, intelligence of even far-distant events reached his ears. It was disconcerting for the governor and commissioners at every conference to hear his praises sung by the Indian speakers, and their dissatisfaction was in itself a problem.

At the conference at Albany in July 1751, Johnson withdrew, and the meaning of his action was duly sensed. A principal purpose of the conference was to end the long-continued war between the Catawbas of the south and the Iroquois. Conrad Weiser, whose journeys from Pennsylvania to Onondaga in 1737, 1743, and 1745 had unsuccessfully broached this problem to the chiefs, was again the emissary of that province. Coming by way of New York, he conferred with Governor Clinton, and also met the Catawba Indian delegates on their way north. In fact he travelled up the Hudson with them on the sloop to Albany, and had a good opportunity to counsel them. He found them friendly and conciliatory, but he had to explain to others that this chance contact did not make him their advocate.[1]

The Catawba conflict was deep-rooted. The Iroquois conquests of the Delawares and Susquehannas had given them jurisdiction over the backcountry Indians of Pennsylvania and Virginia. The addition of the Tuscaroras to the Five Nations had given the longhouse further reasons for keeping open the road to the south. Their ambassadors and representatives, the half kings, asserted their authority by repeated journeys, and hunters and warriors travelled the trails along the Allegheny Mountains, as white men pushed farther westward. One of these trails, stretching from the Genesee River in New York, through Pennsylvania west of the mountains but east of the forks of the Ohio, and into Virginia, was known as the Catawba Path. On this (also known as Warriors Path) war parties moved north and south, frequently clashing as they met, plundering and foraging the countryside.[2]

The Catawbas, living to the westward of the Carolinas, were friendly to the colonies and settlers there and served as a buffer between them and the more war-like Shawnees and Cherokees. When attacked by their enemies and almost in danger of extinction, the Catawbas fell back upon the southern frontiers, raiding, robbing, and killing the inhabitants. So the governor of South Carolina sought to end the war, and sent his representative, William Bull, to Albany. It was also suggested that this Indian war was stimulated by the French, who would like to see the Indian allies of the English colonies at loggerheads, or perhaps destroy each other.[3]

The Catawbas at Albany put on a good show. Weiser conducted them before the assembled delegates of the colonies and of the Six Nations. "The[y] Came along Singing with their Collabashes dressed with feders [feathers] in their hands, they Continued Singing for a while after they Sat down." The calumet was passed around and smoked, and "the Catawba King Stood Up & Spoke, but appeared to be very Much daunted and Could Make no hand of it." It was difficult for the inter-preter to "English it." Finally, Weiser was forced to give the substance of it to the Mohawks.[4]

The Catawbas were willing to make a lasting peace, but the Six Nations speaker said it was customary first for them to bring the prisoners whom they held, and then the Six Nations would release prisoners. The Catawbas replied that two or more of the Six Nations people should come to the Catawbas and then the prisoners would be sent back. But, no, said the Six Nations, this is never done; you must send up your prisoners. Next year, promised the Catawbas, they would do this. And they must come by water, said the Six Nations speaker, for the subject nations are widespread, it would take time to inform them of the truce, and the emissaries might be murdered on the way.[5]

There were other discordant notes. French influence was suspected and feared—apparently for good reason, for Weiser noted on July 2:

This day above twenthy Canoes arrived with french Indians they Came loaded with Beavers, they the french Indians went and paid their Compliment to Govr. Clinton, as did the Chiefes of the Six nations afterwards. . . . [Weiser] Spent the Evening with Mr. Stevens the provincial Interpreter and some of the Chiefes of the Mohocks, to wit Heinry, Nickes, Abram & others. they asked what Buisness the french Indians had in Albany at this time and said that the Govr of Canada would not Suffer the Mohocks in Canada, he would tell them to be gone by Such an Hour or Suffer Imprisement, they Said further that they Could not open their heart to the Govr. of n-york in the presence of those Indians, but it is well known that the french praying Indians are all or Most all Mohocks and are allways Kindly received in the Mohocks Country.[6]

The Dutch merchants of Albany and the Indian commissioners, whose interests were identical, were doing nothing to stop this trade. Nickus had just returned from captivity in Canada, from which he had been ransomed, and these pinpricks rankled. Repeatedly the Mohawks asked that Johnson be reinstated in the manage-ment of their affairs; they told Clinton to have the king do this, but the governor made no promise.

We desire Collo Johnson may be Reinstated; for as there is Some of the Six Nations gone to Canada, about the French Building a fort at Oniagara; unless your Excellency Appoints Some person for us to go to, you Cannot Expect to hear what Answer they Bring.[7]

Presents were given, many speeches of condolence were made, and the governor rather abruptly left for New York. Weiser left the Indians well disposed toward Pennsylvania, but the projected peace was not fulfilled. Before word could reach the warriors, more killings took place along the Warrior's Path, and the Six Nations were reported again vowing to destroy the Catawbas. Governor Glen urged the Hagler King of the Catawbas to keep his warriors at home, where they could stand guard over their women and children and defend them from "the French and Northern Indians."[8]

In the meantime serious threats were being made by the French against the western Indians. If the Six Nations could not be won over, perhaps the farther Indians could. The governors of Canada were reviving their claim to the Ohio Valley, and in the summer of 1749 the expedition of Céleron de Blainville went via the lakes and Niagara to the Ohio River. At river junctions and other points he planted lead plates and attached metal signs to trees asserting the claims of the king of France. He also intended to punish a tribe which in 1748 had killed fifteen Frenchmen.[9] Johnson gave the Ohio Indians timely warning so that Céleron and his forces found them ready and hostile, and he decided to try diplomacy rather than force. The English rejoiced that the Indians remained in their interest; the French blamed their attitude on the English traders. Johnson's report to Clinton gave a graphic description of

the harsh reception & Usage they gave the French Generall or Commanding Officer, who went there last Summer with a Body of 500 Men in order to destroy them, but finding them ready to receive him, by Intelligence from me altered his Tune, & told them he came there for their Good, to forbid the English meaning the Philadelphians &ca: Encroaching on them and their Lands; also to Invite them all to Canada in the Spring, to see their Father who waited for them in open Arms; which they all immediately refused with the utmost Indignation, throwing the Belts of Wampum, with which he spoke on the Ground. At his departure some of them fired a Ball at him, which Graz'd along his Ribbs.[10]

Céleron had better luck with some of the other Indians, but, finding them generally oriented toward English traders, he doubted his success. He turned westward, planting more plates, and went as far as Detroit before returning. Far from winning the Indians over, he implanted new suspicions which were promptly utilized by the English. In the West, said Johnson, he had tried to stir up the Ottawas against the English, and this had alarmed the Six Nations.[11]

They [French] succeeded so far as to get 15 Castles of the Ottawawees & ca. to take up the Ax, upon which they made great Entertainments for them, such as Slaughtering Bullocks &ca. then Sung their War Songs, five Sachims of the Mississagees who are firmly attached to the British Interest being present at the time, at Night as the rest were Dancing and merry, they Slipt away, went to their own Castle, told all had past, to their Brethren, who were much Shocked at the News,

Saying in their way they were all Dead; however they were determined to live and Die by the Five Nations according to the old agreement made between them, so Sent an Express immediately to the Senecas with a Belt of Wampum, and 15 bloody Sticks tyed to it, to be sent through all the Nations, & then to your Excellency Warning them and us to be on our Guard, that the French had a design to Cutt them all off this Spring or Summer [1750], which Belt lyes now with me. the Reason of the 15 Bloody Sticks is to shew that there are 15 Castles Joined the French to spill their Blood. It has alarmed the five Nations prodigiously and no less all the Inhabitants on the Mohawks River.[12]

As he had done many times before, Johnson implored the governor to give the Six Nations substantial evidence of support, to parade the militia ("How shocking a thing it is that even our Militia cannot be review'd, having no Militia Act"), and to face up to the French menace. But he was only told of the complacency of the Assembly, while they congratulated themselves on the rebuff given to Céleron.

Johnson took upon himself to do what he could, but his patience was wearing thin.

The Women of both [Mohawk] Castles came to Me, & beg'd I would repair the Stockados round their Castles, where several are decayed & pulled down, & to have Irons and Locks put to all the Gates thereof, which I immediately got done, & promised them all the assistance in my power, even my House for a Refuge in Case of Need, which pleased them much.[13]

Clinton conveyed Johnson's report to Governor James Hamilton of Pennsylvania for these encroachments were on the soil of that province, but he was unmoved. "I can not venture to put the Province to a considerable Expence without receiving some stronger evidence of the necessity of it, than Coll Johnsons letter to the Governor of another Province."[14] Clinton said to the Lords of Trade that Governor Hamilton was so confident of the Ohio Indian nations' attachment to the British interest that he was not apprehensive, "but I think by our situation and the Correspondence the five Nations have with the distant Nations I can be better informed than he can be."[15]

Now there came to Johnson's hands one of the lead plates which the French were using to sanction their claim to the Ohio Valley. It was stolen, he said, by one of the Indians from "Jean Ceur [Joncaire], the French Interpreter, at Niagara, on his way to the River Ohio." On December 4, 1750, a Cayuga sachem presented it at a conference at Mount Johnson, and wished to know what the writing meant. Joncaire, he said, had gone that summer to the Ohio Valley, to stay three years and to build a trading house at the carrying place between the Ohio and Lake Erie.[16]

This presented a wonderful opportunity for Johnson. He praised the Indians for their attachment to the English and reminded them of the advantages they enjoyed in the trade with Pennsylvania and Virginia traders, whose prices were so much better than those of the French. The French, their enemy, were now trying to take all this from them. "But their Scheme, now laid against you, & yours . . . is worse than all the rest, as will appear by their own writing here on this Plate." He gave the substance of the inscription, "with some necessary additions," and with a belt of wampum sent the message to all the other nations. The sachem responded heartily. "Brother Corlear & Warraghiyagee. I have with great attention & surprise, heard you repeat the substance of that Devilish Writing which I brought you & also with pleasure noticed your just remarks thereon, which really agree with my own sentiments on it."[17]

The plate was then sent to Clinton and from him to the Lords of Trade, where its presence might strengthen the hand of those favoring a strong policy in behalf of the Indians and against the French.

The rebuff to Céleron gave little comfort as reports came from the north of renewed French activity. The post at Oswego was alert to any threat to its own security, or to that of friendly Indians, and was in a position to observe movements on the lake. There Lieutenant John Lindesay, a good friend of Johnson, reported how he saw the French coming and going and, in 1751, relayed these portents. Three Frenchmen, in February, told him of Joncaire's place on the Ohio, where he intended to build a fort; in April Joncaire's brother (Philippe Thomas de Joncaire, brother of Chabert) "came here in his way to Niagara, and said he was to command the new Fort on the carrying place above Niagara"; and in May a Missisauga canoe brought news of an army passing "Cataracque" for this purpose.[18] Finally July 10, Ottrowana, a Cayuga chief, told of his negotiating a treaty with the Missisaugas, but that at Cadaracqui the French "were building a large ship, which was to have three Masts, and that some there told him when fitted, was designed to come and take this place [Oswego]. That he saw the six Cannon, designed for said purpose, three yards long with a wide Bore."[19]

French traders passing Oswego spread stories of strong forces being prepared to go to the Ohio country, to garrison posts and to control the Indians. The French governor, Jonquière, carrying on the policies of his predecessor, justified all these excursions, the claims of Céleron, and the right of the French traders in this area in a letter to Governor Clinton, all of which the latter denied.[20] But the French did not make a concerted effort until the arrival of Governor Marquis Duquesne in 1752. Some Canadians, in fact, such as the acting governor, Longueuil, hesitated to stir up trouble in that quarter.[21] With the help of the able Intendant Bigot, Duquesne made preparations for the notable expedition of 1753, commanded by the veteran Sieur de Marin. Early in February 1753, an advance guard of some two hundred and fifty men, including workmen, set out and succeeded in building a fort and garrison at Presque Isle on Lake Erie.[22] A year later Johnson was to have a firsthand report of this from Stephen Coffin, a prisoner of the French, who had chosen to go along as a soldier and then deserted to Oswego on the return trip.[23]

When in April 1753, Marin's force of two thousand men left the St. Lawrence for the Ohio country, the Indians rushed to Johnson with the news.

"Last night I was alarm'd about 12 of the Clock by two Conajoharie Indians accompanied by a great many Mohawks, who came whooping & hollowing in a frightfull manner." They brought wampum from the Six Nations to acquaint him that within forty-eight hours two of their young men hunting near "Swegaachey below Cadaraghqui" saw a great many French and Indians marching, well equipped for war. They judged there were about twelve hundred men besides bateaumen. They left spies to see whether the French took the road south, which would menace their castles. When it had passed, however, they learned that the expedition was against the Twightwees of Ohio. They asked that the governor at once warn the Ohio Indians lest they be surprised. Johnson, to reassure them, dispatched his letter to Clinton "by one of my own people on Horseback in their presence."[24]

On May 15 the officers at Oswego reported the passing of "thirty odd French Canoes," and they were told this was a part of Marin's army of six thousand, with five hundred Indians. Not all Indians would fight, however, and many were employed to hunt and supply the army. It was confirmed that the French meant to build forts at several points. And the Six Nations were very uneasy at the prospect.[25]

The French expedition reached Niagara, passed the portage around the falls, and joined the advance contingent at the post of Presque Isle on Lake Erie. Soon they constructed a portage to French Creek and built Fort Le Boeuf, the first outpost on the Ohio. The Indians appeared friendly, but in September the half king Tanacharison, the representative of the Iroquois, came to Presque Isle and warned the French commander not to take their lands. He asked that the French not build forts on their land of the Belle Rivière. This was brusquely turned down by Marin, who intended to proceed with the other forts he had been commissioned to erect. He knew that the Indians could do little to stop his forces.[26] What the Indians could not accomplish, however, the forces of nature could. Sickness, difficulties of supply, and low water in the streams prevented further advance. Marin became sick and died. At year's end the French had only two forts of those they had planned. Virginia sent out young George Washington, who, in December 1753, delivered the ultimatum of that province at Fort Le Boeuf. This, too, was rejected by the French, but they were well informed that both the Indians and the English regarded them as invaders.[27]

Disgusted with their efforts to find any sympathy among the Albany commissioners, and alarmed by the French aggression in Ohio, even though they were told that the French had no designs on their castles, the Mohawks now resolved to go to New York to see Clinton and the Council in person.[28] On June 12, 1753, seventeen Mohawks of the Canajoharie Castle appeared at Fort George for a conference. Governor Clinton and the Council, including Johnson, were assisted by Peter Wraxall, the secretary for Indian affairs, and William Printup, interpreter. After renewing the chain, professing loyalty, and noting how their affairs had been neglected, they reproached the government for its weakness in the defense of Albany and their castles. With mounting indignation they upbraided the English for inaction in the face of French threats, while they asked Indians to oppose the French unassisted. Now they again reviewed the several cases of land grabs at their expense and demanded to know what was to be done. Clinton's reply was weak and ineffectual: the commissioners were now in charge of their affairs; another meeting would be held in Albany; there were not enough members of the Council present; and he could not give a full answer on the several land grievances.

Hendrick, now fully aroused, scornfully rejected these excuses. "All what we have desired to be done for our Good is not granted which makes our hearts ache very much. . . . You tell us that we shall be redressed at Albany, but we know them so well we will not trust to them, for they are no people but Devils, so we rather desire you'l say Nothing shall be done for us . . . as soon as we come home we will send up a Belt of Wampum to our Brothers the 5 Nations to acquaint them the Covenant Chain is broken between you and us. So brother you are not to expect to hear of me any more, and Brother we desire to hear no more of you." And with that the Indians stalked away.[29]

As an elder statesman who had endured much, Hendrick was not to be trifled with, and he well knew the impact of his dramatic speech. Yet he was criticized for his action by the other tribes and by the whites, who agreed that he had acted badly. William Johnson had sat quietly in the Council and heard it all, and one cannot doubt that he knew what was to follow. Clinton had no alternative; he had only to go to Johnson to mollify the discontents. What concessions he made, what the Council agreed to, what was done to sidetrack the Albany commissioners does not appear in the record. Johnson was given a new commission to deal with the Mohawks and with the council of the longhouse at Onondaga. He went directly home and summoned the Mohawks and Canajoharies to come down to him.

The third day they arrived at my House to the Number of 250 great & small. They gave me their usual Salute wh. is fireing all their Guns. after getting them all quarters, they mett, then Hendrick rose up & desired to speak a few Words first before I begun, which are as follows. Brother Warraghiyagey on receipt of your Message (by our Brothers ye. Mohawks) our Hearts laughed for Joy to hear our only Brother was again impowered to treat with the Five Nations, and manage their Affairs, we then Agreed unanimously to go down, & hear you speak, but had the Governour desired the Commissioners of Albany to Invite us down, we would not move a Foot, nor hear them at all.[30]

In four days at his house Johnson handled many problems and so well arranged affairs that the whole aspect of Indian affairs was changed.

I have not only Joined or welded the Chain again and made it as Strong & bright as ever. but have also timely prevented the warriours of both Castles goeing to Warr against the Catabaws, and Stopped above a Dozen Familys goeing to Canada being all ready for a March, the reason the latter gave me for their leaving this place, was that they must inevitably perish for want if they stay'd here, upon wh. I gave them a small matter of provision for the present, and promised them more which I hope I may be enabled to perform, as a breach of promise in such a Case especially at this time must be verry Ill taken. had I known their wants (when at York) as well as now should have laid out a good part of the Money for provisions as nothing could be more acceptable.[31]

With no clear directive from governor or council, Johnson could not employ the Indians against the French, nor could he hope to restrain them in provocative acts, except by persuasion. Here, indeed, imperial policy was hanging in the balance. Clinton was about to give place to a new governor with new instructions from home. But to Johnson the course for Indian policy was clear. Could he expect the plans which he had formulated and so often expounded to be accepted at home?

I have considered the takeing the Ax out of their hands at this time would not be proper, and have asked their opinion about it, they agreed wth. me and said that were it to be done now, as the French are at War with their Brothers at Ohio, & Elsewhere, that it would be like tying their Hands, while their people were knocked in the Head, & begged it might not be done at this Juncture. wherefore I thought it my Duty to acquaint Your Excellency of it, and know how I am to act in that affair, being part of my Instructions, and also inserted in my Commission. If I may give my opinion, I think it best to be done when the Govr. Meets them at Albany, provided it be then peace. It will be verry necessary to make Sachims now when I go up in Everry Nation (as there are severall dead) of those who are most hearty in our Interest. for which purpose I should want at least Eight or ten Meddalls. which if approved of, the Sooner they were Sent up the better, I assure Your Excellency that by doeing so, the French have gained a great many to their Interest. and must daily more, if we do not the Same at least.[32]

Several Seneca, Onondaga, and Oneida sachems were at Johnson's house, and he assured them that he would soon meet all the nations at Onondaga.

Now that French invasion of the Ohio Valley was a reality, Governor Hamilton of Pennsylvania, who had brushed aside Johnson's earlier warning, called upon the venerable Conrad Weiser to make another diplomatic mission to Onondaga. It was an unhappy and fruitless journey for old Conrad, who was unable to deliver his letter to Clinton in New York, and did not get the latter's letter advising him of Johnson's new commission. At Albany he conferred with the discredited Indian commissioners and tried to negotiate for the return of Pennsylvania prisoners from Canada. Then he journeyed to Johnson's, where he arrived August 11. Already Johnson had made great advances in improving relations. By virtue of his former friendships, Weiser held long discourse with the sachems and recorded their views in his journal—Hendrick "Henry Peters . . . (he that made so much Noise at New York)," . . . Abraham, "an old Acquaintance of Mine, . . . the Most sincere Indian of that Nation," and others. Thus he obtained some answers to the questions Governor Hamilton had propounded in his instructions.[33]

Johnson received Weiser warmly and extended his usual generous hospitality. But Weiser's conferences were held in his presence, and he had no intention of letting the old interpreter take the negotiations out of his hands. He gently informed him of his plans and showed him his new commission from the governor. Weiser explained in his journal.

Coll. Johnson shewed me his Commission and Instruction, which he had from the Governor of New York under the Broad Seal of that Government. I judged thereby that he did not want my Company [to Onondaga], because he never asked me to go with him, or proceed on my Journey. I had told him before that I had set out from Philadelphia to go to Onondago by Governor Hamilton's Order, but as he had such a Commission (having been informed by the Way) I thought my Journey to Onondago would be needless. He said he left it to me, but I perceived some Coolness in him as to my going; I thought it was best not to proceed any further at this time, but to return.[34]

If this was intended as a rebuff, it was done with such charm and finesse as to leave no rancor, and Conrad could conclude his three-day visit with some satisfaction.

The Coll. has been very kind to me, and entertained me and my Son very handsomely during my Stay, and was open and free in all Discourses to me, and would have me to change now and then a Letter with him, and whenever I came to the

Mohocks Country to make his House my Home, and offered to do all the Service to the Province of Pennsylvania and myself that he possibly could in Indian affairs.[35]

It was not so, however, when he reached New York on his return. The ailing Clinton, about to give up his office, was curt and petulant, blaming Weiser for his failure to wait for his instructions, and snubbing him when he sought to take formal leave. It was considered both as an affront to the agent as well as the province of Pennsylvania, and left a bad taste.[36]

Weiser noted in his journal that the Senecas, the westernmost of the Six Nations, upon hearing of the French in the Ohio Valley "sent a Message to their Brother Col. Johnson to ask how long they had to live, and what was the Intention of the French. They thought the Coll. must know, and begged earnestly to be informed how things were." They were told that they must now resist the French in Ohio, not to permit them to build forts or to take the land of the Six Nations. If they did not, "it would be over with the Six Nations, and their Union would signify nothing more.... They must now stand up and shew that they are a People of Note, or lose all."[37]

The meeting at Onondaga, September 8-10, 1753, was intended to cement relations between New York and the Six Nations, and to pave the way for a meeting in Albany to meet the French challenge. It was marked by recognition of all the forms of Indian diplomacy and by oratory filled with the symbolism of peace and friendship. Johnson was met one mile before he reached the Onondaga castle and was welcomed by the Red Head, a chief sachem. In his address to the "General Convention of the Six Nations" Johnson first condoled the loss of three of the principal sachems with three wampum belts and three stroud blankets. He told them that the governor was sick and was soon leaving and that a new governor was expected who would then meet them with the usual presents. He regretted to find "the Road hither so grown up with Weeds for want of being used and your Fire almost Expiring at Onondago." For they well knew the saying of their ancestors "that when the Fire was out here, you would be no longer a People." Having cleared the road and renewed the fire he "Swept clean all your Rooms with a New white Wing." The "fine Shady Tree, which was Planted by Our Forefathers for your Ease and Shelter" was leaning due to northerly winds; it had to be set upright with widespread roots so that no winds could shake it. They must insure this by not going to Canada or consenting to the French descent on the Ohio.[38]

He urged the Onondagas to follow the old custom of reporting news from all quarters direct; not to let it go from castle to castle and thus be distorted. To the Senecas, the Western Door of the Six Nations, he urged an easy communication with Onondaga, and that they do their utmost to win the western tribes to their interest. For the Oneidas, he set up their "Stone Strait," to remove from it all moss and dirt, and asked them to care for the Tuscaroras, their children, and the Skaniadaradighronos (Nanticokes or Conoys) lately come into the alliance. And to the Cayugas, he urged that they not live scattered and listen to the French, but unite in their castles. He added that he was grieved to hear some men had brought in scalps of Catawbas, in violation of their agreement, and urged the return of prisoners and no further hostilities. As for the rum trade, about which they were concerned, "The Proclamation forbidding Rum to be Sold any where among you, excepted Osswego, is Published."[39]

Two days later the Red Head came to Johnson's camp on Lake Onondaga, where he properly replied to all points and gave the consent of the Nations, save for one or two mild reservations. They would stay away from the French in Canada, "tho' we did not conceive we had done so much Amiss in going thither, when we Observe that you White People pray, and we have no nearer Place to learn to Pray, and have our Children Baptized then that." It was not with their consent that the French committed hostilities in Ohio, but "we don't know what you Christians French, and English together intend we are so hemm'd in by both, that we have hardly a Hunting place left, in a little while, if we find a Bear in a Tree, there will immediately Appear an Owner for the Land to Challenge the Property, and hinder us from killing it which is our livelyhood." As for the prohibition of the rum trade why not at Oswego also? To this Johnson replied that the French sold rum at Niagara and until it was forbidden, they must sell at Oswego.[40]

These, indeed, were minor points. They hoped their Brother would now come frequently and keep up with them a mutual correspondence.

These episodes in the Indian country and the visit of the sachems to New York appeared but straws in the wind. But they were affecting the councils of several colonies and were being reported home. And from these little steps, strides were being made toward major moves in the great game of imperial politics. Clashes between troops and Indians in the back country of America were leading to a general war.

XII

THE ALBANY CONGRESS

When the seventeen Mohawks led by King Hendrick stalked out of the meeting in New York in June 1753, announcing the breaking of the Covenant Chain, they were denounced for their presumption by Colonel Johnson and by the sachems at Onondaga. Again Hendrick had acted badly, said Johnson, and the Mohawks had no right to speak for the whole confederacy. But the wily old chief, a veteran of many such encounters and wise in the ways of the white men, knew what he was doing. Only by such a shock could the government of New York be brought to its senses. The minutes of the meeting were sent to Whitehall and there set in train a series of events which were momentous not only for New York but for America.

The Lords of Trade had received voluminous accounts of conditions in America. Two years before, the learned Cadwallader Colden had sent such a survey, which undoubtedly impressed those who read it.[1] Yet the plaints of Governor Clinton, at war with the Assembly, were often cancelled by rival claims. Now this announcement of the breaking of the Indian alliance, just when the French menace in the Ohio Valley was arousing both colonials and the military leaders at home, was plainly understood. The rift had to be mended, and the provinces must cooperate to this end.

The time was ripe, too, for decisive action. The ailing Governor Clinton was retiring, and a new governor was to be sent to New York. Let him be the means of a provincial settlement with the Indians. Instructions were drawn up for Sir Danvers Osborne, newly appointed governor, to call together the colonial representatives of the provinces concerned for an "interview" with the Six Nations, to join in a treaty in the name of His Majesty. Since Hendrick had made so clear the abhorrence of the Indians for the Albany commissioners, it was suggested that this meeting be held at Onondaga, the seat of the confederacy.[2]

Young Sir Danvers was a poor instrument for such a policy. Possessing no qualifications save good family and connections—he was the brother-in-law of Lord Halifax, head of the Board of Trade—he had received the office as a political plum. Unaware of his serious indisposition and melancholy, the people of New York hailed his arrival on October 10 with high hopes. Two days later they learned with consternation of his suicide, "for on friday the 12th about seven of the Clock in the morning he was found in the lower part of Mr Murrays Garden (at whose house he lodged till the Fort was fitted up for his Reception) strangled in his Hand-kerchief."[3] The tragedy, however, brought to the governor's office a much abler man.

Chief Justice James De Lancey was the archenemy of Governor Clinton and had not aided his Indian policy. Hence when De Lancey had obtained appointment as lieutenant governor, Clinton had withheld his commission until the arrival of the new governor. De Lancey now lost no time in taking over the office. The Council had asked for Sir Danvers's instructions then in the keeping of his secretary, Thomas Pownall; but Pownall quite correctly reserved them for the hands of the governor. It was somewhat ironic that De Lancey now became the agent of the strong Indian policy advocated by Clinton and Johnson.[4] He soon made up with the latter.

On September 18, 1753, the Lords of Trade had written their instructions to the governor of New York, and on the same date letters were sent to the governors of Virginia, Massachusetts, Pennsylvania, New Jersey, New Hampshire, and Maryland, advising them of the forthcoming interview with the Six Nations. The purpose was a general treaty, and all were urged to send delegates of character and integrity who should be well acquainted with Indian affairs.[5]

Upon receipt of these instructions Governor De Lancey informed the Lords of his plans, that the Six Nations had been somewhat mollified by Colonel Johnson's meeting with them at Onondaga in July, and that he proposed to carry out the further instructions. On December 11, he transmitted the call for the interview to the several colonies, setting the date as June 14, 1754, and the place at Albany.[6] He explained to the Lords his choice of Albany, since this seemed to go against the instructions:

I had appointed [the interview] to be at Albany on the fourteenth of June next that being the most proper and usual place of holding General Conferences with the Indians and where they have had a Fire burning from the earliest settlement of this Country and is a place of the greatest consequence to the defense of these Counties being situated on the highest part of Hudsons River which is navigable for vessells of any considerable Burthen . . . the Indians by coming down to Albany upon all their publick Busness, and applications to the Government here contract habitudes & acquire friendships with some of the Inhabitants a kind of rights of Hospitality and if treated with any kind of prudence will always be willing and ready to protect and defend the place, where they have so long had a fire burning.[7]

As for Onondaga, it had been the custom for the governors to hold a meeting there every other year, and notice had been given of Colonel Johnson's meeting there in July. For the New York delegates, Albany was convenient; Colonel Johnson lived nearby in the county, and three other members of the Council would be there on circuit. The call had stressed the importance of an able interpreter, but De Lancey remarked that the interpreter for New York was "very meanly qualified." Therefore, he proposed to Pennsylvania that Mr. Weiser should be brought with their delegation.[8]

De Lancey, speaking for New York, conceived the interview as primarily for the purpose of repairing the unhappy breach with the Six Nations and the fortification of the frontier of New York, for which the other provinces were to give aid. Governor Dinwiddie of Virginia apparently shared this view; he replied that his province was preparing its own meeting with the Six Nations and southern Indians in May and that he was convinced that "the Assembly of this Province will be very backward in sending Commissioners to Albany." At the same time he hoped to have aid for the campaigns on Virginia's frontier.[9]

Pennsylvania responded with alacrity, not only because of her concern with the frontiers, but also because this offered an opportunity to deal directly with the Six Nations for a land grant and to oppose the pretensions of Connecticut speculators for land in the Wyoming Valley. Two of her delegation, Benjamin Franklin and Richard Peters, were experienced in dealing with Indians; and, as requested by De Lancey, Conrad Weiser was sent as interpreter.[10] Franklin, however, was chiefly concerned with the plan for colonial union and brought with him a document referred to as "Short Hints toward a Scheme for Uniting the Northern Colonies" as a basis for discussion.[11]

The Reverend Richard Peters, Secretary of Pennsylvania, but an Anglican clergyman, exerted influence through his Sunday sermons in the English church. One so impressed the Congress that it ordered it to be printed.[12] Isaac Norris had served at the Albany conference with Indians in 1745 and represented the conservative Quakers. And John Penn, grandson of the founder of Pennsylvania, later to be its governor, was a second member from the provincial council.[13]

Governor William Shirley of Massachusetts had taken the lead in colonial defense, and he now expressed the interest of his government in the possibility that at this meeting some form of colonial unity might be evolved and asked that delegates be empowered to act in this matter.[14] Thomas Hutchinson, a Massachusetts delegate, also brought a plan for union.[15] Elisha Williams of the Connecticut delegation was a former head of Yale College and a Congregational clergyman who preached to the Albany delegates from the pulpit of the Dutch church. The Connecticut delegates were conservative and not inclined toward colonial union.[16]

Although New York had issued the call and was host, its Assembly had commissioned no delegates. Governor De Lancey served as presiding officer, and four members of the Council, including Johnson, sat with the others and served on committees. The New Englanders were punctilious about credentials and questioned the New Yorkers for their lack of qualification. The official record did not refer to them as "Commissioners," but as the governor and members of the Council of New York.[17]

Visiting delegations arriving in Albany in June 1754 found no such hospitality as might have been offered by one of the colonial capitals. It was really a frontier town, with its principal buildings clustered near the river. Fort Frederick, with its ramparts and barracks, reminded them of its nearness to hostile territory. Indians, blanketed and with beads in their ears and noses, roamed the streets while soldiers on many occasions billeted in houses.[18] Sloops from New York landed the Pennsylvania commissioners at the waterfront, and those from New England crossed the river by ferry from Greenbush after their overland journey.[19] Lodgings for the visitors were found in the houses of the principal citizens and there they met the others or perhaps held business sessions. The New Hampshire group, through the efforts of Colonel Jacob Wendell of Boston, found lodging at Jacob Lansing's. Here they were visited by others and were soon invited to dine with Lieutenant Governor De Lancey. "Near Twenty Gentlemen Dined there; a Handsom Entertainment, good wine & Arrak Punch." Later they dined with Colonel Schuyler at the Flats, with Colonel Cuyler, and with Mr. Beechman. This was in addition to the official entertainment.[20]

Walking about the town they remarked the old Dutch church at the foot of Jonkers [now State] Street, while nearby stood the scene of their meetings, the Court House [now the corner of Broadway and Hudson Avenue]. Climbing the hill toward the fort, they observed the English church, with a new bell in its steeple, and not far distant were the palisades of the stockade. The western gate toward Schenectady was watched for Indians from the Mohawk castles. The delay of the Indians in arriving gave opportunity to ride out to the Cohoes Falls, a noteworthy spectacle for sightseers. When the Indians began to arrive they were a curious sight: "After Diner [we] walk up the hill on the back of the Town to View the Indians."[21]

Weather often affects the feelings of negotiators and the temper of the meeting. That at Albany in June and July 1754, as reported by Atkinson, was indeed remarkable. Summer heat was broken by numerous thundershowers and followed by high winds. One such storm was nearly a disaster.

The Rain that fell on Sunday &ca. Caused Such a flood that water Encreased near about 14 foot in Perpindicular & welld over the Banks of the River, Drowned all the Corn & Grain &ce on the Inner [Inter] Vale, Came into the Cyty, & was in Some places even with the Top Pallosaidoes, Drove near a Dozen Sloops from their moorings & Carryd Down Stream Eleven miles from Scenactada, only fill the river with rubbish & fleeted Of many Piles of boards.[22]

It was feared that all the corn and grain was ruined, but in a few days the river fell about six feet.

It was not until June 19, five days after the date set, that the first official session was held in the Court House.[23] The previous day Governor De Lancey had sent notices to the commissioners at their lodgings and they now proceeded to present their "Commissions." It was discovered that the Indians had been delayed, so there was time to decide matters of policy and protocol.

The Govr told us yesterday at Dinner that he had recd a Letter from the Interpreter [Arent Stevens] that had the Conducting the Indians to Town that they had Spent a ... Day or Two in Condoling the Loss of a Sachem & Expected an other Day to be spent on the Same Occasion when they got to the Next Tribe So that they Should not be in Town before Wednesday or Thursday.[24]

The usual deliberation with which the Six Nations carried on their diplomacy was being observed, and Hendrick and the other sachems were not to be hurried. On Thursday, the 20th, about twenty Indians appeared. On Saturday about two hundred arrived, and proceedings were adjourned until Monday. On Wednesday, the 26th, the Indians were not ready to receive the speech of the governor, "the Upper Castle of the Mohawks not being yet come in"; and the next day the meeting voted its impatience. Having drawn up in committee the address to the Indians, they "unanimously Agreed upon & Voted and Calculated an additional Paragraph ... to tell them that the Commissioners & Sundry Tribes of Indians had been waiting near 14 Days to open the Congress & hoped they would be more punctual for the future. This was on Accot of Hendrick & the Cononjiro Indians not coming in." On Friday "Hndrick & the Indians of his tribe arrived & twas Thot best to make the Speach on the morrow ... "[25]

Thus the commissioners were well impressed that the Indians were sticklers for form and propriety. Lest there be offense on this score, when the address was drawn up by a committee, to be delivered by Governor De Lancey, it should be concerned with the subjects, "the Particular Iddoms or Diction might be Left, as they were very Peculiar, to those that sheuld deliver the Same to the Indians."[26]

Atkinson wrote:

We had *no Dispute abt Superiority* but was by the Govr Desired to walk in & *take Places as we thot Proper.* There was a Back Seet for the Se[creta]ry Sot in & 2 rows of Seets under it & four Each End which with a Seet In the front Enclosed a Large Table. *The Govr & his Council* Sat und[er] the Sery at the Table, *Massa [chusetts] & New Hampr* opposite, *Philadelphia* [Pennsylvania], *road Island & Mary Land* at one End, *Connecticut* at the other.[27]

De Lancey, too, was haughty and punctilious about his rôle as president of the congress. He allowed the committees to wait upon him formally when they were ready to report; and he raised the question of his presence when the report was read and debated. He was to deliver the address to the Indians on behalf of the congress.

Here arose A motion about the Seats the Commissioners were to take at the Interview and after Several Propositions, as that those Governments that had been Longest in attending the Treaty, heretofore those that been at the Largest Expence &ca, The Kings Governmts before the Charter Govts &ca, but at Last it was upon a motion of his Honrs *Determined that the Commissioners Should take Place according to the Situation of yr respective Governmts begining* either at the North or South. Finally 'twas determined *to begin at the North.*[28]

Next a proper setting had to be arranged for the meeting with the Indians. There was not room to accommodate them in the Court House, where the commissioners had been sitting, so an outdoor gathering was arranged before the door of the governor. Atkinson reported what must have been a striking scene:

The Governr Acquainted us that the Indians were ready to hear what we had to Say to them. We Accordingly went to the Place appointed, which was before the Govrs Door, where were about 10 rows of boards. Each row would hold abt 20 Indians. Opposite & between the Indians & the Govr House were placed a row of Chairs, the Lt Govr & Council of New York Seated in the Center, at the Extream End on far right hand the Massa, next N.H., then Connecticut, then the Govr &ca, next on the Left hand road Island, then Pennsilvania, & on the Extream Maryland. The Govr read the Speach Paragraph by Paragraph which was Interpreted by the

N. York Interpreter. At the Delivery of Each belt they Signifyed their understanding of Each Paragraph by a kind of universal Huzzah. When the great or Chain belt was Delivered on this occasion, they Signifyed their understanding or Consent by Such a Huzzah repeated Seven Times over for every Tribe. Thus finished the Speach. The Indians made a Long Pause & then Hendrick rose & repeated the Substance of Speach & Said they would Consider of & answer it on monday.[29]

The speech delivered by De Lancey was a composite of complaints and compromises, the result of several days wrangling by the delegates. At first there were meetings of the Albany commissioners of Indian affairs, already discredited by the Mohawks, but consulted by De Lancey. They wanted a protest made to the practice of the Oneidas in interfering with the progress of traders. This was ruled out as of local concern. Pennsylvania stressed the sufferings of captives on the frontiers; Massachusetts related at length her great expense for defense; others thought the address should be general, not concerned with local issues. When all these matters had been considered, the draft was turned over to a committee, including Johnson and Hutchinson, to put it in form. In the end it was bound to be ineffective.[30]

In contrast the reply by Hendrick, when the assembly with the Indians was reconvened, was pointed, well reasoned, and dramatic. He did not mince words. He had long been fluent in the English tongue and was experienced in this sort of meeting, as well as in the oratory so loved by his people. His mixture of Indian form and politeness with the brutal frankness which he deemed necessary on this occasion must have put the delegates to shame. No one else equalled his force and eloquence. Even without the impressive manner of its delivery, as printed in the cold type of the official report, it is moving; given the occasion and the setting it must rank as one of the great addresses of Indian history.[31]

When all were seated in the outdoor meeting, Abraham, sachem of the Upper Castle of the Mohawks, rose and asked if the governor of New York and the commissioners of the other governments were ready. Then Hendrick, brother of Abraham, rose and spoke for the Six Nations. With dignity and deliberation he delivered his prologue: "Brother Corlaer, and Brothers of the other Governments." He mentioned the earlier meeting, he listed the colonies represented; he recognized that the King had called them, that Virginia and South Carolina wished to be present. He now welcomed the Chain Belt given by the Governor:

This Chain Belt is of very great importance to our united Nations, and all our Allies, we will therefore take it to Onondaga, where our Council Fire always burns, and keep it so securely that neither Thunder nor Lightning shall break it; there we will consult over it, ... In the mean time we desire, that you will strengthen yourselves, and bring as many into this Covenant Chain as you possibly can.—We do now solemnly renew and brighten the Covenant Chain with our Brethren here present, and all our other absent Brethren on the Continent.[32]

Next he took up the statement of the governor that they were living in a dispersed manner; it was true, and as for their brethren living at Oswegatchie, in Canada, they had tried to bring them back, but in vain. For "the Govr of Canada is like a wicked deluding spirit." Then came a clever bit of stage business, as he turned from approval to reproach.

You have asked us the reason of our living in this dispersed manner. The reason is, your neglecting us for these three years past (then taking a stick and throwing it behind his back) you have thus thrown us behind your back, and disregarded us, whereas the French are a subtle and vigilant people, ever using their utmost endeavours to seduce and bring our people over to them.[33]

Here he paused and gave a belt of wampum. Then as to the encroachments of the French they had made a strict enquiry and found that the French had done this, and built forts, without the Indians' consent. But he raised a new issue:

Brethren—The Govr of Virginia, and the Govr of Canada are both quarrelling about lands which belong to us, and such a quarel as this may end in our destruction; they fight who shall have the land. The Govrs of Virginia and Pennsylvania have made paths thro' our Country to trade and built houses without acquainting us with it, they should first have asked our consent to build there, as was done when Oswego was built.[34]

This reproach was followed by another belt "to clear away all Clouds" which hung over them, and to bring union and friendship. Then with voice rising with increased emphasis, and with all the fire and feeling of which he was capable, Hendrick launched into a diatribe which must have startled and shaken his hearers. Even as we now read it, the words crackle, and the eloquence of the speaker shows through. If this speech suffered any in transcription, we can only imagine what the original was like.

Brethren. This is the ancient place of Treaty where the Fire of Friendship always used to burn, and 'tis now three years since we have been called to any publick Treaty here; Tis true there are Commissrs here, but they have never invited us to smoak with them, [by which they mean the Commissrs had never invited them to any conference], but the Indians of Canada, come frequently and smoak here, which is for the sake of their Beaver, but we hate them [meaning the French Indians] we have not as yet confirmed the peace with them. Tis your fault Brethren that we are not strengthened by conquest, for we would have gone and taken Crown Point, but you hindered us; we had concluded to go and take it, but we were told it was too late, and that the Ice would not bear us; instead of this, you burnt your own Forts at Seraghtoga and run away from it, which was a shame & a scandal to you. Look about your Country & see, you have no Fortifications about you, no, not even to this City, tis but one Step from Canada hither, and the French may easily come and turn you out of your doors.

Brethren. You desire us to speak from the bottom of our hearts, and we shall do it. Look about you and see all these houses full of Beaver, and the money is all gone to Canada, likewise powder, lead and guns, which the French now make use of at Ohio.

Brethren. The goods which go from hence to Oswego, go from thence to Ohio which further enables the French to carry on their designs at the Ohio.

Brethren. You were desirous that we should open our minds, and our hearts to you; look at the French, they are Men, they are fortifying everywhere—but, we are ashamed to say it, you are all like women bare and open without any fortifications.[35]

There was only silence on the part of the assembly as Hendrick sat down. Now, his brother, Abraham, arose and voiced the Indians' dissatisfaction that Colonel Johnson, who had given up the management of their affairs three years ago, had not been reinstated as they had requested of Governor Clinton. The latter had said he would refer it to the King.

We long waited in expectation of this being done, but hearing no more of it, we embrace this opportunity of laying this Belt before all our Brethren here present, and desire them that Coll: Johnson may be reinstated and have the Management of Indian Affairs, for we all lived happy, whilst they were under his management, for we love him, and he us, and he has always been our good, and trusty Friend.

Brethren. I forgot something. We think our request about Coll: Johnson which Govr Clinton promised to carry to the King our Father is drowned in the sea.

Abraham turned and faced the Albany commissioners of Indian affairs and bade them to take notice. "The fire here," he said, "is burnt out."[36]

To answer these charges was not easy; the committee which drafted the first address was asked to form a reply. Then Conrad Weiser, whose friendship with the Six Nations was well known, was called upon to describe the policies of Virginia and Pennsylvania, to reiterate the French aggression and the measures taken for defense. Governor De Lancey replied to the charges of neglect by New York; he could not restore Colonel Johnson, but lamely promised to try the Indian commissioners another year. Martin Kellogg, the interpreter for Massachusetts, told of the French and Indian aggression on their frontiers, and the efforts made by Governor Shirley.[37]

Dissatisfaction with these replies became evident when Hendrick again spoke July 5. The Nations were particularly insistent about the need for the help of Johnson; they were fearful of the French encroachment on their lands, demanded immediate action for defense. Here it seems particularly incongruous that the interview was called to urge upon the Indians the need for defense, yet while the commissioners were debating a governmental union of the provinces, the Indians were impatient for them to take action. They were even concerned for the safety of Johnson, whom they regarded as the key man in this time of crisis, for they said "if he fails us, we die."[38]

Brethren. We put you in mind in our former speech of the defenceless state of your Frontiers, particularly of this City, [of Schenectady] and of the Country of the Five Nations. You told us yesterday you were consulting about securing both, yourselves & us. We beg you will resolve upon something speedily. You are not safe from danger one day. The French have their hatchet in their hands, both, at Ohio and in two places in New England.

We dont know but this very night they may attack us. One of the principal reasons why we desire, you will be speedy in these matters is, that since Coll. Johnson has been in this City, there has been a French Indian at his house, who took measure of the wall round it and made very narrow observations on every thing thereabouts. We think him (Coll: Johnson) in very great danger, because the French will take more than ordinary pains either to kill him, or to make him prisoner, upon account of his great interest among us, and being also one of the

Five Nations (Coll: Johnson is one of their Sachems). Upon this they gave four strings of Wampum.[39]

There could be no doubting the deep concern of the Mohawks, their fear of the French, and their desire for some positive action on their frontiers. Nor could there be any question about their reliance upon William Johnson and of his capacity and influence in dealing with them. Many were present who would remember this impassioned plea and who later would turn to Johnson for the solution of Indian problems.[40] Now he was called upon to make answer and to appease them. On July 10, a committee met at Johnson's house to consider the building of the forts which the Indians desired. Atkinson, one of the committee, wrote: "Came to A Conclusion of the Number Necessary for the frontiers of all the Collonies. Sat till 12 o'clock." The next day the report was made, and the meeting broke up.[41]

Meanwhile there were dissatisfactions in other quarters. The Stockbridge Indians had appeared early and had asked for attention. De Lancey replied that they were not usually treated at the Albany sessions, but the minutes of the Indian commissioners proved him wrong. He persisted that he had no funds for their presents, and it was concluded that they were wards of Massachusetts. Likewise a few of the Scaticook (Schaghticoke), like the Stockbridge known as River Indians, protested injuries done to them in matters of land and the rum trade and had to be appeased.[42]

A major controversy arose, however, over the plea of Pennsylvania for the definition of her frontiers by a grant of land, and this was coupled with the claims of the Connecticut speculators for the upper Susquehanna Valley. Obviously, this was not a principal objective of the interview, but it was a chief concern of the Pennsylvania commissioners, and they pressed it before the congress.

Having well in mind what they sought from the congress, they came well heeled with pieces of eight, and Weiser had advised them in the purchase of presents in New York. He had likewise sounded out the half king Shickellamy about the proposed purchase. The Connecticut delegates and their missionaries with the Stockbridge and Susquehanna Indians were their opponents. It was necessary to deal quickly; the Pennsylvanians arrived in Albany before any of the Indians and began to treat with the leading chiefs as they appeared. Weiser collared one Gachradodon, a Cayuga chief, and won his consent by a present of one hundred pieces of eight (£40 in New York currency). Some Oneidas and Senecas were also won for the purchase before Hendrick and the Mohawks came on the scene. And Hendrick had to be reckoned with; he insisted that the purchase go no further than the Allegheny hills and that the western branch of the Susquehanna should not be included.[43]

After Hendricks's impassioned speech to the general session, July 5, John Penn for Pennsylvania told of the proposed purchase of lands below 42°.[44] De Lancey suggested that this was a concern of Pennsylvania and the Six Nations and should not be a part of the general proceedings. It was so agreed over the protest of Pennsylvania. Weiser now managed to get around the protests of Hendrick by going to the other sachems of the Six Nations, and Pennsylvania got the purchase she desired for lands westward to Ohio. This success was celebrated by the Pennsylvanians' giving the Indians a great entertainment at the Court House.[45]

As the parley drew to a close, the Indians' several complaints were given summary treatment. Something would be done about excessive land claims and patents fraudulently made. (Even William Livingston and William Alexander, devisees of Philip Livingston, were brought in to make promises of restitution of lands to the Canajoharie castle). The rum traffic would be controlled, and a church would be built for the Indians of Canajoharie. Forts would be built, and a greater effort would be made by the union of the colonies which would be here effected.[46]

The Six Nations were called upon to receive the King's present as well as those from the several provinces. As the diarist recorded it: "His Honr this afternoon [Friday, July 5] also Delivered the Kings Present to the Indians which was a good assortment & a great Quantity among which were 400 good guns, Some Extraordinary." Some thirty wagons were ordered by the governor for their return, together with provisions. As a final token they expected a treat—a kind of barbecue. "Bespoke a Cow which this morning was brot us Early. We sent for Hendrick; acquainted him thereof. He came & Liked her; Sent Some young fellows Carryed her off & killed her in the camp."[47]

It was all over with amity and apparent good will, but it might well be questioned whether the Indian congress could be termed a success. There was no general treaty such as had been called for by the ministry. The commissioners chose to postpone this as they turned their attention to forming a general union of the colonies. As to the temper of the Indians, their reactions and apparent conclusions, there is the report of Thomas Pownall in a letter to the Earl of Halifax, July 23, 1754. Pownall, the erstwhile secretary of Danvers Osborne, had been present at the invitation of De Lancey. He believed that the delay caused by the Mohawks was due to the fear that their conditions would not be met—that they wanted nothing to do with the Albany commissioners of Indian affairs and sought rather to deal with Johnson. They finally came only with the knowledge that Johnson would be there. Then they wanted to agree on their demands before coming. The dispute over their lands in New York they wanted dealt with by the governor and Council before they entered the general treaty. They doubted that the English would fight in good earnest against the French, while asking them to do so, and hence would prefer neutrality.[48]

Pownall noticed a coolness in the way in which they sounded their "Yo-heigh-eigh" as the "Great Chain," or "Covenant Belt," was delivered. Instead of successive responses for each tribe, according to custom, they did it in unison. "Some say that this was from mere forgetfullness; but that is very unlikely from them who are such strict observers of these forms."[49] Yet from the assurances they received "they took confidence all wd. be well & spoke freely from their heart in their first speech. But being a little dissatisfyed with some matters, & having (as it is saied) receiv'd some private reasons to appear satisfyed with others, You will easily observe in the second that all Sincerity and Reality is sunk into Political Farce & Compliment." The Indians would be sorry to see a general war; and would be glad if the conflict on the Ohio could remain a private quarrel. The Pennsylvania Purchase, they believed, would help to bring this about, for now Pennsylvania would not fight.[50]

The transcript of the treaty also did not reveal the importance which they attached to their plea for Colonel Johnson. "The Belt they gave when they made the proposition about Col. Johnson was as rich & larg a Belt as that which they gave in answer to ye Covenant Belt." Hence, great attention should be given to Johnson's statement on the sentiments of the Indians.[51] And this was more evidence of the need for a strong policy directed by one man.

Benjamin Franklin no doubt expressed the general view in writing to Cadwallader Colden as he returned via New York. He was irked by the "long detention at Albany . . . due to the Indians not appearing punctually," and felt that "Nothing of much importance was transacted with them; at least nothing equal to the expense and trouble of so many colonies."[52]

The Plan of Union, of course, was Franklin's chief interest, and he had high hopes for its acceptance by the assemblies and by the ministry. From one of the early sessions, the formation of a union had been given precedence over any direct action on the frontiers.[53] A committee had been appointed, with Franklin as its leading spirit, to formulate the plan which was then debated, revised, and finally (July 10) given approval. Only the Connecticut commissioners, who had been cool to the idea, had registered opposition.[54] New York, represented by Governor De Lancey, had shown no enthusiasm, and William Johnson—who was devoting himself to the Indian address, replies and negotiations—was not greatly concerned. Both he and Pownall in their comments submitted to the ministry favored a program of fortifications along the frontier concurrent with, or preceding the completion of, union. These statements, a kind of minority report, were given the sanction of the congress, who expressed their thanks to Mr. Pownall and Colonel Johnson.[55]

The apathy of the several assemblies to the Plan of Union and the failure of Parliament to act gave greater emphasis to the alternate proposals for direct action on the frontier and for dealing with the Indians. Recurring difficulties, the dark aspect of the military situation, and dissatisfaction with the temporary settlements at Albany, aroused increasing concern. When parleys fail, the recourse is to men of action.

Franklin and his fellow commissioners left Albany quite unaware that the Connecticut promoters, with their slippery agent John Henry Lydius, were already at work among the Indians undercutting the Pennsylvania purchase. While the Pennsylvanians had negotiated openly with the representatives of the confederacy at Albany, Lydius craftily collected Indian signatures to a deed for the same land. With $1500 to tempt the Indians, he played upon their weaknesses, their avarice, and their love of liquor. James Stevenson, at whose home the Pennsylvania commissioners had been quartered, learned what was going on and had it confirmed by Daniel Claus. They then reported to Secretary Richard Peters and Governor Hamilton.[56] Claus described the methods of Lydius:

. . . he went in the following clandestine manner to work, and with tempting the Inds. he could prevail upon with Plenty of Dollars, got the following subscriptions to his Deed, viz:

Gahikdote, alias Grote Younge, the Head of ye. Senekers, Atsinoughiata, alias ye. Bunt, & Canatsiagaye, 2 Onontaga; those he got after the Treaty was over & the Commissioners gone; suppose when they were drunk. Afterwards, he under a vain Pretence, took a Ride to Canajochery, as he told me himself, when I asked for the Map of Crown Point to get a Copy off, that he had been there to buy a Span of Horses, and by laying down the Bag of Dollars, had Abraham, Nickas, Hendricks Brothers, and Tarraghioris, to sign.

Then he passed in his Way home, the lower Mohawk Castle, & invited 4 of the Sachems to his house, abt. some Business he had to propose to them, and when they came there, he calld one after another in a Room by himself, & laid the Deed before them, & shewed the Subscriptions of the other Nations, & by many false persuasions, with the offer of 20 Dollars each, brought them to sign their Names, which as Tsistarare Canadagaye, Sotsikowano & Gaweghnog.

He also gave a Call to the Oneidoes, & accordingly, a good Many of them who were absent at the Treaty came down, when Lidius treated them plentifully with Victuals and Drink, & then laid 300 Dollars before them, saying that with this he only would acquaint them with his Intent & that if they would consent to his Proposals, he would deliver them 400 pds. More.[57]

The journeys of the Indians in the meantime had caused them to stop at Mount Johnson, where they were reproached for their double dealing and told that this was "a very dishonest & dirty action of Lidius," which would cause "ill consequences between Connecticut and Pennsylvania." They had no defense, and Johnson directed Claus to relay his information to Pennsylvania. Lydius had even tried to persuade the Indians that the lands were in Ohio and did not belong to Pennsylvania.[58] But the boundaries in the deed were between the 41st and 42d parallels, west one hundred and twenty miles from a line six miles east of the Susquehanna River. This was well within the grant to the Pennsylvania proprietors and comprised the area on which the promoters had their eyes. The consideration was £2,000 in New York currency, "in hand paid / 1705 Dollars in all."[59] This news caused great consternation in Philadelphia. Secretary Richard Peters told the governor, Conrad Weiser was consulted, and it was decided that Hendrick should be brought to Philadelphia and through him the Six Nations persuaded to renounce the deed. To accomplish all this they again had recourse to William Johnson, who alone could be depended upon to persuade Hendrick.

Weiser, in spite of this counsel, was suspicious of Hendrick (if he hesitated to come, he was probably involved in the deal), and he wanted Claus instructed to avoid Albany in his route. If Hendrick would not cooperate, they would have to depend on "Shickelimy & Jonathan." And he suspected, too, "that Wicked priest at Canohadsquagy" (Reverend Gideon Hawley, the Presbyterian missionary of Connecticut at Oquaga).[60]

But it was really Johnson who arranged for Hendrick's journey. He explained in his letter to Governor Morris:

I have been honoured with Yours of the 15th. ult. by Mr. Daniel Clause, whom I immediately sent to call Hendrick to my House. Upon his arrival I delivered and interpretted your Honour's Letter or Invitation to him, and urged his waiting upon you immediately, which, when he agreed to, I spoke to him concerning the affair as far as I judged necessary; and I flatter myself it will have a good Effect, He having faithfully promised me to exert himself and use his utmost endeavours for the interest of the Proprietaries against the Connecticut Attempt.

After my expatiating some time on the Injustice of their Proceedings, more especially so after what had passed at Albany last June in Publick, Hendrick then with such warmth disapproved of them, as well as the weakness of those of his Brethren who were seduced by Lyddius, and promised to do all he could to make them revoke or retract what they had so shamefully done, provided I would Assist him and Countenance his Proceedings with the Five Nations, which I assured him I would with all my Interest; upon that He and his Party sett out full of Spirits and in good temper; and I doubt not (from the knowledge of Your Honour's great and well-established Character) of their returning so; and Mr. Peter's great experience and thorough knowledge of Indian affairs as well as of Hendrick's temper and Principalls will contribute much to Your Honour's Ease in accelerating the Affair with them, Who (to those unacquainted with their Ways and tedious forms) must be thought very troublesome and Silly. I have had a great deal of discourse with Hendrick in private about that affair, and also his present Sentiments, which to insert here would make my Letter of too great length for Your Honour to read with Patience; wherefore make bold to refer Your Honour to the Bearer, Mr. Clause, for some Particulars I have communicated to him, as I am convinced of his Sincerity and readiness to Serve that Government on all Occasions.[61]

Hendrick's journey with eleven other sachems under the guardianship of Daniel Claus has been related by the latter. Proceeding via Esopus (Kingston), Minisink, and Bethlehem, they were greeted on the outskirts of Philadelphia by members of the governor's council, then directed through the streets in procession, escorted by the militia, and acclaimed by "Huzza for King Henry" from the crowd. The governor and officials showered Hendrick with attentions during his ten-day visit and won from him promises of aid in undoing the wrong of the Connecticut deed.[62]

Yet the only sure way of maintaining Pennsylvania's right was by action of the longhouse of the Six Nations. Hendrick returned, promising to work for such action in a congress to be called at Mount Johnson, and upon William Johnson again was thrown the responsibility for obtaining such a settlement. Richard Peters in a long letter, with one from Governor Morris, appealed for his aid and acknowledged his great services for the province. He conceded that Pennsylvania had valid claim to the land, from its charter, from treaties of the time of Governor Dongan, and by direct negotiation at Albany; but in the face of the continuing activity by Connecticut, and the threat of conflict, a new treaty was desired. Johnson acceded to the demand, but pressure of other problems and the imminent recourse to arms soon pushed this matter into the background.[63] When Johnson next met the Six Nations it was to solicit their aid in war. The conflict between New England and Pennsylvania over the Wyoming Valley endured and brought much bloodshed in its wake.

XIII

MILITARY CAREER –
FROM COLONEL TO GENERAL

As the commissioners journeyed homeward, exhilarated perhaps by the excursion into political theory and constitution-making, and contemplated the reception of the Plan of Union by their respective assemblies, they well may have had apprehensions of the future. Even if colonial union as a prerequisite to effective action on the frontier could be consummated, it would take months of negotiation and consultation. In the meantime, the more pressing issues of French aggression and Indian dissatisfaction would not wait. The measures recommended by Johnson and Pownall, if done at all, had to be undertaken by the governors. And soon fresh provocations stirred them to action.

From Virginia, where Governor Dinwiddie's concern for his traders on the frontier and his own conference with Indians had prevented a delegation from going to Albany, a new disaster was reported. Young George Washington, whose warning to Fort Duquesne the year before had been so abruptly rejected, was sent in command of three hundred Virginians to relieve the frontier posts. His rout of a small French scouting party only enraged the French, who forced him to capitulate at Fort Necessity. The report of this reverse reached the other colonies hard upon the ending of the Albany congress. On July 22, Governor De Lancey reported it to the Lords of Trade and said that he would call the Assembly on August 20, "when I shall endeavour to prevail on them to give Mr. Dinwiddie Assistance."[1] Goldsbrow Banyar, the secretary, although his information was scanty, on the next day wrote Johnson, and the latter was censorious in his comment.

The Unlucky defeat of our Troops Commanded by Major Washington gave me the Utmost Conscern. I have been always of opinion Since I knew our weakness there, that we should be banged by the French, and that, that would be attended with verry bad consequences. I am afraid we will, now first begin to feel the sore effects of it, for this will not only animate the French, & their Indians, but stagger the resolution of those inclined to Us, if not effectually draw them from our Interest. It will also be a Means of makeing all the out settlers of the Southern Colonies break up, who lie quite exposed, (as well as Us) to the ravages & Cruelty of every little Scalping party of French, and Indians, Who doubtless will now be employed against them. . . .

I wish Washington had acted with prudence & Circumspection requisite in an officer of his Rank, and the trust at that time reposed in him, but (on considering the affair) I cant help Saying he was verry wrong in many respects, and I doubt His being too ambitious of acquiring all the honour, or as much as he could, before the rest Joined him, and giveing too much Credit to the reports or Acc'ts. given by the French deserters, (which did not at all Shew him the Soldier) was the rock on which he Splitt. he should rather have avoided an Engagement until our Troops were all assembled, for Marching by Detachments in such a close country and against such an Enemy, will never do, wh. if you observe Yl. always find it so . . .[2]

He was profoundly moved by the seriousness of the situation and the consequences which he foresaw. Basing his criticism on such reports as he had, which were incomplete, he may have been too harsh in his criticism of Washington. Yet his reasoning was cogent, and he was displaying a grasp of military affairs based on his experience. This outburst was unusual for him, for he concluded, "excuse my saying so much on this subject, my Passion raised by our Misconduct & to say no worse hurried my pen farther than I intended."[3]

Even the frontier of New York was terrified. On August 28, French Indians raided Hoosick, northeast of Albany, burning barns full of grain and carrying off "the few remaining Indians of Scachtacook, being between fifty and sixty in Number Men, Women and Children," who had recently pledged their fidelity.[4]

De Lancey thereupon took steps to defend the area.

I immediately ordered the City of Albany to be inclosed with Stockadoes in the places where wanting, the Blockhouses to be repaired, two hundred Men of each Regiment of Militia of the adjoining Counties to be held in readiness to march, and the whole Regiment in case of need, to the Assistance of Albany. I sent the independent Company posted in Fort George in this City [New York] to Albany, detaining a serjeant & the Invalids to do the Fort duty; and had also directed a fort to be built at a Pass on the Hudson's River about forty miles above Albany, but no Workmen would undertake it on the credit of the Governt.[5]

Now, at last, the ministry in England was becoming aware of the danger and was hearkening to the pleas of colonial governors. The encroachment of the French upon English territory presaged a war which was not yet declared. Fighting on the American frontier would soon embroil Europe, and English prestige was at stake. Moreover, there was beginning in London a realization of the nature of the Indian problem. Some credit for this must no doubt be given to such colonial leaders as Governor Shirley of Massachusetts, who had effectively sponsored expeditions in the last war, and who had devoted themselves to influencing English opinion on the threat to the American colonies. But the more recent representations were also having some effect. The ministry had called for the Albany conference to consider the Indian problem, and they now read the reports of the proceedings.

On October 26, Secretary Robinson informed the American governors that the king was sending to Virginia two regiments of foot of five hundred men each besides officers, to be commanded by Sir Peter Halket and Colonel Dunbar, where they would be augmented by seven hundred men each. In addition, Governor Shirley and Sir William Pepperell were to raise regiments of a thousand men each, of which they were to be commanders.[6]

There followed in November the appointment of General Edward Braddock, commander in chief of the forces in America, with secret instructions for his campaign. His first objective was to dispossess the French from their Ohio River posts in Virginia. Next he was to seize Fort Niagara, cutting the French line, and for this utilizing the regiments of Governor Shirley and Sir William Pepperell. If there were sufficient forces then available, his third objective was Crown Point on the northern frontier and the erection of a fort on Lake Champlain.[7]

Along with the instructions to Braddock for the military campaign, there was direction for the management of Indian affairs. For some time reports had emphasized the need for centralizing authority in Indian relations. Johnson and Pownall had implied the need, and the latter clearly suggested that Johnson was the man. Peter Wraxall, too, as secretary for Indian affairs, had compiled an abridgement of the Indian Records with comment which pointed in this direction. Wraxall's disgust with the Albany commissioners of Indian affairs, their venal self-interest and shortsightedness, made their replacement by a single official a cardinal objective. Hence the Board of Trade was well briefed on this point, and it left no doubt in Braddock's mind.

Subsequently, Thomas Pownall took credit for securing Johnson's appointment; and—challenging this—it has been suggested that Wraxall's *Abridgement,* addressed to the Earl of Halifax, was of prime influence. Pownall was indeed using all his arts and influence with the ministry, but at this time he was still in America, and his influence was largely confined to his report on the congress at Albany. Wraxall, too, first met Johnson at the congress so that he could not have had Johnson's selection in mind when he so industriously digested the Indian Records. And the receipt of his work by the Earl and the ministry was probably too recent to have effected any change in the plans.[8] But there were many who thought that only Johnson could handle the Indians in these difficult times. Banyar expected the governor and Assembly to "make provision for placing the management of Indian Affairs in the Hands of the only Person that has any Influence among them."[9]

Now, while the ministry was deciding that Indian affairs should be committed to one man, Governor Shirley and Thomas Pownall were urging upon Johnson the resumption of his old duties. Their urgent and flattering letters, offering to present his views and recommendations to the ministry, did indeed strike a responsive chord. Johnson replied with a modest review of his services, but insisted that if he were to assume responsibility it should be with a clear understanding of his powers and authority.

Whoever his Majesty may think worthy of such an Important Trust . . . should be vested with as much power as the nature of the thing may admit of, and intirely independent of any American Assemblys Approbation for the payment of money expended in that Service, as that would certainly be the means of frustrateing his Intentions or best endeavours, be them ever so Sanguine.

. . . Should his Majesty deem me worthy of that important trust, and enable me to discharge it properly, by laying aside all other business, and allowing me to choose, and employ such People as I might Judge proper under me, the remainder of my Life Should be entirely devoted to his Service.[10]

No colonial governor was more ingenious in preparing plans or more energetic in their execution than Governor Shirley of Massachusetts. He and Sir William Pepperell had been instructed to raise regiments which would be used for the proposed conquest of Nova Scotia. General Braddock and the regulars had for their first objective the seizure of the Ohio Valley, in which undertaking they were to have the support of Virginia and Pennsylvania. The New England provinces and New York must of necessity protect their own frontiers, and to achieve this end, Shirley now proposed an expedition against Crown Point by forces supplied by New England, New York, and New Jersey. In a letter to Governor De Lancey, again borne and supported by Thomas Pownall, he argued for the importance of this campaign, declared that it would be supported by the Massachusetts Assembly, which, as the "first Mover in this Expedition," had asked him to name the commander. It was indeed diplomatic that he should choose the commander from New York:

The Gentleman I have thought of on this important Occasion is Collonel William Johnson of Mount Johnson in the Mohawk Country whose distinguished Character for the great Influence He hath for Severall Years maintained over the Indians of the Six Nations, is the circumstance, wh. determines me in my Choice, preferably to any Gentleman in my own Governt tho there are not wanting there Officers of Rank, & Experience, out of Whom I could have Nominated one. . . .

. . . Collonel Johnson raised & Commanded a Regiment of Indians in the late intended Expedition against Canada & with regard to his power to engage them now, No Gentleman can Stand in Competition wth. him, besides his Military qualifications for this particular Service, & knowledge of the Country & place against wh. this Expedition is destined, are verry conspicuous.[11]

Johnson was reluctant to accept the honor and command and insisted that his abilities were not equal to the task. He had been nominated, he insisted, chiefly because of his influence among the Indians, and that influence could be exerted just as well in support of another in command, which would be more agreeable to him. As a councillor, he assured Shirley and others that New York's governor and Council would support the plan; he could not be so sure of the Assembly, but he would at once leave New York for home, where he would begin to prepare the Indians for participation. Almost as an afterthought, he added his opinion that it would be more effective in breaking the French power if General Braddock should first attack Niagara. In this, then, he presaged the later Niagara campaign.[12]

Determination of plans for the campaign, however, was to wait upon a conference of governors which General Braddock called to meet him in Annapolis. Shirley was reluctant to make the long journey. He still pressed upon Johnson his selection for the Crown Point command and urged him to begin at once to recruit Indians. Pownall as Shirley's agent conferred with De Lancey in New York, and they urged Johnson also to go to Annapolis as an expert on Indians, and he agreed.[13] Due to delays, the meeting was not held at Annapolis, however, for Braddock had begun to move, and the governors and their attendants finally joined him at his camp at Alexandria.

The governors and Colonel Johnson arrived at Alexandria April 13, and the next day Braddock held his conference.[14]   According to the minutes kept by Shirley, only officials participated: General Edward Braddock; Commodore Augustus Keppel, commander of the fleet; Governor William Shirley of Massachusetts; Governor Robert Dinwiddie of Virginia; Lieutenant Governor James De Lancey of New York; Governor Horatio Sharpe of Maryland; and Governor Robert Hunter Morris of Pennsylvania.[15]   Since Johnson had no official status as yet, he was not one of the group, but in view of his importance in the deliberations and the commission proffered him, it is hard to believe that he was not consulted. Thomas Pownall, it was later asserted, sought to participate but was excluded, and perhaps from this stemmed his later pique with Shirley.[16]

Braddock read his commission and his secret instructions, and immediately encountered opposition to a proposal that the assemblies should contribute to a common fund to defray expenses of the expeditions. The governors well knew that they could not get their refractory assemblies to agree to any such *carte blanche.*[17] There was no disagreeement, however, on the proposition that the Six Nations should be cultivated and secured to the British interest and that Colonel Johnson was the "fittest person" as a negotiator for that purpose. He was to have a fund of £800 supplied him (£500 for the Five Nations and allies, and £300 for the western nations to be given at Oswego).[18]

The proposals of Shirley and Johnson for campaigns against Crown Point and Niagara appear to have been considered, for the decision was in accord with them. In addition to the objective of Fort Duquesne, they agreed to the general's proposal

to attempt the reduction of Crown Point with the forces agreed to be supplied by the provinces of New York, New Jersey, Connecticut, Rhode Island, Massachusetts, and New Hampshire, amounting to four thousand four hundred men; and whether, as they were all Irregulars, they did not think Colonel Johnson a proper man to command this expedition.[19]

Considerable time and attention were given to the matter of the Indians, linking them with the Crown Point expedition, and it was proposed that Johnson be employed as "plenipotentiary to the Six Nations." This he at first declined, due to his unfortunate experience before, but the assurances of General Braddock that £2,000 would be put at his disposal by Shirley, and his confidence in the integrity of the general finally persuaded him. Also a speech was prepared in the name of General Braddock, which Johnson should present to the Indians, and it was thought that his selection, since he was one of their sachems, would incline them to go with him on the expedition and so more fully join them to the British interest. Johnson was given a commission granting him the fullest powers.[20]

The Council also decided that in addition to the Fort Duquesne expedition, an attack would be made on Fort Niagara by way of Oswego. The fort at Oswego, then in a defenseless condition, would be reinforced by two independent companies from New York and by Sir William Pepperell's regiment. Two vessels of sixty tons were to be built there according to draughts to be sent by Commodore Keppel. Ship carpenters were to be obtained from New York and sent out to fell timber for the construction of these vessels. Governor Shirley "having much interest in, and being extremely well acquainted with the Eastern Governments was supposed most capable of removing the principal difficulties attending the expedition to Niagara," and thence was given its command.[21]

Thus there came about the assignments which later were to appear paradoxical. Johnson, a New Yorker, was given command of New England troops against Crown Point; Shirley, from Massachusetts, was to command an expedition whose route spanned the province of New York, much better known to Johnson. Shirley was the first to recommend the Crown Point campaign; Johnson had suggested that against Niagara. But there were other good reasons for the choice. Militia usually preferred a short campaign, and hence the New Englanders were to march the relatively short distance to Crown Point, and regular troops (the standing independent company and the new regiments to be enlisted) were to make the longer march. Moreover it would be relatively easier to enlist Indians from the Mohawk Valley to go against Crown Point. And finally, the Niagara campaign, if successful, offered a prospect of a glorious achievement, very appealing to Shirley.

To persuade William Johnson to accept again the responsibility for Indian affairs, his conditions had to be met, and the conference was liberal in its promise of support. He was to bear a message from General Braddock, in whose name he was to present it to the Six Nations. The sum of £800 was to be placed in his hands immediately for gifts to the Indians, and further funds were not to be lacking.[22] Moreover, his official commission by authority of the King to General Braddock (dated April 15) gave him "sole Management & direction of the Affairs of the Six Nations of Indians & their Allies" with "full Power & Authority to treat & confer with them as often and upon such matters as you shall judge necessary" agreeable to instructions given. "And all Persons to whom the Direction of the Affairs of the said Nations or their Allies have been heretofore committed, and all others whatsover are strictly required & enjoined to cease & forbear acting or intermeddling therein." He was to be assisted by interpreters and by a secretary whom he was to appoint.[23] He immediately enlisted Peter Wraxall as his secretary.

It was Johnson's understanding, too, that a commission as commander of the Crown Point expedition would be issued, but Governor Shirley gave him a commission as major general over the Massachusetts troops and such as had been promised from other provinces, totaling forty-four hundred men. Governor De Lancey of New York followed suit with a similar commission.[24] Hence, he was not only commissioned by the commander in chief, by virtue of his instructions, and with the assent of the governors at Alexandria, but also by New York and Massachusetts. It was indeed a confusing spread of authority for a military commander and was to occasion a number of misunderstandings about whom he should report to.

William Johnson had not sought either commission, yet he well knew the nature of the task of managing Indian affairs and did not dissent from the view that he was the logical man for the job. On the other hand, he repeatedly complained that he was not qualified for the military command and doubted his ability in this field. In this self-evaluation he exhibited a modesty and reticence which was uncommon. Such commands were frequently given to political appointees with even less military experience and were sought for their prestige and influence, if not also for the opportunity for considerable remuneration. Johnson, in fact, had more military experience, though on a small scale, than a number of the other officers appointed. This Shirley had pointed out, as well as the even more important fact of his familiarity with the countryside.[25] But he had never had a large command with ordnance and a supply train, and he had to deal with companies from the several provinces with their own commanders. He was raised from militia colonel to major general, commander in chief of an expedition.

As he journeyed home the newly appointed general began to be concerned with ordnance suitable for his command. At Alexandria he had observed Braddock's equipment, the guns and their carriages, the quantities of supply, and the wagons necessary to their movement.[26] And he also observed, with an eye to emulation, the behavior, conduct, quarters, and deportment of the officers. This was indeed the first professional unit of the British army to undertake an American campaign and it was bound to impress the provincials. Braddock himself was a brilliant example of the veteran soldier, and according to Captain Orme he had charmed the Americans.

At New York Johnson surveyed the ordnance available, and selected what he considered necessary. First on his list were six 18-pounders, fieldpieces with carriage, which he felt to be the very minimum. "Six I shall want if them at Albany be bad." And as soon as he reached Albany he examined "the Cannon & field Pieces designed for me & find everry thing belonging to them rotten, & unfit for service."[27]

But the field cannon were just the beginning of the problem. He would need all sorts of smaller pieces—mortars, "Royals and Cohorns," fuses, bombs, grenades, shot and powder, the gunners tools—and the means of transport.[28] Much would depend on the plan of campaign, the use to be made, and whether or not he was to carry guns to fortify forts to be erected. All of this was vague estimate. What the government would allow and pay for, and what other governments were to contribute, he would learn later.

By the end of April, however, Johnson had worked out his list with Banyar, who compiled an estimate of £10,000 for "the Train and the Stores & Necessaries to be provided at the general Expence of the Colonies engaging in the Design of Building a Fort near the French Fort at Crown Point." This included, too, a "Vessel of abt. 40 Tons to be built imediately on Lake Champlain."[29]

Johnson's thinking along these lines was revealed by his estimates of the cost of transporting the ordnance—"to Horses, & drivers Sufficient to carry them to Crown point in 14 Days at £12 per Day"; and later "Carrying all the Battoes from Hudson's River to the South Bay, Supposeing 800 Battoes at 20s per 800"; and "transportation of the Amunition, provisions, &c. over the Said carrying place allowing Each Battoe to carry 2 Waggon Load."[30]

These plans and estimates, however, were all subject to modification due to the contemporary and parallel plans of the other provinces. For while Johnson was thinking in terms of New York, the prime mover was Massachusetts, and hers was to be the principal contribution in men and supplies.

At Alexandria it had been decided that the Crown Point expedition should have a force of forty-four hundred men, to be provided by the provinces most concerned with defense in that quarter. This number was divided, in accordance with relative population and resources, as follows: New York, eight hundred; Connecticut, a thousand; Massachusetts, fifteen hundred; New Hampshire, five hundred; and Rhode Island, four hundred; and this was supposed to be augmented by two hundred Indians to be raised by Johnson.[31] Furthermore the assembly of New Jersey voted five hundred men under the command of Colonel Peter Schuyler.[32]

This was a sizable command, approaching five thousand men, and General Johnson wrote to the governors of the respective provinces asking for their provision of supplies, transport, and especially engineers and gunners.[33] Since this was entirely a provincial undertaking he was dependent upon the action of assemblies for financial support, even for his salary and equipment.

Herein there developed many headaches for the general, for the several governments had their own conditions and sent their own instructions to the commander. Massachusetts had moved with alacrity, taken early steps to enlist men, made provisions for transport, and alloted special salaries for engineers and gunners.[34] Connecticut was more reluctant; she was to furnish several companies of the New York contingent, for which she wanted to appoint a major. And Connecticut insisted on naming the second in command.[35] The New Hampshire assembly voted the five hundred men of her quota, but no stores or guns; neither would they provide bateaux for transport (their woodsmen preferred to travel by land), and insisted that they march to the Connecticut River and rendezvous near Crown Point.[36]

Johnson had stipulated that as fast as companies should be completed they should be sent to Albany, where they would be disciplined and prepared for service. There he would review them and reject such as were unfit. There, too, stores and bateaux would be prepared for the time of departure. At that time he expected as commander to make decisions:

I find by one part of your instructions you expect I should march to Crown point as soon as a number of men get to Albany, I must beg leave to say I think it of much more consequence to order a Sufficient Number to go before to make the roads passable & then march with the rest & every thing necessary for that service, and not depend upon their being sent after me.[37]

But these forces destined for Crown Point were to be depleted somewhat by the needs of the Niagara expedition, which had not been contemplated when Governor Shirley promoted the former in Massachusetts. Now he became concerned over the strength of forces allotted to him—his own regiment and that of Sir William Pepperell, which were, unlike the levies to Crown Point, to be supplied and supported by Braddock's funds. Each of these was to be of a thousand men, but he discovered after leaving Alexandria that Pepperell's were unlikely to be more than six hundred. On his way home, therefore, he stopped in New Jersey and persuaded

Governor Belcher and the assembly to assign the five hundred men already voted for Crown Point to be joined to his command. In New York he took steps to obtain órdnance and supplies from the stores there, and made it a point to settle matters with the governments in other capitals. Then when he reached Boston he had the Assembly of Massachusetts pass

a vote enabling me to employ as many of the troops rais'd within this Province for the service at Crown Point, as I should think proper in that agst Niagara; leaving 3700 in the whole for Crown Point, and provided the men were willing to go with me and the other Governments concern'd consented to it. Since which I have obtain'd the consent of all the other Governments, but one.[38]

The objection came from Connecticut. But Governor De Lancey and his aides were now particularly concerned over the strength of the forces for Johnson. A good deal of sophistry was employed to show that the reduction in the size of his force would not be serious. The French would sooner lose Crown Point than Niagara, the key to their fur trade and communication; General Braddock's success at Duquesne and the defeat of the French at Niagara would draw forces away from Montreal, thus serving as a diversion; and even after taking Niagara some of Shirley's men could be sent toward Crown Point.[39]

This last idea was ridiculed by Banyar, who queried whether Shirley knew it was five hundred miles between Niagara and Crown Point. He found unconvincing the arguments put forth by Massachusetts for reducing her quota by five hundred.[40] A contrary argument was formally drawn up, as the consensus of Johnson, Lyman, and the other officers. And Johnson was plaintive in his letter to Braddock on May 17.

But Sir, I cannot avoid expressing to you my Uneasy Apprehensions that the Colonies who have engaged themselves to forward & support the Attack wch I am honoured with the Command of will not act with that Vigorous & generous Spirit so very necessary towards its Success in particular & that of the Common Cause in general. I am truly sensible of my own Inability to be at the head of this undertaking, & I am afraid I shall have but few with me to assist & strengthen my Incapacity. None that can be called an Engineer, their Artillery in bad order & no Carriages yet provided, their Shells not fit for Service, No Man of Military Experience that I hear of amongst them. The 500 Men from Jersey under Col. Schuyler are I understand to go to Niagara, not a Company yet marching this way that I hear of, no List of officers appointed yet sent me nor have I any Account of what progress they are making.[41]

To others he expressed a premonition that disagreements might bring about unfortunate divisions; and at this time he felt no ill will toward Shirley.

I will only add, that I dread Confusion, want of Money, & that my hands will be too much tied up. Provincial Quotas will I foresee occasion an argumentative War, and I dread will retard if not destroy our Success. Govr. Shirleys Attack is happily not upon Provincial Funds, & I hope therefore it will be carried on with Vigor & Success. Certain I am of Opinion that General Braddocks Glory & very probably the safety of his Forces will very much depend upon these Diversions being carried on with Spirit & Dispatch.[42]

Braddock was sending him an able engineer, Captain Will Eyre, who arrived in New York May 30 and soon was deeply involved in the squabble for ordnance and supplies. On June 13 he arrived in Albany.[43] Thus one of Johnson's worries was somewhat allayed; Eyre was to double as quartermaster general, however, and he in turn began to complain of shortage of supplies, the depletion of the forces by Shirley's orders, and "the total Neglect of the train." He even thought that it "looks as if it's Success was not now in contemplation among ye great. . . . Hitherto I have been Successfull, and it makes me grave when I consider to be embark'd in so extraordinary an Undertaking."[44]

It was indeed an anomalous situation, out of which harmony could scarcely be expected. Governor Shirley was undoubtedly concerned over his own campaign, and yet as governor of Massachusetts which was contributing heavily to the Crown Point expedition in men and money, and as its first protagonist, he could scarcely have desired to see it languish. Johnson was his appointee, and he had issued both commission and instructions; and he expected Johnson to look to him for his wants and to report directly. Yet the two men were fast becoming rivals. This situation in turn was not a happy one for Johnson. He was respectful to Shirley and well considered his instructions. As he had stated, he was ambitious for success. Yet he had all along protested his feeling of inadequacy. Under these circumstances, it was easy for him to magnify his difficulties and the obstructions in his path. A series of pinpricks soon began to irk him; the complaints of others against Shirley were brought to him; and the prejudices which were occasioned by other events served to feed the flame.

Behind many of the early disagreements lay the ill feeling between Governor Shirley and Lieutenant Governor James De Lancey. Their respective provinces for some years had been at odds over the boundary between them, still unsettled. Furthermore, Shirley had sided with Governor Clinton in the struggle with the De Lancey faction in New York, and they found themselves in opposition over other questions. At Alexandria, in conference with General Braddock, Shirley had played a principal role, and in his own account plans had been made chiefly between Commodore Keppell, Braddock, and himself.[45] But De Lancey was constantly emphasizing in his reports the full support which he and New York were giving to Braddock.

Now Goldsbrow Banyar, deputy secretary of New York, and Johnson's principal informant, being close to De Lancey reported many incidents which were derogatory to Shirley and which implanted suspicion of his intentions. After getting additional troops, Governor Shirley now sought ordnance and supplies from New York, from the same stores that Johnson was to depend upon, and in this he was opposed by De Lancey, who was jealous of the authority which Shirley had over the Crown Point preparations. De Lancey wanted equal power, to grant also a commission and instructions to Johnson, and to have reports from him directly; and he did not intend to let Shirley continue to direct the campaign. As Banyar wrote:

he has no objection to your Instructions but that instead of following *such other Instructions as you may receive from Mr. Shirley*, which Mr. De Lancey says is putting the intire Direction of all the Troops under him, It must be *to act (in such Matters as your Instructions are silent in) by advice of a Council of War.*[46]

Shirley in turn began to question Johnson's authority from Braddock, whether he had a commission, and whether he was given "Impress Warrants," to requisition supplies.[47] Oliver De Lancey's efforts to raise men in Connecticut for the New York contingent and his references to Shirley's influence soon made the rupture between the two governors evident to all. Banyar called Shirley's letter "full of Sly insinuations and greatly to Mr. D's disadvantage," but opined that De Lancey's reply would cause him to "be more sparing of these sorts of Reflections for the future."[48] And De Lancey wrote Governor Morris of Pennsylvania: "The D———ys have thrown all imaginable Obstructions in my Way, and I perceive an open Quarrel with the G———r is unavoidable."[49]

As yet Shirley was cordial to Johnson and assured him of support and that his needs would be met. Yet disagreements were developing, and each felt his own interests were vital. One concern of Johnson was financial support for his Indian policy. Shirley thought it was limited to the £800 for gifts and the £2,000 authorized by Braddock. He also implied that this would supply Indians for the Crown Point expedition, but Johnson construed them as only for his larger assignment. Shirley finally assured him that his drafts would be honored.[50]

It was one of the handicaps under which the Crown Point expedition labored, that when the support as well as authority over the commander was divided among the provinces there was bound to be delay, if not actual neglect. This was well demonstrated by Johnson's trouble in getting his personal needs and those of his staff. A month after his appointment he wrote De Lancey:

I seek I desire no private Emolument to my fortune by the Command but Surely Sir the public should take Care & fix a reasonable Establishment for me, of wch. I see no Footsteps nor have any Intimations concerning it.[51]

The New York Assembly had resolved that the command should be a common charge on all the colonies, and New York should pay her just proportion. Massachusetts, however, the principal backer, acted as though her provisions were sufficient, and on June 7 fixed the salaries for officers; that for the commander in chief was £25 a month. If this was all, Johnson thought, "they were very sparing."[52] But he was more concerned as to provision for his staff and its maintenance.

The Pay set down for me, their Proportion of wh yr Province is to be answerable for, I submit to, but surely your Government doth not intend or suppose these Wages (as they term it) is to supply me with Equipage, with Necessaries, charge of Servants, & the various other expences wch the Command will subject me to. I am far from intending or desiring a Support for a Vain or useless ostentation, but they will I presume think it necessary that I Sustain the Honour conferred upon me with a Decent Dignity; the Troops will naturally expect to see it the officers to feel it. Neither my Policy nor my Spirit will allow me to disgrace the Character I am placed in.

The Province of New Jersey have agreed to give Col. Peter Schuyler who commands but 500 Men £300 in their Curry. for his Table &c. Is not a Secretary, are not Aid de Camps necessary officers about me, is there to be no Establishment for them, they must be always part of my Table.[53]

He assumed that these things would occur to them, that they were omitted in their hurry, and that his "wages" were only for his personal loss of time and fatigue. No pay, not even the most lavish, would compensate him for the loss to his fortune and private affairs, which he endured for the public good.[54]

Shirley's imperious attitude in some other affairs was dictated no doubt by his suspicion and dislike of De Lancey, rather than any wish to oppose Johnson. Yet when these touched upon Indian matters in which Johnson expected to have a free hand, they added to his irritation. Shirley, for example, expected that the Indian officers (those men entrusted with leading the Indians) should be treated and paid like other officers. He even thought the Indians would be organized in companies. Johnson insisted that this service was different, that the risks and hazards were greater, the duties more arduous, and that these men required more pay.[55]

Governor Shirley was especially insistent that the New York government take immediate steps to expel the French Indians from Albany. That these Caghnawagas, who ostensibly were trading with the Dutch merchants of Albany, very likely included French spies among their number was recognized by no one more clearly than by Johnson. De Lancey and the Council referred Shirley's letter to him for action, but he was about to begin negotiations with the Six Nations, to whom these "French Indians" were related, and he feared that action against them might jeopardize his diplomacy. "I am afraid," he wrote to De Lancey, "if the laudible Zeal of Govr. Shirleys measures should now take place with respect to the Cagnawaga Indians, it may breed a Dissatisfaction amongst ours & prejudice my Influence over them, for tis Certain they do look on the Cagnawagas as a part of themselves."[56] His reluctance in this regard was later construed as opposition to Shirley.

Johnson's aides had their own grievances, and these seemed cumulative. Captain Will Eyre, the engineer, who was not happy about the prospects, expressed his feelings, which Johnson tried to mollify.

In regard to Mr. Shirley's Letter, I thank you very kindly for the advice you give me. The Stile of his Epistle, I am so little accustom'd too, made it take the greater Impression. He is the first Genl officer that ever thought my Conduct was Irregular before, and I have served under the most knowing in his Majestys Service, and had the good fortune to be applauded rather than rebuked for my endeavours: I am obliged to you in not considering my zeal in the light that he is pleased to do.[57]

Johnson was still trying to reconcile these disagreements and to forward his expedition. He did not really oppose Governor Shirley or become convinced of his ill will (if such it was) until their agents clashed in recruiting the Indians. This came to light during the conference at Mount Johnson which was about to open.

XIV

INDIAN AUXILIARIES

William Johnson's appointment as sole manager of Indian affairs was a recognition of his position and of his continuing involvement. For the past year he had watched the Six Nations as a barometer indicating the pressure on the frontier and enabling him to forecast the climate for the immediate future. In December 1754, he wrote:

Upon the News of the first engagement at Ohio, Our friend Indians were in high spirits, but the last had a verry different Effect, of which, I have been an Eye, and ear witness to. Soon after the Seeming friendly Interview at Albany last June & imediately on the news of Washington's defeat, above two Hundred of the Six Nations went to Canada, as did also Severall of Both Mohawk Castles, the latter are return'd, the former are not expected untill the Spring, before time I fear many of them will be prevailed on to join the French & go to Ohio, as Severall of them have done last Summer. and those who may return will be so corrupted & poisoned that they Seduce the rest.[1]

Yet he felt that the natural bent of these tribes toward the English gave an opportunity to persuade them by attending to their grievances and by taking steps for their defense. But the behavior of the Six Nations would sway some western Indians, the Shawnees and Twightwees (Miamis), toward the English.[2] Already on behalf of the New York Council Johnson had taken steps to stockade the Mohawk castles. His dealings in behalf of the Pennsylvania government had kept him in touch with their Indians who were tributary to the Six Nations. Now he could work more effectively with increased authority.

No one needed to tell Johnson in this field what should be his first steps. He had insisted upon, and obtained, the right to pick his subordinates. Now before leaving Alexandria he wrote to Peter Wraxall, the New York secretary for Indian affairs, to continue under him. Braddock assented, and Wraxall was summoned to Mount Johnson.[3]

Next he appealed to the one man in Pennsylvania who could help him most, George Croghan, introducing himself and asking Croghan to speak to Scaroyady, the half king, with a belt in his name. It was Johnson's intention to send Indian help to Braddock both from the Pennsylvania tribes and from the Six Nations. Croghan replied cordially, and acceded to Johnson's demands; thus began a relationship between two Irishmen which was to endure for many years.[4]

There was a world of difference between these two products of the Emerald Isle, each of whom had acquired, first through trade and then by diplomacy, a great influence with the Indians. Croghan fled Ireland in 1741, due to a potato famine (three years after Johnson had come to the New World), and found his opportunity on the Pennsylvania frontier. A sharp trader, shrewd speculator, and promoter, he was involved in numerous ventures, becoming the most considerable Indian trader in Pennsylvania. He journeyed widely on the frontier, won the confidence of the Indians, and thus was frequently called upon by the government to furnish supplies or to negotiate with the tribes. His many deals, often too risky or unsound, involved him in huge debts which he was unable to pay, and his failure to meet obligations caused him to be widely suspected or distrusted. Yet no projects on the frontier seemed possible without him. He accompanied Washington and later Braddock, and was present at the latter's defeat and death.

Nothing is known of Croghan's early life. Rough and crude in manner, he did not come from Johnson's social level, and from the first was deferential. But he had an independence of mind and a directness in action which Johnson respected. He also knew and understood Indians in the same way that Johnson did. He had a knack for Indian negotiations, but, unlike Johnson, he was not always able to keep his diplomacy and his trading interests separate. With the outbreak of war, he was to lose thousands of pounds.

Best of all in Johnson's eyes, however, Croghan was a congenial and convivial spirit, a straight-shooter who disliked cant and humbug. Although he dealt with governors and generals, and later sported the title of *Colonel*, he was not adapted to military forms or discipline and disliked the pretense of military rank. His letters, with their original orthography reflecting his Irish brogue, reveal a unique character. To Johnson as to the Indians, he needed no introduction.[5]

From his associates in the militia and in trade Johnson now picked his Indian officers, the men who were to enlist and lead the Indians for him. The qualities of these men he knew; their abilities would warrant the extra pay he had demanded. They were less officers than interpreters and deputies of Johnson. First was John Butler, from Oswego, who was sent off with a small party of Indians to join Braddock. This was more of a token of support than any real help, for the Mohawks refused to stay longer than to "pay their Duty to Yr. Excellency."[6] Others to get commissions were Benjamin Stoddert, Thomas Butler, and Jonathan Stevens; also enlisted was his brother-in-law Matthew Ferrall, now with some experience in westward trading. To Benjamin Stoddert he explained the duties:

If you think it would be worth your while to engage in this Service I would Give You a Captn. Commission to command a party of Indians, they are not to go a Scalping as in the late War, only to March with me where ever I go . . . you should bring as many Indians with you as possible, makeing them promise to go any where with you. . . . Let them bring their Arms . . . the best way to engage Indians, is to Secure in yr. Interest ye. head Warrior who can bring their party along with them.[7]

This was a far cry from Shirley's plan to have the Indians in companies of one hundred with captains, lieutenants, and ensigns. Such a plan would not work and would even subvert the accustomed procedure.

At Mount Johnson preparations threw all in a turmoil. "Since my arrival here," William wrote Banyar on May 20, "no Man liveing has had so much trouble & Hurry." He had met the Mohawk castles' sachems at his home and informed them of his new title and duties as "Sole Manager and Director of Affairs." He had sent two interpreters to call all the Six Nations to a meeting at his house. He learned of some murmurings among the Mohawks when some troops advanced toward Oswego, so he had sent Clement the interpreter with a belt of wampum to Onondaga to allay their fears. He had sent out two Indians to Cadaracqui to learn about the French forces being sent to Ohio. And he sent three Indians and two white men to spy on Crown Point and to learn of the forces there.[8] But the biggest event of all was to be the meeting with the Six Nations and their allies at Mount Johnson.

This was indeed the greatest meeting yet held with the Indians of New York. Over eleven hundred Indians appeared; most were from the two Mohawk castles, but all the Nations were represented, as well as their allies, the Delawares, the Oquagas, the Tiederigroenes, and Skaniadaradighronos. To meet them Johnson assembled an impressive array of aides. With him were Peter Wraxall, secretary for Indian affairs, the Reverend John Ogilvie, missionary to the Mohawks, and four interpreters headed by Daniel Claus. Then there were the Indian officers—captains Stoddert and Butler, Mr. Ferrall, and others.[9]

The formal opening of the conference on June 21 was made when Johnson, superintendent of Indian affairs, made a speech to the nine nations present. It was put into the Indian tongue by Daniel Claus. This speech was an introduction to the treaty, and related the "Journey of Gen. Johnson with the different Governors to General Braddock and his being appointed to the sole management of their affairs." The tree which they had lamented was fallen was now set upright and planted with a firm hand; the embers of the fire which burned at Albany were brought here, to Mount Johnson, and supplied with wood which would never burn out; and they were exhorted to unity and cooperation, that they might enjoy the strength of a bundle of sticks which could not be broken. The speech which General Braddock had sent was mentioned, but not delivered at this time. The Indians' reply would be delivered later.[10]

It was two days before the Indians were ready, for they were far from united, and a great deal of persuasion was used by the friends of the English. French influence was strong at Onondaga and among the western nations, especially with the Cayuga. Hendrick was the ranking sachem, but he realized the danger of too much initiative from the Mohawks. He abdicated his undoubted right to serve as speaker and put forward Kaghswughtioni (Red Head), an Onondaga who had been known for his attachment to the French. By this move he would be brought under Johnson's influence and won over to the English. In his speech Red Head rejoiced in Johnson's appointment; as for the fire at Albany, "it was so low and so bad, that we could not even find a spark to light a pipe at it"; the fire here and at Onondaga they would keep, all others would be kicked away.[11]

The letter written by George Croghan on behalf of Scaroyady for the Pennsylvania tribes was read, telling how they were going to join General Braddock; and Braddock's message to the Six Nations was presented. Now Johnson called upon them to join him in the war.

I am ordered to go myself with a considerable number of your Bretheren from the neighbouring provinces over whom I am appointed to the Chief Command with great guns and other implements of war, to drive the French from their encroachments on your hunting grounds in this Province; if you will be dutiful to the King your Father, if you will be faithful to your Bretheren the English, if you will treat me as your Brother, Go with me. My war kettle is on the Fire, my Canoe is ready to put in the water, my Gun is loaded, my sword by my side, and my Ax is sharpened. I desire and expect you will now take up the Hatchet and join us, your Bretheren against all our Enemies.[12]

The Caghnawagas, he knew, were their brethren, so he promised an effort to treat with them and to make them "sensible of their true interest," that their blood should not be spilt. He also promised for those who would join him to care for their women and children. But, he warned, if they would not follow him he would give up his commission and leave the country. Many other matters were now explained to the Indians in private, with the aid of interpreters, before the speech of General Braddock was read.

Now was action suited to the words, as the appeal was made to all sachems and warriors to take up the hatchet.

When Coll: Johnson threw down the War Belt in General Braddock's name, it was taken up by an Onejda Sachem, when Arent Stevens the Interpreter began the War dance for General Braddock, he then danced one for Coll: Johnson, to both which the Sachems bore the usual Chorus.

Coll: Johnson then ordered a large Tub of punch out, for, to drink the King's health.[13]

Johnson's skill in parley, in dancing, and in feasting with the Indians soon became legendary. Surgeon Williams of Massachusetts then at Albany heard of these feasts and wrote: "Gen. Johnson has about 1100 of the blacks [Indians], little & great, Male and female about him; he has the war dance, when the Indians painted up the General, & an ox was roasted whole & the General with his cutlass went up & slashed off a piece, & each of the Indians took up their axes & followed."[14]

In spite of these demonstrations there were many matters to be settled and difficulties to be ironed out. The Cayugas were closest to the French, and their great sachem and warrior Ottrowana came, with friends who lived north of Lake Ontario, and with a Missisauga sachem. After a long parley they too expressed confidence in Johnson. The latter was now getting impatient and reminded them that he had many duties which called him back to Albany to prepare his expedition. There was the matter of the rum trade, which the sachems protested. Even at the treaty five or six kegs of rum were discovered by William Johnson, which he proceeded to break up. He was sorry for this trade, for it hindered their councils and prevented some from coming.[15]

As to the Caghnawagas and their dealings, he explained that the English had allowed them to come to Albany to trade as brethren of the Mohawks, but it was quite in the power of the English to exclude them. They would be asked to come and join with the others their relatives, and not to help the French, for he did not wish to spill their blood. If they would not, he asked them to stay out of the way; for he could not do less.[16]

As the conference drew to a close and many Indians desired to return home, it was necessary to get specific commitments, and Johnson called upon them to contribute to the various expeditions whose objectives had been described. First he asked that some of their young men go immediately to join General Braddock. Captain Stoddert stood up and was presented as the leader of this group. Next, he asked men to join the Niagara expedition on its way to Oswego.[17]

Bretheren. Your Brother and friend Govr Shirley who is well known to you is now or will in a day or two be at Albany. He is going to Oswego with a great number of Soldiers who are now at Albany and Schenectady. He designs to go to Niagara to prevent the French from sending any more reinforcements to the Ohio, and to open the Road which is now stopped for your and our Bretheren to the Westward to come to Oswego. He expects and I desire you will meet him there and give him that assistance in his undertakings which as bretheren you are bound to do.[18]

I shall in a little time be ready to march with the forces under my command for Crown Point, and I desire you will have some Warriors of each Nation here to attend my directions, and when I send for more that they may be ready to join us.[19]

As for further help to be sent to General Braddock, Johnson was already apprehensive. He had learned that the six young Indians who had been sent to General Braddock had been killed. Hendrick also learned of this, and the speaker, Red Head, answered that they had already fulfilled their obligation, and there were enough southern Indians friendly to the English to supply the need there.[20]

As for the other two expeditions, they preferred to go with Johnson and felt there were others who would join with Shirley.

Brother. In answer to your third Belt we say, are you not our Tree of shelter, and why will you desire us to take shelter under any other Tree, where you go we are ready to follow. However there will be many of our people round about Oswego and near to Niagara, who will join and be ready to assist Govr Shirley.[21]

Nor did they think it urgent for them to answer the call to join Johnson; "as for him there wou'd be Time enough, as he was a heavy Body that cou'd move but Slow [meaning the Army] ; and he might be assured that all the rest of their People wou'd learn where the Tree lean'd [Meaning General Johnson] ."[22]

In spite of these reservations there was apparent harmony and goodwill at the meeting—although the superintendent had to labor mightily in private to keep it so—until the appearance of John Henry Lydius. This insidious character, who had so recently gained a bad name among the Six Nations as agent for the Connecticut speculators, was now officially employed by Massachusetts. He came to Albany commissioned by Shirley as Indian officer for the Niagara expedition. Knowing the man's shady reputation, and that his employment years before had irritated Johnson, Governor Shirley here displayed exceedingly bad judgment. And that he continued to employ Lydius and to back his actions, despite Indian protests, more than anything else produced the break between him and Johnson.

Nearly a month before, while Shirley's carpenters were at work in Albany on their bateaux, Lydius displayed to Johnson his commission from Governor Shirley as colonel of Indians to go to Niagara. At that time Johnson remarked, "I find Shirley thinks of himself, & little of anybody Else." Yet he cooperated loyally and wrote the governor, "I have assured Coll. Lydius & your Excellency may depend, that if the Indians can be brought to act with us against the French, I will endeavour to prevail on a sufft Number to attend your Excellency under his Command."[23]

But the methods of Shirley and Lydius with the Indians were the exact opposite of those used by Johnson. Shirley still clung to the idea that Indians could be employed like white troops, organized in companies, and ordered on service. He supplied funds to Lydius for that purpose, and he seemed to expect Johnson to have Indians at hand to go with him as he requested. Johnson's parleying was all designed to have the Indians act as a group with their own leaders as allies, and with the Indian officers serving as interpreters and advisers. This meant no payment to individual Indians, but strong promises of support and insurance of the protection of their villages and the care of their women and children. He had made this clear in a positive statement to Governor Shirley in his letter of June 19. "To establish the Indians into Companys of 100 Men each with Capts. Lieuts. & Ensigns, is impossible that sort of regularity cannot be obtained amongst those People, their officers must be Interpreters & take Care of them in all respects besides doing their Duty as officers, Ensigns will be needless."[24]

Now on July 3, Lydius, with some of his followers, was present in the meeting at Mount Johnson, and he was recognized by one of the speakers. Conochquiesie, an Oneida sachem, arose and dramatically accused him, at the same time censuring Johnson.

> Brother. You promised us that you would keep this fireplace clean from all filth and that no snake should come into this Council Room.[25] That Man sitting there (pointing to Coll: Lyddius) is a Devil, and has stole our Lands, he takes Indians slyly by the Blanket one at a time, and when they are drunk, puts some money in their Bosoms, and perswades them to sign deeds for our lands upon the Susquehana which we will not ratify nor suffer to be settled by any means.[26]

In his formal reply the following day Johnson took up the matter of Lydius. It was never possible in the course of Indian diplomacy to ignore a point made by a speaker, hence this accusation had to be met.

> Bretheren. I did promise, that I would keep this fireplace free from all filth and did desire, that no snake should come into this Council room. As to Coll: Lyddius, if his coming hither was such an offense to you, I am sorry for it, he came of his own accord without any invitation from me ... If Coll: Lyddius hath done as you represent and which I am affraid is in a great measure true, I think, he is very faulty, and that nobody should attempt to settle Lands upon such unfair purchases.

I will endeavour all in my power that justice may be done you in this affair.[27]

Interpolated in the official record here was an explanation of Lydius's activity in the valley by Peter Wraxall, the secretary, which got both him and Johnson into trouble with Shirley. For Wraxall had written:

Col: Lydius came to Mount Johnson with an Interpreter [employ'd by Govr: Shirley] & several Indians complain'd to Col: Johnson that Lydius had been privately perswading them to go to Niagara wth: him [and Govr: Shirley and] they express'd their Displeasure at this Application of Lydius's; upon w'ch. Col. Johnson spoke to Mr. Lydius [who shew'd him Gov'r: Shirley's Orders for what he had done;] Col. Johnson forbid him & the Interpreter to interfere any further with the Indians, as it had, & would occasion an Uneasiness amongst 'em wch. Might be prejudicial to the Interest in general.[28]

This was all true, but as a note it was a sort of *obiter dictum;* for the Indian was complaining of Lydius's earlier activity in purchasing land of the Indians for Connecticut, whereas Wraxall's note was an attempt to explain his presence and Johnson's attitude toward him.

When Shirley read the report of the conference at Mount Johnson he was furious. He demanded that Johnson expunge his name from the note by Wraxall; he denounced Wraxall, called him unfit and guilty of betrayal of his trust; and he held Johnson responsible for this action and even criticized Johnson's speech to the Indians regarding Lydius. He demanded affidavits and attested copies of letters, and he showed every intention of pursuing the matter to the end.[29]

The meeting was now brought speedily to a close. Red Head, the speaker, spoke highly of "Our Brother Warraghiyagey," whom the King at their request had appointed, and he was confident that now the war would be prosecuted successfully. The Indians expressed their approval with a shout of applause. It was still necessary to meet in private with the Cayugas, to give some extra presents, and to provide for the safe return of the Indians, with provisions for their journey.[30] But Johnson could now write with satisfaction, as he did to Braddock, that the Confederate Nations were all affectionately disposed and that they would remain "firm and unshaken." If present plans were carried out this would be a great factor in turning other Indians toward the English.[31] He had labored mightily toward this end. At the beginning he described his task as "the hardest Struggle ever Man had with them for I will make them turn their coats."[32] A week before the end of the meeting, he told De Lancey:

I am in private working with the Sachems & leading men from morning to night. The Fatigue I have undergone has been too much for me. It still continues & I am scarce able to support it. I am distress'd Where to get victuals for such Numbers, they have destroyed every Green thing upon my Estate, & destroyed all my meadows. I must humour them at this critical juncture.[33]

Now he would have to turn to his other task of preparing his expedition, taking command of the troops arriving in Albany, and organizing the train of supplies. And in the midst of all this came the mounting altercation with Shirley.

General Shirley had been much delayed and was greatly irked by his difficulties in getting men and supplies—a condition common to both expeditions. Yet his advance contingent under Colonel Ellison had gone up the valley, his carpenters were at Albany building bateaux, and others had gone ahead to build at Oswego and to strengthen the fort there. De Lancey had assisted them with supplies, and Johnson had prepared the Indians of the Mohawk Valley for their friendly reception. After several days in New York (July 2–5), Shirley embarked up the river for Albany, where he arrived July 10.[34] Before his arrival he wrote Johnson for an interview. "There are several points for us to settle before I leave that place."[35] They met in Albany the morning of July 15.

There are no records of what passed between the two men on this occasion save for references to it in several letters between them. Their previous meetings had been friendly, and Johnson had to look to Shirley for funds and supplies so that his attitude was no doubt respectful. (He always addressed the governor as "Your Excellency.") There were many details to be handled, for which each needed the help of the other. Yet the needlings and insinuations in three months of correspondence had left their mark, and a certain caution and wariness was no doubt the result. Both men were proud, firm in their convictions as to the importance of their missions and the correctness of their views. Shirley, as governor of Massachusetts and as second in command to Braddock, with the title of major general, regarded himself as Johnson's superior. Johnson, however, felt that his commission to manage Indian affairs gave him freedom of action in that field for which he was responsible only to Braddock or to the Board of Trade. In his commission it was specifically stated that others were not to meddle, and that referred, he believed, both to Shirley and his men.

From what we know of their characters, we would expect Shirley to have been haughty and somewhat imperious. He could be charming and courteous, but he was now a bit peevish, and it was bound to show. Johnson, the master of Indian diplomacy, could be obsequious and considerate, with unlimited patience, capable of concealing his feelings with the greatest composure. Under this exterior, however, there was a quite surprising firmness and resolution. Shirley had seen enough of Johnson the Indian leader that he should have suspected this inward iron beneath the outward calm. But Shirley was in no mood to make concessions.

Johnson's two-week conference with the Indians was reviewed and Shirley pounced upon the reference to him in Wraxall's note. Johnson expressed regret and promised that Shirley's name should be expunged. (He did not agree to delete the note.) Shirley complained that Johnson had not tried to get him any Indians, whereupon Johnson referred to the Indians' reply to him on that score, that none would be needed until the army reached Oswego, to which he had agreed. But to appease Shirley, he asked Indians of three tribes then in Albany to get some Indians to go with the governor.[36]

Johnson, on the other hand, renewed his demand for funds and supplies for his expedition, and Shirley complied with an order for £1,654 and also granted commissions to certain officers in Johnson's train.[37] It probably was not a stormy meeting, but one of guarded sparring. Each withdrew with grievances unsettled, and perhaps seething with resentment.

It was Shirley, however, who kept up the controversy, which suggests that it was he who was most disturbed by the interview. His letter of July 17th was a full bill of particulars in censuring Johnson, questioning his conduct and that of his secretary, doubting his judgment in Indian affairs, and his interpretation of his commission. He was sharp and insistent in his demands upon Johnson, while at the same time denying Johnson's right to send queries to him.[38]

Johnson later spoke of this as "a verry long angry Letter, reproaching, menacing me & grosly abusing Mr. Wraxall. I answered with Spirit but cool & Decent." His immediate answer was but an acknowledgment, saying that he was to leave Albany for four or five days and would take up the various points on his return.[39] Wraxall, who was given the brunt of the blame by Shirley, in the meantime drafted a reply which was to be a full answer. Before it was sent, however, news of Braddock's defeat so chastened them that Johnson contented himself with a brief reiteration of his position.[40] The Wraxall draft has not survived, only his description of it.

I propose to send you said Draught & Govr. Shirleys Letter herewith. In two parts it is warm & I think justly so. first in that where you answer to his desiring attested Copies, in the Light I view it, it carries an Insinuation wch I think it would be a blamable mildness not to take notice of. Secondly where it says if yr. present Command depends wholly on his favr. & authority. The Spirit of his whole Letter carries such an overbearing & Insulting Air with it & he treats you in a stile so Magisterial, that I think your Answer might say more, but cannot less, consistent wth that Independent Spirit wch you are entitled to show him.[41]

Wraxall also suspected that "this Letter of his, may be designed for future & farther Purposes." And Johnson, too, felt that it forecast trouble for them both. "I make no doubt he will endeavour to wreek his Malice upon me & poor Wraxall, who has wrote to Mr Fox to get quit of his Military Commission so I hope he will be clear of the thunder in that Quarter."[42]

In the meantime the activity of Lydius and Shirley's other agents continued unabated, convincing Johnson that Shirley meant to wreck his Indian influence. Reports from Daniel Claus, Arent Stevens, and Matthew Ferrall recounted the disastrous effect which these efforts were having on the Indians, jeopardizing not only his followers, but the Indian interest in general.

During the Indian conference at Mount Johnson, Lydius, Joseph Kellogg,[43] and Isaac Staats were present (according to their affidavits submitted to Shirley). Lydius had spoken to some Indians about going to Niagara, and he had asked Staats to get some Stockbridge Indians. Johnson, who was still in the midst of his negotiations, summoned Lydius and Staats, who were guests at his table, and told them not to deal with the Indians. Lydius asserted that he had authority from General Shirley; the others were directed by Lydius. Lydius belonged to the "Tribe of the Tortoise," several of whom informed him that they would go with him to Niagara. It was this activity which alarmed Johnson and which occasioned the note by Wraxall.[44]

If Shirley was depending upon Johnson at this time to get Indians for his expedition, they were working at cross purposes. Lydius and his men might enlist the same Indians who had agreed to go with Johnson. And Staats asserted that

General Johnson then offered him a Captain's commission if he would enlist Stock-bridge Indians for Crown Point. This seems unlikely after Staats had been forbidden to speak to them; it is more likely that Johnson merely offered him a commission.[45] Now Shirley in his letter of July 17th demanded a specific number of Indians to be supplied him by Johnson.

> I depended upon your having engag'd some Indians to have proceeded wth. my Regiment from Schenectady to Niagara, when I sent you my letter by Col: Ellison, and must own I was greatly disappointed at the Accts. he gave me from time to time, of the Answers he receiv'd from you.

> Your Opinion that there is no Occasion for any Indians to join me 'till my Arrival at Oswego, is singular; all persons besides, whom I have consulted in this Affair are of different Sentiments; I am so myself.

> ... I think it necessary for his Majesty's Service, that I should have a Party of sixty or seventy Indians to escort me from Schenectady; & as I shall proceed from thence in a Short time, I must desire forthwith to know what I am to depend upon from you in this point: upon wch. you will be pleas'd to give me an explicit Answer.[46]

Shirley, who had earlier expressed such confidence in Johnson's judgment in Indian affairs, now refused to accept his assurances or those of the Indians them-selves. Earlier, in fact, he had written Johnson from Boston (May 24): "You will not forget to engage some good Indians to meet me at Oswego."[47] The Indians had told Johnson that there would be Indians near to Oswego, and there was no real need of an escort through friendly country. Shirley's secretary, William Alexander, who had managed procurement in New York for the expedition, and who came to Albany and sent ship carpenters on to Oswego by bateaux, found no difficulty or need for a guard for them. Each bateau had two men with firearms. "This is all the Guard it is possible to get for the Carpenters (for there are no troops left here [Albany May 27,]) and I am in hopes it will be sufficient, for the People of this Country are daily passing betwixt this and Oswego without any Apprehension of Danger that way."[48]

It was always easier to get Indians to go on a short campaign, and they preferred to travel by themselves rather than to accompany troops, with whom there was always danger of friction. Thus the Mohawks preferred the relatively short distance toward Lake George and Crown Point, and they chose to meet Johnson's troops on the way. Shirley would be travelling with a regiment, and there was little danger that a few Indians would attack a large contingent of men. Johnson was later to warn his own commanders: "If due regularity be preserved neither in Marching nor in Camp can a few Indians do any Mischief to a Body of Men & indeed they will not attempt it, but they will never miss taking advantage of Disorder & rash Confusion."[49] There might have been scattered parties of hostile French Indians somewhere along the route to Oswego, but not in such numbers as to endanger a regiment of troops. But Shirley had an *idée fixe* and he was determined to make it an issue.

It was the continued activity of Shirley's agents in the Mohawk Valley, however—interfering with Indians who were committed to go to Crown Point and disrupting the arrangements which Johnson so painstakingly had made—that drove him into outright suspicion of and hostility to the general.

Frustrated by Johnson and the Indians at the conference, Lydius now sought out persons in Albany and Schenectady to use as his agents. Among these were several traders, John Vischer (Fisher or Visger), Martinius Lydius, and one Bleecker (or Blicker), and a Captain Van Schaick. With plenty of money to offer as bribes and promises of regular pay, they enticed the Indians into houses and then pressed them to go to Niagara. At Albany the influential Cayuga sachem, Ottrowana, was so approached, along with Abraham and Aaron, who had agreed to go with Johnson.[50] At Schenectady several Indians, including a Missisauga sachem, were seized and carried into a house to be persuaded.[51]

Not the least active in this work was "Billy" Alexander, Shirley's secretary and advance agent. At the home of John B. Van Eps in Schenectady he offered Daniel Claus a lieutenancy, plus an allowance for Indian service (as interpreter), if he would go to Niagara, and urged him to break away from Johnson. Alexander then approached Arent Stevens, Johnson's interpreter, told him that Johnson could not raise his salary, thus seeking to make him dissatisfied and implying that Shirley would pay him more. Stevens dutifully reported this to Johnson, and added: "He used all Arguments to persuade me to go to the Castle to speak to those Mohawk Indians in Govr. Shirleys favor, which had any inclination to Join him, which I absolutely refused because I had no such orders from you."[52]

With troops in the valley it was possible to use the methods of the press gang. Even two of Johnson's servants were thus seized, as Ferrall related:

Mr. Allexander Prest Jemmey and Wat Uppon their return home they tould him they were your Servants and was to go to Crown point along with you he said he did not Care for you yourself must go where some ever Govenor Shirley orders you they brought them before Govenour Shirley who order'd Jemmey in to one of the Battows he went in her for about a mile and then run a way from her home.[53]

News of these extraordinary exertions in the valley disturbed Johnson, first because they upset the Indians, who perceived that there were divided counsels among the English, instead of the sole management of which they had received assurances. Secondly, they introduced the recruitment of Indians through bribes and payment of money, which was contrary to Johnson's plan, and therefore subversive to his arrangements. And thirdly, the competition for the same Indians threatened his own plans for the Crown Point campaign. Since there was to be an immediate confrontation near Crown Point where French auxiliaries and scouts would have to be offset by Indians in the English interest, his need was far more urgent than any use of Indians by Shirley between Schenectady and Oswego. His discouragement was compounded when he learned of the disaster of Braddock's defeat.[54] On July 29, he again wrote Shirley, not stressing minor points of disagreement but arguing for the larger aims of both.

If the Expedition under my Command is to go forwards, I must have Indians or I can promise myself no Success but the reverse. In the present Sittuation of Affairs, it appears to me of the last Importance that the Management of our Affairs with the Indians should be conducted with the utmost harmony & in the most uniform manner. The Proceedings wch have lately taken place & are asserted to have Your Excellencys Countenance have given me a great deal of Concern, as I am persuaded they tended to distract & hurt the common Interest, & will undoubtedly if persevered in be of fatal Consequence & defeat the very Ends proposed.

I am of Opinion that An Attack upon Niagara & securing that important Pass is now more than ever necessary, & that no Delay be suffered wch. can possibly be avoided. [*I shall most readily concur with the whole weight of my Indian Interest to forward & promote that Service wch.*]I continue to think dos not require the assistance of any considerable Number of Indians as the Opperations will be chiefly conducted by Water.

And I make no doubt Your Excellency would have found in & about Oswego as many Indians ready to help you as would be realy necessary, whether it will be so now, as the News I fear is got that way by this time, is doubtful.

Without Indians tis in vain to expect Success from our Expedition. And how they will behave in general under the present Circumstances, I cannot pretend to assertain.

I pray God assist & direct your Excellencys Detirminations. . . .[55]

Shirley of course was profoundly disturbed by the news of Braddock's defeat, which he received on leaving Albany. In addition to the palpable effect upon the Indians and the damage to the morale of the troops, he had suffered a personal loss in the death of his eldest son, William. And he was now heir to the command of the American forces. He appealed to the governors for reinforcements for both expeditions; he pondered the question of where to order the troops of Braddock, now under Colonel Dunbar; and he worried over where the French forces might now be directed. Friends made him more apprehensive of an Indian attack, making him redouble his efforts to get Indians.[56] But he now had a trump card in his dispute with Johnson.

Shirley's progress up the Mohawk gave him personally an opportunity to hold meetings with the Indian tribes, to assert his authority, and to plead for their participation in his expedition. Passing by the Lower Castle, he stopped at the Upper (Canajoharie), where he recalled his acquaintance with the venerable sachem Hendrick, Johnson's best friend and ally. Daniel Claus and Johnson's other Indian officers learned of the meeting and hurried over to repair the damage. Claus related that

he, suspecting that the same Intrigues would be carried on as was at the Lower Mohk. Town proceeded with all Expedition to Canajoharie and Arriving at King Henrys House where he lodged found that Genl. Shirley had already had a Counsel with the Indns. & Henry & his two Brothers Abraham & Nicklas just come from it after his arrival & Henry immediately communicated every particular to Mr. Claus; the Chief purpose of the Meeting was that General Shirley after loading Henry & his Brothers (who had the whole village at his nod as well as the 6 Nations) with cash & presents, giving Henery a Captns. Commissn, & his Brothers Lieuts. & their wives a Number of Spanish Dollars. He in the strongest manner invited them to accompany him, well knowing the rest of the Indns must follow many of whom were likewise bribed, telling them that He was an older Acquaintance of theirs having had Interviews with them at Albany before Colo. Johnson came to America, & hoped they would not set aside their old Friendship but share his Fate the ensuing Expedition against Niagara etc. &c K. Henery showed Mr. Claus the belt of Wampum & the pargament Commissions that were given on the occasion and asked his Opinion and Advice how to act in the Affair & whether Colo. or Sr. Wm. Johnson would allow him his Captns. pay to support his family during his Absence, the same Question was asked by the Brothers Abraham & Nicklas.[57]

Claus chided them with not being loyal to Johnson and the agreements which had been made in the council, saying that it was unfair for Shirley to upset these arrangements in his absence. He told them that they knew they could depend upon Johnson in money matters, but

Genl. Shirley only made Tools of them by Bribery & fair promises while he stood in need of them after wch. they perhaps would never see him again, when [while] Genl. Johnson was among them and in all probability would live and die among them and have it in his power to show them many Favors & Services &c.[58]

Claus was not only an interpreter and agent of Johnson, but had lived with Hendrick, whom he was accustomed to call his father. The Indians were now influenced not only to repudiate any promises to Shirley but to warn the rest of the Six Nations. Claus continued:

This Talk had its Effect & these Chiefs called a private Council in which it was agreed that a running Messenger should be sent to the 6 Nations Country with a large Belt of Wampum to apprize them of Genl. Shirley's approach with his Suit of Indn. Officers whom the six Nations were strictly enjoined not to notice or give Ear to if called together or regard any of their words, as their Design & Insinuations were bad and proceeded from a bad Heart at the Instigation of ye D———l, to annule the Resolutions they had agreed upon in full Council abt. the Distribution of their Warrs. & thereby occasion Confusion & Disagreement. That they the Mohawks to a Man were determined to join Genl. Johnson and as they were the Seniors of the Confederacy they expected they would listen to their advice and follow their example.

Accordingly a Runner dispatched wth. a large Belt of Wampum, the Result of wch. was that the Six Nations in general accepted the Message and promised to follow Sr. Wm. Johnson and Genl. Shirley had not 50 Indians wth. him tho Mr. Lydius, Fisher from Scheny. and other Indn. Traders as above mentioned declared they would have all the 5 Natns. Inds. to a Man.[59]

Two days after Shirley's meeting at the Mohawk castle, three Indians were in Albany reporting these claims to Johnson. For Shirley informed them that he was to get twenty of their warriors, of which they had not been told; and that Johnson had been allowed £5,000 for the Indians. Had he not promised them ten shillings a day for going on the outscout, and £5 apiece if they returned successful? When the Indians said no, they knew nothing of such pay, "John Fisher & the rest looked at one another & smiled." Thus it was implied that Johnson was not playing fair with the Indians. Furthermore, Shirley said that "these doings of General Johnson seemed very Strange to him, as it was him raised Gen. Johnson to the Post he was in now." The Indians were also troubled that Shirley had taken away the men who were working on their forts, and that he "stopped all the Waggons that was pressed for General Johnson upon the River."[60]

Johnson answered them that only six Mohawks had been promised by him to Shirley.

It was not Govr. Shirley who raised me up, it was as I told you at our Public Meeting, by the King your Fathers directions to General Braddock. Govr. Shirley has lodged no Money in my hands—the Money I received for mannaging your Affairs, was put into my hands by General Braddock, he having a Power from the King your Father for so doing. If Govr. Shirley told you I had orders to Allow you 10 Shillings per day or to give you £5 per Man after your return, he imposed on you, for I never had any such Orders.

All my Promises I will faithfully fulfill to You, as I have always done, and you may depend upon it, that those who remain true to their Engagements & go with me, I will always remember & do everything for them in my power . . .[61]

Shirley had left Albany with thirty Stockbridge Indians; at Schenectady he had managed to get ten more, and at the Mohawk castles he had persuaded "eight of their young men who were not engaged with General Johnson." At the Oneida carrying place he sent messengers to the several nations apprising them of his march and asking them to join him at Oswego. "Soon after my arrival at Oswego Several of the Sachems and Warriors of the Oneidas met me, as did a few days after, almost all the Onondaga Sachems, and a Considerable Number of their warriors; and I had reason to Expect a large Number of the Senecas."[62]

Thus, in spite of earlier contentions, was borne out Johnson's opinion that Shirley needed no great escort, and that he would obtain sufficient Indians at Oswego.

Johnson's discouragement over his own expedition in July and early August was compounded by what he believed to be the sabotaging of his Indian diplomacy. The arrival of Shirley in Albany and the subsequent controversy had multiplied his duties and concerns.[63] It was hard for him to believe that the governor who had proposed and backed the Crown Point expedition did not want its success; but it was difficult to accept Shirley's opposition and intervention in all his Indian plans. He had been chosen for the Crown Point expedition because of his Indian influence and his probable use of the Indians on that campaign. Now after months of ticklish negotiation he found Shirley's men in the Mohawk Valley using every effort to take these Indians from him. He finally concluded that there was an intention to undermine his Indian influence.

Besides all these Matters Mr. Shirleys Proceedings with regard to the Indians have been so unexpected & Extraordinary, he has brought a new Scene of trouble, Employment & vexation upon me & thrown the Indians into the utmost Confusion. Lydius is his Indian Premier, and under him are a Number of Agents, working with Money and by every kind of Artifice to destroy my Influence, to overset the Measures agreed upon at our Meeting & to turn the Indians from the Crown Point to the Niagara Expedition.[64]

To this De Lancey, on receipt of news of Braddock's defeat and death, noted the probable loss of Indian support:

This astonishing & most Tragical Event puts it out I am affraid of all our Powers by any means whatsoever to prevail on the Indians to join us, nay I very much fear their self Preservation may influence the greatest part of them to join our Enemies against us. This is the great Evil I fear and the worse side of the Picture. I make no doubt the French have sent their Emissaries with Trophies & Agravated Accts. of our Defeat to our Indians & that these are already arrived amongst the upper Nations.

If the Crown Point Expedition must be stopped & unless we get Indians to Assist us I think it would be madness to Attempt it as we now are, the best Measures wch in that Case Occur to me are that I should go thro all the Nations or try to get some of their most leading Men to meet me at Onondaga, lay matters before them, use all the Arguments & Influence I am master of to prevent the Dissolution of our Indian Connexions. . . .[65]

With hopes that the war would be vigorously prosecuted on all fronts, with suggestions and plans for the several theaters of war, and even with a suggestion for a "Grand Council" of the colonies to deliberate on the crisis, Johnson now turned to his own preparations.

When I was up at My house last I dispatched the Indian officers amongst the Several upper Nations with marching Orders to set out with all possible Dispatch & meet me at the Carrying Place. The Two Mohock Castles except 5 Scoundrels whom Govr. Shirleys Agents had debauched promised me they would join me to a Man. I sent to the Acquawgas & Two chief Mohock Indians to the Westenhack & some River Indians to come. I expect several parties are already on their way to join Genl. Lyman at Seraghtoge if he should not be got to the Carrying place.

I have now some of the most leading Men of three upper Nations with me to whom I have communicated our Misfortune at the Ohio pretty nearly in its true Light. they assure me they will stand by their Engagements & I am now fitting them out with Arms &c. I cannot but flatter myself, if Govr. Shirley's Proceedings who will not be controuled by my reasonings, does not throw things into confusion, but that the Indians will for the most part stand by us.[66]

The controversy with Shirley was not over. The foregoing events were in late July and early August. For a month Johnson was fully occupied by the campaign. Then on September 3, he was to write a full and detailed complaint against Shirley to the Board of Trade. His whole career as Indian diplomat, his influence with the Indians and his future, too, he believed were at stake. Thus he was bitter and severe. Historians and biographers who have taken this statement, without knowing the sequence of events, have blamed him for his attack upon Shirley, placing him in the wrong as initiator of the dispute. (For additional information about this dispute, see Appendix II.)

At this time, however, no one knew what was to be the outcome of the campaigns. Johnson's later success and the sequel has placed all in a different light. In fairness, it is better now to consider the campaign against Crown Point.

XV

THE ADVANCE TO LAKE GEORGE

Albany, which had been host the year before to the intercolonial congress, and where large contingents of Indians had gathered on various occasions, was not unaccustomed to military expeditions with all their truck and followers. Fort Frederick, a gloomy and not-so-formidable pile on the hill overlooking the river, contained a small garrison with officers and boasted but a few pieces of artillery. Military officers were put up at a few taverns or in some of the private houses. Distinguished visitors might be guests of the Van Rensselaers, Schuylers, or Douws, while larger groups resorted to camps nearby or constructed lodges for themselves.

In the spring of 1755 there was a hum of activity as two expeditions were to make Albany their base. Massachusetts had begun early preparations in the raising of troops and in plans for their transport. While some of Shirley's men marched to Rhode Island and then came by water to New York, plans were made to build bateaux there for use above Albany. Connecticut, too, had some bateaux built in New York, but more were to be constructed by carpenters sent to Albany. As Shirley's regulars arrived under Colonel Ellison, they made preparations to embark by bateaux at Schenectady for the journey to Oswego.

Since General Johnson was engaged with the Indians, he left to Captain Eyre, engineer and quartermaster, the task of receiving the provincial troops in Albany. Eyre surveyed the surrounding countryside for a suitable place for an encampment. Johnson suggested the east side of the river, on the land of "Col. Rentzlaer" as most desirable, for it would be easier to keep the soldiers from visiting Albany. If that were not available, Eyre was to examine the land behind the fort, "but as far from the road as possible." He found that Van Rensselaer's land, which was formerly used for encampment, was "now under Corn." But there was space for eight hundred or a thousand men below on the lands of "Mr. Dow." Further up the river on the Flats, he felt, as many as two thousand might be encamped. Johnson favored the former location, fearing that an encampment on the Flats might signify to the enemy the intention to march north; whereas troops encamped to the south of Albany would be as likely intended for Oswego.[1]

On June 24, the Connecticut and Rhode Island troops were arriving, and Eyre was busy placing them on these private properties. Not only did he have the problem of consent for such occupation, but he had to discipline the men, instruct their officers (for all of these were irregulars with little drill), and see that they did not carouse in town or prey upon nearby farms. As more New England troops arrived his problems increased.

If it should not be possible to find ground on the east side of the River for all the Troops, would you have any objection to have the remainder encamped a little below the ferry house on ye. Pasture opposite to Col. Ransler's, or above the Town, in a large field belonging to Mrs Ransler? for its impossible to fix them together behind the fort, the ground is so hilly & broken, except they are placed by Companies.[2]

Johnson approved all of these measures, though he still favored the east side, since he hoped thereby to keep men from the town. He wanted them to be actively employed and sober, for there was no greater enemy of military welfare than "Intemperance & Idleness."[3]   Each day there were new arrivals, filling up the quotas, and now Johnson issued "General Orders" for discipline and proper exercises:

That a Captain's Command be every day detached to reconnoitre for 2 or 3 miles round the Encampment . . . That a Captains Guard mount for each Regt and that the Centinals be posted so as not only to prevent any surprise from the Enemy, but to preserve Peace & good order amongst the Soldiers . . . to let none pass over the River without orders from the officer of the Guard . . . That no Rum be upon any Acct suffered to be brougnt into Camp or sold to the Men, that whatever shall be discovered be immediately staved & the offenders punished by a Court Martial.[4]

Finally he could report to Braddock that most of the quotas were complete; New York was one of the last to fulfill—there were three hundred from Connecticut hired for New York, three hundred more from Albany County—but two companies were yet to be supplied. More Connecticut companies were to come. New Hampshire troops, of course, were not to come but to join forces near the lakes.[5]

Despite these measures the Massachusetts regiments were scattered above and below Albany along the river for seven or eight miles. Each New England regiment had its own commissary, and each had stores and supplies for varying lengths of time. Some articles were in short supply; there was only one kettle for every fifteen men, not enough for the proper freshening and boiling of salt meat. The surgeon reported insufficient medicines, and as the men did not take proper care, and were unused to military life, they came down with fevers and fluxes.[6]

Ammunition was also in short supply, and as for muskets, they were all "of difft. Bores & sorts." As time passed, week after week in camp, with no word of marching orders, the men became disgruntled; was this to be "another Canada expedition" they asked. When word finally came of marching orders there was "a more cheerful countenance in the Mens phizzes."[7]

General Johnson's assumption of command of the provincial forces in Albany was a step of major significance, but it was fraught with uncertainty, and there were many pitfalls. He had often expressed his feeling of inadequacy and his lack of preparation for the task. He knew something of the delays, the obstructionism, and the irresponsibility of colonial legislatures, and he feared for the lack of financial support and of the necessary provisions and armament. He already had discovered that the two campaigns were competing and were at cross-purposes. Yet a major test for him would come when he exercised command.

He was not lacking counsel—generally from persons with less experience. Goldsbrow Banyar, his New York correspondent, dealt with everything from supplies to strategy. Some warned him of dangers to his own safety, or cautioned against rashness or surprise. None was as comprehensive, however, as the recorder, his fellow councilman, Archibald Kennedy, who drew up a code of "Hints for a Commanding Officer." What use Johnson made of this is not known, but he kept the paper and may have referred to it, or on occasion reflected upon these maxims. Some were trite, some a bit absurd, while others were the expression of thoughtful men with good intentions and may well have been highly regarded. Certainly, Johnson did not resent the advice, and as he went to meet his men, the following may have guided him:

Let nothing ruffle your Temper, be always cool, happen what will.

Let no disappointment cool your Courage, but on the Contrary exert yourself the more, disappointments create experience, and this is an officer.

At no time shew any diffidence or fear in your Countenance.

By all means get the esteem and affection of your officers and Men, but they ought at the same time to know you Command; there is a difference between power and authority.

Distinguish a brave man, and reward a gallant action upon the spot.

Be careful of your sick men, and visit them some times your self.

Prayers have often a good effect, especially among New England men, a well gifted New England Parson, might therefore be a usefull implement.

A General officer must keep a good Table.[8]

Many of these points were well taken, and were exemplified in no small degree by the general. In some—that he should keep a good table, for example—he needed no urging.

Upon arrival, General Johnson was at pains to acquaint himself with his officers. Colonel Seth Pomeroy of Massachusetts was then in town and noted in his diary: "I supt with him yt night at Lanlord Lattridg's. Stay'd with him Till about 11 of ye Clock was well Pleas'd with his Company." The next day he considered going to the camp, but decided to invite General Lyman and the colonels to meet him in Albany. Then on July 9, he reviewed the troops encamped below Albany, mustered in regimental order, and expressed his pleasure.[9]

He was to learn more of the proper conduct of an officer, both by precept and example, when Governor (or General, whichever title seemed more impressive)

Shirley arrived on July 10. Colonel Pomeroy related the events of two days:

> Thursday 10th Governor Shirley came to Town with Several officers and 2 Companies of Soldiers for his army—at his arival the Cannon in the Fort were Discharg'd, the Field officers that were in Town waited upon the Governor & Drank glass of wine with him.
>
> Friday 11th. Governor Shirley Invited General Johnson & the Field officers of Crown point Expedition to Dine with him (viz. ye Colls.). We accordingly waited upon him and was well Entertained.[10]

The tensions and disagreements then developing between Johnson and Shirley were not allowed to disturb the appearance of good relations. Colonel Pomeroy had been a faithful attendant at divine service in the Anglican church (St. Peter's) both morning and afternoon on the sabbath while in Albany. He usually commented favorably on the preaching of the Reverend John Ogilvie. Now he noted on the 13th that in "ye forenoon Governor Shirley & General Johnson was their Serm well adapted to ye. ocation."[11]

Although each New England regiment had its chaplain, Johnson did not have to seek New England parsons while the troops were in Albany. Both the Reverend John Ogilvie and Dominie Frelinghuysen of the Dutch church preached to the men and officers, and Ogilvie as chaplain to the garrison ministered to the needs of the troops. In fact, Ogilvie so impressed General Shirley that he was asked to accompany the Niagara expedition as chaplain; yet the Indians whom he had served had asked him to go along with them, and as they were all going to Crown Point he was obliged to turn down the general's offer for fear of giving offense to the Indians. He found his greatest service, however, both as missionary and as agent of Johnson, by remaining in Albany.[12]

New England chaplains were earnest men who endured all of the trials of the troops and some besides while performing a useful, if somewhat thankless, task. The irregularity of the troops, their lack of discipline combined with some unusual temptations, all tended to lower morale. Nor did they receive the full support of the officers. The Reverend William Williams, "our mouth to God," as one soldier called him, stuck to his regiment and delivered two sermons on one sabbath day when General Lyman decreed that all men should work on the roads, "But his hearers were fue." And the following year a chaplain of Lyman's troops complained that his office was ineffectual, that the general did not attend services and allowed his men to violate the sabbath.[13]

As his forces increased day by day, although still short of their quotas and lacking much in supply, General Johnson had to plan his campaign. Expeditions into frontier America were formidable chiefly because of the physical task of road-building and transport. If a sufficient force with artillery could be brought before a wilderness outpost it could usually be taken. Fortifications were not strong enough, nor their garrisons large enough to resist. The greatest dangers were to be faced on the march, from hostile raiding Indians or a surprise by an enemy. Hence came the desire for Indian allies and scouts. And for a like reason, it was better to have a respectable force, which would be less likely to be attacked.[14]

Thus while officials and the public urged and expected Johnson to make an early start toward Crown Point, he hesitated until the troops were ready. This readiness was in most minds related to the transport. Bateau building had gone on apace. With each province providing its own boats, there was considerable variety. Connecticut, displaying Yankee ingenuity, built bateaux of various sizes so that they could be put in nests and brought from New York on provision sloops. Yet in Albany it was discovered that some were too small to be of use.[15] By June 19, Johnson found that boats for Shirley had been finished, and he now hoped that the same people in Albany and Schenectady who had done the work might build a hundred bateaux for him. Usable timber and boards were left over. At that time there were fifty carpenters from Boston in Albany making two hundred bateaux for the Massachusetts regiments.[16] Yet even by mid-July the Massachusetts regiments were not ready. Surgeon Williams wrote:

Our Battoes not yet Complete; hope they will be finished this week; No train of artillery yet arrived, that is Mortars, shells, cannon, shot, &c. I very much fear the consequences of our long stay here. Things look with a dark aspect. I am often urging the necessity of our speedy march, but what can we do? Move we can't till such time as our stores arrive, Neither will the General suffer it, he says, till two thirds are ready, or a suitable force to oppose their Army should they attack us, as they doubtless will if their numbers are superior, which they can know by their Indians who will view us every day, & if they should Cut off our first detachment they may defeat the expedition.[17]

Although much stress was placed on the use of bateaux, it was also quite necessary to use land transport, to have wagons for portages, and where water was shallow, and for them roads had to be made. Furthermore troops would have to march much of the way. The first stage of the advance would be up the Hudson from Albany to the "House of Lydius," later Fort Edward, where began the Carrying Place. So Johnson decided to send out General Lyman in advance to build a road and to cache the stores. On July 17, he gave orders to Lyman, directing him and his company of Connecticut men to join the Massachusetts men encamped at the Flats, and to go north from there.

From the Flatts to Col. Lydius's, you are to open the Road twenty five to thirty feet wide where it will possibly admit of it, to have the Trees, Logs & all obstructions cleared away, the Stumps trimed close, Bridges well repaired where necessary & good Ones made where wanted, on the whole as good a Road made for Carriage as possible, . . .[18]

He was advised to guard against "Sudden & lurking attacks of the Enemy," to keep his men disciplined and sentries and scouts alert. At the same time Johnson would send Indians, always with one or two whites, to reconnoiter toward Crown Point. Since these "Friend Indians" might cross the path of some of the New England forces, they were to be distinguished by a "red Fillet round their Heads." For should one of these accidentally be killed by the English it might destroy the usefulness of the Indians. And if one of them should fall into the hands of the English troops, Johnson had directed them "to call out Warighajage wch is my Indian name."[19]

Johnson now hoped, if no enemy regular troops were encountered, that thirty-two hundred men would rendezvous at the Carrying Place. There he would also have his Indian auxiliaries, and the forces would be able to advance on Crown Point.[20]

His hope of surprising the French fort, or of reaching it without meeting the enemy was shattered by news of Braddock's defeat. Early reports of the battle on the Monongahela had been quite indefinite, and some even held out hopes of a victory. But on July 28, the details of the defeat reached Albany and spread consternation in all quarters. The morale of the troops, the hopes of the populace, and the plans of the leaders were bound to be affected. And no one knew exactly how this news would strike the Indians.[21]

Could the original plans be carried out? Now there was concern about the safety of Albany; a few days earlier Shirley had written back to Johnson that if he were confronted by superior force and obliged to give up his plan, he should fall back upon Albany and prepare for the defense of the Province of New York.[22] Banyar in New York, reflecting the concern of government circles, wondered if the Indians could somehow be kept in alliance; "I know a certain degree of Truth is necessary to keep up your Influence with them," but "if they abandon us now in a time of danger, . . . they may go to the Devil for aught I Care."[23] Although strategists might well have reconsidered the proposals adopted at Alexandria, now that the French had all the plans, New York could not think of it.

I cannot give way to the thought that Genl Braddock will stop either of your operations. they are both more necessary now than ever, Mr. Shirley's to Snatch from the French the use they might make of this Victory, which we shall effect by taking & securing that now more than ever important Pass. Yours is still more necessary because our immediate Safety is concerned in it, which is not the Case as to the other, If Crown Point is not secured what are we to expect from the French, but an attack on Albany, they'l not be content with the Amusement of setting their Indians upon us.[24]

The Council, too, asked the governor to recall the two independent companies sent with Braddock, to garrison the New York forts. And they wanted troops from the south and from Nova Scotia sent to Albany to back up the campaigns now begun.[25] In fact, the bad news spurred all the provincial governments to ask for new levies, and when later requests came from Johnson they were ready to act.[26]

To Johnson at Albany, soon to be on the march, these were not academic questions. He well knew the Indians could not long be deceived; he made a frank statement of the situation to the sachems, at the same time exacting their pledge of support. When finally some Indians returned from Pennsylvania with all the lurid details of the English failure told in their own terms, they had been forewarned. He had no authority in making strategy; yet he opined that now Shirley would do better to attack Cadaracqui (Fort Frontenac), rather than to attempt the attack on Fort Niagara.[27] But Shirley was also committed to his campaign. As for Johnson's own campaign, he would redouble his caution and send out more scouts and reconnoitering parties to watch for the French movements.

When General Lyman received orders to march and to begin road building toward the Carrying Place, there were some twenty-six hundred effective men in camp near Albany. Yet many of the companies for one reason or another were unready, and when he set out from Schuyler's the Flats, on July 19, he had only his own and two of the Massachusetts regiments, about twelve hundred men. They were accompanied by "about 20 of the Dutch Waggons" with stores.[28] Somewhat later bateaux were loaded and "Set out in good Earnest for Crown Point," making six miles their first day. For ten days they labored making frequent "Carrys" around rapids or falls, lightening bateaux better to navigate in shallow streams or against the current, and at times sending back work parties to mend bridges and clear roads. At the "great falls" a ladder was constructed over which to tow the heavy boats. Thus it was indeed an amphibious operation.[29]

Although the original order presumed a road all the way from the Flats to the "House of Lydius," this was evidently not accomplished. There was a kind of road along the river which was somewhat serviceable, and Lyman's men labored heroically to widen this, to build bridges, to make it suitable for wagons. But many of the stores and supplies could be floated along, and later contingents relied upon the water transport. In fact Lyman at Stillwater July 25 wrote back to Johnson regarding the roads.

I have Sent out Severall Parties to build Bridges & Clear Roads they Tell me they have Prepared ye Road 3 miles South & 2 miles North and Expect by monday next Shall be Ready to set out for Saratoga. . . .

I would Propose to your Honr. Whether if we make a good Wagon Road & Clear abt. 30 feet wide for ye men to Travel it will not be Sufficient which may be done with vastly more ease than to Cut down all ye Trees & Small bushes which if we do we must make Such a Pile or heap of Timber in the Thickest Places in ye woods that will be a Compleat fort for ye Indians to Ly behind & fire on the army & by Cutting ye Small Low bushes Which grow abt. 3 feet high the Troops will be more Expos'd by the Stubs than by Leaving them Standing. . . . You must undoubtedly depend on Wagons to transport your Artilery & Baggage for ye water is so Low & Rapid it Kills ye men [to] wade up & work So hard as they must To do it.[30]

He asked that the men still at the Flats be employed to clear the road as far as Half Moon. Johnson agreed to this modification of his order, but commented that he saw little danger of attack between Albany and the Carrying Place.[31]

Colonel Ruggles's company had arrived with Lyman the 24th, "but tired with ye fateigues of Rowing up the River which is very Low & Rapid & Battoes are of but Little Service." While Johnson was impatient for others to move, three Massachusetts regiments, of colonels Titcomb, Goodrich, and E. Williams, were still at the Flats on August 3, protesting that they were not ready and that "Battoes were all leaky & unfit for Service." They did not reach the Carrying Place until the rest of the troops with Johnson and some Indians arrived on August 14.[32]

Among the problems which troubled Johnson and delayed his own march to the Carrying Place was that of the New Hampshire company. Five hundred men had been voted by the assembly of that province, but little else in the way of support. No bateaux or transport had been provided, so that the men had to march overland and join the other forces near Crown Point. Moreover, their funds were in paper

2. *Smithstown House,* County Meath, Ireland.
Home of the Johnson family in Ireland.
Photo by the author.

3. *Sir Peter Warren.* Portrait painted by Thomas Hudson.
Courtesy of the National Maritime Museum, Greenwich England.

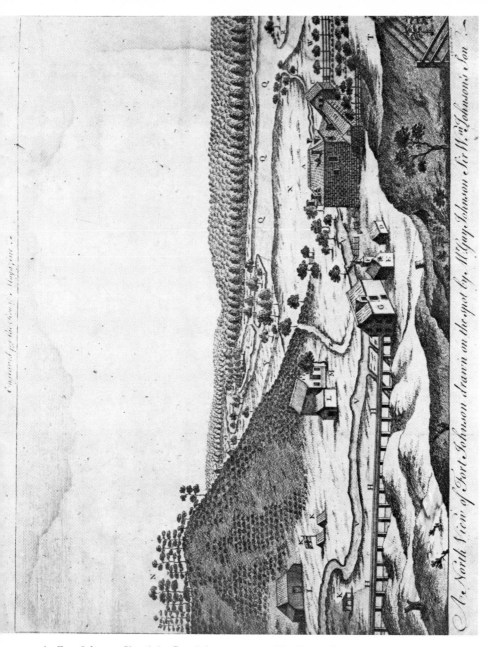

4. *Fort Johnson.* Sketch by Guy Johnson, engraved by Hulett. Published in the *Royal Magazine* (London, 1759).

Key: (A) – The House, or Fort Johnson. (B) – Wall and ramparts. (C) – Blockhouse in the corner, on the front, and barracks that flank the gate; the same on the other side. (D) – Cooper's house. (E) – Bake house. (F) – Pigeon house. (G) – Mill. (H) – Aqueduct from mill dams to the mill. (I) – Indian council house. (K) – Indian encampments. (L) – Sheep house; but now there is a blockhouse built there. (M) – Very large barn and stables. (N) – Mount Johnson, very high and steep. (O) – House where Sir William Johnson lived before he moved (Jan. 1749–50) into the main house. (P) – Barn (Q) – Mohawk River. (R) – Part of an island opposite to the fort, 100 acres. (S) – Thirteen smaller islands belonging to Sir William Johnson. (T) – Another blockhouse, to defend the back of the house. (V) – Creek that runs by the fort into the river. (W) – Garden. (X) – Fine pastures. (Y) – Corn fields. (Z) – Road to Schenectady.

5. *Peter Wraxall.* Portrait owned by Mrs. W. S. Moore,
of New York City and Hull's Cove, Maine.

6. *The Reverend John Ogilvie.* Engraving by Duthie, from the painting by Copley, in the possession of Trinity Church, New York City.
Documentary History of the State of New York, Volume 4.

7. *Thomas Pownall.* From an engraving by Earlom, after the painting by Cotes.

8. *William Shirley*. From the portrait by Thomas Hudson.

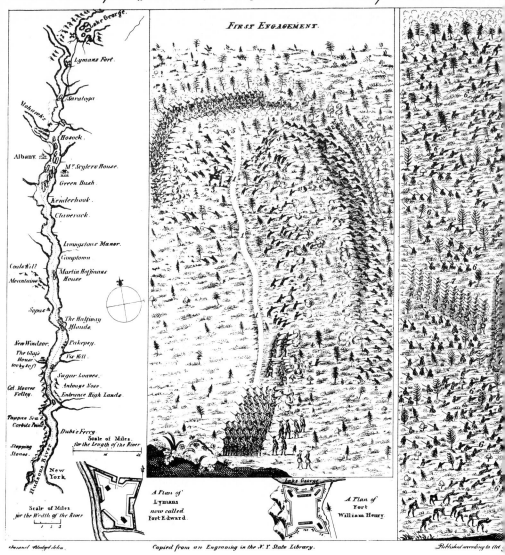

9. *A Prospective View of the Battle Fought Near Lake George, Sept. 8, 1755.*
Engraving by Jeffreys, London, 1756. From the original published with the
pamphlet of Samuel Blodget. Courtesy of the New York State Library.
See Appendix III.

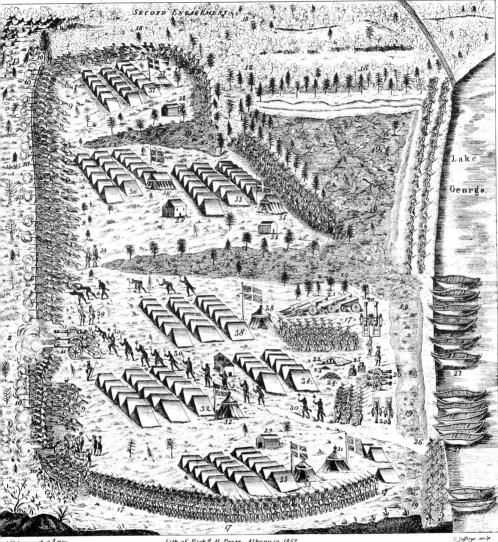

on the 8.th of Sep.t 1755, between 2000 English, with 250 Mohawks.

were victorious captivating the French Gen.l with a Number of his Men, killing 700 & putting the rest to flight.

SECOND ENGAGEMENT

Lake
George.

nt February the ? d 1756.   Lith. of Rich.d H. Pease, Albany in 1852.   T. Jefferys sculp.

The brave old 𝓗𝓮𝓷𝓭𝓻𝓲𝓬𝓴 *the great* S.ACHE.M *or Chief of the* 𝓜𝓸𝓱𝓪𝔀𝓴 *Indians. one of the* Six Nations *now in Alliance with, & Subject to the* King *of* Great Britain. Sold by Eliz. Bakewell opposite Birchin Lane in Cornhill.

10. *Brave Old Hendrick.* Engraving published in London, c. 1740.
Courtesy of the Albany Institute of History and Art.

11. *Sir John Johnson.* Sir William's son and heir.
Portrait painted in 1772 by John Mare. In Johnson Hall.

12. *Sir William Johnson.* Copy by E. L. Mooney,
of the lost original by Thomas McIlworth, painted at Johnson Hall in 1763.
Courtesy of the New-York Historical Society.

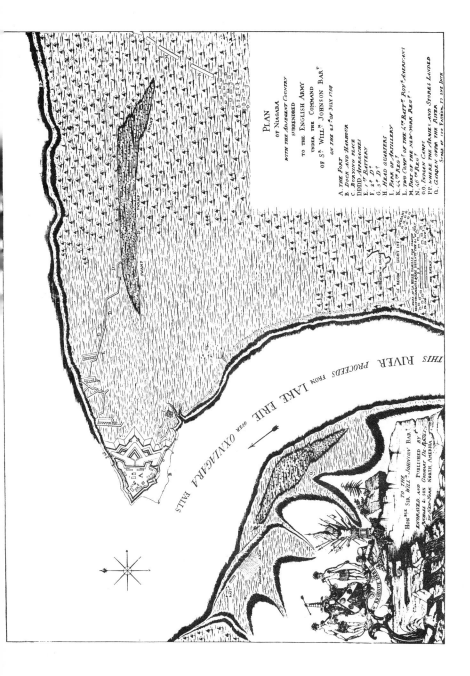

13. *Plan of Niagara, with the Adjacent Country, Surrendered to the English Army
under the Command of Sr. Willm. Johnson, Bart. on the 25th of July 1759.*
Engraved by De Bruls, New York. Published in 1762. Dedicated to
Sir William with his coat-of-arms. Printed in *Johnson Papers*, Vol. 3.
Complete map in New-York Historical Society.

14. *Original Patent of Sir William Johnson,* creating a hereditary baronetcy for himself and his family. Owned by James W. Johnson, Spokane, Washington, a direct lineal descendant of Sir William, and his son Sir John Johnson.

15. *Indian Council at Johnson Hall.* Painting by E. L. Henry.
Owned by the Knox Gelatine Company, Johnstown.
Courtesy of the Albany Institute of History and Art.

currency, which would be of no use after they crossed the Connecticut River. Johnson disliked the idea of their being separated; he would not know where they would meet him and felt that it was risky for a small force. But he was assured that these were all woodsmen, inured to fatigue, who might be most useful, and Colonel Blanchard was highly recommended. When the company was delayed in starting and for some time no word of their whereabouts had come to the general, he fumed with disgust. It seemed that they would arrive with nothing in the way of provisions or supplies, and there were no funds for that purpose. "A Strange System of Conduct theirs!"[33]

Finally the New Hampshire men reached the Flats, and word came from Governor Benning Wentworth that £500 sterling had been voted for their supply at Albany. Johnson ordered the merchants there and the commissaries of Massachusetts to issue them supplies on credit. And when they finally joined the others they would be provisioned from the common stores. Colonel Blanchard and his men arrived at the Carrying Place after Lyman and Johnson had marched ahead.[34]

The Indians in the meantime were swarming to Mount Johnson, where they were outfitted, although some preferred to follow Johnson to Albany. Some brought their wives and families, who either had to be sent back or cared for. This task fell upon the Reverend John Ogilvie in Albany, who on Johnson's order sent off two wagons with the Indian women to Schenectady, and found lodging in Albany for the family of Ottrowana, the Cayuga sachem.[35] Johnson ordered most of the Indians to proceed via Saratoga to the Carrying Place, where they would join General Lyman. He had some fifty Indians with him at Albany who marched with the remaining troops on August 9.[36]

Up to this time the general had received frequent letters urging him to march, pressing for action and wondering at the delay. Finally he gave vent to his own feelings in a letter to John Watts.

Let no one imagine any time is lost & let not People's Imaginations & wishes out run Possibilities. . . . No one is more sensible than I am of the Importance of Dispatch, & the most Sanguine dos not burn with more Impatience. I cannot be every where. I give strict orders, I entreat, I animate.[37]

His arrival at the Carrying Place with the Mohawks on August 14 made an impression on the New England troops. The diarist Gilbert wrote:

My pen is not abel to Describe the odiesnes of Their Dress. They had Juels in their noses, Their fases painted with all Colours . . . in ye evening ye Mohocks had a Janiel [general] Dance and They had ye eyes of many to view There with great Admiration.[38]

Now the troops rejoiced that when the last division arrived, with supplies, an advance would soon be ordered. But the larger contingent of Indians was yet to come, and if delays caused impatience and fretting among the whites, the Indians were even more troublesome.

Tho I have at present not quite 60 Inds with me, yet that tedious particularity which is their Character at all times, & their insatiable thirst of Rum takes up more of my time & gives me more constant Uneasiness, than all the affairs of the Army would otherwise do.

imagine that you see my Tent from Morning to night crowded with Indians, with officers &c. all impatient to be heard, each thinking his own affairs more important than the others. I obliged to hear all whilst my Pen & ink lies suspended. this is the real Picture tho but faintly drawn of my Life every day, wch I assure you renders it miserable & almost intollerable & tis in no ones power to relieve Me.[39]

In the meantime, at Mount Johnson, the Indian officers and interpreters—Daniel Claus, Matthew Ferrall, John Butler, and Benjamin Stoddert—prepared the warriors, supplying their needs and mending their weapons. As Claus remembered it later, there were over four hundred. "King Henry led the van with Mr. Claus and passing thro the country everybody allowed that the Body of Inds. the finest Sight they ever saw."[40] Such indeed must have been the emotion in the breasts of those who had doubted whether the Indians would go. They may have started all together, but they arrived at different times: Stoddert, Hendrick's brother, and some young warriors on the 23d; Ferrall, Butler, and old Hendrick with some two hundred, the 25th; and others straggled in to total some three hundred.[41] Moreover, they required constant mollification, for they learned of the Ohio defeat and that the Caghnawagas had declared for the French. To these provocations Johnson added "Genrl. Shirleys Violent proceedings," all of which "renders our Indians not only very cold but many of 'em most provokingly Insolent wch at present I must bear with Silence."[42]

There were now nearly three thousand men at the Carrying Place, and General Johnson decided to erect a fort. Captain Eyre drew up a plan, and the work was begun. It was to be a palisaded work with bastions on three sides, enclosing the log trading house of Lydius and taking advantage of the steep river bank for security on the fourth side of the rectangle. Intended to contain three hundred men as a garrison, it looked too ambitious to many of the men and officers, who felt that there was not time for its completion. On August 18 Johnson held a council of war which endorsed the plan if it should not delay the advance; but the men were uneasy and murmured at being so employed; hence the bastions were not finished to the desired height. Yet the general felt that it was serviceable as a base or a retreat; and Eyre thought it was sufficient so that three or four hundred men could hold out against an attack by fifteen hundred, if they had no cannon.[43]

There was by now a sufficient concentration of men and guns there, even after the main body went on the march, to make it a deterrent to the enemy. French intelligence from a captured English soldier revealed that five or six hundred men were encamped outside the fort; that armament (though not yet in place) consisted of eight "brass pieces," which were 8- or 10-pounders, twenty mortars throwing six- or twelve-inch shells, and that some twenty-five iron thirty-twos or forty-twos were expected. The soldier thought fifteen hundred French could not take it.[44]

It was a common custom for a fortification to be given the name of the officer in charge, and so after Johnson left, the men began calling this Fort Lyman.

Whether this was justified, since it was ordered by Johnson and largely built by Eyre, it may have irked the general to see one of his subordinates so prematurely honored. A month later, when this title appeared on a dateline of a dispatch, Johnson quickly renamed it *"Fort Edward*, in honr. to the Second Prince of the Blood of that Name."[45]

Gratifying as it must have been to Johnson to have a sizable force with Indian auxiliaries at an advance post, he was far from happy with the temper of his men. There were really no very good reasons for the discontent which prevailed. The weather was good in August and September, warm with occasional showers. Supplies were now adequate with sufficient provisions. But a series of minor complaints had to be dealt with tactfully, for these irregulars were hard to satisfy and unused to discipline.

In Lyman's first letter from his march he complained vehemently to Johnson that the New York and Rhode Island companies were bringing along women, which gave "very great uneasiness to ye New England Troops." If allowed, he said, it would make it impossible to raise more troops in New England and "would be Sacrificeing all our Carracter in the Places where we Live." Some officers said the soldiers would "either mob or privately destroy 'em." Lyman thought they were of no use, and "I cant doubt but you will order 'em all to be Left behind."[46]

Johnson's reply was sympathetic and conciliatory.

As to bad Women following or being harboured in our Camp I shall discountenance it to the utmost of my Power. As to Men's Wives while they behave Decently they are suffered in all Camps & thought necessary to Wash & mend. Immoralities of all kinds I will use my utmost power to suppress & chastize.[47]

Apparently some women remained, for nearly a month later, August 18, Lyman brought the question up in a council of war, and a resolution was passed that "all the Women in the Camp should be removed from the same & forbid to return." They were thereupon sent back to Albany.[48]

There was difficulty, too, over the rum traffic, which was forbidden, and especially from sutlers supplying the Indians. An allowance of a gill a day was made for each soldier, which had to be extended to Indians. When rations fell short, and the colonel refused to give the men "our Back Lowance of Rum," thirty men marched off; they were caught four miles from camp, brought back, and disciplined. And Johnson imprisoned a Connecticut captain on suspicion of "selling the Store Rum to Indians."[49]

Connecticut troops were rebellious about their pay, and at the Flats held up their march two days. "They absolutely refused to strike their Tents untill their Billeting was paid." Later they threatened mutiny if not paid monthly while in the field. Their officers thought that while in the forest they had no need for cash, but they stuck to the letter of the act of Assembly and forced the leaders to send to Albany for money. They also insisted on having the same fresh meat—"Beeves and Sheep"—when others got them. After Johnson left the Carrying Place the men there gave increasing trouble:"they have Quarrelled with each other . . . blows have passed, & some are wounded." Desertions became more frequent; the sick increased; wagoners were taking off without warning; and commissaries "were full of frivolous scruples, wh. is the mildest I can say of it."[50]

Desertions were frequent and there was a tendency to be lenient in punishment. Favoritism and concessions were known, and officers, many of whom were but recently from civilian life, were little better than the men. Irritated and plagued with greater problems, Johnson was almost in despair.

> In short there is not through the Troops in general due Subordination kept up. The officers are most of them low weak People, who have neither the ability nor Inclination to maintain a necessary Superiority. some of them I believe are sorry Fellows & rather join with than restrain their Men. . . .

> The Indians are perpetually Drunk, their Insolence is scarce to be borne at these times—they give me not a Moments rest or leisure. . . .

> What with the trouble I have with the Indians & that disorderly management there is among the Troops, I am almost distracted. I have neither rest night nor day, nor a comfortable thinking hour to myself. Our Sick increase our Men impatient to have the affair ended & most of the officers little better, yet they will not carry things on with that order & application necessary to forward our Proceedings. I would exert Authority but I cannot be sufficiently seconded.[51]

Before Johnson arrived and began building the fort, Lyman had sent road-building details forward to prepare the way for the anticipated march to Wood Creek or South Bay, whence all plans envisaged a fleet of bateaux, even building a larger vessel, for the navigation of the lake. Surgeon Williams reported that in two days three hundred men had "cleared a road thirty feet wide, about 8 miles, or two thirds of the way to Wood Creek." But the general now sent out reconnoitering parties to consider the advisability of marching toward Lake St. Sacrament. Why had not this been done before, queried Williams.[52] Now, on August 18, a council of war endorsed the route to South Bay and approved a force of fifteen hundred men under General Lyman to "Cut a road." There it was intended to build a fortification.[53]

Johnson was apprehensive, for the Indians were restive. Repeated attempts had been made through the Mohawks to neutralize the Caghnawagas. The last embassy sent out on August 21 had returned a negative answer. The Caghnawagas replied that "the French Priests by throwing Water upon our Heads, subject us to the Will of the Governor of Canada." They acknowledged the warning of "Brother Warraghiyagey," but they could not comply with his request that they stand out of the way, "for the French & we are one Blood, & where they are to dye we must dye also."[54]

This was very discouraging. Johnson and the council of war asked the provinces for reinforcements, and while most were quick and ready to comply, Governor Wentworth of New Hampshire felt that his government had done all it could. "General Johnson's demand For an Additional force at this late hour, makes me doubtfull of our success."[55]

To make matters worse the Indians and scouts to the northward now reported that the French were approaching in considerable numbers. A council of war was held to hear the story of the four Mohawks who had gone to the French Indians.

It appears that the French are all in motion in Canada towards Crown Point; that the Road from Montreal to St John's is constantly crowded with carriages passing to and fro' with provisions and stores to be dispatched by the Brigantine, and one smaller vessel up Lake Champlain to Crown Point, which vessels are constantly employed therein; that the Enemy flinging up new works at Crown Point and every body there busily employed. The said Indians further inform, that there appeared to them a great plenty of provisions, that three Men-of-War from Europe had arrived at Quebeck with provisions, arms, cloathing & 6000 Troops which the French said were designed for Crown Point.

That the Govr of Canada was calling in all the Indians settled around that Country, who these Indians do not doubt will readily and warmly join the French, and will with the Cagnawagees amount to a very considerable Number. That the French Govr at Montreal told them, he waited impatiently for Genl Johnson and his Troops, and should be very glad to see him, that he should have ready to oppose him 8000 Men besides Indians. That the French have had pretty exact intelligence of all our motions from the Marching of the first division from Albany. But if we marched by the way of the wood Creek, they designed to attack us at South Bay, if by the way of Lake St Sacrament at Tieonderoga, that when these Indians past by Crown Point, there were not above 100 Men there, and two hundred more on their way from St John's, but that by this time, they doubted not they are greatly encreased, and daily arriving as also the Indians.[56]

In view of this information the general asked the council of war, "which way towards Crown point, from this place they would advise a Road should be cut, for the March and embarkation of the Army, and whether that Road should be immediately set about." It was the unanimous opinion that "the Road to Lake St Sacrament appears to them the most eligible"; that two thousand men and half the artillery and stores should be sent.[57] "Allowing for the natural Boastings and Vapour of the French to our Indians," it still appeared that the English might be outnumbered by the French; and the French might have more Indians. Immediate steps had to be taken to prevent their taking the advanced positions. Two days after the council of war, August 24, Johnson wrote that he planned to start the following day with the "first Division of about 1500 Men & some Indians & a few Field Peices for Lake St Sacrament." Lyman was to follow as soon as the New Hampshire troops arrived.[58]

At last the army was on the move. Six or eight cannon at the fort were shot off to signal the event; fifteen hundred men, about forty Indians, "with two Field pieces in front and an Iron Mortar," set off at four o'clock, and by evening had travelled four miles. They moved cautiously for fear of an ambush, although preceded by road-makers clearing the way. Wagons trundled along carrying stores, and with no enemy in sight it was a pleasant journey. Hemlock brush shelters housed them at night; deer were shot to add venison to their larder. Colonel Pomeroy recorded how on the second day after advancing four or five miles they "Stopt Eat Peace ham Baken [bacon] Bread & Cheese Druk [drank] Some fresh Lemon Punch & ye Best of wine with General Johnson and some of ye Field officers."[59]

The last day of the march was quite as pleasant.

Set out about 8 of ye Clock with our army having Early Sent about 400 to Cut yt way about noon Stopt & Din'd with General Johnson by a small Brook under a Tree Eat a good Dinner of Cold Boyld & roast venison Drunk good fresh Lemon Punch & wine.— We Came to the Lake about 4 of ye clock.[60]

Set like a jewel in the mountains between forested slopes and dotted with islands, this lake is one of America's beauty spots. But Johnson and his soldiers had little time for comment on the scenery. They reached the end of the lake, which was thickly wooded, "where no house was ever before built nor a rod of land cleared." They immediately began clearing land for a camp and soon had an "intervail," a space between two small inlets and marshland, a bit rocky but a firm footing for a defensive work. As soon as Captain Eyre arrived a defensive fort was to be laid out. In the meantime Indian scouts fanned out to the northward in search of an approaching enemy.[61]

If Johnson said nothing of the scenic setting, he was alert to all the political and strategic importance of the site. "This Lake," he wrote, "called Lake St. Sacrament by the French, I have called Lake George not only in honour to his Majesty but to assertain his Dominion here."[62] As soon as possible he intended to make use of the water route north.

When the Battoes (certain small Boats so called) are brought from the last Fort I caused to be built at the Great Carrying Place abt 17 Miles from hence, I propose to go down this Lake with a part of the Army and take post at the end of it about 50 miles from hence at a pass called Tionderogue abt 15 miles from Crown Point, there wait the coming up of the rest of the Army & then attack Crown Point.[63]

The greater part of the Indians with their officers—Butler, Ferrall, Stoddert—and the interpreter Claus arrived the next day. There were now two hundred, and gradual additions increased the number in a few days to near three hundred. Though the soldiers often viewed the auxiliaries with misgivings, there was some comfort in having numbers allied with them, and their coming was hailed by salutes. "Ye Indians fir'd of there guns at ye Entrance of our Camps with our Cannon we fir'd 2 Rounds."[64]

Finally over the newly cleared road wagons came rolling, toiling slowly with their teams and sweating wagoners, bumping over rocks, roots, and stumps and miring in marsh and mud. "About 150 loaded with stores and artillery" came the night of the 31st, and more followed each day. On September 3, came "about 200 Wagons . . . Load chiefly with battoes." There were some six hundred bateaux expected. Meanwhile wagons were returning, but many wagoners deserted or proved unreliable.[65]

On September 3, the New Hampshire troops having arrived at the Carrying Place, Generals Lyman and Titcomb came up, followed by more artillery and supplies. Life at the camp took on some semblance of military regularity. Scouting parties went out each day—thirty, forty, or fifty English with four or five Indians—some on the land and sometimes over the lake. But no sign of an enemy was reported, and Ticonderoga was found to be not fortified.[66]

The morale of the men was not neglected as New England chaplains preached both to the men and to the Indians.

In ye forenoon Mr. Williams Preach'd a Sermon to Indians by an Interpreter—In the afternoon one to the English In the Camp; at 5 of ye Clock Mr. Newel a young Gentleman In Rhod Island Government a Chaplin of Capt. Babcocks Preach'd a very good Sermon from Christ Sermon In ye Mount Love your Enemies.[67]

The Mohawks, a number of whom were communicants of the Church of England, missed having their missionary, John Ogilvie, but did not lack for attention. Johnson later reported to the Society for the Propagation of the Gospel that "Good Old Abraham performed Divine Service every morning & evening."[68]

The French ministry was not unmindful of the military activity of the British. Learning of the dispatch of regulars under Braddock to Virginia, the French in the spring of 1755 took steps to reinforce their posts on the American frontier. They had reports that the walls of Fort St. Frederic at Crown Point and of Fort Niagara were crumbling, and that defenses were weak. It might even be necessary to relocate the forts. The garrisons were not strong, so it was planned to send six battalions of regulars as a reinforcement. The aim was defensive; there probably was no hope of an extended invasion or conquest. And as yet there was no declared war between Britain and France.[69]

Hence on May 3, 1755, a fleet of twenty ships, with a convoy of frigates, departed from the port of Brest. Six batallions, some three thousand men, were under the command of Maréchal de Camp (Major General) Baron de Dieskau,[70] a veteran soldier, and with him sailed the new governor, M. de Vaudreuil.[71] In spite of the strength of the convoy, however, two ships became separated and were captured off the coast of Newfoundland by the British fleet of Admiral Boscawen. The rest of the troops were united at Quebec.[72]

General Dieskau had detailed instructions for his command, but he was subordinate to the governor, with whom, in council of war, strategy and the plans of campaigns were to be formulated. Vaudreuil had enough information of British plans to be somewhat worried. He knew that Fort St. Frederic and Fort Niagara were weak and probably could not withstand an attack; he feared what might happen at Fort Duquesne when Braddock and his regulars reached it. But he believed that Oswego (Chouaguen), in spite of British reinforcement, could be taken. So this became Dieskau's objective, and soon two regiments (Guienne and Béarn) were sent ahead to Fort Frontenac. Later they would be joined by Dieskau and the rest, to surprise Oswego from across the lake.[73]

All these plans were to be changed, however, when on August 13, there came news of Braddock's defeat of July 9 on the Monongahela. Braddock's papers, captured on the field of battle, laid bare to the French the entire strategy of the English. They now knew the details of all the plans drawn up at Alexandria, and the proposed strength of each expedition. Dieskau gloated, "We are as well acquainted as themselves with all their treacheries." He wanted to go ahead with his seizure of Oswego, but Vaudreuil and the Council ruled otherwise. Fort Duquesne was safe, and there seemed no immediate danger to Fort Niagara. Shirley at Oswego, faced by a French force across the lake at Fort Frontenac, would not dare to move. But Crown Point was not far from the advance of the English under Johnson; and if it fell the route would be open to Montreal. So Dieskau was to take his army up the Richelieu River to Lake Champlain and Crown Point. From there he could expect little trouble in defeating the inexperienced militia under Johnson. The siege of Oswego could wait until next year.[74]

French sloops, brigs, and bateaux were plying the waters from the Three Rivers to Fort Chambly and over the blue expanse of Lake Champlain to Fort St. Frederic, carrying Dieskau's battalions of three thousand men and supplies. The increased activity over this route was not unobserved by scouts who had reported to Johnson. Of this force, one thousand were French regulars from the battalions of La Reine and Languedoc; sixteen hundred were Canadian militia and recruits; and there were Indians estimated from five hundred to seven hundred. At Fort St. Frederic there was a garrison of one hundred and fifty men.[75]

General Dieskau had reason to be proud of his command. In each of the two battalions of regulars he had formed an elite corps, a company of grenadiers. He was a soldier of the German school of Marshal Saxe, insistent upon discipline and official punctilio. It was even complained that he would not speak to common officers and was disdainful of the provincials.[76] Yet he was assured that his Canadians, some of whom were veterans of campaigns on the Ohio, were more than a match for the English. Their leaders were Jean Hugues Péan, a henchman of the Intendant Bigot, who had commanded the French invasion of the Ohio Valley in 1753, and François Le Mercier, engineer and artillerist, his cousin and associate in command. Another veteran of the wilderness fighting, Legardeur de Saint-Pierre, was in charge of the Indians. It was he who turned back young George Washington with the letter of Governor Dinwiddie at the Forks of the Ohio.[77]

In contrast Dieskau was told that the English militia were the poorest kind of soldiers. At Montreal he wrote with confidence, "the troops are in the best disposition possible, and panting only for the attack. All I fear is, that the enemy, who imagine all our troops to have gone on the expedition against Chouaguen, will beat a retreat on learning that we are on the march."[78] At Crown Point, however, he was constantly troubled by the Indians. He suspected the fidelity of the Iroquois, "both of the Sault St Louis [Caghnawagas] and of the Lake of the Two Mountains whose number exceeded 300, composing half of the Indians that had been given to me."[79] These were being worked upon by their relatives of the Six Nations, unsuccessfully it seemed to the English, but their indecision was crucial. They were the best fighters, the leaders, and they seemed to dominate the Abenakis.

After ten days at Fort St. Frederic, Dieskau learned from scouts that the English were at the Great Carrying Place, in numbers "about 3000," and were building a fort there, already pretty well advanced. "I immediately resolved to go forward and to post myself in an advantageous place, either to wait for the enemy, should he advance, or to anticipate him myself, by going in quest of him." Thus the French army was moved up the lake and on September 2 encamped at the "Falls of St. Sacrement" (Ticonderoga), which the French named Carillon. Here the Abenakis, who had been prowling ahead, brought in an English prisoner: and from him Dieskau learned that Johnson had marched toward Lake St. Sacrament, and that there were only five hundred men left at "Fort Lydius," although more were expected.[80]

Dieskau now made a crucial, perhaps a fatal, decision for which he was later blamed. He violated his instructions from Vaudreuil by dividing his army. He thought by moving quickly with a smaller, unencumbered force, he could surprise and destroy the fort, and then having cut off Johnson's supply, he would have him at his mercy.

I determined to leave the main body of the army where I was [at Carillon], and to take with me a picked force (*corps d'élite*) march rapidly and surprise Fort Lidius, and capture the 500 men encamped without its walls. My detachment was composed of 600 Indians, 600 Canadians and 200 Regulars belonging to La Reine and Languedoc regiments. It was four days' journey by water and across the woods to Lidius.[81]

Leaving at noon, September 4, they journeyed by water and encamped three leagues from Carillon; the next day they reached South Bay whence they would have to march through the woods. The Indians now complained through St. Pierre that the general was leaving half his army behind, that his canoes were ungarded, and that he was not sending out scouts. They could not understand the bold tactics of *coup de main*; they wanted to be cautions and to follow the wilderness rule of stealth and secrecy. Dieskau finally agreed to have two hundred men sent from Carillon to guard the boats, and to send out scouts. He told the Indians that he had enough men to beat the enemy; but they were making him think about his boats.[82]

The Iroquois were now beginning to direct operations. On the 6th they forced a delay while their scouts went ahead to reconnoiter. These reported the following day, the 7th, and gave assurance of the weakness of the fort. Dieskau wanted forced marches, but there were more delays. One eyewitness wrote:

On Sunday the 7th after hearing mass and a long exhortation to the savages, Monsieur de Dieskau started out in three columns. At 9 o'clock we arrived [   ] of the river where it was necessary to fell some trees in order to get across. At one o'clock in the afternoon we found ourselves within three leagues of Fort Lydius. The savages refused to go on any further, wishing to hold a council which lasted until four o'clock in the afternoon.[83]

At this council the Iroquois argued that they preferred not to attack the fort, but would prefer to attack the English camp. The fort they said was in English territory, but the camp was not. Perhaps they feared the guns of the fort, which the French learned were unmounted, and they did not know that Johnson had cannon. Dieskau was impatient and told them that they need only serve as flankers to act as a diverson; if they would not go the Abenakis would, and he would march without them. Finally they agreed to go, but slyly found means, as the general thought, to frustrate his design.[84]

Mine was a combined movement. I was to arrive at nightfall at that fort and rush to the attack; but the Iroquois, who took the lead on the march, under the pretence of zeal, caused a wrong direction to be taken; and when I was informed of the circumstance, it was no longer time to apply a remedy, so that at nightfull I was yet a league from that fort on the road leading from it to Lake St. Sacrament.[85]

Thus the Indians had maneuvered the French force over to the road which led from the Carrying Place to the camp on the lake. Now it required only an incident to divert the attack to the camp. And it was soon supplied. The events were related by a participant.

Some of the Indian scouts noticed a horseman who was coming from the camp on the lake. He was going to Fort Lydius. They yelled to him to stop and on his refusal they fired four shots which killed the man and the horse. He was found to be carrying a letter from Colonel Johnson to the commander of Fort Lydius by which he was informing the latter that a large French detachment was marching toward Lydius, to attack it at the latest next day at noon.

The rest of the savages took some prisoners and a score of wagons that were bringing boats and goods to Lake St. Sacrament. Some of the wagon drivers escaped and crossed the river by swimming. We spent the night in this place

That evening the savages held a council, with the general present, during which they refused to march to Fort Lydius and proposed going to attack the English on Lake St. Sacrament, where the prisoners were reporting that there were 3,500 men. As Monsieur de Dieskau could not make any impression on them, he decided to do as they wished.[86]

Dieskau's account, written shortly afterward, asserts that after intercepting Johnson's message to the fort and getting further information from the prisoners, he called the Indians together and gave them their choice of attacking the fort or the camp, and that the Iroquois chose to attack the camp.[87] In the official report of Vaudreuil, however, General Dieskau upon learning the conditions "had concluded on proceeding to Lake St. Sacrament; that the more English there were, the more of them would he kill; and that after the expedition, he would go and summon the fort to surrender."[88]

The next morning, September 8, the French marched up the good road, which Johnson's men had built, to the lake. An the same time a small party of English and Indians were marching south. Upon the events of this day hung the fate of armies and of men.

XVI

THE BATTLE AT LAKE GEORGE

For ten days the camp at the head of Lake George teemed with activity. The ring of axes, the clatter of timber, and the hammering of the carpenters broke the accustomed stillness of the forest. Set among the wooded mountains, the beautiful lake seemed a world in itself. The only word of danger, of a warlike force, would come from the scouts, quietly slipping away through the forest and as unobtrusively returning to report. Day after day, however, more wagons laden with supplies, guns, and bateaux bumped over the road from the south and rumbled up to the camp. With each addition there had to be more clearing, more shelters of bark or lean-tos, as the population increased; and with every transport, coming and going, the road became more of a highway. This was indeed a base camp; from here it was expected a fleet of bateaux was to carry the army down the lake, to portage again to Lake Champlain, and then to invest Fort St. Frederic.

As a base camp it was bound to be fortified, and the engineer, Captain Eyre, on his arrival was to select a site for a fort. Finally a council of war approved his design for a picketed fort with room for a garrison of one hundred men.[1]

In laying out the camp the general had given little thought to its defense. His principal consideration had been convenience for transport and nearness to the water where the army would embark. Yet he had selected some high and rocky ground, an instinctive preference which was to prove of great advantage. Sentries were posted, however, and daily scouting parties fanned out toward the enemy— that is, in the direction of Crown Point.

Sunday, the seventh of September, was marked by sabbath prayers and sermons. Then early in the afternoon three Indians who had been scouting for several days returned with news of the enemy. The leader, Thick Lawrence, went directly to the general's tent.

He said . . . that he discovered a large Body of the Enemy coming from South bay and seemingly directing their March towards Fort Edward and they marched in three columns [from] the Impression of each Column made in the ground he guessed to be between 6 or 700.[2]

Johnson immediately called a council of war, to which he invited the Indian sachems. Hendrick, who had the whole story from the Indians on scout, narrated the intelligence with his accustomed eloquence.

Brors. When we first set out from hence we went to South Bay where we spied the Tracts of 2 Men wch we followed & came to the Tracts of 3 more wch we pursued & in Journey towards Evening (3 Nights ago) we heard 6 Guns fired & we proceeded on our Journey till Night & in the morning the day before Yesterday we heard so many Guns fired that we could not count them, upon wch. we counselled together & thought this Army must be proceeding by way of Wood Creek, but upon going that road we found we were mistaken for there were no tracts that way, upon wch we turned back towards South Bay in our road found three large Roads made by a great Body of Men Yesterday wch we judge were marching towards the Carrying Place & we hereupon made all possible Dispatch hither to acquaint you herewith, as we expect there may be an Attack made at the Carrg. Place either to day or this Night.[3]

It was agreed that two warning dispatches should be immediately sent off to Colonel Blanchard at the Carrying Place; that scouting parties should be sent out from the troops, guards doubled, and all men ordered "to lay on their Arms all Night."[4] Now appeared the first hero of the war; according to Claus, no New England man would volunteer for the dangerous role of courier to the threatened fort. But one

Jacob Adams of the New Yorkers offered himself, he was equipped with Sr. Wm. Johnson's horse & Furniture, when he came within 2 short miles of Fort Edward he found himself in the midst of the french Army & was called to stop, but he depending on the Swiftness of his horse thought he would force his way thro' but soon was fired at, knocked off the horse & the Dispatches found upon him.[5]

The second dispatch was sent off about half an hour later (dated four o'clock) by two Indians and two soldiers going afoot. They at twelve o'clock that night returned with news that the French were four miles from the Carrying Place; they heard gunfire and a cry which they took to be Adams's. Blanchard was urged to retire into the fort with his men, "to defend the Troops under your Command & preserve the Provisions and Stores."[6] But the warning was unnecessary; had the French attacked the fort, it is quite possible that Blanchard with his New Yorkers and New Hampshire men, spoiling for a fight, could have held out until Johnson's relief arrived.

The council of war now debated how best to foil the French design. Some preferred to strike behind the enemy at his base of supply. The French had left their boats at South Bay, so it was resolved to send five hundred men there to destroy them, while another five hundred would then be sent to help the beleaguered fort. When the Indians learned of this they demurred. As Claus remembered it, Hendrick and the other chiefs replied to the general "that if he was to divide his small Force so as not to be able to co-operate he would be undone and his Indns. would leave the Army, but if he would keep his Army together and send a sufficient Body towards Fort Edward," the Indians would follow him. They believed that such a force would cause the fort to rally, and that it would be strong enough to defeat the enemy. So the English, like the French, were compelled by their Indians to attack their way.[7]

The next morning, September 8th, the camp was mustered by beating to arms. As Johnson recorded it

I called a Council of War, who gave it as their opinion, and in wch the Indians were Extreamly Urgent, That 1000 men should be detached, and a Number of their People would go with them in order to Catch the Enemy in their retreat from the other Camp, either as Victors or defeated in their Designs. The 1000 men were detached under the Command of Colo. Williams of one of the Boston Regiments with Upwards of 200 Indians. They marched between 8 & 9 OClock . . .[8]

In addition to Colonel Ephraim Williams with his Massachusetts company, there was Colonel Nathan Whiting with the Connecticut troops, while Colonel Edward Cole of Rhode Island brought up the rear. "Old Hendrick King of ye Six Nations before with Colo Williams the Indians Some afore some in ye Middle & Some in ye reare so Intermixed Through."[9]

They went on the now heavily traversed route to the Carrying Place. They were glad at last, so they thought, to see action. As one witness reported,

Conol Williams had ye Command of ye Scout & So they marched off Cheerfully. They marched two or three Miles and Sat down to Refresh Them Selves & Som of Their head officers sent Back for their Comisions [?] Then They ware Drawn up five or Six Deep & So marched on But ye Mohocks marched in a Single file before Them.[10]

Though called a scout, this was in reality a relief expedition bent upon going quickly over the road which supply wagons had been travelling safely for days. They relied on their information that the enemy was near the fort and neglected to send out scouts before them. They were committing the same error as did Braddock with such disastrous results. For this they were censured by Peter Wraxall, who shortly after wrote, "Our people were surprised, by neglecting to have advanced, & flank Guards."[11]

The French army in the meantime had set off at daybreak, marching in three columns over the "fine road which the English had opened." The French regulars marched in the center, the general at the head of his troops; the Canadians marched on the right, the Indians on the left. "Each column was about 30 paces apart, so that the Canadians and Indians were obliged to advance through the woods and on the mountains to preserve that order of march, which seriously fatigued them." Dieskau, the disciplinarian, made a fine show, even on this forest highway. He knew, however, that he was approaching the enemy with every step, and his Indians were out ahead. Soon they told him that they had seen the English camp, that there was a considerable force and that it was entrenched. Dieskau marched on.[12]

Shortly scouts brought in two English captives, possibly wagoners, certainly not men of the army, who told him that the English and the Indians were on the march, coming to the relief of the fort. They also confirmed to the scouts that the camp was entrenched, with twelve cannon. Dieskau now called a halt, regrouped his forces, and prepared an ambush.[13]

The Canadians and Indians laid down their kit so as to be lighter; he made them all pass to the left of the road, where they ambuscaded, in order not to be seen by the enemy, and to admit of the latter being engaged all at once. M. de Dieskau occupied the road with his troops. He had given orders that the Regulars should fire first, whereupon all the Canadians and Indians were to rush on the enemy.[14]

Dieskau later referred to this as a *cul de sac* and said that if his orders had been followed not a man of the English would have escaped.[15] Blodget depicted the ambush as in the form of a hook, the Indians and the Canadians forming a curved line of about half a mile on the right, but only half of that on the left. The terrain was advantageous, providing cover for the ambush and a narrow defile in which to trap the marchers.

On the Left of the Road, all along the Line they had placed themselves in, they had the advantage of being covered with a thick growth of Brush and Trees, such as is common to swampy Land as this was; On the Right, they were all along defended, as with a Breastwork, by a continued Eminence, filled with Rocks, and Trees, and Shrubs as high as a Man's Breast.[16]

The English marched into the trap, and it seems that their Indians were of little help in detecting it for they, too, and especially Hendrick, were victims. On the other hand, the French claimed that the English had some warning from the Indians. Writing afterwards, the French blamed the Indians, and any other circumstance, for their lack of success.[17] But the English were so surprised as to be nearly completely routed with the heavier losses. That they were able to fight at all, and managed a retreat, was blamed upon the Indians.

Dieskau wanted his soldiers to fire a devastating volley first, after which the Canadians and Indians would close on the flanks. This did not suit the Indians, who for long had been promised their quarry. And as usual they upset the French plan. Dieskau remarked bitterly, "This was the moment of treachery." It was the Iroquois, of course, the Caghnawagas, who had relatives among the Mohawks. The French said they yelled a warning, or prematurely showed themselves.[18]

Daniel Claus gave a delightful version of the Indian exchange, an elaboration of the briefer statement he made immediately afterward:

They had not marched 4 Miles before the Indians were challenged in ye Iroquois Tongue who they were; upon which Henery replied, We are the six confederate Indn. Nations the Heads & Superiors of all Indn. nations of the Continent of America. Whereupon the French Indian answered, we are the 7 confederate Indn. Nations of Canada & we come in conjunction with our Father the King of France's Troops to fight his Enemies the English without the least Intention to quarrel or trespass against any Indn Nation. We therefore desire you will keep out of the way lest we transgress & involve ourselves in a War among ourselves, whereupon K. Henery answered that they, the 6 Nations, came to assist their Brethn. the English agst. the French who were encroaching upon the Territories of the English as well as Indians on the Ohio. And it was their place rather to join them, or at least follow their advice & keep out of Harm's way &c. Upon which one of Henery's young Warriors fired upon the french Indian that spoke behind the Bushes.[19]

Firing now became general. The English were thrown into disorder, especially in the front ranks and among the Indians in the lead, who sought to take cover.[20]

Colonel Williams and his men with sure instinct scrambled for a "rocky eminence" to the right; but the Indians and Canadians, "having unhappily got the Possession of it, rose up from the Rocks, and Shrubs, and from behind Trees, when our men came within sure Reach of their Guns, and made a considerable Slaughter among them. The trees were thinly scattered where our men were thus fired upon, and the Shrubs but low; However, they made the best use of them they could, and continued Fighting here for some time with the greatest resolution."[21] Colonel Williams was soon picked off, as were some of the French leaders, notably Saint Pierre, commanding the French Indians.

By this time the fight became very fierce on both sides. The advanced party of *Indians* behaved with the utmost intrepidity; but perceiving they should be surrounded, and destroyed, they gave way; and as they passed by our men, they told them of their danger, and advised to a retreat. They [the troops] went on notwithstanding, fighting with undaunted courage and resolution; but finding themselves over-powered with numbers, and almost encircled, they quitted the ground, firing as they gave back with constancy and fury. Five or six Hundred of them retreated with such dexterity, and vigorous exertment, that the return of this *detachment* to the camp was hereby rendered, in a manner, safe and easy.[22]

Colonel Whiting's company, being in the rear, had time to rally and to manage a slow retreat, with constant firing at the enemy. As Colonel Pomeroy told it, "a very hansom retreet they made by continuing there fire & then retreeting a little & then rise and give them a brisk Fire So Continued till they came within 3/4 of a mile of our Camp."[23]   Even the French later commended the orderly and effective retreat which thus prevented a full rout.

The engagement lasted for an hour and a half,[24] and while the fighting went on, to cover the retreat, large groups fled down the road toward the camp. Peter Wraxall had harsh words for those who turned from the fight, yet this behavior on the part of men who thus got their first taste of battle is not unique.

The rest did not advance, or make any Motions to sustain the Front, upon which They were beat back, a Panick took Place, & the whole fled in a disorderly Manner towards the Camp. The Enemy pursued, and kept firing upon the nearest Fugitives. Our People run into Camp with all the Marks of Horror & Fear in their Countenances, exagerating the Number of the Enemy, this infected the Troops in Camp.[25]

Johnson now reported the reaction at the camp.

In about an Hour And a half afterwards we heard a heavy firing, and all the Marks of a Warm Engagement, wch we Judged was about 3 or 4 Miles from us: We beat to Arms, and got our men all in readiness; the fire Approached nearer, upon wch I judged our People were Retreating, and Detached Lieut. Colo. Cole with about 300 men to Cover their Retreat; About 10 OClock some of our men in the rear, and some Indians of Said Party came running into Camp, And Acquainted us that our Men were retreating, that the Enemy were to Strong for them; The Whole Party that escalped returned to us in large Bodies.[26]

Although the retreat was achieved, the engagement appeared to be a disaster. Colonel Williams and most of the officers of his company were killed in the attack; and the Indians at the front had suffered heavily, losing two of their chiefs, Hendrick and Nickus, while several of the Indian officers—Captain Benjamin Stoddert, Captain Jonathan Stevens, and Captain Matthew Ferrall, Johnson's brother-in-law—were killed.[27] Yet it was quite difficult at the time to get a fair estimate of the losses; and afterwards it was not clear how many who were casualties in later engagements were in the first. In the hasty retreat, dead and wounded were left by the roadside, some to reach safety or to be listed as missing, others, both French and English, to fall a prey to the savagery of the Indians, who scalped and stripped the bodies until their identity was lost.[28]

The loss of Colonel Ephraim Williams,[29] widely known and respected, with several relatives among the troops, was keenly felt. His company lost forty-one killed, twenty-six wounded, and three missing, most of them in this engagement. The French Indians were furious over the loss of their commander, Saint Pierre, and nothing could atone among the Mohawks for the falling of the great Hendrick.

There was some mystery about how he came to his end. After the engagement, he was reported as fallen; since he had been mounted and in the van, it was assumed that he had fallen in the first volley. He had been provided a horse (presumably by Johnson), and one account says that it was shot under him and that he was then bayonetted.[30] If this had happened it very likely would have been observed. Johnson the next day wrote, "Old Hendrick, the great Mohawk Sachim, we fear is kill'd."[31] He seemed to have no certain knowledge. Claus on September 11, writing Richard Peters, to whom Hendrick was well known, said "our Common Loss is Henry my Father."[32] No other details were given then, but in after years Claus reconstructed the story. Perhaps he was now telling the truth, for he had a high regard for Hendrick, with whom he had lived to learn the Mohawk tongue.

Henery being on Horseback lit off his horse & being heavy old man as grey headed as Silver was soon left in the rear & attempting to gain the Camp on the left where he thought [he] would meet with no Enemy, unluckily not far from Camp fell in with the french Indns. Baggage Gard of Young Lads & women who haveing no fire arms, sta'd [stabbed] him in the Back with a Spear or Bayonet, some pretend to say it was committed by a Squaw, the Lads being too young to attempt it, & by the Manner of his being scalped it is probable a woman did it, as the scalp being taken off not larger than an English Crown.[33]

The doggedness of the English retreat, together with the vigor of their fire, somewhat disorganized the enemy. The French Indians were chastened by their losses and had no desire to pursue and attack the main body of the English, and they missed the leadership of Saint Pierre. In fact, their Iroquois tried to make the Abenakis release some of their Mohawk prisoners. And it was Indian custom, once they had had an action, to collect plunder and trophies before fighting again. A number of Canadians, too, could not follow the march but were "so fatigued that they were *hors de combat*."[34]

These difficulties, especially the disputes of the Indians, made the French call a halt one half mile from the camp. "This happy Halt," wrote Wraxall, "in all

Probability saved Us, or the French General would have continued his Pursuit, & I am afraid entered with the last of our flying Men, before our Troops recovered from their Consternation."[35] Yet General Dieskau, confident of the superiority of his picked men and chagrined by the behavior of his Indians, resolved when he saw the camp to march upon it with men in formation and with fixed bayonets. He made no reconnaissance and was unaware of the nature of the entrenchments.[36] In his own words, "as I was near the enemy's camp, and in front of the cannon, I marched forward with 200 Regulars to Capture it, [expecting] that the Canadians would not abandon me, and that the Indians would perhaps return; but in vain."[37]

Within the camp there was frantic activity as preparations were made for the attack. It was no easy task since the wounded were arriving, too, along with troops fleeing in panic. The camp was a mere clearing in the forest, open on three sides, the fourth being the lakefront, where boats were moored. It was thus exposed to flank attack, but any body of men in formation could be expected on the road from the south. The only defense was from felled trees forming a kind of breast-work, and now more trees were placed and joined with bateaux and "a number of Albany provision waggons laid on their sides and ranged in a line, minutes before the French attack. In some places these entrenchments were but a foot high."[38]

General Johnson ranged his men along this barricade, the Connecticut troops under Lyman facing the road; the Massachusetts regiments with colonels Titcomb, Ruggles, and Pomeroy on the right. Some five hundred men were held in the rear of the camp as reserves. There too the larger cannon were set facing in three directions; but on an eminence to the left was placed a field piece (twelve-pounder) in good position to rake the open road. And facing the oncoming column were three heavier cannon. The swamps and gully to the right hemmed in the camp on that quarter.[39]

Johnson and his aides rallied the men for the impending attack. Wraxall wrote:

Our General harangued & did all in his Power to animate our People, I rode along the Line from Regiment to Regiment, decreased [discounted] the Enemy's Numbers, promised them a cheap Victory if they behaved with Spirit, begun a Huzza which took & they planted themselves at the Breast Work just as the Enemy appeared in Sight; some of the Officers, but not many, seconded my Endeavours.[40]

Between eleven-thirty and twelve noon,[41] the enemy hove in sight of the camp. The French grenadiers of La Reine and Languedoc marched in regular formation, six abreast, their white coats and fixed bayonets gleaming in the sun. "They made a Small halt about 150 Yards from our breast work, when the regular Troops . . . made the Grand and Center Attack." At 20 rods (110 yards), they fired in platoons, then filed to right and left, "but it did no great Execution being at too great a Distance and our men defended by the Breast Work. . . . The Canadeans and Indians Squatted and dispersed on our Flancks."[42]

Now the fieldpieces opened fire with good effect on the massed regulars, eventually forcing them to disperse and to try a flank action with some cover. Captain Will Eyre, the engineer, directed the artillery, for which he received special commendation from the general. And a veteran gunner, Captain Boyle, who had lost one hand as a naval gunner on a privateer, gloried in the carnage. "Our artillery," he said, "made Lanes, Streets and Alleys thro' their Army."[43] The French thought they silenced the artillery by picking off "all those who were working the guns," from their higher positions. But Johnson referred to the "warm and constant fire," which put the enemy in disorder; and Surgeon Williams believed the artillery "saved us." Its roar was heard as far away as Saratoga. A south wind caused a cloud of smoke to envelop the camp, obscuring the battle.[44]

Fighting now became general; the raw and undisciplined soldiers had to be prodded and encouraged. General Johnson was obliged "to Expose himself greatly in Action, . . . he was soe hoarse in the Engagemt. with calling to the Troops & running along the Lines, as not to be able to speak untill he got a Lemon & sucked the Juice."[45] The Connecticut men faced the first attack. General Lyman said the bullets whistled all about him, but he was untouched, even though he once ran through the field to have the men hold their fire.[46]

The regulars held their ground and order for a while, but in the face of the artillery and warm fire, they sought cover. The French and Canadians from the first, on right and left were concealing themselves behind trees and shrubs, giving but a small mark for the musketry.[47] After two hours

their fire became more Scattered and Unequal; and the Enemy's fire on our Left grew very faint; they moved then to the right of Our Encampment. and Attacked Colo. Ruggles, Colo. Williams, and Colo. Titcomb's Regiments, where they Maintained a very Warm fire for near an hour, Still keeping up their fire in the other Parts of our Line, tho not very Strong. The three regts. on the Right Supported the Attack very resolutely, and kept a Constant and Strong fire upon the Enemy. This Attack failing, and the Artillery Still Playing along the line, we found their fire very weak, with Several Intervals. This was about 4 oClock, when our men and the Indians jump'd over the breast Work, Pursued the Enemy, Slaughtered numbers, and took Several Prisoners.[48]

The gunner reported that after trying for two hours on the right flank, the enemy again tried the front and "thought to come in on the rear of our army; but the General perceiving danger, ordered me to throw some shells, which accordingly I did, and some 32 pounders which soon made them shift births; they retreated in sad disorder, and with shoults of Victory we got the day."[49] The French collapse was largely due to the loss of their leader. During the fray General Dieskau had removed fifty paces to one side the better to observe the battle; while there he received a shot in the leg. Chevalier de Montreuil rushed to him and stanched his wound; but then Dieskau received another ball in his knee. Two Canadians came to his aid, and one of these was killed. Dieskau ordered de Montreuil to go, to command the troops. He did so, but only in time to order a retreat. Refusing to let his servants remove him, Dieskau was captured by the advancing English and Indians. The French made an orderly retreat, by platoons, but did not inform the Canadians or Indians. Fortunately for them, the English did not pursue.[50]

The Indian allies of the English had played little part in this engagement, but they now entered the camp from the rear and spread out to capture and scalp the retreating enemy. Enraged by their own losses, they scalped and plundered, slaying the wounded and helpless, as the French defeat became a rout. With difficulty Johnson and his men saved the life of Dieskau and brought him captive to Johnson's tent.[51]

Although victory was in their grasp, the English, having suffered heavy losses— among them a number of officers—and having many wounded—including General Johnson—seemed unable to follow up the retreat. Wraxall accounted for it as follows:

When the enemy was beat off and flying, a Trial was made to pursue, but Men & several Officers were backward. However, I don't know but a Pursuit might have been dangerous to Us. The Day was declining—The Rout of the Enemy not Certain —The Country all a Wood,—our Men greatly fatigued, provided neither with Bayonets or Swords, undisciplined, & not very high spirited. These Reasons (for my Opinion was asked) induce me to think we had better be content with the fortunate Repulse we had given the Enemy, and before Night put every thing in Order and Security, for the Prisoners said they had 1000 Men more who were expected on their March to reinforce them.[52]

There were no adequate preparations for care of casualties, and the presence in the camp of the dead, dying, and wounded was bound to produce havoc and consternation. Surgeon Williams gave a graphic account.

The Wounded were brought in very fast, & it was with the utmost difficulty that their wounds could be dressed fast enough, even in the most superficial manner, having in about three hours near forty men to be dressed, & Dr. Pynchon, his mate & *Billy* (one of his students) & myself were all to do it, my mate being at Fort Lyman attending on divers sick men there. The bullets flew like hail-stones about our ears all the time of dressing, as we had not a place prepared of safety, to dress the wounded in, but through God's goodness we received no hurt any more than the bark of the trees & chips flying in our faces by accidental shots, which were something frequent. Our tent was shot through in divers places, which we thought best to leave & retire a few rods behind a shelter of a log house, which so loose laid as to let the balls through very often.[53]

Early in the action, while encouraging the men and directing the disposition of the troops, General Johnson received a ball in his thigh. Wraxall, who was near him, thought he saw the ball enter, and feared it was mortal; but in spite of pain, Johnson "kept the field"; then, seeing him grow stiff, Wraxall led him to his tent to have his wound dressed. Several accounts indicate that he directed the action after receiving his wound; and he himself said it was dressed just before Dieskau was brought in, about six o'clock.[54] Seeing the suffering of many whose wounds were more serious, or fatal, and knowing that many of his officers were among the dead, Johnson minimized his wound. But the ball was not removed and plagued him the rest of his life. In fact, he was unwell for the rest of the campaign.

Colonel Blanchard, commanding the fort at the Carrying Place, learned of the battle from a scouting party which came within the sound of guns. Having been spared so narrowly from a direct attack, he was not able to send a reinforcement. Not knowing how the battle went, he dared not leave the fort unprotected, so he sent out a detachment of 120 New Hampshire men and 90 New Yorkers under the command of Captain William Maginnis.[55] They met the enemy, some 300 Canadians and Indians, returning from the battle to the place where they had dropped their packs. Some of their Indians were engaged in scalping and looting. The French said they were ambushed; Johnson said the French attacked. Lyman said the "Yorkers and New Hampshire men attacked and drove them from their Baggage, took it, and all their blankets, Victuals, Powder, &c. Killed a Number, and took some Captives, and then returned well to the Camp."[56] This was forest fighting, and the fresh New Hampshire men were in their element. The fighting raged for two hours, from about five until seven o'clock. Most of the French were killed; Baron de Longueil, now in command of their Indians, had been wounded and was reported missing. Those who escaped now joined the retreating Canadians in the woods. The loss of the English was reported as only two killed, eleven wounded, and five missing. But Captain Maginnis was mortally wounded and was borne to the fort on a horse litter.[57]

Although Wraxall called this "the only considerable honor on our side," it was more of a *coup de grâce*, for "the Enemy were vanquished troops and had fled from the attack at the Camp."[58] These troops after sundown joined the regulars in the mountains and began the long trek to their canoes, then to Carillon, bearing their wounded, and thence to the protection of the guns at Fort St. Frederic. Both sides were exhausted.[59]

The next day General Johnson held a council of war, took stock of his losses and those of the enemy, and wrote his official account of the victory. It was indeed a victory, though the excited and somewhat exaggerated reports of participants tended to magnify the forces, the losses, and the action. "Such a Battle," wrote Colonel Pomeroy, "It is Judg'd by all I have heard was never known in America."[60] This was echoed by General Lyman: "I believe there Never was a heavier nor hotter Fight in this Country, and I believe Men never behaved better than the Province and Connecticut Soldiers, who alone were attacked."[61]

The official report of the casualties under Johnson's command was 120 killed, 801 wounded, and 62 missing. Some of the wounded, of course, were not to recover, and some of the missing were doubtless killed or died later. Of the allied Indians, 32 were killed or missing, including "Hendrick the Great Mohock Sachem & another great Sachim of the said Castle (Nickus)," and 12 wounded. Of special concern was the great mortality of the officers: two colonels (Titcomb and Ephraim Williams), five captains (Elisha Hawley and Maginnis, listed as wounded, died shortly from wounds); and eleven commissioned officers. In addition four Indian officers, not included in the regimental list, were killed in the morning engagement.[62]

At the time, the English felt they had inflicted as heavy or heavier losses on the enemy, but the French governor reported "100 men killed and 130 wounded, all included." Presumably this included Canadians but not Indians. It does not mention the missing or prisoners. After the battle Wraxall said, "We have about 25 prisoners" and "Our Indians have taken off near 70 Scalps."[63]

But the capture of General Dieskau, with his aide-de-camp Bernier and with his maps and papers, was of considerable moment. From him and other prisoners

Johnson learned the details of the French expedition, its aims and its strength, just as the French had learned from Braddock. Moreover, it was a personal triumph of some magnitude. Dieskau was a distinguished soldier, sent to command all the French troops in America, and his loss badly disconcerted the French command. It was the source of much gratification in the English colonies, the best evidence of the English triumph.

More soberly regarded, Johnson had won the battle, but his drive to Crown Point was halted. The provincial authorities now expected him to push onward toward his objective. This of course was not easily done, for his men had suffered losses equal to the enemy, and the Indians' losses in their own eyes were considerable. On the other hand, the expedition, which was expected only to capture the fort at Crown Point and its garrison, had been forced to meet the counterthrust of the main French army. While Dieskau's fourteen hundred men, a picked force, was only half of his army, Johnson's was superior in numbers; yet the number facing the French at any one engagement was not great. Even when the camp was attacked, perhaps only half of the men were engaged. Had Dieskau attacked Fort Edward, he would have outnumbered the garrison. But comparison of numbers is unsatisfactory; Dieskau had regulars of the French army and French-Canadian veterans of the Ohio campaigns. Johnson's men were all raw recruits, newly enlisted, and wholly inexperienced. And he had far fewer Indians than did the French. The real results of the battle must be measured in the larger context of the war.

It must have been a hurried meeting which Johnson had with his officers the next day. What measures, he asked them, in view of the present state of the army and the information gained from prisoners, would they advise. It was unanimously decided that the governments who had supplied troops should be informed by "Express"; "One general Letter to be sent to the Province of Massachusetts Bay, giving as Summary an Account as time & Circumstances will permit of the Engagement of Yesterday & of the Intelligence derived from it & the present State of this Army, and that we employ our time in securing ourselves here in the best manner possible."[64]

The general's immediate report of the battle, written out by Peter Wraxall for the several governors at the direction of the council of war, was a communiqué of the first importance. It was widely printed and served as the basis for other reports. It was lavishly praised and also criticized for what it said and what it omitted. Johnson several days later explained that it was written under pressure, at different times, while another attack was expected (two alarms during the writing), when they were "fatigued both in Body and Mind." Under such circumstances, "it was both difficult to collect and pen a distinct and exact Relation." Yet he had reviewed it and found it to be "in the main as just & full an Account as I can give."[65]

Not only the contents but the manner of his sending this letter were criticized. With but one secretary (Wraxall), who in the midst of such confusion had scarce time to make five separate copies for the governors, Johnson added a memo on the outside of the letter to Lieutenant Governor Phips of Massachusetts, to make a copy for General Shirley. Perhaps this note was intended for Wraxall, but in Albany it was seen by James Stevenson, who opened the missive and sent on a copy to General Shirley at Oswego.[66] Now commander in chief, and fretting at his own inaction, Shirley was angered and took Johnson severely to task for not informing him first and directly. "What could be your Reason for postponing my being acqainted with these Matters which I ought to have known as soon as possible, . . . seems difficult to say."[67]

Likewise, the Massachusetts Assembly, while it "could find no fault with the conduct of the general in the field," were not pleased by his "distinguishing New York in his Correspondence" and sending prisoners—including General Dieskau—there thought it was more convenient and easier transportation by water.[68]

Plagued by many new problems and the discontent of his men, and suffering from his wound and illness, General Johnson was irked by these petty complaints of protocol (though he could expect little else from Shirley), and he replied sharply in letters to Lieutenant Governor Phips and Thomas Hutchinson. "As no Establishment was made, to enable me to carry on the diffusive Correspondence wch seems to be expected from me, it has been & is impossible for me to fulfill those Expectations."[69] He also wrote:

Whatever Papers I have sent to the Govt. of New York, I did it with no other View, than as a Method of the most eligible Conveniency to get them transmitted your way. From selfish or Ambitious Views, I make my Court to no Govt. having no political Schemes to carry, & resting every future Plan of my Life on a Private Bottom. A Lesson wch. mortifying Experience has taught me.[70]

Another dispute arose over the letter which Peter Wraxall wrote to Governor De Lancey and which immediately was published in the *New York Gazette*, September 18, 1755. Johnson explained that this was a "Scrawl hurried over," with no intention of publication, "a composition of parts of his & of another wrote from this army." Since Wraxall had a civil appointment from the governor, he felt obliged to keep him informed. But he had already incurred the displeasure of Shirley, and the letter which appeared over his name seemed semiofficial. Another, perhaps revised, version appeared later.[71] Another letter which looked official was that written by General Lyman the day after the battle; it appeared in the *Connecticut Gazette* on September 20 and was reprinted in the New York papers.[72]

All of these early reports, while rejoicing in the victory, expressed concern over the safety of the army and the possibility that the French might soon attack again. "We are apprehensive & our Indians very much so, that the French will make a more formidable attack upon us and bring Artillery up the Lake," wrote Wraxall.[73] General Lyman, who later was credited with being bolder and urging an advance while Johnson held back, now wrote: "I expect their whole Strength against us here shortly."[74] And Captain Eyre, in writing to Shirley on September 10, reiterated this fear that "the Enemy by all Accounts are very formidable, & I think it not improbable, they will pay us another Visit soon; if they can seize and take our Work at the Carrying Place, I fear it would be attended with bad Consequences, as it would cut off our retreat and Communication with Albany, and totally stop our Reinforcements and Provisions from Joining us."[75]

This fear for the Carrying Place as a base of communication prompted Johnson on September 14 to send back three Connecticut companies for its defense. Protection of the camp at Lake George depended chiefly upon the "picketed fort" already begun under Captain Eyre's direction. Johnson and his engineer had favored a "stronger Fortification" with earthen bastions, but the Council decided on palisaded work because "the troops had an aversion to digging." Some wanted to move the camp to the fort site, but this suggestion was considered premature, and the breastworks of the camp were strengthened.[76]

There was a general demand for reinforcements, and there was a certain unanimity in the feeling that this would make possible the advance on Crown Point. That this did not transpire can only be explained by examining the events and conditions following the battle.[77]

XVII

AFTERMATH OF BATTLE

Success in battle redounded to the credit of the commanding officer, who became the man of the hour. In the widespread rejoicing at the defeat of the French, and their humiliation in the capture of their general, General Johnson was acclaimed as a military leader and the architect of victory. Congratulations poured in from governors and from the public, mixed only with praise for the brave troops who so nobly justified the hopes of their respective governments. For the moment an undercurrent of dissent and criticism was forgotten, for there had been suspicion and jealousy of this frontier leader of Indians in the minds of many New Englanders. But his good humor, generosity, and good sense had caused some of the officers to change their attitudes, and he had grown in their esteem. Under great provocation he had kept his head, and somehow this conglomeration of militia had come to be an army under one command. Now the men in general not only accepted his leadership but gloried in the victory which he had brought them. Surgeon Williams, who had served through the campaign and who as a noncombatant was better able to judge than most officers, now penned a flattering judgment, reflecting the change of opinion of at least one New Englander.

I must say he is a complete gentleman, & willing to oblige & please all men, familiar & free of access to the lowest Centinel, a gentleman of uncommon smart sense & even temper; Never yet saw him in a ruffle, or use any bad language—in short I was never so disappointed [disillusioned] in a person in the idea I had of him before I came from home, in my life; to sum it up he is almost universally beloved & esteemed by officers & soldiers as a second Marlborough for coolness of head & warmness of heart.[1]

"The name of Johnson," wrote William Williams from the Mohawk Valley, "will always be dear to New England."[2] This acclaim, however, was not unmixed with the hope of further advance and even greater victory. With the congratulations of the governors came the assurances of reinforcements for the campaign. "I congratulate you on the victory you have obtained over the French. I hope this will prove the prelude to greater success," wrote James De Lancey.[3] While some expressed concern for his wound, his health, and his recovery, it was believed that now he could count on the enthusiastic support of the several assemblies.

Governor Stephen Hopkins of Rhode Island gloated that the defeat of Braddock had been avenged; he noted that three hundred and fifty additional men had been raised in "this small colony" and that large reinforcements would be forthcoming from the others. And he lavished praise upon Johnson for his good judgment.

We all rejoice, yea we rejoice much at your Success, yet are not half so much pleased with that as with your Conduct and Bravery. We esteem it a sure Earnest of further Successes that you are able to obtain certain Intelligences and not be surprised or deceived. We are not more encouraged by your Ardor to engage, than by your Judgement to retreat, as on one Hand Success can add Nothing to your Courage, so on the other we hope it will take Nothing from your Caution.[4]

The chorus of approval from the governors was a bit marred by the tone of General Shirley's letter of September 19. This, as noted above, first took Johnson to task for not reporting directly and immediately to him. Then as commander in chief he called upon Johnson to advance, as soon as reinforcements were received from New England, to Ticonderoga and thence to take Crown Point.

Then he figured Johnson would have four thousand men and two hundred Indians; his men would be flushed with success while the French would be demoralized by their defeat and their losses (about a thousand, leaving them but seven hundred men); and Ticonderoga was reported as not yet fortified. Furthermore, Shirley doubted the figures given by the French general on the strength of his army; he figured that with all their reported losses the number able to oppose Johnson "can't amount to Near the number wch. you seem to think are there." And he discounted the idea that the enemy might make "a more Formidable Attack very Shortly," with artillery.[5]

I suppose that Artillery must be brought from Crown point or Tenonderoge; and if the French should imagine, that you design to attempt nothing further this Campaigne than building the Stockaded Fort, you propose, I think it probable enough, that they would make you a Visit at your Camp with Cannon; in which Case I doubt your Fort, when built, would not Stand long.[6]

In sum, Shirley wanted Johnson to proceed at once, without consideration for any delays or objections; he assumed he would have sufficient information to justify this demand; he doubted the French strength; but at the same time he disapproved of Johnson's building a fort, which he thought could not stand. There was here no commendation for previous steps or action, or for the behavior of officers or men. In a final paragraph he tersely expressed concern for Johnson's wound—"that the Ball is by this time extracted from your Thigh, & your Wound in a fair Way of healing: I congratulate you upon your Success hitherto, & wish it may be increased in the remaining operations of the Campaigne."[7]

From many miles away with only the written word from which to judge, it was easy to say "advance!" But for the men in camp, just recovering from the shock of battle, grieving for their dead, nursing their wounds, and reconstructing their shattered defenses, there were many things to do. With the best of resolution there were grievous conditions to face. Colonel Seth Pomeroy, who reflected all of these, wrote on the day after the battle: "Our people are out Burying ye Dead now . . . we Design to make a Stand here till we have a sufficient Reinforcement what number yt must be I Cant tell but they Determine to stop us before we get to Crown Point."[8]

Some twenty-five French prisoners, according to Johnson, were brought to camp. Like their leader, they felt themselves lucky to escape the fury of the Indians whose hands itched for their tomahawks and that retribution which only a French scalp, or a prisoner, would satisfy. A few prisoners had to be granted the Indians, to replace their own losses, but twenty were taken via Fort Edward and through Albany to New York.[9]

Not only the Indians but some of the soldiers turned upon the captives. It was rumored and widely believed that the French had used poisoned bullets (some said they were chewed; others that the lead was "rolled up with a solution of copper and yellow arsenic") which produced a mortification of the wound and in some cases death in convulsions. Baron Dieskau on his honor denied the charge and asserted if such were used they must have been by the Canadians or Indians.[10] Johnson accepted his statement; but according to Claus, General Lyman pressed the matter, and notwithstanding the entreaties of others not to molest a prisoner in such pain and suffering "came every day for several days parading with two large Musquateer Cartridge Boxes slung across his Body & a French Musket on his Shoulder."[11]

The principal prize of the victory of course was the captured general, Baron Dieskau, but it was difficult to keep him from being a sacrifice to the vengeance of the Indians. Even as the Baron lay wounded on the field an English soldier, taking no chances as he said, shot him again through the loins. Luckily for him, he persuaded his captors to take him to the general's tent. There Johnson directed that his wounds be attended by a surgeon even before his own wound was dressed.[12] Now the Indians invaded the tent and demanded that he be given them to torture, to atone for the loss of Hendrick and other chiefs who had been killed. Johnson was able to persuade them to leave the French general to him, but constant guard and surveillance were necessary to protect him as long as he remained in camp. Daniel Claus related his own experiences with the general, with whom he was able to converse in his native German.[13]

General Johnson was impressed with the high rank and military distinction of his captive and resolved to treat him in accordance with military protocol. Moreover, he was a gentleman by birth and breeding and therefore deserving of proper treatment. His papers had been taken, and from them and by interrogation it was possible to learn from him the strength and plans of the enemy.

Due to his serious multiple wounds it was doubted whether the Baron would live, but after nine days it was considered feasible to move him. On September 17 he was transported on a litter with an escort to Fort Edward, whence he could be moved by bateau to Albany. He was provided with a military escort or guard and accompanied by Dr. Middleton, the surgeon who had been called to attend General Johnson. The latter gave strict orders that crowds or the mob were not to annoy him with "their impertinence and ill-mannered curiosity." From Fort Edward to Albany the escort of fifty men was commanded by Captain Philip Schuyler, who was directed to lodge the Baron in Johnson's Albany house. With him went his aide-de-camp, Bernier, upon whom the guard was told to keep a watchful eye for any treachery. A French-speaking soldier went along as interpreter.[14]

While in Albany not only was the Baron housed by General Johnson, but his sister Catty, the widow of Captain Ferrall, kept the house and nursed him to better health. To be thus indebted both to General Johnson and to the grieving widow of a victim of his army was almost too much for the courtly Baron. Though she was kind and solicitous, and gave no sign of her loss and grief, he was acutely conscious of her position and generous in his praise. It was one reason, he said, why he wished to be moved to New York.[15] Finally, on October 17, the Baron and his aide with "the complement of a guard of Regulars," sailed on a sloop for New York. There he was commended by Johnson to the distinguished Dr. Magra, who was somehow offended by Bernier, and then he was entrusted to the care of Dr. Richard Shuckburgh, the army surgeon. Dieskau later blamed the "bad surgeons" in New York, but by January 1756 he found himself out of danger and appealing to Governor Hardy to be sent to England. There he sought cure at Bath for several years.[16]

Johnson's care for Dieskau, his humanity in restraining the Indians, and his courtesy toward the vanquished leader were widely noted and commended both in the provinces and abroad. These showed at least that this leader of Indians and commander of provincial irregulars was no barbarian but the equal of Europeans, not only in fighting but in the amenities of military life. They built up his reputation abroad and served to justify later the honors and acclaim which came his way.

While concerning himself with his wounded prisoner, restraining the Indians, and issuing orders at the close of the battle, General Johnson was suffering from the wound in his thigh. Its severity and the extent of his incapacity have been the subject of much debate as was whether he was thereby removed from the command, so that it devolved upon General Lyman, whose friends—the enemies of Johnson—later claimed for him principal credit for the victory. Since this contention was the result of later rivalries and recriminations and is supported by no firsthand testimony, it must be rejected here.[17]

It was early in the fighting, after he had directed the disposition of troops, the placing of cannon, and had rallied the retreating troops from the first engagement that Johnson received the ball in his thigh. Wraxall testified that he saw it happen; thought it was in his back and might be mortal; noticed that the general stiffened; and led him from the field. There was at once no one to care for him, and Dr. Middleton was sent for. Testimony varies as to whether Johnson was able to act after his wound, or remained the whole time in his tent. In the first published version of Wraxall's letter, he "kept the Field, altho' in great pain."[18] Writing later, Daniel Claus said little of Johnson's wound, but referred to his "still keeping the troops at the Breastwork," after the capture of Dieskau and that "it was now late Genl. Johnson came in from the Lines to see how the french Genl. did."[19] Colonel Pomeroy the next day wrote, "General Johnson shot In the Thigh not Brook [broke] Majr. General Lyman well both behaved with stediness & resolution."[20]

On the next day, as noted, Johnson was actively directing affairs from his tent, dispatching reports and holding a council of war. "My Wound wch is in my Thigh is very Painfull, the Ball is lodg'd and Cannot be got out, by which means I am to my Mortification Confined to my Tent."[21] Soon he was walking about and eventually the pain from the wound ceased, but the rigors of camp life, exposure, and the constant strain of his command again laid him low.[22]

By October 1 he was suffering from a violent pain and inflammation in the side of his head, which settled in his ear. It was accompanied by fever, gave him "inexpressible torment," and soon again confined him to his bed. From the description of symptoms this may have been an ear infection, aggravated by cold and exposure, and possibly mastoiditis. The surgeons took drastic steps; he was "bled, blistered & purged," and as a result was extremely weak; he had very little sleep and little nourishment. He was incapable of writing but dictated to Peter Wraxall. This continued for three weeks; then on October 22, he ventured from his tent, caught cold, and had a recurrence of the violent pain in his ear, which kept him awake. Two days later he was better and hoped to get out in a few days. On November 1 he had been venturing out for a few days, but "with caution." Hence for almost the entire month of October he was a very sick man. That he was able through this time to continue in command and to transact business was only due to his determination and stamina. He finally was compelled to ask General Lyman to preside at the council of war, to consider the proposals which he submitted.[23]

Of immediate concern to the general after the battle was the attitude of the Indian allies. Having been brought on the campaign by his personal efforts and depending so much on him for leadership, their behavior was a real test of influence. Now they had suffered severely in casualties, almost all in the first engagement. The loss of Hendrick and other sachems was a terrific blow to their morale. Wraxall said they were "very much enraged, but not in so high spirits as I could wish."[24] Lyman, who had little use for Indians, commented on their losses and added, "I hope the Indians will now be mad enough."[25] Others were concerned, too, for their constancy.

Johnson's feelings were mixed. He felt a real sense of loss for Hendrick, an old friend and faithfull ally, who for many years had been a source of his strength among the Mohawks. There were others, like Abraham, of course, who were his friends, but none commanded such respect among both Indians and whites. His fame had been widely known and his death was lamented, even in England. Wise counsellor—his interposition may have turned the course of history on this occasion—he also leaned heavily on Johnson. Not even the blandishments of General Shirley, who had tried to win him over with money and a captain's commission, could shake his loyalty to Brother Warraghiyagey. And in death he would not be forsaken; for many years Johnson provided a pension for his widow.[26]

The general well knew that it was difficult to keep the Indians on a long campaign, and that after one engagement, especially if they had losses, it was their

custom to take time to mourn their dead and to perform the ceremony of condolence. But if he were to go forward he needed their help. Now they were
drifting away, and so he called a formal conference with them at the camp, with the
officers and interpreters present. The Oneida speaker said they had responded to
his call and had destroyed their enemies; now they were determined to return to
their homes and families. Johnson remonstrated that there had been but one day
of fighting; they were only halfway on their expedition, and he was resolved to
continue. What could be the reasons for not fulfilling their promises and engagements? He had covered the graves of their dead with black strouds, and he expressed sorrow for their losses, as for those of the English. He placed no restraint
upon them, but with a belt of wampum asked that they honor their engagements. It
was of no avail. Even the Mohawk speakers told him their return home was not to be
avoided. But they assured him that later they would return, with "fresh people
with them." They gave back his belt but said there was no "coldness of heart,"
for they expected to return with fresh vigor. There was another reason. Since the
sword was now drawn between them and the French Indians, they feared for the
safety of their homes and castles, and intended to put "their affairs in a proper
Posture & their People on their Guard."[27]

So most of the Indians left the camp and travelled homeward; on their way they
met some other parties on the road to join the army, and these they turned back.[28]
There was some comfort for the English in the knowledge that the French Indians
had been alienated, and that the French forces, by their defeat, had lost the confidence of their own Indians. The military victory and the Mohawks' losses had
"more effectually wounded the French influence among them, and by their
influence will more weaken it among the other Confederate Nations, than any other
Event wch. could be expected."[29]

When the new governor, Sir Charles Hardy, came to Albany, he sent the
Reverend John Ogilvie with an interpreter to the Mohawk castles to persuade them
to rejoin the army. Ogilvie spent a week condoling their losses, covering their
graves, and urging their warriors to return, but he found a great "Backwardness."
They were a small nation and their losses were heavy, said the sachems of the
Lower Castle, and they refused to venture again. At Canajoharie, the Upper Castle,
there was more willingness, and some warriors were ready to set out, saying that
they considered it their duty. Perhaps twenty or thirty could be expected.[30]

By the end of September, however, save for a few loyal individuals, there seemed
no hope for much Indian support. Banyar reported that the old women of the
council were set against their men going again.[31]

In New England, however, the news of the victory was hailed as an augury of
further success, the reinforcements sought by the general were eagerly voted, and
enlistments were stimulated. Soon the fresh troops were arriving at Albany and
awaiting orders to march to Lake George.[32] Fresh supplies of provisions were
also voted, and some communities showed their loyalty by gifts to the cause.
Outstanding was the action of Suffolk County, Long Island, in sending one
thousand sheep. This was widely heralded, but proved to be less of a boon than
anticipated. After they were driven part of the way north, it was found impractical

to deliver them on the hoof and they were exchanged for "14 Oxen, the Sheep being reduced in Numbers by the Carelessness of the Drivers."[33]

It was generally believed that with these new levies, Johnson would be able soon to push on for the taking of Crown Point. But it was often overlooked that by greatly increasing the size of his army they were increasing its needs in every way—food, armament, transport, and housing. Some of the new troops came ill prepared or badly outfitted. In contrast with one report that they came "upon horses, two upon each horse, well accoutred and armed," Banyar found them arriving in Albany without sufficient supply. "I saw about 1000 Connt. Men drawn up before the Govrs. door this Morning, they make a difficulty of marching yet . . . they might eat up your Provs. I told some of their officers to do as the French did carry 10 or 15 days Provs. in their Sacks. Some Voluntiers came on horseback I hear from Boston." General Johnson noted too that "Reinforcements particularly from Connecticut are coming thick upon us, by fresh Numbers they are Welcome, but as hungry Guests who with our old People consume Provisions as fast as the Waggons bring them . . . [they will] retard us."[34]

There was great misconception of the conditions at the Lake George camp. Shirley expected that the men were exhilarated by victory and therefore in a mood to advance. Testimony of officers and men, however, showed a great weariness, reaction from the battle losses, and a desire to regain strength before proceeding. Johnson retorted to Shirley frankly:

To my great Mortification, I must confess to you, that Notwithstanding the Providential repulse we gave to the Enemy, Our Troops are so far from being invigorated thereby or filled with any Additional Ardor for pursuing the Main Plan, that the reverse of this has been evidently the Case almost ever since. The [   ] resolute & obstinate Attack made upon our Breast work in the Face of our Cannon seems to have given our Troops a dread of the Enemy. We have had wet & cold days since, the Men are thinly [clad] ill bedded & Tented were pretty much fatigued by the Engagement by the false alarms & precautions taken afterwards, Bad weather, [   ] Life to wch they are wholly Strangers, Sickness since the 8. greatly increases amongst; Winter at no great Distance, Family tyes, In short all [these] Causes put together, have so influenced our Men that they are by no Means inclined to proceed further & I have reason to believe many of their officers of the same Mind.[35]

Earlier he had written Governor Phips that he had no more than "between 18 and 1900 Men fit for duty." Some one hundred and fifty had then arrived from Massachusetts, but this was a far cry from the three thousand or more on which others counted.[36] These were the stark realities as seen at the camp. This was not pleasant news for those exerting themselves to support the campaign; and new problems and obstacles to its promotion were developing.

Of course griping and complaining on the part of troops is a concomitant of every military operation, but when troops are irregulars, popularly led, and enlisted for short or indefinite terms, it becomes a major problem of discipline. Insubordination and mutiny easily followed. Johnson rightly blamed most of his troubles in this respect on the diffuse responsibility and irregularity of the commands.

At Fort Edward the conflict between New Yorkers and New England men, which emerged in quarrels before the battle, now got worse. One solution was to transfer some of them to the Lake George camp. For there were two parties, and the New England men complained of Colonel Cockroft, the New Yorker, in command. There was "Cursing, Damning, Swearing and drinking engrossing the Chief of the Time." There were so many invalids that the colonel ordered them stripped "of all the Cloathing given them by the province" and sent off; Johnson had to modify this that they not be sent out naked. Yet he well understood the problem, that sickness was possibly malingering to escape work. When there was complaint that a surgeon would not care for some, or give them fresh provisions, he was firm. "If they pretend Sickness to cover Laziness as I am convinced numbers here do, I applaud the Surgeons Honesty, & to such I would Order no Work no Victuals."[37]

Conditions undoubtedly were bad; provisions were in short supply, often only a few days in advance, and officers therefore had to cut rations. Minor complaints— that blankets were lost, that rum and flour were not sufficient, that they "Want a Sauce to their Meat, wch. they are used to and cannot live without it,"—became the pretext for drastic steps.[38] Officers supported or condoned these complaints. Several were not sympathetic with work on the forts and did not compel their men to do what was ordered. As time went on threats of mutiny and actual mutiny appeared.

While this clamor went on in camp, General Johnson expostulated with the commissaries, the governors, and others that an adequate train of supply be furnished if anything were to be expected from his army. They were shocked when he ordered that regiments of reinforcement be detained in Albany, because there was not sufficient supply in camp. The number of wagons was far below that required and was decreasing as wagoners deserted the service. And the building of boats for the advance, as well as for supply, was lagging.[39]

General Johnson hoped to make the provincial governments realize the situation. They in turn sought a closer relationship with the general. New York now had a new governor in Sir Charles Hardy, who arrived on September 2 and immediately showed great interest in the campaign. A naval officer, son of a distinguished admiral, and himself recently knighted, the governor had a real interest in military affairs. With several advisers he journeyed to Albany, arriving there September 20, and took steps to increase the flow of supplies to Lake George. As noted above, he sent the Reverend Mr. Ogilvie to the Indian castles, and he devoted himself to getting wagons for transport, but in this he encountered great difficulty. General Johnson hoped that Governor Hardy would visit the camp and see for himself the conditions there.[40] But it became clear that such was not to be. Sir Charles expressed a desire to see the general, but Johnson's severe illness prevented him from travelling. Therefore he commissioned his aide-de-camp, Peter Wraxall, to present his case to the governor.[41]

Wraxall was sent to Albany with a letter of instructions and a portfolio of sixteen documents. He had become Johnson's right-hand man, a very trusted friend and, as his secretary, an almost indispensable aide. He could personally explain the documents and clarify all points from his own knowledge. Moreover, Johnson wanted him to tour the capitals of the other provinces supporting the expedition and report to their governors. Due to his illness, and in view of the division of opinion in his councils of war, this seemed his only recourse.[42]

Wraxall carried out his mission to Albany with satisfaction to Johnson, brought a personal message to Johnson's sister Catty, and made a good impression on the governor, to whom he gave a glowing account of the general. If anything, he overplayed his hand in describing the difficulties at the camp. Sir Charles did not approve of his continuing on to the other governments, for he said it would tend to discourage them and put Johnson in a bad light.[43] General Shirley, when told of Wraxall's trip, disapproved for other reasons: it would take too long before he could report and would therefore delay the expedition. Moreover, he had for some time held a personal grievance against Wraxall, told Johnson that he did not trust his secretary, and now summarily ordered him to join his company at Oswego. It is hard to view this action of Shirley's as anything but spite; he had no particular need for Wraxall and merely sought to remove him from Johnson's staff. Sir Charles saw this clearly enough and backed Wraxall in his refusal, noting that the public service would suffer it he were to abandon his duties with Johnson.[44]

But the governor and his advisers gave Wraxall a rough time. They brushed away many of the complaints; ridiculed the doctor's reports; doubted the correctness of the report on wagons ("I found I touched a sore place"); doubted Captain Eyre's view of the enemy's artillery; thought the intelligence reports of Robert Rogers unreliable—he should be sent again. "I told them I did not believe another Man in the Army would go, try if there is not, was replyed"; they found the councils of war reports too short and not explicit; Johnson should make them answer specific questions; if orders to build boats and forts were not obeyed, this should be reported to the governments. But Sir Charles was all for more vigor in sending supplies, and he was fully behind Johnson in desiring that work be continued on the two forts. If nothing else, Wraxall had established an important liaison for Johnson, to whom Sir Charles was very favorably disposed. Nor was his time wasted in cultivating friendship with Banyar and others about the governor.[45]

Johnson was now convinced that his difficulties stemmed from the diffusion of authority over his command. He was beholden to five governments and the commander in chief. General Shirley could order him to advance, but could not provide him with the men or supplies which came from the provinces. He could issue orders, but they were not carried out by colonels whose appointments came from their governors, or even from a popular choice of their companies. Johnson wanted to fill the vacancies occasioned by the death of his officers in battle from the best men in the army, but Governor Phips insisted that seniority in the several companies should be observed. Johnson had already expressed disillusionment with some of the officers. He now declared that most of the evils were due to the system.

Sure I am, that the popular channel thro wch. this army in general [en]rolld its officers, was a Capital defect in its Original Construction & wch. has given me inexpressable Vexation & almost constant Obstructions in carrying that little command wch. I have been able to do. A Popular Choice in Military Life & that by new Levies is founded in Ignorance, & will be guided by Caprice, such officers will in all probability be like the heads of a Mob, who must support their preheminence [sic] by unworthy Condesensions, & Indulgences subversive of order & of the very Existence of an Army.

After Assuring you Sir that there are several officers in this Army worthy of the Rank they bear, I will also assure you that there are very many under the Rank of Field officers who are in no respect but by their commissns. superior to any of the Men they command, nay that are utterly incapable of Acting in the posts wch have fallen to their Lot.[46]

He was an amateur soldier, a civilian in military command, but he believed that an army could only be run on military rules and discipline.

For my own Share, I was not bred to Military Life, nor do I claim the knowledge of an experienced officer. I have held myself quite indifft. to the Ceremonials, & only been attentive to essential parts of Discipline. All my Orders if inspected will I believe be found, both easy to be understood & as easily obeyed, yet they have in very few Instances been duly complied with, & many daily & Notoriously Violated. If I am asked why I did not enforce my Authority supposing I had wch. I think I had not the requisite powers to do it. I answer the Evil was too general to admit of a Remedy, it was radical in the Constitution & could not be conquered but by a Dissolution. General Court Martials & Regimental Ones have been held but with a Success suitable to the Fabric which occasioned them.[47]

Courts-martial had been held every few days, considering matters both trivial and consequential—crimes, infractions of discipline, gossip, and the serious questions of supply and courses of action. They were criticized for their evasion, and Wraxall told the governor that those who opposed the general's views in private would not express themselves in council. "Mentioned L[yman] & R[uggles] saying whatever their private Opinion they would not give it in Council against proceeding."[48] Johnson said in an early letter to Shirley, "My Council of War are playing Politicks upon me."[49] Those who because they were from New England, or because they disliked the type of work, did not want to build the fort, rallied around General Lyman, who was a leader of the opposition. When rumors circulated by the faction reached his ears, the general moved to spike them. At a council of war on September 27, he laid it on the line.

The General acquainted this Council of War that One Henry Cooke of Major General Lymans Regt. asserted to Capt. Wraxall that the Expedition to Crown Point was not to go forward this year, for that General Johnson pulled General Lyman back who was for proceeding forward, and that he had heard this from above 100 Persons in this Camp upon wch Capt. Wraxall as Aid de Camp to General Johnson thought it prudent to order the fellow into Confinement, where he now is.

The General then told this Council that he apprehended the circulation of such Groundless False & Malicious Reports would have a tendency to over throw this Expedition & to injure his Character & he must therefore desire this Council of War to the utmost of their power to repress the Growth of such Scandalous Un-truths, and as they have for the Major part been Eye Witnesses to the whole of his Conduct to this Day relative to his Command of the Army, that they would declare their Opinion of his Conduct relative to the above Charge & inform him whether he has neglected any or if there are any further Measures in his power to pursue or Order wch. may Contribute to Expedite the present Expedition against Crown Point.[50]

With General Lyman present, the council declared the words spoken by Henry Cooke to be "false and Groundless," and asserted that General Johnson had done all he could to promote the expedition.[51] Another rumor had been spread reflecting on the conduct of Captain Eyre and his artillery in the engagement, and this too was labeled as "False Malicious Scandalous and Groundless." An ill feeling, or disagreement had arisen between General Lyman and Captain Eyre, who had always been a staunch supporter of the general.[52]

Such conditions would seem to reflect upon the commanding officer as well as upon others, but to have concealed them or to have minimized their importance would have created a false impression everywhere.

Since Wraxall had been unable to carry Johnson's reports to the other provinces, it was decided to send certain officers back to their respective governments. Lieutenant Colonel Pitkin was selected by General Lyman to go to Massachusetts, and Colonel Ruggles was sent to Connecticut. In the meantime, General Shirley had requested the governments to appoint commissioners to meet him in Albany when he came from Oswego. This did not suit the Massachusetts Assembly, but they commissioned Oliver Partridge to go to Albany to make inquiries about the state of the campaign. He met Colonel Ruggles on his journey and found Governor Hardy and his staff in Albany, but there was no meeting of minds.[53]

Efforts were being made to move men and supplies, but there was no real concept of conditions at the camp. There the principal concern of men and officers seemed to be how soon they could get home, be discharged from the service, or at least get to Albany. On October 8, Surgeon Williams wrote, "I supposed the Expedition to Crown Point for this year was at an end. But our recruits begin to come in daily, & the road is full of men & provisions."[54]

Governor Shirley at Oswego wrote little of the conditions which dictated the inactivity of his force and his decision to abandon the attempt on Fort Niagara. There were substantial reasons for his caution: the lateness of the season and the consequent risks of stormy waters on the lake (although some blamed this upon the general's delay in reaching Oswego); the threat to the security of the forts at Oswego from the French across the lake, especially if he left behind only a small garrison; and the probability that if he succeeded in demolishing or taking Fort Niagara it would be difficult for him to hold it. Finally he called a council of war which advised the postponement of the attempt until next year.[55]

It was not only the Crown Point campaign which he wished to consider with commissioners at Albany. As the successor of Braddock as commander in chief, he hoped to assert his authority and to make provision for the campaigns of 1756 on all fronts. He had ordered Colonel Dunbar and his troops to Albany either to assist against Crown Point, or in the event of Johnson's failure to serve as the defense of that city. And he expected further to fortify the Indian country of the Six Nations against any French attack.[56] Thus General Shirley was not just coming to Albany with the aim of curbing Johnson and countering his authority or command, but the steps he took were on such a collision course.

On his journey up to Oswego General Shirley had held Indian conferences at which he had tried to raise his Indian auxiliaries but in which he also spoke as commander in chief. Now, on his return to Albany by whaleboat (by which he hoped to show the serviceability of this craft for his next campaign), he held conferences with the Indians and told them their castles would be protected by forts constructed there and to be garrisoned by his regular troops. When he informed Governor Hardy of this plan, however, he met objection. Hardy had learned from the Indians that they preferred to keep only the troops already garrisoned there, and he suggested that this matter should fall in the province of General Johnson, who had a commission from Braddock for the management of Indian affairs.[57]

Shirley left Oswego October 24 and arrived in Albany November 4. Meanwhile his troops were coming down and being quartered in Albany, and he had problems with his own command. It was a weak and dispirited army, too, which had little to show for its efforts. According to the missionary Gideon Hawley, many were of a "vile character" who deserted and made a bad impression on the Indians.[58]

Shirley was eager to turn his attention to other matters, and he had an ill-concealed hope that Johnson would prove a failure as commander. Writing to Secretary Robinson, October 5, he asserted Johnson had as many as eight thousand men, but he had reason to think that the outcome of the campaign "will be a disatisfactory one to all the colonies of New England, as well as to myself." At this time Johnson's effectives were only three thousand.[59]

The commissioners from Connecticut and Massachusetts were repeatedly told of the conditions at camp and the indifference of the troops. But the resolution and determination of General Shirley overcame their doubts and won them for a more optimistic view. On November 17, at a meeting in Shirley's lodgings, it was "recommend[ed] as the Opinion and Advise ... of the Members of this Meeting that the Army under the Command of Major Genl. Johnson, do advance against the Enemy, and attempt to remove them from their encroachments as far as they are able this season."[60]

When this resolution reached Johnson he laid it before the council of war, remarking that it was "next to an absolute Order for this Army proceeding forthwith against the Enemy." Shirley's accompanying letter, however, implied his doubts. He demanded that Johnson tell him "by the Return of this Express as soon as possible what Number of Men you shall think necessary to employ in the Attempt, wch. you shall forthwith make against the Enemy, in case you determine to make one"; what artillery he proposed to use, the number of men his bateaux could carry over the lake and what provisions he had for the attempt. This put Johnson on the spot, and he asked the council of war for their resolution. They were unanimous that it was "not advseable," and repeated the reasons given before: the advanced season and difficulties of a winter campaign, inadequate supplies of clothing and shelter for such a campaign, and insufficient transport and lack of provisions.[61]

Far more compelling than these, however, was the deteriorating morale of the men. Enlistments were expiring, the New Hampshire men had left, and when the Connecticut troops threatened to march off, it was feared that others would not go on scouts. Their monthly pay was overdue, their provisions were short, and they could be mollified only for brief periods. Some groups had marched off, and then been brought back. Officers in private admitted the condition, but in public or in council dared not assert it. General Lyman in particular, said Johnson, glossed over his apprehensions. But the officers generally believed "if the Men were ordered to go forward the greatest part of them would flatly refuse."[62]

And yet plans to make some sort of an advance against the enemy had been pressed by the general, although short of an attack upon the forts. Much of the argument concerned the enemy's strength and his positions, so that scouts and small reconnoitering parties were sent out almost daily. Many of the provincials were not suited for this kind of work, however, and their reports were unsatisfactory or conflicting. And the Indians, who were best adapted for the scouting with their knowledge of the country, had not returned in any force and were usually used in conjunction with rangers.[63] Thus Johnson found his chief support among the frontier irregulars, of whom Captain Robert Rogers of New Hampshire was outstanding.

Rogers had enlisted in the New Hampshire company of Colonel Blanchard. During the battle of September 8 he had been out on scout, so had no part in the third engagement in which the New Hampshire men had fought. But his forays up the lake in pursuit of stray captives and his daring infiltration to within sixty rods of the enemy's camp to gain intelligence supplied the general with information then relayed to the Council in Albany.[64] This was questioned, because it was unpalatable; but Rogers had been warmly supported by Wraxall. Then Johnson wrote Governor Hardy

of Capt. Rodgers whose Bravery & Veracity stands very clear in my Opinion & of all who know him, tho his Reg. is gone he remains here a Volunteer, & is the most active Man in our Army. Tomorrow he proposes to set off with two or three picked Men take a review if he can of Tionderogo & proceed to Crown Point for a Prisr. . . . I have mentioned Capt. Rodgers more particularly as I have Understood some Insinuations have been made to his Disadvantage I believe him to be as brave & as honest a Man as any I have equal knowledge of, & both myself & all the Army are convinced that he has distinguished himself since he has been among us, superior to most, inferior to none of his Rank in these Troops.[65]

On his scout of October 14, referred to by Johnson, Rogers with four men reached Crown Point, lay ambushed sixty rods from the fort, which he judged to have a garrison of five hundred, caught and scalped a Frenchman, and then went on to Ticonderoga, where he reported about two thousand men.[66] This was the kind of intelligence on which Johnson could rely; too often scouts feared to approach the camp closely and gave vague and unreliable reports.

On October 30, General Johnson went before the council of war with a proposal to send a force to cut off the French advance camp, which his scouts estimated had no more than eighty men. There were eighty-five bateaux fit for use, and the plan seemed feasible. If successful, the exploit would encourage Indian support, raise the reputation of the army, weaken the French, and reduce the danger from their scalping parties. But the council voted it "not adviseable," and preferred to wait upon further reports from Captain Rogers. "The men were all possessed of a firm

Persuasion that we were to proceed no further this Fall, that finishing the Fort was to be their last Labour."[67]

When two Indians came back and excitedly recorded their surprise to find the French encampment "so large they had never seen the like and the Encampt. at this Lake was nothing in Comparison" the caution seemed well founded.[68] But a later scout by Daniel Claus and Lieutenant Richard Rogers found the French abandoning their outposts. There was no smoke, and the place seemed desolate. It was now late in November; the hardships of the scout were great, and the weather forced an early return.[69] The time for a decisive action had passed.

On November 20, a meeting at Albany of General Shirley, Governor Hardy, Lieutenant Governor De Lancey, some members of the New York Council, and the commissioners from Massachusetts and Connecticut, agreed that the army under General Johnson's command, save for about six hundred to garrison the forts, should be discharged. The commissioners, then about to set off for the lake, were to decide in a council with field officers and the general what numbers should be detained and how divided between Fort William Henry and Fort Edward. The meeting here further decided that these garrisons should be subsisted and paid by the provinces in the following proportion: Massachusetts Bay, 185; Connecticut, 154; New York, 123; New Hampshire, 77; and Rhode Island, 61.[70]

Setting off the following day, the commissioners of the three provinces were provided an escort to Fort Edward at the Carrying Place, where Johnson was asked to have them met and escorted by fifty men. They were also accompanied by twenty-five wagons of supplies. At Fort Edward, Colonel Gridley informed them of the precarious state of the troops in the camp.[71] The New York commissioners bore a letter from Governor Hardy to Johnson which strongly implied that on carrying out these affairs he was to leave the camp and to devote himself to his commission for Indian affairs.[72]

The council of war met the commissioners November 24–26 at Fort William Henry with full attendance. General Johnson laid before them the directive from Albany. The number of men to garrison the two forts was set at 750—430 at Fort William Henry and 320 at Fort Edward—and the proportions as adopted at Albany were to be followed. Lyman and three other officers objected that these numbers were too heavy for their respective governments. The men selected were to form detachments, and their officers were designated.[73]

That Fort William Henry was at all in readiness, although much remained to be done, was due to the determination of Johnson in the face of official opposition and downright obstruction on the part of men and officers. General Shirley had opposed it from the start, saying that a picketed, or stockaded, camp was enough and that Fort Edward would be more defensible.[74] The council of war took the same position, and the men were reluctant to do the extra work. They also preferred to think that this was a temporary stop in the campaign.[75] But Captain Eyre as engineer had laid out the plan for a fort on the lake in what he considered a defensible position. And as time went on without advance the plan seemed more feasible. Governor Hardy came out strongly for a "more respectable Fort than a picketed one," and the council of war finally on September 29 approved.[76] But the men and officers, to the point of mutiny, held up the works and delayed construction. Officers questioned its value and location and the general's motives. Johnson wrote warmly to Governor Fitch of Connecticut.

As to the Fort building here, whatever insinuations have been made to your Honour to the contrary, I am convinced the ground is the most Advantageous of any wch could be chosen here & has not within 370 paces of it any rising Ground wch commands it, and that distance is not within Battery in Breach.[77]

On the same day on which he wrote this letter he wrote one to Hardy which showed that his exasperation had reached its zenith. He then had four thousand men fit for duty, of whom not more than three to five hundred had been at work on the fort, although the council of war had stipulated seven hundred when there were only twenty-six hundred fit for duty. In this he had not been supported by but a few of the officers. It was time for a showdown.

I have issued out this Morning a fresh order in the most peremptory manner for 1/3 of each Regt. in camp to go upon the Works. I am determined if this order is disobeyed by only one [or] two Cols. to put them under arrest, if too general I shall be almost tempted to leave the Command of the Army to Genl. Lyman & make a Remonstrance upon it. Genl. Lyman has always been a great Enemy to this Fort & dos every thing in his Power to throw cold water upon it. Says tis only beneficial to New York, will be disapproved by the other Govts. who will not consent to Garrison it, &c.[78]

Hence the fort was far from being completed when the council ordered that it be garrisoned by a detachment of the several provinces. Although the quota was four hundred and thirty men, the barracks would house scarce half that number; tents and temporary huts would have to be used while the garrison continued to labor on the barracks and the works.[79] Johnson's orders to the commander, Colonel Jonathan Bagley, directed him to complete the works as laid out by the engineer, Captain Eyre; to level the old camp lest it be used as an ambush by an enemy; to put the place in readiness in the event of an attack, following the advices of Captain Eyre; to send out "constant Scouting Parties round you of about 6 or 7. And if any of our allied Indians should come to the Fort to receive them kindly and Friendly."[80]

Thus Johnson on leaving Lake George hoped that the defensive measures which he had fathered would be adequate to contain the enemy. The forces, alas, were far below the quota assigned. Colonel Bagley reported that he lacked 196 of the more than 400 allotted him. And there were also shortages in materials and supplies. Johnson ordered 113 men to be sent up from Fort Edward to meet the quota.[81]

Fort Edward at the Carrying Place had been started at the outset of the campaign, first by Lyman, enclosing the old "house of Lydius." It was the way station for the transport of supplies from Albany and therefore of importance in the line of communication. Having escaped the French attack, it contained a small garrison after the battle. Captain Eyre as engineer had drawn up plans for its works and barracks, and its officers and men had worked upon them when time permitted. But it was constantly losing its men and supplies to the advance post at Lake

George. Now, as General Johnson himself stopped there on his journey back to Albany, he gave attention to the condition of the fort.[82]

Fort Edward had labored under the same difficulties as Fort William Henry—the disinclination of the men to do the work, the changing personnel, and the shortage in this case of tools and building materials. The barracks were the chief concern, for with winter approaching the men needed comfortable shelters. Two stories in height with stone chimneys, they presented a definite objective—there was not as much desire to work on the bastions and earthworks. On November 28, Johnson gave an encouraging report to Shirley. "The Barracks for this Fort are not finished but when compleated will contain & that commodiously the Garrison for this Fort, were all the Materials at hand & the Men to work briskly they might be compleated in about a Fortnights time."[83]

Colonel Nathan Whiting was given command of the detachment to be stationed here, and his orders were like those sent to Colonel Bagley. And he, too, found his contingent short of the allotted quota. He was seventy-five short of the number stipulated. Worse, however, was his lack of men to finish the building.[84]

I dont find I have above ten or twelve Carpenters & but two Sawyers & them borrowed of Col Bagley. They I immagine are gone to the other fort with their Comrades: What a bad Situation the fort is in, & what want of every thing you perfectly know.[85]

As these irregular contingents were disbanded and their men, save those designated for the garrisons, filtered back to their homes, there were judgments pro and con. It was hard not to apologize for the failure to advance in nearly three months. Governor Hardy, returning to New York, wrote to the Lords of Trade:

The miscarriage of this Expedition is owing to many circumstances but principally to a want of care in carrying up a proper quantity of Provisions in Store at Lake George, before the arrival of the whole body of reinforcements raised after the battle on the 8th of September last.[86]

He then recounted his own efforts to provide supplies and their transportation, but he added also that reinforcement of the French forts and the advancing winter season had made the council of war unanimous in their decision. However, Hardy felt that the expedition had not been without its great achievement.

I shall only beg leave to observe to you, that though the Army under the Command of General Johnson has not been able to reach Crown Point this year they have advanced the Frontiers of His Majesty's Dominions by building two very respectable Forts, at the Expence of the Provinces.[87]

General Johnson on reaching Albany wrote to the several governors in his own defense, anticipating or refuting criticism, and assessing the achievement of their forces.

I think myself obliged to observe to you—that altho the Sanguine Hopes & over-eager Expectations of the Governments concerned, are disappointed, and which I am informed have been in a great measure nursed & strengthened by some of our own Corps from (as I apprehend political & selfish Motives)—in spight of the Envy or Malice of others. I say in opposition to These or any other Causes of public Discontent, I think my self obliged to observe to You Gentlemen, that our Army hath had the honour by the singular favour of Divine Providence, of defeating some part of that formidable & ambitious Plan which was concerted at the Court of France & put into the hands of the Baron Dieskau to execute. a Plan Gentlemen, which had not this army been the chosen Instrument of putting into Confusion, would very probably not only have destroyed all our other Military Operations, have totally lost us all our remaining Indian Allies, but have plunged these Northern Colonies into the most calamitous sittuation & opened Streams of Blood from every vein.[88]

Following this line of thought, the letter was somewhat plaintive rather than apologetic; it commended some officers and men—particularly Peter Wraxall, William Eyre, and Beamsly Glaser, who had assumed extraordinary duties without additional pay[89]—and laid the principal blame on a system which made efficient command impossible. This was his valedictory as commander.

I have to the utmost extent of my Abilities faithfully & Diligently discharged the Trust reposed in me. . . . I look upon my Command as now at an End & my Authority no longer to exist. If I am herein mistaken, I must beg to surrender my Commission as Major General & Commander in chief of the Provincial Forces on the Expedition against Crown Point, and to declare my disinclination to act any longer in that Capacity.[90]

XVIII

FAME AND CONTROVERSY

While General Johnson at Lake George was suffering, both physically and mentally, with as frustrating an experience as ever befell a commander in the field, his fame abroad was soaring. It was the first notable British success after a series of defeats; the capture of General Dieskau atoned for the loss of Braddock and was a blow to French prestige.[1] Furthermore, Johnson, an inexperienced provincial with irregular troops, had succeeded while professional soldiers with regulars had failed. He was acclaimed as a near genius, the "heaven-sent" general, and his skill, diplomacy, and humanity were toasted. His reported uncanny power over the Indian tribes added a romantic glamor to the hero. His own account of the battle and those which followed added new luster. An Irish friend wrote that his "glorious victory" over the "perfidious French" caused "our whole kingdom to be overjoyed." But they "could expect no less from the nephew of the Brave Sir Peter Warren." And the former governor, George Clinton, noted that "your name is up on every Occasion in the House of Commons."[2]

In the colonies the victory was a spur to enlistments and renewed the flow of troops to join the campaign. It was a boon to the morale of the frontier settlements, so shaken by Braddock's defeat, and bolstered the self-esteem of the provincial governments. Governors showered the commander with effusive letters of thanks and congratulation.[3] Colonial cities burst into celebration and quite naturally acclaimed the general. When the news reached New York City, the "Fort fired for Joy; and was answered by the *Sphinx* in the Harbour."[4] Sir Charles Hardy, the new governor, left for Albany, where on October 2 he participated in a day of public thanksgiving.[5] And in Charleston, South Carolina, the printer of the *Gazette* noted the public reaction to the victory.

As soon as the above News became publick, the Gloom that sat on our Countenances, since the Defeat of the late brave General Braddock, was instantly removed and a universal Joy took Place; And all the Vessels in the Harbour immediately hoisted their Colours, and fired continual Rounds of Cannon, till Night, when several of them were ornamented with Lights; At Night a greater Number of the

Houses in Town were illuminated than has been known for many Years, and every where nothing was to be heard, but Rejoicing and loyal Toasts, with *Long live victorious JOHNSON.* In short, our Joy was too great to be expressed.[6]

Johnson's friends were quick to note his mounting fame and to urge upon him a public rôle. He was now vindicated in his measures and strengthened in his official position, while his opponents or detractors were confounded. His friends saw an opportunity for his future preferment and sought to capitalize on his rising fortunes. Goldsbrow Banyar, the deputy secretary, reported the goodwill of Governor Hardy as the latter departed for Albany. "I find your character and Consequence are both well known at home, and Sr Charles makes no doubt of the Ministrys getting you an appointment equal to your great Merit."[7]

But Thomas Pownall, a friend since the days of the Albany Congress, a persistent correspondent in search of geographical and ethnic data, and a political intriguer of ambition and resourcefulness, sought to be both his mentor and personal agent.

There are two things upon which every Man must rest his Merits, one his own Right Conduct ye other the Reality of his Freinds, ye First is in your own Breast & You will command it.—The Other give me leave to assure You off, Your Interest in this latter is & shall be secured. I have receivd such Accts from England as will putt it into my Power to be of Service to You. if I go home I can more Particularly. if I stay here I shall have Instructions to appear at ye next Congress as a Principal for ye Govr of NJersey, to which it has pleasd His Majesty to appoint me Lt Govr. with a Destination (at ye same time) to ye Govr. on a Vacancy. Do not Lett Your personal Courage carry You beyond what is ye Duty of a General.[8]

Banyar, Pownall, Richard Shuckburgh, and Peter Wraxall urged Johnson to write directly to the ministry in his own behalf, saying that his messages might be conveyed by Pownall, whose brother John was secretary to the Lords of Trade. Peter Wraxall was formulating his representations as to Indian affairs.[9]

Johnson meanwhile was so preoccupied with the problems of his command, his illness, and his thoughts of Indian affairs, that he had little concern for his own preferment. What he wanted above all was to separate himself from this impossible conjunction of command and Indian affairs, and to follow his own destiny as he saw it. But he could not escape the logic of his actions; his previous remonstrances and his controversy with Shirley had projected him into the maelstrom of ministerial politics.

At Albany, December 1-4, General Johnson had dispatched his orders to the commanders of the forts, his resignation from his military command to the governors, and invitations to the Indian tribes to meet him immediately at his house for a conference.[10] This latter action was pressed upon him by the importunities of the Indians. Their castles and settlements were menaced by the French, whose agents were moving among them, and they asked for assurances from the English. They demanded fulfillment of promises to fortify them with defenses and garrisons. Moreover, reports from Pennsylvania of depredations on the frontier had reached Governor Hardy, and he asked that Johnson use his influence with the Six Nations to check their dependents.[11]

Now, too, he wanted to return to his home, which much needed his attention.

Mount Johnson had been renamed "Fort Johnson" and wore the aspect of a military outpost. In wartime, barracks there had housed a company, and Banyar now asked if he wanted another. A blockhouse flanked the gate, and a low parapet provided emplacements for small cannon. Other blockhouses were provided later.[12] It was suggested that an attack might come from the north, and Pownall with his knowledge of geography suggested that a picketed fort with magazine might be built there as an outwork.[13]

In the midst of all these concerns came repeated requests to present himself in the city of New York. Governor Hardy wanted him to report there "as soon as possible after you have met and conversed with the principal Sachems and leading men of the six Nations." General Shirley on leaving Albany for New York requested that Johnson come to see him there before he left about December 7, stating that if he did not come then, "it will be necessary for me to see you at Boston as soon as may be."[14] Both requests Johnson found quite impractical. Then his friends—Pownall, Wraxall and Banyar—urged him to come speedily. "A reception from many friends here is intended you, wch will do you great honour & give the Attorney Genl. great Chagrin."[15] Already some were thinking of how such a visit might become a triumph for him and counter the efforts of the opposition.

They intend on your arival to have 6 of their Capital Mercht. Men haled out in Batalia in the Stream to proclaim it in so audable a Manner as the Sound thereof shall be both grating & Irksome to the few here whose private piques or late Contracted dirty party Prejudices would wish you a different reception & lest your Modesty should induce you to shun a complimt. of this kind they beg the favour yr. permission & of your acquainting them when you are within a few Miles of this City to the End their attempt may be conducted with such Decency & regularity as may make it ornamental both to themselves & Country—[16]

Criticism of Johnson ranged from the statement that he had failed to take his objective, Crown Point, to the suggestion that the whole battle was overplayed and not a victory at all. Partisans of Shirley and the New England governments sought to diminish his reputation lest it be used to elevate his friends and their enemies. Some newspapers slyly insinuated that he could not compare with other victorious generals: "I can tell you the Story of *another* General, who undertook a March of about One Hundred and ten-Miles.—His march was very cautious and very *slow*—for in five Months he advanc'd about sixty Miles, and in that Time his Army consum'd as much Bread and Meat as almost caus'd a Famine, and then *decamp'd for Want of Provisions.*" He was not a New England man and was unlike General Pepperell, who "never call'd a Council of War to know whether it was proper to proceed or not, for he knew his Orders."[17]

In reply Johnson's friends published laudatory verses.

> To Major General Johnson
> With ev'ry Patriot Virtue Crown'd
> Disdain the Lye by Malice spread;
> The Shafts that strive thy *FAME* to Wound,
> Hiss unregarded o'er thy head.[18]

If Johnson could let these barbs fly unobserved, he was not so sure about the steps taken by General Shirley. On September 3, he had sent to the ministry his severe charges against Shirley's interference with his Indian policy. The severity and bitterness of his words then have caused some to believe that he started the quarrel with Shirley, who had not yet reported his disagreement with Johnson. But this was the acme of his resentment against the commander, containing a demand for freedom in Indian policy or to be relieved entirely of it. His charges against his superior while in the field, when the issue of his own campaign was in doubt, were most indiscreet. A more cautious person would have avoided such a wholesale indictment. Had he failed at Lake George, he would have been pilloried for his indiscretion. "I am under no doubt that he is become my inveterate enemy and that the whole weight of his Power & abilities will be exerted to blast if he can my Character."[19] Smarting, then, under repeated provocative incidents in the field of Indian relations (which he considered his own), he lashed out against one of the ablest politicians in the colonies. He might well expect retaliation.

Hence, when on December 7, Shirley sent him a new and revised commission to conduct Indian affairs he suspected an underlying motive. Shirley had decided to curb Johnson's power over the Indians by placing him directly under his orders, and by deleting the phrase "sole management" from his commission. If Johnson refused to accept the appointment, which he rather anticipated, he would replace him with Conrad Weiser. This was his declared intention.[20] Shirley also demanded to know whether Johnson had received a royal commission.

You will let me know by the return of this express whether you have received any other Commission than that from the late General Braddock relative to the care of the Indians and how far I may depend upon your acting under the inclosed Commission and proceeding in the Service I now direct you to go upon, that in case you may decline it, I may otherwise provide against His Majesty's Service being disappointed by that means.[21]

Johnson hesitated; Shirley became insistent upon an immediate reply. Governor Hardy pressed Johnson to accept the new commission lest Indian affairs should suffer if he withdrew.[22] Johnson was in the midst of negotiations, and new instructions with a diminution of authority presented him with a dilemma, which he reported to the Lords of Trade. This letter may have influenced his later appointment.

By my military engagemts I have not been able to be at my own House, or in the Indian Country one day these four months, and now I am last got home, and am just entering into the administration of Indian affairs, so as to form and conduct them to the extent of my knowledge and abilities for the good of His Majestys service, I am again obstructed and every thing put to a stand by Genll Shirleys sending me a new commission and Instruction for the management of Indian Affairs and ordering me to attend him either at New York or Boston, the least of which is 200 miles distant from hence; this journey I am but ill quallified for, upon account of my wound the effects of which I still feel.[23]

Johnson frankly admitted that he had no other commission than that from General Braddock, although "I have this long time been told there was a Commission from his Majesty for me, and that it was sent by the late General Braddock, but I never received any, nor pay for the one I had of him, alltho I have neglected all my own business, on account of it and suffered much thereby."[24] He had some intimation that a new commission from England was coming. Now rather than serve with restricted powers, he insisted that a new commission was not necessary and that he should be permitted to serve under the one he had. The upshot of it was that Shirley, rather than disrupt negotiations in progress, allowed this point if Johnson would admit his power to give instructions. But it required a trip to New York to iron this out.[25]

General Shirley had a concept for the campaigns of 1756 which was imperial in scope. It was consistent with his earlier schemes for an all-out attack on French Canada, for which he had worked as peace commissioner in Paris in 1750-52.[26] If adopted, it would sweep away all criticism of his failure at Oswego, and would overshadow the limited success of Johnson. He came to New York on December 2 to press for its adoption. But the cool reception which he received made him redouble his exertions. Governor Hardy was now a critic of Shirley, if not his enemy; he was at dinner when Shirley arrived, and there was a delay of an hour before the customary guns of salute were heard. Shirley repaired to the home of his secretary, William Alexander, and gathered around him kindred spirits—the Livingstons (William, Philip, and Robert R.) and William Smith. Exuding the charm for which he was celebrated, Shirley impressed upon all his grasp of imperial politics, in which he was an experienced negotiator. "General entertained us with a Narrative of the Conduct of the French Commissioners at Paris relating to the settlement of Limits according to the Treaty of Aix La Chapelle, . . . Then he opened his view of the Importance of Oswego & the Lake, that he designed against Frontenac and La Gallette where he proposed to build a Strong Fort on an Island."[27]

This plan of making Fort Frontenac, Oswego, and the St. Lawrence the objective of his campaign was adopted by the council of war composed of governors and officers that met on December 12-13. Fearful of the influence of Hardy, he sent for Governor Robert Hunter Morris of Pennsylvania; and he excluded from the meeting Thomas Pownall (who as lieutenant governor of New Jersey sought to represent Governor Belcher) and James De Lancey of the opposing faction.[28]

Shirley also began a pamphlet war in support of his project. The celebrated mapmaker, Lewis Evans, in June 1755 issued his "Map of the Middle Colonies," which he dedicated to Thomas Pownall in "Gratitude for his Great Assistance." This was enough to make Evans an opponent of Shirley, but in the accompanying *Analysis* and description he emphasized the importance of the Ohio Valley and the backcountry for the future of America, rather than the area about its lakes, where attacks might exhaust the strength of the provinces. Although published before Shirley's plan was known, it was conceived to be in opposition to his ideas. Hence Shirley planted a newspaper attack upon Evans, specifically for calling Frontenac and the territory north of Lake Ontario French. The ideas were Shirley's but the letter was written by William Smith and was printed in Gaines's *New York Mercury*, January 5, 1756.[29]

The sequel was Evans's *Analysis No. 2*, which was not only a defense of his views, but an attack upon Shirley, his campaigns, conduct, and reputation. Subsequently he was sued in the New York Court for a libel on Governor Morris of Pennsylvania; he had been befriended by Benjamin Franklin and was regarded as of the anti-proprietary party. Thrown into jail and unable to furnish bail (although that was later provided by Oliver De Lancey), Evans died before he could be brought to trial or released.[30]

Before leaving New York for Boston, General Shirley dispatched to London with his plans Captain Staats Long Morris, an aide as well as a nephew of Governor Morris of Pennsylvania, and Major John Rutherford, a member of his council of war. There they were to be confronted with the ubiquitous Thomas Pownall.[31]

Thus it was to offset Shirley's faction that Pownall and the De Lanceys held the celebration in honor of Johnson. His friends and wellwishers in New York were numerous and had expressed their desire to do him honor. And they did not conceal their pleasure in thus embarrassing Shirley. William Smith, the unfriendly diarist, said "Twas a party Business to put Contempt upon Mr. Shirley . . . Oliver De Lancey's House and those who were no Friends of Shirley illuminated their Houses in the Evening."[32] It was on December 30 that Johnson arrived, and the events of the occasion were described in the press.

Last Tuesday Major General *JOHNSON* arrived here from Albany: About 6 Miles out of Town, he was met by a considerable Number of Gentlemen on Horseback, who conducted him to the King's Arms Tavern, where most of the Principal Inhabitants were assembled to Congratulate him on his safe Arrival; The Ships in the Harbour saluted him as he passed the Streets, amidst the Acclamation's of the People. At Night the City was beautifully illuminated, and the general joy displayed on this Occasion, evidenced the highest Gratitude of the People for the singular Services this Gentleman has done his Country in the late Expedition.[33]

Smith noted that the cavalcade included "Several Coaches, Chairs and Horsemen," while Daniel Claus, who accompanied Johnson, said he was escorted to his lodgings. The festivities of the night were such that Johnson found himself in no condition to meet General Shirley the next day. He then received an invitation to be his guest at dinner.[34]

More important, no doubt, than this eighteenth-century counterpart of a "ticker-tape" welcome were the private counsels in which Johnson had a part. Daniel Claus described the small group who gathered in Johnson's room—"his most intimate friends . . . such as Govr. Pownall of the Jerseys, Colo. Oliver DeLancey, Mr. [John] Watts, Mr. Secretary [Goldsbrow] Banyar of the Provce. & Capt. [Peter] Wraxall."[35]

As if Johnson were not sufficiently aware of the differences between him and General Shirley, and of the latter's enmity toward him, Claus related:

Govr. Pownall told Genl. Johnson in confidence that altho he had been so well rec'd just now (and made so successful a campn.) that General Shirley & party were his declared Enemies and going to make serious & heavy Complaints against Him laying the whole Blame upon Him for not having done anything in their Expedn. agst Niagara on Acct. of his having sent a Belt of Wampum to the Six Nation's clandestinely that not a man of them would join General Shirley's Expedn.; which accordingly was the Case & he had no Indians & without whom he could not pretend to go on with his Troops & that he Genl. Johnson had diametrically acted contrary to his orders Instructions of which he should officially acquaint the Kings Ministers.[36]

Claus went on that Johnson heatedly denied this, that he had no knowledge of such; and was told that Shirley had the very belts of wampum sent to the Six Nations advising them not to join him; then when Johnson again denied there was such a belt, Claus spoke up and revealed how he had persuaded the tribes and King Hendrick not to follow Shirley, but to go with Johnson. The company was astonished at Claus's revelation and agreed that to clear this up an affidavit should be made and sent with Johnson's report to the ministry, thus to forestall Shirley's criticism.[37]

This story has been much quoted and, coupled with the assertions of the writer of the *Review*, has been interpreted to substantiate the charge of a "cabal" against Shirley. But it is dubious in many of its details. It seems incredible that Johnson could have been unaware of the sending of the belt by the Mohawks; or that Claus had no opportunity (he was with him a great deal in the intervening months) to inform him; or that the Indians would have kept him ignorant of the facts. Certainly it was not necessary at this late date for Pownall to tell him that Shirley was his enemy; Johnson had said so vehemently several times, as in his letter to the Board of Trade above cited. Also Claus's statement that his revelation in an affidavit was put in the official report of the campaign is not borne out by the facts, nor was it included in material submitted to the ministry. And Claus failed to mention the principal issue between Johnson and Shirley, the new commission.[38]

That this informal group made plans to promote Johnson's interest, and to counteract the moves of the opposition, is quite obvious. Yet it was no more an insidious cabal, as the opposition asserted, than the group of Shirley's friends who met at "Billy" Alexander's. Johnson asked Peter Wraxall to draw up a statement of his views and the condition of Indian affairs to be presented to the ministry. But he soon met with Governor Shirley, on the latter's invitation, and they came to an agreement as to the commission and their future cooperation.[39]

The issues between the factions were next taken to London. Shirley's agents, Major John Rutherford and Captain Staats Morris, sailed on December 25; and on February 8, Thomas Pownall left on a long-deferred journey.[40] Presenting opposite points of view on many issues, these agents greatly perplexed the Board of Trade, but eventually the ideas of Pownall prevailed.

Pownall had found his position as lieutenant governor of New Jersey irksome and unrewarding, and he was angling for a new appointment. Ambitious, and convinced of his ability to influence the government, he had been planning his journey as early as October, when he approached Johnson. A persistent correspondent through these trying months, he gave ear to Johnson's complaints and offered to present his views of Indian affairs to the ministry. On the one hand he plied Johnson with queries on geography, ethnology, and the etymology of Indian words;

on the other he expressed his complete understanding of Johnson's thoughts on Indian administration. If only the heads of topics were given him, he said, he could explain Johnson's plans and measures. His fertile mind produced a variety of schemes which he was indefatigable in promoting. Believing that to be "well heard & to have weight is to talk with precision & punctuality so as to be understood & to be depended upon," he was well prepared and fortified with recommendations and papers.[41] Johnson wrote the Board of Trade on January 17, commending "Mr. Pownall who I find is going to England as he knows every particular of my Sentiments & is also perfectly acquainted with Indian affairs."[42] On military affairs he was commended to the ministry by Sir John St. Clair, deputy quartermaster general. And on Pennsylvania politics he posed a triple threat; he was a friend of Evans, Franklin, and Isaac Norris for his views on geography and the frontier; he was denounced by Richard Peters and William Allen for his attitude toward the proprietors; and he was a candidate for the governorship to succeed Morris.[43]

A prolific writer and pamphleteer, Pownall early conceived of that method of promoting Johnson's interest. In October he had written:

I can see no Impropriety if You think it Proper (but before 'tis done I will take Advice from Home,) to have published Your Late Treaty. The Benefit of Which Mr. Wraxal is intitled to & should have. It will sell so as to raise more money than wd. appear at first sight. I will take ye. Trouble to see it done, & will (without putting my name in public) write a Preface to it pointing out ye. Leading Matters to it in ye. former state of Indian Politics, together with a Short Account of ye. Indians their Govt., their Method of Treaties &c. Give me Your answer to this, I mean to make it point out Your Services by an Induction of ye. strongest sort.— & to putt your Interest on a Right bottom.—[44]

Upon his arrival in England, Pownall found that the situation had changed in his favor. Already Shirley had been superseded by the appointment of a professional soldier, John Campbell, Earl of Loudoun, to command the forces in America. Johnson had been singled out for honors, and his aides had been rewarded or promoted. The principal concern of the ministry was now military policy, the commission and instructions to be given Lord Loudoun. On these Pownall and Shirley's agents represented opposite views, but Pownall had a decided advantage. Better prepared than they with pertinent information, he also had influential friends at court, his brother John and the Earl of Halifax. So Pownall routed his rivals, and when Loudoun finally reached America he had with him Pownall as "Secretary Extraordinary." Young William, son of Dr. Samuel Johnson of Kings College, said the ministry were perplexed by the conflicting opinions, but that "Morris, finding Shirley's side the weakest, began to turn about and contradict many things which he had before affirmed."[45] Morris's disappointing report, which reached Shirley April 16, was softened only by the rumor that he was to receive the governorship of Jamaica.[46] So the way was cleared for successors in both of Shirley's offices.

Much as Pownall desired to be of service to Johnson abroad, he learned upon his arrival in London that both honors and administrative authority were already bestowed.[47] The graphic reports of the battle of Lake George, as well as the persuasive accounts of Indian affairs of the past summer, had greatly impressed the ministry. Popular response to the victory and repeated testimonials to the general's valor, wisdom, and character had so enhanced his reputation as to demand public recognition. His laurels were still green when in November his honors were gazetted in London: "Whitehall, Nov, 18, 1755. The King has been pleased to grant unto Wm. Johnson of New York, America, Esqr. and his heirs male the dignity of a Baronet of Great Britain."[48] A letter from Secretary Robinson, dated November 11, noted that Johnson's "printed circular letter, containing an account of the success of His Majesty's arms in the Action near Lake George on the 8th Septr. and the gallant behaviour of the Troops under your command, has been laid before the King." He further commended on behalf of the King "the great and eminent service you have performed"; "the prudence, Judgment and precaution, which you showed in sending to the New England Governments before the action, for reinforcements"; and the vigorous action of the colonies in sending troops to his support. Finally, the Secretary had "the particular satisfaction of having it in charge to acquaint you, that the King has been graciously pleased to confer upon you, as a distinguishing mark of His Royal favour and approbation of your conduct, the dignity of a Baronet of Great Brittain; and the patent will be accordingly transmitted you by the first convenient opportunity."[49]

This letter did not reach Johnson until the following March 20, but news of the honor was heard in Philadelphia and New York, February 2-3.[50] At the time of the London announcement, the outcome of his campaign was unknown and it was rumored that "if he returns victorious from Crown Point, he will be invested with the Order of the Bath."[51]

The patent, which made the title official, was dated November 27, but was even longer in reaching America, arriving with Colonel Daniel Webb in June 1756. No doubt the new baronet was a bit bewildered by the terminology and style of this significant piece of parchment so beautifully illuminated and decorated with the portrait of His Majesty George II.[52] He might well have glowed with pride as he read of himself—"Our Trusty and Welbeloved Subject William Johnson of Our Colony of New York in America Esquire (a Man Eminent for ffamily Inheritance Estate and Integrity of Manners)." Perhaps he was puzzled, as many have been since, to find no reference here to his military service, or his management of Indian affairs for which he was so commended by the Board of Trade. Instead he was cited as one "who generously and freely gave and ffurnished to Us an Ayd and Supply large enough to Maintain and Support Thirty Men in Our ffoot Companies in Our Said Kingdom of Ireland to continue for three whole Years for the Defence of our said Kingdom and Especially for the Security of the Plantation of our said Province of Ulster."[53]

Little did William Johnson care about Northern Ireland—he showed too little concern even for his own family in County Meath—but he was now blessed with the arms of Ulster. He and his heirs male, they and their descendants, "shall and may bear either in Canton in their Coat of Arms or in an Escutchion at their pleasure the Arms of Ulster (to wit) an Hand Gules or a Bloody Hand in a ffield Argent." He was later to make for himself a coat of arms, not without the "bloody hand."[54]

More important for the future were the definitions of rank and precedence, that he, his wives and those of his male heirs, and descendants should enjoy; the wives were to be called *"Lady, Madam* and *Dame."* And—often overlooked by biographers, but not by the principals—was the promise that "Wee our Heirs and Successors will create and make the first born Son or Heir Male Apparent begotten of the Body of the said William Johnson and of the Bodies of his Heirs Male aforesaid and Every one of them a Knight as soon as he shall attain the age of one and Twenty years although in a Lifetime of his ffather or Grandfather"; upon proper notice being given.[55] While his spouse never used the title of "Lady," or "Dame," his son was to claim his title so provided.

As the second American to receive the title *Baronet*, Sir William Johnson was immediately a personage of eminence and heightened influence. But it is evident that his American friends and partisans had little to do with his gaining this distinction. The views of others, the reports of governors, and the continuing emphasis upon the frontier and the Indian menace in dispatches gave added weight to Johnson's reports on Indian affairs. His lengthy missives to the Board of Trade, while they were still plaintive about his differences with Shirley, were eloquent in their outline of drastic reforms and new measures. To these the ministry were in a receptive mood. They already had determined upon some professionalizing of the American forces (a professional soldier at their head with new levies to be recruited in Europe), and Johnson's denunciation of the ineffectiveness of colonial levies was in accord with this decision.[56]

The need for more effective handling of Indian affairs was also apparent. Shirley and Johnson agreed upon this; they disagreed upon methods and the seat of authority. Here Johnson had the advantage of successful experience, while Shirley was on the defensive. Moreover, Johnson was not seeking a place, but was threatening to turn over such authority as he had, if his demands were not met. His attitude became known to the ministry through his own dispatches as well as from other sources. To sustain his position and to promote his claims, Johnson asked Peter Wraxall to draw up the document termed "Some Thoughts Upon the British Indian Interest," which was completed on January 9, 1756. But this was too late to influence the ministry. On January 20, the "Inner Cabinet," including such key figures as Newcastle, Halifax, Admiral Anson, Henry Fox, and Sir Thomas Robinson, decided upon a unified command under a professional soldier, and two superintendents of Indian affairs.[57] Johnson's commission was dated February 17, 1756.

George the Second ... by these Presents constitute & appoint You to be Colonel of Our Faithfull Subjects, and allies, the Six united Nations of Indians, & their Confederates, in the Northern Parts of North America, ... and We do also constitute & appoint You Our Sole Agent and Superintendent of the said Indians and their Affairs, with the Annual Salary of Six hundred Pounds Sterling, payable Qarterly.[58]

Thus were the principal points of Johnson's recommendations, Pownall's elaborations, and the Wraxall thesis provided for. Johnson was still subject to orders from the commander in chief, from whom he was to receive his funds and his salary.

But he now had a royal appointment, and as Secretary Pownall explained the commission, "the whole management of this Branch of the Service will be left entirely to your Discretion."[59]   Furthermore, the commission as "Colonel of the Six Nations" insured his having military status with the salary which went therewith. To complete his honors and the recognition of his services, Parliament in February voted him, in the words of Secretary Fox, "£5000, as a reward for your long and faithful services in North America." This was no doubt in part a recognition of his financial losses and his expenditures on Indian Affairs.[60]

News of Johnson's honors and appointments and of Shirley's replacement as commander reached America at about the same time, and were linked together in the popular mind. Moreover, the aides whom Johnson had commended were promoted or rewarded, and Shirley's adherents were out of favor. "Both Captain Eyres and Mr. Wraxall get their Promotions in consideration of their Service in the last campaign with you," wrote Banyar. But Major John Rutherford's recommendations for military appointments were set aside to make way for German officers. "Mr. Rutherford says he found himself and other Field Officers nominated by General Shirley broke."[61]

Partisans of Shirley said this was due to the way in which "the Action at L. George had been magnified in England into almost a decisive victory." The diarist William Smith commented bitterly: "Shirley its said in great Contempt in England. Johnson highly esteemed—Ayre who was with him as Engineer made a Major Wraxall Secy. Capt. of Rutherford's Company, & yet the Battle at Lake George was a poor Business.—"[62]

Hence Johnson has often been regarded as the nemesis of Shirley. While it is true that the long and bitter controversy between them had its effect in England, as it did in America on the conduct of Indian affairs, it was not the sole cause of Shirley's fall. Neither were the intrigues nor the legitimate opposition of Johnson's friends decisive. Some factors contributing to his declining popularity were his own fault.

As commander, Shirley's imperious attitude and insistent demands had procured for him many influential enemies. In addition to those who were definitely pro-Johnson (Pownall, Banyar, and the De Lanceys), he alienated some who might have taken his side and who had no love for his enemies. Sir Charles Hardy as governor of New York might logically have opposed the De Lanceys. But he resented Shirley's treatment of him in making appointments in New York, and his attempt to handle Indian affairs in the Mohawk Valley.[63]   By November Hardy was denouncing Shirley to Lord Halifax:

I have had many Conversations with Mr. *Shirley*, whom I left at *Albany*, and I must take leave to say I never met his Equal to transact Business with, Let me entreat your Lordship not wholly to give Ear to his Representations, and however hard the task is to reflect on any Gentleman, the honour & respect I have for your Lordship oblige me to inform you that *I fear he is no better than an artful Deceiver* ready to advance anything in his Representations of Things as Facts, when he is perhaps *more a Stranger to the Facts he asserts than those he lays them before.* . . . *The Scene of Confusion* I left him in at Albany, is hardly to be Credited.[64]

Former Governor George Clinton, who while in New York was intimate with Shirley, in February 1756 congratulated Johnson and even claimed credit for advancing Johnson's cause. Yet he denounced De Lancey and Peter Wraxall adding, "I have no Sort of regard for Shirley."[65] Although Shirley had returned to Boston with great acclaim and popularity undimmed, for his cause was that of Massachusetts, his policies were suspected in the southern provinces. Pennsylvania, harassed by the Indians on the frontier, blamed her exposed position on Braddock's defeat and Shirley's order for Colonel Dunbar's troops to go to Albany. A Boston letter in April 1756 showed that this feeling had reached New England.

We apprehend it has been no small Blott in Mr. Shirleys Escutcheon, his drawing the Troops from the Southward, and as the Consequences have proved so bad, it is not improbable the Gentn in favour of the Colony of Virginia, which is so dear to the Crown, have made a Party against him at home. I believe this news is no small Chagrin to the Governor, and has I believe compounded [confounded] many designs & Schemes he probably might have laid.[66]

Shirley was to suffer criticism and controversy in the months ahead over his accounts and the award of military contracts, on which his successor, Lord Loudoun, was a chief complainant. But none of these issues so blackened his reputation as the furor aroused over the discovery by British intelligence of some letters between the French ambassador, the Duc de Mirepoix, and someone in Pennsylvania who had knowledge of military plans. With no evidence whatever, an imputation was bruited about that Shirley had been careless with military secrets. Secret orders were discovered in the letters from Shirley to Johnson regarding Pennsylvania, of which the ministry had not been told. Secretary Fox said, "I don't suspect Shirley of Treachery, but I have no doubt of his having great Schemes, and that he trusts the execution of Traitors, and that he ought not to stay in North America." Cumberland wanted to have Shirley brought home a prisoner, and the ministry agreed upon his recall. Secretary Fox softened the blow in his blunt letter ordering Shirley to England immediately, on the pretext that he could give useful information on American affairs.[67]

After their conciliatory meeting in New York in January 1756, Johnson and Shirley cooperated to some degree in the military measures then under way and in Johnson's handling of the Indians. Yet Johnson complained that Shirley's agents were not withdrawn from the Indian country; and Shirley and his supporters continued their pinpricks and sniping at the New Yorker and his friends.[68] As late as April 1756, Banyar reported that Shirley had criticized Johnson for his proceedings with the Indians "in your own Name and not in the Kings." In an early letter to Johnson, Shirley wrote,

I have not seen any of the Gorgetts, which you have distributed among the Indians, but I am told that instead of the King's Arms you have caus'd a Cypher of your own Name to be engrav'd on the Front; as these presents are made with the King's money, Sir, and to create in the Indians a Dependance upon his Majesty, and not merely a personal attachment to yourself, you will excuse me If I note the Impropriety of your ommitting the King's Arms.[69]

Even as late as May 28, 1756, Johnson wrote the Lords of Trade:

Tho' I have reasons to believe I have lost Genl. Shirley's Friendship & Confidence wch. I wish myself honoured with for the good of His Majesty's Service so far as it is connected with my Department; yet he hath of late silenced those agents he set up in Opposition to me & of whose Conduct I complained of to Your Lordships.[70]

With the departure of Shirley, Johnson had no reason for concern or malice. But the campaign to vindicate Shirley kept alive earlier charges against Sir William. While inconclusive hearings were held in London regarding Shirley's finances and contracts, his aides were busy writing tracts in his defense. Most notorious of these was the oft-cited *Review of the Military Operations in North America*,[71] which was published in April 1757. Ostensibly a factual relation, it was an ill-disguised polemic which denounced Pownall, De Lancey, and Johnson, imputing to them dastardly schemes and a "cabal" against Shirley. It was widely read, and copies were sent to America. Secretary John Pownall was incensed by the charges against his brother. He compelled William Alexander to admit that he had taken the tract to the printer, but was not its author. A friend in America, presumably William Livingston, was the author, but Alexander offered to back up the charges, and even said he had softened some of them. He did back down on one assertion about Pownall.[72] Mr. Charles, the New York agent in London, wrote that it had "a virulency against several private characters . . . very indecent."[73]

Somewhat later William Alexander composed a defense of Shirley, much milder in tone, in which there was no such virulence against Pownall and Johnson and which, in its omissions, raised doubts of the charges in the earlier tract. The popularity of Johnson, his eminent friends, and the need for a little diplomacy undoubtedly dictated the approach. *The Conduct of Major Gen. Shirley, Late General and Commander in Chief of his Majesty's Forces in North America Briefly Stated* emphasized Shirley's responsibility for the conduct of the war, and gave many details of his campaigns. Since Alexander accompanied him and was a witness of much that transpired, it is a kind of testimonial evidence of Shirley's worth, his motives and his services. The author, faced now with a *fait accompli* in Shirley's removal, stated, "It is not intended to veil Miscarriage, which Mr. Shirley may have been guilty of during his late Command, with Merit; which might be claimed for him from his former Services."[74] Alexander soon turned from the controversy to claim the title of "Lord Stirling," in which he was not entirely successful.

Granting his responsibility for much that happened, one cannot but regret the succession of misfortunes which dogged Shirley. The loss of two sons in the American campaigns, the collapse of his military plans largely due to factors beyond his control, and his supersession by commanders who could do no better, evoke some sympathy. Imputations of treachery and malfeasance could not be sustained. Shirley had performed heroic services for the defense of the colonies; but he was not a military leader, and he lacked many qualities which would have smoothed his path. He was an astute politician who had risen through successful intrigue and manipulation. Jealous of his position and power, he conceived a dislike of Johnson which drove him to many petty and invidious acts, which Johnson could not ignore. He had a grand conception of American destiny, but little sympathy with the Indians, so he could not understand Johnson's viewpoint. Temperamentally different, with divergent aims, they used different tactics, with opposite results. Ill advised as was Shirley's course, he seemed incapable of self-criticism or of a dispassionate view of those who disagreed. Called the ablest of American colonial governors, he failed when he essayed a larger role. If his fall was a victory for Johnson, it was one which could give Johnson little gratification. The serious problems on which they disagreed still remained.[75]

XIX

THE FATE OF GENERALS, 1756

Fears and apprehensions of insecurity which gripped the frontier in the fall of 1755 were disconcerting to both settlers and Indians. The French invasion had impressed the Indians, had unsettled their confidence in the English, and even roused a fear of French retaliation for their part in English defense. After such a reverse as Braddock's in July, English settlers moved to more populous centers, strengthened their defenses, and increased their supply of arms. Governments seemed impotent, their leaders afraid to move, and the words of the king's representatives carried little conviction. Complaints, rumors, and finally reports of barbarities committed by the natives flooded the stream of intelligence. Hence there were problems aplenty for the Superintendent of Indian Affairs when he returned to the Mohawk in December.

On his way home from Lake George, Johnson had summoned the Mohawks to meet him at Fort Johnson. Governor Hardy and General Shirley pressed him to gain support there for the English policies, and the Mohawks were eager to lay their troubles before him and to ask his help. From his own point of view, it was vital to reaffirm his role as manager of their affairs, the one man on whom they could rely for help and protection. He was criticized for this personal relationship, but it was the core of his strength as mediator and diplomat. As Warraghiyagey, "doer of great things," his capacity for leadership was tremendous. He could not afford to fail his charges or to lose their confidence. Yet, in his absence, others had been active in either supplanting him or weakening his influence.

Shirley's agents, whose intrigues had moved him to criticize the general, were still in the Indian country. One of them, John Van Seice, was reportedly holding daily meetings among the Onondagas; interpreters, many of whom were hired by Shirley, were sending messages to his secretary, William Alexander; and John Bradstreet, whom Shirley had put in charge of his transport plans, was regarded by Governor Hardy as Shirley's chief Indian agent.[1]

Emboldened by the confused state of affairs, French agents were more intrusive than ever. Through traders, especially in rum, they sought to entice Indians to

Canada and to bring them under French influence. Now Johnson reported to Governor Hardy:

I am credibly informed he [John Abeel, Albany trader] has lately Supplied a French officer & Interpreter Called Jean cure in Indian Sinuchsis at that place [Seneca country] wth. Rum & other Merchandise for a present wch Said Sinuchsis gave the Indians after treating with them. nay by ye. power of his Rum prevailed on an Indian called the Grote Younge & others to go with him to Canada.[2]

This "Jean Cure" was Philippe Thomas de Joncaire, eldest son of that Louis Thomas Joncaire, Sieur de Chabert, who had done so much to spread French influence among the Iroquois earlier in the century. He had been sent among the Iroquois by Vaudreuil after the defeat at Lake George.[3] Johnson took steps to thwart or even capture Joncaire.

I have this Day offered two French Men who have lived in this province some Years, & traded there Each a Commission in ye. Indian Service in Case they would bring Said Jean ceur down a Prisoner. they have undertaken it, & expect they will Succeed. I shall endeavour to prevent his tampering further with them . . .[4]

To prevent the Iroquois from going over to the French, he sought to enlist their warriors for the English campaign. "I have great hopes many Indians will Join us in the Spring if we push Matters vigourously." Messages were sent out to all the Confederate nations, and to the more distant dependent tribes, even those north of Lake Ontario, "the Mississagaw and Chipawais." He was optimistic of their "kind acceptance" of his words and that his influence would be felt, for by previous contacts he believed they were receptive.[5]

Now at Fort Johnson he exhorted his "brethren of the Mohawks, Senecas, Oneidas and Tuscaroras" to intervene with their cousins the Delawares, Shawnees, and River Indians, committing hostilities in the southern part of the province, and in the Jerseys and Pennsylvania.

I must desire you will, without loss of time, reprimand them for what they have already done, prevent their doing any more mischief, and insist on their turning their Arms with us against the French and their Indians; both your and our common enemy, and that without loss of time. This is what you engaged to do at the general meeting last June at my house. I am surprised you have not done it before, and I expect you will now do it without loss of time; if not, we will endeavour to put a stop to their barbarities, and do ourselves that justice the law of nature allows.[6]

They agreed readily to comply, expressing great concern, and promising to "forward your message through all the nations, and use all arguments in our power for their exerting themselves on this important occasion."[7] Messengers were sent forth, but when they returned the next month they gave no hope of relief. They related the course of the quarrel, what had been done on both sides, but were unable to learn the cause. The Delaware war parties would continue to go out.[8]

Pennsylvania's traditional policy of peace and friendship with the Indians, as initiated by William Penn, was in danger of being abandoned. The Delawares, dependent upon the Six Nations and kept at peace through negotiations with the half king, had long been docile and friendly. They had been called "women" by the imperious orators of the Six Nations, but now began to show stirrings of independence. They remembered being cheated by the white man in the notorious Walking Purchase of 1737, when clever agents had stretched a vague grant into a vast land claim. They now witnessed a New England group, the Susquehanna Company, invading their lands at Wyoming. And they were ripe for French propaganda. Once-friendly Indians began to listen to the persuasion of the French. Teedyuscung, the Moravian convert and orator, who was styled "King of the Delawares," heard the siren voices and seemed eager to throw off the yoke of the confederacy.[9] Since Braddock's defeat the English appeared weak and the French strong. Here was an opportunity to assert himself. Sporadic murders and destruction on the frontier which had caused alarm in the summer and fall now burgeoned into a frontier war. "We have accounts that the whole Body of Indians is against us," wrote Richard Peters. Few Indians appeared for the governor's conference, and no one seemed ready to fight; so he thought the only hope was assistance from the southern Indians, or some warriors from the Six Nations. He fretted that promised help or relief had not been sent.[10]

In this emergency, however, Pennsylvania was distraught with factions who could not agree upon policy. The frontiersmen and popular party demanded action, a military force against the Indians, and the raising of funds for defense. The Proprietary was resisting attempts to place taxes upon his lands; and the Quakers, who were influential in the Assembly, were opposed to the use of force or any appropriations for military purposes. Hence every effort would be made to bring peace by diplomacy. Since the Indians would not come to a conference, an embassy must be sent to the Delawares themselves.[11]

In December two stalwart warriors who had marched with Braddock, Scaroyady and Andrew Montour, began their journey up the Susquehanna to Wyoming.[12] At every Indian village they parleyed, persuaded, and threatened the Delawares with ill consequences if they persisted in hostilities. Some listened and gave heed, but those who had set foot on the warpath were loath to turn back. Then eighty Delaware warriors arrived, determined on their course, and threatened those who opposed them. Scaroyady and his party dared not separate or go back, for their own lives were in danger. After the war party left they continued on up the river stopping at every Indian village. At Diahoga (Tioga) they met the messengers sent down at the behest of Johnson. At Oquaga they found the missionary Gideon Hawley with a village of Oneidas and Tuscaroras. And finally they reached the Mohawk, at Fort Johnson, where a conference was being prepared.[13]

Having delivered their message and assisted Johnson with his conference, Scaroyady and Montour then returned to Philadelphia by way of Albany and New York. They were highly praised by Peters "for undertaking this dangerous journey and executing their orders so well and faithfully." Daniel Claus, still regarded as in the service of Pennsylvania, was provided with funds and directed to escort them, while the governor and Council awaited their report.[14]

Since the mission had failed to deter the Delaware warriors, Governor Morris and his advisers decided to resort to war. While Conrad Weiser and Scaroyady assented, agreeing that Pennsylvania had been patient and that the Delawares should be punished, the friendly Indians were in a precarious position. Scaroyady informed the governor that he and several others, with their women and children, were departing for Onondaga, to be with their own people.[15] Along with them went Daniel Claus and George Croghan, who now threw in their lot with the negotiations begun by Johnson. Claus wrote him of their decision:

And [to] acquaint your honr. in the Name of Skaronyade Mr. Montour and all the Indians that were last Summer with Genl. Braddock, and at present in this City [Philadelphia], that they were resolved to quitt this Government and live among their friends the Six Nations since times were so troublesome at Ohio they are twenty odd in Number Men Women and Children. − captn George Croghan, and John Davison are likewise coming that Way, the former left this place last Wednesday in Order to Settle his affairs at Aukwik, and is to be back next Saturday, when We I hope Shall Set off for the Mohawks.

Govr Morris is Striving to give me a Captns Commission in the Provincials under Colo Clapham a N: E: [sic] Man to go to the frontiers and build Forts at Shamokin &ca, NB: The party is to consist of 400 Men only, but I can not conceive how that will be consistent with me as I plainly foresee Indian affairs must drop in this Province as there will be no Indians.[16]

Thus Claus broke with Pennsylvania, although he protested to Peters that he would "always consider himself as in the service of the Proprietaries, and, at any time when wanted, he would chearfully come and do their Business." His chief objection to further service now was that "he would disoblige the Indians, who expected him to join with them this campaign, to revenge Hendrick's Death." But the Governor "took this Refusal amiss," believed him insincere, "and would not after this admit him to his Sight."[17]

As he arrived in Albany from New York January 27, Johnson was handed an express from Fort Johnson and the Indian country. A bombastic French general at Niagara had boasted to the Senecas there that the French proposed soon to take Oswego. The Onondagas were frightened "we See Death before our Eyes" and turned to the English for help. Johnson relayed this information to Shirley and Governor Hardy and set off for Fort Johnson, "Where I understand there are a good Many Indians from Susquahana Mett, the Five Nations are not yet arrived, they are verry much alarmed at the Menaces of the French and I expect will be asking great things to be done for them."[18]

It was more than two weeks before all of the Six Nations Indians arrived at Fort Johnson. Severe winter weather, making travel difficult, and their custom of condoling losses at all villages en route, occasioned some delay. In the meantime Johnson with a considerable entourage engaged in preliminaries with the Oneidas, Tuscaroras, and some Susquehanna River Indians. There were the useful Reverend John Ogilvie, catering to Indian spiritual needs in their own tongue (he baptized two children of Scaroyady), and the Reverend Gideon Hawley, who came up from Oquaga. There were eight army officers, who were aided by "Several Indian officers [among them Captain John Butler] and other gentlemen"; and three interpreters were listed, not including Arent Stevens, William Printup, and Daniel Claus, who could serve in that capacity. But "General Johnson," still so called, or "Brother Warraghiyagey" to the Indians, played the chief role.[19]

The Design of this Conference [wrote Ogilvie] is to make an Acknowledgment to them for yr. late Behaviour at the Lake [George], & to engage them for the next Sumer's Operaons. And to know what yr. Sentiments are with Regard to the barbarous Murders committed by the *Delawares Shawanas* &c. on the Frontiers of Pennsylvania.[20]

The condolence ceremony, the covering of the graves of the dead, and the sweeping away of all dirt from the council room with a clean white wing were followed by more substantial consolation.

Six French prisoners, some of those who were taken at the late battle, near Lake George, were delivered with great ceremony to the Indians, in order to replace the following Indians, who were killed in that battle, viz. Tayanoga, alias Hendrick Tarraghiyoris; Waniacoone of Canajoharee; Skahyowio Onienkoto of the Mohawks; Nica-anawa Skaronyade's son; and Cayadanora, a Tuscarora.

They received the prisoners with the greatest marks of gratitude and satisfaction; every nation giving the shout of approbation, and then carried off the prisoners to their respective families.[21]

Thanks for their help at Lake George was followed by the rhetorical question: "How much greater might our success have been! . . . had more of your warriors appeared in the field on that important day, had all our force been united."[22]

Now Warraghiyagey referred to the appeal from the governor of Pennsylvania—"the shocking news of (your nephews) the Delawares and Shawanese falling upon your brethren of Pennsylvania, Maryland and Virginia in the most cruel and treacherous manner, killing and barbarously butchering the innocent defenceless people, who lived on the frontiers of the said governments." What had they done to restrain their nephews and to stop these barbarities, as he had requested? The governor of Pennsylvania had sent to them their friends, Scaroyady and Andrew Montour, to receive their answer.[23]

When Red Head, the Onondaga speaker, replied, he was cool and somewhat indecisive. They had sent messengers; but were not the Delawares under the care of Onas, the governor of Pennsylvania, and in "the circle of his arms?" If he had taken care of them as he ought, the French would not have taken advantage of his neglect; had proper measures been taken, they would have been faithful to the English.[24] Sharply did Warraghiyagey answer him. This was the principal reason for calling them here at this season; he was sorry they were "not so hearty in the affair," for upon its outcome much depended. He urged them to "settle this affair before you leave this place."[25]

Finally, it was necessary to bring them to the support of the military affairs of the English. General Shirley was in supreme command, and he planned a vigorous campaign in the spring, for which their aid was needed. French threats to steal Oswego showed that they must keep open the road that way. Forts would be built to defend their castles, and soldiers would be garrisoned there. And Warraghiyagey proposed to meet the Indians at Oswego in the spring. He trusted that they would honor their old engagements and be faithful to the English.[26]

Then to seal and confirm all promises there was given a large belt of wampum, with an emblem of the Six Nations "joined hand in hand with us"; and at the end of Johnson's summary of advice he gave "the largest pipe in America, made on purpose."

Take this pipe to your great council-chamber at Onondago, let it hang there in view; and should you be wavering in your minds at any time, take and smoke out of it, and think of my advice given with it, and you will recover and think properly.[27]

There was another belt, the largest ever given, with the sun shining on figures of the Six Nations; and gifts to some warriors and sachems of silver gorgets. At the very end was a "handsome publick present" from the government, worth £1,085 in New York currency, or £620 sterling.[28] Indeed, no efforts had been spared to make the congress a success. And the Reverend Mr. Ogilvie was impressed: "There never was a better & more promising Appearance at a Treaty than this. The six united Nations give us all the Assurance possible, that they will join in our public Measures."[29]

But the outcome was not acceptable in Pennsylvania, where the ravages of the French and Indians on the frontier continued, and where the reports of Scaroyady and Montour promised no relief. Pressured by the popular party, yet over the protests of the Quakers and some of the Indians, the governor on April 14 issued a formal declaration of war on the Delawares. This was followed by offers of a bounty for scalps of £30, and a reward of £50 for a prisoner.[30]

News of this was shocking to Johnson, who looked toward future meetings to bring about peace and especially to a meeting at Onondaga in the summer. This seemed to undercut his efforts and to belie his protestations to the Indians.

What will the Delawares & Shawanese think of such Opposition & contradiction in our Conduct? how shall I behave at the approaching Meeting at Onondaga, not only to those Indians, but to the 6 Nations? These Hostile Measures wch. Mr Morris has entered into, is throwing all our Schemes into Confusion, & must naturally give the 6 Nations such Impressions & the French such advantages to work on against us, that I tremble for the Consequences.[31]

This to Shirley and a like protest to Hardy were relayed to Morris, who soon began to backwater. Secretary Peters smoothed over the affront by saying no new parties had gone out; exception had been made of the friendly Indians; and the move was necessary "to animate our own people." He hoped Sir William would see it in a better light.[32] Morris vacillated, and even allowed a delegation of Quakers to meet with the half king (who was asked by Morris to take a war belt to the Six Nations) and to assure him that they, descendants of William Penn, were opposed to the war. Such contradiction confused the Indians and weakened the position of the government.[33] Finally, since Johnson was preparing for a great conference at Onondaga,

Pennsylvania at last declared a suspension of hostilities for thirty days, until the outcome was known.[34]

Of more immediate concern to Johnson and the Six Nations was the defense of the Mohawk Valley. On his return from Oswego, General Shirley had assured the several castles that they would be defended by garrisons of troops. A fort had recently been built at the Canajoharie Castle, and now the other nations (Oneidas, Onondagas, Tuscaroras, Cayugas, and Senecas) asked Warraghiyagey for stockaded forts, with troops, officers, and interpreters. Johnson agreed to have these forts built and made several contracts for their construction.[35] The nature of these is revealed by instructions given to a carpenter for a fort for the Senecas.

This Fort is to be one hundred & fifty feet Square—the Logs to be either of Pine or Oak, Sixteen feet long, four feet of which to be set in the Ground well rammed & pounded; two sides of each Log to be squared so as they may stand close to each other, proper loop Holes to be cut at four feet distance, the heights from the ground to be left to the Indians. Two good block Houses to be built at either of the opposite Corners, each block House to be twenty four feet square below, the upper part above the Beams to project a Foot so as men may fire down upon the Enemy.[36]

Building such forts was an essential step in defense, one which the French had not overlooked; for the Indians in asking for them showed their reliance upon the English, and the presence of troops would insure their cooperation. Without such protection for their homes and families, no warriors would go forth to fight. Yet construction was made difficult, if not impossible, while the valley was fraught with fears of enemy invasion.[37]

In addition to such fortification, there were the two English forts at the Carrying Place, guarding the transport route to Oswego, and serving as storehouses for supplies. Each of these was laid out as a fortification, had a garrison, and was named for its commander. At the head of navigation on the Mohawk stood Fort Williams (Captain William Williams); and at the other end of the carry, some four miles away, stood Fort Bull (Lieutenant Bull) where bateaux were reloaded to proceed through Oneida Lake and down the Oswego River to Lake Ontario.[38] Backing up these outposts in the absence of any regular troops was the Albany County militia commanded by Colonel Johnson. But these could be counted on for only limited terms of service or short expeditions.[39]

From William Williams came a stream of letters, relaying rumors, reports of scouts, and apprehensions of danger from the French. He was unhappy in his post and appeared on poor terms with the Indians, with whom he had little sympathy. From such "intelligence" Johnson had difficulty in sifting out the true situation.[40] Thus on March 14, Williams reported a large army of the French with three hundred Indians was heading for Oneida. Colonel Johnson led a thousand hastily recruited militia on a march to the German Flats. There he learned from Williams that it was a false alarm. Johnson's alacrity in meeting this emergency was praised by General Shirley, and the show of force impressed the Indians.[41] Hence the three-day march had not been in vain.

The French, well aware of English preparations to support Fort Ontario with ammunition and supplies, decided that the best way to counter these plans was to break the supply line. For this purpose they dispatched from Montreal an expedition of between three and four hundred men led by Lieutenant de Lery. Arriving undetected at the Great Carrying Place on March 27, they attacked Fort Bull, where a garrison of some sixty men was overwhelmed. Again the French Indians whooped so that the defenders had time to shut the gate and offer some resistance. But the attackers within an hour broke down the gate, fired the wooden fort, and massacred most of the garrison.[42]

Learning of the invasion, Johnson marched with five hundred militia and with Mohawk Indians but arrived too late and viewed a ghastly scene where the fort stood.

I found the Enemy withdrawn So Went over with my Party, and above 100 Oneidaes, & Tuscarora's Who Met me there; to the Fort which the Enemy had distroyed. I found within the Fort twenty three Soldiers, two Women, and one Battoe Man, Some burnt almost to Ashes, others most Inhumanly Butchered, and all Scalped, without the Fort, I found three Soldiers Scalped, who I think were blown over by the powder which was in the Magazine, as they were verry much Scorched. about 200 Yards from the Fort. . . . Mr. Bulls Party could make no great defence as there was not one Port hole to fire thorough in all the Fort, nor a Flanker, or Bastion of any kind, wh. the Enemy well Seeing, fired in between the Pickets at our People, they Cutt a Hole in ye gate for Said purpose, then Cutt the Wooden Hinges by which the gate hung and threw it down, so rushed in I imagine. the Whole Number killed & missing is 62 thirty of which I found and buried. They distroyed everry thing in the Fort, and about it. also 20 Battoe load of Provisions which had been carried over for Osswego, Cutt what Battoes were there to peices, also Sleds Harness &ca. and took almost all the Horses they had there.[43]

The loss of Fort Bull was a blow to morale, for the French told the Indians that their place of rendezvous was only two days away, whence they could return much stronger, and even destroy "the whole 5 Nations." The French, fearing Colonel Johnson who had once beaten them, dared not attack Fort Williams, but might at any time strike at the supply line.[44]

Shirley had appointed Captain John Bradstreet, an energetic officer, to procure a fleet of bateaux, and he even conceived that the bateaumen, who were to be armed, would constitute a kind of army. The flow of men and supplies toward Oswego had begun, but now Bradstreet reported that his bateaumen were so intimidated by what had happened at the Carrying Place, that they were deserting daily. The rough bateaumen, quite undisciplined, were causing trouble with the Indians; and Bradstreet asked for guards to accompany the fleet of bateaux to Oswego. Thereupon Johnson sent Captain Thomas Butler to muster the Mohawks and other Indians to serve as guards. To be effective, however, such Indian guards needed a number of rangers to accompany them.[45] Both Bradstreet and Shirley depended upon Johnson and the Indians to see that supplies went through, and blamed him for any failure.[46]

The plan for a great meeting at Oswego had now been abandoned for one at Onondaga where the Six Nations had invited their offending cousins, the Delawares and Shawnees. This seemed all the more important, for in addition to checking the aggression in Pennsylvania there was the need to secure the route to Oswego, and to counteract French influence. The raids of the French and their Indians had even rendered the Mohawk Valley dangerous, and the Mohawks questioned whether Warraghiyagey would be safe in making the trip. Only the Onondaga insisted upon it. There were threats against his life, but the risk of offending the Onondagas and the hope of some positive achievement convinced him to make the trip. A strong guard would be necessary for Fort Johnson in his absence (some ten Indian families were protected there), and he asked for an escort through the valley. "Not only in point of Security but to strengthen my Consequence at this Onondaga Meeting, I must desire Your Excellency will order me a Guard of an Officer 3 Subalterns & 100 Men."[47]

No effort was spared to make this a prestigious meeting, with abundant supplies of presents, arms, and rum. As the entourage approached Onondaga it was met by messengers, announcement was made of its coming, and the formalities of condolence for chiefs who had died, especially Red Head, were arranged. "Then Sr William marched on at the Head of the Sachems singing the condoling song which contains the names, laws & customs of their renowned ancestors, and praying to god that their deceased Brother might be blessed with happiness in his other state." There was another halt in sight of the castle, where the head sachems and warriors placed themselves across the road in the form of a half moon, and for an hour sang the condoling song. Then they shook hands.[48]

Then Sir William marched on at the Head of the Warriors the Sachems falling into the Rear and continued singing their condoling song. On entering the castle Sir Wm was saluted by all the Indians firing their Guns, which was returned by all the Whites and Indians who attended Sr William. The Sachems proceeded to a green Bower adjoining to the deceased Sachems House prepared on purpose, and after they were seated they sent for Sr William.[49]

Suspicions of the extent of French influence, the poison of their intrigues and of their infiltration among the Iroquois were confirmed by the reports of Indians returned from Canada.[50] They were now exhorted by Brother Warraghiyagey to mend their ways, to reject the invitations of the deceitful French, and to join with their English brothers when called upon to fight. They conceded their errors and promised if possible to bring their allies into the English interest. Of special importance was the protection of the supply route to Oswego. Since the present water route was tedious and dangerous, Johnson won the Indians' consent to cutting "a Road to Oswego through their Country with their promise of Assisting in laying it out, and also for building a Fort at Oswego Falls, 12 Miles from Oswego." This was to forestall the French, who had declared their intention to seize the falls and to build a fort there. Now the Indians also engaged to protect supplies en route to Oswego; but the projected overland route had to be abandoned.[51]

Disappointing, however, was the failure of the chiefs of the Delawares and Shawnees to appear until the proceedings were about over. Finally on July 2, the Delaware "King" arrived. Presents were already being distributed, and rum was flowing, so Sir William told the Delaware and Shawnees that he would rather invite them to his home, and the Onondaga meeting was adjourned.[52]

At Fort Johnson on July 9 began the negotiations with the chiefs of the Shawnees and Delawares. They confessed that their people had been deluded by the French; some Delawares had engaged in hostilities. But Nutimus, "king" of the Delawares, was reluctant to give a "determinate" answer. Johnson insisted that only a firm declaration would be acceptable. He used pressure and cajoled; the Makikanders, River Indians, who had been brought to Fort Johnson to be armed and clothed, were an object lesson of the value of his favor. Finally the Delaware king agreed to all of Johnson's demands on behalf of his own people on Susquehanna, at Tioga; he could not speak for the Ohio Delawares, but he would ask them to follow the example of the Six Nations. Then both chiefs accepted the war belt and sang the war song "with singular zeal and warmth."[53]

Now Johnson played his trump card. After a brief consultation with the six nation sachems he formally took off the petticoats from the Delawares. "I do in the name of the Great King of England your Father, declare, that henceforward you are to be considered as Men by all your Bretheren the English and no longer as women." He hoped the Six Nations, too, would remove this invidious distinction; he concluded by awarding the chiefs medals and silver gorgets.[54]

Then, as a fitting climax, "having this morning [July 11] received his Majestys Patent creating him a Baronet of Great Britain together with his Commission as sole Agent and Superintendant of the affairs of the 6 Nations & acquainted all the Indians present with it, and shewed them the said Patent and Commission upon which they gave a loud & unanimous shout." Henceforth in all Indian records he was known as "Sir William." "A Tub of Punch was then brought in and Sir William drank His Majestys health, and success to his arms, afterwards Prosperity and Harmony to the 6 Nations and all their Allies."[55]

His mission accomplished, Sir William returned to the comparative safety of Fort Johnson. But the rigors of travel, constant negotiations and ceremonial, as well as the anxiety caused by the French, had taken their toll. He was "very much fatigued and in a bad state of health." And Peter Wraxall, who had been ailing in New York for months, started on the journey but became sick and turned back; he wrote up the minutes later.[56] Yet it was all quite worth the effort if engagements were kept.

It was indeed an important negotiation. For the first time Johnson had taken upon himself not only responsibility for the Six Nations, but also negotiation with the chiefs of their dependent allies. And he had gained their promise of friendship and cooperation in war on the French. He may have overstepped his authority in removing the appellation of "women" from the Delawares, for this was a sign of their dependence which the council of the Six Nations refused to ratify.[57] Yet he had them pledge to take up the war belt and to join in campaigns to come, and the Nations had also agreed to cut a road through their lands to Oswego. But all these gains depended on the English playing their part, in pressing their offensive against the French, in building forts in all the castles of the Mohawk Valley, and in caring for the needs of the Indians. Any faltering or failure would undermine it all.[58]

At this juncture, all eyes turned toward the newly appointed commander in chief. Since early April brought news of his appointment, Lord Loudoun had been eagerly awaited in America. The long delay after his selection before his arrival, or even before the arrival of his troops, seemed hard to comprehend. In the interim Shirley had continued to act as commander, until he should be officially relieved. Thus he went on with his plans for the year's campaigns, made appointments, and arranged contracts for supplies. These measures seemed necessary and commendable, even though his every act might be superseded or reversed by his successors. To what extent he was justified in so doing no one could say, but that he would be held responsible there was no doubt.

Lord Loudoun's appointment had been deliberate and well considered and was generally approved. As an experienced professional soldier he was expected to reorganize and make more efficient the American operations. His high rank and his considerable wealth and social standing brought prestige to the American commander, now even more significant with the imminent declaration of war. Furthermore, he was to bring newly raised regiments of regulars to replace the haphazard American provincial levies. These were the Scotch Fusileers and the Highlanders. A new regiment, called the Royal American, was to be recruited here, but with German and British officers. These units required preliminary planning and preparations which held up their departure, for Loudoun was a precisionist. "Thus did this master of army paper work, this general of the pen, lay his plans for operations in a country which had never known a well ordered campaign."[59]

Two major generals, Daniel Webb and James Abercromby, were chosen to precede Lord Loudoun in America and to assume command until his arrival. Shirley was officially relieved by Major General Webb on June 8. Since the regiments from England, however, did not come for a month, Webb had little to do and Abercromby little more; most matters waited upon the coming of the general. Shirley in the meantime had moved quietly to Albany, "without any ceremony—not a gun fired he has dismissed his Guard only two Senterys.—[while] the new Generals Coach and Servants are arrived at New York."[60]

The arrival of Lord Loudoun in New York, July 23, 1756, was a momentous event. Benjamin Franklin had been invited by his friend Thomas Pownall, now "Secretary Extraordinary" to the general, to be on hand, and because of the delay waited in New York for five weeks. Shirley of course was there, and the governor and council of the province.

Lord Loudoun made a good first impression. Peter Wraxall went down to represent Sir William Johnson and wrote:

This Morning abt. 4 o Clock Ld. Loudoun came up (silently) in a Pilot Boat—he saw Company abt. 12. I went to make my bow with Multitude. . . . I am to wait on him between 7 & 8 this Evening. His Countenance is full of Candor, his Eyes Sprightly & good Humoured, he is short, strong made & seems disposed & fit for Action, he lets himself down with great ease & affability.[61]

Benjamin Franklin, despite his long wait, was pleased, for he had several fruitful conferences with the general and thought he might do him some service. "He seems to me," he wrote, "very well fitted for the Charge he has undertaken."[62]

Everyone sought to pay court to "My Lord," but Wraxall finally got his audience:

Such a scene of hurry, what can I say of it! My Lord is to set off this Morning or this day—he has been so crouded that till last night no getting near him—however he then sent for me. he opened with Military Matters about my Company. Next about Oswego on this Subject I mentioned the Article of Rum, its great Plenty—private Sale—prejudice both to Indian Service & Troops. Bradstreet reported to be concerned—Kings Battoes said to have been made use of last year for private trade. William's at Carrying place, & him at Fort Hunter.—[63]

Wraxall was impressed with the numerous entourage and made a friendly contact with an aide, Captain Cunninghame. The latter offered to find a place for him "to be near My Lord & be in his Family." But Peter was loyal to Sir William, with whom he had hopes of appointment as Indian secretary. But Secretary Extraordinary Pownall was indeed the key man.

Mr. Pownall is I understand to have the Govt. of Boston on Mr. Shirley's departure. he (Mr. P) received me very civilly, but there is that something, wch. flows from the Heart, wch. I thought wanting, he asked very kindly after you . . . I asked Pownall about Secretary p. for Ind. Affairs. he said the Choice & Sallary would rest with you. what Pownall is with regard to Ld. Loudoun, Cuninghame told me this Morning he knew not, but said he soon woud know. . . . Pownall seems thoughtful & loaded with Cogitation. the Boston People (I hear) begin to Yelp against him. Mr. Shirley paid his visit at one oClock. Oliver [De Lancey] sticks close & runs about for him (Ld. Lou) . . . Cuninghame is first Aid de Camp & if Pownall dont interfere will be chief man. he has but one Aid de Camp more as yet, I fancy [Roger] Morris will come in . . ."[64]

Sir William's service, merits, and ideas were extolled to Loudoun not only by Wraxall and Pownall, but by Governor Hardy and others. In a mood to be critical of Shirley, Loudoun found Johnson's ideas on the use of the militia agreed with his own. He was unacquainted with Indian affairs, though dubious about their great expense, and therefore willing to listen to the acknowledged expert in that field. Sir William, for his part, was content to wait upon the plans, and the forces, of the new commander. Yet he knew the value of time, which the European commanders seemed to neglect in the American theater, and he saw frontier defense steadily deteriorating. The gains made by his conference at Onondaga might be quickly lost through mismanagement or untoward events. The Indians were constantly reporting threats to their security from the French, who sought to break the English supply line to Oswego. An Oneida who returned from Canada said the French planned to build a fort at Oswego Falls to prevent supplies going to Oswego, and to build another fort at the west end of Oneida Lake, whence they could attack German Flats, "Sr. William Johnson's house; kill or take him and Ravage that Part of the Mohawk River."[65] While there was recognizable bombast in such boasting, the reports unsettled the Indians and required recognition.

One method of securing the Indian allegiance and of restoring confidence was the garrisoning of their forts. Shirley had promised this, and, while the Indians preferred colonial militia, now regiments of regulars were sent to posts on the Mohawk. These garrisons were often of doubtful value when the Redcoats' behavior toward the natives became insolent and rude.[66] A crisis occurred early in August, when one Jerry, a Tuscarora, a known rascal and murderer whose record extended back to the Braddock expedition, was seized by the Schenectady garrison. Not only was he killed, but his head was cut off and exhibited on a pole in the camp. Colonel Gage tried to play down the atrocity, but the Indians seized upon it as a *cause célèbre*. It mattered not that he richly deserved punishment; the action could not be defended. Loudoun wished to discipline the soldiers. Sir William dealt with it in his own way, to quiet the Indians and to make amends. Yet Jerry's nation showed their resentment by sulking when they were next called down.[67]

The plight of the garrison at Oswego now became a matter of concern. Since the destruction of Fort Bull, the fleet of bateaux under Captain John Bradstreet had continued to carry supplies and ammunition down the Oswego River. But reports from Captain Williams at the Carrying Place stressed the jeopardy of their route. And Colonel Mercer, commanding at Oswego, reported shortages in supply, sporadic killing of his workmen, and rumors of imminent attack.[68] Shirley and his aides had drawn up plans for reinforcing Oswego, completing the forts, and building a fleet there to control the waters of Lake Ontario. He ordered Patrick Mackellar, an engineer, to journey with Bradstreet to Oswego to examine and report upon the fortifications and to direct their completion. Mackellar arrived at Oswego on May 16 and was appalled. Fort Oswego had only three guns mounted, which could not be fired for fear of bringing down the cracked and crumbling walls. The town was exposed to attack and the fortifications were badly laid out. Fort Ontario on the east side of the river was stockaded but had no loopholes, and was badly planned. Mackellar undertook to direct work on the defenses, but found most of the men employed in building the shipping, which was given priority. Not until July 1 could he get men to work at the fortifications. Apparently, in spite of the Indians and raids on the communication, the officers did not expect a land attack.[69] Not only were the defenses weak; the garrison was sickly, poorly provisioned, and morale was low.[70]

Much emphasis was put upon the success of Bradstreet's bateaux and his corps of armed bateaumen. The convoys were large—as many as six hundred bateaux in one—and their deliveries were important, so the French spied upon their movement. At Niaouré Bay they had a force of nine hundred men under de Villiers, which sought to harass the English. On July 3 a large convoy led by Bradstreet was returning from Oswego, had gotten nine miles up the river when it was surprised by de Villiers's force of four hundred. Bradstreet and six men got to an island and fought off a superior force. Others were engaged by the French in a swamp, and the fighting raged for three hours. Bradstreet reported the repulse of the enemy, the saving of the convoy, and a considerable loss in the attacking party. He admitted losses of sixty to seventy men (at least forty killed and twenty-four wounded on the first report). French reports listed only a few casualties, but claimed many British killed and a number of prisoners.[71]

News of this bold attack, evidence of increasing pressure from the French and the likelihood of more raids, worried the English command. Work was hastened on the defenses at Oswego, but progress was slow. And worse still was the delay and indecision in Loudoun's command.

The French in Canada were now under the vigorous leadership of the Marquis de Montcalm, who had replaced Dieskau. Montcalm felt that the main British thrust must come from Fort William Henry, directed at the nearly completed new Fort Carillon (Ticonderoga). He decided to create a diversion by attacking Oswego and perhaps destroying the forts there. For this post was a thorn in the side, an obstacle in the way of communication to the westward, and a threat to Frontenac and French Canada.[72]

Montcalm left Frontenac with his first troops on August 4; the rendezvous of the three divisions was at Niaouré Bay—la Sarre and Guyenne were joined there by the Béarn batallion brought east from Niagara—thirteen hundred men were to be joined by colonials and Indians to make a force of three thousand. Moving secretly by night and hiding in bays during the day, the troops escaped detection by the English until on August 11 they were within a quarter of a league of Fort Ontario. There they landed and began entrenchments for the siege. Digging their parallel trenches in the accepted siege pattern, the French fully expected a stubborn resistance. English boats observed them from off shore. Fire opened from the forts; quite as abruptly within a few hours it ceased. The French watched as the British evacuated Fort Ontario on the east shore and carried what they could to Fort George across the river. They abandoned eight cannon and four mortars. French grenadiers occupied Fort Ontario. On the 14th the French under Rigaud forded the river and brought guns to bear on Fort George; they also had the advantage of the height from Fort Ontario. Since English firing had been brisk, the French were surprised to see the white flag run up as two officers asked for terms. Bougainville was sent over to give the terms of surrender. The victory seemed easy, for the French expected the forts to sustain a prolonged siege.[73]

The demoralization of the British defenders was complete. Colonel Mercer, the commander, had been killed by a cannon shot. Lieutenant Littlehales, succeeding him, felt that resistance was futile. Women as well as men pleaded with him to capitulate. The long period of neglect, starvation rations, sickness, weakness, and mismanagement had taken its toll.

It was a cheap victory also, for Montcalm wrote:

There were, on our side about thirty men killed or wounded; on that of the English about 150, including several soldiers, who wishing to escape across the woods fell, into the hands of the Indians. The number of prisoners was nearly 1700 men; to wit Shirley's and Pepperell's regiments, arrived from Old England and who were at the battle of Fontenoy, a detachment of Schuyler's regiment, Militia of the country, about 80 officers, among whom were two artillery, two engineers and 12 nave officers. We captured, also, 7 vessels of war; one of 18 guns, one of 14, one of 10, one of 8, three mounted with patereros [swivels], 200 barges or bateaux, 7 pieces of bronze, 48 of iron, 14 mortars, 5 howitzers, 47 patereros [swivels], a quantity of bullets [shot], bombs, balls, powder and a Considerable pile of provisions.[74]

The prisoners were transported to Montreal; the forts were demolished and set on fire, and on August 21, the French departed. They had no intention of holding the forts.

Thus, in a brief campaign the French had gained control of a strategic post, command of the waters of Lake Ontario, and a great influence over the Indians.

The fall of Oswego was a tremendous blow to British prestige.[75]

When news of the attack upon Oswego reached Sir William in Albany on August 20, he took immediate steps to organize relief. Hastening up the Mohawk, he rallied a thousand militiamen and issued a call for Indians to come to their support. He was ordered by General Loudoun to join these with the forces under Major General Webb at the German Flats as a relief expedition. When he arrived at German Flats on August 24, however, he was struck down by an attack of "the bloody flux" (dysentery) and was confined to his bed, unable to go further. George Croghan and Thomas Butler then gathered the Indians to go with Webb's forces. The latter got as far as the Carrying Place before learning of the fall of Oswego. Scouts told of the destruction of forts and gave a dismal picture of the carnage; the Indians now held back. The Onondagas advised Webb to turn back. Blaming the Indians, Webb decided to return to German Flats. On his retreat he destroyed the Indian forts and cut down trees to encumber the creek, thus making it clear that the English were abandoning the Carrying Place. The Indians were convinced that the English could not save their frontier and were filled with forebodings.[76]

Conceiving the Oswego expedition as a diversion, destroying rather than holding the forts, and soon withdrawing, the French had no intention of a further advance to the Mohawk. Yet it was to their advantage to spread the idea among the Indians in the hope of weakening their attachment to the English. Hence they used Nickas, a chief warrior of the Oneidas who was at Oswego as a scout and whose life they spared, to carry their warning.

Child you shant die; I want you to carry a Message for me thro' the Castle of the 5 Nations . . . That the French General told said Indian that he was now going to take Oswego from the English and he would give it again to the 6 Nations who were the right owners of it, and after he had done that he would go up the River and look for English Battoes with the Provisions and destroy the people who came with them after which he would proceed to the Oneida carrying place and destroy what he had left standing there since last spring and therefore he warned all his children of the 6 Nations to keep away from the carrying Place or they would be hurt and they did not want to hurt them. After he had finished at the carrying Place he would proceed down the Mohawk River and destroy every thing as he went along as far as Sir William Johnson's where he would strike off thro' the woods to Lake George, and there meet another General in conjunction with whom he would destroy Fort William Henry & then he knew the English would beg Peace.[77]

The threat to attack Johnson's house was not new. Many Indians of all tribes were constantly passing on the Mohawk, and Daniel Claus reported on August 3 that some three hundred in the French interest were reputed to have a scheme "to cut off your honours House," after which three thousand would descend on the settlements. These "Stranger Indians" had said "it would be nothing at all to Scale the Walls of this house and Kill everyBody in it without firing a Gun."[78]

On August 9, Sir William issued orders to Lieutenant Alexander Turnbull of the 42d regiment at Schenectady, who was to head a party to garrison Fort Johnson.

You will in the Day time keep one Sentry on the Eminence to the Northward of the House, who upon Seeing the Enemy advance, is to fire his peice & retreat to the Fort. Another Sentry to be posted at the gate of the Fort on the outside who is also to enter the Fort on the advanced Sentrys alarming him. . . .

In Case of an attack, the 2 Bastions to be properly manned, the Curtains also, there mixing some of my People wth. Yours. The remainder of My People to Man the Dwelling House & fight from thence, makeing Use of the four Wall peices, & Musquetoons out of the Window fitted for them.

Whenever an alarm is given by the advanced Sentry, you will order three Pattereroes [pedreros] to be imediately fired that being the Signall I have given to the Mohawks, & on their approach near the Fort when challenged, they are to Answer George as Distinct as they Can, then to be admitted if practicable.

When there are no Indians here the Gates to be Locked at 8 o Clock in ye. evening and opened at Six In the Morning: first looking round about to See that all is Safe & clear—the advanced Sentry to be posted Everry Day.[79]

In spite of these threats, the fears of the Mohawks for their security and the obvious intent of the French now to dominate the Iroquois tribes, Sir William was convinced, both by logic and from his Indian intelligence, that the next objective would be Lake George.

I must own I cannot think the French will make any considerable attempt this way, notwithstanding the many accounts we have that they intend it. I am of opinion it is only to keep us at Home here, while they are executing their Plan the other Way, by all accounts their whole strength is now bent towards Lake George.[80]

His Indian scouts reported the buildup of the French forces at Carillon and on the lakes, and this information was relayed to General Loudoun.[81] The general, however, lately arriving to take personal command found the New England expedition already committed to the attack upon Crown Point. Massachusetts had taken the lead in raising forces which were thought sufficient for a successful assault on the French stronghold. Ten thousand men were expected, but somewhat less than this number were finally assembled under the command of General John Winslow. While New York had furnished some, the greater support voted by the Bay Colony gave her the commander and direction of the campaign. Lest there be any diversion, it was specifically prescribed by the General Court that these troops should not serve west of Schenectady or below Albany. It was also specified that the men should be under their own officers (i.e., not under the regulars), for there had been considerable friction between troops and commanders in previous campaigns in Nova Scotia and at Lake George.[82] Thus the expedition seemed to exclude the regulars, but the fall of Oswego and renewed warnings of French advances made some reinforcement by regular troops highly desirable.

Loudoun now decided to take over the Crown Point expedition and notified Winslow of his intention. The latter balked, but when ordered to come to Albany by the commander in chief had no other recourse. He agreed to have the regular troops back up his rather than join them. Hence Loudoun decided to concentrate the regulars at Fort Edward, leaving the provincials holding Fort William Henry.[83]

By October he reported:

I have now at Fort Edward Maj. Genl. Abercrombie with the 42d, 44th, & 48th Regiments, and 500 of the Royal Americans, under Lieutenant Colonel Bouquet at Saratoga; . . .
It looks odd on the Map, to see the *Provincials* advanced before the Troops; but I look on *Fort Edward* as the likeliest Post to be attacked, and if that is taken Fort William Henry, with all the people there, falls of Course; therefore I have chose to be there with the Troops.[84]

This was indeed a rationalization of an illogical and unpleasant situation; Loudoun comforted himself with a false optimism. "As both Encampments are fortified, and Covered by Forts, with plenty of Cannon; I imagine they [the French] must find it a very difficult Affair, to Force us; and I think if they try it; they will repent it."[85] Thus he practically abandoned the idea of offense.

Sir William countered with as strong language as he dared in opposing the views of the commander:

I am of Opinion The French are Sending all the Force they can towards Lake George and intend to Strike a Blow, which may put an end to this Campaign.
If they attack Fort William Hennery first, it will certainly be with the Regulars. and I imagine the Irregulars, & Indians who will be verry numerous, and expert in ye. Woods will be employed to Cutt of the Communication between the two Forts, and perhaps between Albany & Fort Edward.
Your Lordship will pardon the freedom I take in Giveing my opinion so freely.[86]

Sir William not only repeatedly urged the imminent danger to Fort William Henry, but took measures to supply militia, rangers, and Indians, while he kept out scouts in that direction. On October 1, he wrote:

I have kept Partys of the Militia scouting ever since the Regiment moved from the German Flatts, and intend to have that service constantly kept on, untill it may be found unnecessary. I have ordered the Militia of Schenectady to do the same, by wh. means I hope we shall be able to prevent their stealing a March upon us. . . . I sent Mr. Croghan and Capt.n Funda one of the Indians officers two officers two Days ago from here with a Party of near Eighty Men Consisting of near fifty Delawares, the rest Six Nations, and five Rangers. He is to March with them directly to Fort Edward through the Woods from Schenectady, there join the Rest, and receive Major Genrl. Abercrombies Commands. I impatiently wait the arrival of the Six Nations, & Oghuagoes. . . .[87]

The French were indeed building up their forces at Fort St. Frederic (Crown Point) and Carillon (Ticonderoga). By September they had over five thousand; and there were detachments of Canadians and Indians who were sent out as scouts and on raids. The size of the English Garrisons at Fort Edward and Fort William Henry and movements of Johnson's Indians and rangers were duly reported. Considerable work was done on the fortifications of Carillon, for the French were prepared for an attack. On the other hand they did not feel strong enough to send an expedition to seize the English forts. So there were brief raids of small parties, the capture of prisoners, and the fighting of these raiders as they met or were able to overpower each other in the forest. The French Indians alternately held back or insisted upon their modes of fighting, which irked the French soldiers and altered their plans. As the season wore on and winter weather approached, it became evident that no major attack could be made. Each side waited for the other to withdraw. The French realized that they were handicapped by their long water supply route to Montreal, which would soon be closed by snow and ice. Finally on October 25, the regiments were ordered into winter quarters, and Montcalm departed northward.[88]

The rangers and Indians sent out in parties by the English had thus served as a deterrent to French action, and had kept the commanders informed. But the inability of the regulars and militia to cooperate in a concerted action precluded any English offensive. Then, the enlistments of the militia were running out, so on November 11, Winslow turned over command of the fort to Major Eyre, and led his men to Albany, where they were soon followed by the rest of the New England provincials. Thus the expedition was abandoned.[89]

While Loudoun was being frustrated in his efforts to merge the colonials and the regulars on the Crown Point campaign, Sir William for the first time was asserting his authority as superintendent of Indian affairs for the whole northern district. It was difficult during the pressure of the campaigns to distinguish his rôle as colonel of militia, raising troops and employing rangers for defense, and his management of Indians, who were needed for auxiliaries, for scouting, and as a source of intelligence. Now the threats to the Pennsylvania and Virginia frontier demanded his attention.

At this time, too, there appeared on the scene the newly appointed superintendent for the southern colonies, Edmund Atkin. Although ostensibly the opposite number to Sir William, he was an unknown quantity who had little qualification for the post. He arrived in New York October 6, and met Loudoun when the general came down from Fort Edward in November. He followed Sir William to Fort Johnson, where he observed Indian negotiations for ten days. He wrote that he and Sir William discussed their problems and planned future cooperation. But for some time he was largely engaged in pressing Loudoun for his salary, for his supply of Indian presents, and in trying to assert the limits of his authority. Loudoun became so irritated by this conduct that he lost faith in Atkin and turned to others to carry out his directions.[90]

George Croghan had responded with alacrity when troops and Indians were wanted for Fort Edward. But the Pennsylvania trader was a man of many talents, and his ingenuity had many outlets. He offered his services directly to Loudoun to raise frontier troops; he claimed he could raise four or five hundred woodsmen from Pennsylvania. But Loudoun had used him to distribute Indian presents and wrote to ask Sir William if he would not be more useful in Indian diplomacy. Loudoun was troubled about Croghan's character. Sir William replied a bit evasively that Peter Wraxall, who had known him in Pennsylvania, could give a better account of his character. Yet, he added, "I believe Him an Honest Man, but a little indiscreet."[91] Whatever his faults, he could be used to advantage in the area he knew best.

In the fall of 1756, Pennsylvania's Indian relations were sorely in need of direction. The frontier situation called for firmness and decision in government, and that was sadly lacking. The provincial assembly, dominated by the Quakers, would not directly support the war, to the disgust of the ministry, who felt that a new governor, a military man, was required. Hence they chose Captain William Denny to succeed Governor Morris. In the meantime the Quakers had recognized the Indian "king of the Delawares," Teedyuscung, as the spokesman for Indian grievances. This unusual character, a perennial drunkard though the ward of Moravian missionaries, an eloquent orator in the Delaware tongue, but an unstable and pliant puppet in the hands of others, complicated the problem. Both governors, Morris and Denny, held conferences with him, wherein he brought up many old grievances.[92] But they were now reminded that Indian affairs were in the hands of Sir William.

Sir William was irked by the crosspurposes of the Pennsylvania situation. Teedyuscung, with Quaker support, was trying to make the Delawares independent of the Six Nations, even threatening to join the French. The Quakers used the Indians to raise up old issues against the proprietors (like the old Walking Purchase of 1737), to embarrass the governor. And Governor Denny proved to be a vacillating and weak instrument, capitulating first to the Indians and then to the Quakers. So the superintendent sent George Croghan to Pennsylvania as his deputy with full instructions and authority. This was a shock to Pennsylvanians like Secretary Richard Peters, who knew too well Croghan's devious record as trader and land speculator. "How can I give credit to a man, who has told so many lies in Mr. Hockley's and other affairs to such a degree that I question whether he means a word he says."[93]

Yet Croghan was cautious, conciliatory, and diplomatic in order to win the support of all sides. He handled the Indian presents and even dealt successfully with some Cherokee warriors on the western frontier, although they were from the southern district. He won his point that another conference should be called at Easton, under Sir William's authority, to settle the question of Teedyuscung's charges. The proprietors in England resented these imputations of unfair dealing by them in the past, and even Croghan's suggestion that it would be politic of them to abandon Pennsylvania's 1754 land purchases and to stop building forts in the Indian country. No questions had been settled, but Croghan had made a strong case for the handling of all issues by Sir William's department.[94]

At a meeting of colonial governors and military officers in Philadelphia on March 14, General Loudoun had gained support for his next campaign. Not he but William Pitt had decided that a major attack should be made on Louisbourg or Quebec. Loudoun assembled sixteen regiments, close to fifteen thousand men, at New York, whence transports took them to Halifax. He was accompanied by Sir Charles Hardy, who resigned his governorship to revert to his naval profession as second in command to Admiral Holburne. While the British fleet, joining the transports in Halifax, was imposing, totaling nearly a hundred vessels, its slowness in assembling allowed the French to prepare the defense of Louisbourg. When the British looked into the harbor they discovered seventeen French warships waiting for them, not to mention the strong land forces for the defense of the fortress. A council of war decided that it would be foolhardy to engage this force. The French would not come out to engage in a naval battle, and soon the British fleet was struck by a hurricane, which destroyed or sank a number of ships. So at the end of August the fleet withdrew, and General Loudoun returned to New York.[95]

XX

THE FATE OF GENERALS, 1757–58

The diversion of Loudoun with so many of the regular troops left Fort William Henry and Fort Edward to be defended by small garrisons, provincials, rangers, and Indians. Through the long winter of 1756–57, Major Will Eyre, the engineer, was in command at Fort William Henry with about four hundred regulars, of whom only three hundred were fit for duty. Another small garrison held Fort Edward, while major generals Abercromby and Webb were at Albany. Winter weather seemed to preclude a major attack; Montclam had retired to Montreal, but the French kept considerable garrisons at Crown Point and Ticonderoga, where they continued to build up the works. They were supplied by convoys of sleighs upon the lake. From these respective garrisons, raids and scouting parties of limited numbers could be dispatched. The English likewise had no intention of attacking the French forts but sought to harass them by probes into their territory of small parties of rangers and Indians. Captain Robert Rogers now became famous for his daring, resourcefulness, and intrepidity in such ventures.

In January, Rogers with only seventy-four rangers marched over the ice up the lake, then on snowshoes overland until he could strike Lake Champlain below Ticonderoga. Halfway between that fort and Crown Point he intercepted a French convoy; the rangers seized three sleds and six horses but became aware that this was a part of a larger convoy, which would be more than they could handle. Realizing that French reinforcements were pursuing them, the rangers took off through the woods but were ambushed and compelled to fight a rearguard action. It was raining, and there was deep snow, which gave some advantage to the rangers on snowshoes. Though outnumbered two to one, crippled by the loss of several officers, and twice wounded himself, Rogers succeeded in reaching Fort William Henry, with the loss of fourteen men. The French narrative of the engagement admitted the loss of fourteen killed and twenty-seven wounded.[1] While this sort of raid accomplished little, it harassed the enemy and hampered his plans and preparations.

In March 1757, while a most severe winter held Lake George in its frozen grip, the French apparently made a serious attempt to take Fort William Henry. A detachment of sixteen hundred men commanded by Rigaud de Vaudreuil, governor of Trois-Rivières and brother of the governor general, set out up the lake over the ice. They were planning a surprise and were equipped with scaling ladders with which they hoped to seize the fort. In spite of their secrecy and caution, however, their approach was detected by English sentinels, and the garrison was alerted. On March 20, the fort was invested on all sides, and the French Indians were sent out to cut off the communication with Fort Edward. Now the French commander tried to intimidate the defenders; he paraded his whole force across the ice before the fort, and sent an emissary to demand its surrender. Major Eyre assembled his officers to consider the proposal, thus gaining time to empty his outer storehouses and to prepare his defense. He replied that he intended to defend the fort. The French were able to burn and destroy the outbuildings, the huts of the rangers, the bateaux (some frozen in the ice), and the waterfront structures. But they were not able to scale the fort. Snow began to fall, and soon a heavy storm forced their withdrawal. So serious was their predicament that they suffered much and lost considerable equipment on their hazardous return. A French writer called the raid partially successful; but Bougainville, the diarist, was severe in his criticism. The size of the force was too much for a mere raid, he wrote; and if escalation was intended, surprise was essential. The English rejoiced that the attempt had failed.[2]

The very day of the siege (March 20), Sir William received letters informing him of the attack on Fort William Henry. He immediately called the militia to muster at Fort Johnson, and sent messages to the Indians to meet him early the next day. In the evening he "sang his War Song" and made a speech to the Six Nations. The Indian Records noted:

Monday Morning
Sir William marched with the Six Nations, some Mohocks, then ready & the militia to Schenectady, from thence with the highland Regt. to half Moon on Tuesday.
Wensday he got to Seraghtoga & Thursday Evening to Fort Edward with the Militia who were then about 1200—and 60 Indians—the certain Account then came that the French had abandoned the Attack.[3]

After waiting another day at Fort Edward for confirmation, Sir William set off on Saturday to return and "got to his House about 5 a Clock Sunday Morning having rode all night, as he had several Accounts the Enemy were coming to attack the German Flatts."[4] Again the militia and Indians had responded with alacrity when danger threatened.

There was little reason, however, to consider this reverse as anything but a temporary check to the French menace to the forts. The size of their garrisons was increased with warmer weather, and the English in turn again built up their forces. They replaced the burned bateaux with others, and again sought to command the waters of Lake George. Yet their hopes were soon dashed. On July 24, an English force of three hundred and fifty men of the New Jersey Regiment, under Colonel John Parker, advancing up the lake in twenty-two barges were surprised by an ambush of four hundred French and Indians and nearly wiped out. Only two barges escaped capture or sinking, and some hundred and fifty men were killed; one hundred and sixty prisoners were claimed by the French. It was a major disaster and a serious loss for the English. A year later when the English passed Sabbath Day Point they remembered Parker and his men, and noted still there the "melancholy remains both in the water and on the shore."[5]

This disaster was a severe shock to the English morale, for they anticipated that the French would soon follow up this succcess with aggressive action. Now, rather belatedly, the English gave attention to their defenses and to plans for reinforcement. This was the responsibility of General Webb in Albany, who now moved to the garrison at Fort Edward.

The defenses of Fort William Henry against a large-scale enemy attack had long been recognized as inadequate. Begun by Sir William in September 1755, it was first thought of as a base for expeditions against Crown Point rather than as a permanent outpost. Work on it under the direction of Colonel Eyre had been sporadic. In June 1756 it was visited by Colonel Harry Gordon, an engineer with much experience in Western campaigns, who made a full report of its condition and recommended measures to put it into a proper state for defense.

The plan of Fort William Henry was the orthodox square of four bastions in the style of Vauban. Its location on the shore of the lake, however, was both its weakness and its strength. Near the launching docks for bateaux and barges, a convenience in sending out expeditions, it was open for a winter attack from that quarter. On the east side was a morass; on the west were gardens and open ground, while some three hundred yards farther away was high ground which would give advantage to an attacking party. On high ground on the other side lay the encampment of supporting troops, and from that point ran the road to Fort Edward. The barracks within the fort could hold three or four hundred men.

Colonel Gordon envisioned an attack from the west side and recommended raising "the Faces exposed to the rising Ground three Foot higher"; and a strengthening of the bastion on that side by a ravelin, or advanced gun position, and by supporting trenches, communications and redoubts. Without this, he said, the French could throw shells in from the higher ground, make trenches within 280 yards, and establish batteries to make a breach in the walls and earthworks.[6] But, amidst the various attacks and counter attacks, boatbuilding, and shifts of command, little was done along these lines.

Late in July, 1757, James Furniss, an English military inspector of ordnance, made a visit to Fort William Henry from Fort Edward, accompanied by General Webb. As they set out on July 29 they learned of the loss of Colonel Parker's men a few days before. Furniss reported on the conditions as he found them:

On our Arrival we found six Companys of the 35th Regiment Commanded by Lieut. Col. Monro with the Remnants of the New Jersey [Parker's] Regiment and some New Hampshire Troops amounting to one thousand men encamped at a Distance from the Fort under a Hill in such a Manner that they might easily have been cut off. It was therefore judged necessary to remove this Encampment as soon as possible and to take Possession of an Eminence, which was set about the next Day, and a Breast Work of Logs erected.[7]

Furniss found that his duty in checking the supply of powder—a great part was "Extreamly bad"—compelled him to stay when General Webb with his escort of five hundred men returned to Fort Edward on the 31st. On August 2, a reinforcement of one thousand men, with field pieces, under the command of Lieutenant Colonel Young, came from Fort Edward. Firing heard from up the lake that evening gave the first indication of a French attack. The next morning the boats of the French army were seen coming down the lake, and the alarm was sounded.[8]

This time the French were making an all-out attack with a large expedition. Their previous attempts had taught them the value of surprise, to prevent the fort from receiving adequate help to repel an attack, for the small garrison could not stand a long siege or heavy bombardment. And they were bringing sufficient force, they felt, to counterbalance whatever the English could assemble.

The French had been building up their strength at Crown Point and at Ticonderoga. Here were assembled the troops for the expedition, and here were collected the Indians who were thought to be such an essential part of the advance. The French could draw their Indians from a vast area; here were 820 of the domesticated Indians—Algonkins (Abenakis), Iroquois (Hurons, Lake of the Two Mountains, some from Detroit and Lorette)—who were subject to some control. Then there were 979 of the far western Indians (Ottawas, Chippewas, Mississaugas, Pottawattomies, Menominees, Miamis, Winnebagoes, Foxes, Sacs, and Delawares), more ferocious, over whom they had less control. According to Bougainville, the Indians presented constant difficulties, and their barbarity could not be restrained.[9]

The Royal army was commanded by Major General Montcalm, who was seconded by Chevalier de Lévis, brigadier. It was composed of the regulars of the brigades of La Reine, La Sarre and Royal Rousillon (three thousand), and there were nearly three thousand of the colonial troops and militia. In all an army of eight thousand men was assembled at the foot of Lake George.[10]

A fleet of two hundred and fifty bateaux was provided which could carry only half the army. Many of the Indians swarmed about on the water in some hundred and fifty birchbark canoes. So the remainder of the force under de Lévis, less a few hundred left to guard supplies and the portage, marched overland to rendezvous at the Bay of Ganaouskie, four leagues from Fort William Henry. Then on August 3 they came together to plan the attack.[11]

The advance came at daybreak. Chevalier de Lévis with his men took a position to the southward to cut off all communication or reinforcement from Fort Edward. Bourlamaque pitched camp and began to build fortifications to the westward—trenches, fascines, and gabions, placement for artillery pieces to invest the fort. A siege was expected, but Montcalm first tried to intimidate the defenders. Under a flag of truce he sent a message advising surrender, for he could now restrain the savages and make them observe a capitulation; but if Indians were killed, this would be out of his power, and resistance would only delay the surrender and subject the garrison to suffering. Colonel Monro returned the spirited answer that "while one log of the Fort remained upon another, or he had a man to fight, he would defend it."[12]

While the French pressed on with their siege tactics, creeping closer with their trenches and opening new batteries of guns, the English defenders countered with fairly effective fire and put the fort in a defensive position. There were four hundred men within the fort, whose cannon were frequently effective, and the camp had six fieldpieces in action. There were also occasional skirmishes and sniping in the woods. Twice rangers got through with messages for General Webb. Colonel Monro confidently expected help from Webb and the forces at Fort Edward; this indeed was his only hope for raising the siege. That the fort was lost was due to the failure of reinforcements.[13]

General Webb had at Fort Edward some four thousand men. Additional militia and Indians had been called for, and belated appeals had been sent to the governments of New England. Yet the only aid given to Fort William Henry was the thousand men under Colonel Young, who marched on July 30. None came after the siege began, although Monro asserted that some had been promised. Webb underestimated his potential strength, accepted an exaggerated claim of a prisoner that the French had eleven thousand, and concluded that the odds were against him. He coldly informed Colonel Monro that he could not send help; and thus he incurred the blame for the disaster and tragedy which followed.[14]

Sir William Johnson learned from General Webb of the danger to Fort William Henry on August 1, when the story of the loss of Parker's men was recounted. Immediately he took steps to supply both militia and Indians in accord with his standing orders from General Loudoun. The Indian Records are eloquent concerning his vigorous response.

. . . Gen Webb was convinced by the Enemys Motions that an Attack upon Fort William Henry was their Design & therefore desired Sir William to raise all the Militia upon this River except the Flatts and with as many Indians as he could muster together, to march himself & join him as soon as possible at Fort Edward, that on the Enemy's Approach they might jointly make such a stand as with the Assistance of Heaven might frustrate the Designs of the Enemy. Sir William told them all he was resolved to go & join the General with all the Militia he could Muster & threw a War Belt to them desiring they would join His Majestys Arms.[15]

The Indians replied that they would drop the other matters they came to see him about and would assist him, if he provided arms, ammunition, and clothing for them. This Sir William promised, and then "sent away a black Belt to the Schoharys & Susquahannas, another to the Connojoharys Oneidas & Tuscarores inviting them to come & join him."[16]

2 Augt As many as were present of the difft. Nations were armed & fitted out, also several Mohocks, the rest they said would be here the next day, also the Connojoharys. When they arrived Sir William ordered an Ox to be dressed for their War Dance & the next day set off with near 100. several more followed the 2d. & 3d. Day to the Amount of 180 in the Whole. they arrived at Fort Edward Saturday Morning about 9 a Clock 6 Augt. with about 1500 Militia. 46 of the Stockbridge Indians joined Sir William the 9 who were very serviceable scouting.[17]

Sir William acted as promptly in giving orders to the militia. He wrote General Webb on August 1, at six o'clock.

I instantly Issued My Orders to the two Lieut. Collos. of the Militia. Ranslear [Van Rensselaer] at Albany is to detach as many Men from the first Battallion as he and ye Comdg. officer there may Judge Sufficient for ye. defence of that Place, and March the remdr. to Join you. Lt. Collo. Glen is to order Boats Canoes &ca: to Nestigamy [Niskayuna] and Join me with those of the 2d. Battallion from this River & Indians there tomorrow or next day at furthest, if my Health will permit me to go. It could not have happened at a worse time, as the People are all busy with their Harvest, wh. must now Suffer. I have my hands & Head full with some delegates from ye. Cherokee Nation & Severall from the Southward here also. ...[18]

In spite of all his business, his ill health, and the inopportune time, Sir William inspired the Indians with his vigorous preparations, urged on the militia who responded to his call, and even added a final word of encouragement to his superior.

If the Militia from New England will but come time enough, & those of the lower Countrys & here together wth. Indians can be got in so short a time, I doubt not but you may be able to give the Mosrs. [Monsieurs] un coup Mortel wh.God grant. ...[19]

Having reached Fort Edward with militia and Indians at fever pitch, awaiting the commands of General Webb, Sir William was scarcely prepared for the abject abandonment of relief by that miserable commander. He well knew the whole situation, for his Indian scouts were all through the woods. With Indians and militia both depending upon him he knew the risks of battle, but he also knew the consequences of defeat, which would permeate the frontier like an infection. Webb was but a general in a strange country; Sir William's power, his property, his whole estate and influence might be at stake. And he had a personal interest in Fort William Henry, which he had established and named two years before.

The Indian Records are mute upon, and Sir William drew a veil over, the events which followed. But there must have been many witnesses of the dramatic scene when he confronted General Webb, after the latter had resolved not to relieve the fort. The French learned of it through the Iroquois Indians, whose regard for Sir William endured through this show of spirit and leadership so much in contrast with the inaction of the general.

Some months later Bougainville wrote a correspondent that the tale had come to him from the western Indians, who had it from their Mohawk brothers, how Sir William Johnson had gone into a towering rage at General Webb. Johnson, he wrote, had arrived at Fort Edward with the provincials, and at the head of his Indians, all in war paint like his followers, tomahawk at his side and spear in hand. He proposed to General Webb that they march at once on the French lines. Webb replied that he would do no such thing, that he did not wish to expose himself to a complete defeat in woods still wet with English blood. Johnson retorted that these very shores of Lake George would be as fatal to Montcalm as they had been to Dieskau, that French bones would cover this battlefield, and as for himself, he swore by his spear and tomahawk he would conquer or die. General Webb was not moved. Johnson then called to witness the Celtic [British] lion, tore off one of his leggings and hurled it at Webb's feet. "You won't do it?" he cried. "No." Tore off the other legging. "You won't?" Threw down his loincloth. "You won't?" Threw his shirt, tomahawk, and spear down and galloped off with his troop, who had followed the example of their leader. "Where, oh, where," wrote Bougainville, "is there a Homer to depict such a heroic scene."[20]

Although he had three appeals from Colonel Monro, General Webb by a letter dated August 4, at noon, informed the commander that there would be no help. "He did not think it prudent to attempt a junction, or to assist you, 'till reinforced by the militia of the Colonies." Instead of relying upon his own scouts, Webb magnified the risk by citing a French prisoner who claimed the enemy controlled the area five miles this side of Fort William Henry, that they numbered eleven thousand, and had "a large train of artillery and mortars." Hence, the letter went on, "in case he should be so unfortunate from the delays of the militia not to have it in his power to give you timely Assistance, you might be able to make the best terms left in your power." In other words, the garrison was told to go it alone.[21]

Inept and unwise as was this letter, its effect was compounded when it fell into French hands. One messenger was captured and another was killed; the letter was found in the vest of the slain man and was carried by the Indians to Montcalm. And well may that wily general have smiled when he read it. He would make full use of it for his own ends. First he used it to galvanize the French; they determined "to expedite still more the construction of the batteries. The number of workers was increased, " to complete works necessary for the final bombardment before help arrived.

Next Montcalm revealed the contents of Webb's letter to the Indians, telling them of his plans and of the likelihood that the English would soon surrender. The restless savages were thus mollified for a while. Finally, under a flag of truce he sent Bougainville to deliver the letter to Colonel Monro and to demand his surrender. There was the usual protocol, Montcalm saying how he wished to treat like a gentleman, and Monro thanking him for his consideration. But again the fort commander declared his determination to resist. Although their hopes for relief had been dashed, Monro and his men were resolute. "It was surprising," he wrote later, "to see a handful of men, with all hopes of Succour cut off, behave with so much resolution as they afterwards did."[22]

For two days more the garrison held out, until the men were worn down and many of their guns had given out. The engineer estimated that only twenty-four more hours of resistance was possible. By August 9, the French trenches had reached the garden, and their guns were in a position to do increased damage. Finally, after consultation with his officers, Colonel Monro sent out a white flag and asked for terms of capitulation.[23] The French thereupon dictated the following terms:

That the garrison of the fort and the troops of the intrenched camp to the number of 2,000 men, shall march out with the honors of war, carrying away arms and baggage, and take with them one cannon, out of respect for the gallant defence they have made.

That they will not serve during 18 months against his Most Christian Majesty [the French King] and his allies.

That within 4 months from this date they shall send back to Carillon the prisoners they have taken from the French and their allies, on the territory of North America since the commencement of the war.

That they shall leave in the ramparts, arsenal and magazines, all the artillery, ammunition, provisions and other effects that are there.[24]

Montcalm rejoiced that he had taken in the fort "36 pieces of ordnance, 2,500 shot, 545 shell, 36 thousand weight of powder, 350 thousand rations, some other provisions and some merchandise; two sloops in the harbor, two on the stocks, 4 large flat bateaux and eight barges." Moreover the cost had been light, for he claimed only thirteen men killed and forty wounded, while the English, he said, lost two hundred.[25]

All along Montcalm had been apprehensive of the conduct of the Indians and of his ability to control them. He had informed them of Webb's letter, and he held council with them to explain the terms of surrender and to gain their approval. But even before the fort came into French hands the Indians began pillaging; they fell upon some of the sick and wounded in the hospital, whom they scalped and killed. The French tried to stave in all the casks of wine, brandy, and liquors, but the Indians found some, which added to their frenzy. Montcalm feared trouble when the prisoners were to be marched to Fort Edward; he once ordered them sent in the evening and then countermanded the order. At ten o'clock on the morning of the 10th, the prisoners began their march with an escort of regulars.[26] Accounts differ as to just what happened then. The eyewitness account of Furniss is factual:

On the 10th early in the Morning when we were preparing to march, the Savages surrounded us, took my Horses which I had given to carry off the Gun, got over the Breast Work, and began to plunder. At all Events the French Troops who we thought were sent to protect us, were of no Assistance, and advised giving up our Effects rather than dispute with the Savages who would not be satisfied untill they had got all the Baggage, this 'tho contrary to the Capitulation (to prevent worse Consequences) was complied with, as the Officers and Soldiers immediately delivered every Thing up to them, except their Arms and the Clouths on our Backs, which we hoped they would suffer us to carry off. Instead of which they took our Hats, and Swords from us, and began to strip us, on which it was thought proper to march out as soon as possible, the Savages [having] taken the Drums, Halberds, and even the Firelocks from the Soldiers.

This unexpected Treatment so contrary to the Terms of the Capitulation, surprised us so much, and struck so great a Panick into the Troops, who knew not where it would end, that all Efforts proved ineffectual to prevent their running away, in a very confused and irregular Manner, which gave the Savages an Opportunity of scalping many who were so unlucky to be in the rear or made the Resistance.

The sick and wounded felt the first Stroke of their Barbarity whom they scalped before they could get out of the Breastwork. The Savages pursued about four Miles, and made several Prisoners, amongst whom I was one, at three Miles Distance, by two of them & carried back towards Fort William Henry, but was luckily retaken by a French Guard, who sent an Officer and Twenty Men with me into the Fort, where I found Lieut. Colonel Monro, and several Officers. some of which had been made Prisoners, and others had surrendered themselves to a French Post about a Mile from the Fort to protect them from the Cruelty of the Savages.[27]

Montcalm and his officers had rushed out when they heard the tumult and did their best to control the Indians, at the risk of their lives; but, as Bougainville exclaimed, "who in the world could restrain 2000 Indians of 32 different Nations, when they have drunk liquor!" French officers herded into the fort some of the prisoners and clothed the naked, even giving up their own clothes. Yet the result was a shameful massacre of an estimated two hundred men and women, sick and wounded, who were helpless victims. A number of others were carried off by the Indians as captives to Montreal. Grateful for their rescue, some of the English praised the efforts of the French officers, but everyone realized that this episode was a black mark upon the honor of the victors.[28]

Several days later the English prisoners remaining were escorted safely to Fort Edward. Montcalm quickly wrote to Generals Webb and Loudoun explaining the massacre, relating his efforts to stop it, and advising that it should not be considered in any way as a pretext for not carrying out the terms of the surrender. In fact, he asserted, any infraction of the terms would be met with reprisals.[29]

So the French tried to minimize the massacre and its importance; Montcalm contended that "what would be an infraction in Europe, cannot be so regarded in America."[30] They blamed the English for giving rum to the Indians and asserted that if the prisoners had shown firmness, instead of giving in or running, the disaster would have been less. But primarily they contended that the Indians were uncontrollable. They related many examples of barbarity and cannibalism to illustrate this view. The savages were a necessary evil.[31]

To the English this all had a hollow ring. The massacre had occurred under the very eyes of the French general and before three thousand of his regular troops. It was in defiance of the promised escort. It did little good to plead the nature of the savage; the French were responsible for the numbers and the character of those they enlisted, and surely they must shoulder the blame. The English press reported that the French "most perfidiously let their Indian bloodhounds loose upon the people" and recorded the gory atrocities committed.[32]

The consequences of the episode were many. It may have had weight in deterring the French from proceeding to attack Fort Edward, which their orders required them to do. Their Indians had now returned to Canada, but there were other factors—shortage of food and munitions, fatigue of the men, and the desire of the colonials to return for the harvests. The English fully expected Fort Edward to be attacked. All of the militia called to succour Fort William Henry were converging there, where a much greater force would await the French.[33]

Hence the victors contented themselves with the burning and demolition of the fort, which they had completed by the 15th. Considerable effort was required to raze the well-built breastworks. Two row-galleys were burned at the water's edge. Leaving little behind, Montcalm's army departed on the 16th, and returned to Montreal.[34] The spoliation of many fresh graves by the French Indians in search of further plunder and scalps was said to have given them the smallpox infection, from which many died.[35] This was regarded by the English as a kind of retribution for the massacre.

Although Fort Edward was spared, the destruction of Fort William Henry, the massacre, and heavy loss in men and munitions, coupled with failures elsewhere, were severe shocks to the English. The press reproached the ministry, as well as the commanders in the field. In America the frontier was apprehensive of future blows. If the French could strike so effectively where troops were massed, what protection could be expected at other points?[36] Morale dropped; the Indians became lukewarm or defected. Sir William had to resort to extreme measures even to keep the good will of old friends.

> . . . The loss of Fort Wm Henry & the victory lately gained by the enemy at Lake George, together with our disappointments from Halifax and my Lord Loudoun's return with the troops from thence and the French receiving Succors of troops & stores at Quebec has very much cooled the ardor of those Indians who were disposed to be active & rendered us of less consequence in the eyes of others. . . .
> The two Mohock Castles have hitherto stuck firm to us, tho at a very expensive praemium since the loss of Fort William Henry, they have renewed to me the strongest assurances of their zeal & fidelity & I think they are sincere tho' our present sittuation makes them very mercenary & some of them as well as the other Nations, not a little insolent.[37]

General Webb's responsibility for the debacle seemed conclusive. He was censured in Colonel Monro's report on three counts: that he did not promptly send information, which he had, of the French advance; that he admitted that Fort William Henry was more likely to be attacked than Fort Edward, yet he kept a larger force at the latter and denied the former adequate support; and that when he promised a thousand men on July 30, they were not sent until August 2, and further requested reinforcements were denied. By August 6, Webb's aide wrote, he had five thousand men, with the militia who were marching to relief with the hope of victory.[38] His failure on several occasions to take the most logical steps for the support of the fort, can only be explained by his gross incompetence. That in turn was partly due to his physical condition. He was subject to fits of the palsy which left him weak and demoralized. Why under these circumstances he was left in command is indeed a puzzle. Perhaps some blame should fall on General Loudoun, whose absence from the field gave the golden opportunity for the French offensive. And in true military fashion this is where the official condemnation fell. Loudoun's recall was no longer in doubt.[39]

The fiasco of the Louisbourg expedition and the loss of Fort William Henry which followed hard upon it were enough to end Loudoun's career in America. Yet his recall was quite as much determined by the change in the ministry in England; William Pitt had succeeded Cumberland, who had favored Loudoun. Pitt had ordered the Louisbourg expedition and was chagrined at its failure. He now charged that Loudoun had no plans for the year 1758, and denounced his handling of American affairs. In a sharp letter of December 30, he ordered Loudoun home and told him to hand over the command to Major General Abercromby.[40]

From the first, Loudoun as a severe critic of Shirley, whom he had sent home to explain his accounts, had been friendly to Sir William. He allowed the superintendent much freedom in his organizing of the Indian department. Sir William for his part sympathized with Loudoun's efforts at reorganizing and coordinating the colonial forces with the regulars. He had had his own troubles with the independence of the New England troops. Yet Loudoun had shown no regard for Sir William's insistence on the danger at Lake George, which was now all too evident.

Reporting on the return of Loudoun to Albany in October, Banyar wrote to Sir William that Loudoun was displeased with the Six Nations and dissatisfied with the handling of their affairs. Sir William was too ill to meet Loudoun in Albany, but a long letter from the general, December 25, revealed a disturbing attitude. Loudoun would cast off the Six Nations as allies and rely on his own efforts to enlist "domiciliated Indians"; at the same time he would ask for all the Indian intelligence Sir William could supply, protesting his confidence in him and denying any intention of interference. Minor differences had arisen over Loudoun's use of Peter Wraxall, the Indian secretary, while in New York, and over Croghan as Sir William's deputy.[41] Sir William was disturbed that Loudoun seemed to lack comprehension of his rôle. What Loudoun failed to understand was that the series of English defeats, culminating in the fall of Fort William Henry, along with French attacks on the Mohawk Valley settlements, had undermined English influence with the Indians. The most heroic efforts of those in charge of Indian affairs had to be devoted to keeping their good will.

Major General James Abercromby, who had served with Loudoun from the time of his selection, was made commander in chief upon Loudoun's recall. When this news reached America Sir William wrote promptly to congratulate the new commander and to renew his several requests and demands, with which Abercromby was not unfamiliar. He emphasized the need for arms and other supplies to equip Indians, which could be bought more cheaply in England; he sought the release of Captain Wraxall from his regiment in New York to serve him as Indian secretary; he asked for permission to continue his correspondence with Lord Howe, the brilliant field officer who was so quickly adapting his men to frontier fighting; and he finally asked a warrant for his salary, which had not been paid in three years.[42]

Abercromby's reply was cordial and conciliatory on all points. He recognized the significance of Indian affairs; he would seek to obtain supplies, and when possible would release Captain Wraxall from his duties. He mentioned especially, however, that he would need as many Indians as possible raised for the attack upon Crown Point, which he was ordered to make this summer.[43] Sir William promptly proposed several measures in line with the commander's requests: Croghan was to be sent to Pennsylvania both to help pacify Indians there and to seek their aid; a party of Mohawks would scout toward Canada; and messengers would be sent to the Six Nations to enlist their support for the campaign. He thought he could "bring a pritty considerable Body of Indians into the Feild." But he had conditions. "It would greatly encourage the Indians If there were about a hundred of the briskest young men from this part of the country to join them," for scouting, bringing intelligence, being under the present Indian officers, and being paid as rangers.

Also needed would be "a good number of proper light arms for the Indians, also middle sized Pistolls, & Cutlasses." A good armorer would be necessary to repair their arms. If there should be a lack of this equipment, not only would their aid be lost, but they might "turn against us."[44]

Since the help of the Indians depended so much upon their temper, the condition of their affairs, and their attitude toward the French, Sir William prepared a lengthy review of Indian affairs from 1755 to the present and went to Albany to explain matters to the general in person. All was in suspense due to an impending meeting of the tribes at Onondaga. Should this gathering favor the English, Johnson thought, he could bring "4 or 500 Indians" into the field; but if it should propose a neutrality, he might just possibly muster three hundred Indians to go to Lake George; should the meeting favor the French, he could not say whether any would join him, or how far such a hostile influence might pervade. Furthermore, he had to state that "the Indians in general are so devoted to & debauched by Rum, that all Business with them is thrown into confusion by it & my transactions with them unspeakably impeded."[45]

The task of recruiting the Indians was taken up with vigor; Indian officers were sent out with belts, Sir William's message, to the various nations, while other Indians were brought to the council room at Fort Johnson. Captain Jelles Fonda journeyed to the Oneidas and intended to carry the belt to the Onondagas, too, but was advised to hold back. Captain Thomas Butler went to the Canajoharies, while John Butler carried word to the Stockbridge Indians and the Mohegans. John Lottridge was sent to the Schoharie Indians.[46] At Fort Johnson Sir William reminded the Six Nations that he could fix their arms, caulk their bateaux, and clothe them from the King's supplies only if they would join him on the campaign. He assured them that he would go with them in person, for many would follow if he would lead.[47]

In the meantime Sir William in his capacity as commander of the Albany County militia issued orders for their mustering at Schenectady and Albany, but since he was so involved with the Indians he turned the details of this operation over to Colonel Jacob Glen. The response might have been good but for the diffusion of the available manpower. As he wrote Abercromby June 1, "the Militia on this River [Mohawk] are almost all drawn off by the Battoe, Ranging Service, Provincial Levies &c. [so that] the remainder make up but an inconsiderable Body." His own Indian officers and rangers also drew from this resource.[48]

Hence when Sir William finally reported to Abercromby on June 22 that the Indians were coming or reported on the way, that he needed six or seven days longer, and he should be given "positive Orders when I must march to join you," Abercromby blew up. He expressed surprise that his demands had not been recognized, that he was "being deprived of your Aid & Assistance with the Indians at Your Back, which we stand much in need of." He had been assembling the largest force ever raised in America for such an expedition. He now displayed resolution:

I propose to be at the Lake on Monday the 26th: & to get every thing a-float with all possible Dispatch; So that you have not a day to lose in joining us; & if we should fall down the Lake, I shall leave Boats for you to follow.—Let me know what number you can bring. Forward those in readiness, with your Indian Officers, & come with the last Column yourself; You know best their Trim, & take your own Method.[49]

Stung by this sharp order, Sir William replied courteously but with spirit.

If I have failed herein, it hath not been owing to Intention, but to the misfortune of my being involved in a Service which cannot, or at least which I cannot, put upon a Footing of Certainty & Punctuality.

On Thursday I will march from hence with such Indians I can prevail on to go with me; what number that will be, I cannot be certain of, I believe about 200, and that more will follow me. . . .

I assure you, Sir, upon my honour, that you cannot be more impatient for my joining you with the Indians, than I have been, & am, to do so. I am as much perplexed as you are displeased at the Delay, & your Displeasure adds to my Perplexity.[50]

The Indians were not easy to assemble at this time. It was reported that they were short of provisions; they had taken to drinking and some were not sober enough to come. Some two hundred accompanied Sir William and reached a camp ten miles from Fort Edward on July 5. About a day's march behind came Croghan with a hundred more. Daniel Claus, Montour, and other Indian officers rounded up additional Indians, who appeared by the time the forces were engaged to make the total four hundred and fifty.[51]

Less than five hundred Indians seems an insignificant element in the army of fifteen thousand which was being assembled at Lake George. But in all wilderness campaigns and marches they were essential for scouting, for intelligence, to make raids and to capture prisoners, and to counteract and frustrate the similar activities of the enemy Indians. Without them the commander felt a chink in his armor. In battle they were likely to be on the periphery, scalping and looting and perhaps out of control, as were the Indians of the French at Fort William Henry. Sometimes the English, like the French, considered them but a necessary evil.

In assembling the unusually large force for the campaign, Abercromby was chiefly aided by the energetic Brigadier General Lord Howe. Sent over the previous year by William Pitt to invigorate the army, George Augustus, Viscount Howe, a man of thirty-three years, was the ideal commander. First a colonel of the Royal Americans, he was promoted and given command of the 55th Regiment. Howe spent some time observing the Mohawk frontier in 1757. He met and corresponded with Sir William about the use of Indians, and there was mutual respect. Unlike so many regular commanders, he learned from the frontiersmen and copied their methods.[52] In May a Boston writer described him:

I need not inform you how justly Lord Howe is celebrated here for his robust Soldier-like Constitution, his bold, enterprising Spirit, and every other military accomplishment; with how much Care he has been forming his regular Troops to the Method of Bush-fighting all Season, so that he has now, it is said, made them as dexterous at it almost as the Rangers.—In order to do this, he has ordered all the coats of his Regiment to be cut short, to make them as light as possible; and has sacrificed a fine Head of Hair of his own, as an Example to the Soldiers, which they have followed, so that not a man is to be seen with his own Hair. The Strength of his Constitution enables him to undergo all Hardships, and it is his opinion that every Officer ought to do the same, and to live and fare like the Common men.— To this End he has forbidden the Officers all supernumerary Baggage, when they march into the Enemy's country, as being only a useless Encumbrance to the Army, has allowed them only so much Cloaths as may be sufficient; and no Provisions, but those which proceed from the Commissioners. . . . His Soldiers love and fear him, and are willing to comply with his Commands, because he first sets them an Example. What great things might not a few officers like Lord Howe effect, with an Army of such men.[53]

Howe marched with 3,000 men and was at Lake George on June 19.[54] Other regulars, including the Royal Americans and the Highland Scots of the Black Watch, brought the total at embarkation time to 6,367. Provincials from Massachusetts, Connecticut, Rhode Island, New Jersey, and New York—including Rogers's rangers and Bradstreet's bateaumen—numbered 9,024. This army was ready to embark via the water route down the lake on July 5, in 900 bateaux, 135 whaleboats, and some rafts to carry the artillery.[55]

What a scene was presented as this unusual flotilla blackened the waters of the peaceful lake at daybreak and slowly rowed and poled its way some twenty-five miles down to Sabbath Day Point, which they reached at five P.M. Here, only twelve miles from the enemy, the army paused, and some units landed on the shore. They waited until eleven o'clock, and then resumed their journey under cover of darkness. Yet at this stop they had been observed by French scouts, and when they encamped the next morning the enemy were aware of the danger. Only a mile away from the English army, the French encampment of a few hundred men became alarmed and prepared to return to the Fort. The English now sent out a small force of fifteen hundred men under Lord Howe to feel out the approaches to the fort. Seeking an Indian path through the woods, they accidently fell upon the French force of three hundred men. In a brisk skirmish the French were routed with some loss. But the English suffered most grievously, for with the first volley Lord Howe was killed, and with his death the soul and spirit of the English army went also. All mourned the youthful commander, whose body was sent back to Albany with honors, but the greatest loss was his inspired but sensible leadership. Now all decisions had to be made by Abercromby, who proved quite unequal to the task.[56]

The next day, July 7, was one of preparation for battle. The French abandoned their camp at the saw mill, destroyed the bridge over the creek, and withdrew to the fort. Colonel John Bradstreet led an English force which rebuilt the bridge and then occupied the camping place, now only two miles from Ticonderoga.[57]

Montcalm, in command of Fort Carillon (Ticonderoga), had long anticipated the English advance and had vainly warned Governor Vaudreuil of the danger of an attack for which he felt himself unprepared. He had asked for more troops; he had no Indians, since the French had economized on their food distribution; and now he discovered that he would be greatly outnumbered. All day on July 7, his entire command, officers and men, were engaged in building entrenchments on the height west of the fort. Trees were felled, their branches stripped and pointed to form a kind of *chevaux de frise* or abatis, with earthworks to protect the defenders. This stretched from the river side to the ravine or cliff side of Lake Champlain. Behind these barriers the army could make its stand outside the walls of the fort. In the evening the French were cheered by the arrival of some 400 picked men under Chevalier de Lévis. Yet the French could still only claim 3,250 men for defense. Through their industry, however, they had erected a formidable barrier to the attacking army.[58]

Abercromby now lost all sense of discretion. He feared that the fort would be reinforced, so he wanted to attack at once and thus overwhelm the enemy by weight of numbers. He sent an engineer to observe the French works from a nearby elevation; the latter gave an incorrect report of the height and strength of the abatis. Why did Abercromby not rely upon his scouts, rangers, and Indians for this intelligence? Conventional tactics for reducing a fort would dictate a siege, especially when the attackers had the advantage and the use of artillery to wear down the defenders. It was also logical to send a force to cut off supplies and reinforcement. But Abercromby did none of these things. Instead he resolved upon a frontal assault, and struck where the French were best prepared to receive him. Even if he had succeeded in forcing the abatis, he would still have had to attack the fort itself.[59]

At daybreak on July 8, orders were given for storming the French lines; picquets, the light infantry, the rangers, and bateaumen moved first, and were followed by the regulars and militia. "The piquets were to begin the attack, sustained by the grenadiers, and they by the battalions: The whole were ordered to march up briskly, rush upon the enemy's fire, and not to give theirs until they were within the enemy's breast-work." A critic later said the advance was not all at once, but in files, upon which the enemy could center their fire. Abercromby naïvely reported that "unfortunately they found the intrenchments not only much stronger than had been represented . . . but likewise the ground before it covered with felled trees, the branches pointed outwards, which so fatigued and retarded the advancing of the troops that, notwithstanding all their intrepidity and bravery, . . . we sustained so considerable a loss, without any prospect of better success, that it was no longer prudent to remain before it." It was a suicidal venture, for while the English were slowed by the obstacles and completely exposed, the French were hidden and able to mow down the attackers. After one hour the outcome was evident, but no orders came to withdraw until four hours of fighting had brought the English nearly two thousand casualties. The dead and wounded covered the field when Abercromby ordered a retreat to camp of the night before. The next day he ordered a return to the camp on the lake.[60]

The French fully expected Abercromby to return to the attack on the 9th. They manned the abatis at daybreak, but soon were informed that the enemy had withdrawn. Great was their joy and relief, for a prolonged siege would have been hard for them to sustain. The English troops were shaken by their heavy losses, but were not without resolution and spirit. They were shocked when Abercromby decided to abandon the campaign.

What will our posterity say [wrote one man] when they will learn that 14,000 men kept up and sustained, for six consecutive hours, with a courage truly heroic, a triple fire from the enemy at an intrenchment impregnable to small arms, without the slightest hope of carrying it?. . . Our loss in Regulars was 1,500 men killed and wounded; the Provincials lost in all only about 600 men. The enemy cannot have lost over one hundred. . . . . We retreated that evening and during the night to the Landing Place, and what crowns our misfortune and surpasses all belief, on the morning of the 9th everything was embarked and gone, to return whence we came, having still 12,000 fighting men in good health, and divers good intrenched camps. We arrived on the same day at Fort Wm. Henry.[61]

Abercromby's supreme effort had not only proved costly beyond all belief, but it had been abandoned with nothing achieved. His attempt to take the fort by assault, so futile and ill-advised, had ended in failure and was not followed by siege or any further attempt on the part of his strong forces. He thus lost the respect of the army and the confidence of the government. His recall was inevitable.[62]

While there has been criticism of the rôle played by Johnson and his Indians in this battle, it is hard to see what more they could have done. They took up the position on Rattlesnake Mountain to which they were assigned, and they fired upon the defenders at work on their abatis, as the French noted. Like all such auxiliaries they waited for opportunities to cut off stray parties, to cut supply lines, or to harass the enemy during a siege which never came. They could be of little use in the frontal attack. Like Sir William, the Indians were stunned by the catastrophe. The collapse of the campaign left them nothing to do but return to their homes. Again it would fall upon Sir William to explain away this defeat, so hard to reconcile with his promises to them.[63]

Lacking any plans of his own, and being forced into defensive measures at Lake George and Fort Edward, Abercromby now harkened to suggestions of others. Major Robert Rogers and his rangers combed the wilderness to the northward and by their forays somewhat contained the French.[64] Colonel John Bradstreet, who had performed so remarkably in providing whaleboats, bateaux, and their manpower in transporting the great army, now reverted to his scheme to attack Fort Frontenac. In March he had proposed to Loudoun "an attempt against Cadaraqui" with "800 Battoe Men or Rangers," who would be eager for a service involving the security of their own area. Information brought by Indian scouts revealed not only the danger of French raids upon the Mohawk Valley, but that there were boats, munitions, and supplies at Cadaracqui destined for such raids or for Niagara.[65] Brigadier General John Stanwix had been sent to the Mohawk, and on June 25 Sir William had suggested

that if a strong Body of Troops could speedily take Post at the German Flatts, and about 600 be detached as a grand scout to the Oneida Carrying Place, their march thither would be very soon carried to Oswego, Fort Frontenac or Sweigachie, and if the Enemy had any Designs on foot, as I am apt to believe their Force consists cheifly of Indians, it would I think confound & over-awe them, & not improbably, cause the Indians to withdraw.[66]

Now it seemed this plan was to be adopted. Colonel Bradstreet with some three thousand men, chiefly colonials, was sent to join Stanwix, and Sir William was asked to provide Indians for the expedition. He made an appeal to the several nations and dispatched his Indian officers—captains John and Thomas Butler and John Lottridge—to enlist the warriors. A sum of £500 was given to Thomas Butler for the service; Lottridge was given instructions for the march as far as Oswego, but told to keep secret the purpose or destination. When Bradstreet and Stanwix reached German Flats, Sir William had a guard of seventy Indians ready to accompany them to the Oneida Carrying Place. The Indian response was good; contingents came from each of the Six Nations, and their officers were later commended for their part in the enterprise. The rangers and Indians served as scouts, led the vanguard on the march, and preceded the other boats down the lake. They were assigned flanking duties during the siege, holding a hill position. Lest they be mistaken for the enemy, each of the Indians were a piece of red gimp in his hair.[67]

Bradstreet left the Carrying Place with about three thousand men, "with a train of artillery, Mortars, Shells, &c." He followed the route well known to him and the bateaumen who had supplied the ill-fated fort at Oswego. From there the whaleboats and bateaux hugged the shores of Lake Ontario, or took refuge near the islands, fearing the winds and heavy seas which often prevailed on the lake. From a nearby island they were able to take the fort completely by surprise. Although Fort Frontenac had long been an important post for the French, its defenses were weak, and its garrison was relatively small. French critics had frequently noted its vulnerability.[68]

The fort of Frontenack was a Regular Square Built on the Entrance into the Lake Ontario On the West Side of the River. It was Built of Stone and lined about fifteen feet high had all Round a platform of timber Boarded with thick plank on which their Cannon was mounted the Embrazures were too narrow to Admitt many of the Cannon to be brought to bear on One point.
The Situation was bad for it Stood in a Low place And Rising Ground N West of it, and Little Hollows by Which we made our Approaches with So Little Loss, the first Day we made no Entrenchment but behind one of these Little Heights fired our Cannon upon them.[69]

Bradstreet knew that the garrison was weak, but he did not make Abercromby's mistake of relying upon superior numbers. Hence he was able to win a cheap victory and to take the fort without the loss of a man. A few days later Colonel Thomas Butler, one of the Indian officers, reported the action.

26th Eairley in the morning Landed our Cannon. &c: Drew them Near the Fort upon which we fired & they at us, which lasted the whole day & not one of our people hurt. in the night we Got two intrenchmts Made within 200 yards of the Enemys Fort. the Enemy fired very briskly with Cannon & Small arms at us all this night little fire from us. onely once in a while a bumb.
27th our Cannon &c played at the Fort very briskly which the Monsrs finding to hot Came out to Capitulate & about twelve oClock we took possession. Spent the Remainder of the day in destroying the Fort. Shiping &c.. the latter of which were nine. not one Escaped.[70]

Bradstreet was efficient and methodical in his treatment of both fort and captives. With his small expeditionary force and limited number of boats he could not carry off a great deal. As Clinton described it, they "broke trunnions of cannon, broke down the wall of the Fort and Burn'd all the houses Barracks & Buildings in and about it." All was a "heap of Rubbish, By this we paid them for the Demolition of Oswego." [71]

There was a great quantity of military stores and supplies intended for western posts. One vessel richly loaded attempted to escape but was caught. Seven of the nine vessels were burned, the others were used to transport the loot to Oswego. It was a great satisfaction to recover an English ship taken at Oswego, and to retake material captured from General Braddock in 1755. The value of the loot was estimated at £70,000. [72]

The Indians were restrained and properly paid off. Generous terms were accorded the prisoners, about a hundred and twenty of whom were sent down the river to Montreal to be exchanged for English prisoners. Noyan, the commander, was traded for Colonel Peter Schuyler. It was impossible for Bradstreet to carry his prisoners back, and even some of the captured supplies had to be left or destroyed at Oswego. The return trip, upstream and by portage around the falls, was "slavery" to the exhausted troops. [73]

The taking of Fort Frontenac was a brilliant stroke, for its loss not only hurt the French prestige and morale through the whole frontier, but it cut in two their communication with the West. The English were now masters of the waters of Lake Ontario. This victory helped to atone for the failure at Ticonderoga and was a great boon to the sagging morale of the English in the Mohawk Valley.

News of Bradstreet's victory was widely hailed and joyously celebrated. At Abercromby's camp it came after word of the fall of Louisbourg to Amherst, but it received far greater acclaim, with prayers, massing of troops, the firing of salvos, and with three large bonfires on the mountains. It meant the removal of the French threat and was followed by the departure of Montcalm for Montreal. Indians were dispatched with the news to encourage Forbes on his campaign against Fort Duquesne. Sir William wrote Abercromby, "I am of opinion the Destruction of Fort Frontenac, of the Vessells, Provisions &c. there will fix the 5 Nations firmer to our Interest, & tend to destroy what Interest the French had amongst them." [74]

Then early in December came reports of the arrival at Fort Edward of Colonel Peter Schuyler with 114 prisoners released at Montreal. These were loud in their praise of their deliverer, Bradstreet. [75] Both Bradstreet and General Amherst were acclaimed when they reached the camp at Lake George, where the general reviewed the troops. Shortly thereafter Abercromby left for Albany; news of his being superseded by General Amherst did not reach America until December. By then, too, came word of the abandonment of Fort Duquesne by the French and its occupation by General Forbes on November 25. This still further raised the hopes of the English in America. [76]

The loss of Fort Frontenac hit the French like a thunderbolt. Coming almost simultaneously with the fall of Louisbourg, it deprived them of any initiative for campaigns that year. Losing their influence with the Iroquois and affecting the morale of their Indian allies, it forced them to reconsider a strike at Oswego or the Mohawk which the British had feared. The loss of supplies, munitions, artillery, and shipping was considerable. Their western supply line was cut, and their supremacy on the waters of Lake Ontario was ended. The morose Montcalm, long a critic of French policies, now saw Niagara endangered and feared the fall of all Canada.[77]

Relations of the English with the Indians, on the other hand, greatly improved and thus were expected to enhance the prospects of treaty negotiations to be held at Easton, Pennsylvania, in the fall.[78] Pennsylvania's Indian relations were complicated by conflicting policies of the weak governor, the proprietary party, and leading Quakers. The latter had pushed forward Teedyuscung, to make extreme demands and to play a large rôle at Easton. Governor Denny hoped to make this a great meeting, inviting the governors of several states and asking Sir William to take charge of the negotiations. Abercromby viewed the meeting as crucial in its probable effect upon the campaign in western Pennsylvania. Yet he left to Sir William the decision as to whether his presence was more necessary on the Mohawk with the Six Nations.[79]

Sir William had little stomach for involving himself in Pennsylvania's internecine squabbles. He was incensed when Quaker leaders proposed to invite Cayugas and Senecas only, and not the leaders of the Six Nations. He regarded Teedyuscung's presumption in speaking for eighteen nations as "an excess of Vanity & a head made giddy by . . . the Courtship which has been paid to him"; and thought him "inebriated with the Notice which has been taken of him at Philadelphia." He decided he could not leave the Mohawk at a crucial time and so delegated George Croghan to represent him.[80]

Croghan was an old hand at Pennsylvania politics but was not favorably regarded by many officials there. Now he acted circumspectly in accordance with Sir William's directions. He was instructed to look after the British interest and to "avoid entering into the views of any Particular person or Party."[81] Sir William sent a messenger with a belt to the Six Nations and persuaded them to send a strong delegation of their leading chiefs—Nickus, Red Head, and The Belt. A Delaware, Joseph Peppy, carried a belt from the Six Nations to the Delaware tribes. Like Croghan, they were all to report to Sir William.[82]

When the Easton meeting convened on September 21, there were three hundred Indians present; the Six Nations delegates did not come until October. Pennsylvania was well represented by interpreter Conrad Weiser, Secretary Richard Peters, Israel Pemberton of the Quaker party, and on October 7 by the governor and Council. Extreme claims of the Delawares for land were discredited by the behavior of Teedyuscung, who backed down after being denounced by the Onondaga Nickus. They were compelled to respect the authority of "their Uncles" the Six Nations and to make peace. The treaty repudiated the deed of 1754 made at Albany, and returned to the Six Nations the land west of the Appalachians. Croghan was praised by Denny for his "peculiar address" in achieving His Majesty's interest and in thwarting the faction.[83] Sir William credited the Six Nations for the successful outcome.

To the Zeal & mediation of the Delegates of the Six Nations, the favorable Event of that Treaty is in great measure owing, and from which there is abundant reason to hope, the Indian Interest in those parts will be restored to its former Strength and the Designs of the Enemy with regard to the Indians in that Quarter be in a great Measure frustrated. . . .

My Deputy Mr. Croghan writes me he is set off with 50 Indian Warriors who were at this Treaty to join Brigr. Forbes in his Operations against the Enemy, and this upon a short Summons.[84]

XXI

NIAGARA
KEY TO THE CONTINENT, 1759

Successes at Louisbourg, Frontenac, and Fort Duquesne gave the English high hopes for 1759. William Pitt now gave close attention to the American theater of war and chose his generals from those who had proved their worth. His instructions to Jeffery Amherst, new commander in chief, were explicit on measures to take Quebec and Montreal. For this task he picked the dashing James Wolfe to lead an army of twelve thousand men. The invasion of Canada from New York he gave to Amherst himself, but left the strategy to the general. Finally he paid some attention to Oswego and Fort Niagara on Lake Ontario, as a means of cutting the supply line to the west.[1]

Amherst had his first real contact with the New York area when he journeyed from Boston to Albany and New York in May. In New York he found a detailed plan for the campaigns, with distribution of forces, outlined by chief engineer James Montresor. This would assign fifteen hundred men to march to Oneida, Fort Stanwix, of whom four thousand would go to Frontenac (Cadaracqui) if the French had refortified the spot, and then down the St. Lawrence to La Galette. Oswego would be held by five hundred men, while two thousand (five hundred boatmen, five hundred rangers and provincials, and a thousand regulars) would "shape their course for Niagara." This small force might not capture the fort immediately but would summon it to surrender, since the English would have taken La Galette and were on their way to Montreal. The enemy here, thought Montresor, would not dare to hold out, knowing of the loss of Fort Duquesne in their rear. Hence Niagara was conceived as a minor branch of the overall strategy.[2]

That the Niagara campaign acquired larger proportions was directly due to Sir William and the Indians. After assuming command and informing Sir William of his reliance upon him for Indian support, Amherst was somewhat aghast at the superintendent's request for "four or five thousand pounds Sterling" to arm the Indians. He had not used Indians in his earlier campaigns, and he had the soldier's distrust of the savages. He did order four hundred "good light arms such as Indians use," however, and he told Sir William that the strong garrison at Fort Stanwix would guarantee the safety of the region.[3] The changed climate of Indian relations and the prospects of the meeting in the spring, however, enabled Johnson to promise strong Indian support for the Niagara venture.

If an Expedition was designed against Niagara, or elsewhere, thro' the Country of the Six Nations, I shou'd be able to prevail upon the greater Part if not the whole of them, to join His Majesty's Arms; This Circumstance I thought it my Duty to acquaint your Excellency with, in Case such as Expedition was in Agitation.[4]

Amherst replied that "at the Same time that our future Operations are carried on elsewhere I Shall not lose Sight of the Expedition you Mention."[5]

In April a general conference with the Six Nations was held at Canajoharie, the Upper Castle, although the Mohawks wanted it at Fort Johnson. The prevalence of yellow fever, however, dictated a change, and Sir William made his headquarters at Brant's house. His taking this year of Molly Brant as mistress of his house made this hospitality the more agreeable. The usual protocol was observed, a great feast was furnished the Indians, and various difficulties were straightened out. Prisoners were delivered, the murder of a trader (one McMichael) was explained, the outcome of the Easton conference was reported, and relations with the French were reviewed.[6]

Then Sir William informed the Indians of the call of General Amherst for their aid in the forthcoming campaigns, to which the chiefs responded in the most dramatic and emphatic manner.

In the Evening the Carcasses of 2 oxen having been boil'd in five large Kettles & laid out in pieces according to the Indian manner, all the Indians assembled & the Sachems and Warriors being seated in 2 Lines opposite to the several fires kindled in the Center, The Old Belt a great Seneca Sachim and Warrior rose up, with a Belt of Wampum in his hand, & acquainted Sir Willm & the several Nations there present that he was authorized by ye Chenussio Indians (one of the most considerable of the Seneca Towns, near to Niagara) publicly to declare at this war feast that they heartily concurred in the Resolutions of joining the English against the French, which all the confederate Nations at this Meeting, had avowed to Sir Wm. Johnson & that 26 of their warriors now present determined when they left their country not to return till they had seen the face ot the enemy, that they would now go down to Sir William's house & from thence march to what Quarter he should judge proper. And they now further made known to Sr Willm Johnson, & all the Confederate Nations present, that the Chenussio Indians did last winter determine among themselves to commence hostilities against the French, & as Niagara was built in their Country they gave it up and will assist the English in destroying it, & desire that the English would assemble, with all possible speed, & proceed to the reduction of it, as Dispatch herein will greatly contribute to facilitate the success: That the Chenussio Indians have kept these their Resolutions a Secret not only to the whole Confederacy but to the Drunkard himself the Head of the whole Seneca Nation, reserving the publication thereof to this Meeting of all the Nations, & added that, in their opinion, the Reduction of Niagara would be a proper plaister to heal all the wounds we complain'd of.[7]

Three days later, April 21, three sachems waited upon Sir William and his party to say that all the Nations in council had concurred in urging the Niagara campaign to be undertaken as soon as possible. They also "Gave a Belt with the Figure of

Niagara at the end of it, & Sir William's name worked thereon." He replied heartily and assured them he would convey this message to the general and return his answer.[8]

The next day Sir William's letter to Amherst urged the general to take up the request of the Indians, and he made specific his own ideas and plans on the subject. "I am so much persuaded of their Sincerity herein, that I think 800 Indians, if not more, would join me."

The French, by the Intelligence I have Sent to Brigr. Gage, have I believe, by this time, Two Armed Vessels upon Lake Ontario, and I apprehend they are the only Interruption, of Consequence, We should meet with in our Way to Niagara, & that the Fort would be no very difficult Conquest, as I Could Invest it with Indians to favour the Attack, and with them Cut off all Succours from coming to it.

Your Excellency will permit me to Say, that I am of Opinion the Reduction of Niagara will Overset the whole French Indian Interest, and Trade, and throw it into Our hands, if this Conquest be properly improved, and that if You should put this Plan in Execution, no Time should be lost, as the Transportation to Lake Ontario grows more & more difficult as the Summer Advances.[9]

Amherst received Sir William's letters as he was about to leave New York, and replied immediately upon reaching Albany on May 3. He asked for a conference in Schenectady the next day at ten A.M. This was the first meeting of the two. Johnson came primed with fresh Indian intelligence which Amherst sought. The general asked for more information regarding the upper St. Lawrence at La Galette. He also wanted a sketch map of Niagara and the fort, which Johnson sent him the next day.[10]

The tall, lean general with the hawklike visage was at the crest of his popularity, and his reputation lent him prestige. He had seen little of the frontier and felt he had much to learn from the other man whose unusual skill and rapport with the Indians were already a legend. Perhaps he expected a rough frontiersman; if so, he was surprised by the courtly bearing and strong face and figure of this Irish trader who had become a king's officer and soldier. Amherst, like most soldiers, distrusted the Indians, but he was ready to learn and he seemed impressed. Johnson reported to Peter Wraxall that he had been received "politely."[11]

Upon his return to Albany, Amherst took steps to provide arms for four hundred Indians. Then on May 7 he wrote that he "had now determined with myself the Expedition to Oswego and Niagara, and that the Corps for that service should consist of Abercromby's, Lt. General Murray's, 4th Battn. of the Royal Americans and the 2680 New York provincials and that Br. General Prideaux should have the command and be joyned by all the Indians under Sir Wm. Johnson."[12] His letter informing Sir William of his plans, however, was dated May 19, but he credited the assurance of Indian assistance, which "determined me to pursue the plan I had before formed for an Enterprise against Niagara." He noted that the forces to be commanded by Prideaux, regular and provincial, were already encamped along the Mohawk, or ordered to Schenectady. The eight hundred or so Indians Johnson had promised were to be collected, but "without nevertheless acquainting them, that Niagara is the object in View," lest the enemy be informed.

This request in view of the information Johnson gave of the Indians' zeal for that objective was difficult to accept or to carry out.[13]

Prior to receiving this explicit commitment, Sir William had written the Lords of Trade regarding his proposals, and even more optimistically outlined the prospects:

I am persuaded I could join his Majesty's troops that way with the main body of the Warriors of the five Nations together with many others of their Allies and Dependants, and that by taking proper measures I could not only prevail on those Indians of the five Nations who have been debauched by the French from their respective settlements to go and live under their protection at La Gallette on the River St. Lawrence to abandon the French Interest and return to their native Towns; but that I could also prevent many if not most of those Northern and Western Indians who form the Ottawawa confederacy from joining the French against us, and which they have hitherto done. Nay, I flatter myself I could prevail on many of the aforesaid Indians to join with us in our operations from Lake Ontario. . . .

The Reduction of Niagara, and if well conducted I think we cannot fail of success, will be in the light I view it a point of inestimable advantage to the security and welfare of these His Majesty's Dominions, and if the Conquest is rightly improved, will throw such an extensive Indian Trade and Interest, (for they are inseparable) into our hands, as will in my humble opinion oversett all those ambitious and lucrative schemes which the French have projected and in pursuit of which they were interrupted by the present war in this part of the world.

Whilst the French are in possession of Niagara in vain will our repossession of Oswego, and reestablishing an Indian Trade there enable us to hold the Ballance from them either in Indian Interest or Trade.

The many nations of Westward Indians in comparison with whom the Six nations are but a handful must pass by Niagara in order to come to Oswego, where the French stop them and their goods, secure them by negotiations and engross their Trade. This we felt for some years before the War began when very few of those Indians came to trade with us to Oswego, and latterly the chief trade there was rather carried on wth. the French than Indians. by which means our enemies procured assortments and supplies of Goods from us to support their Trade at and from Niagara.[14]

While Amherst stated that Prideaux was "fully provided with Everything requisite to Warrant the Success of this Undertaking," Johnson still needed a great deal. He was to join Prideaux at Oswego with the number of Indians he could collect. Four days later Amherst wrote, that "Two Hundred of the best and lightest Arms (of the Carbine kind) come out from England . . . I now send you for the Use of your Indians." Finally, after Johnson had met with Prideaux, the latter prevailed upon Amherst to send for the Indian service a warrant for £3,000 sterling. "I have given him everything he has asked of me," the general wrote in his journal.[15]

Indian officers were now sent out to recruit the warriors. Thomas Butler was unwell and unable to campaign, but his influence was used; two young men, William Hare and Hendrick Nellis, were appointed lieutenants of Indians. Jelles Fonda was also unwell, but expected to go. George Croghan and Andrew Montour ranged to the southward. Mohawks, Oneidas, and those living on the Susquehanna River were to meet Sir William at Fort Stanwix. Those further west (Onondagas, Cayugas, and Senecas) were directed to join the expedition at Oswego.[16]

Brigadier General John Prideaux was an experienced officer, made a colonel in 1758, and given his brigadier's rank as he set out on this campaign. He reached Schenectady on May 15 and was joined by Johnson the next day. Together they went as far as Fort Hendrick (Canajoharie), where they met the first group of Mohawk warriors. Already in whaleboats and bateaux, the troops were moving up the river. In addition to the regulars of the 44th and 46th regiments, and two battalions of the 60th, Royal Americans, there was a small train of royal artillery— "insignificant," Sir William later called it. Prideaux also found fault with the artillery, and its personnel had to be bolstered with men from other companies. The militia was much less than the 2,560 expected and probably comprised somewhat more than 1,000 men, while the regulars finally numbered 2,200.[17]

Although he was not in command of the expedition, Sir William's personal party was considerable. He had learned from his earlier experiences, and he intended to maintain the full prestige of his office and rank. In addition to Indian officers above mentioned, he brought along others on whom he could depend. Daniel Claus did service as interpreter, and the Reverend John Ogilvie could serve in that capacity, too, or as chaplain for the troops. He preached sermons to the soldiers on the sabbath. John Johnson, Sir William's son, who had been at Lake George, was a member of the party. Nephew Guy Johnson, who had arrived in America from Ireland in 1756, did such good service in the campaign that he was recommended to General Amherst for preferment later. Missing from the group, however, was Peter Wraxall, Indian secretary, who was ill and had returned to New York. He died there July 11.

Although the route was well known to Sir William and he was in friendly Indian country, this was no pleasure trip. When the auxiliaries joined the column, or converged on it at Oswego, there was much to do to manage them, to dispense arms and supplies, and to coordinate their movements with the army. They were sent out as couriers and spies and brought in much-needed information.

As the boats moved up the Mohawk they made stops at night at Fort Johnson, Herkimer's, Oriskany, and a general rendezvous at Little Falls. Here there was some delay for the portage and road making, and some difficulty was encountered in transporting the artillery and supplies. Another major stop was at Fort Stanwix (Rome), where the portage began for Wood Creek and Oneida Lake. Here more Indians joined Sir William, bringing their total to four hundred. They set out from the fort led by the general and Sir William, with the band playing on the ramparts. It was to Yates "a fine sight."[18]

The business of transport and supply required men of many talents. Captains were asked to report "Masons, Sawyers, Bricklayers, Wheel-wrights, Cutlers, Carpenters, house & ship joiners, Turners, Black Smiths, Gun Smiths, White smiths, Tent makers, Bakers, Brewers & coller makers." As the expedition set out on the waters of Oneida Lake, the whaleboats took the lead, and three columns were formed. The next day they encamped at Three Rivers (where the Seneca joins the Oneida to form the Oswego). A principal obstacle was to be the rapids and the Great Falls of the Oswego River. A call went out for returns of all the men who had ever gone over the Oswego Falls. Great caution was taken as the boats shot the rifts, and guards were posted against the loss of men and supplies, or for fear of an attack. Rum was issued to the men during these special exertions, but care was taken about the rum when more Indians were expected.[19]

On June 27, Oswego was reached, and a camp was prepared near the site of the old fortifications, on both sides of the river. Brush and grass were cleared away, cattle were pastured and foraged, and carpenters were set to work. Likewise here the boats were caulked and prepared for the journey on the lake. Sailors and ship carpenters were weeded out of the personnel; and the better, more able-bodied men were selected for the next journey. Seven days' rations were issued for the lake voyage; four days only for those assigned to remain. The camp was to be fortified and held as a protection in the rear. Finally, on June 30, orders were given to embark in the morning. Early on Sunday, July 1, the whaleboats and bateaux, heavily laden with stores, artillery, and the soldiery in their proper order, set forth along the shore of Lake Ontario. By nightfall they had reached a cove later known as Sodus, without untoward event.[20]

The main body of the army, the 44th and 46th regiments, grenadiers and provincials, was commanded by General Prideaux. Sir William at this point had assembled some six hundred Indians; some had joined the entourage below Oswego. Along the way, as they neared the Seneca country, four hundred more were expected. They were serving as scouts and were sometimes far from the main body of the troops, ranging along the shore.[21]

Colonel John Haldimand was left at Oswego, along with five hundred of the 4th Battalion and five hundred and twenty effectives of the New York Regiment. They worked with gabions and fascines to create a breastwork for defense. Unknown to them at the time, the French were preparing an attack. After their loss of Fort Frontenac the French had built two sloops at the end of the lake.[22] These had not reached a point where their crews could observe the English arrival or departure from Oswego; but on June 24, Chevalier La Corne set out from Isle Galot, on the lake near the St. Lawrence River, with about fifteen hundred men and over a hundred Indians. On July 4, late in the evening, this French force arrived at a cove two miles from Oswego. Apparently learning of Prideaux's departure, they planned a surprise attack, which began at seven on the morning of July 5. The Indians shouted and tried to cut off some men who were cutting wood for the breastworks, but a detachment of pickets protected them. The English hurriedly brought their provisions behind their lines, threw up more improvised breastworks and prepared for the attack. They saved their fire until the enemy was near and made it effective. They had three pieces of artillery, while the French had none. When they saw that their fire was ineffective, the French withdrew. The next morning they tried again; they cut loose and fired the bateaux at the water's edge, but were driven off. The defending force was stronger than they expected, and their losses were heavy. The French commander, La Corne, was wounded, and the head of their Indians was killed. They ran to their boats and gave up the attempt. The English losses were three men killed and sixteen wounded, among them was the engineer Sowers.[23]

In the meantime Prideaux and Johnson had made progress. On July 4, they put in at Prideaux Bay, as they called it, and on the 5th at an inlet called Johnson Creek.[24] Then on July 6, they made a final landing four miles from Niagara. Although the French at Niagara had a schooner under Captain La Force cruising along the lake shore, the English had landed undetected. A Canajoharie Indian party sent out by Sir William brought in a French prisoner, a hunter from the fort. The French were alerted when one of their scouting parties fired upon the Indians. The next morning they saw seven barges on the lake and realized that the English were there in force. The French schooner began firing at the camp and so delayed operations that no entrenchments were dug for two days.[25]

Captain Pierre Pouchot was the commandant of Fort Niagara and largely responsible for its defenses. The original building erected by the French in 1725 – 26 as a trading house, but built strongly as a fort, had fallen into disrepair. Stephen Coffen, a prisoner of the French being returned from Ohio in 1753, found it "a very poor rotten old wooden Fort with 25 men in it."[26] Pouchot had distinguished himself as a military engineer by building the fortifications at Fort Frontenac. Since Niagara had been threatened by Shirley in 1755, Montcalm sent him there to strengthen and build up the fort. He found there a garrison of only sixty Canadians and no defensive outworks. He drew up plans, but said these were derided by unsympathetic officers, who thought they would take four years to complete. Then in 1756 he was put in command of the fort with a regiment of Béarn regulars. Hence he was able to carry out his plans. Upon his return to Montreal the following year, he reported great success in bringing the defenses "to their present perfection," though with few men and at little cost. There remained to be done only some sodding of the parapets, and of the "scarps and counterscarps of the ditches" to make them more secure and permanent. "There are now," he reported, "two large barracks, one church, one powder magazine, one store for provisions and merchandise. Barracks will have to be built in the course of the winter to lodge one hundred men additional." Pouchot also on orders from Vaudreuil and aided by Chabert Joncaire, tried to neutralize the Iroquois and claimed to have succeeded in embroiling them with the English. He was given an Indian name, and this experience as well as his engineering success made him a natural choice to return as commandant in 1759. In the meantime he had served with Montcalm in the defense of Ticonderoga in 1758.[27]

The fort's defenses were now in good condition and presented a far more difficult problem in its capture than either Johnson or Amherst had imagined. Located on the point of land between the mouth of the Niagara River and the shore of Lake Ontario, it was a natural fortress. The banks on the river side could be climbed with difficulty; the lake side was perpendicular. Across the land, like the base of a triangle, Pouchot had constructed a hornwork according to the accepted designs of Vauban. An angular demilune (halfmoon) was flanked by two lunettes, providing bastions which could command the approach of the enemy. The earthworks formed a sloping parapet, separated from the bastions by a moat, or cut, while the bastions had banquettes from which soldiers could fire with small arms. A broad covered way would hold guns which could fire through gaps in the picketed summit of the parapet. Upon his return, Pouchot had the earthworks faced with sodding: sods cut in the form of bricks were stacked and laced together with wooden stakes to prevent erosion and to resist bombardment.[28]

M. Pouchot had just completed the raising of the ramparts. The bastion batteries which were in barbet, were not yet finished; they were constructed of barrels filled with earth. On his arrival, he set men to work at oak blindages, 14 inches square and 15 feet long, with which he lined the rear of the large house on the lake side, the quarter most sheltered, in order to build an hospital there. Along the faces of the powder magazine he constructed, for the protection of the walls and to serve as casemates, a vast storehouse in pieces joined by a pinnacle at their summit, and in this house he placed the arms and armorers. 'Twill be remarked that such a work is excellent for field forts in wooded countries, and can easily serve for barracks and magazines. The shell falling only on an oblique plain, does it little injury, because such construction is very solid.[29]

The garrison now consisted of 486 men: 149 regulars from the regiments of La Sarre, Royal Roussillon, Guienne, and Béarn; 183 colonials; 133 militia; and 21 gunners. There were 39 employees, 5 of whom were women "who with two Douville ladies attended the hospital, sewed up gun cartridges and made earth bags."[30] Thus it was indeed a formidable fort which the English had to conquer.

The landing place was happily selected for the protection of the English forces. The only sizable indentation of the shore before the fort, its steep banks afforded a hiding place and the broad lagoon, the *petit marais* or little marsh, was a good place to draw up the whaleboats and bateaux. Here they could be guarded and shielded from the enemy until needed again. It was only after they were safely ashore that the French corvette came close enough to begin firing, but this did hinder the operations of unloading and making camp. A trail was found leading westward and on this the English moved nearly a mile toward a swamp which stretched another mile toward the fort. Behind this natural barrier they build their camp, and from this base they would begin the siege. With the French corvette hovering off shore and periodically throwing shells, the English labored inland to transport their boats and supplies and to erect the base camp.[31]

The location and layout of the English camp are well shown on the map drawn by engineer George Demler and engraved and published in New York. This indicates that about a quarter mile from the shore were lined up: the park of artillery; the 44th Regiment; two companies of the 4th Batallion, Royal Americans; part of the New York Regiment; the 46th Regiment; and in less regular groups, the Indian huts to the north and south. Headquarters were a short distance behind. The terrain was heavily forested, but one trail went to the lake shore while another path went southwesterly to the Niagara River.[32]

There was preliminary skirmishing, and efforts were made on each side to determine the other's strength and weakness. The French corvette kept up its shelling from the lake and was able to observe the English camp; La Force, its commander, judged the camp to contain three or four thousand men. Indian scouts were seen and fired at. All of this firing did little damage.[33] The English sent off their Indians, the grenadiers, and light infantry to reconnoiter. The French met them with a sally which was soon repulsed. One man was wounded by a cannonball, an Indian boy was killed, and five prisoners were taken. From this encounter the estimate was made that the French had one hundred regulars, five hundred Canadians, and about thirty Indians. General Prideaux reported "a fort very regularly fortified and the situation very advantageous [to the French] exclusive of a superiority of artillery and plenty of ammunition."[34] A detachment of men was sent over the trail to the Niagara River where the French observed them at La Belle Famille. Perhaps they were opening a trench there; before long scouts were on the west side of the river. After two days they were ready to proceed with the business of the besieger.[35] But first there was to be the call to surrender and the notice of the attackers' intention, with the formal courtesy of the art of war. Pouchot reported the incident:

About ten o'clock [July 9], a white flag was displayed in the clearance. M. Pouchot sent to reconnoitre it with precaution. A Captain of the Royal Americans was conducted to him with eyes blindfolded. He was led through the thickest and densest brushwood, and handed to the Commandant, after the bandage was removed from his eyes, a letter from Brigadier Prideaux, stating that as the King of England had invested him with the government of Niagara, M. Pouchot had to surrender the place to him; if not, he would oblige him to do so by superior force which accompanied him. M. Pouchot answered that he did not understand English; that he had no reply to give. Yet he perfectly understood the letter. The officer insisted on the great force he had. M. Pouchot replied that the King had confided that place to him; that he was in a position to defend it, and was in hopes that M. Prideaux would never enter it, and that before he became acquainted with them, he should at least assuredly gain their esteem. He had breakfast furnished to the young officer, and had him sent back with eyes blindfolded, to the place whence he had been brought.[36]

The emissary may have been Walter Rutherford, who in a letter dated July 14, said, "I drank an excellent Bottle of Claret and a glass of liquor with the commandant, *que je crois être bon soldat et Homme d'Esprit.*"[37]

Although he was overwhelmingly outnumbered, Pouchot had hopes of being reinforced from the west and from the two posts up the river. On July 7, he had advised Chabert Joncaire at the trading post, the *Magazin Royal*, below the falls, if he saw signs of the enemy to abandon the place and to take his people and goods across the river for safety. The next day he warned Chabert that there were forty men in the woods nearby. These may have been English who had been sent that way to cut brush for fortification. Hence the building was abandoned and burned— either by the French or by Johnson's Indians as was later claimed. Some seventy persons, several women and Indians, fled to the west side of the river near Chippewa (Chenondac) Creek. Later, with Philippe Joncaire, elder brother of Chabert, they found their way across and into the fort. A few Indians came there, too, but others fled when they saw the trading post in flames. Although they had brought some horses and cattle, these extra persons were no great addition to the fort's personnel. Later Johnson's Indians seized the fort above the falls, which had also been destroyed by the French.[38]

Now that the camp was established and well guarded, the English began the formal investiture of the fort. Following the siegecraft of Vauban, engineers planned an approach of trenches in a zigzag line, beginning just east of the swamp and moving northwesterly toward the lake. The workers were protected by fascines and gabions built up as an earthwork on the fort side of the trench: from four to five hundred men each day were employed in making fascines (bundles of twigs from four and a half to nine feet in length) or gabions (loosely woven basketlike cylinders two feet in diameter and three and a half feet long), which were then filled with earth from the trenches. When the approach trench was far enough advanced, a parallel was constructed. This was a wide trench parallel to the face of the fort in which batteries of cannon and mortars were set up and from which fire could be directed at the fort. Gradually, as sappers pushed forward the trenches and as new parallels were opened, the fortification could be brought under heavier bombardment. Care was taken to protect the entrenchers, since sharpshooters on the fort's bastions sought to pick off stray or exposed men, to harass the work parties, and to impede the work.[39]

On July 10, the French discovered the first parallel at more than three hundred toises (a thousand feet) from the fort, on low ground where the approach emerged from the swamp. On the 12th, a pile of earth some two hundred toises (seven hundred feet) away appeared to be the location of a second battery of six mortars, and on the 14th a work only forty or fifty toises (one hundred and seventy-five feet) away from the covered way was the location for a mortar battery. While they continued to batter the English line and the fire was hot, the French learned on the 15th of a new battery; the bombardment with a great many more shells went on, and they were told that a battery of fifteen guns would soon open up. There was an occasional respite due to rain or fog, but such conditions were of more help to the besiegers, who could then work more easily without observation.[40] On the 19th Pouchot wrote:

The enemy were observed to have made about 30 toises of work in advance, parallel to the bank of the lake, by a double sap, whence they opened a zigzag boyau [cut] almost equal to the front between these two batteries. They merely perfected it through the day, and kept up a hot fire from cannon, mortars and howitzers. We answered them very briskly from our artillery.[41]

The English appear to have made three parallels, the last within close range of of the fort. Twice they made false starts on trenches which had to be given up; the engineers were blamed for this. The chief engineer, Williams, was wounded, and responsibility fell upon George Demler, the later map maker. Major Rutherford, writing to Haldimand, spoke of "shocking Delays thro' the incapacity of our Engineers."[42]

The French were doing all they could to hamper the siege works. On July 11, a sortie of sixty men reached the English trench and forced the besiegers to fall back, as they were caught off guard. More of the garrison poured out of the covered way and a hand-to-hand battle was nearly precipitated. But the English rallied their superior numbers, and the French, fearing that they might be engaged by the entire English army, fell back to the fort, covered by their artillery fire. After this the entire garrison were stationed at posts which they kept round the clock, with only short reliefs for sleep in the day time. Then they lay on beaver pelts, fully clothed and ready for action.[43]

Captain Pouchot had boasted of his good Indian relations and his hopes for Indian support, but these proved most disappointing. Joncaire, Chabert's brother, was sent to enlist the Missisaugas (Missisakis), but returned with only one. Then Kendae, the Iroquois chief who had come to the fort with Chabert, offered to go to his people of the Six Nations who were with the English to persuade them to give up the fight. Pouchot allowed this embassy, and Kendae brought back from the English camp two deputies to confer with the commandant. These listened to the pleas of Pouchot: that he was their friend and had never deceived them, that they had given him an Indian name, and that he was surprised the Iroquois were with the English and would meddle in the English-French quarrel. He concluded by pointing out how he expected to chastise the English and that all the upper nations were coming to his support. The Missisaugas and Pottawattomies present pledged their support to the French. The two deputies were sent back blindfolded. They appeared convinced, and their replies the next day were that they would quit the English and would camp near La Belle Famille and remain quiet. There had been a suspension of fire during these parleys, during which the English had opened another trench. "This proved a lesson for M. Pouchot." He doubted the sincerity of the pledges. The reproof to the Iroquois by the deputies had been delivered in the presence of Sir William Johnson. "Johnson smiled and regarded this reproof as a joke." The English were using the negotiations for their own advantage. They were working on the western Indians, Ottawas and others, to make them disgusted with the French. As the bombardment of the fort intensified, some of his Indians besought Pouchot to let them retire outside, lest some "kettles" (bombs) fall on their heads. He had to persuade them to remain in the fort. He concluded that their attachment was thin, and that they might falter or lean toward the stronger side.[44]

Things were not going well for the French. The corvette carried messages to Montreal and Quebec and sought to learn what had happened at Oswego; on the 13th Indians reported La Corne's defeat there by the English. The corvette also went to Toronto for supplies. The English fire was getting hotter. On the 17th, when a battery of two cannon and two howitzers was set up directly across the river from the fort, a new danger appeared. A canoe with French Indians trying to run past the fort had one of its paddles shot off by a cannonball. The English lobbed one cannonball down the chimney of the commandant's quarters; it rolled out of the fireplace and down by the side of his bed, where he was lying. This was indeed a reminder that the fort was in danger.[45]

July 20 was a sad day for the attackers and perhaps the turning point of the siege. As the English trenches came closer, those who manned them were subject to more intensive fire. Colonel John Johnston of the New York Regiment, called by one writer "the best man in the army," was laying out an entrenchment when he was killed by a musket ball.[46] Two hours later an accident took the life of General John Prideaux. Always critical of the artillery, the general was passing by one of the mortars, a cohorn, when it was fired by a careless gunner. The shell exploded as it left the mouth of the mortar, and a piece struck the general in the head. Highly regarded by his fellow officers and superiors, Prideaux had brought the expedition to the verge of victory. Somewhat dour and dubious of the prospects earlier, he had seen the trenches advanced to "within 140 yards of the covered way" of the enemy. Operations were now taken over by Sir William Johnson as second in command, by whom the campaign plans were assiduously carried out.[47]

The assumption of command by Sir William was carried on without a hitch, although some questions were raised. Since Lieutenant Colonel Haldimand, the second-ranking man of the expedition in the regular army, was at Oswego, there was no one else on the spot. Moreover, while Sir William was directly in command of the Indians, he had been a principal mover and consultant of the expedition, and his resourcefulness and ability as a leader were generally recognized. His action was immediate and decisive. The next day he issued the following order:

Sir William Johnsons orders. the command of the army devolving [upon] the death of the late General Prideaux (on me I trust) that as I am determined to persevere in the same just and vigorous manners [measures], which was carried on by the Deceased General, that the troops will exert themselves to the utmost and act with the same laudable spirit which they have hitherto shown an[d] of which I shall not fail to acquaint his excellency General Amherst. The business we are upon being nearly finished the completing of which will be easily effected by the continuance of the same measures and the utmost exertion of our abilities, all orders given therefore by the late general to be punctually obeyed.[48]

At the same time he wrote Haldimand: "As the Command devolves on me, I would have You imediately Join the Army here, without Loss of time, and forward that Letter to Genl. Amherst by Express." The next day, Sir William had time to read Prideaux's instructions and orders from General Amherst and other papers, and rescinded his order for Haldimand to join him. He explained his decision thus:

When I wrote you last night, I had not seen General Amhersts Orders or Instructions to the Late Brigdr. Prideaux with regard to Your Destination, and as I also find by yours of the 17th Inst. to Brigdr. Prideaux, that your presence there is necessary, on Severall Acctts. I now Countermand the Orders I sent you last night, and will do the best I can here, with the few Feild Officers I have left, and wish You may, as I doubt not you will be able to keep your ground, agst. any Number the Enemy may Send that way. I am Sorry You are so circumstanced, as I find by Yours You are, and wish it were in my power to reinforce You, or assist you in any shape, but as Everry thing necessary for such an Expedition as this, is so verry deficcient and the place so much Stronger than I imagined. It is not in my power to Send you any relief, altho my Inclination would readily lead me to it.[49]

It was the opinion of some that Haldimand was entitled to the command. Allan Macleane, writing to him on the 21st, expressed that view and hoped he would come, regardless of Sir William's second letter.

Yesternight there was an express sent for you which gave me great joy; for tho' Sir Willm. Johnson is a very worthy man he knows little about Generalship and he has nobody can help him for our Engineers god damn them Dembler has showed himself a fool & blockhead

I was a little surprised to find this night a resolution taken of countermanding your coming here; if you are sett off before this Express comes for God sake come and save us, and as the command of this army is your due and belongs to you, if you come I believe we may take the place, if not God have mercy on us. I can tell you at meeting at who's instigation this counter order was sent, but I hope it will not hinder your coming to us.[50]

If Sir William had any doubt of his right to the command he did not show it and later asserted his title when Haldimand appeared on the scene. By then, however, he was a victorious commander with successful operations behind him. There was a contemporary story that Prideaux had designated Sir William before his death. A letter from Albany, July 29, said: "General Johnson took Command, by Virtue of a written Order found in the General's Pocket after his Death."[51] If such was the case, Sir William never mentioned it. Haldimand, however, must have started for Niagara immediately, for he was there on the 28th, as Sir William reported in his letter to General Amherst, asserting his right to the command. "Lt. Colo. Haldimand Arrived here, in order to take on him the Command, but as I have His Majesty's Commission as a Colonel since the year 1756, I did not chuse to give it up to him; however We have Settled it in such a manner, that no dispute may Arise untill Your Excellency's Opinion is known, being both equally inclined to carry on the Service as far as in our Power."[52] As colonel of the Six Nations by royal appointment he outranked a lieutenant colonel, even though he was a provincial. It was a claim the regulars had always disputed.

Like the other regulars, Amherst distrusted the military ability of Johnson and immediately ordered Brigadier General Thomas Gage to succeed to the command. Gage, however, was at Ticonderoga and had to make the long journey westward. He finally took command at Oswego on August 15. Amherst in his journal expressed his hopes and fears:

This is unlucky [death of Prideaux]; indeed, the loss of a good Officer a good man may overturn all the intended operations on that side but as they were advanced to within 140 yards of the covered way I hope Sir Wm. Johnson will pursue the same plan as begun by Mr. Prideaux and success cannot fail. I immediately ordered Br. Gen. Gage to set out for Oswego to take command for future operations which are of the greatest consequence to the general Plan of reducing Canada & might fail on Sir Wms (Sir Wm. Johnson) and Colonel Haldimand's disputing the Command.[53]

There need not have been concern about Sir William's pressing the attack. His letter to Haldimand on the 21st stated his resolution:

I am in hopes by tomorrow Morning to have a Battery of 6 Guns opened within 140 yards of the Enemys Covered Way, by wh. I hope to bring them to my Terms, if not, I shall be obliged to go greater lengths, and attempt an Escalade, as I am determined to take the place if possible.[54]

A French observer marked the English trenches moving nearer, and finally a fourth parallel only a hundred yards away. The French kept up their sniping at the works. A pause in the bombardment indicated that the English were moving up the heavy guns. Both sides were expending their ammunition in desperation; the

English wanted to force an early victory, since their provisions were running low; the French hoped to stave off disaster.[55]

Orders became Explicit: "As the work draws nigh to the Fort, much depends on the goodness of the Fashenes & Gabions; . . . make them of small wood & perfectly Tite." Constant watch and readiness were demanded lest there be a surge from the fort. An appeal was made for even greater exertions since the loss of the general and Colonel Johnston. Still they had to guard against any defections. "An officer and 200 men always to be posted at the Tail of the trenches to prevent any Schulker from quitting the trenches without leave from an officer."[56]

The defenders of the fort were now facing a desperate situation. The enemy's fire was doing even greater damage and execution, and the toll of killed and wounded increased. There was danger of fire from hot shot, and heavy cannonading was breaching the bastions. Pouchot's journal is eloquent in its description of heroic efforts in the face of danger and of the worsening condition of the fort.

About nine o'clock in the morning [of the 22d] they began to throw red hot shot from the battery on the other side of the river. The battery where they had placed their heaviest guns did the same. By the precaution that M. Pouchot had taken, of having casks full of water before all the buildings, and parties of carpenters ready with axes to cut away the places exposed to the flames, the fire did not commit any ravages, although it started in several spots, even in the magazines of merchandize, and this is still more remarkable from the buildings being all of wood. . . ."[57]

English fire was concentrated on the lake side, where it effectively dismounted the cannon and howitzers and ruined the bastion, tearing holes in turf and sodding. Frantically the French threw bags of earth into the breach, but their supply was limited. Not only were bags torn and used up, but there was shortage of wadding for cannon. Mattresses were taken from the beds, straw was used, and finally even the linen.[58] The night of the 22d and 23d the firing continued as Pouchot related.

We replied to them from our fort, but our arms were in so bad a condition that among ten guns scarcely one could be used, and on the next day there remained not more than a hundred fit for use, notwithstanding all the repairs daily made. Seven smiths or armorers were daily employed in mending them. The women, as we have said, attended the wounded and sick, or worked sewing cartridges or sacks for earth.[59]

The only hope lay in the imminent arrival of relief from the west. When Pouchot was sent to Niagara with the purpose of backing up the French further west and maintaining the line of French forts, Vaudreuil conceived the possibility of another English attempt to take Niagara. In that event, his orders were for De Lignery at Fort Machault (Venango) and Aubry at Detroit to bring their troops and Indians to support Pouchot.[60] Now the courier sent to Chabert on July 7 carried letters for the western posts demanding this aid. Aubry had three hundred French soldiers, and as he marched or voyaged the length of Lake Erie to meet De Lignery, he recruited some six hundred Indians. At Fort Machault, De Lignery was having a grand council with a thousand Indians. After abandoning Fort Duquesne, he relied on them to bolster his defense or to attack the English there. Now he had to tell them that the English and the Iroquois under Sir William were besieging Niagara. He asked them to join him to save that post and to keep the English from their lands. When these forces were joined they floated down the lake from Presque Isle and entered the Niagara River. On July 22, they sent a message to Pouchot that they were six hundred French and a thousand Indians and that they felt capable of defeating the enemy. This seemed like an imposing army, "who when passing the little rapid at the outlet of Lake Erie resembled a floating island, so black was the river with bateaux and canoes."[61]

The wilderness outposts as far as the Mississippi had been stripped for recruits for this forlorn hope of France in the heart of the continent. Among the 600 or more French were traders and *coureurs de bois* who had left their Indian families on distant prairies, or in the forests of Michigan and Wisconsin, to rally for the preservation of Niagara. There were officers not unknown to the Court of France, some whose names are on the rolls of the pathfinders of America where their wilderness service had covered many years. Here, too, were half-breed and the Indians of far tribes, a thousand strong in paint, grease and feathers, whose favorite weapons were the scalping knife and tomahawk, who had never seen, much less shared in, "civilized" warfare.[62]

Perhaps the French had reason to be confident. No earlier flotilla on the waters of Lake Erie had equalled this. Their progress had been remarkable, and as they were propelled by the rapid current of the river their destination was soon to be reached. On July 23, Pouchot received two letters from De Lignery which stated that he had reached the Great [Navy] Island. He asked which route he should now take. In his earlier letter Pouchot had estimated the English strength as from four to five thousand exclusive of Indians and had warned of a direct encounter, suggesting the west side of the river. He now replied to De Lignery in a missive, four copies of which were sent out by Indians, in which he repeated his earlier advice. The English, he explained, were distributed before the fort in trenches, in camp behind the swamp guarding their bateaux, and at a battery on the west side of the river opposite the fort. The latter were no more than two thousand and could not be readily reinforced. Therefore if the French could defeat them, it would be possible to reach and support the fort.[63]

These letters exchanged between Pouchot and De Lignery had passed through the English lines, and their contents were known to Sir William. The messengers had even tarried with the Six Nations Indians and had tried to persuade them to retire and not to fight against the French. The Six Nations had received five belts and had said that they would not meddle. The French appeared confident and chose not to follow Pouchot's advice.[64]

In spite of these French efforts, Sir William knew that he could rely upon the Indians pledged to his campaign, who had earlier expressed their feelings about the French. He had managed to keep their strength between 900 and one thousand, and he had given them assurances of their reward when the English won. The Indians had witnessed the steady progress of the siege and could not have been ignorant of the growing weakness of the fort, and of the plight of its defenders.

Hence Sir William possessed full knowledge of the enemy's plans and movements and took steps to intercept their advance. On the 23d he deployed a small company to take a position at La Belle Famille. These were under the command of twenty-seven-year-old Captain James De Lancey (son of the lieutenant governor), who wrote a vivid account of the action:

The 23d I was sent with 150 of the light Infantry to encamp near the River close to the Road leading from the Falls to the Fort, in order to prevent the enemy's throwing any Succour into the Fort and alarm the Rest of the Troops, who were about a mile distant from us, in case they attempted it. That night and the next morning I threw up a breast work in the Front of my Camp and about 6 O'Clock I sent a Serjeant & Ten Men to a Camp we had on the other side of the River opposite to the Fort, for a six pounder ordered to be placed in the front of my Camp, they were obliged to go a mile up the River to the Boats, as soon as they got to the Boats they were attacked by the enemy and all taken or killed.[65]

The French scouts who had attacked and killed these men put their heads on poles and sought to arouse their Indians to fight. But again they wanted to parley, and when they were denied that privilege, according to Pouchot, only "thirty of the most resolute followed M. Marin" when the French attacked.[66] Captain De Lancey quickly reported the incident, and Sir William soon had another picket there, to be followed by troops and Indians under Colonel Eyre Massy. De Lancey continued:

I immediately sent a Serjeant to Sir William to acquaint him that the Enemy were coming and in ten Minutes I was joined by three pickets of 50 each who were that morning ordered to reinforce me, about a quarter of an hour after Lt. Colonel Massey arrived with 150 of the 46th with which and the picket of the 44th he drew up on the Right of me, and the other two pickets on the left, about 100 Indians went to the left of the whole in order to fall on the Enemy's Flank.[67]

Now some of the Iroquois went to the French Indians to persuade them not to fight; the French said they did not want to fight with the Indians, but with the English. These parleys helped to delay the action and probably gave the English time to get ready their defenses and to raise their abatis.

The French troops made an assault upon the right; English infantry were told to hold their fire until it could be effective, which they did so well that the French fell back. They then tried the left side, and were repulsed again. As they fell back they dropped to one knee and kept up a return fire. After about half an hour, the firing let up, and the English saw an opportunity to attack.[68] Captain De Lancey wrote:

I found the Enemy's fire slacken, upon which I sent to Col. Massey to desire he would let me leave the Breast work and rush in on the enemy which he granted, desired I would move slow and advance with his party on the Right, we jumped over the Breastwork and Rushed in on the Enemy, who immediately gave way, they then Endeavoured to Flank us on the left, but I ordered a party from the Right to move to the left which they did, and with them I pushed forwards to the enemy, who falling in with the party which was on my left immediately ran away as fast as they could, and never offered to rally afterwards, a few of them remained behind and exchanged a few shot with us, and were either taken or killed.[69]

From the bastion of the Five Nations at the fort, Pouchot and his aide observed the entrenchments of fallen trees, saw the English defiling from their camp, and threw some shot at them. He was too far away to see much, but heard the musketry and saw some Indians with a white flag–which he fired upon, fearing a ruse. When all was over he thought it but a small affair; perhaps Marin and the Indians had come up to reconnoiter and had then gone back. One of his Onondagas had asked to be allowed to join the French Indians, went through the lines and then came back to report the rout of the French. Pouchot could scarcely believe it. He ordered firing on the English entrenchments, but it caused such a fusillade in reply, killing a number of men, that even that was halted.[70]

The French Indians did little to help the assault and drifted away when the English counterattacked. The Six Nations, who were several hundred in number and occupied the left flank, however, went into action. In Captain De Lancey's words, "Our Indians as soon as they saw the Enemy give way pursued them very briskly and took and killed great numbers of them, we pursued about five Miles and then returned, we took several prisoners in our return under the bank of the River."[71]

As Pouchot helplessly awaited the outcome of the action, he allowed a sortie of a hundred and fifty men prepared to attack the English entrenchments, as a diversion. But Sir William had wisely prepared for such an event by having the 44th regiment under Lieutenant Colonel Farquhar posted for defense. When the French rose on the palisades, "the whole trench at once appeared full of men, who showed themselves stripped to the waist, with companies of grenadiers at the head of the trenches." The sortie was abandoned, but cannon fire was renewed, which made the English take cover.[72]

Slowly the extent of the debacle was impressed upon the commandant. The fighting had begun at nine A.M. and went on for an hour. The pursuit and dispersal of the French, the seizure of captives and booty, took the rest of the morning. It was two o'clock when the Onondaga returned to the fort.

He related the whole of our disaster, which we could scarcely believe, and we thought the English had invented the account. He told us that all had fled, that Mm. Aubry, de Lignery, de Montigny and de Repentigni were prisoners and wounded, and that the rest of our officers and soldiers had been killed. We hope this man was telling a lie.[73]

The French concluded that Johnson had prepared an ambuscade into which they had fallen. Sir William at four o'clock sent a messenger with a demand for the surrender of the fort.

Although Pouchot had been informed of the defeat and the capture of the French officers, he feigned ignorance and demanded proof. He tried to avoid blame for the capitulation and to justify whatever action he had to take. While Major Hervey waited for the commandant's answer, a French officer was sent to the English camp, where he was shown De Lignery, wounded, and other officers "in an arbor near Colonel Johnson's tent." He returned and reported to Pouchot. The latter called in his officers and reviewed the condition of the fort and the garrison.

The morale of the latter was broken; German recruits were threatening mutiny. It was evident that an English attack upon the fort could not be withstood. Losses had been heavy, and there was now no hope for any help from outside. With great reluctance Pouchot agreed to surrender, but he sought to get his own terms. He asked to march out with the honors of war and to have the entire garrison sent to Montreal. Johnson politely refused, and said he was "not master of the conditions." The garrison, irked by this delay and punctilio, showed their concern. By daybreak Pouchot had given in and accepted the English conditions. He could not have done otherwise.[74]

The capitulation provided for the surrender of the fort to the English, together with military stores, arms, and ammunition, including the vessels and boats which were there. The French garrison was to march out "with their arms and baggage, drums beating, and match lighted at both ends, and a small piece of cannon." Immediately they were to embark in vessels which would carry them to Oswego, and then as prisoners to New York. They were to lay down their arms, but keep their baggage. Noncombatants, women and children, were to be provided means to go to Montreal; sick and wounded would go when they were able to travel to join the rest. Indians in the fort would be allowed to depart, quietly and quickly.[75]

There was much concern over possible "insult," "reprisal," or mistreatment of the garrison by the Indians. The French feared, and some of the English desired, a revenge for the massacre at Fort William Henry two years before. But Sir William undertook to control the Indians and to protect the prisoners. This was difficult to do, for the Indians had been promised rewards and were ready to embark upon looting and revelry. They wanted their share and payment for their services. Hence they were kept from the fort until the garrison marched out to embark immediately. Some French officers were seized by the Indians in the battle, and these Sir William ransomed by paying £160 and by what he called "good works." They had taken other prisoners, who could not be rescued. On the 27th, Sir William said he "divided among the several nations, the prisoners and scalps, amounting to two hundred and forty six, of which ninety-six were prisoners."[76]

When it came to looting, the Indians could not be denied; as soon as the fort was opened, they swarmed in, gathering up whatever they could lay their hands upon. One report said that the Indians obtained loot to the "value of 300 £ per man." Once satisfied, however, they could be sent home, and they soon departed. Although Pouchot reported incidents, he conceded that Johnson had controlled his charges well. There was no massacre, and the French were able to leave safely.[77]

M. Pouchot gave a dinner to Colonel Johnson and some officers. After dinner these officers helped themselves to all the utensils and movables. The Indians had the discretion to take nothing in the house where all the officers lodged, until they had gone out. But soon after their departure, they took everything, even to the iron work and hinges of the doors, and broke whatever they could not carry off. They pillaged the magazine of the king's goods, of which there were still about five or six hundred peltries. We had used many of them for merlons for the batteries. They broke open and wasted all the barrels of flour.[78]

On the 25th, the weather was stormy, so that not even a bateau could be launched, but on the afternoon of the 26th, the garrison marched out to the beach, guns on shoulders, drums beating, and with two large cannon at the head of the column. As soon as they reached the bateaux, they laid down their arms and embarked, although the water was rough with high waves. They would go via Oswego to Fort Stanwix and thence down the Mohawk and Hudson rivers to New York.[79]

XXII

VICTORY AND THE WEST

With the capitulation of Fort Niagara and the departure of its garrison as prisoners of war, the immediate problems had been met. Most of the Indians had departed. Sir William now had time to reflect on the outcome of the campaign, the extent of the victory, and its probable consequences. His first duty was to report to his superiors the essential facts of the situation. As soon as he had a free moment, on the 25th, he dictated a letter to General Amherst, recounting the action and the resulting victory; this was dispatched with Lieutenant Moncrieffe to Oswego. By this messenger, too, Haldimand would receive the news. The letter was delivered to Amherst at Ticonderoga on August 5. The first flush of victory was evident in Amherst's cordial reply, his forwarding the news home, and his commendation of the successful commander.[1]

Along with the joyful news, however, went the sobering details. The surrendered garrison numbered "607 men and 11 officers, besides a number of women and children." Some thirty officers were captured at La Belle Famille, but three of these had escaped. The French troops who first fled the field went to an island above the falls, where 150 men had been left guarding the boats. These, with the garrisons of forts Presque Isle and Machault, later retired to Detroit. Pouchot recorded that "of 400 men 250 were killed, almost all Colonials." In the defense of the fort itself, "109 men were killed or wounded."[2]

Compared with these figures, the English losses were slight. They reported 60 killed (including 5 officers, notably Prideaux and Johnston) and 118 wounded. Only 3 Indians were known to have been killed and 5 wounded during the siege.[3] Sir William was commended for "his inclination to put a stop to the further effusion of human blood" in compelling the fort to surrender without an assault.[4]

Fort Niagara itself, the greatest prize, now became an English stronghold. It was larger and its defenses were more extensive than Sir William had thought. The captured ammunition and supplies were considerable, but it might require a thousand men to defend in wartime. The posts above and below the falls had been destroyed, either by the French or by the Indians.[5] Sir William had a drawing or plan of the fort made to send to the general and to Governor De Lancey in New York. Later he had a fine engraving made of engineer Demler's plan of the siege, which was published in New York in 1762.[6]

Nor were the military consequences of the victory neglected. On the same day, Sir William wrote General Stanwix on the Ohio, informing him that the fort had fallen and that by the defeat of the enemy's relief expedition his own position was improved. "This is an Event that I imagine will be of great Consequence to Your Expedition *as they* [the relief forces] *were intended to oppose your army had they not been called by Express to the relief of this Fort.*" Moreover, Indian intelligence gave information that the forts at Presque Isle, Le Boeuf, and Venango were poorly armed and weakly defended. "I shall Garrison this place agreable to General Amherst's Instructions to General Prideaux," wrote Johnson, "till the Arrival of Some of your Troops, who I find are Intended to Garrison this Fort."[7]

When news of Niagara came to the English armies, Amherst was still before Ticonderoga, and Wolfe had yet to take Quebec. What an uplift this gave their prospects! Captain Charles Lee of the 44th Regiment, writing from Niagara, August 9, described it in superlatives.

Our happy reduction of this important Fort of Niagara, which is to the English Nation a most glorious and solidly advantageous acquisition, by its strength most formidable, & by its situation absolute Empress of the Inland parts of North America, commanding the two great Lakes, Erie, Ontario; the River Ohio, all the upper nations of Indians, and consequently engrossing the whole Fur trade, cutting off the communication between Canada & Mississippi, & thus defeating their favorite and long projected scheme of forming a chain round our Colonies, so as in time to have joustled us into the Sea.[8]

It seemed incredible to Lee that so small a force, "a mere handful of men, 2,000 only from the body of the Army, with 1000 Indians of the Six Nations," could have done so much. He also noted, "Our artillery was trifling & bad; our Engineers (as usual) execrably ignorant," the Indians wavering, and due to the death of General Prideaux the command fell to "Sir Wm. Johnston [*sic*], a very good and valuable man, but utterly a stranger to military affairs."[9] So grudgingly did the military admit any credit to Sir William, or his wards, the Indians.

Not so to the public at large, however, who a second time proclaimed Johnson a hero. There was rejoicing on the Mohawk and in Albany. A Boston paper held the victory would "crown with Laurels the ever deserving JOHNSON." One report said gentlemen in New York planned to give him a "medal in gold worth 500 £." Horace Walpole wrote how such victories as those in America would have been celebrated in Greece and Rome. "If we did but call Sir William Johnson 'Gulielmus Johnsonus Niagaricus,' and Amherst 'Galfridus Amhersta Ticonderogicus,' we should be quoted a thousand years hence as the pattern of valor, virtue, and disinterestedness."[10]

Such instant fame, however, was to be eclipsed by the more dramatic and mortal stroke of Wolfe in taking Quebec. More relevant to Johnson's reputation was the somewhat disputed role of the Indians in the victory. Their essential service in preparing for and carrying out the march to Oswego, and in the besieging of the fort have been noted. Nor can it be denied that in scouting, bringing intelligence, and serving as eyes and ears of the army they did well. When it came to fighting, however, military men gave them little credit. Colonel Massy, who commanded at La Belle Famille, was irked by frequent mention of the Indians' help and stated that they were "all the time running off toward our camp." "As I hear the Indians have got great credit on that day, in Europe, I think I would not do justice the Regiment [46th] I had the honor to Command, if I wou'd allow Savages, who behav'd most dastardly, to take that Honour, which is deservedly due, to such of His Majesty's Troops, as were in that Action."[11]

One writer said all but the Mohawks "stood Neuter" at the first attack to see which way the battle would go; when they saw how the French gave way, they fell upon them "like so many Butchers with their Tomahawks and long Knives" and so killed many, which barbarities may have atoned for Fort William Henry.[12] Daniel Claus, who was present as interpreter and aide, later wrote that the expedition "must inevitably have miscarried were it not for a Body of near 1000 Six Nats. Indians & their Confederates under the Command of . . . Sr. Wm. Johnson."[13] The initial reports of Johnson and the letter of Captain De Lancey gave full credit to the Indians in this battle.

The commander had little time to think of fame and credits, however, for there was much to be done. The fort had to be occupied. Prisoners had been dispatched with an escort for New York, but sick and wounded had to be cared for or sent home. Nearby posts formerly held by the enemy had to be surveyed and perhaps occupied. Defenses had to be constructed. Most important of all for Johnson, the Indians of the west had to be conciliated or controlled, and perhaps the fur trade could now be directed into English hands. As Caesar wrote of himself in his *Gallic War*, all these things had to be done by him at the same time.

On July 28, the Indian allies departed, "set off in boats with a deal of plunder for their several countries." Then General Prideaux and Colonel Johnston were formally buried in the chapel. Sir William was the chief mourner. The arrival of Colonel Haldimand, claiming the command, was a test which Sir William disposed of diplomatically as related above. Until Amherst's "pleasure was known," he would vigorously deal with the many problems confronting him. To change over now would jeopardize much. Surely no one else would deal with the Indians, but Johnson resolved to "settle with the general how far my limits extend, for taking care of or managing Indian affairs, that I may regulate my passes and Indian trade."[14]

A party under Lieutenant Turbutt Francis was sent off "in Three Whale Boats, across the Lake to Toronto in order to make discovery whether the Enemy were there, that in that Case I might Send a Body of Men to take and destroy it." After four days, on July 30, the party returned and reported the place abandoned and the buildings burned. A lone Chippewa Indian was brought back for information and future negotiation.[15]

Then, on August 1, there was a confrontation with a remnant of the French from Lake Erie. Sir William's journal gives a graphic account.

August 1st, 1759. I went to see Niagara Falls with Colonel Haldimand, Mr. Ogilvie, and several officers, escorted by three companies of the light infantry. Arrived there about 11 o'clock; in my way at the thither end of the carrying place, I met a flag of truce from Presque Isle, desiring to know the number of officers I had in my hands, from the action of the 24th and begging I would advance them anything they might want, they being men of fortune and credit. One letter was from the commandant of Presque Isle named Chevalier Poitneuf, the other from Mons. De Couagne, who came with the flag of truce with 9 men and Indians. I ordered them to stay in the woods, and left Mr. Rogers with a guard with him, until I sent a message to them and provisions.[16]

This was Johnson's first visit to the falls, and he and his staff were no doubt impressed by the grandeur and power of the cataract. He would come again with more leisure for sight-seeing. The next day he replied to the chevalier and provided him with an escort to his boats. The trader, Jean Baptiste de Couagne, proved a fortunate contact and was hired to remain at Niagara as interpreter. He was to continue in the Indian service for many years.[17]

Now Colonel Haldimand and Captain Williamore were dispatched for Oswego. They were to make ready that post for the return of the troops in a few days, as well as to send off the French women with an escort to La Galette. The latter, though under a flag of truce, were to spy out the land and make observations, but were stopped by the French before reaching their destination.[18]

Colonel Massy commanded the escort of about three hundred men who set out with over six hundred French prisoners destined for New York. These included Pouchot and the officers of the garrison, as well as Joncaire, Villars, and Marin. Others who were wounded or sick remained to be taken along to Oswego later, and then sent to Fort Stanwix with the English wounded. The press reported the arrival of these prisoners in Schenectady, Albany, and finally in New York. A few escaped at Fort Herkimer, and eight were drowned (with four New Yorkers) when a boat capsized. Yet they were well treated, as even Pouchot testified. It was something of a sensation to have these celebrated prisoners, who had faced Braddock on the Ohio and were well known for their hostile activities. Although intended to be sent to England, some were exchanged and returned to French service in this country.[19]

With the capture or emasculation of all the French western forts except Detroit, the principal danger in that quarter lay with the Indians, their former allies. Sir William had held out the hope that the fall of Fort Niagara would deliver the western Indians and their trade into English hands. He now took steps to insure that result. Failure to follow up this advantage might leave the Indians under French influence.

The Chippewa sachem Tequakareigh was won over by belts of wampum and presents of clothing, an English medal and silver gorget in place of the French emblems he was wearing. He was made the bearer of the English message to the Missisaugas residing near Toronto: that the English wished their friendship, that they planned meetings with them, and proposed to open up a profitable trade with a large assortment of goods in the spring.[20]

A Chenussio (Seneca) chief related that after the battle the Ottawas held a council at the falls and considered whether to go to speak to the English. Instead they tried to make peace with the Senecas, who reminded them of their earlier errors. At the falls these Indians or their emissaries could see the French interpreter, De Couagne, now employed by Sir William. By the end of August a numerous assembly, "upwards of eleven hundred" Indians, was convened at Niagara.[21]

Sir William gave serious attention to the defense, repair, and protection of the fort. He planned soon to depart for Oswego with all the troops save those needed for its garrison. These, however, would need new supplies of provisions and a means of controlling the waters of the lake for their own security. More artillery and ammunition were needed to equal that of the French boats on the lake, and he proposed to build two new schooners in the good harbor at Niagara. On July 31 he reported to General Amherst that there were only "1584 Effectives" and that in a few days he would embark for Oswego leaving "a Garrison here, Consisting of 600 of the 44th and 100 Yorkers under the Command of Lt. Colo. Farquhar."[22]

It was a crucial decision. Just how much should be left at Niagara and what should he take with him to Oswego? Would this army be expected to carry on further down the St. Lawrence, and how many reinforcements could be expected? He still counted on General Stanwix's troops coming to Niagara. Until relieved he would be in command of the troops at Oswego. On the 29th, his journal reflected these concerns.

> 29th, I gave the French officers shoes, stockings, and blankets I wrote by De Normandy to Oswego for all the ship carpenters to come here, to build 2 vessels of 18 guns each, and to bring all the naval stores, and as much provision, as they can, along as soon as may be; the house carpenters [at Oswego] then to repair the battoes and make a number of oars, paddles, &c., against I get there; a detachment from the York regiment to come with the convoy.[23]

He was also contemplating the building of a fort at Oswego, to replace Haldimand's camp, and asked for more carpenters. The journey of the major portion of the command to Oswego was fraught with risks, from the weather, from the French schooners, and because of the considerable baggage involved. Then there were sick and wounded men in hospital boats. The flotilla consisted of twenty-six boats for the troops and thirty artillery boats, which also carried ten men each. Strict orders were given for discipline and quiet (no one to fire his piece) en route, and they were to row both night and day. They embarked on the 4th and arrived at Oswego the 7th, in two hours less than three days.[24]

> Saturday August 4th.—I was to embark at 5 o'clock in the morning with the troops &c., for Oswego, but the two French schooners appearing off harbor prevented our embarkation until 5 in the evening, when I left Colonel Farquhar everything in charge; also some Indian goods to give occasionally to such Indians as might come upon business to him. Then set off with all the Yorkers except one company; all the light Infantry, and grenadiers, and the general's company of the 44th regiment, and arrived at Oswego, Tuesday, about 3 o'clock P.M. with everything safe.[25]

For nine days at Oswego, Sir William was in command and gave his attention to several serious problems: The bulk of the forces of the expedition were now uncertain of their status, and there was a breakdown of discipline. He decided to apply strictly the articles of war; he sought to break up the prevalent gambling (gaming) of the troops, and he looked into other abuses. Twenty-one French prisoners were sent down to Fort Stanwix with an escort, along with some of the sick and wounded. He wondered what had become of the troops being sent up, and where the orders were he expected when he reached Oswego. Oswego was more than a camp now; it was a military outpost and a link in the support of Fort Niagara.[26]

He dispatched a letter to Amherst, reviewing the situation and asking for orders.

I must beg leave to Remind your Excellency of the necessity there will be for a Respectable Work here, as the Supplying of Niagara depends entirely on this Post, and should either of our Other Expeditions happen to fail, the Enemy will undoubtedly use all Efforts to Send an Army for the Reduction of this Place, by which Niagara must of Course fall, and they again be in a possession of the Lake, and Open the Communication to the Westward and Louisiana which they have so long had in View—Capt. Sowers, Engineer, has sent your Excellency a Plan for a Pentagon, which is Judged the best for the ground We intend to Occupy; We are now busy in felling bringing in Loggs, and Levelling the Ground for the foundation untill Your Excellency's Approbation of the Plan is known.—[27]

Every day the troops were employed at the works, weather permitting. Vistas were cut through the woods to the lake, and as logs were cut some blockhouses were erected to protect the workers from possible attack. When General Gage arrived the ground had been prepared and the pentagon was formally laid out. The fort became Gage's chief interest, and by late October barracks were ready to be occupied. Eventually it was to garrison five hundred men.[28]

Lake navigation, so necessary for the supply of Niagara, became more difficult and hazardous as the season advanced. Sailors and ship carpenters were asked to come up from Oneida. Whaleboats and bateaux left at Irondequoit were sent for. French vessels were sometimes sighted but they kept their distance. In spite of the shortage at Oswego, and the delay of the support from Fort Stanwix, the schooner was sent out in stormy weather on August 15, fully loaded to provision the Niagara garrison.[29]

Then, amid other concerns, Sir William turned to his principal charge, the Indians. Most of the Indians at Niagara had gone home with their plunder, prisoners, and scalps. Was there need for more of them at Oswego? he asked General Amherst. This question had to wait upon the arrival of General Gage and his party, with orders and instructions.

Thursday 16th.—Brigadier General Gage arrived here in the afternoon with 300 drafts for the 3 regiments here. I gave up the command to him, and General Amherst's instructions to the late Brigadier Prideaux, also his last letter Do., which I received on my way from Niagara. He then showed me a letter or two he received from General Amherst, with orders to proceed to this place, and take the command. Also to proceed to Niagara, if not yet taken. If taken and the troops returned, then to proceed to La Galette and take post there, which (in case General Wolfe should be defeated) would make a frontier, with Niagara, Oswego, and Crown Point. . . . General Gage brought up about 140 barrels of provisions, only, with this reinforcement. We have now about 3 weeks' provisions here for the whole—the New Hampshire regiment coming by land with cattle.[30]

Brigadier Gage was an urbane and experienced officer whose career had not been marked by distinction, although he had served in Flanders, Scotland, and Ireland. In America he had been with Braddock at the Fort Duquesne debacle, for which he might have received some blame, and was with Abercromby at Ticonderoga. Obtaining his colonelcy, he had organized the 80th Regiment as "Gage's Chasseurs." Then in 1758 while in New York and New Jersey he met the socially prominent Margaret Kemble, whom he married in December. The next year his bride followed him to Albany. He had had hopes of heading the Niagara campaign, which was given to Prideaux; he now succeeded to this command. Gage was not anxious to jeopardize his promising career by such injudicious actions as those of Braddock or Abercromby. After reading Amherst's instructions, he told Sir William that he thought it "impracticable" to establish a post at La Galette in so short a time. Later he was to add that "his honor was as dear to him as General Amherst's could be to him, and [he] did not understand running his head against a wall, or attempting impossibilities."[31]

In calling for an expedition down the river, Amherst asked again for "Johnson's Indians" as auxiliaries and scouts. Since they had nearly all gone home from Niagara with their plunder, prisoners, and scalps, a new recruitment had to be undertaken. For this Sir William called upon his Indian officers and interpreters to go again among the Six Nations. From his home on the Mohawk River, Captain John Butler went to the Mohawk and Canajoharie castles. Captain Jelles Fonda, Lieutenant Hare, and interpreters were sent to the Onondagas "with a black belt of wampum to speak with," and Captain John Lottridge visited the Senecas and Cayugas. The old sachems, Bunt and Red Head, and interpreters Printup and Clement threw their influence into persuasion. There was considerable reluctance to overcome, and many questions were asked. Why did Warraghiyagey want them to go on a campaign so soon after that at Niagara? What about the promised trade at Niagara? Butler found himself "very ill treated" at the upper Oneida town, where hostile rumors had been spread. Nevertheless on August 25, about seventy Senecas and Chenussios arrived. Fifty of a promised hundred Onondagas came the next day, and, by August 30, there were over two hundred Indians at Oswego. Some eighty-four Cayugas were on their way on September 3, but halted to take advantage of a plentiful supply of game. Then their chief Ottrawana's daughter was killed, and they all turned back. Sir William sent Captain Lottridge, Lieutenant Hare, and Red Head with a Cayuga Indian to join the condolence ceremony. He hoped they could be brought up in six days. It was September 18, two weeks after they started, before they arrived.[32]

Impatient for action, the Indians were a constant problem for Sir William. He fitted out small parties (eight to twelve) to go scalping, to scout for information and to bring back prisoners. They reported that two hundred French had abandoned Cadaracqui, were concentrating on Isle Galot, and that the schooners were active. When two French vessels were sighted on the lake, a plan was laid to attack or waylay them. Captain Parker with two hundred and fifty volunteers set out in whaleboats on September 9 with that in view. He also took a few Indians and an interpreter. On the 12th, one boat returned with prisoners and information on the strength of the enemy. While these raids made no permanent gains, they sounded out the enemy and by their harassment put him on the defensive. Red Head provided a map of the river.[33] All of these implied an attack upon La Galette, but General Gage withheld his orders for such an attempt.

After a few days in Oswego, General Gage began to develop his conditions for the assault on La Galette. He would need artillery vessels and adequate provisions. He would need to leave three hundred men at Oswego and he would need a convoy. He consulted Colonels Haldimand and Massy. On August 18, Sir William gave his opinion that "our going to La Galette and destroying it was practicable, and might favor General Amherst's designs, but to remain there was impossible on account of provisions, and being too late to make [such] a respectable work there, as the French would not be able to take." Haldimand concurred and things seemed to rest upon such a proposal.[34] Then the general began to hedge. He did not want the Indians told of any plans. He confided his fears and concern very frankly to Sir William, and he was critical of Amherst, who was not pushing for all of Canada, and hence this expedition would be of little help. After all, "this little army had done more than his, and if they could finish a fort here this season, supply this and Niagara with sufficient provisions, they would carry a very fine point." This was on September 6, and five days later he told Sir William "that he entirely gave up all thoughts of prceeding to La Galette, but desired I would keep it very private."[35]

While Gage was thus rationalizing his inaction, Sir William became convinced that some sort of attack on La Galette was necessary and began to press his views, gaining some support from Haldimand and Massy. He had been asked to stop the Cayugas and other Indians from coming, and he pondered how to direct them and to reconcile the change of plan.

I told the general that our going and destroying La Galette, would be the means of drawing all the Swegatchie Indians away from the French [interest], and that if we did not attempt it now, it might be the means of riveting them more firmly in it. Besides that, our destroying La Galette, might make us masters of the French vessels, which then would be out of the way of any relief.[36]

Gage said it would depend on General Wolfe; next he wrote Amherst that with his forces it was all he could do "to make this post tenantable by the latter end of October, and bring up provision for it and Niagara." He threatened Bradstreet that without more provisions, Niagara would have to be abandoned. As for La Galette, he clung to reports of French prisoners that the enemy were "very strongly intrenched there, with numbers superior to ours."[37] Yet he did not turn down Sir William's proposals, and even asked him for his further thoughts. At the risk of the General's displeasure, Sir William pressed the issue.

I . . . spoke with Colonel Massey upon the subject, who said he would gladly go in case I went. I told him I was resolved to go if allowed, and would go directly and throw myself in the general's way, expecting he will ask me my opinion. I did so several times, even to the tent door, with his aid-de-camp and brigadier major, but he avoided talking with me on the subject.[38]

The next day he wrote, "I intend this day to ask the general for 600 men, to go to La Galette, as the Indians here and there, both, are desirous of it. If he will not agree to it, I shall then desire liberty to go home." A few days later he observed, "since I gave my opinion for going to La Galette, the general is not free or friendly with me, but rather shuns me."[39]

News of Wolfe's taking Quebec, or of Amherst's advance above Crown Point, came too late to affect Gage's decision. When Amherst learned of Gage's failure to make an attempt at La Galette he was sharp in his criticism. Gage was told that now he should complete the fort and the one at Fort Stanwix. He was visibly shaken by Amherst's displeasure. The latter also noted in his letter to Sir William, that if he had known that "this very Essential Operation should not have taken place" he might have used Johnson's Indians on the Crown Point campaign. Now it was too late in the season, and all that remained was to dismiss the Indians and return home.[40]

And well might the ambitious Gage have been concerned. Amherst reiterated his criticism in reporting to Prime Minister Pitt, who concurred and repeated this view to the King in his approval of Amherst's plans and conduct. In fact, he noted that Gage's decision not to attack La Galette was made a full month before Amherst judged that the season was too late. Pitt felt that Amherst's advance up Lake Champlain was more difficult, and had no complaint of the commander in chief's deliberate campaign.[41]

Historians have been inclined to excuse Gage, as they have been more critical of Amherst's Fabian tactics. Gage's forces were not large; communication on the lake was precarious, and the river would be difficult to navigate when they were returning upstream.[42] Yet the record of Johnson's diary shows Gage to have prejudged the proposal and to have opposed it from the start. He was justifying by every means available his early decision. Even when Johnson offered a different kind of attack, with only six hundred men, he refused. He preferred to devote all his resources to building the fort.

Sir William's impatience was partly due to his responsibility for the Indians, who became suspicious of the general. On September 23, some Onondagas on arriving said they were told "at the falls" that no expedition was going forward and they might well return. Sir William had to give an evasive answer, as he was directed to do by Gage. He tried to turn their attention to trade and to the necessity of holding Niagara. The Onondaga chiefs Daniel, Belt, and Silver Heels left on the 27th. Scouting parties were still out. Finally on October 10, Gage consented to tell the Indians that "the season of the year was so far advanced, and so much work to be done here to finish the fort, that he did not intend to proceed further this campaign, and that they might return to their respective habitations and country." Sir William the next day held a general meeting with the Indians to mollify them and to thank them for their services, to discharge them, but to call upon them for future good relations with the English. After some further dealings there was nothing more to do but prepare for his own return to the Mohawk Valley.[43]

The day before, October 8, a scout returning from La Galette brought news of the fall of Quebec and of the deaths of Wolfe and Montcalm. General Gage dispatched an express to General Amherst with the news.[44] Sir William now turned his thoughts to the journey home and other concerns. After giving up the command, he took up his correspondence with his bouwmaster about affairs at Fort Johnson; he wrote to daughter Nancy, the titular head of the household; and he sent an imperative direction to Molly Brant, his new consort, not to follow him to Oswego, as she proposed to do. He had enough trouble with discipline and he had discouraged the presence of other women at camp. Other letters went to merchants, to his factor in London, and to his relatives and friends. He wrote a letter to Amherst to promote the claims of his nephew Guy Johnson for a commission. This eventually procured for Guy a lieutenancy in the Independent Companies of New York.[45]

Nor had the days at Oswego, waiting for reports and arguing over delays, been entirely unhappy. The boredom was broken by short expeditions of exploration along the lakeshore as far as Sodus, and up the creeks which flowed into the lake. Colonel Massy and Guy went along as they fished and shot ducks. The officers, the General, Colonels Haldimand, Massy, Graham, and some others dined with Sir William. On the feast day, September 29th, he and the general had a "Michaelmas goose." On the eve of departure, "I supped with Colonel Massey, when all the company were very merry."[46] With him on the journey home were his personal party, Guy, his son John, the Reverend John Ogilvie, interpreters, and Indian officers. Only John Lottridge of the latter group was left to care for the Indian relations at Oswego, to supervise the Indian trade there, and to keep in touch with Niagara. The party stopped briefly at Three Rivers, where some of the Indians left for their respective Habitations. At Fort Stanwix an escort was provided for the remainder of the trip, but it was hardly necessary. From Canajoharie and the other castles the Indians flocked to Fort Johnson to bring their greetings and problems, to seek aid, and to speak for future favors. Sir William was soon in the midst of Indian affairs ranging from Pennsylvania to the far west.[47]

Most urgent was his rendering of his account of Indian expenses for the past year (November 1758 – December 1759), including the campaign, which reached a grand total of £17,072, New York currency. To balance this he had £1,142 left from Abercromby's campaign and three payments in March and May totaling £8,000 sterling (at a rate of approximately 3/5, this meant some £(13,712) leaving a balance still due him of £2,214 New York currency. This he submitted to General Amherst in a letter of December 8. In addition, he would need £2,000 sterling for the payment of Indian officers, bateaumen, and others on the last campaign. These obligations were promptly recognized and provided for by warrants from the general.[48]

In another category was his own remuneration as colonel of the Six Nations or as commander of the expedition since the death of Prideaux. Amherst disclaimed any authority over this, and in fact seemed to imply that there was no provision for it.[49] Sir William reacted sharply in his letter of March 7, 1760:

. . . I find you are of Opinion, I am not entitled to any pay as a Military Officer. I cant help observeing to your Excellency, that I made but little doubt of it myself as you did not blame my conduct in Assumeing my Rank in the Military last campaign at Niagara, as well as for many other reasons which I shall not now trouble your Excellency with. this, I shall only add, that in the year 1746 by virtue of the then Governor of New Yorks Commissn to me as Coll of the Six Nations of Inds. I recd Coll's Pay at Home then I had not quarter the trouble, fatigue, or expense I now have and I can assure You Sir that my present pay (which I look upon to be only for the Civil appointment) is not adequate to the expense I am oblidged to be at in executing even that.[50]

Already at Oswego on October 20, he had written his London agent, William Baker, that he intended to give him power of attorney to obtain his pay since 1756.[51] The profits of war surely did not come in prompt salary payments, yet the crown and its agents expected continuous employment by him in handling the Indians. Not having received any official appointment as commander after the death of Prideaux, he had little hopes for recompense for his most valuable service and for the risk which he took in assuming command.

One other matter of the Indian service plagued him. Since the ill health and death of Peter Wraxall had left vacant the office of Indian secretary, Dr. Richard Shuckburgh, a military surgeon attached to the Independent Companies of New York, had acted very competently in that capacity. He had attended all Indian conferences and had kept the Indian Records. Furthermore, he was a congenial spirit, had spent much time in the Indian country, and Sir William wanted him to continue. So now he commended him to Amherst, and he later formally asked the Lords of Trade to appoint him officially, and so give him the salary of the office. But this wish, too, was to fall on deaf ears. At the end of 1760, Shuckburgh was remanded to his military duties.[52] Having attended to such matters, Sir William could well have used a period of rest, but the urgency of Indian affairs prevented any relaxation.

The tenuous connection of Niagara with Oswego, upon which it depended for both supplies and trade, showed the precarious state of affairs. To insure the good will of the Indians, the English had to open the trade at the Niagara post. Traders were now applying for permission to go there, and Sir William issued licenses. Yet there was a danger that corrupt or irresponsible traders would overcharge and cheat the natives and so jeopardize the English position. The French, meanwhile, would seize upon any advantage to frustrate the English effort to win over the western Indians.[53]

From western Pennsylvania George Croghan as Sir William's deputy sent a series of reports describing the Indian mood, the good effects of the English victories, and the opportunities for winning the west. He was critical of the English officers, however, who distrusted the Indians and cut down on funds for gifts. General Stanwix, like Gage at Oswego, wanted to sit tight and perfect his fortifications at Fort Pitt instead of seizing the abandoned posts of the French or sending the promised relief to Fort Niagara. In the meantime, the French were zealously restoring their line of communications in the Illinois country and strengthening Fort Detroit. In spite of English gains and hopes, Croghan despaired of their efforts to win over the natives to a point where he was about to give up. "We have conquered the Continent, it is True We may say We have beat the French; but we have nothing to boast from the War with the Natives, yet it is thought every Penny, thrown away, that is given them, which Obliges me to think the Service very disagreeable tho' I will by no means Resign without your Consent and Approbation."[54]

Sir William in February 1760 warmly approved of his deputy's measures and endorsed his reports to Stanwix and Amherst. He held out hopes of successful negotiations with the Indians, which would contribute to military operations against the French. Yet it was the next spring before Croghan got Sir William's long-delayed letter, and then a new campaign was being planned.[55]

News of English successes in the fall of 1759—the capture of Quebec, Prince Ferdinand of Brunswick's victory at Minden, and the defeat of the French navy off Portugal by Admiral Boscawen—came too late to spur the campaigns to the northward. Amherst received Gage's report of the fall of Quebec on October 18 and concluded that now Vaudreuil would concentrate the French army at Montreal. He immediately decided "to decline my operation and get back to Crown Point, where I hear the works go on slowly." The French were strongly entrenched at Isle aux Noix, his troops were clamoring to go home—some were deserting—and he resolved to retire to Albany. The brilliant commando raid of Major Robert Rogers in destroying the Indian village of St. Francis on the St. Lawrence on October 6, so damaging to French morale, thus lost its effect for the season.[56]

Confronted with freezing weather, and suffering from the cold, Amherst's army retired to Albany, where he met Sir William on December 2. The provincials were straggling home, so the general marched with the regulars to New York.[57] There he had orders from William Pitt to formulate plans for taking Canada next year. He conceived a three-pronged attack, but this time the major thrust would be down the St. Lawrence from Oswego. Colonel Haviland would lead the forces from Crown Point down the Richelieu, and Major Murray could press from Quebec toward Montreal from the east. He would want Indian auxiliaries to accompany his march to Oswego and as guides and scouts along the St. Lawrence. These would be indispensable as pilots through the dangerous rapids toward Montreal.[58]

On February 23, Amherst wrote Sir William "to use all Your Influence with the Several Tribes and Nations of Indians, in Amity with Us, and to bring as many into the Field as You can possibly prevail on to Join His Majesty's Arms. . . . that You will have them ready, as Early as possible to Act in Conjunction with His Troops in such Enterprise and Attempts . . . which I shall hereafter apprise You of." He also wanted the Indian superintendent "to Exert Yourself to the utmost in bringing over to His Majesty's Interests all such, or as many as possible, of the Enemy Indians."[59]

Johnson accepted the task but reminded the general that his success would depend upon many circumstances. The Six Nations, due to the failure of their crops, were in "a famishing condition," and there was urgent need for provisions, pork, pease, and flour. There was also a great lack of wagons and bateaux to transport this food, which could be temporarily laid up in his house. For this, and for the clothing and arms necessary to prepare for the campaign, he would need a warrant for £5,000 sterling. The warrant was granted, although the military chest was empty; for the present Sir William had again to rely upon his own credit.[60]

He was optimistic about the English interest among the Indians, although the French from La Galette were seeking to infiltrate the Onondagas and other tribes, and to win back their affections. The Indians always listened to such overtures, however much they might distrust them. Johnson held several conferences and sent among the tribes his trusted Indian officers John Butler and Jelles Fonda. He relied upon John Lottridge at Oswego to deal with those formerly under the French who now wanted to come and trade but were distrusted by the commandant, Colonel Haldimand.[61]

General Amherst spent the spring months assembling his forces and expediting their transport. First he ordered two regiments of regulars to strengthen Murray before Montreal on the St. Lawrence. He allotted two regiments of regulars, the Independent Companies of New York, the provincials from New England, rangers, and Indians to comprise a force of thirty-four hundred men to go the Champlain route under Haviland. The rest of the regulars, provincials and Indians would go up the Mohawk and then rendezvous at Oswego. These included four regiments, the 4th Battalion of the Royal Americans, two of the Royal Highlanders, six companies of Montgomeries, and provincials from Connecticut, New York, and New Jersey. When assembled at Oswego, this army consisted of nearly ten thousand men.[62] It was more than twice the force that marched to Niagara and three times that of Gage at Oswego the year before. The logistics of this army with its supplies presented no mean problem.

Amherst arrived in Albany May 8. He summoned Sir William to meet him in Schenectady, and noted in his journal:

12th. I met Sr Wm Johnson at Schenectady. He promised the Indians would be ready, did not doubt we should have as many at least as last Campaign, was uneasy himself at not having proper Rank in the Army tho' he did not wish or pretend to be a military man, but because some People had talked as though he had no Rank at all. Wished to be paid as Colonel, for the £600 p year was not sufficient to bear his expenses & could not be meant for his taking the Field.[63]

Sir William was uneasy also lest the campaign should be too late. Provincial troops arriving at Albany were set to work on the transport of provisions and stores. It was late in June before the General was ready to follow them up the river. On June 24 he left Gage in charge at Albany, "crossed the River, & went on the North side 18 miles to Sr Wm Johnsons, dined there & in the evening four miles to Clements & passed the River to Fort Hunter." Fort Johnson was a way station on the route and was jammed with supplies to be forwarded. Amherst commented that it was "very badly situated, commanded entirely by hills." It was not as well fortified as Fort Hunter but had a blockhouse and cannon, and Sir William sought for it a small garrison.[64]

Bringing Indians into the campaign depended heavily upon their receiving badly needed provisions, for many were starving. The provisions had to be transported to centers for distribution; to do this required bateaux and the cooperation of the deputy quartermasters. When in April the transport broke down, the provisions overflowed the warehouses, and some were sent back to Albany. This caused Sir William to boil over with indignation, and he wrote to Gage with unwonted heat.

The good of the Service, & regard for my own Credit oblidge me to repeat to you the necessity of having that affair settled, so that the service may not be wantonly obstructed by a Set of low lived Self Interested, and overbearing Depty Q Masters, most of them, if not all, I am Convinced would sacrifice the Interest of their King & Country, to gratify their resentment. *this is notorious.*[65]

Later he tangled with Amherst over a demand for oilcloths to protect corn from the weather and to prevent its spoiling. The general had cancelled the order, for he claimed earlier oilcloths had not been used. Now the provisions, corn and pork particularly, had to be carried to Oswego and to be distributed among the Senecas. Not only the warriors, but their families, too, had to be cared for, if they were to take the field.[66]

Even the troops found the travelling slow and toilsome. After arriving at Lake Ontario, one wrote; "the Navigation was bad in the Mohawk River, the Water being swift, and in many Places so low that we were obliged to get our Batteaus over by lifting by main Strength; the Wood Creek was still Worse; it was full of Logs, and the Water so low, that we were obliged to lift over the Logs; I was eight days going the length of the Creek, which is not 40 miles." Low water and swift current and rapids also plagued them the 60 miles down the Onondaga River to Oswego. [67]

Amherst arrived at Oswego July 9 and laid out the encampment near the fort. Men were set to work on the fort's defenses, and sailors were sent to Niagara for two ships. The French had a brig and schooner on the lake which had to be watched. The English snows were larger vessels and tried to catch the French if they came near the river. On July 23 Amherst noted that "Sr Wm Johnson arrived with his Indians." There were about 500 Indians with him at Oneida Lake; Senecas and Cayugas joined them at Three Rivers. These stops had occasioned delay. Now the most of the Six Nations were here, and by August 5 their number was 1,330 men, women, and children, of whom 600 or 700 were warriors. At times these were troublesome, especially when drunk, but Sir William could control them. On the 29th, Amherst noted "a little disturbance at night between the Indians and some of our people, but Sir Wm Johnson quelled it without any harm done."[68]

Although the general often expressed doubts about the Indians, he went to some lengths to cultivate them.

August 1st. To please the Indians I desired them to christen the Snow and took all the Chiefs on board in the afternoon, as they had told Sr Wm Johnson they would like to have her called ONONDAGA. I had a large flag made with an Onondaga Indian painted on it. This was hoisted just as I christened the Snow by breaking a bottle at the head. Then Gages Regt fired a volley. The Fort fired a gun & the R Highlanders fired a volley & the ONONDAGA answered it with 9 guns. All this pleased the Indians extremely & I made them some speeches by Sr Wm Johnson. Gave them Punch & they were greatly delighted with the whole, promised to be fast friends & said they were ready to go with me.[69]

Some idea of the size of these vessels may be gained from the statement that the *Onondaga* mounted four nine-pounders and carried a hundred sailors, while the *Mohawk* mounted sixteen six-pounders and carried ninety sailors.[70]

It was likewise very important for Sir William to neutralize and if possible to win over the several tribes of Indians who lived along the St. Lawrence, and who were now slipping from their French allegiance. Those who had come to Oswego to trade had been cautiously encouraged by Lottridge, although Haldimand was apprehensive and wanted strict orders as to their treatment. Pouchot's efforts to hold them had proved abortive. Now the arrival of English forces impressed these natives, and they were ready to listen to English persuasion and promises. They would even be treated as a part of the confederacy of the Six Nations.[71]

Finally on August 10 Amherst was ready to advance with his full force, but he was tormented by rough weather and other incidents.

The General beat at Peep of day & the Tents were struck & with the camp necessaries all loaded, the Assembly [was beat] half an hour after, & the whole embarked. . . . The order of rowing was Gen Gages (Regt) the advanced Guard covering the Front of Columns. The Indians coasted on the right of the Artillery which formed the right column, that their batteaus might be ready to run on shore if a storm arose.[72]

For fear of heavy winds and rough water on the lake, Gage turned back and set out again the following day. A number of Indians were so drunk that Butler and Fonda stayed with them until they were sober enough to travel. On the second day they had caught up with Sir William. Camping on islands at night, hugging the shore and being very wary of French vessels or hostile Indians, the army finally reached Cadaracqui, site of former Fort Frontenac. Some of the boats were not very seaworthy and were heavily loaded; artillery boats carried twelve barrels of pork, fourteen of flour, and twenty men each. Many of the men were sick, yet they made from fifteen to thirty miles per day.[73]

Amherst was impressed as they "passed Islands innumerable [the Thousand Islands] a most romantick Prospect." He looked in vain for the three ships of Captain Loring, but when he sighted a French vessel on the 16th, which fired a warning shot, he decided to attack. The next day five row galleys, each with a twelve-pounder or a howitzer, engaged the French schooner, although it had more cannon and a crew of one hundred. There was little wind and the sailing vessel could not maneuver well upstream, so the galleys closed in like dogs on a cornered deer. The *Ottawa* was badly battered; three of her men were killed and twelve were wounded, and she surrendered. She was boarded, her crew taken prisoners, and she became the first prize. Later she was repaired, reconditioned and named the *Williamson* (after the leader of the attackers) to become an auxilliary vessel of the English.[74]

To oppose the expected English advance down the river, and to delay its junction with the forces converging on Montreal, the French had built Fort Lévis, on Isle Royale, a little below La Galette (Oswegatchie). The latter had now been abandoned as untenable, and the Indians of La Présentation had drifted away, some had congregated on Isle Picquet nearby. Command of Fort Lévis had been given in March to Captain Pouchot, who had surrendered Niagara the year before. With characteristic energy and technical skill, he had constructed barracks, bastions, and magazines and had raised ramparts to implant cannon commanding the river on both sides. By cultivating the neighboring Indians he learned of the English move-ments, and he also kept in touch with the French schooner on the lake, which was watching the English advance. With a garrison of three hundred men, the fort presented a considerable obstacle to the English.[75]

General Amherst now analyzed the situation and proceeded methodically to take the fort. On the 18th, lest he give Pouchot more time to prepare, he moved his troops and boats down the river. Indian officers Fonda and Lottridge had reconnoitered the day before. The north shore was farther from the fort, so he sent General Gage with an advance guard on that side to get below and to seize Isle Galot. On the south shore the boats could row under cover of islands until nearly in range; they then ran under enemy fire, losing one row galley, but seized the two islands which the enemy had now left, and took positions along the shore. For three days they built embrasures and set up shore batteries to fire upon the fort. The French harassed them as much as possible, but saved their fire for the impend-ing attack. Captain Loring's two vessels now arrived and Amherst thought to use them for a closer bombardment. On the 23d the vessels were ordered to run by the fort; they used their anchors to hold them in position but received such a heavy fire from the fort that their cables were cut, and they were badly mauled. Pouchot had fired grape and iron fragments to cut the cables. The *Mohawk* ran aground, and the *Onondaga,* (Captain Loring), was sunk while exposed to the fort. Amherst decided to give up this plan. For the next two days the firing went on from shore batteries while Pouchot saved his fire.[76]

While this plan of attack had failed, the fall of the fort was inevitable. The besiegers greatly outnumbered the defenders, and the fort was suffering. On the 25th Pouchot, pressured by his own men, asked for a parley and finally consented to a capitulation. Three companies of grenadiers under Colonel Massy, who had commanded at La Belle Famille, marched in and occupied the fort. The garrison of 291 (12 having been killed) became prisoners of war.[77]

It seemed like a repetition of the year before to Captain Pouchot. As he was conducted to General Amherst, he recognized officers whom he had seen at Niagara and New York, and even some of the Indian chiefs, his former friends who had deserted him. He must have thought, too, that Sir William Johnson and his Indians were again his undoing. But this time the canny Frenchman was fighting a rear-guard action. He had successfully held up the English advance for a week before giving up Fort Lévis. He was not losing a very strategic post or the key to the continent this time. When Amherst sought to learn from him the French designs or their condition he was evasive, and he magnified the difficulties of descending the St. Lawrence rapids.[78]

Amherst now set about repairing and fortifying Fort Lévis, which he named Fort William Augustus. He also had the boats repaired and got ready to descend the rapids, not without some trepidation. Perhaps he could have reached Montreal sooner had he bypassed the fort with his main army and thus arrived before Murray or Haviland, which was what the French feared. But the English advance, if slow, was inexorable.[79]

The six or seven hundred Indians whom Sir William brought along of course played little part in the siege. Yet they had scoured the shores to bring in information through prisoners or their contacts with other tribes. With the Indian officers, Fonda, Hare, Lottridge, and Nelles, they made scouting forays near the fort and down the river, which were indeed useful. They rightly felt that they should have some part in the capture and division of the spoil, but Amherst, fearing violent reprisals on the French, denied them access to the fort. While they protested, Sir William strove mightily to hold them in check. When denied fresh captives, Amherst wrote, "The Indians scratched up the dead bodys and scalped them as if it had been the greatest feast to them." Finally, a great many, as Sir William rather mildly put it later, "thro' some disgust left us." In fact, twenty whaleboats filled with Indians started home, and there was little that he could do about it. He concluded that those who remained were the best and most desirable. Amherst wrote testily, "I should have sent to have taken their whaleboats away." He did little to appease them.[80]

Always foresighted, Sir William was now fully engaged in conferences with the Canadian Indians. Delegations came to him with information and offers to help. At the Indian village of Aughquisasne the French priest offered his help in keeping the Indians quiet. Better than dealing with these scattered adherents of the enemy, however, was a general peace which he sought to negotiate with the nine nations in an all-day conference. These not only prevented their helping the French, but smoothed the way for the journey downstream without opposition.[81] As he later explained,

the Peace which I settled with the 9 Nations . . . was productive of such good consequences that some of these Indians joined us, & went upon Partys for Prisoners &c whilst the rest preserved so strict a neutrality that we passed all the dangerous Rapids, and the whole way without the least opposition, & by that means came so near to the other two Armies, that the Enemy could attempt nothing further without an imminent risque of the City & inhabitants.[82]

Passage down the river, begun on August 31, was an ordeal more from the bad weather, violent rain, and turbulent rapids than from enemy opposition. Boats had to go in single file, and many of the troops were put on shore to march around the rapids. At the Cedars, Chevalier de la Corne had four hundred troops, but he marched off to Montreal on hearing of the English approach. On September 4, the worst rapids were encountered; although French or Indian pilots were on each boat, many capsized and sank while the men floundered, were tossed on the rocks, were pulled in by others, or went to the bottom. "We lost 84 men, 20 batteaus of Regts., 17 of Artillery, 17 whaleboats, one Row Galley, a quantity of Artillery Stores & some Guns, that I hope may be recovered," Amherst reported. Sir William rode a whaleboat with five French Indians (Caghnawagas) as rowers.[83]

On September 6, the small flotilla came out on the placid waters of Lake St. Francis. Meeting with only token opposition, the troops landed on the west end of of the island of Montreal and encamped. The next day a messenger from Vaudreuil indicated that the French wished a cessation of arms. They anticipated news from the peace negotiations in Europe. General Amherst, expecting the forces of

General Murray and Colonel Haviland, who arrived on the 8th, demanded surrender, to which the beleaguered Vaudreuil agreed. Amherst congratulated himself upon the favorable outcome of the campaign. "Never three Armys, setting out from different & very distant Parts from each other joyned in the Center as was intended, better than we did."[84]

Although dictated, the capitulation was fair. French troops who surrendered were to return to France and not again to serve in the war; the French inhabitants were to retain their possessions and to receive good treatment; English troops, except those necessary for occupation, were to be withdrawn, along with their Indian allies. French efforts to forestall Indian reprisals by some conditions were turned down, for the English insisted that their Indians had behaved well and had committed no cruelties. In fact, under Sir William's orders the Indians had brought in four hundred prisoners safely and turned them over without violence. The city was formally occupied when the grenadiers and light infantry marched in under the command of Colonel Haldimand.[85]

Montreal, which had suffered privations during the siege and was now faced with occupation by the English troops, presented a dour and dismal aspect. The inhabitants were resigned and depressed; the Indians lingered in the neighborhood expecting gifts; and the French soldiery calmly awaited their fate. Amherst acted quickly to clear the city. On September 9, he ordered the provincial troops to march to Chambly and thence on to Crown Point. Commanders were detailed to go with detachments to garrison Fort Stanwix, Fort William Augustus (formerly Fort Lévis), and Fort Ontario at Oswego, while engineers were sent to repair their fortifications. The French prisoners, troops and officers, including Captain Pouchot, were sent southward as soon as possible toward New York, whence they were to be sent home on English ships.[86]

Sir William and the Indians of the expedition were also to return home by the Champlain-Lake George route, but it was the end of September before they had all left Montreal. In the meantime there was much to be done to establish English rule among the Canadian Indians. In this he was so ably assisted by Daniel Claus that he decided to leave him in charge. Claus mollified the Indians with supplies and gifts, although he was greatly hampered in this by the parsimony of General Amherst. He adjusted disputes, cared for prisoners and refugees, and tried to regulate trade. Traders and sutlers who had followed the army were now doing well.[87] Other traders came from Albany, some of whom were unscrupulous, and compounded the difficulties. Claus wrote on November 20, that Thomas Wilson, whom Sir William had permitted to take a cargo of goods up from Albany, reported receiving £400 currency the first day. Ready cash was a problem, but the resumption of trade was praised.

All things are quiet and easy here & the People of this Town seemingly well pleased with their New Mastrs. if they only had the Argent blanc [silver], the Country People have the Advantage in selling their Produce for cash and will sooner oblige the English in selling them things cheaper tho the others have sometimes Silver to pay, which vexes them greatly.[88]

Claus found some help in dealing with the Abenaki Indians of the nearby mission through the Jesuit priest Père Roubaud, and Sir William sanctioned their relief. Amherst, however, suspected Roubaud and would deny him any aid. Claus deplored the hostile attitude of the military toward his Indian policy.[89] On the other hand, Amherst encouraged the Anglican missionary and chaplain, the Reverend John Ogilvie, who settled in Montreal with his family. Good friend of Sir William and valued for his work among the Mohawks, Ogilvie could serve the Canadian Indians with services in their own language. The first Anglican in Montreal, he organized an English congregation, in addition to the military, and thus was credited with establishing English worship in the city. For this he was highly commended by the Society for the Propagation of the Gospel, to whom he reported.[90]

Sir William's journey to Albany in eleven days (September 29–October 10) was in good weather and the Indians with him were generally well behaved. The exceptions were a few who got to the "Posts all drunk and Naked" and Silver Heels, who murdered "Moses of Canajoharie." He found that troops destined for Halifax had sailed from Albany the day before, and "this Town is quite Empty and dead like." This was surely a contrast with the hurry and bustle when troops had been mustered there for the campaigns and were encamped on both sides of the river. But the people of Albany had not been indifferent to the victories or to Sir William's part in them. They had demonstrated for three days in September when they heard of the fall of Montreal, and recalled that September 8, the day of its capitulation, was the fifth anniversary of Sir William's victory at Lake George.[91]

The next day he returned to Fort Johnson, weary and nursing a sore leg (perhaps the one which suffered the wound at Lake George), which prevented his conferring with Amherst at Albany. He was ready for a rest and surcease from his heavy responsibilities. Soon he composed a lengthy report of his stewardship since 1755, which he sent to Prime Minister William Pitt. He was proud, but not boastful, of his achievements, both military and in the management of Indian affairs, and solicitous for a proper future care for the latter. He now sought to give up these responsibilities and to return to his private affairs.

Permit me to add that having now discharged my Duty during the War to the utmost of my Ability, I should be glad to be freed from the discharge of an Office so fatigueing, in which I have greatly impaired my constitution, & neglected my concerns in this Country, which I would willingly apply the remainder of my life to retrieve.[92]

A life of bucolic ease at Fort Johnson, however, was not for Sir William. There were many concerns for him to attend to after his long absence in the field, and he was tired and ill. His brother Warren spent the winter with him, and kept a journal recording his impressions and observations.[93]

Warren was much impressed by the Mohawk Indians, Sir William's charges, although he reported their numbers greatly depleted. They had recently lost many through an epidemic, or some kind of fever. In December he accompanied Sir William to Canajoharie, where they attended an Indian council, "very Solemn &

decent in form of an House of Lords & Commons." At a council in March, Warren "had . . . the honour, at Fort Johnson, to be made a chief Sachem, or Prince, in a grand Council of the Six Nations, being the first white Man ever admitted to that Rank (my brother excepted) amongst them." Then he was pleased to add, "They look upon me, as their great Mate, being Brother to Sir William, & having besides their own good Opinion of me."[94]

During this winter Sir William told his brother of his exploits and narrow escapes: at Niagara, a tree near him was riddled by fourteen balls; walking home through a snow squall once he survived only by clinging to the tail of a big dog; he told of his difficulties with his Dutch neighbors, and of the riotous conflicts between Dutch and Irish. Warren recalled "a great Meeting at my Brother's House [on March 17] to drink St. Patrick, & most got vastly drunk." He also told of the price put on Sir William's head by the French. These were footnotes to history.[95]

XXIII

DETROIT AND EXPANSION

Reports from Pennsylvania and the west now raised new questions and problems in Indian relations. News of the successes of British arms in the east must be conveyed to western lands, where a new order would have to be established. While diplomats in Europe negotiated a peace, America remained to be pacified, for a settlement on paper would mean nothing if old alliances and conflicts continued.

Shortly after the fall of Montreal, Amherst took steps to subdue the west. On September 12, he ordered Major Robert Rogers to lead a small force of rangers to accept the capitulation of Detroit and the other western posts held by the French. He would bear letters of Vaudreuil which would direct the commandant at Detroit to surrender according to the terms of the capitulation. The noted ranger was a proper choice for this mission, since he and his men were accustomed to wilderness travel in all seasons and were resourceful in overcoming difficulties which might daunt the military. He would be joined on the way, however, by troops and commanders to occupy the French posts after their surrender.[1]

With two companies of rangers (two hundred men) in fifteen whaleboats, Rogers left Montreal on September 13. He went up the St. Lawrence to Fort William Augustus, La Galette, and Fort Frontenac. Thence he crossed Lake Ontario along its northern shore to Toronto, and then down to Fort Niagara. It was October 5 when he reached Presque Isle on Lake Erie, from where as ordered he journeyed south to receive orders from General Monckton at Fort Pitt. He got back to Lake Erie October 30, and was joined by Captain Donald Campbell with a company of Royal Americans who were to garrison the fort when it surrendered. George Croghan, the Indian agent representing Sir William, also joined him there bearing Monckton's orders. On November 4, the reinforced expedition sailed from Presque Isle along the southern shore of Lake Erie toward Detroit. Forty men, led by a ranger, went overland with a number of bullocks for provision along the way.[2]

Croghan, under orders from Sir William, soon encountered some Ottawa Indians, who proved to be friendly. He had previously dealt with these Indians, and he now secured their good will by presents and promises. Word of the changed course of the war had reached them, and they were ready to welcome the transfer of the western posts to the English. Nearer to Detroit he also conferred with some Wyandots and Pottawattomies and found them friendly. French emissaries were displeased with the Indians' welcome of the English, however, and tried to delay their arrival. Approaching Rogers, these French demanded proof of the surrender of Montreal. On November 28, Captain Campbell went under a flag of truce to Captain Bellestre and showed him the orders. The next day the troops landed at Detroit, Rogers received the capitulation, and a detachment of regulars under Captain Campbell took over the fort. The French *habitants* and militia pledged their allegiance to the English, while French officers and men were sent off as prisoners to Pittsburgh.[3]

Following the orders of Amherst and Monckton, parties were sent out to seize and garrison the outposts of Fort Miami on the Maumee River (present Fort Wayne, Indiana) and Ouiatenon (present Lafayette, Indiana) on the Wabash. Major Rogers with Andrew Montour and some Indians sought to reach Fort Michilimackinac on the northern straits, but were forced to turn back when they encountered heavy snows and ice on the lake. It was late December, so Rogers returned with the remainder of his command to Pittsburgh, where he arrived January 21, 1761. It has been a long and arduous journey in cold weather, and a credit to all who participated. It had officially established the English claim to the western posts and to supervision of the western Indians.[4]

Much of the credit for the success of the expedition, however, should be given to George Croghan for neutralizing the Indians. Sir William later wrote: "The westeren Indians would not have suffered us to take possession of Detroit, but from the precaution I took in sending Mr. Croghan to prepare them for it."[5] Yet a great deal remained to be done before the country was pacified. Thousands of Indians and scores of tribes had not been reached or convinced of English rule. Many Indians and traders would revert to their old allegiance and former habits of intercourse at the first opportunity. Throughout the winter, reports of the new country and its problems trickled in to Sir William at Fort Johnson.

General Amherst was greatly pleased that the Rogers mission had been so successful and that Croghan had mollified the Indians. He now anticipated a fruitful trade, for Detroit was said to abound in furs, and thought that he could take steps to improve the advantageous situation. "I propose to appoint a Person of knowledge, & probity to be Governor at the Detroit, with Directions to open a free and fair Trade between the Subjects & the Indians, giving to each such Advantages, as Shall make it their respective Interests to deal fairly & honestly by each Other, and at the same time to reap reasonable profits." He asked Sir William for suggestions for cultivating these good relations and trade, what commodities should be sent, and what constituted a fair profit for the trader.[6]

To this request Sir William replied cordially, with a full list of commodities and some rather pointed hints as to how affairs should be conducted. There should be on the part of post commanders a "Steady, Uniform, and friendly Conduct" toward the Indians. A system of rules, regulations, or laws governing trade should be drawn up and enforced. "It has always been Customary; it is very necessary, and will always be Expected by the Indians that the Commanding Officer of Every Post have it in his power to supply them in Case of Necessity with a Little Cloathing, Some arms & Ammunition to hunt with; also some provisions on their Journey homewards, as well as a smith to repair their arms & working utencils &ca." Croghan had been obliged to give the Indians "a great Deal of Goods by way of presents for their good behavior, and to others for Service," while with Rogers. He submitted a bill of £586.10.6 for these.[7]

To this Amherst registered several objections and announced his Indian policy. To him Croghan's expenses seemed high, his gifts "very bountiful." "Services must be rewarded; it has ever been a maxim with me; but as to purchasing the good behavior either of Indians, or any Others, is what I do not understand; when men of what race soever behave ill, they must be punished but not bribed." Yet if Sir William found Croghan's charges justified he should discharge his draft. Amherst also demurred at supplying arms and powder. That might be all right in cases of necessity, "but when the Intended Trade is once Established they will be able to supply themselves with these, from the Traders, for their furrs, I do not see why the Crown should be put to that Expence.—I am not neither [sic] for giving them any Provisions; when they find they can get it on Asking for, they will grow remiss in their hunting, which should Industriously be avoided; for so long as their minds are intent on business they will not have leisure to hatch mischief." As for rewards, he was having a Montreal medal struck off to be given to all Indians who had served there, which when hung about their necks would give them freedom of access to forts and trading posts.[8]

Sir William approved of the medals and was glad to distribute them to the Indians who had served on the late campaign. But he felt it dangerous to keep the Indians from any posts where they had normally traded. He confided to Daniel Claus that, "Inter nos, he is not at all a friend of Inds. wh. I am afraid may have bad consequences."[9]

To this optimistic view of the west, Croghan and Sir William gave cautious assent, if certain conditions were met. While Detroit offered prospects of trade, it was now in desperate need of help. The French troops who had retreated there in 1759 had plundered the inhabitants and left them destitute of provisions and cattle. The sale of liquor had been forbidden by Monckton, as advised by Croghan, so that they had little except what was brought from Niagara. Some of the French had retreated to the Mississippi Valley and there sought to stir up the Indians against the English. An Ottawa informed Croghan that these proposed a junction with the Cherokees and Creeks to drive the English out. But the Ottawas would not join their former enemies in this plan.[10]

There was to be, wrote Croghan, "a greatt Meeting of all ye. Westren Nations att Detroit Next Spring by their own appointment to wh. ye. Six Nations are Invited & I think they Should attend." This would give an opportunity for those friendly to the English to have a voice. Croghan had brought to Fort Pitt forty-two English prisoners from Detroit; but now he had little to do and so appealed to Sir William. The latter suggested to Amherst that his deputy be sent to this meeting. Amherst had urged Croghan to cut down his list of assistants and his expenses and seemed reluctant to give him new orders. Finally the Irishman used all his blarney to get himself sent to the Mohawk Valley. He asked Johnson if "Yr. honour Intends to keep Me heer Till I grow Gray"; "give me Leve to go Onst to Fort Johnson that I may have the Plesher of Seeing you Onst there in yr. Country Sete in yr. Woods."[11]

Fears of impending trouble with the western Indians mounted. At a meeting with the Six Nations in March, Sir William heard rumors of the Creeks and Cherokees rising; the Iroquois had long been enemies of the southern Indians, but now feared that the English might destroy them. It was clear to Sir William that Croghan and Montour were needed to escort the Six Nations deputies to Detroit and to supervise the meeting there. They were ordered to come to Fort Johnson for that purpose.[12] Then to complicate the problem the governor of Pennsylvania called a meeting with the Delawares at Philadelphia to deal with earlier land frauds, and also invited the Six Nations chiefs there. Richard Peters wrote to Sir William that those chiefs were wanted who had been at the Albany congress and had been witnesses of the frauds perpetrated there. He also suggested that Daniel Claus return to serve Pennsylvania.[13]

General Amherst seemed inclined to go to Detroit himself and began to importune Sir William to attend him. He sent for the Indian superintendent to meet him in Albany on June 1, when plans were discussed although not announced. A week later Amherst decided he could not go, but would send Sir William as head of the delegation. At the same time he chose Major Henry Gladwin to go as military governor of Detroit with three hundred troops. It now became incumbent upon Johnson to plan the expedition, to contract for gifts and supplies, and to pave the way by friendly relations with all the Indians concerned.[14]

Hence when Sir William discovered that the Philadelphia meeting would take chiefs from the Six Nations, he feared the effect upon the great meeting at Detroit and took steps to counteract it. "If the Indians are not stopped & brought back to Detroit," he wrote Amherst, "the end of my going there will not at all be answered, wherefore I now send Mr. Croghan back by the way of Pitsborough, that he may let all Indians whom he may meet going to Philadelphia or elsewhere, know of my being on my way to Detroit, in order to settle all affairs with the Indians in them parts."[15]

Having put Sir William in full charge of the expedition to settle all things with the Indians, Amherst could not deny him full authority, supplies, and an adequate entourage.

I Shall not Attempt to point out to You the Measure that you will take with the Several Indian Nations; the thorough Knowledge that You have of them, with the Zeal, Judgment, & Abilities, which You have so often Exerted for His Majesty's Service, will now best Guide You, in doing Everything that may be Conducive thereto; And You wil please to give Captain Campbell, the Officer Commanding at the Détroit, all such Orders & Instructions, as You Judge necessary for permitting and Continuing an Open and free Trade, with the Indian Nations; . . .
When I had the pleasure of Seeing you here [Albany], I Acquainted You I should Order Three Hundred Men of Gage's, under the Command of Major Gladwin to Explore the Upper Lakes, & to Assist Captain Campbell in the Relief of the out

posts, in Case the Latter part is not already Effected. . . .

I send orders to Capt: Waters [*sic*, William Walters], who was Directed to take some Artillery to Oswego, to Quit that Service, and to be ready to Attend You;. . . When You Arrive at Oswego, You will be pleased to Continue him, with his Detachment, with You, or to take any others, in his room as you shall Judge proper.[16]

Sir William would indeed like aides and assistants of his own choosing to go with him; but Claus and Ogilvie were in Montreal, Witham Marsh, the official Indian secretary, was sick in New York; and there, too, was Dr. Richard Schuckburgh, who had served so well in the interim. So he asked the general to allow his nephew, Lieutenant Guy Johnson, to leave his company in New York and to act as his secretary. His nineteen-year-old son "Johnny," already a veteran of two campaigns, would be a personal aide.[17] These, with thirty-eight men under Captain Walters, would make up his party. They would have five bateaux from Schenectady to carry them up the Mohawk and to Oswego. There Sir William asked that a whaleboat be provided for use on the lake. The transport of sufficient provisions, supplies, and gifts was essential.[18]

When it came to the size and nature of the cargo of Indian gifts and supplies, Amherst was again critical. He thought Sir William's proposal "really a large Sum," and counselled frugality, though of course Sir William was the best judge. But he thought "Strowds may be taken off, Which is a very heavy Article, and the Other things are Sufficient to please them"; and as for "Powder, lead, & Flints," they should get them at the posts, or may already have enough.[19]

This kind of criticism irked Sir William, and he replied with some firmness.

When I made out the list of goods for a Present to be given ye. Westeren & other Nations of Indians, who will attend a Meeting at Detroit, I do assure You Sir, I used all the frugality, which I Judged the good of the Service, & the end intended thereby would admit of, and as I observed to your Excellency in my letter at that time, that taking less would be doing nothing. I cant help being of the same opinion still, and as to Strowds, it is the main Article next to Amunition, . . .

but this I am to observe to You Sir, and you may depend upon it, that unless all our Old, as well as New Indian Allies are allowed Amunition for their livelyhood or hunting, all Treaties held with, or Presents made to them will never secure their friendship, for they will in such case ever be Jealous of Us, as I find they are a good deal so already, by reason of their not being able to get, or purchase any from Us.[20]

Amherst's confidence in the success of the mission was somewhat shaken by reports of French intrigue in the west and of the opposition to be expected from the Indians. These came to him from General Gage at Montreal. Then Sir William indicated that these western Indians showed, partly due to French influence but also due to English coolness and indifference, "a great jealousy and uneasiness." He was "very apprehensive that something not right is brewing, and that very privately among them. I do not only mean the Six Nations. I fear it is too general." Amherst's reply was, "If it is Mischief, it will fall on their own Heads, with a Powerful and Heavy Hand." They should learn from the defeat of the Cherokee to the south, and he trusted to the forces under Campbell and Gladwin.[21]

Preparations were finally concluded, the five bateaux loaded, the boatmen assigned, and the military engaged to follow. The trip up the Mohawk through friendly country, which Sir William had traversed so many times, promised to be pleasant. He began his personal journal with the entry: "Sunday, July 5, 1761.— I set off from Fort Johnson for Detroit, accompanied only by son John Johnson and Lieut. Guy Johnson of the Independents."[22]

For five days good progress was made. Stops at Canajoharie, German Flats [Herkimer], Oriskany, and Fort Stanwix meant calls upon friends and officers, and conferences with Mohawk, Oneida, and Tuscarora Indians. The bateaux lagged behind, and one night, not having tents, the party slept in the open without cover. Then, due to the lowness of the water, boats had to be dragged a large part of the way. At Fort Stanwix there was a portage to Wood Creek, where dams and sluices had been constructed to give sufficient water to float bateaux. But even this was insufficient for the heavily laden bateaux, and only the smallest could get through. Sir William determined to push on with a whaleboat and leave the baggage to follow later.[23]

Meetings with the Indians had been ceremonious and friendly: condolences had been performed, the medals sent by Amherst were awarded; relations with Pennsylvania and the proposed meeting at Detroit were explained. The Reverend Samson Occom, the Indian preacher who had come along, was commended to the Oneidas, with whom he proposed to work as a Christian teacher. Being one of their own he was well received.[24]

Sir William had just begun his slow progress through Wood Creek when he was overtaken by Colonel Will Eyre, bringing letters from General Amherst, and an enclosure from Captain Donald Campbell at Detroit. The latter gave information of an Indian plot for a widespread uprising against the English. A Wyandot interpreter informed Campbell of the design which had been carried to Sandusky by two Seneca deputies of the Six Nations. The Captain had confronted the Wyandots with the information and had taken steps to frustrate the plot. Shortly after this Sir William was overtaken by two Mohawk messengers who confirmed the story, saying they had learned of the purpose of the two Senecas and wished to warn him.[25]

The Six Nations chiefs now renewed their pleas for Sir William to turn back and not to proceed into the hostile country. He in turn queried every gathering of Indians from this time forth as to their knowledge of or complicity in the plot, which they always denied. He could now urge how much more necessary it was for him to treat with the several Indian tribes, and he used this suspicion and inquiry to obtain further resolutions of friendship and cooperation.[26]

Proceeding across Oneida Lake, the party stopped at Fort Brewerton, commanded by Captain Baugh, with some New York companies encamped nearby. Thence going down the Onondaga River to Three Rivers and to Oswego Falls, they arrived at Oswego the 19th, at one o'clock. Here the fort was under the command of Major Alexander Duncan, and the party dined with him and his officers. Here, too, were more Indians, several Onondaga chiefs, and some Swegatchie and Missisaugas from farther north. More medals were distributed to those who had been to Canada the year before, and further condolences, pleas, and explanations were made. Why go to Detroit, a chief asked, when the principal council fire was at Onondaga? Why did not more of them go to Detroit, Sir William countered; and why did some of their people leave him last year so unceremoniously at Isle Royale? He must go westward because now his authority extended over many more territories and Indians, who traded at Pittsburgh, Detroit, and in Canada. The Indians should stay at peace, reject all bad counsels and the vile schemes of the plotters, and in return they would enjoy a good trade and have smiths and interpreters to care for them.[27]

From Oswego the small party—Sir William, John and Guy Johnson, and a Lieutenant Irwin—embarked on a former French schooner, renamed the *Anson*, the 21st for Niagara, where they arrived the 24th. Here at Fort Niagara was Major Walters with the troops who were to accompany him, but there now ensued a long wait for the bateaux loaded with their equipment and supplies. It was late on August 9, before the boats arrived from Oswego, a trip which took them eleven days.[28]

Nevertheless, the stay at Fort Niagara, while Sir William fretted over the absence of the boats, was not entirely unpleasant or unprofitable. Comfortable quarters were prepared for him, and he enjoyed convivial table companions. Traders and military officers arrived and departed, and Indians called and sought him out. Major Gladwin arrived with his detachment of Gage's infantry destined for Detroit. Sir William conferred with him and decided on the numbers to garrison the western posts. Colonel Eyre and party started back for Oswego and carried letters, while others left for Detroit. There were intrigues and courts-martial which involved the fort's personnel. There were boats a-building, and some parties went out to explore the neighboring streams. With Guy and John, Sir William made trips to the landing place of 1759, the *petit marais*, which held memories of their campaign, and at other times they surveyed the carrying place below the falls. Finally, they visited the falls, and the site of Joncaire's post at little Niagara. Mr. Demler gave Sir William a map of Niagara and its environs. Land speculators were now casting covetous eyes on desirable locations. But over all these activities there was the necessity of pressing preparations and getting the expedition off for Detroit.[29]

Meanwhile, meetings with Senecas and the other Indians gave Sir William a chance to query them about their discontent and any knowledge of the plot. It seemed inconceivable that, with their many lines of communication and their sensitivity to undercurrents, they could be as innocent and ignorant as they protested. New details of the intrigue now came to light. The two messengers were Kayashuta and Tahaiadoris, the latter the Indian son of Chabert Joncaire, the French agent in whose name their appeals were made. Sir William felt that the plans, once discovered, would be dropped. The Senecas were now called upon to show by their presence at Detroit their dissociation from such villainy.[30]

Hampered by much rainy weather, the party took a week getting all the baggage and provisions over the portage and around the falls. First the goods were taken across the river opposite the fort and prepared for the trip upstream. Casks were repaired and strouds and other material were partially dried. They were unloaded at the carrying place below the falls. It was a rugged terrain with no easy journey to the higher ground, and there were not enough wagons, so that some loads were dragged slowly over the route. Just above the falls was Little Niagara, the former post of Joncaire, and here again the goods were prepared to reembark. On the large island in the river was a small shipyard where boats were building. There Gladwin and his troops were finally getting ready, and some of Sir William's boats were being repaired. More rain held up the work, but after two days it cleared, and orders were given to embark. Major Walters was now sick with the gout and had to stay behind. Gladwin and his men had left earlier. This time the party had thirteen bateaux, including four for the Royal Americans, and there was one birchbark canoe with some Mohawks.[31]

Anxious to get on with his business at Detroit, Sir William found the Lake Erie voyage "a tedious passage of 15 days." The first few days were clear with favorable winds so that some days nearly forty miles were covered. But at other times there were high seas and rugged shores, and there were promontories to be crossed rather than skirted. Following the south shore as advised, they dared not venture too far from land. Some days the troop boats lagged behind. French traders were met coming from Detroit who brought them news, both good and bad. The Indians and others were friendly and expectant. Croghan had arrived from Pittsburgh, but the cattle supposed to have been brought overland for provision had not been available.[32]

There was little company or entertainment, so that when a message from Niagara overtook them with good news of the war they made the most of it. The diary entry spoke volumes.

25th. [August] . . . At 10 o'clock Tom. Lottridge arrived here from Niagara, which he left the 21st inst., and brought me a large packet from General Amherst, with news of the surrender of Belle Isle to his Britannic Majesty, the 7th of June last; also an account of our defeating the Cherokees the tenth of last July, and burning fifteen of their towns; also an account of the reduction of Pondicherry in the East Indies. On which I gave orders for the Royal Americans and Yorkers, at three o'clock to be in arms, and fire three volleys, and give three cheers; after which each man is to have a dram to drink his majesty's health. I also acquainted the Indians with the news, who were greatly pleased at it. All the officers dined and spent the afternoon with me, and Mr. Gambling [Gamelin], the Frenchman, who got very drunk this night, and told me several things very openly.[33]

Surely this picture of this handful of men on the shore of the great lake, weeks away from their settlements in the east, making the welkin ring with volleys of musketry and their shouted toasts, drinking and celebrating the king's health and victories in the far corners of the earth, is one to remember. The dusky natives, whose own habits of self-congratulation over warlike deeds were often violent orgies, could well understand and partake in the rejoicing.

M. Gamelin had informed Sir William both as to the temper of the Indians and the French and of the character of the settlement. He offered to accompany the party, even proffered the use of his house. Sir William, with considerable experience in protocol, knew the value of a prestigious entrance and proper attention to the social graces. He wrote in his journal while still en route his intention "To give diversions at Detroit to the Indians, and also to the French, of the best sort, balls, etc." Now he sent word ahead to Croghan to meet them about six miles downriver from Detroit with horses.[34]

For ten miles along the Detroit River were the houses and farms of the *habitants*, interspersed here and there with Indian villages. Facing the river, these farms ran back a narrow strip for two miles or more. But their occupants were traders, artisans, and soldiers rather than farmers.[35] Johnson took note of the country as he prepared for a reception which he knew awaited. Various writers have referred to his triumphal entrance. It had indeed to be worthy of the crown's highest official in the west, who bore good news and the promise of better days to come.

Thursday. 3d. . . . Embarked at 7 o'clock, and on our way passed several fine islands and drowned meadows. About twelve, came to the house of Mr. Jarves [Louis Gervais] of the militia, which is the best house I have seen in the neighborhood. Eat some melon there, and set off for Detroit, which is but a league from said house. Opposite to the Huron town and Pottawattamie village, saw Mr. Groghan and St. Martin, the interpreter, with horses expecting us.

On coming farther, the Indian towns drew out and began to fire with cannon and small arms, which I returned by three volleys from the Royal American detachment; then went on shore and rode to town through a number of settlements. All along the road was met by Indians, and near the town, by the inhabitants, traders, &c. When I came to the verge of the fort, the cannon thereof were fired, and the officers of the garrison with those of Gage's Light Infantry received me, and brought me to see my quarters, which is the house of the late commandant Mr. Belestre, the best in the place.[36]

Then he called on Captain Campbell and was introduced to the other officers and some French gentlemen, no doubt of the "best sort." Finding Major Gladwin was very ill with a fever, he called at his quarters, too. Having fulfilled all the formal obligations, he supped with Captain Campbell. At his suggestion, the next day there was held another *feu de joie*, with more volleys of arms and cannon, to celebrate the victories of the King's arms.[37]

After his long and protracted journey, which had taken nearly two months since leaving Fort Johnson, Sir William was glad to have for a short while the comforts of a residence in a settled community. While Detroit was far out on the frontier, it had a community and social life which gave it warmth and character. As Peckham described it:

The *habitants* of the Detroit River were a convivial lot. Life was hard, but the people were robust and vivacious. Practically every adult could dance and play cards. Everybody could talk and did: they "have no talent for silence," as one observer noted; it was both a cause and an effect of their warm hospitality. To Croghan's surprise, they could all talk some Indian language. They played the Indian game which today is called lacrosse. They held foot races and canoe races. Their church was close to them; Sundays were days for dressing up and the numerous saints' days were occasions for celebrations.[38]

Now to this post, which the year before had lost its French garrison, came the detachment of three hundred men under Major Gladwin, and the smaller party of Sir William. It was indeed a time for celebration of victories and for the welcoming of distinguished guests. At the same time, droves of Indians of many tribes were converging on the settlement for the forthcoming parley. Traders and sutlers saw in all this opportunities for profit and gain; there would be many exchanges of gifts and presents from well-stocked bateaux. And the center and focus of most of the activity would be the crown's superintendent of Indian affairs.

The two weeks' stay in Detroit was filled with a round of visits, conferences, administrative decisions, Indian pow-wows, private consultations, and concern with presents and supplies. Interspersed with all of these there was a lively social life, which put a severe strain on Sir William and his aides. Theirs was a mission fraught with the greatest consequence for the English colonies, and particularly for the frontier. A vast area would either be controlled, opened up for trade, and governed, or would be lost to the intrigues and divisions of former enemies, greedy traders, and discontented savages. Great questions hung in the balance. Could peace be brought to this vast wilderness so recently torn by conflict? Could the arm of government hold sway over so large a country? Could a small and scattered white population and many diverse native tribes be given a measure of control?

The coming of the military posed an immediate problem. Amherst's orders to Major Gladwin were to explore the great lakes—Huron, Michigan, and perhaps Superior—which already were included in the capitulation, and to relieve the rangers left at the several outposts the previous year with small detachments from his command. In doing this he was specifically enjoined to consult with Sir William Johnson, to take his orders, and to give him any assistance he might require.[39]

Major Gladwin was an officer of some experience in American campaigns. He had been with Braddock in 1755, and had accompanied Amherst against Montreal; his regiment, the 80th of Light Armed Foot, was given command of the captured Fort Lévis. Having left a hundred men there, he had sailed up the river across Lake Ontario to Oswego, and thence to Niagara, whence he had preceded Sir William to Detroit. Gladwin was a man of great capacity, courage, and determination, as his subsequent career fully proved. But he was now very sick with a fever, perhaps malaria, and must necessarily rely heavily upon Sir William.[40]

This, then, was the first order of business. On his second day, Sir William with Captain Campbell called on Gladwin at his quarters, "and there we settled about the garrisoning the several posts in the best manner we possibly could, considering the bad situation of affairs, viz: the lateness of the season, the badness of the boats, and above all the scarcity of provisions and ammunition." It would be necessary to send a party back to Niagara for further supplies. They decided to send an officer and thirty men each for the posts of Miamis, St. Joseph, Ouiatanon, and La Baye, with provisions for ten months. These were subsequently detailed and supplied so that they set off on September 9. The previous day Sir William had drawn up for them orders and instructions for their conduct of the posts. They were to insure a good understanding with the Indians, an open and fair trade (but under the control of the post), and to provide the services of interpreters and smiths. The traders were all required to carry a passport from Sir William.[41]

By the next day social amenities were being observed in earnest. In the morning, the principal French inhabitants of Detroit, led by their priest, made a formal call to pay their respects and to seek protection. They were given "assurances of his Majesty's protection, while they continued to behave as good subjects. Then gave them rusk and shrub in plenty, which they made very good use of, and went away extremely well pleased."[42]

At dinner Sir William had not only Campbell, but eight or ten other officers, as well as two French officers who had been his prisoners at Niagara. While drinking they were interrupted by a delegation of fifty Huron women, old and young, introduced by Mr. Croghan. This feminine visitation was an indication of the power of the matriarchy in Indian society. It was duly and respectfully regarded by Sir William. "After saluting them, I ordered them a glass of wine and some biscuit, and drank their healths. They then told me, they had brought me some corn, the produce of their land, which they begged I would accept of. In return I ordered them a beef for their nation, which pleased them much. At parting they shook hands again, and bid farewell."[43]

But the social season really began the following evening when Captain Campbell gave a ball for the ladies to present Sir William. There were twenty ladies, no doubt the most outstanding of the post in social rank, dress, and pulchritude. A number were French, some wives of officers or traders. One in particular made an impression, indicated by several laconic entries in Sir William's diary. "I opened the ball with Mademoiselle Curie—a fine girl. We danced until five o'clock next morning."[44]

The lady whose French name Sir William had trouble with was Angélique Cuillerier dit Beaubien, the acknowledged belle of Detroit. It was indeed proper and customary for the guest of honor to escort the "belle of the ball" in the opening cotillion. To assume that he danced with her alone would be incorrect. Many a ball in New York or Philadelphia began at eight P.M. and continued until five o'clock in the morning, and this frontier assemblage was not to be outdone. Colonial balls often included in addition to the more formal and polite English dances, French and country dances, and certainly these could be expected on this occasion.[45]

Indian affairs occupied most of Sir William's time and attention for the following week, but as negotiations seemed to be nearing a conclusion he again turned to his social obligations. On September 13, "At 10 o'clock, Captain Campbell came to introduce some of the town ladies to me at my quarters, whom I received and treated with cakes, wine and cordial." Could these have been some who had not attended the first ball, and did they suggest their desire for further festivities? At least the next day he had "all the principal inhabitants to dine with me." It was a very convivial affair. "The French gentlemen and the two priests who dined with us got very merry. I invited them all to a ball to-morrow night, which I am to give to the ladies."[46]

This was indeed a farewell function. He had settled his accounts and was trying to wind up the Indian negotiations. This ball was given by him in his quarters and in it he took pride. With his usual economy of words he summarized: "In the evening, the ladies and gentlemen all assembled at my quarters, danced the whole night until 7 o'clock in the morning, when all parted very much pleased and happy,

. . .; there never was so brilliant an assembly here before." Of course he led off with Angélique as before. As he squired the attractive French girl, just half his age, were there romantic stirrings in the heart of the baronet? Was this something of a flirtation, or a sign of philandering, as some biographers have suggested? His note that he "promised to write Mademoiselle Curie as soon as possible my sentiments," surely does not imply a continuing correspondence. Rather this was a memo in his diary to make the proper response to one who had so brilliantly graced his ball. He would never see her again.[47]

Perhaps Sir William, soon on his way home and troubled by ill health and many problems, both public and private, put aside thoughts of the vivacious mademoiselle. She had not forgotten him, however, and a year later, in June 1762, she was called to his attention by none other than Captain Donald Campbell. Again she was the belle of the ball and she could not forget the earlier resplendent occasion. "I gave a Ball on the Kings Birthday," wrote Campbell, "where a certain acquaintance of yours appeared to great advantage. She never neglects an opportunity of asking about the general, what says she, is there noe Indian Councils to be held here this Summer—I think by her talk Sir William had promised to return to Detroit. She desired I would present you her best compliments." A few months later, in November, Gladwin too conveyed her interest to Sir William, who responded politely though with some warmth. "I have not forgot the powerfull Effect of the Charms of the Lady who honours me with a place in her remembrance, & should be very happy in any opportunity which might offer of paying her my Devoirs."[48]

The spirited Angélique did not pine for long, nor was her influence confined to the ballroom. In 1765 she married James Sterling, a prosperous Irish trader who had settled at Detroit. Through him, or through her father, she may have been the secret informant of Major Gladwin, who helped to thwart the treachery of Pontiac.[49]

Meanwhile preparations had been going on for the great meeting of the many Indian tribes. Talks with chiefs, the settlement of minor grievances, and customary visits had taken up much of Sir William's time. Some larger groups had waited upon him and received assurances of the forthcoming meeting. The Ottawas who were nearby made a speech "on the begging order," but were mollified by promises and a belt of wampum. Reports came in of the approach of the more distant tribes, and some of the Mohawks were delayed beyond the date set, which was September 9.[50]

In keeping with so large a meeting, many gifts and presents would be expected; in fact much would be extremely necessary. Sir William became concerned, since on examination of the goods brought it was found that many were "rotten and ruined by the badness of the boats, for want of a sufficient number of cloths, &c. so that I shall have to replace them." Provisions, too, were short because an expected supply from Fort Pitt did not come, and more cattle had to be purchased. One of the store boats being brought down by Montour was reported lost.[51]

On the eve of the great meeting Sir William spent some time putting finishing touches on his opening speech. An officer briefed the two interpreters in French upon the substance of the speech, lest they not understand his English. It was concluded that no building was large enough for the expected throng, so that seats were arranged out of doors. Following the example of earlier meetings, these would be in a semicircle with a place at the center reserved for the superintendent, surrounded by his aides, the crown officers, assistants, interpreters, and some observers.[52]

Promptly at 10 A.M. on September 9, a gun was fired to summon the assemblage in the appointed place. When all were ready, Sir William, accompanied by Captain Campbell and other officers, walked to his seat. Close by sat his deputy George Croghan and his secretary Guy Johnson. The military included two captains, two lieutenants, two ensigns from Gage's regiment, and two lieutenants from the Royal Americans. The official interpreters were M. Le Bute for the Ottawa, and M. St. Martin for the Huron. Printup, interpreter for the Mohawks, sat "only as an observer," as did John Johnson. Formality was observed, for the Indians had to be impressed by the solemnity of the occasion. The minutes recorded sachems and warriors from the following nations: "Wiandots, Saguenays, Ottawas, Chipeweighs, Powtewatamis, Kickapous, Twightwees, Delawares, Shawanese, Mohicons, Mohocks, Oneidas & Senecas."[53]

Sir William's opening address to the Indians, over which he had so labored, was a model of diplomacy. It began with the customary ceremony of condolence. He wiped away the tears from their eyes for their losses in the wars, but reminded them of English blood also shed, which he would also wipe away, that there would be no offense or obstruction which would prevent a clear passage to their hearts. He plucked out the hatchet with which they were struck and applied "a healing salve to the wound." With a belt of wampum he symbolically buried the bones of those lost and leveled the ground over their graves.[54] He then set forth his authority and his mission.

Brethren
The great King George my Master being graciously pleased some years ago to appoint me to the Sole management & Care of all his Indian Allies in the Northern parts of North America directed me to light up a large Council fire at my House in the Mohocks Country for all Nations of Indians in amity with his Subjects, or who were inclined to put themselves under his Royal protection to come thereto, and receive the benefit thereof. This fire yields such a friendly warmth that many Nations have since assembled thereto, and daily partake of its influence—I have therefore now brought a brand thereof with me to the place with which I here kindle up a large Council fire made of such Wood as shall burn bright & be unextinguishable, whose kindly Warmth shall be felt in, and shall extend to the most remote Nations, and shall induce all Indians, even from the setting of the Sun to come hither and partake thereof.—[55]

He next commended the western Indians for their friendly reception of Mr. Croghan and of the forces sent to take over the French posts. He praised their wisdom in rejecting the war belt sent among them, and told them how this had been disavowed by all the nations he had met on his way. He referred to the "Just War" waged by the British in defense of their lawful claims, and mentioned the success of their arms. Then he sought to explain the blessings which this now brought to their people under proper conditions.[56]

The happy period being now arrived which has freed you from the Calamitys of War & enabled you to enjoy your long desired tranquillity, His Majesty allways attentive to the Welfare of his Subjects and Allies is now resolved to shew you the mild use which he purposes to make of his Victorys by Cultivating the arts of peace, repairing the ruins and devastation usually attendant on War, & establishing harmony and concord throughout all his dominions—For these purposes am I sent by the General & Commander in Chief to renew in his Majesty's Name the friend-ship formerly subsisting between you and us, to give assurances of his clemency and favour to all such Nations of Indians as are desirous to come under his Royal pro-tection, as well as to acquaint you that his Majesty will promote to the utmost an extensive plentifull commerce on the most Equitable terms between his Subjects & all Indians who are willing to entitle themselves thereto, & partake of his Royal Clemency by entring into an offensive and Defensive Alliance with the British Crown.—[57]

He assured the Indians that it was not His Majesty's purpose to deprive them of their lands or property. The English troops would occupy the captured posts for protection and security, and to insure an extensive commerce among them. He urged them to regard the officers and troops among them "as Brethren," and as allies with whom they should live in friendship. On the other hand, he adjured them as to their future behavior. They had wisely surrendered to Mr. Croghan the year before English prisoners who were among them; they would be expected to yield any others still held. There were English complaints daily of "your stealing His Majesty's Horses, & those of the Traders who bring goods to dispose of amongst you." This behavior they should abandon as it is unbecoming their character as men. They had been wise in earlier conferences before his arrival in making peace among the several nations. He now offered his assistance "to make the road of peace even, broad, and easy for travelling as far as the Setting of the Sun."[58]

Nickus, the Canajoharie sachem, spoke warmly on behalf of the Six Nations, endorsing what Sir William had said. Then the conference broke up for the day while the western leaders prepared to answer. Some thirty Hurons and Ottawas came to Johnson's quarters and said that tribes from the south of Lake Erie were coming and that they did not want to discuss the war belt publicly. Sir William insisted, however, that the plot had to be brought out into the open, and to this they finally agreed. Then they asked that two guns be fired to summon the meeting on the morrow.[59]

On the next day replies were made in turn by chiefs of the Hurons, Ottawas, and Chippewas, reiterating the ceremonial words and commenting approvingly upon Sir William's speech. As for their behavior, they disapproved of the stealing of horses, they had given up all "slaves" or prisoners, and they rejected the "Bad Birds" sent among them. In good diplomatic fashion, the Huron speaker countered with his own complaints. He was glad the King had no intention of taking their lands, which they had once feared. Also, many Indians had frequently been ill-used by the sol-diers and inhabitants of Detroit, and he asked that this be prevented. Finally he referred to the conditions of trade, the dearness of goods, and the scarcity of am-munition; goods so dear they could not afford them, and powder so sparingly sold they might have to give up hunting, and would be unable to provide for themselves and families. He asked for cheaper goods and enough powder for their hunting.[60]

Two speakers had pointed at Kayashota, the Seneca messenger, as the culprit who had brought the war belt. Now Kanaghragait, the White Mingo, also a Seneca, asked for a return to the council meeting to air the whole business. Kayashota "with great oratory and resolution endeavored to clear himself." He claimed he had not been told the purpose of the journey by his companion before they reached the Wyandots. He was immediately and angrily contradicted by others. Adariaghta, a Huron chief, "confronted him and the White Mingo, and discovered everything which had passed. Upon which the White Mingo told them that they had come several times to him at Ohio, and pressed him and others living there to fall on the English, which he as often refused." A great altercation ensued, whereupon Sir William tried to pour oil on the troubled waters. "I got up, and desired that they would not go to too great lengths, being now joined in stricter friendship and alliance than ever. Left them liquor and broke up the meeting, telling them I intended next day delivering them some goods, &c., which I had brought up for their use." He asked them to be punctual and come as soon as the cannon was fired.[61]

The gift had been a matter of major concern. Would there be enough, since some things had been lost and others damaged en route? How could the five hundred Indians, the several nations and chieftains, be satisfied and yet treated fairly? Early in the morning on the 11th, George Croghan set about cutting up the present and making proper divisions thereof for the several nations. He more than anyone could weigh their claims, estimate their importance, and satisfy their desires. The goods were finally divided into nine parcels, one for each of the nations represented, whereupon they were asked "to make an equal distribution amongst you." In addition individual gifts were doled out privately where they were expected and would do the most good. Following this, an ox was roasted and a feast provided.[62]

The general meeting was over, but several tribes tarried for separate meetings with Sir William. He obtained from the Chippewas assurance of their loyalty and rejection of such overtures as the Senecas had made. Three Huron chiefs in a separate conference were recognized as head of the Ottawa confederacy, which would serve in the west as had the Iroquois in the east. There would be a council fire at Detroit where the Ottawas, Hurons, Chippewas, and Pottawattomies would gather, whence they would send a calumet to the Six Nations in token of peace and friendship. These chiefs received presents which greatly pleased them. "Nickus, the Mohawk, desired I would take home the pipe, belts, and strings and deliver them to the sachems of the two Mohawk Castles." Thereby it was hoped that the Covenant Chain which had bound the English and the Six Nations might also hold the western confederacy. This promised future friendship and cooperation.[63]

The principal work having been done, efforts were made to bring the meeting to a close and to speed the departure of Sir William and his party. Farewells were said with some additional gifts and words of counsel. Regulations to govern the Indian trade at Detroit and the several posts were issued to Captain Campbell. The two interpreters, Saint Martin and La Bute, were given $100 each, and Doctor Anthony, the post surgeon, was paid off. Departure on the 17th was marked by a frantic exchange of gifts and visits.[64]

Thursday 17th.—I counted out and delivered to Mr. Croghan some silver works, viz; one hundred and fifty ear-bobs, two hundred brooches or breast buckles, and ninety large crosses all of silver, to send to Ensign Gorrel of the Royal Americans, posted at La Bay on Lake Michigan, in order to purchase therewith some curious skins and furs for General Amherst and myself. Also gave Mr. Croghan some silver works as a present for himself to the amount of about forty pounds—he having given me many presents of Indian kind. This day I am to give an answer to what the Indians said yesterday, and to set off, if I can, after visiting Major Gladwin, Irwin, &c.

I set off about 4 o'clock in my boat, when the guns of the fort were fired. Arrived at the Huron castle soon, where the Indians were drawn up and saluted. Encamped here; visited the Priest Pierre Pottie [Pothier] ; took a ride with Captain Jarvis in his chair; supped with St. Martin, the Jesuit, La Bute, &c., and went to the Huron's council room, where they had every thing in good order and three fires burning. I here delivered them an answer to what they had said the day before, as will appear by the minutes of this day. Then broke up.[65]

The formal meeting at the Huron village with the Indians who lived about Detroit was a kind of repetition of earlier speeches, complaints, and assurances. They praised Sir William's discourse, yet sought further concessions in trade; they pledged friendship, alliance, and that they would make war against the Cherokees. They would keep the covenant chain and live in amity with the Mohawks and with the English in America. They thanked Sir William for spending the night at their castle and wished him a pleasant journey.[66]

Captain Campbell and several officers came over from Detroit to bid them farewell, as did also several French *habitants*, traders, and the priest. For six miles they were carried in three chairs to the home of "Captain Jarvis," where Mme. Gervais gave them breakfast. Then they embarked in their boats. As the last traders and settlers waved them on their way, the party relaxed, observed the shoreline and islands, and contemplated the import of all that had transpired. To his diary Sir William confided: "The Indians and inhabitants were all very kind, and extremely pleased with all that was done at this meeting. We left their country with the greatest credit."[67]

Time alone would tell whether this supreme effort was indeed a success, for much depended upon subsequent acts, attitudes, the course of trade, and the advance of settlers into the Indian country. As in all diplomacy there could be no assurance that fair words and promises represented sincere intention, or that alliances bound either by paper documents or wampum belts would be honored and carried out. Sir William was too experienced in these matters not to recognize how precarious was any peace. But he could see some positive gains. French-oriented Indians and *habitants* by these conferences and good offices had been brought to a friendly cooperation with the English. They were made to accept the English garrisons and traders in their midst. And a serious threat to the English, the Seneca plot, had been thwarted and repudiated by those concerned. For a time, at least, the euphoria of the King's largesse would be felt.

Some steps were taken immediately to make the most of the advantageous situation. George Croghan was ordered to return to Fort Pitt, where he would report to General Monckton and render an account of expenses. There he was to engage a smith to go to Detroit for a period of a year, to service the arms and utensils of the Indians. And he was to forward to Detroit a supply of hoes, "a couple of hundred of the middling sort," for weeding the Indian corn, with directions for their equitable distribution.[68]

The return voyage of six weeks, lacking the expectation and the Indian conferences of the trip out, was tedious and uncomfortable. The autumnal rains and high winds troubled the boats, hindering their progress. Camps at times were flooded by the high waters, and exposure to the rain and cold was severe. To make matters worse, Sir William began to experience a return of his old ailments and suffered extremely. The first day he took a dose of electuary; but his cough persisted, and he ran out of this medicine. He may have had a recurrence of pleurisy, which he had suffered from a few years before. Exposure and a little walking aggravated the old wound in his right thigh, which pained him through the night. "I never passed so bad a night in my life." The next night was just as bad; he spent a whole day in bed while the winds blew and the sea was too rough to embark. "I was very bad all this day and night with pains in my thigh and downwards, so that I could not walk or sleep a wink." This went on for days as he purged with physic and tried some liquors. By October 15, the pains abated somewhat, but the cough continued. After leaving Oswego and the lakes he tried to walk some at the landings, but this only increased his pain. But he was able to go hunting for a few hours. Heavy rains came again, however, as the party negotiated the rivers, portaged around the Oswego falls and over the Oneida carrying place. There was some trouble at the latter when the sluices failed to work, but higher water helped their progress. Now in more familiar country, Sir William could spend nights at the forts on Oneida Lake, at Fort Stanwix, and at the houses of friends on the Mohawk; at Conrad Frank's at Burnet's Field, and at Brant's at Canajoharie. At last, on the frosty morning of October 30, came the last leg of the journey. With great relief he penned the last words of his diary: "arrived at my house about half after seven at night, where I found all my family well; so ended my tour—Gloria Dei Soli."[69]

After a few days rest he sent off a letter to General Amherst which epitomized the results of the expedition. The official minutes would be prepared by Guy Johnson, recorded in the Indian Records, and sent on later. Guy was now doing the work of the Indian secretary, Witham Marsh, who was ill in New York.[70] If Sir William was overly sanguine, it was of a piece with his positive and conciliatory attitude. He had not only to appease the Indians, but to convince an unsympathetic commander of both the virtue of his methods and the efficacy of his expenditures. The success which he hoped for and which the country sorely needed would depend upon the acceptance of his terms and the carrying out of all obligations.

It is with great Satisfaction I now Inform your Excellency, that I have left the Western Indians Extremely well Disposed towards the English; and I am of Opinion that matters are Settled on so stable a foundation there, that unless greatly Irritated thereto they will never break the Peace Established with them; And there now only remains to Compleat Every thing by Calling down the Six Nations to a meeting, and Settling all matters with them, which I doubt not being readily able to do, and will immediately set about it, if your Excellency Approves of it.[71]

XXIV

THE MOHAWK SETTLEMENT

Weary and weakened by the illness which had plagued his return journey, Sir William longed for a period of rest and recuperation. Public services he had been performing for months to the neglect of his private affairs, and while there was satisfaction in his achievement and some pride in his commanding position as superintendent, he looked for the relative calm and orderly cultivation of his lands and business. He had written Claus on August 9, "My going on this tour is a vast hindrance to my settling my land and improvement."[1]

Success had commended him to many for political preferment, and indeed both his position and abilities made this extremely likely. Many men in a similar position would have tried for some valuable plum in the nation's gift. His friend Thomas Pownall had offered aid to secure for him the governorship of the province of New York, after De Lancey's death. Shuckburgh in New York wrote that it was the consensus there that he might have "whatever you pleas'd to Signifie to ye Ministry."[2]   It was indeed flattering to have such sentiments expressed by men of influence.

His reply to these, however, acknowledged the honor but modestly protested his "inability for the execution of so important a Trust." He was firmly convinced that "the Settleing of my Lands requireing my Presence and daily encouragement in these parts, it would not at all answer for me. besides I have hitherto had the most fatiguing and disagreeable Service I now propose to retire and spend the remdr. of my Days more tranquile."[3]

Alas for such hopes of retirement, the mere supervision of valley Indians, not to mention the problems arising from the north and west, would give him little time for idle reflection or bucolic ease. His interest and intervention were sought and expected at every turn. He had announced on his return that he would meet with the Six Nations soon, and he bore messages, belts, and a calumet to present to them from the western confederacy. But the principal issue appeared to be the Indian lands, and this in turn involved one of his chief interests, the settlement of the country.

(297)

The return of peace and security to the frontier was bound to revive hopes for the occupation of unsettled and undeveloped land. Campaigners, soldiers, officers, merchants, and traders now had a new vision of the wealth of the country. On his tour Sir William had been approached by those who sought his aid in acquiring or settling lands along the lakes and on the Niagara or Detroit rivers. He could not help himself from casting appraising eyes upon the desirable islands, the likely sites, and the promising bottomlands which were visited.[4] What possibilities were there for trade, frontier villages, and future estates in this wild country now taken over by the English! Although he had much to do at home, and he had vast tracts yet to develop, he too felt the urge to pioneer once more in new lands.

Such prospects, however, must be tempered by the realization that the country was not yet completely pacified; there were unresolved questions dealing with the French *habitants*, Indian relations, fortifications, and the regulation of trade. Moreover, the Indians who now seemed so docile were worried by the advance of settlement. And, turning from the western wilderness, he found the same problems close at hand in the Mohawk Valley.

Just prior to his western expedition, he was approached by the Mohawks, who asked for greater security in their farms and villages. Much reduced in numbers, they felt helpless to prevent the encroachment of settlers on their lands and were alarmed as new steps were taken by speculators in obtaining Indian deeds. Repeatedly they had protested the greed and land grabbing of the white man, who had used fraud and treachery to lay claim to vast tracts of their lands and who always seemed to gain more by surveys and legal trickery.

Two patents were notorious and became constant irritants in Indian relations. The Kayaderosseras Patent of 1704 claimed a huge area of perhaps eight hundred thousand acres of Saratoga between the Hudson and Mohawk rivers. Initially only £60 was to be given as a consideration, and the Indians contended that only a small sale was intended. It was also said that the Indians were never paid and no surveys made, so that the conditions of the patent were not met. But the original thirteen patentees divided and resold their claims, for which some had made considerable payments. Sir William and other officials contested these claims on behalf of the Indians, but with little success, for many years.[5]

A more immediate threat was the Livingston Patent, obtained by the elder Philip Livingston, to Indian lands along the Mohawk. Knowing that his patent embraced some Indian farms and villages, Livingston hired one Edward Collins to survey the land. Collins, it was reported later, one night went forth with a few companions in a canoe and took observations which were the basis of the claim. The "moonlight survey" was so surreptitious that even his companions were not fully aware of it, and the Indians were hoodwinked. Settlers on these lands continued to pay rent to the Indians.[6]

Now speculators appeared with purchases from the Livingston heirs and sought licenses from the Council of the province. These entitled them to negotiate with the Indians, whom they often defrauded. Most notorious for his villany was Ury Klock, who, Sir William charged, brought Indians to his home to get them drunk and then had them sign deeds. Thus, idle and irresponsible Indians were made the instruments of his designs, and these deeds were put before the Council in New York for approval. Other persons, perhaps unwittingly, were drawn into his schemes and thus had an interest in such action. Henry Wendell was sharply reproved by Sir William because his mother-in-law, Mrs. McGin, became so involved. Another whose actions were condemned was Mrs. Eve Pickerd, a mulatto woman who ran a tavern on the Canajoharie flats. Her children enticed three Indians, "the drunkenest Rascals in the whole castle," from a horse race on the ice into her house and while there had them sign deeds. The next day the Indians declared that they knew nothing of what they had done.[7]

Alarmed by such incidents, the Mohawks asked that their holdings be defined and that a stop be made to incursions on their farmlands. They begged Sir William "to let them know their Bounds, or what Lands they are still Masters, or owners of in these parts." Sir William thereupon urged Alexander Colden, the surveyor general of the province, to make "(on account of the Crown) an Exact & full Survey of all the Patents, & Lands taken up on both sides of the Mohawk River, from Schenectady to Fort Stanwix." By this means he could tell the Indians what was still theirs, for this would be the best possible method to allay their fears.[8]

Sir William also wrote urgently to Lieutenant Governor Cadwallader Colden, who was far more understanding and sympathetic than was the late Governor De Lancey, not to grant any more patents in this area. Colden affirmed his policy, going back to 1736, and also to recent rules of the crown in these matters.[9] But regardless of legal restrictions and obstacles, the speculators were bound to continue their intrigues and to take advantage of the vagueness of surveys, and of the maze of land petitions, deeds, and patents.

Under these circumstances the Indians concluded to do what in modern parlance would be called, "If you can't beat them, join them." If they could not prevent the preemption of their lands any other way, they would give them away. Rather than have villains evict them, they would throw themselves upon one whom they could trust, their friend and counsellor and honorary sachem, Warraghiyagey. Warren Johnson was visiting Fort Johnson at the time and recorded the event.

Decemr. the 20th [1760] I Sett out from Fort Johnson, with Sir Willm. for Canajoharie, where we arrived that Night, . . . the three Days following we were admitted to their [the Mohawk's] Councils which were very Solemn & decent in the form of an House of Lords & Commons. On the Second Day they unanimously gave Sir William a Gift of 100,000 Acres of Land or thereabouts, that is 16 by 10 Miles & reckoned the very best in the Country opposite Fort Hendrick, & 36 Miles from Fort Johnson.[10]

Shortly afterwards Sir William wrote a full account of the gift to Banyar, the provincial secretary, asking him to take steps for its legal approval.

The Indians of Conojohare in full Council Sent me a Message some time ago, & desired I would come up to their Castle, haveing something of Moment to communicate to me, on my Arrival the whole Castle mett in form, and let me know that they had unanimously resolved to make me a present of a considerable Tract of Land, & desired a Deed of gift might be drawn for that purpose. I thanked them for their good Will shown towards me, and told them I could not draw one then, but would consider of it. in a few days after, abt. fifteen of them deputised by the rest came to my House, and executed a Deed of gift for a Tract of Land on the North Side of the Mohawk River wh. they desired I would Send up to their Castle that the rest might Sign it wh. I accordingly did. this Grant includes all the Lands as yet unpattented between the Creeks called Takahyuharonwe, & Tinghtoghraron, the former falls into ye. Mohawk River opposite almost to Fort Hendrick, the latter at Burnets feild, from the Mohawk River as it Runs, to a line wh. is to be Run from the North Westerly Corner of the Rear line of a Tract of Land (last Autumn) laid out or surveyed for Mrs. McGin &ca. to the Canada Kill or Creek at Burnets feild, wh. Rear line is to be the Same Course of Sd. Mrs. Mc.Gins Rear Line, & will make the length from the Mohawk River to Sd. Line abt. 13 Miles, containing abt. 40 Thousand Acres—for wh. I would willingly get out a Pattent as Soon as I could, and for that End, I would be glad You would take, or direct the proper Steps.[11]

He stated that he had "no other view in desireing this than to be able to See, or have Common Justice done to ye. Inds." Later he disclaimed any intention of getting lands which belonged to others, but that the Indians wanted to dispose of this rather than see it fall into the hands of Ury Klock. While it was obviously a gift and he said nothing of any payment at this time, two years later he wrote Pownall that he knew the Indians' wants and that it was customary to give something in return, so he immediately made them a present of "1200 Dollars or £480 Currency."[12]

Convinced of his own rectitude and good motives, Sir William could not see that he was a bit disingenuous, nor that others would regard this as just another speculative venture on his part. Yet he knew that it was contrary to the rule requiring a license from the government before getting an Indian deed. He expressed surprise when Banyar replied, raising objections. Others, including the hated Klock, had already obtained licenses to purchase these lands, and they had been crafty enough to include members of the Council among the potential patentees. In fact, Banyar himself, and the surveyor general, Alexander Colden, each had an interest. Furthermore, Banyar questioned whether the Indians had a right to give away their lands (crown lands) to anyone they pleased regardless of any license. He hoped Sir William would accommodate himself to the other claims and give up any advantage save an equal share.[13]

Sir William was angry: he felt he was being badly treated, and he was incensed that others, including some of whom he had a bad opinion, were holding up his grant. He felt it was an outrageous proposal that he should give up half of his grant to these others. Likewise, he knew that although he could not obtain the grant without government help, the others without his approval had no chance of getting an Indian deed. He sent down a list of forty names to enter on his patent and peremptorily ordered Banyar to take steps, or, if he did not, to turn the affair over to someone who would.[14]

Banyar was much disturbed by his old friend's anger and suspicions and hastened to justify his position. Indeed, some claims to that area, in which he too was concerned, went back to 1754. What could he do when members of the council who had to ratify all the licenses were concerned? Would it not be better to come to an agreement? Rather than to incur Sir William's wrath, both he and Alexander Colden agreed to give up their claims and to serve as intermediaries.[15]

There was a hiatus in the argument while Sir William was away on his trip to Detroit, but on his return he sought a compromise. He made an offer by which the other claimants might pay him £300 and obtain ten thousand acres; this they rejected as being much more than he had probably paid for the whole. He viewed it as conceding them a portion of his grant. They wished to be treated as equals. There was some dickering over the more desirable riverfront lands and those in the backcountry. Finally Sir William agreed to take either twenty thousand near the river or forty thousand further back, while the others paid him £600. Just as this seemed agreeable to all, new instructions came from the crown to the governors restricting the sale of Indian lands. Sir William held that his grant, having come before this, was not affected. Banyar and the Council held that the new restrictions did apply and wanted to divide the area into three separate patents of twenty thousand acres each. This would deny the validity of the Indians' deed to Sir William while recognizing the licenses of the others, and this Sir William would not accept. Hence he informed Banyar that this put an end to his agreement.[16]

Now Lieutenant Governor Colden took up the issue on Sir William's behalf. He wrote the Lords of Trade, March 1, 1762, explaining the Indians' gift to Sir William, the refusal of the Council to grant him a license, and that the Indians had then refused to sell any of their lands. This had created an impasse. In 1765, after the Indian uprising, Colden again took up Sir William's claim with the Board of Trade, and strongly urged that it be given royal sanction, recognizing Sir William's services thereby, and that the Indians had given it to him out of gratitude upon the ending of the war.[17] By this time both the political situation and the aspect of Indian affairs were much altered. Hence the Board of Trade did nothing. With the help of friends at court and after much lobbying, the Canajoharie Patent was finally confirmed in 1769, and due to the unusual circumstances was generally called "the Royal Grant."[18]

The furor caused by this controversy appears unseemly in that none of the speculators, least of all Sir William, really needed this land. He already had a great deal and was not averse to taking additional portions as legitimate perquisites of his office. He was frank in admitting this to Banyar. "I make it a Rule to be concerned where I can, because I look upon this to be the principal advantage arising from the Office I sustain." The latter quite as frankly reminded him, in connection with a proposed purchase of Susquehanna lands, that he "meant then a very great share for yourself, more perhaps than you'l now want; as your attention in point of Settlement, is taken up nearer home." On the other hand he was vexed that his opponents and critics "have been pleased to say, that I have and am engrossing too much Land in these parts." In fact, he was not like so many others who acquired claims merely to hold for future profit. "I am the only person in these parts who (far from preventing) takes measures for Settling the Lands which I purchase by the encouragement of industrious people to whom I grant Lotts on the most reasonable terms."[19]

The Lands wh. I possess were pattented by others, and afterwards purchased by me, except one Tract which you [Banyar] know adjoining that wh. you were concerned in, but supposing I had made great purchases in these parts, with the consent of the proprietors, & to their satisfaction, I cant see the least reason why they, or any others should envy me, as my motive is the Settling the Country, wh. I have been promoting all the War at a very considerable expence, and risque, and as I never spared any pains to do all I possibly could for the protection of the Inhabitants (who were it not for me would not have remained on their Lands either this, or the last War) I think I have at least as good a right to purchase and add to what I already have perrilously acquired, & maintained in these parts, as any man in it.[20]

Settlement of the land, laying out new areas on the frontier, their support and protection were indeed his passion. Neither war nor hardship could check his determination to proceed with a development which he had at heart. Behind Fort Johnson, on the rising backcountry north of the Mohawk, he saw great possibilities for the future. This was the tract of some fifty thousand acres known as Kingsborough and was covered by two patents. Some of it he had purchased of earlier holders.[21] Here he would bring in settlers and encourage them to cultivate the land. Here, too, would be his future home and country seat. It was vast enough for unrestricted expansion into the backcountry. It would be suitable for his business interests, adaptable for Indian negotiations, and perhaps for the jurisdiction of a barony or manor. Only the future would tell.

Early in 1760 he wrote a letter from this development with the dateline "Castle Cumberland." With his penchant for royal names, he thus honored the second son of George II, a military hero and the conqueror of the Pretender. That he later changed the name of his seat to "Johnson Hall" after the accession of George III could have been due to the altered reputation of the Duke of Cumberland.[22] Here he spent much of his time while not on public service for the next three years.[23] The progress of its settlement and cultivation was his proudest boast. This he accomplished in spite of the rigors of the frontier, the threat of warfare, and his diversion to Indian affairs.

Early in 1760, Sir William visited the new tract, but soon thereafter he was off on his campaign to Canada. But his overseer Thomas Flood, in spite of drought, harvested hay and wheat, ran a sawmill, and carried on the construction of buildings. Brother Warren was present when work at the new location was begun early the next spring (1761). He reported in April that "Castle cumber Land & about, it is a very fine rich black soil, & they are now preparing to sow their Spring grain." To Claus in Canada Sir William wrote in March, "This improvement goes on very well. You would scarce know it now." Claus in turn expressed his "great Satisfaction and Surprise," and added that he had learned of several gentlemen "what fine and great improvements you have made at Kingsborough since last year, and I am convinced it will be a new Place to me whenever I have the Pleasure to see it." By June of that year there was further progress. "I am busy clearing Land at Denis Maddins, also, where I propose please God to build Mills for use of ye. upper part of the Pattent—I have but about 50 Familys Settled as yet, but expect many more next Fall.—"[24]

On the eve of the Niagara campaign, Samson Occom, the Indian preacher who came up the Mohawk to join the party, found "Sir William at his Farm Seven Miles out off the Road in the Wilderness." Earlier that spring twenty Canajoharie chiefs

came in sleds to confer with him at Castle Cumberland. Thus it was back from the
river but not too far for easy access even in bad weather. His headquarters there
was but "a small Lodge in the Wild Woods," so that in the winter of 1762 he wrote
that he proposed building "a good dwelling House next spring on my new
Patent."[25]

While on the Detroit journey he jotted memoranda for the improvement of this
estate:

> To settle all my affairs when I get home, with regard to land, settling tenants
> &c. . . .
> To have my books and all my accounts properly settled; and all my tenants'
> accounts adjusted regularly and put into one book.
> To sow the several seeds I pick up in my way to Detroit. . . .
> Little summer houses to build in my gardens when I get home.[26]

The seeds referred to were "like Piony," and herbs, and "seed of a weed good
for the flux." Now his correspondence was filled with requests for seeds and
plantings. From Claus in Canada he sought those not available locally, "a parcel of
the best Garden Seeds of every kind for me, so that I may try them out next
Spring, in my new Garden, wh. is 2 Acres and near a half without Root or Stump."
From other correspondents in New York he sought melon seeds, potatoes, "a
peculiar kind of Beet root," and "all the extraordinary kind of Seeds I can
procure." Again he asked for fruit trees and grape vines. He was so absorbed in
this that one friend joked about it. "You put me in mind of the Antediluvian
Shalum that lived in Mount Terza, that covered the Country with trees of his own
planting—so you are taking down the old Forrests and planting a new of Fruit
Trees."[27]

All of this interest in farming was productive, however, and elicited unusual
comment. Brother Warren was properly impressed by farm products so different
from Ireland. "Barley sowed here in May, may be cut in six weeks; Buckwheat in
June; Indian corn the 1st of May, . . . Trees are in blossom, and Asparagus very
plenty the 15th of April Inst."[28] Witham Marsh was rhapsodically complimentary
on things sent to New York.

> The Kegg, with Potatoes, was sent to Mr. Darlington; and tho' the water-melon, and
> some of the first were spoiled, yet the Frow preserved all the remains, & the
> Husband swears that the whole Town can't shew any ones so good as your
> smallest—what would he say if had a Barrel of the largest? Why out-puff (but with
> propriety) the Puffs of all Puffers here, who are no small number! At my Club, to
> be sure I have not expatiated at all about the produce of your matchless Garden,
> and the remainder of your Farm! Oh the Oats, &c. . .[29]

Livestock was collected and imported. Horses and cows were ordered from
Canada also, although their transportation posed a problem. Sheep were imported
from the West Indies in return for exports. Husbandry was to be followed, for the
breed of horses was not of the best, either for saddle or draft. From Canada, too,
Sir William wanted a breed of wild geese: "Send me 4 Geese & 2 Ganders for
Breed." Cows were small. Bullocks were used for plowing.[30]

The principal boast of this development, however, was not his own land, but the increase of his tenantry in spite of adverse conditions. In two years the fifty families had increased to a hundred, largely due to his own exertions.

Altho' my Lands lay on the Frontiers here, & much more open to the Incursions of all the Enemies parties than any other, I nevertheless at a Considerable Expence established above 100 Familys thereon during the heat of the War, furnishing them with Cattle, provisions & money to encourage them to remain thereon, at a time when all the Neighbourhood were abandoning their Settlements, which they would have left to a Man to the great detriment of the province, if not induced to the contrary by my own example & that of my Tenants, for which purpose I spent all the time in which I was not on the publick service, in a small Lodge in the Wild Woods amongst them.[31]

Many of these tenants were German immigrants, too poor to pay him any rent or to take out leases. They were Calvinists (Reformed) and Lutherans but could not afford a minister, so Sir William helped them to support an itinerant preacher who held services in one of his barns. He even made two gifts of land, of fifty acres each, to enable them to erect churches.[32] Thus he set the pattern for the paternalism in settlement which would greatly enhance his power and influence in the Mohawk Valley.

While the master was so much of the time in the field or on his new development, Fort Johnson witnessed a number of changes. Since the death of Catherine in 1759, Mary Brant, more commonly called "Molly," had served as housekeeper and mistress. In the next few years her rôle became increasingly important. As Sir William's consort she was the mother of a growing family, and the dominant personality in his absence. One can only conjecture the emotions and tensions as she moved in, not just as housekeeper but as a replacement for the mother of the white children. "Granny," if she was indeed the mother of Catherine, was relegated to the role of governess. If Nancy, the eldest girl, had served for a while as housekeeper, as Witham Marsh indicated, she soon abdicated.[33]

Legend has it that Sir William saw a young Indian girl at a militia muster, who asked one of the mounted officers if she might ride behind him. Jokingly he said yes, whereupon "she leaped upon the crupper with the agility of a gazelle. The horse sprang off at full speed, and clinging to the officer, her blanket flying, and her dark tresses streaming in the wind, she flew about the parade ground swift as an arrow, to the infinite merriment of the collected multitude." Whereupon Colonel Johnson, admiring her spirit, took her off to Fort Johnson.[34]

No doubt as a young girl Molly was attractive and may have come to Johnson's attention then, but by the time she took over the affairs of the house she was fairly mature. She was probably born in the Mohawk Valley in 1736, and hence would have been twenty-three in 1759.[35] Of her earlier life we have little knowledge. Daniel Claus wrote that on his return journey from Philadelphia in 1754, a certain captain at Albany "fell in love with Ms. Mary Brant who was then pretty likely, not havg had the small pox."[36] This implies that later she did have the smallpox, and if so probably during the epidemic which hit the Mohawks and Canajoharies in 1757.[37] Even if disfigured thereby, she possessed charm and spirit. While carrying her first child by Sir William, which was born the following month, she wanted to follow her man on his campaign against Niagara. He had to write her from Oswego in August 1759, not to come.[38] Her second child, a girl, was born in 1761, and a third in 1763. Sir William was proud of his half-breed children, whom he treated with great consideration, and was always deferential to Molly. Many writers have speculated that he might have married her in an Indian ceremony, but of this there is no evidence. She apparently accepted her dual role of mistress and housekeeper with no complaint.

On the other hand there is much evidence of Molly's active participation in and direction of the affairs of the Johnson menage. Contemporary accounts show her shopping or making purchases for the household and its entertainment. Visitors mentioned her in their thank-you notes and sent her gifts.[39] Even distinguished and noble guests treated her as an equal and commented upon her presence and courtesy. Lord Adam Gordon after a visit in 1765 wrote, "My Love to Molly & thanks for her good Breakfast."[40] Lady Susan O'Brien, who visited the Johnsons at the same time, was quoted as saying that Molly was "a well bred and pleasant lady," who (according to Stone) "in many a ramble with her ladyship in the green-wood, proved a delightful companion."[41]

Molly's influence and persuasion in dealing with her people, so consequential in later life, was evident while she lived with Sir William and was a tremendous asset. Little Peter, an Oquaga chief, after a period of mourning sent the special thanks of his family. "My wife & her Sister Salute Miss Molly and all your family."[42] James Stevenson of Albany married an Indian woman and by her had a "young warrior" living among the Senecas. Molly and Sir William interceded to get his boy from the tribe, for which he repeatedly praised them. "My compliments to Molly & thank her for the pains she has taken relative to the Child."[43] While some of her influence in such affairs may have been derived from her status with Warraghiyagey—Sir William as a sachem—it may not have come from any previous matriarchal inheritance from her parentage. If so, it is an even greater tribute to her personality.[44]

Somewhat reluctantly, Sir William was beginning to realize that his children were growing up. "Johnny," as he still called his twenty-year-old son, had been his companion on campaigns and expeditions. He was used to frontier life and rural pleasures and was a favorite with his father. His very closeness caused him to be treated as a child. The two girls, however, remained at Fort Johnson while their father was in the field or tending his estate. It is hard to conceive that they could have enjoyed, or resented, the seclusion related by the garrulous Mrs. Grant.[45] They might well have partaken of the generous entertainment provided visitors and strangers, the surprising "custom" described by their Uncle Warren. Among such visitors were young military officers whose eyes could not but notice the burgeoning maturity of the young ladies. Nancy, the eldest child, in the spring of 1761 was just twenty-one, well beyond the age when women began to think of marriage. She was but sixteen in 1756 when the young German aide to her father had already begun to court her. In view of her father's expressed surprise, this probably went on *sub rosa*.

Daniel Claus told of his emotions when Sir William, acknowledging his debt and gratitude for the services of the young man during the Lake George campaign and after, besought him to make a request of anything which could be given him. Overwhelmed by this generous offer and its implications, Daniel was speechless. He made a bow, mumbled his thanks for the compliment and asked for time to consider. "His mind was so agitated and surprized upon the Occasion that he retired to his Room to sit down at a Loss what to say or do."[46]

The first Object that presented itself to his Mind was a certain young Lady he paid his Addresses to for some time past who seemd not to be averse to them & Mr. Claus flattered himself that Sir Wms. Consent was only wanting to complete the Matter, made that the first Object of his request from Sir Wm. & proposed the Matter first to her. She told Mr. Claus that all the objection she had was that she thought it rather too early to change her Condition particularly at a Time of War wch. was uncertain how it might turn out, desiring Mr. Claus to put it off to a more convenient & quiet time. He was quite satisfied with her Discourse upon the Occasion and dropd. thoughts of saying anything then to Sr Wm.[47]

Shortly thereafter the purchase of a military commission came up, for which Sir William generously offered to advance £1500 Sterling. It was not until 1761, however, that Lieutenant Claus was offered a captaincy in Haldimand's 60th Regiment, and sought the financial aid thus proffered.[48]

Having spent the winter in Montreal, serving as deputy for Canadian Indians and performing numerous errands for Sir William, Daniel now bethought himself of his lady fair. With a captain's commission he would be much more eligible as a husband, but his feelings were mixed. If he took the commission he would be expected to join his regiment and give up his duties as deputy. The military life looked less attractive than the possibility of continuing in the Indian service. He wrote Sir William that "under your Management [as] I always hoped for, and wished to have the Pleasure of making one of your Family." This admission let the cat out of the bag, so he came straight to the point.

To be more open in my Sentiments I beg leave to mention to you that I always had and ever shall have a Sincere Regard and Esteem for Miss Nancy your elder Daughter, who likewise was kind enough as not to discourage me therein, wherefore I should before now have asked your Consent and Approbation to marry her, had it not been for the troublesome times we hitherto sustained, but that Period being at last come I embraced this opportunity of doing it now, and from your natural Goodness flatter myself a favourable Answer.[49]

It was late March, and Claus hoped soon, when Lake Champlain opened and before the Indians returned from hunting, to get a month's leave to return to Fort Johnson. But, alas for such hopes. When Sir William's reply, dated May 1, Castle Cumberland, arrived in Montreal, it quashed his plans. He had thrown himself on Johnson's advice as to whether to purchase the commission. That was decided and that he should stay with his regiment as expected by the general. Furthermore, his proposal of marriage was not taken kindly.[50]

Your proposal of Marriage surprises me a great deal, haveing never had the least hint of the kind dropped or mentioned to me before, so that it really seems to me verry extraordinary & precipitate; beside, it is giveing me a bad impression of my Daughters regard for, & Duty towards me, whom I think she should consult in a case which concerns her happiness so nearly. it shall ever be a maxim with me to give a Child as great liberty in the choice of a Wife or Husband as is consistent with the Duty they owe to a Parent, in whose power it is to make them happy with their own industry [afterwards]. if they exceed that indulgence, and will act independent (which seems now to be the case with my Daughter, as you represent it) then I think all expectations, as well as parental regard are forfeited.—I have always had a regard for You, and believe you are sensible of it, from the notice I have on occasions taken of You. that alone, should have weighed with You, or any Man of Honour, and be a bar to prevent the carrying on any private intrigue in my Family. had you moved the Affair to me, before you had made your inclinations known to some others, as I find, is the case, it would have been more in Character of a Gentleman & Freind. I have not yet spoke to her on the Subject, but intend it as soon as I go to the House, & when I find out her Sentiments or inclination shall be better able to say more to you on the affair. . .[51]

Poor Daniel. Not only were his behavior and intentions questioned, but he had placed Nancy in jeopardy with her father. What would be the scene and the issue when her father confronted her with doubts as to her filial duty. Whatever elation he could experience in acquiring his captaincy was clouded by Sir William's statement in the postscript that he could not assure him of continuance in the Indian service. The general gave him no answer or indication that the office would last, and Amherst had a low opinion of Indians.[52]

Claus's letter of explanation protested the interpretation placed upon his letter, and especially denied any impropriety or intrigue on the part of Nancy. She had always shown the highest regard and duty towards her parents. He also denied that he had consulted others, or that Nancy had made any commitment to him.

That I sounded Miss Nancys Disposition towards me before I asked your consent, I dont deny, and if that may be deemed dishonorable it was not done with any disrespectfull Design, and hope you will attribute it to my Inexperience in those Cases and forgive me, all I meant in my Letter by meeting with no Discouragement on her side was that I flattered myself not to be disagreeable, and perhaps would not meet with a Refusal from her after obtaining your consent, for I assure you Sir with Truth that I never had nor expected any positive answer from her on that head, wch. you will find when you speak to her.[53]

This avowal, Sir William admitted, cleared up the "Ill impression" of his letter, as well as "the uneasiness which it gave me since on different accts." (on Nancy's part) However, "I would not have you make any advances that way until your arrival here whenever it may be. the General is not for Your Stirring from thence as You will find by my last Letter from Albany."[54]

It was nearly a year before Daniel Claus was able to return to Fort Johnson. He arrived there March 24, bearing official communications, reports of his Indian conferences, and complaints from the Canadian Indians, and was soon deeply involved in Indian affairs.[55] Arrangements were quickly made for the wedding, however, and he and Nancy were married on April 13, 1762. There being no Anglican clergyman available near Fort Johnson, the ceremony was performed by a

Lutheran clergyman, Mr. N. Shults, but "agreeable to the Form as directed by the Church of England." Present, and witnesses, were, "Sir William Johnson, Bart., Mr. John Johnson, Miss Mary Johnson, Mr. Guy Johnson, Lt. Gullin of Indpts. Comdg. at Fort Hunter & Messrs. Fran. & Ferl. Wade."[56]

If there was a honeymoon trip, it was not an extended one. Claus was shortly engaged in meetings with the Indians, and on May 11 was sent off again to Montreal, while Nancy remained at Fort Johnson. His tour of duty there lasted until the winter; he returned in time for the birth of a daughter, Catherine, January 22, 1763. Sir William hailed the new arrival as "a fine Child of ye. best or Female Kind." The little family was to remain a part of the Johnson menage.[57]

Sir William's younger daughter, Mary, usually called "Polly," was not without suitors. Now about sixteen or seventeen, she too had attracted the attention of young officers. Ensign John Carden had asked for Polly's hand and had been refused, when he once again made his appeal to her father from far-away Martinique. Perhaps like Claus, he felt it was safer at a distance, and that his report of the military action in the West Indies would give him new prestige. These letters must indicate something of the proper course for suitors or at least the formidable protection of the baronet which made the young swains timorous and obsequious. At least Carden did not make the mistake of approaching the lady first.

> I now mention one thing which I hope wont give offence and if you will Consent will get leave to go to your house which is to give me your Daughter as a wife which you refus'd me before but hope you wont now Miss Molly [Polly]. I hope you wont take it ill my making such a request but the vast regard I have for [you?] obliges me to desire her for my wife. I begg if you dont think it loosing time you will let me hear from you as it will give me great pleasure to hear you are well. . .
> I begg you will consent to my request & make me a happy man which I must be if I am so fortunate as to have her for my wife. I desire no money with her. [   ] I begg you will comply.[58]

That he had no better luck this time was due to the fact that another had the inside track. At what time her cousin Guy became a suitor is not known. As Indian secretary *pro tem*, he was in constant attendance on Sir William at home as well as in the field. He was giving great satisfaction as a scribe, so much so that the superintendent asked that he should be given the position so much of the time neglected by the ailing Witham Marsh. But General Amherst could not do anything in that way while Marsh hung on to the title. He even now suggested Dr. Shuckburgh, whom Sir William had mentioned earlier. There was a possibility too, that Guy could be recalled to his regiment.[59]

Guy undoubtedly had talent and ability. He wrote a good hand, sketched some, and as a draftsman could provide very useful maps and charts.[60] As Johnson's nephew he had been given recommendations and pushed forward in the dispatches. He was gaining experience and knowledge of Indian diplomacy which was to serve well. He would continue as deputy if Sir William had his way. There was nothing like keeping things in the family. Polly's marriage to Guy probably took place in January 1763. Its consummation was proudly announced by Sir William in the letter which told of the birth of his granddaughter.[61]

While both his sisters were married, what sort of a career was open for Johnny? He was indeed the heir and favorite of his father, who was inclined to be indulgent. He took the boy along on his campaigns and expeditions and lost no opportunity to probe his tastes and to encourage his development. John appeared to like the outdoor life of the frontier or of a military career, but his father had to look out for his education. At the beginning of the war in 1755-56, he would have chosen the army, but Sir William insisted that he go to school, and in 1757 sent him to attend the Academy in Philadelphia (later to become the University of Pennsylvania). He was enrolled in the fall of that year by the provost, William Smith, and attended sporadically for three years.[62] In May 1759, Peter Wraxall wrote from New York, relaying information from the Philadelphia merchant Francis Wade.

Mr. Wade's brother from Philadelphia dined with me yesterday. he tells me your son is in good Health that the masters of the Academy give a very good Character of his Progress in Learning. I find he is yet backward in writing and Ciphering as he has not hitherto been much put to it; in my opinion it is full time he should & it is too important a part of his Education to be delayed, also Merchts. accounts which are very necessary to every Gentleman for the regulation of his own private affairs, he gives me a good Character of his sobriety & virtuous Inclination & that he is constant at Church every Sunday.[63]

On one occasion, at least, possibly when he wanted to go along on one of his father's expeditions, John came home from Philadelphia sooner than expected. He thus braved the parental wrath or discipline, but was not treated harshly therefor.[64]

Perhaps the young man was acquiring more of the characteristics of a frontiersman than of the son of a country gentleman. George Croghan, who liked the lad and would have rather made him a countryman, joked about his tastes after his return from Detroit. "I . . . make no Doubt butt Capt. Johnson [John was a captain in the New York militia] by this time has a good Relish for parchmale [dried corn meal] & Wild Ducks & Despises Rost Beeff."[65]

A military career was opened for John without any of the difficulties which Claus encountered. Colonel Haldimand wrote from Montreal in March 1762 that there was a commission for sale in his battalion, and he offered it to Sir William's son "If you destine him for military service and he has a liking for it." General Amherst would have been glad to comply and to facilitate the matter, but now John had second thoughts. Or was he just too diffident about a career of any sort? At least on this occasion Sir William gave him rein:

In the beginning of the War he was very desireous of going into the Army, but his Youth then and not haveing finished his Learning prevented my indulging his inclination, and now he says, as the War is near at an End, he does not think it would look well for him to enter into the Army.—and as he is come to the years of discretion I allow him his own turn of Mind.[66]

Hence John remained at Fort Johnson, enjoying the country life and the company of his relatives and friends in the rapidly growing estate and settlements at Kingsborough. He was not ambitious, but others viewed his position as heir and prospective baronet with some misgivings. Finally, his father was persuaded to send him on a grand tour to the mother country, to develop as a man of the world, to "wear off the rusticity of a country education," and perhaps to find him a lady worthy of his station.[67]

Ever present in the Johnson menage were Indians. Along with Molly and her growing family were two half-bred Mohawks, illegitimate sons of Sir William, who must have had the free run of the place. Like other half-breeds, they probably spent their early years with their mother's people. Now, probably in their teens, they could enjoy some of the privileges of the household. William, Tagawirunte (later called William of Canajoharie), was probably the "little Will" referred to in a letter of 1750; an infant then, he would have been eleven or twelve in the 1760s, and about sixteen or seventeen when he was sent away to school. There are fewer references to "Young Brant," Kaghnaghtago, but the two were associated and treated equally in Sir William's will. Nothing is known of their mothers.[68]

At the request of Eleazar Wheelock, who was soliciting support as well as students, several Indian lads were selected to attend the Indian charity school at Lebanon, Connecticut (later New Hampshire). One of these was William, who early displayed the temper which made him a problem child and a violent young man. Sir William wrote, "concerning William, whose Temper I know to be very warm. I have advised that if he continues to be troublesome, and to break the decorum of your School that he had best be sent back, he doubtless deserved to be used with severity and I am fully persuaded of your care and good intentions towards him."[69]

Joseph, the brother of Molly Brant, may well have been the playmate of the other Indian boys. When he was sent to Wheelock in 1761, he was most promising and well behaved. "Joseph appears to be a considerate, Modest and manly spirited youth. I am much pleased with him."[70] It was only natural that Sir William showed greater favor to Molly's children, who grew up in his household. They were to be educated in his church and school. Peter, the eldest, was sent to Montreal and to Philadelphia to study. They had every opportunity to develop their talents.

Somewhat below the status of these half-breeds were other Indians who were transients or occasional residents at Fort Johnson or Castle Cumberland. There was also a full complement of servants and slaves as part of the Johnson menage. In addition to Negroes, there were a few "panis," Indian slaves acquired by purchase. These along with all the regular members of the household would be ensconced in the new establishment at Kingsborough.

XXV

THE BUILDING OF JOHNSON HALL

The valley of the Mohawk, like that of the Hudson, is straight and narrow. At some points there are headlands, and the hills rise abruptly, while the bottom-lands suitable for cultivation are not broad. A military observer in 1767 found these features worthy of comment: "The banks of the river are well settled, and the soil in the flatts is very fine, but the breadth of these flatts in the broadest parts do not exceed a mile from the river to the mountains, none of which are very high. The mountains are barren, covered with brush and a few straggling trees." Just as the Hudson reminded European travellers of the Rhine, so did the Mohawk appeal to early visitors. Lord Adam Gordon said the country reminded him of Westmorland "on the banks of the Tay above Perth." Viewing the valley as a place for settlement, he called it "a narrow vale or Strath, of excellent Soil, hemm'd in on both sides with high ground, uncultivated and covered with Timber, but exceedingly pleasant to the Eye, and cut by a thousand little Brooks descending rapidly from above."[1] Another observer a few years later confirmed this judgment with respect to the lands near Fort Johnson. "The Breadth of the Flats on each side of the River from Schenectady . . . may be from 100 to 300 yards; the road very level and good; the Upland in general is no other than Pine Barrens both Strong and Hilly."[2]

Sir William loved this valley, which had been his home for twenty-five years, but he fully realized that these features put limitations upon its future development. The hills rose abruptly behind Fort Johnson, and Kayaderosseras Creek tumbled over rocks in its sharp descent, providing power for its mill. The trail followed the winding course of the stream to the uplands some two hundred feet higher. As one climbed to where the trail leveled on a kind of plateau, he sensed that he was entering a new terrain; the barrens gave way to rolling hills, the air became a bit thinner, and there was a feeling of open spaces. The mists and the fog which often hung over the river valley were less evident, and the air was cooler. For the frontiersman here was the challenge of the vast country to the northward. For the farmer here was good soil calling for clearing and cultivation.

There has been much speculation as to why Sir William Johnson chose his new location. His reasons for so doing were no doubt many and varied. But as time went on there was no doubt of the wisdom of his decision.[3] Jeptha Simms, who knew the country well and collected its folklore, supposed that Johnson was attracted by the opportunity for hunting and fishing afforded by the adjacent woods and streams. He especially described the "Sacandaga vlaie, a body of from ten to thirteen thousand acres of drowned lands. This immense marsh extends east and west about six miles . . . the greatest portion is in [the town of] Broadalbin, where it is widest, being perhaps a mile or more in width." Through the great marsh ran a fine stream, the Vlaie Creek, sometimes called the Little Sacandaga, and by the Indians named Kennyetto, or "little water." In his later years Sir William did enjoy the hunting and fishing in this wilderness. At this time, however, he was concerned with settlement, with cultivation and farms, and with the erection of buildings.[4]

The site of Johnson Hall was a small eminence not far from a little stream, the Cayadutta, a tributary of Canada Creek flowing into the Mohawk. Here there was made a clearing in the forest where land was under cultivation as early as 1760–61. Then Warren Johnson had commented upon its fertility, and Daniel Claus had noted the progress of the farm. At first the only structure was a hideout in the woods, but this was soon complemented by barns, outbuildings, and by temporary houses for tenants and laborers. One of the first had to be a sawmill on the creek. Work was going on apace when the name was changed from "Castle Cumberland" to "Johnson Hall."[5] It was a happy choice. The term "castle," long used to describe the Indian villages, would seem inappropriate. "Fort" fitted his old home when it was fortified during the recent fighting, and it was an honored name. Perhaps "hall" indicated the hopes for expansive entertaining in a happier period of peace. It came to symbolize the hospitality of Sir William on the New York frontier.

Having resolved to build a new mansion in the winter of 1762–63, Sir William considered the kind of house he could and should erect to serve his purposes. It would have to be larger than Fort Johnson, spacious enough for his entertaining both social and official, and imposing enough to sustain the pretensions of the great landlord. He was entertaining thoughts of a manorial establishment, the proper seat for his New York baronetcy. He was well aware of the kind of homes built by the Livingstons and Van Rensselaers along the Hudson, although he would not imitate them. He could have seen something of the mansion, "The Pastures," which Philip Schuyler was erecting in Albany. Yet it is more than likely that his mind dwelt upon the country seats of the English and Irish gentry. In fact his floor plan was to resemble that of the house of his uncle, Peter Warren, "Warrenstown" near his father's home in Ireland.[6] Yet the square plan with central hall was common to most of the houses of the period.

Sir William was not hidebound by previous examples or custom. He was a man who could be original and did not fear innovation. In all things accustomed to being self-reliant, resourceful and independent, he was capable of making his own plans and using his own ideas. This was the day of the capable man of many parts who dared enter new fields. Moreover there were no professional architects available. All he needed was a capable builder and skilled workmen.

For a carpenter he turned to Samuel Fuller of Schenectady, who had been working on the Anglican church there in which he was interested. Fuller had first come to this area from Needham, Massachusetts, in March 1758. As a carpenter he had been engaged in various jobs, including building boats and houses for Abercromby's army. He worked for the army and in the navy yard at Halifax, but returned to this area in 1761. He had brought other carpenters from New England to assist him on such projects as the church.[7] So Sir William was well aware of his capabilities before approaching him early in 1763 about building his own house. In the course of his other works at the site he had been gathering materials for his house. He well knew the difficulties to be encountered and wanted no delay. His letter to Fuller was dated January 5, 1763.

Sir

I here with send you a Plan of the House I intend to build early in the Spring, and shall be glad to have a Bill of Scantlin, or the dimensions of all the timber wh. will be requisite for it, and that in two or three days time if possible as I shall delay beginning to square the timber until then. Therefore expect you will not fail sending it by that time, and verry exact.—[8]

The detailed specifications which followed showed that Sir William had been carefully working up the plan himself. His conception had been worked out and a rough plan drawn. But he was not a builder, and he wanted Fuller to carry out his designs.

The House is to be 55 feet long from outside to Outside, four Rooms on a floor of abt. 18 feet Square, with a Hall in the Middle of the House 18 feet Wide thro the House, with a good Staircase at ye. end thereof on one side of the Back Door, as many Windows in the rear as in the Front of the House, the first Story to be 12 feet high from Beam to Beam. The next as it will not be a full Story to be 8 feet from ye. floor to the Ceiling—
A large Cellar under ye. whole House with 2 Fire places.—I would not have the Roof so heavy as that in the Inclosed Plan. As I imagine this Discription may sufficiently enable You to make out the Quantity of Timber necessary for such a House, I need not add further on that Head. I would willingly have a draft from You on the same Plan with the best kind of Roof you can make, also the lowest rate You will work for the whole Season that is until next Fall.—
Pray let me have the Acctt. of the Timber, and Yr. proposal as to pay before next Sunday if possible, as I intend to begin Squareing next Monday—[9]

The plan which he enclosed has not survived; perhaps when Fuller worked it over he did return it as requested, but working plans receive hard usage. The builder must have responded and entered into discussion of terms as well as plans, for some six weeks later he and Sir William signed a contract.

This Day I agreed with Mr. Samuel Fuller now of Schenectady, Carpenter in ye. following Manner Vizt.—He is to direct the building of my House at Johnson Hall, and Assist to finish it agreable to my Plan, for which he is to receive from me Eight Shillings New York Currency per Day Meat Drink & Lodging dureing the time. in Case He finds Tools for any of the rest of the Workmen dureing the time they are at Work at Said House, or any other for me and that they agree to allow him anything per Day for the use of the Same, I will on their order pay to Said Samuel Fuller what they agree for the loan of the Same.

WM. JOHNSON
SAMUEL FULLER[10]

Sir William made it clear that it was to be according to his plan, but that Fuller was to direct the work. He employed the men, kept a record of their time and expenses, including meat and drink, and an allowance for the use of their tools, which was then submitted for payment.[11] Sir William apparently kept a close watch over the operation whenever he could, but as it turned out he was to be extremely busy this year with public affairs.

Gathering material for construction was soon under way, for logs could be cut, taken to the sawmill, and "squared" in winter with snow on the ground. Then it was easier to transport them by sleighs over the river ice and through the forest trails.[12] This was a preoccupation which appealed to Sir William, and he wrote of it with relish to Witham Marsh on February 4.

You would be surprised to see how I am swallowed up to the Head & ears in Mortar Stone and Timber wh. are all intended for the House I purpose building next summer. I have had for this Month past thirty & forty sleds a day brideing [riding] ye. same so that it cannot be said I was without some kind of company. We have snow here now abt. 3 feet deep, and more daily falling wh. (altho a gloomy prospect) makes ye. Country alive with their flying slideing machines.[13]

It was an especially severe winter with a great deal of snow, which prevented the digging of foundations until late in the spring. By April 15, a letter to Darlington mentioned the "house that is building" but predicted that snow would "linger 10 days longer in the woods."[14] Fuller and his men, however, were busy repairing and remodeling Sir William's first house on the Mohawk for occupancy by Daniel Claus and his bride, when the former could return from Montreal. From March 15 until April 17, the carpenter's accounts related to work on the Mohawk, variously referred to as "Capt. Clouse house," "the house Mr. Farell Wade begon to bild," and "the house beloe the fort."[15]

Sir William tried to oversee the work, and most of the time this spring he was at Johnson Hall, where he dated his correspondence. But business and Indian affairs took him away so that on May 8 he wrote from Fort Johnson to Fuller.

My reason for comeing here this Day was to agree with the Workmen whom You intend taking into the Woods with You, and as I had not an opertunity of Seeing you or them, I leave this paper to let you know that I am determined to give no more than five Shillings per Day to any whom you may employ for my Work; if they will not agree to that, I desire you will not bring them with You. Neither will I give more to any (yourself Excepted) who work at Cap't Clau's House. What I have promised you shall be paid.[16]

Perhaps they had already gone into the woods and he was irked to have missed them. At any rate the next day Fuller and two of his men came to the Hall, and shortly more were brought up from the work on the "house below." The large timbers and beams had been squared and were ready, and the next step was framing the house. This meant fitting the joists and beams to form a frame which would when ready be raised into place. At the same time work was being done on barns and outbuildings—the framing of "the Shay house" and of "the long house"; and on May 14 all hands joined in "helping to Rays [raise] the Cotch [coach] house."[17]

From this time the work went on apace with ten or eleven men working each day. The work of framing required 105½ man-days, but when the ground flooring was in, the raising of the structure took but three days—June 2 through 4. Fuller's journal relates what each man did each day and thus gives a graphic picture of the carpenter's craft when all work was done at the site—making pins (dowels), "huing [hewing] the hip Rafters," boarding the sides, making sash frames, making and fitting doors, making shutters, and finally finishing the interior rooms.[18]

In the course of construction certain changes could be made, and thus the style of the roof was left to Fuller—"the best kind of roof you can make."—in Sir William's first letter. In June Fuller made a memorandum of dimensions in which this was taken into account.

Sir Wm. Johnson Hous
    54 feet 6 Inches long 37 feet 6 Inches wid from out to out the Coving projects 1 foot 2 Inches the flat on the top of the house 36 feet 6 inches by 19 feet 6 Inches Rises but 2 feet 7 Inches leaves a Ridg on the top of the hous 16 feet 9 Inches long the lore [lower] or first Pitch of the Rough [roof] flys 10 feet 2 Inches and Rises 9 feet 4 Inches 8 Inches a low [allow] between the first and Second pitch for the Cornishing.[19]

This describes what is known as a hip roof, with a ridge along the top, which was much favored by the builders of that day. Fuller, and perhaps Sir William, too, had the "Builders Companion" volumes, published in England, which seemed to guide the carpenters and had much influence on colonial taste in architecture.[20]

Another feature which received much attention from architects was what Fuller called the "frontespeace," the formal entrance. This usually reflected the Greek temple idea, and added class and prestige to any structure. Although double doors of normal size are to be found in Fort Johnson, Johnson Hall was entered by a broad single door, of simple style but pleasing dimensions. The exterior, too, reflected in its dimensions and balance Sir William's taste for classic simplicity. Shutters were provided for the windows in front and back, and on the sides or ends; dummy windows with shutters decorated the plain wall. A door of equal size at the back, below the staircase, was to face the formal gardens and led to the question later as to which was really the front of the house. Another classic feature, new and distinctive in this region, was the Palladian window at the landing between the floors.[21] It provided an impressive view of the garden and estate.

Thus in early June with the structure taking shape and progress being noted toward its completion every day, Sir William glowed with satisfaction. He was always a builder, who gained his greatest pleasure from seeing the country develop, new farms and houses settled and built, and new and useful institutions erected. His orderly and constructive mind was willingly devoted to all progressive projects. He was impatient with interruptions which impeded the work, yet such were constantly occurring. To a traveller who stopped at Fort Johnson and was disappointed in not finding him there he replied:

I . . . do assure you it would have given me great pleasure to have had your company at the Hall, wh. is about 2 hours ride from ye Fort & where I am building and improveing as fast as I can, endeavouring to make up for the time I spent in ye service without pay or promotion.[22]

He was in fact conducting much business at the site, although the house was not ready for occupancy. Numerous references to other buildings indicate that they were occupied. Perhaps he lived first in the bouwmaster's house, the home of his overseer or estate manager, which was also being improved. Then there were the coach house, the "shay" house, mills (at first a sawmill and later a gristmill), and stables. To house the workmen there were other temporary buildings, and two years later a traveller reported the "superbe and elegant edifice" was "surrounded with little buildings for the accomodation of the Indians, when down upon treaties or conferences with him."[23]

Indian conferences were first held at Johnson Hall in April 1762, a full year before the house was built. Coming to a new site for their council fire, the Indians complained of the bad roads and difficulty in travelling. They met in the open and there were inconveniences. Sir William was unable to consult the volume of Indian Records for details of treaties, for it was at his other house, Fort Johnson.[24] In the spring of 1763, however, there must have been a building large enough for meeting indoors, for each time mention is made of assembling in "ye. Council Room." Perhaps one of the large barns or carriage houses was thus used until the Hall was finished, for during these sessions the carpenters continued work on the Hall.[25]

By September 11, however, the house could be occupied and in the Indian Records of that date he proudly announced: "All the Nations present being assembled in my new House, they Sent to Acquaint me that they had yet something to say to me." Henceforth the "Council Room" seems to have been in the house, and perhaps the wide hall was so used. During a stay of several days the Indian delegates were assigned ground for an encampment and were supplied with provisions, drink, pipes, and tobacco.[26]

It is no wonder that visitors during these times found Johnson Hall a scene of confusion. The activities of building, farming, and living in this wilderness outpost were interspersed with the solemn conclaves of these numerous delegations; their comings and goings, freely entering and leaving the buildings, and at times with some pageantry.

Septr. 17th, A M—The Caghnawagas being ready to depart assembled in the Summer house in the Garden, and 10 of their Warriors being naked, painted & feather'd (one of whom had a Drum on his back made of a Cag covered with Skin) marched in Slow order in two Ranks, Singing their Song accordg. to the *Ottawa Custom*, Tom Wildman in the Rere Tank beating the Drum with one Stick, and the rest accompanying it with Notched Sticks which they Struck to good time on their Axes—

In this manner they proceeded to the House where they entered, [& then] when Tom Wildman advanced before the rest, & Sung his War Song, which he twice repeated, after which Sir Wm. gave them some Liquor, Pipes, Tobacco, and Paint whereupon they returned back in the same order—

The occasion of this Ceremony was to shew Sir Wm. that they had approved of what he said, & had taken up the Axe against our Enemies.[27]

The frequency of these Indian conferences and visits was of course increased by the alarming news of the uprisings in the west. Sir William was soon deeply involved in correspondence, messages to and from the Indian tribes relating thereto, and the measures to be taken by the English in meeting the crisis. While the events of May and June on the western frontier at first seemed remote and isolated, their import was shortly realized and even the building operations were affected. While friendly Indians were all about and the Six Nations were generally well disposed, there was the possibility of hostiles sending spies and emissaries and even making attempts on Sir William's life.

Wed. 27th [July, 1763]. abt. 9 at night We had an Alarm here occasioned by 2 of the Wenches haveing Seen an Indian Skulking abt. the House with a Lancet in his hand, & run away on being discovered. I had all my People under Arms the whole night. this day begun to fortify my House.—[28]

The next day the carpenters were diverted from work on the house to making pickets and gates for a kind of palisade around the house. There is some question as to just how much of a fortification or fort was constructed. The Fuller journal refers to work on "the fort," and a few other references imply that there was a separate building with emplaced guns.[29] On July 31,

Nickus of Oneida my great freind & his Family arrived here and encamped by the Brick Kill. . . . he told me that he & his Family were come to me for Shelter, being threatened by those who are now in Arms agst us, as they knew his attachment to me.—

thursday 4th.—He erected a House under the Guns of my Fort which I built on the Inds. declaring War agst. us, and on Acctt. of the many threats thrown out agst. my Person.[30]

Subsequently General Amherst advised that a guard of twelve men be sent from Fort Stanwix to serve as a garrison at Johnson Hall. Just how extensive this fortification was is a matter of speculation. It apparently was hastily thrown up in a few days, and was designed more to discourage unfriendly skulkers than to withstand a formal attack.[31]

Despite these diversions and their inconvenience, the carpenters labored on. The brick kilns on the premises supplied materials for walls and fireplaces. Sir William specified two fireplaces for his basement, and the two chimneys provided a fireplace in each of the eight principal rooms. The exterior, by some quirk of the builders, sought to simulate stone by rustication (the cutting of the clapboards to resemble stone blocks). These may have been painted gray and even sanded to resemble stone.[32]

The long central hallway, occupying one-third of the house, could have been the scene of Indian gatherings and later of social events. It offered few comforts and probably held little furniture, but the broad staircase with its landing at the Palladian window made an impressive appearance from the entrance, and gave a sweeping view from the stair. The dark carved mahogany rail and balusters were an effective decoration. This had all been stipulated in Sir William's original order, and no doubt fulfilled his ideas.[33]

Full occupation of the Hall as living quarters would depend upon its completion by the carpenters, which was announced in a letter to Witham Marsh in December. That worthy congratulated Sir William thereupon, and upon the consequent "riddance of the cursed hammerers." There remained the papering of the walls, doubtless delayed due to the dampness of the plastering. But the implication of these scant references is that removal of the Johnson entourage to the new residence was by then fully effected.[34]

The furnishing of the fine new mansion was of course a paramount concern of the baronet. For two years he had been writing about the development of this estate, and whenever opportunity offered he picked up appropriate items. His letters to Daniel Claus asked for items from Canada, and he was constantly sending requests to his factors or agents in New York.[35] Of course, he would remove many things from Fort Johnson, but since that house was still to be kept running, and finally was turned over for occupancy by his son John, it could not be stripped. Most of his newly purchased furniture came from New York, and hence illuminating references are noted in the invoices of both merchants and skippers of sloops. In 1760, Captain Van Bergen brought up six mahogany chairs, which are thought to be some of the fine Chippendale which have survived. William Darlington of New York in October of 1763 listed one pair of sconces, one pair of blankets, carpets, glasses, decanters, and andirons. From one cabinetmaker, Thomas Brookman, "eight cases of furniture" were put on the sloop of Captain Marselius. Another, John Macomb, built bedsteads which were then forwarded via John Van Eps of Schenectady.[36]

The furnishing of the Hall, after such essentials as carpets, beds, and the larger pieces, went on continuously in the years that followed. The best craftsmen were called upon and patronized. Records of purchases and some survivals supply interesting details of the life and activities of the Hall. While these make an interesting study in themselves, they are mentioned here only as they relate to the life of Sir William and his family.

Henceforth the negotiations and business of the superintendent of Indian affairs, the management of the estate, and the progress of settlement and development of the land are inextricably mixed in the accounts and papers of the baronet. References to building construction, brickmaking, masonry, additions, and repairs could apply to outbuildings, new houses, shops, and offices, on or removed from the Hall grounds.[37] Observers from time to time noted the presence of many such structures, offices, storehouses, and workhouses, which suggest a bustling community. Guy Johnson testified much later that "there were many out offices which were exceedingly well built." Palisades enclosed a "court yard" where Sir William sat sometimes, and where he could hold Indian conferences. When peace was restored in later years, construction and settlement increased, and the grounds were further planted and beautified. In 1775 the cleared land around Johnson Hall amounted to six hundred acres, and at that time was estimated to be worth not less than £4,000.[38] It would be inaccurate, however, to compare the Hall of 1763, when just completed, with the many buildings and additions of the years which followed.

The rapid succession of events, the issues of Indian relations, and the critical judgments and administrative decisions which required his attention now dominated Sir William's life and work. It is surprising that in the midst of such concerns he could continue to play the role of landed squire and patron. On the other hand, he had lived in critical times before and had always exhibited the greatest capacity and resourcefulness. He did not turn his back upon the work of construction and settlement which he had started, but his attention was perforce diverted to the larger sphere. From this new vantage point he directed or helped to mold the Indian policies of the colonies. His remaining years were to be devoted to maintaining the peace in that British Empire which the Indian wars had helped to create and which was shattered by the American Revolution.[39]

APPENDIXES

I

FICTIONS AND FORGERIES IN AUGUSTUS C. BUELL'S
SIR WILLIAM JOHNSON (NEW YORK: D. APPLETON COMPANY, 1903)

In several articles, principally in "Myths and Legends of Sir William Johnson" and "Augustus C. Buell, Fraudulent Historian," the author has pointed out the character of this biography. Yet Buell's statements frequently appear and plague the student, and nothing short of a complete catalog will serve to scotch these stories and make it clear to future students to what extent Buell has colored and infiltrated biographies and histories.

Early Life in Ireland and on the Mohawk.
Buell alone wrote fully of Sir William's early life.
P. 4: "Warrenpoint, County Down," as birthplace is wrong.
Pp. 4 - 5: Story of Christopher Johnson, cripple, schoolmaster, and officer in the army is fiction. See Pound, *Johnson*, pp. 26 - 27; accepted by Reid, *Old Fort Johnson*, pp. 5-6.
Pp. 6-9: Stories of youth, schooling, and relationship to Sir Peter Warren are fiction. Diary of Sir Peter Warren, his "log ashore," is fiction. Repeated in Reid, *Old Fort Johnson*, p. 6, and Seymour, *Lords of the Valley*, pp. 2-3.
P. 8: Statement that Sir Peter Warren "had purchased under Royal Grant a large tract of land in the colony of New York" is untrue. This instance is given by U. P. Hedrick, *History of Agriculture in the State of New York* (1933) as an example of a royal grant.
P. 9: Johnson's journey to New York, 1737 - 38, his route, and his winter with Lady Warren are fiction. A novel by John Tebbel, *The Conqueror* (New York, 1951), used this as the basis for an illicit liaison of Johnson with his aunt.
P. 10: "Warrensbush," "Waren's Bush" in Simms, *History of Schoharie County*, is incorrect for Warrensburgh. That Johnson remained there five years is untrue. Home on the north side of the river was built in 1739.
Pp. 11 - 12: Corrections by Buell of the dates for Sir Peter Warren given by W. L. Stone are all incorrect. Disposal of Warren's land is fiction.

P. 15: George Clinton's correspondence with Johnson, 1741-43. Earliest letters between them were in 1746.

Pp. 16-17: Story of "Katherine Weisenburg." Buell follows Simms, *History of Schoharie County*, pp. 109-10, on the purchase of his wife by Johnson, but invents Katherine's father, "Jacob Weisenburg, a Lutheran clergyman." Cites Reid for the marriage ceremony performed by Barclay. Dates for the birth of Johnson's children are all incorrect. Removal from log house to stone mansion "Mount Johnson" in 1743. Details are imaginary.

Pp. 18-19: Story of laborers brought from County Down, with Johnson's father as agent; story of German refugees in New York and their settlement on the "Johnstown Tract," arranged for in New York by Warren Johnson, "an officer of the British navy then on shore duty in New York," 160 souls settled: all fiction, but quoted on Buell's authority in Francis W. Halsey, ed., *A Tour of Four Great Rivers* (1906), p. xlix. Halsey was an able historian but a friend of Buell.

Pp. 19-22: Settlement and fort at Oquaga in 1744: details of the village and its inhabitants, the building of the post by Ezra Buell (an ancestor of Augustus), who was the first manager of the post, his relief there by John Butler, and the quoted application of Johnson to the governor for a license—these are all fictitious. There was no Buell employed by Johnson in all the *Johnson Papers*.

P. 23: Capital supplied by Stephen and James De Lancey at low interest for Johnson; his discharge of the loan through Peter Warren. All Buell.

Pp. 23-24: Letter of Warren Johnson, September 13, 1747. Badly garbled version of the letter in the *Johnson Papers*, 1-116. It makes Warren captain of a frigate, he was actually in the British army. See my "Myths and Legends."

Pp. 25-26: Beginning of Johnson's public career "as master or referee" in land litigation of George Klock and Peter Van Braam is an invention of Buell. Statement that Johnson acted as interpreter and that after 1740 he never employed an interpreter is untrue.

Pp. 26-27: Statement that after 1743, when Peter Schuyler retired, Johnson succeeded him on the board of Indian commissioners: Peter Schuyler died in 1724, and Johnson was never a member of the board. Story that Jacob Weisenburg, Lutheran minister of Schenectady and father of Catherine, was placed on the board due to a requirement of the law that one must be a clergyman, is all fiction. There is no record of such a minister, nor was a "Rev. Mr. Van Ness, a Dutch Reformed pastor of Albany," on the board.

Pp. 27-29: Account of the clerical influence on the board of Indian commissioners and of the consequent enforcement of the laws against selling rum to the Indians, and of the imprisonment of twenty-six culprits in the Albany jail is all fiction. Authorities for this quoted, the journal of John Sammons and the papers of the Reverend John Barclay, are unknown.

P. 29: Quotation of Johnson on the Indians in a letter to Governor Clinton in 1744 is a forgery. Pound, *Johnson*, p. 98, found this letter interesting but unbelievable. Johnson's appointment to command militia in 1744: should be 1748. King's magistrate in 1745: he was justice of the peace.

Pp. 30-31: Importation of horses from England (Irish hunters, Suffolk stallions, and of cattle from Hereford and Devonshire); importation of English and Merino sheep: records of Johnson's horses and cattle show American origin until Sir John brought home some horses in 1767. Merino sheep were not introduced to America until the nineteenth century. Yet this account of Sir William's importation is given without authority in U. P. Hedrick, *History of Agriculture in New York State,* (New York, 1933, reprint 1966), p. 360, and has been accepted by writers on agriculture. Hedrick, however, omitted mention of Merino sheep.

P. 31: There is no basis for the statements about the rate of his clearing land, nor for the number of his tenants in 1746. That Johnson had no slaves until 1747 when he bought nineteen from a Dutchess County estate is untrue. He brought some slaves with him from Boston, and there is no record of the large purchase. This story is repeated in Hedrick, *History of Agriculture*, p. 80.

P. 33: Landing force at Louisbourg "commanded by Warren Johnson of the twenty-gun ship Avon, and brother of Sir William." Warren Johnson was in the army and commanded a company, but saw no action at Louisbourg.

P. 34: There was no royal warrant for Johnson's conduct of Indian affairs.

Pp. 35–39: Details of the campaigns and war to 1748 are furnished by Buell and are not based on fact.

Pp. 40–41: Johnson's reorganization of the militia and the quotation from Governor Clinton are fictional.

Pp. 41–42: The roads built to carry wagons and artillery have no basis. Johnson had no camp at the end of Lake George at that time.

Pp. 43–45: Episode of the artist "Mrs. Julia Grant" and her quoted description of Johnson is fiction (See my "Myths and Legends.") No such person has been discovered, nor has anyone seen her journal as listed in Buell's bibliography. Quotation copied in Seymour, *Lords of the Valley*, p. 49; in Lydekker, *The Faithful Mohawks*, p. 26n. The whole episode, with the artist as a character, is used in Margaret Widdemer's novel, *Lady of the Mohawk.*

Pp. 46–47: His wife "Katherine" died in 1745. This agrees with Stone, but is not correct. Care of children by a Dutch widow is fiction, but parallels the tale of Mrs. Anne Grant in *Memoirs of an American Lady.* For "Mrs. Barclay" as governess there is no evidence. Footnote, commenting upon Parkman's bias, makes assertions about Catherine Weisenburg which are not supported.

P. 49: "Brant Manuscripts," authority for statements on the Brants, are unknown.

Pp. 49–51: "Legends" about the Brants, "Nicklaus Brant," Abraham, and the "bleached out" Indians are all fiction.

Pp. 51–54: Story of the Indian girl Caroline, second spouse of Sir William, is attributed to W. Max Reid of Amsterdam; this was originated by Reid, embellished by Buell, and stated as fact. For analysis and proof of falsity see my "Sir William Johnson's Wives." That Caroline was Johnson's wife has been accepted by numerous writers, including Pound, *Johnson*, pp. 135 – 37, 419 – 21; Seymour, *Lords of the Valley*, pp. 15, 64–65; and *Dictionary of American Biography*, 10:127.

P. 54: Story of the death of William of Canajoharie at Oriskany. See Pound, *Johnson*, pp. 422-23.

Pp. 53–56: Stories of Caroline's children, their marriages and families, are all fictitious, as are the stories about the Brants.

Pp. 58-59: Quotation from Wheelock is a forgery.

Pp. 59-62: Argument over Sir William's motives in marrying Indian women, even the quotation from Griffis (which cannot be checked), is all Buell.

Pp. 62-67: Story of a grand council of the governors and Indians at Albany after 1748 is a fictitious amalgam of vague ideas about the later congress of 1754. Quotation from Stone cannot be located and must be considered pure Buell. Hiokato, Seneca husband of Mary Jemison, introduced here is out of place geographically and chronologically. Anecdote of Hiokato on p. 72 is fictitious.

P. 68: Footnote on the Montours is confusing and inaccurate. Andrew (André) and Henry Montour were the same. Note on Joncaire is also confusing and inaccurate.

Pp. 70-72: Episode of rifle making and of gunsmiths brought to Johnstown is fictitious. This has bothered students of early gunmaking.

P. 73-76: Stories of the Colonial Assembly in which Sir William was attacked by a "Mr. Hardenburgh" and the former's challenge are fiction. Letter of Sir William on duelling is a forgery; there is no such letter. See my analysis in "Myths and Legends of Sir William Johnson."

Pp. 78-81: Indian protest to the governor on Sir William's resignation with the words of Hendrick is fictitious, as are the words of "Jean Montour."

Pp. 85-89: Stories of Johnson's visit to the Seneca capital at Genesee Falls in December 1753, meeting with Hiokato and Joncaire, are false. Johnson made no such journey and had no such contacts with Hiokato and Joncaire.

Pp. 89-92: Account of the Albany Congress of 1754 is so full of errors and fictions as to be completely false. Buell did not use the full record of this in the Colonial Documents and missed the point of the meeting and of Johnson's part in it.

Pp. 102-6: Family of Joncaire. This confusing family is still further confused here by incorrect names, dates, and other details. Correcting Parkman, Buell invents details which are far from the truth. For clarification see Severance, *Old Frontier of France.*

Pp. 109-12: French in the Ohio Valley: omits mention of Céleron de Blainville and the lead plates of 1749, and says first knowledge by the English of French encroachment came when Captain Joncaire established Venango in 1753.

P. 125: Appointment of Johnson by Braddock to supervise Indian affairs is given as March 1755, with no mention of the Alexandria conference of April (until p. 135) where it occurred.

P. 128: Story of Joncaire's accident which made it impossible for him to command the Indians is fiction.

P. 129: Indians present at Braddock's defeat include Pontiac and Anasthose, said to be the grandson of Count Frontenac. Quotes Joncaire's journal, which is said to be prejudiced because he was captain of marine. Here Buell confuses the two Joncaire brothers. The journal is fictitious.

P. 131: "Joncaire recognized at 'Government House' in Quebec as commander of French and Indian forces in the Ohio Valley. He was over seventy years old at the time." Here again he confused the elder Joncaire (d. 1739) with Daniel Chabert and his brother, Philippe Thomas, Captain of Marine, neither of whom commanded the Indians or French.

Pp. 131-32: Footnote tells of Sir William's council with Indians at Niagara in 1766 to make peace after Pontiac's War. In fact, he was at Niagara in 1764 and made the peace at Oswego in 1766. Hence the long quotation from Sir William's journal with his opinion of the Joncaires is all a forgery, and again misnames and garbles the Joncaires.

P. 136: Quoted letter of Sir William to the Duke of Cumberland is a forgery.

Pp. 135-41: Story of the Seneca Indians, assembled by Hiokato and Montour, who did not come to Lake George due to Braddock's defeat, is all fiction. Details of Johnson's troops and their march are incorrect. Story of Joseph Brant and the fowling piece presented by Sir William is fiction. That Sir William had built a road seven years before from Lake George to Fort Edward is untrue.

Pp. 149-50: Story that four companies of New Hampshire provincials under the command of John Stark filled the breach and repulsed the flower of the French army is fiction. The New Hampshire companies at Ford Edward were commanded by Blanchard. John Stark was probably with Rogers on scout and therefore not at Lake George. The New Hampshire men were in the third engagement, which is not mentioned by Buell.

Pp. 150-52: Very detailed story of Sir William's wound is invented: that he was on his horse, that the bullet was from an Indian's gun, the course of the bullet, lodging in his back, and that it was easily removed. He was standing; the bullet, or ball, entered his thigh, and it was never removed.

Pp. 152-53: Lyman's request to advance to Crown Point turned down by Sir William: this story originated with Lyman's partisans and enemies of Sir William and has been repeated by Dwight, Parkman, and Stone, but has been disproved. See my article, "Hero of Lake George: Johnson or Lyman?"

P. 155: Statement that New England colonies showed no disposition to reinforce Johnson is untrue. They sent almost too much. That Johnson was promoted to the rank of major general in the British regular army is untrue; he was made a colonel.

P. 157: That not a single officer of the British regular army was there is untrue. The engineer Will Eyre was one.

P. 158: That Colonel Lyman succeeded to the command after Sir William left, and was then promoted to brigadier general is untrue. Colonel Bagley succeeded to the command of Fort William Henry, and Colonel Whiting to that of Fort Edward.

Pp. 158-59: That the elder Brant succeeded Hendrick as head of the Indians at Lake George and was father-in-law of Sir William since Mary Brant came to his household the year before: Molly Brant appears to have come to Johnson in 1759. That Hendrick's place as "senior chief" of the Iroquois confederacy was an elective position, vacant for twenty years until Joseph Brant was chosen chief to fill it in 1775: this is fiction; Joseph was never a chief of the confederacy.

P. 159: Sir William in January 1756 "fully recovered from his wounds, went to New York City to lay his annual report before the governor. . . ." He went for other reasons and was not fully recovered.

P. 160: Sir William's salary as £600 is correct, but there was no "like amount for official expenses."

P. 161: Footnote about Shirley. Quoted letter of Sir William to Amherst about Shirley is a forgery.

P. 163: "Abercrombie" is a common misspelling for Abercromby. That Loudoun had little knowledge of warfare is untrue.

Pp. 166–67: The long quotation of Sir Willian on General Webb is a fiction.

P. 169: That Pontiac commanded the Indians under Moncalm at Oswego is untrue.

P. 170: That the women and children of Oswego were sent to Onondaga Castle under a guard of French regulars is untrue.

P. 171: The attack on Fort William Henry in March 1757 was not led by Montcalm.

Pp. 172–73: The story of relations of Johnson and Webb is filled with errors. "Stark's Rangers" with Sir William is an invention. The well-known massacre of hundreds by the Indians at Fort William Henry is not mentioned; only that Montcalm's Indians "scalped several of Webb's soldiers," which is untrue.

P. 176: "Nicklaus Brant" with Sir William at German Flats is a misnomer.

Pp. 177–78: Long letter of Sir William to the Duke of Cumberland criticizing the military in America is a forgery.

P. 183: Conversation of Sir William in conference with Amherst is an invention.

P. 186: Prideaux's words to Sir William are invention, as are Sir William's in reply.

Pp. 188–90: Battle of La Belle Famille, not so called here: figures on personnel are too high; Sir William did not lead the advance; Indian chiefs mentioned (Hiokato, Jean Montour, Onasdego, and Nicklaus Brant), and Joseph Brant as "lieutenant in the Canajoharie company of Mohawks" are all of Buell's concoction. Details of the battle, "led by Sir William in person," are contrary to the known facts.

Pp. 190–91: Quote of Sir William's threat that if French did not surrender he might not be able to restrain the Indians is an invention. French commander "Pouchet": Buell could have had access to Pouchot's *Memoir of the Late War,* but does not mention it or list it in his bibliography.

Pp. 192–93: Story of Sir William's entertaining Prideaux at Mount Johnson with his quoted estimate of the general is all fiction.

Pp. 199–200: Footnote is filled with fantastic untruths about Indians and their leaders: that the Indians were organized in military regiments and companies, that these were led by "Brant (Nicklaus)," Hiokato, Captain Montour, and Young Cornplanter; that there were two companies of rangers under John Stark.

Pp. 205–06: Anecdote of Sir William offering Amherst Seneca Indians as "provost guard" in Montreal, with quoted letter, is fictitious. Sir William's departure with thirteen hundred Indians to Oswego; he went with a smaller group down to Albany. That Indians received the same pay and allowances as provincial troops is untrue; also that each Indian received a blanket from French stores.

P. 207, note: That Pontiac met Rogers and Stark at Detroit in 1760. See discussion of Pontiac, *supra.* Buell again puts Stark on the expedition, although Rogers's detailed account does not mention him.

P. 208: Proposal of Amherst to seize Louisiana with regulars by water and by four thousand provincial troops from Fort Pitt down the Mississippi under Sir William is fiction.

Pp. 210–12: Sir William's outlining of British policy toward Canada to Amherst which was adopted by the ministry is contrary to fact. That he and Amherst were "the closest of friends confiding absolutely in each other's judgment," is quite untrue; they differed radically on Indian policy.

Pp. 216-17: Account of St. Martin as Jesuit historian of New France (his book in Buell's bibliography) is imaginary. He was a merchant and interpreter.

P. 220: Colonel Claus in charge of Canadian Indians with headquarters at Detroit; Claus was stationed at Montreal. Guy Johnson in charge of Iroquois and Canadian Indians east of Ottawa, with headquarters at Oswego: there was no headquarters at Oswego.

P. 221: Manor house, Johnson Hall, built 1761-62. House was built in 1763.

P. 222: Sir William's family, "Charlotte and Caroline Johnson, his half-breed daughters by Caroline Hendrick"; "Sir William's half-breed son by Caroline Hendrick, young William Johnson, . . . lived at Canajoharie with his uncle 'Little Abe.'" The fiction of Caroline has been exposed in my article, "Sir William Johnson's Wives."

P. 223, and note: Anecdote of Sir William Johnson as related by Joseph Brant is fiction. That the Pontiac uprising took Sir William off his guard: He had been receiving warnings from Gladwin and others, which he sent on to Amherst.

P. 225: Croghan was real commandant at Fort Pitt. He was only Indian deputy at the time.

Pp. 228-32: Long quotation of a memoir of Lord Amherst describing his plan for a concerted attack upon the Senecas apparently fiction. Hanging of two recalcitrant Seneca chiefs at Onondaga Castle is fiction.

Pp. 233-34: Grand council at Niagara after the Oswego meeting in 1766. Sir William returned directly to Johnson Hall.

P. 235: Naming by Sir William of Colonel Thomas Polk of Mecklenburg, North Carolina, as deputy over the southern tribes: Sir William did not have authority over the southern tribes.

Pp. 236-41: Sir William directed by British government to build a road from the upper Mohawk to Niagara; surveying party organized by Sir William, including his half-breed son, William, who was learning surveying; among others named was Ezra Buell—whose quoted Narrative and description of "Old Castle Town," Seneca settlement on the site of Geneva, is a concoction of Buell, the author. Story of a gunsmith Dreppard put there by Sir William in 1759 is a fiction.

Pp. 242-43: Sir William's estimates of the numbers of the Indians in the various tribes is wrong and much exaggerated. He did make such a report, but these are not his figures.

Pp. 242-43: Quotation is a forgery.

P. 243: Treaty of "Colonel Polk," deputy with the Creeks, is false.

Pp. 244-45: Ezra Buell's notes as assistant to surveyor Simon Metcalf, on the Fort Stanwix line, are an apparent fiction.

Pp. 246-48: Details of Sir William's land grants are inaccurate, although the general impression given is correct.

Pp. 248-49: Dates for Molly Brant's children are inaccurate. Quotation of General Schuyler on Mary Brant is a forgery.

Pp. 249-51: Detailed story of Sir William's introduction of riflemakers from Lancaster, Pennsylvania, to Johnstown, with names of gunsmiths—Palm brothers, Henry Hawkins, and John Folleck—is fiction. Writers on gunmaking in America have listed some of these, but have been unable to find their work. Late in life Sir William sought a Pennsylvania rifle, saying none were made locally. For documentation see my "Augustus C. Buell, Fraudulent Historian."

P. 260: That Sir William used Latin fluently and made notes in Latin on his correspondence is not born out by the extensive *Johnson Papers.*

P. 261: Quotes of Sir William's sayings were obviously not recorded.

Pp. 264-65: Quotes of conversations with Sir William are fiction.

Pp. 266-68: Quotation of Daniel Claus's statement on Molly Brant during the Revolution is a garbled approximation of Claus's statement in the Haldimand papers. Buell said he got it from Reid, but he dressed it up or remembered it without checking. Twice it refers to Molly's home "at Danube" (Herkimer County) which was not so named until 1817. Claus died in 1787.

Pp. 270-71: Sir William's death. Details of Indian conference and the hour of death are incorrect. Last words to Joseph Brant—"control your people! I am going away"—are Buell's invention, but they have been widely quoted by other writers who thus accepted Buell's idea that Sir William "bequeathed his mantle to Joseph Brant" and thus propelled Brant to his leadership in the Revolution. There is no evidence that Brant was present, or even that he was so trusted by Sir William, who made provision for Guy Johnson to succeed him as Indian superintendent. Cf. Pound, *Johnson,* p. 455; Codman Hislop, *The Mohawk,* (1949) pp. 153-54; John J. Vrooman, *Clarissa Putman of Tribes Hill* (1950)—a novel but with a conscientious attempt at accuracy.

P. 271: Story of Sir John's ride from Fort Johnson told by Stone, 2:377, without authority, is here embellished with the introduction of young William of Canajoharie as the messenger and with details about the horses.

Appendix. Works Consulted: Buell's bibliography is as remarkable for its omissions as for its garbled titles and fictitious works. Four are entitled "Life of Sir William Johnson": Stone, Griffis, Claus (?) and Anon.; he did not bother to get the correct titles for the first two; the other two are imaginary. Among titles which are still unknown or unidentified and which must be considered pure Buell are: "Narrative of Ezra Buell"; "Eight Years in America. Journal of an Officer's Wife. Mrs. Julia Grant."; "Rites and Social Customs of the Iroquois (By a daughter of Sir William Johnson) Mrs. Kerr"; "Public Correspondence of Sir William Johnson. Sir John Johnson"; "The Montours, Mother, Sons and Grandsons. Mackenzie"; "Diary of Admiral Sir Peter Warren. Navy Records Society, England"; "Memoir of Comte de Frontenac. By his Grandson."

There are a number of other entries which suggest that the writer may have seen or heard of some titles which he could not quote, like: "Journal of Jean François Joncaire"; "Journal of Father Joliet"; "Journal of Father Moline"; "Journal of Captain Orme"; "Reports of the Marquis Duquesne. Operations in New France, 1752-1755"; "The Holy Cross in America. Collection of Narratives of Jesuit Fathers"; "Voyage to North America in 1772. Peter Kalm." Some of these claim research by Buell in sources which are nonexistent or have been seen by no others.

Finally, one looks in vain for the obvious sources or titles then in print on which all other writers depended: O'Callaghan's *Documentary History of the State of New York*: (Albany, 1849–50); Simms's *Trappers* (1850) and *Frontiersmen*, (1882–83); the *Orderly Book of Sir John Johnson*, edited by W. L. Stone (Albany, 1882); the *Journals of Major Robert Rogers* (London, 1765); and Pouchot's *Memoir Upon the Late War* (Roxbury, Mass, 1866). As one writer has said, how can one put any trust in such an author.

II

THE SHIRLEY CONTROVERSY

The dispute with General Shirley over the recruitment of Indians and the ill feeling between him and Johnson have been treated thus fully, because most historical accounts have given an interpretation of this unfavorable to Johnson. Shirley's biographer, John A. Schutz, refers to "Johnson's unreasonable conduct," his refusal "to obey the orders of the General's second-in-command, thus forcing Shirley to hire agents to bargain with Indians"; and his "asserting an independence in Indian Affairs that seemed ridiculous even to his friends, who cautioned him against challenging Shirley's right to parley with the Indians." Schutz, *Shirley*, pp. 207. (The documentation for this last is Johnson's letter to De Lancey, which fails to support the assertion.)

Lawrence H. Gipson in his monumental *British Empire before the Revolution* treats these campaigns in Volume 6, *The Great War for the Empire–The Years of Defeat, 1754–57*, Chapter 6, "Niagara and Crown Point." Dr. Gipson, who is a great admirer of Shirley, has been less than fair to Johnson. He speaks of Johnson's preference for his own campaign and adds that this "human weakness" was "combined with insubordination." He goes on to say that Johnson's "resistance to Shirley's efforts to secure an Indian escort was unreasonable and even reprehensible," as shown by the attack on stores by five hundred French Indians at the Carrying Place the previous April (p. 147).

The relation given in Chapter 14 is the best answer to these charges. Observation of the chronology of the controversy shows that Johnson's hostility to Shirley did not come until he had extreme provocation. Both Gipson and Schutz use statements of Johnson's which came late in the controversy to prove his hostility. Schutz's claim that Shirley was "forced" by Johnson's unwillingness to recruit his own Indians is disproved by the Lydius episode, even before Johnson had finished his conference at Mount Johnson. Both assume that Johnson was unreasonable in wishing to direct all Indian recruitment, whereas his commission from Braddock gave him that right (although questioned by Shirley) and forbade all others to interfere.

Other writers have misrepresented Johnson's attitude as saying to Shirley that he did not need Indians. It is quite obvious to the reader that Johnson was willing to admit Shirley's use of Indians to be obtained at Oswego or Onondaga, but that he did not need an escort of Indians through friendly country; and as shown above, Shirley's secretary supported this with the statement that carpenters and small groups had journeyed to Oswego without danger. On this episode Gipson relies heavily upon *A Review of Military Operations in North America*, which is a biased polemic, and an attack upon Johnson in defense of Shirley. On matters of interpretation and on many facts it is quite unreliable. For example, the writer [William Livingston] asserts (p. 99) that due to Johnson no Indians joined Shirley at Schenectady, in the Mohawk country, or at Oswego. Shirley's own report and that of his secretary, however, detailed the number of Indians which he found at each place.

It would seem that the unusual nature of the Indian problem, and the reputation which even Shirley attributed to Johnson's understanding and influence, would have been sufficient reason for following Johnson's advice. One can only understand the issue, however, if he weighs all the factors involved. Thus Schutz and Gipson failed to consider the effect of the practice of Shirley and Lydius in recruiting Indians with money and promises of wages, as opposed to Johnson's group diplomacy, dealing with sachems in councils. Nor have they considered, in defending Shirley's demand for an escort from Schenectady, that Johnson, himself, did not expect all his Indians to accompany him, but to meet him en route, at the Carrying Place. In his 1759 campaign with Prideaux to Niagara, he likewise had the Indians meet the troops at Oswego. It was extremely difficult to keep the Indians with the troops on so long a journey. They frequently made an additional burden upon the transport. Critics and later writers referred to "Johnson's Indians," as though they were a military unit capable of being sent here and there. This was not the case, as Johnson told Shirley it was useless to organize them into companies; they had to be won and led by persuasion.

III

CONTEMPORARY ACCOUNTS OF THE BATTLE OF LAKE GEORGE

So confused and conflicting are many of the eyewitness accounts of the battle of Lake George that it is an exercise in historical criticism to weigh and sift the evidence. Observers, in their excitement, are usually not precise or accurate and frequently are restricted in their points of view. Their views are subjective and represent their reactions to conditions and the problems of the moment more than an objective appraisal of the occurrences. Yet these are extremely important in reconstructing the story of the day's happenings. The same persons, however, when writing later with calmer reflection and the benefit of other information, will tell a different story. This is to be noted in several accounts of this battle.

Basic to all later accounts is the letter composed by General Johnson and sent to the several governors.[1] Probably dictated to Captain Wraxall, at different times as he said, it represents his own observation as commander, no doubt with the collaboration of his aides. It attempted to be a fair and comprehensive report, but notes the secondhand information of the first and third engagements not in his purview. Later Johnson noted some small errors and made corrections, but in the main he felt that it was correct. It was severely criticized later for failure to mention Major General Lyman as second in command; Captain Eyre was commended for his direction of the artillery. The view that he thus unfairly denied Lyman credit as commander after his being wounded seems unjustified, and the letter remains the best and fullest of the early accounts.[2]

Also hurriedly composed and rushed into print was Peter Wraxall's letter to Governor De Lancey, dated September 10, and printed in the *New York Gazette*, September 18, 1755. As indicated above, Wraxall and Johnson found this an unauthorized and garbled version. The letter as published in the London Documents (*DR* 6:1003-4) had significant differences. It may have been that the personal mentions of General Lyman and of Captain Eyre were not in the original; these may have occasioned the dispute. On September 27, 1755, Wraxall wrote a long letter to Henry Fox in London, reviewing the events of the campaign in summary form. This, coming nearly three weeks after the event, was critical, influenced perhaps by the disagreements then prevalent, and had as its purpose the outlining of a course of action for the conduct of the war.[3]

Daniel Claus dispatched a letter dated September 11, 1755, to Richard Peters in Philadelphia, with immediate comment upon the battle and especially on the death of Hendrick.[4] Years later (probably in the 1780s) he composed his autobiographical *Narrative*; and in the Claus Papers are narratives with anecdotes of Hendrick and of Joseph Brant. These later essays are more critical and sophisticated and are influenced by subsequent events.[5] Other personal letters or journals of Seth Pomeroy, General Lyman, Surgeon Williams, or Gunner Boyle are illuminating but make no effort to be comprehensive.

From the French side the most important records are those in the Paris Documents, from the French War Department. Here are the letters and the report of General Dieskau concerning his defeat and his defense of his conduct; the report of Governor Vaudreuil to M. de Machault, with the journal of Dieskau's expedition and criticism of his conduct; and the report of M. de Montreuil, with special details on the wounding and capture of Dieskau. Finally there is a curious document from this source: "Dialogue between Marshal Saxe and Baron de Dieskau in the Elysian Fields." This appears to be a defense of his conduct by Dieskau and was probably written by him or by an aide with his collaboration. While details vary, it agrees pretty well with Dieskau's report and seeks to refute Vaudreuil's criticism.[6]

Contrasting with these are two published accounts, which compared the testimony of eyewitnesses with Johnson's letter. Written a short while after the event, they have the benefit of reflection and later judgment, and their authors were able to make some correction in details.

Of first importance is *A Prospective-Plan of the Battle near Lake George on the Eighth Day of September, 1755. With an Explanation thereof; Containing A full, tho' short, History of that important Affair. By Samuel Blodget, Occasionally at the Camp when the Battle was fought.* (Boston, New-England: Printed by Richard Draper, for the author, MDCCLV). Samuel Blodget enlisted with Colonel Blanchard's New Hampshire regiment, but then became a sutler and thus, as he wrote, was not a combatant.[7] The principal feature of this work was the pictorial plan or diagram showing the first and second engagements, the layout of the camp and the disposition of men and artillery. There were also marginal plans of the Hudson River and of Fort Edward and Fort William Henry. The long descriptive caption under the map was not too accurate in that it gave the numbers engaged as "2000 English with 250 Mohawks" and "2500 French and Indians"; and that "the English were victorious captivating the French Genl. with a Number of his Men killing 700 & putting the rest to flight." Various parts of the plan were keyed by numbers to an explanatory text, which in itself was a description of the battle. The formalized and too regular layout of the plan implies that it was a reconstruction later from descriptions and observation. According to an "Advertisement," this was issued in Boston, November 10, 1755,[8] just two months after the battle. And on January 7, 1756, Blodget transmitted a copy to General Johnson with his respects and apology. Already, it appears, the battle and its conduct were a matter of controversy, for the author maintains that he has set down the facts "without the Least partialeti; which I think there is much Need of in Vindication of your Honour." For since his return from the camp he had met "Newmorous and Groundless odd Questions," and he tried to satisfy "numbers of people that has misunderstood the Conduct of affairs."[9]

The comments in the Blodget text must be considered with other eyewitness accounts. For Blodget, unlike most observers, recorded his qualifications and point of view.

I was myself present in the Camp; and though I could not be in the *Front*, the *Rear*, and on either Wing, at the same Time, yet being an independent Person, not belonging to the Army, I had, it maybe, as good an Opportunity as any Person Whatever to observe the whole Management on both Sides; especially as I took my Post at the Eminence where the *Field-Piece* was planted, from whence I could, with Advantage, view the Action, in all its Parts, from the Beginning to the End of it; Though I must confess, the thick *Smoke*, which arose from the Discharge of so many Guns, on both Sides, rendered the Sight less clear, than I could have wished; and I was often interrupted by taking Care, that the Guards, beginning at the above Eminence, kept to Order, and attended to Duty.

As to the Fight of the Detachment of which Col. Williams had the Chief Command [first engagement], I am beholden to others, but of the best Character in the Army, for the Account I have given of it; and I received it immediately from their Mouths; Though I was myself well acquainted with the Ground upon which they fought, and viewed the Dead as they lay after the Battle was over.

What I have said of the last [third] Engagement, also in which a Party of our Men from Lyman's Fort drove off the Ground, and routed, double the Number of the Enemy, I had from those that were present at it, best able and most disposed, to represent the Matter as it really was.

I have not, therefore, confined myself with my own Observations, but made it my Business to converse with those at Camp, who were most capable of enabling me to give a fair, and full Account of the Transactions of this Memorable Day.

He may have made minor errors, but he had "No sinister end to serve," and was not conscious of any bias. Thus he had the attitude of a good journalist out to inform the public.

The second published account was in the nature of a pamphlet tract written by the Reverend Charles Chauncy (1705–87), a distinguished Boston clergyman, whose aim was not only to inform but to influence opinion on behalf of the New England military effort. Earlier in the year 1755 he had published a *Letter to a Friend . . .* describing and commenting upon the defeat of Braddock. Now he issued *A Second Letter to a Friend, Giving a more particular Narrative of the Defeat of the French Army at Lake George, By the New-England Troops, than has yet been published, Representing also the vast Importance of this Conquest to the American-British Colonies. To which is added Such an Account of what the New-England Governments have done to carry into Effect this Design against Crown-Point, as will shew the Necessity of their being help'd by Great Britain, in point of Money.*[10] The first letter had been dated August 25; the second was dated Boston, September 29, 1755. In the three weeks since the battle, the writer had diligently gathered and compared testimony brought from the field as well as the published letters. First he commented on that of the general to the governors.

And if you have seen this letter, you must be pleased with it, and conceive a high opinion of the General's Merit. Perhaps, the best bred *regulars* could not have disposed matters, under like circumstances, with greater wisdom—And the vein of modesty that runs thro' his whole narrative cannot but recommend him to all who are capable of discernment.

He also mentioned the letter of General Lyman, but without any special comment for his rôle or command. Then he obtained much information from Major Hore (Hoare) who had come to Boston as special emissary from the camp at Lake George to Governor Phips. One of his informants had timed the engagement by observing his watch; and he, or another, had surveyed the field with measurements after the battle, thus correcting Johnson on the distances.

As in his former letter, he exhibited a strong New England bias; Massachusetts had of course contributed the most, done the most fighting, and suffered the greatest losses. Other provinces, especially New York and those to the southward, were chided for their lack of support. He magnified the victory and urged immediate and greater exertions.

NOTES

ABBREVIATIONS

DAB	*Dictionary of American Biography*
DCB	*Dictionary of Canadian Biography*
DH	*Documentary History of the State of New York*
DNB	*Dictionary of National Biography*
DR	*Documents Relative to the Colonial History of the State of New York*
JP	*Johnson Papers*
N. Y. Histo. Soc.	New-York Historical Society
NYSL	New York State Library
Pa. Arch.	*Pennsylvania Archives*
Pa. Col. Rec.	*Pennsylvania Colonial Records*
PRO	Public Record Office, London
WA	*Wraxall's Abridgment of the New York Indian Records*

CHAPTER 1: IRISH BACKGROUND

1. Richard Pococke, *Tour in Ireland in 1752*, George T. Stokes, ed. (Dublin, 1891), p. 177. Bishop Pococke saw Tara as it was in the mid-eighteenth century. The Hill of Tara has become the subject of historical and archeological investigation, barely begun when the author visited the place in 1963.
2. Manuscript pedigree of the Johnsons, formerly owned by Sir Gordon Johnson, Montreal.
3. *Ibid.*
4. Quoted by L. H. Gipson, *British Empire before the American Revolution*, 15 vols. (New York, 1936–70), 1:217.
5. Franz V. Recum, *The Families of Warren and Johnson of Warrenstown, County Meath* (New York, 1950), p. 3.
6. Constantia Maxwell, *Dublin under the Georges, 1714-1830* (London, 1936), p. 28. See also her *Country and Town in Ireland under the Georges* (London, 1940).
7. Samuel Madden, *Reflections and Resolutions Proper for the Gentlemen of Ireland* (Dublin, 1738; reprinted 1816), pp. 10–11, 15, 26–27.
8. *Ibid.* p. 20.
9. *Ibid.* pp. 22-23.
10. *Ibid.* pp. 10–11.
11. Deed, Earl of Fingall to Christopher Johnson, Registered July 15, 1736. Registry of Deeds, Dublin.
12. Arthur Young, *A Tour of Ireland made in the years 1776, 1777, 1778* (London, 1780), pp. 37, 45; 74–76.
13. *Ibid.* pp. 74, 75.
14. *Ibid.* p. 77.
15. All biographers have assumed that Smithstown, home of Christopher Johnson, was a village. Edith M. Fox, in an excellent master's thesis at Cornell, 1945, "William Johnson's Early Career as a Frontier Landlord and Trader," made a determined effort to locate this village on contemporary maps. She located a hamlet of 15 houses and 122 inhabitants in a topographical dictionary of 1838, "in the Fore Mountains," thirty-six miles from Dublin. This was a poor neighborhood ten miles from Quilca, where Jonathan Swift's boyhood was spent. Thus Smithstown was equated with Quilca, and the conclusion was drawn that William

Johnson came from such a miserable cottage as was so graphically described by Swift in his letters and by his biographers.

The argument was taken over in the most recent biography of Johnson, *Mohawk Baronet*, by J. T. Flexner, pp. 7–10. This paints the background of the Johnsons in Ireland as one of poverty and squalor, and their home a cotter's hut. Having misread the deed to Smithstown, Flexner also wrote of Johnson's mill; the deed referred to the mill of the Earl of Fingall. Mrs. Fox had not seen the Christopher Johnson deed and had not visited Ireland.

Smithstown was not a village, but a country seat near the village of Dunshaughlin (mentioned in *Johnson Papers*, 1:244–45), about twenty miles from Dublin. Warrenstown was the seat of the Warren family, two miles from Smithstown. Both Smithstown House and Warrenstown House are located on a map in *Memorial Atlas of Ireland*, showing provinces, baronies, parishes, etc. (L. J. Richards & Co., Philadelphia, 1901). Warrenstown House still stands, although altered and added to by the Catholic order which occupies it. It was visited by the author in 1963.

The practice of naming estates "-town" or "-burg" may be seen in Peter Warren's Warrensburgh on the Mohawk, and in Daniel Claus's later calling his house Williamsburgh.

16. *JP* 1:21.

17. Franz V. Recum, *Familes of Warren and Johnson,* supplies details on the family. Four of the sisters of Sir William Johnson are mentioned in the will, *JP* 12:1071. They were Anne (Dease), Bridget (Sterling), Frances (Plunket), and Ellis (Fitsimmons). Catherine, who married Matthew Farrell, and came to America with him, died in 1755. The informative letter of Warren Johnson on family affairs, Feb. 14, 1750/1, *JP* 1:319–20, mentions sisters "Ferrell Fanny, & Polley" at home. "Polly" may have been the nickname for either Ellis or Bridget.

18. Martha J. Lamb and Mrs. Burton Harrison, *History of the City of New York*, 3 vols. (New York, 1877–96), 1:588. I. N. Philps Stokes, *Iconography of Manhattan Island, 1498–1909*, 6 vols. (New York, 1915–28), 3; 4:552, 559, 562.

19. Cadwallader Colden Papers, N. Y. Hist. Soc., *Collections*, 1918 (Daniel Horsmanden to C. Colden, July 23, 1736), 2:152.

20. George Clarke to Sec'y Popple, May 28, 1736. *DR* 6:61.

21. The romanticists have elaborated a tale of a frustrated love affair because of which William Johnson fled to America. Highly embellished with dialogue by W. Max Reid, *The Story of Old Fort Johnson* (New York, 1906), pp. 2–5, it was repeated, but doubted, by Pound, pp. 27–29. Flora Warren Seymour, *Lords of the Valley*, p. 2, had him exiled "for his youthful errors and turbulences." Earlier it was stated by William Elliot Griffis, *Sir William Johnson*, p. 12, that his marriage had been thwarted by his parents. Evidently he had this from an informant among the Johnson descendants, possibly Mrs. Bowes, but there is still much reason for doubting. There is no evidence of such a motive or escapade in the family letters, even when they became censorious, as Lady Warren's did. There is no hint on the part of brother Warren of such a heartthrob left behind. Hence it must be classified among the legends.

22. *JP* 1:907.

23. Account against Estate of Sir Peter Warren, May 15, 1754. *JP* 13:28–33.

CHAPTER 2: TO THE MOHAWK VALLEY

1. The principal source of information for this is the account Sir William rendered against the estate of Sir Peter Warren, March 15, 1754. Warren Papers. *JP* 13:28–33.

2. *Ibid.* "To a large Cask Charg'd £19.10 Boston Money, never used, and lyes on the Farm / Blocks for pulling up trees charged £8 .. 17 .. 1 Bostn. Money in his Acct. never used & are on the Farm."

3. *Ibid.* Previous biographers have assumed that Johnson came up the Hudson. Lacking any information, Buell, pp. 9–10 (see Appendix I), described Johnson's voyage over, his landing in New York, his winter at the home of his aunt and uncle, where he made plans and got supplies, and his going up with a sloopload of supplies in the spring of 1738. Other writers have fallen for the story.

4. *DR* 6:65. *Boston Gazette*, June 12, 19, 26; July 24; August 10. On October 16 (*ibid.*) it was announced in Boston that Mrs. Warren, "Lady of Peter Warren Esq. commander of His Majestys Ship Squirrel was safely delivered of a daughter."

5. Used by Phineas Stevens in 1752. Newton D. Mereness, *Travels in the American Colonies* (New York, 1916), pp. 305–6. See map by Robert Treat Paine (1755), Massachusetts Historical Society, printed in *Bulletin of the Fort Ticonderoga Museum*, 10, no. 4 (February 1960): 263.

6. Used by Nathaniel Wheelwright, "Nathaniel Wheelwright's Canadian Journey, 1753–54," *ibid.* pp. 260–61; and shown on the map of Paine, *ibid.* Lord Adam Gordon in 1765 travelled this route from Albany to Boston and found the roads were then good most of the way. Mereness, *op. cit.* pp. 447–49.

7. *JP* 13:3.

8. Claverack, the Lower Manor, had been conveyed by the patroon to his younger brother Hendrick in 1704. The residence of the latter, where he died in 1740, was Fort Crailo. The

patroon–his proper title since the time of Governor Dongan was "Lord of the Manor"–now lived north of Albany on the west side of the river. See Cuyler Reynolds, *Albany Chronicles* (Albany, 1906), pp. 171, 205, 222.

9. Warren Johnson Journal, 1760–61, *JP* 13:184, 211.
10. Adolph B. Benson, ed., *Peter Kalm's Travels in North America,* English version of 1770 (New York, 1937), 1:341–42.
11. Carl Bridenbaugh, ed., *Gentleman's Progress: The Itinerarium of Dr. Alexander Hamilton, 1744* (Chapel Hill, 1948), p. 66.
12. *Kalm's Travels,* 1:343, 346.
13. *JP* 13:187.
14. *Ibid.*
15. Mereness, *Travels,* p. 417.
16. Boston, September 2, 1738. *JP* 9:1.
17. Francis W. Halsey, ed., *A Tour of Four Great Rivers* (Journal of Richard Smith, 1769) (New York, 1906; reprinted 1964), p. 22.
18. *Kalm's Travels,* 1:333.
19. Lord Adam wrote in 1765, but this stretch from Schenectady to Fort Johnson had not changed much. Mereness, *Travels,* p. 417.
20. Peter Warren's tract purchased of Mrs. Cosby has been called Warrensburg, Warrensburgh, Warrensborough, and Warrensbush. The last, a Dutch form sometimes used along the valley, was not likely to be adopted by Johnson. The first may be confused with a later place named in northern New York. Johnson himself used the longer form.
21. *JP* 1:907. The best study of these lands has been made by Edith Mead Fox, "William Johnson's Early Career" (Cornell University master's thesis, 1945), pp. 34–38. It is based upon the Warren Papers, N. Y. Hist. Soc., and other land papers.
22. Edith M. Fox, *Land Speculation in the Mohawk Country* (Ithaca, N. Y. 1949), pp. 39–41. *JP* 1:16–18; 9:2; 13:3.
23. November 20, 1738. *JP* 13:2.
24. *JP* 13:3.
25. *JP* 1:8.
26. *JP* 1:7.
27. Account against Estate of Sir Peter Warren, *JP* 13:30.
28. *JP* 13:2 (November 20, 1735).
29. *JP* 1:5.
30. *JP* 1:8. Simms's informants told of sixteen families of immigrants brought in by Johnson in 1740 who settled on lands of Henry Shelp, west of Fort Hunter, town of Glen; they had cleared land and settled, but when war broke out between the New York and Canadian Indians, "the chicken-hearted pioneers, then numbering eighteen or twenty families, returned to the Emerald Isle." Jeptha R. Simms, *History of Schoharie County and Border Wars of New York* (Albany, 1845), p. 136. This is apparently the basis for the embellished legend in Buell, p. 18, that in 1741, Johnson brought in sixty Scotch-Irish families recruited by his father in County Down, for whom he paid all expenses and for whom he had houses built, and that he released them from indentures and allotted them long leases at nominal rental. This story was accepted by F. W. Halsey, ed., *Four Great Rivers,* p. xix; and on his authority by Ruth L. Higgins, *Expansion in New York, with Special Reference to the Eighteenth Century* (Columbus, Ohio, 1931). Edith M. Fox, in her thesis, concluded from her study of the Warren Papers that this was an exaggeration (p. 73). It appears to be a fiction based on legend.
31. November 20, 1738. *JP* 13:2–3.
32. Account of March 15, 1754. *JP* 13:28–33. See also Susan Warren's letter, April 24, 1741, and William's reply, May 11, 1741. This also mentions pork being sent, and Negro servants from Warrensburgh, one to serve as a coachman. *JP* 13:4–6.
33. November 20, 1738. *JP* 13:1–3.
34. *JP* 1:5–6.
35. *JP* 9:1.
36. *JP* 13:3.
37. *JP* 1:7.

CHAPTER 3: WILLIAM JOHNSON, MERCHANT

1. *Kalm's Travels,* 1:232, 343.
2. *JP* 1:5.
3. *JP* 1:4.
4. *JP* 1:30, 31, 37.
5. *JP* 1:9–10.
6. *JP* 1:50–51. "Gammon" was a ham or shoulder of pork, sometimes a flitch of bacon. "Firkins" were small wooden casks of varying size.

7. *JP* 1:24.

8. *Kalm's Travels*, 1:342. See also Thomas Elliot Norton, *The Fur Trade in Colonial New York, 1686-1776* (Madison, Wis., 1974).

9. *Kalm's Travels*, 1:343.

10. *JP* 1:7.

11. Oquaga (Onoquago and various other spellings. See *Johnson Calendar*, p. 639.) was an Indian village near the present site of Windsor, N. Y. Its importance as a center for the Oquaga Indians and as a junction on the Susquehanna trade route was long recognized. The settlement there endured until it was destroyed during the Revolution.

This reference to Johnson's early venture into Indian trade there has been exploited by several writers, but without documentation. Buell, pp. 19-22 (see Appendix I), elaborated a story of a trading post built there by Johnson, even supplying dimensions. F. W. Halsey, ed., *A Tour of Four Great Rivers*, p. lvi, accepted Buell's statement. Pound, *Johnson*, p. 45, accepts the idea of a post, as does Seymour, *Lords of the Valley*, p. 8. Edith M. Fox, in "William Johnson," p. 98 doubted that there was a post or fort as described by Buell. If a building or fortification had been erected there, other than Indian dwellings, it no doubt would have been noted by such later visitors as Gideon Hawley in 1753 or Richard Smith in 1769, who kept journals. Hence it is likely that the trade there was carried on by agents, with no permanent post.

12. Cadwallader Colden, *The History of the Five Indian Nations of Canada* (London, 1747), pt. 3, pp. 42-43, Letter of J[ames] A[lexander] Esq. to Mr. P[eter] C[ollinson], New York, 1740.

13. *Ibid.*, preface of pt. 2, p. iv.

14. "Witham Marshe's Journal," Massachusetts Historical Society, *Collections* (1800), p. 184.

15. *JP* 1:18.

16. *JP* 1:19. There is no record of the result of this summons.

17. *JP* 1:23, 50, 183.

18. J. R. Simms, *History of Schoharie County*, pp. 138-39, quoting Joseph Spraker.

19. *DH* 2:326-27.

20. Lewis H. Morgan, *League of the HO-DE'-NO-SAU-NEE, or Iroquois* (Rochester, N. Y., 1851), pp. 417-18.

21. Francis Grant, "Journal from New York to Canada, 1767," *New York History*, 13 (April-July 1932): 188-89.

22. John Bartram, *Observations* (London, 1751), pp. 46-47.

23. Grant, *loc. cit.* p. 190. Some discrepancy in the estimated measurements for the river and the height of Oswego Falls.

24. *Kalm's Travels*, 1:342-43.

25. *Ponteach: or the Savages of America, A Tragedy* (London, 1766), pp. 4-5.

26. *JP* 1:7.

CHAPTER 4: THE IROQUOIS

1. He wrote Peter Warren, July 24, 1749: "My Scituation among the Indians, & integrity to them, made those poor Savages Seek to me, so that I have a Superior Interest with them, which Sort of Interest is the most advantagious to this Province, and to all the Neighbouring, & requires their Cheifest Policy to Cultivate, and Mantain." *JP* 1:239.

2. Some historians oversimplified this initial hostile contact to a pattern of enmity which controlled future relations of the French and the Iroquois. John Fiske, *The Discovery of America* (Boston, 1892), 2:530-31, said it resulted in a "permanent alliance" between the Five Nations and the Dutch and English, "one of the great cardinal facts of American History down to 1763." But the influence of French Catholic missionaries in central New York and the establishment of a colony of Iroquois "praying Indians," the Caghnawagas, on the St. Lawrence, are evidence to the contrary. The career of Sir William Johnson shows that the English could not, without extreme exertions, depend on the friendship of the Iroquois, or on their being hostile to the French. Cf. George T. Hunt, *The Wars of the Iroquois, a Study in Intertribal Trade Relations* (Madison, Wis., 1940; reprinted 1960), p. 69: "In those years the Iroquois, who were later led by the Mohawks, were not conquerers. Being at a disadvantage in inter-tribal warfare they tried ceaselessly to make a permanent arrangement by treaty, and nothing could be farther from the truth than the ancient assumption that Champlain's skirmishes produced a lasting enmity."

3. Cf. L. H. Morgan, *League of the HO-DE'-NO-SAU-NEE, or Iroquois*. Later scholarship and more critical writing has modified many of Morgan's conclusions. See George T. Hunt, *The Wars of the Iroquois*, pp. 6-12, 66-68. For a sympathetic retelling of the legend, see Paul A. W. Wallace, *The White Roots of Peace* (Philadelphia, 1946).

4. William A. Ritchie, *Indian History of New York State*, vol. 2, *The Iroquoian Tribes* (Albany, 1953), p. 14.

5. See Hunt, *Wars of the Iroquois*, pp. 66–68. There has been some criticism of this as economic determinism. Whether or not one accepts the Hunt thesis, the historical evidence which he mustered has effectively undermined older theories.

6. *Ibid*. pp. 32–37.

7. *Ibid*. pp. 38ff. P. A. W. Wallace, "The Iroquois: A Brief Outline of their History," *Pennsylvania History*, 23 (January 1956): 19–22; Hunt, *The Wars of the Iroquois*, p. 83.

8. Hunt, *The Wars of the Iroquois*, pp. 82–86ff. Allen W. Trelease, "The Iroquois and the Western Fur Trade," *Mississippi Valley Historical Review*, 49 (June 1962): 32–51, has questioned the importance of the middleman rôle of the Iroquois as expounded by Hunt.

9. J F. Jameson, ed., *Narratives of New Netherland, 1609-1664* (New York, 1909); A. C. Flick, ed., *History of the State of New York* (New York, 1933), 1:286–93; 317–20.

10. *DR*, vol. 3 *passim*; 156n.; A. J. F. Van Laer, ed., *Van Rensselaer Bowier MSS*. (Albany, 1908), p. 817.

11. Charles H. McIlwain, ed., *An Abridgment of the Indian Affairs Contained in Four Folio Volumes, Transacted in the Colony of New York, from the Year 1678 to the Year 1751, by Peter Wraxall*, Harvard Historical Studies, vol. 21 (Cambridge, 1915), p. 155. (Commonly referred to as "Wraxall's Abridgement of the New York Indian Records" and hereafter cited as *WA*.) Peter Wraxall, later Indian secretary, was a biased observer, but his unfavorable opinion of the interpreter was based on firsthand knowledge.

12. *DR*, vol. 3 *passim*. *DAB* 16:476–77, sketch of Peter Schuyler by R. E. Day.

13. The visit of the "four kings" has produced quite a literature, both at that time and since. For a full treatment see Richmond P. Bond, *Queen Anne's American Kings* (Oxford, 1952). The many copies of the portraits of the sachems are treated in R. W. G. Vail, "Portraits of 'The Four Kings of Canada,' A Bibliographical Footnote," in *To Dr. R.* (Philadelphia, 1946), pp. 216–26. These writings point out that the Indians were not "kings" but sachems; they were not "of Canada," but Iroquois of the Mohawk Valley. Hence there arose many false conceptions, widely held, of the nature of these aborigines. For a hostile view of Schuyler and the project, see N. Y. Hist. Soc., *Collections*, 1868, 1:199–200. The Reverend Thomas Barclay, an Anglican missionary, stated that only Hendrick was a sachem. *DH* 3:899.

14. The religious articles and silver for the Mohawks were used in Queen Anne's Chapel at Fort Hunter and were carried by the Mohawks to Canada; they are now in the chapel of the reservation in Brantford, Ontario. There was no chapel among the Onondagas in 1710, so that the mission at Albany accepted the gift, and the silver communion service is now in St. Peter's Episcopal Church, Albany.

15. Cf. Lawrence H. Leder, *Robert Livingston, 1654-1728, and the Politics of New York* (Chapel Hill, 1961). Also Leder, ed., *The Livingston Indian Records, 1666-1723* (Gettysburg, Pa., 1956). See also John A. Krout, "Robert Livingston," *DAB* 11:318–19.

16. Wayne E. Stevens, "Thomas Dongan," *DAB* 5:364–65.

17. Cadwallader Colden, *History of the Five Indian Nations of Canada*, pt. 3, pp. 44–52; *WA* pp. 10–14.

18. *DH* 1:33–55. Cf. "Isaac Jogues," by Louise Phelps Kellogg, *DAB* 10:74–75.

19. P. A. W. Wallace, "The Iroquois," 24–25.

20. Allen W. Trelease, *Indian Affairs in Colonial New York, the Seventeenth Century* (Ithaca, N. Y., 1960), pp. 252–53. The name *Caghnawaga*, meaning "on the rapids," was equally appropriate for the St. Lawrence River town. William Martin Beauchamp, *Aboriginal Place Names of New York*, New York State Museum Bulletin 108 (Albany, 1907), pp. 122, 264.

21. *WA* pp. lxiv–lxv. Cadwallader Colden, *History of the Five Indian Nations of Canada*, pt. 3, p. 52n.

22. *DH* 1:155–56.

23. Edward Channing, *History of the United States*, 6 vols. (New York, 1905–26), 2:152.

24. P. A. W. Wallace, *Indians in Pennsylvania* (Harrisburg, 1961), pp. 100–102, has a good summary of the Montreal Treaty of 1701.

25. Anthony F. C. Wallace, "Origins of Iroquois Neutrality: The Grand Settlement of 1701," *Pennsylvania History*, 24 (July 1957): 223–35.

26. *WA*, pp. 82–87.

27. *Ibid*. p. 86.

28. Three French agents of the Joncaire family have greatly confused writers on this period (including Parkman), as they were baffling to their contemporaries. Louis Thomas de Joncaire, Sieur de Chabert (1670–1739), the elder here mentioned, in 1706 married Madelaine de Guay of Montreal, and two of their ten children followed in the father's footsteps. The eldest son, Philippe Thomas de Joncaire (born 1707), was living among the Senecas in 1744, was in the Ohio country 1753–55, and was with his brother at the surrender of Niagara in 1759, referred to as "Capt. de la Marine." Daniel Joncaire, Sieur de Chabert et Clausonne (1716–1771), often referred to as "Chabert," succeeded to his father's place and influence as a French agent among the Iroquois, and thus was an opponent of Sir William Johnson. He will be mentioned more fully in the following pages.

The confusion becomes greater with the many variant spellings of the name: Jean Coeur,

Jonkeur, Jonquere, and Joncour are only a few of the more obvious. Both father and son Daniel were known as Chabert (also rendered Chabiere and Shebear).

29. Frank H. Severance, *An Old Frontier of France* (New York, 1917), 2 vols., has two excellent chapters on the elder Joncaire, 2:146–196.

30. *WA* pp. 90–92.

31. *WA* pp.107–17.

32. *WA* p. 119.

33. *WA* pp. 123–28. Severance, *Old Frontier of France,* 1:183–87. The site is in the present town of Lewiston.

34. *WA* pp. 128–33.

35. *WA* pp. lxv, 152–54. Severance, *Old Frontier of France*, 1:217ff.

36. Severance, *Old Frontier of France*, 1:225–50, describes in detail the building of Fort Niagara.

37. *DH* 1:443–59.

38. Colden, *History of the Five Indian Nations of Canada* pt. 3, pp. 42–43. A letter from New York dated 1740.

39. *WA* pp. 180–81.

40. *WA* p. 189.

41. *WA* pp. 213–15.

42. *WA* p. 216.

CHAPTER 5: DOMESTIC AFFAIRS

1. J. R. Simms, *History of Schoharie County,* p. 69. This highly colored yarn had many flaws, as I pointed out in my article, "Myths and Legends of Sir William Johnson," *New York History,* January 1953. Simms first had the wrong name for the girl and had her bound to a valley settler. This now seems impossible. Other details of the story as he told them are pure folklore.

2. This important bit of evidence has escaped all biographers until now. It came to my attention from the listing of "Genealogical Data from Zenger's New York Journal," in the *N. Y. Genealogical and Biographical Record,* January 1965, but that was a one-line listing which omitted the important details. The advertisement was printed in *The Arts and Crafts in New York, 1726–1776* (N. Y. Hist. Soc., New York, 1938), p. 337, under the head of "costume," with the all-important name of the servant omitted.

3. Captain Richard Langdon was a freeman of the city of New York. From abstracts of wills it is learned that he had a wife Anne, and in 1755 a daughter Ann was the wife of Richard Ayscough. The latter was a doctor on Johnson's 1755 campaign. N. Y. Hist. Soc., *Collections,* 18 (1885): 130, 29 (1896): 381, 400. Langdon's ship *Oswego* was frequently noted in maritime news. She arrived in New York from London, November 6, 1738, which would have been the latest voyage on which Catherine Weisenberg could have arrived. *New York Weekly Journal,* 1738–39. *New York Gazette,* November 6, 1738.

4. "Register of Baptisms Marriages Communicants & Funerals begun by Henry Barclay at Fort Hunter January 26th 1734/5." Original in New York Historical Society. Photostat in NYSL. Hereafter referred to as Fort Hunter Register.

5. Claus Papers, vol. 23. Fort Hunter Register, p. 24. Papers of the Commissioners of Forfeiture, NYSL.

6. Fort Hunter Register, p. 38. There were no entries by Barclay in November or December 1741. Claus Papers, vol. 19. Obituary in *Montreal Gazette,* January 9, 1830.

7. Fort Hunter Register.

8. *JP* 1:14.

9. William L. Stone, *Life and Times of Sir William Johnson, Bart.,* 1:189–90. *JP* 1:42. *DH* 2:785. Daniel Campbell Accounts, in *JP* 13:354. *Johnson Calendar,* p. 98. For fuller discussion of Catherine's status as wife, and of her death, see the writer's "Sir William Johnson's Wives," *New York History,* January 1957. There is considerable parallel in the cases of Deborah Read, the wife of Benjamin Franklin, and Catherine Weisenberg. Neither was formally married, but each served faithfully as wife. While both Franklin and Johnson begot illegitimate children, their consorts did not complain but quite dutifully (especially in Deborah's case) harbored and raised the bastards. See Carl Van Doren, *Benjamin Franklin* (New York, 1938), pp. 93–94, and Carl L. Becker, "Benjamin Franklin," in *DAB.*

It is highly debatable whether Sir William Johnson ever was legally married. The legalists argue that he must have been, for how else could he have passed on his title? There is the direct distinction in his will between his wife Catherine, and his housekeeper, Mary Brant. There is a letter of Daniel Claus to John Johnson, July 3, 1776, Claus Papers, suggesting that the record of Sir William's "Marriage and lawful issue" may be completed in the Herald's Office in London "for you by sending an attested copy of his marriage certificate, the Issue by that Marriage, and Your Marriage and Issue with a Copy of the Arms." This suggests that in the knowledge of his son-in-law such a certificate did exist.

10. *JP* 1:179. John Catherwood wrote, August 8, 1748, "I hope you have got rid of your Family and that you have been fully Sated with the joys of their Music."
11. Letters of John Johnson to D. Claus, May 13, June 4, August 2, October 12, 1766. Claus Papers. From these references it appears that Sir William wrote to his son the details of the grandmother's illness.
12. *JP* 1:249.
13. *Memoirs of An American Lady* (London, 1808), 2:56-64. This work of reminiscence, the literary production of a woman of fifty-two, written in Scotland many years after the events described, based on recollections of a childhood when she was only thirteen, has no validity as a firsthand account. Mrs. Anne Mac Vicar Grant (1755-1838) was brought to Albany from Scotland in 1758 by her mother, who was the wife of an officer. She visited the family of Colonel Philip Schuyler and his wife Margarita, the "American Lady" of the book. She returned to England in 1768 (when she was thirteen), and in 1807 wrote the book about America.
  She was vague and misinformed on many points. She made Philip, rather than Peter, Schuyler the shepherd of the "four Kings" who visited England. Johnson was made superintendent of Indian affairs at the behest of the Schuylers. The Johnson homes were "Johnson Castle" and Johnson Hall, the latter a summer home on the river. Her story of the upbringing of the Johnson daughters was of a period before her arrival in America at the age of three, and hence was hearsay from the start. But her glowing prose, her convincing description of William Johnson, and especially her charming description of the care of the two daughters is classic fiction.
  The governess was given a name, Mrs. Barclay (or Barkley), widow of a nonconformist minister by Buell, p. 48. See Appendix I.
14. *JP* 1:13.
15. *JP* 1:89. See also Bryan Flood to Patrick Flood, June 5, 1741. *JP* 1:15.
16. *JP* 1:778.
17. *JP* 1:41, 52-53, 58-59, 63, 66, 69, 74.
18. *JP* 1:258. Warren was to make another visit to his brother in America, 1760-61.
19. Warren Johnson. *JP* 1:319.
20. *JP* 1:931. For mention of their deaths, see *JP* 2:393-94, 426.
21. *JP* 1:34-35, 257. Flexner, p. 98, confuses this man with Johnson's brother-in-law Matthew.
22. Cf. papers in possession of a descendant, William H. Van Voast of Johnstown, New York. Statement of Robert Adems in Johnson Scrapbook (in the possession of Sir John Paley Johnson). Also Jeptha R. Simms, *Frontiersmen of New York*, 2 vols. (Albany, 1882-83), 1:252-55. *JP* 1:931, and 245. Robert Adems later settled down as a merchant in Johnstown.
23. See account of Jane Watson, a servant. *JP* 1:39.
24. *JP* 13:11.
25. Account against Estate of Sir Peter Warren, *JP* 13:29-33. These were valued at about £40 each.
26. *JP* 1:229-30; 9:3.
27. *JP* 13:4-6.
28. *JP* 1:39.
29. Claus Memorial, Claus Papers, vol. 14, *JP* 1:240.
30. Purchased in 1741 or 1742 from Joseph Clement, the lot contained 900-1,000 acres, according to testimony in the Loyalist Claims, A. O. Public Record Office. Testimony of Guy Johnson and Sir. John. Others called it a mile square (640 acres) extending one mile along the river. The boundaries were in dispute, resulting in litigation with Clement. *Ibid*. and *JP* 1:240.
31. Richard Smith, in F. W. Halsey, ed., *A Tour of Four Great Rivers*, p. 25, reported that in 1769 all three Johnson places on the river were "situate at the Foot of Hills very steep, barren and rocky having narrow Strips of Bottom Ground."
32. *JP* 1:197.
33. *JP* 1:198.
34. *JP* 13:205. Other materials ordered listed, *JP* 1:220-23.
35. *JP* 1:240; 13:209.
36. *JP* 13:186, 199.
37. *JP* 1:240.
38. *JP* 9:37.
39. *DH* 1:532.
40. *The Royal Magazine* (London) 1759. It is captioned: "A North View of Fort Johnson drawn on the spot by Mr. Guy Johnson Sir Wm. Johnson's Son." Guy, of course, was his nephew. Reprinted, with the original key, in *JP* 1:260-61. For the blockhouses, see *JP* 10:77.
  No doubt Fort Johnson was much further improved after it became the residence of Sir John Johnson and was described by him in his testimonial before the Loyalist Claims Commission. (In 1769, when Richard Smith rode by on the river, the fortifications of the wartime period had been removed.)

"Fort Johnson a large Stone House 62 Feet in Front & 32 Stories high 4 Rooms on a floor & a Hall 12 feet wide thro' the whole & 2 Stone Wings 1 Story high abt. 30 feet long & 18 deep. good cellar under the whole a Grist & Saw Mill wt. 14 Saws well framed Barns & sundry smaller Buildgs. for cattle, a well built Stone Stable wt. 8 Stalls Room for Carrgs., & a large hay loft the whole worth . . . £2500 . . ."

Guy Johnson's testimony added: "Abt 30 acres was fine Meadow—There was no other Material part not cleared a good deal of Wood was cut down as there were Saw Mills upon the Estate." Loyalist Claims, A. O. Public Office, London.

41. *JP* 9:120–21.
42. *JP* 13:195.
43. *JP* 13:195–96.
44. *JP* 13:197–98, 207–8. In spite of changes on the banks, deepening of the channel, and locks for barge canal boats, a sudden thaw and breakup of ice in the Mohawk River still can be momentous, and considerable damage can be done by the crush of ice.
45. *JP* 9-340–41.
46. *JP* 13:185.
47. *DH* 3:1039.
48. *JP* 1:374.
49. *JP* 1:197–98.
50. *JP* 1:205. Some writers have cited these references in support of the supposed loose life of the Johnson menage. If they do indicate such behavior, they also carry some recognition of a sense of decorum.
51. *JP* 1:82.
52. *JP* 13:207.
53. *JP* 1:271–73.
54. *JP* 1:240.
55. *JP* 9:36. During the French and Indian War, Johnson sent there the wounded Baron Dieskau, accompanied by Doctor Middleton, where he was nursed by Catty (Johnson) Ferrall. *JP* 2:46, 47; 184. Later he complained to Abercromby that troops had been billeted in his Albany house, and that General Loudoun had ordered them removed. "Notwithstanding which, I fear there are Some Men Billeted there now, and in the best Room I have, which I ordered Mrs. Miller Some time ago to have cleaned out, and put in order again I went down. besides I have always a good many Stores in that House which may not be Safe with Soldiers in it, there being but an old Woman to take care of them." *JP* 2:760–61.

CHAPTER 6: MILITARY ADVENTURES

1. *Gentleman's Magazine* (London), 26 (1756): 404.
2. Cadwallader Colden, *History of the Five Indian Nations of Canada*, pt. 3, pp. 42–43.
3. *WA* pp. 194–95.
4. *WA* pp. 220–21.
5. *WA* pp. 227–28, 231.
6. *WA* pp. 233–34. Also *DR* 6:264–66. He had as early as October 1743 urged the fortification of Oswego. *DR* 2:249–50.
7. *JP* 1:22.
8. *DR* 6:268.
9. *DR* 6:249–50.
10. Colden Papers, N. Y. Hist. Soc., *Collections*, 1935, 9:302.
11. Lamb and Harrison, *History of New York*, 1:589–90.
12. Colden Papers, N. Y. Hist. Soc., *Collections*, 1935, 9:302, *DR* 6:348. See Stanley Nider Katz, *Newcastle's New York: Anglo-American Politics, 1732–1753* (Cambridge, Mass., 1968), pp. 25–26, 33–36, 57, for Governor Clinton and his disputes with De Lancey.
13. *JP* 1:49. Pound, *Johnson*, p. 109, surmised the personal meeting between Johnson and Clinton.
14. *JP* 1:70.
15. *JP* 1:51; 13:9–12. To J. Glen, May 28, 1747, September 7, 1748; *JP* 9:6–7.
16. *JP* 13:10. September 8, 1748.
17. *JP* 9:32–33.
18. *JP* 1:6–7.
19. See Pound, *Johnson*, p. 20; Claus Papers, vol. 14. Testimonial of Daniel Claus; Warren Johnson Journal, *JP* 13:192. The name first appears in the documents April 25, 1747, when Johnson appears at an Indian conference held by Clinton. *DR* 6:360.
20. Johnson's rise to prominence among the Indians was not as sudden as some writers have implied. He did not burst forth, full-panoplied like Athena from the head of Zeus, when he led the Indians to Albany as described by Colden. (See below.) Neither does there appear to have been any adoption, with ceremony, as "blood brother," in the terms of the romanticists.

Flexner, *Mohawk Baronet,* p. 40, has drawn an unwarranted inference in comparing Johnson's "adoption" to that of a captive prisoner taken by the Indians to replace one of their own men. There is no evidence that Johnson was ever adopted into an Indian family.
21. *JP* 1:42.
22. P. A. W. Wallace, *Conrad Weiser, Friend of Colonist and Mohawk, 1696-1760* (Philadelphia, 1945), pp. 17-18.
23. See John Wolfe Lydekker, *The Faithful Mohawks* (New York, 1938), pp. 1-41. Useful, because based on the records of the Society for the Propagation of the Gospel in England.
24. Colden, *History of the Five Indian Nations of Canada,* introduction, pp. 3-4. "I have been told by old Men in New England, who remembered the time when the *Mohawks* made War on their *Indians,* that as soon as a single Mohawk was discover'd in the Country, their Indians raised a Cry from Hill to Hill, *A Mohawk! A Mohawk!* upon which they fled like Sheep before wolves, without attempting to make the least Resistance, whatever odds were on their Side. . . . All the Nations round them, have for many Years, intirely submitted to them and pay a yearly Tribute to them in *Wampum;* they dare neither make War nor Peace, without consent of the *Mohawks.*"
25. *JP* 1:237n. See *DAB* 7:532-33. The author has contributed a fuller and more critical biographical sketch of Hendrick, "Theyanoguin," to the *DCB,* 3:622-24.
26. *DR* 4:281, 364, 462, 472, 533, 730-31, *et passim.* Also *DR* 5:279, 358, 569.
27. Albert Bushnell Hart, ed., *Hamilton's Itinerarium* (St. Louis, 1907), pp. 137-38 (with facsimile of part of this extract). This was a limited edition. CF. Carl Bridenbaugh, ed., *Gentleman's Progress,* pp. 112-13. This is valuable for its careful editing and fuller notes.
28. P. A. W. Wallace, *Conrad Weiser,* pp. 39-174, *passim.*
29. Colden *History of the Five Indian Nations of Canada,* pp. 87-152; Wallace, *Conrad Weiser,* pp. 175-96. See also "Witham Marshe's Journal of the Treaty . . . at Lancaster in June 1744," Massachusetts Historical Society, *Collections* (1800), pp. 171-201.
30. Colden, *History of the Five Indian Nations of Canada,* pt. 3, pp. 138-44.
31. P. A. W. Wallace, *Conrad Weiser,* pp. 217-19.
32. P. A. W. Wallace, *Conrad Weiser,* pp. 217-28. Of the Albany traders' help to the enemy they told Weiser: "They have sold many Barrells of Gunpowder, last Fall to the French, fetched by some of the praying Indians gone up ye. Mohawks river, & a great deal by Sarractoga, which enabled the French to fight against the English."
33. *DR* 6:268, 275-88. Cadwallader Colden Letters and Papers, N. Y. Hist. Soc., *Collections,* 1935, 68:20-21.
34. P. A. W. Wallace, *Conrad Weiser,* pp. 226-28.
35. *DR* 6:289-305.
36. *DR* 6:293.
37. "Journal of Isaac Norris, During a Trip to Albany in 1745," *Pennsylvania Magazine,* 27 (1903): 20-28. Norris was one of the two Quaker delegates from Pennsylvania. P. A. W. Wallace, *Conrad Weiser,* pp. 229-30.
38. *DR* 6:296-305; "Journal of Isaac Norris." pp. 25-26.
39. P. A. W. Wallace, *Conrad Weiser,* pp. 230-31.
40. *DR* 6:306.
41. *WA* p. 244.
42. *WA* p. 245.
43. Colden, *History of the Five Indian Nations of Canada,* pt. 3, pp. 192-93.
44. *WA* pp. 246-47.
45. *WA* p. 246.
46. *DR* 6:309-10. Writing to Newcastle, June 10, 1746, Clinton begged to be allowed to return to England with his family. He was disappointed in his position; the climate was fatal to one of his family; his son with an ague had to be sent away for a change of air; and he himself "having very much impaired my hearing and eyesight," needed to return to recover his health.
47. Colden, *History of the Five Indian Nations,* pt. 3, pp. 155-56.
48. *JP* 1:40-41. This letter to Colonel John Roberts was dated in the *Calendar,* p. 11, October 24, 1745. Since Roberts was not appointed to the command of the expedition until July 1746, the date is probably in error. If the date were 1745, it would be the first instance of Johnson's being used as an agent of the government with the Mohawks.
49. *JP* 9:4.
50. *JP* 9:4-5.
51. Colden, *History of the Five Indian Nations,* pt. 3, p. 159.
52. *Ibid.* pp. 161-62.
53. *Ibid.* p. 161.
54. *Ibid.* p. 163.
55. *Ibid.* pp. 163-64.
56. *Ibid.* p. 164. The Indian salute was made by each firing his piece at the ground as he passed the fort.
57. *WA* p. 248 n. 1.

58. *Ibid.*
59. Colden, *History of the Five Indian Nations,* pt. 3, p. 165.
60. In commenting on this episode, biographers have tended to emphasize Johnson's display of himself in Indian dress and paint, rather than his achievement in turning the minds of the chiefs from hostility to active support of the English. Yet conformity with Indian custom on the part of white negotiators had been practiced for decades. The Joncaires lived among the Indians, took Indian wives, and looked upon this as a part of their rôle. Even governors had adopted Indian forms of oratory, their metaphors, the condolence ceremony, and the use of wampum as a symbol. The Jesuit Father Lemoine harangued the Indians in their own manner; "I was full two hours making my whole speech, talking like a Chief and walking about like an actor on a stage, as is their custom." *DH* 1:38–39. Johnson was to take such a part in later times, too, as we shall see, but he wore many hats, and this was only one aspect of his versatility.
61. Colden, *History of the Five Indian Nations,* pp. 184–87.
62. *Ibid.* pp. 188–89.
63. *JP* 1:59.
64. *JP* 1:60–61.
65. *Ibid.*
66. *DR* 6:314. Colden, *History of the Five Indian Nations*, pp. 195–96.
67. *JP* 1:64; *DR* 6:314.
68. *DR* 6:341, 343, 349, 363. For the condition and plight of these troops, see Stanley McCrory Pargellis, "The Four Independent Companies of New York," in *Essays in Colonial History Presented to Charles McLean Andrews by His Students* (New Haven, 1931), pp. 96–123. Governor Clinton advanced money for payment of troops out of his own funds, but he also reaped considerable profit from commissions and exchange (p. 117).
69. *JP* 1:73–74.

CHAPTER 7: INDIAN DIPLOMACY

1. *JP* 1:80.
2. *JP* 1:80–82. Clinton wrote that the Council thought it not proper "to put rewards for Scalping or taking poor women or children Prisiners in it, but the Assembly has assured me the Money shall be paid when it so happens, If ye Indians insist upon it." *JP* 1:87.
3. *JP* 1:81; 94–95.
4. *JP* 1:108–9.
5. *Ibid.*
6. *JP* 1:110–11.
7. *JP* 1:86, 113.
8. *DR* 6:389.
9. *DR* 6:390. His date of return is approximate. George Clinton heard of it on September 13, in an express from Colonel Roberts at Albany.
10. *DR* 6:384–85.
11. *DR* 6:397.
12. *DH* 2:618. He may have been in New York the previous hear. Cf. *JP* 1:xvii.
13. *JP* 1:108.
14. *DH* 2:618.
15. *Ibid.* His brother Warren was much concerned for his safety. *JP* 1:116.
16. *JP* 1:146–48.
17. *DR* 6:362.
18. *JP* 1:149–50. Clinton's official order to make the journey and hold the conference for this purpose was dated March 18, 1748. *JP* 1:151–52.
19. *JP* 1:153. April 9, 1748. To John Catherwood, secretary to the governor.
20. *JP* 1:155–56.
21. *JP* 1:157.
22. *JP* 1:157–62.
23. *JP* 1:162–65.
24. *DR* 6:438. See also *WA* p. 249.
25. *JP* 9:36–37.
26. *JP* 9:37.
27. *JP* 9:39.
28. *JP* 9:47–49.
29. *JP* 9:73–74.
30. *DR* 6:361–62.
31. *Ibid.*
32. *JP* 1:78.
33. *JP* 1:139, 144, 148, 154, 166–67. In the meantime, his authority was being questioned by the invidious Edward Collins, who displayed a letter in which Clinton said he was sorry he

could not appoint Collins. Even his good friend Lieutenant Colonel Jacob Glen of Schenectady, frustrated by Schuyler's neglect, found it hard to meet Johnson's requirements, which he admitted were correct, and insisted on resigning his commission. *JP* 9:11-14; 13:11-12.

34. *JP* 1:90-92, 114; *DR* 6:650.

35. William Smith, *The History of the Late Province of New York, from Its Discovery to the Appointment of Governor Colden in 1762*, 2 vols. (New York, 1830), 2:120. Smith of course reflected the Protestant fears of the effect of his marriage. Peter Kalm, writing about 1750, visited the site of Lydius's house and told of its being a trading house, and of its destruction. *Kalm's Travels*, 2:360-61. Lydius was born in 1693; his wife was Genevieve Massé, born in Canada, where she lived until she was twenty-seven (see their affidavits in 1750, *DR* 6:569). His involvement with Johnson in 1754-55 is treated later. In 1776 he went to England, where he died in 1791. See *JP* 1:645.

36. *DR* 6:385.

37. *JP* 9:76-77. For the attitude of the commissioners, see *DR* 6:362-63.

38. *DR* 6:432.

39. *JP* 9:15-31. See also the bill of exchange dated November 5, 1748, for £2,836, drawn on William Pitt, as paymaster; it noted that his first and second of the same tenor had not been paid. *JP* 1:35.

40. *JP* 1:72. He also asked for something additional for his personal services and for the delay in payment.

41. *JP* 9:44. He added: "I've heard that Coll Johnson has recommended Mr. Lydius to be Secretary for Indian affairs but I doubt of his being equal to this task.

42. *JP* 9:66.

43. *JP* 9:78.

44. *DR* 6:739.

45. *JP* 1:340.

46. *JP* 1:341-42.

47. *JP* 1:342-43.

48. *JP* 1:344.

CHAPTER 8: PROVINCIAL POLITICS

1. William Smith, *History of the Province of New York*, 2:100n.

2. *JP* 13:3.

3. Lamb and Harrison, *History of New York*, 1:531-32 and note. This lists seven children of Stephen De Lancey. This work, inaccurate in some details, is especially concerned with the families of New York. See also Dixon Ryan Fox, *Caleb Heathcote, Gentleman Colonist* (New York, 1926), pp. 276, 278.

4. Lamb and Harrison, *History of New York*, 1:530-32, 615-16. Here is printed from the manuscript source James De Lancey's map of his Bowery farm.

5. William Smith, *History of the Province of New York*, 2:344-45. William Smith, Sr., father of the historian, was his only rival as a university-educated jurist. Hence Smith Jr.'s comment may be biased. "Mr. De Lancey's genius exceeded his erudition. His knowledge of law, history and husbandry excepted, the rest of his learning consisted only of the small share of classical knowledge which he acquired at Cambridge and by a good memory retained. He was too indolent for profound researches in the law; but what he had read he could produce in an instant, for with a tenacious memory, he had an uncommon vivacity; his first thought was always the best; he seemed to draw no advantages from meditation; and it was to this promptness that he owed his reputation. He delivered his opinions with art, brevity, and yet with perspicacity." William Livingston, *A Review of the Military Operations in North America*, Massachusetts Historical Society, *Collections*, (1800), p. 79, a hostile tract, conceded that "His uncommon vivacity, with the semblance of affability and ease; his adroitness in jest, with a show of Condescension to his inferiors, wonderfully facilitated his progress."

6. Lamb and Harrison, *History of New York*, 1:615-16.

7. Clinton to Duke of Bedford, August 15, 1748. *DR* 6:429.

8. *DR* 6:286. To Duke of Newcastle, November 30, 1747, *DR* 6:414.

9. William Livingston, *loc. cit.*, p. 79. William Smith, *History of the Province of New York*, 2:100.

10. *DR* 6:312-13.

11. John A. Schutz, *William Shirley, King's Governor of Massachusetts* (Chapel Hill, 1961), pp. 138-39. Colden to Shirley, August 22, 1748. Colden Papers, N. Y. Hist. Soc., *Collections*, (1920), 4:73-74.

12. *DR* 6:430.

13. *DR* 6:313, 330-31.

14. *DR* 6:429.

15. Smith wrote of the Assembly of 1752: "It may gratify the curiosity of the reader to know, that of the members of this Assembly, Mr. Chief Justice De Lancey was nephew to Colonel Beekman, brother to Peter De Lancey, brother-in-law to John Watts, cousin to Philip Verplank and John Baptist Van Rensselaer; that Mr. Jones, the speaker, Mr. Richard, Mr. Walton, Mr. Cruger, Mr. Philipse, Mr. Winne, and Mr. Le Count were of his most intimate acquaintances, that these twelve of the twenty seven which composed the whole house, held his character in highest esteem. Of the remaining fifteen he only wanted one [?] to gain a majority under his influence, than which nothing was more certain; for except Mr. Livingston, who represented his own manor, there was not among the rest a man of education or abilities qualified for the station they were in; they were in general farmers, and directed by one or more of the twelve members above named." William Smith, *History of the Province of New York*, 2:170–71.

16. *DR* 6:414. William Smith, *History of the Province of New York*, 2:100n., notes that Philip Schuyler, Indian commissioner, attached himself to De Lancey, and hence Johnson turned to Clinton. Clinton seems to have been more antagonized by the Livingstons.

17. To Peter Warren, July 24, 1749. *JP* 1:238–39. This is an autographed draft; the crossed-out portions were written before he had seen De Lancey (he had been in New York eight days), the final part after twelve days.

18. *Ibid*. 1:240.

19. *JP* 1:238.

20. William Smith, *History of the Province of New York*, 2:124–33.

21. *DR* 6:414.

22. *JP* 1:269, 273–74, 282.

23. *JP* 1:316.

24. *JP* 1:344; *DR* 6:724.

25. Edgar A. Werner, *Civil List and Constitutional History of the Colony and State of New York* (Albany, 1884), pp. 67–68.

26. *JP* 1:30, 32.

27. *JP* 9:56.

28. *JP* 1:293.

29. *Ibid*.

30. Philip Schuyler and Hans Hansen represented Albany County in the 26th Colonial Assembly, September 4–November 24, 1740; May 30–June 6; October 1–November 25, 1751, when it was dissolved.

31. *JP* 1:293–94.

32. *JP* 9:70–71.

33. *JP* 1:301–2.

34. John Ayscough, sheriff, who wrote for Clinton, January 3, 1752; *JP* 9:86.

35. *Ibid*.

36. *JP* 1:362–63.

37. *JP* 9:89, 90, 92; 1:364.

38. *JP* 9:89–91.

CHAPTER 9: FAMILY PROBLEMS

1. *JP* 1:88–89. In April 1744, reporting the death of his mother, Susan Warren relayed his father's complaint that "you don't write him." *JP* 1:21. This letter of 1747 indicates that William wrote his father circa 1745, i.e., after his mother's death.

2. *JP* 1:258.

3. *JP* 1:116, 319–20. Later Warren was able to get his commission with the aid of a loan from Uncle Peter. *JP* 1:258; 2:425.

4. *DNB*, 20:876–77.

5. *JP* 1:117.

6. *DNB*, 20:876–77. In 1751 Clinton heard a rumor that Admiral Warren's commission to succeed him had been made out. *DR* 6:712. See Stanley Nider Katz, *Newcastle's New York, Anglo-American Politics, 1732–1753* (Cambridge, Mass., 1968), pp. 210–12; 220–25.

7. *DNB*, 20:876–77.

8. *JP* 1:258. Franz V. Recum, *Families of Warren and Johnson*, pp. 2–3, 5, gives some added data about Warren's property. While in London he had a country seat at Westbury, Hampshire. Leases in the Registry of Deeds, Dublin, show the Warren family at various times to have held lands at Corbane, Ballinglassin, and Moorestown. Those at Corbane were leased to Henry Rowley in 1723.

9. *JP* 1:319–20.

10. *JP* 1:370–71. Knockmark was the parish for Warrenstown. Lady Warren later erected a monument to Peter Warren in Westminster Abbey. In her will she directed that his body was to be disinterred and buried with hers in a vault. F. V. Recum, *Families of Warren and Johnson*, p. 3.

11. Sir Peter Warren's will, printed in *JP* 13:19-23. The will was probated October 30, 1752. The will of 1746 is in Warren Papers, New-York Historical Society.
12. *JP* 1:907-8. Oliver De Lancey (1718-85), a younger brother of the chief justice, was also a merchant associated with John Watts and an active politician with his brother.
13. *JP* 13:19-23. Peter Warren had also made loans to his nephews John Johnson and Warren Johnson for which he took their bonds, "not with an intent to be paid but to make them diligent," and these he now cancelled in his will.
14. Warren Papers, New-York Historical Society. In his earlier will Sir Peter cancelled William Johnson's debt, provided he gave Warren Johnson one thousand pounds; William was also given "one hundred guineas to buy a ring."
15. *JP* 1:907.
16. *JP* 1:907-8. See Julian Gwyn, "Private Credit in Colonial New York: The Warren Portfolio, 1731-1795," *New York History*, 54, no. 3 (July 1973): 269-93. This lists the Warren investments in America including the three bonds of William Johnson.
17. *JP* 13:28-33. Warren's account against Johnson was for £6,830 . . 9 . . 5½ (corrected £6,820 . . 9 . . 5½), of which the original account was for £4,097 . . 3 . . 0½. Three bonds with interest totaled £2,365 . . 3 . . 5, which were balanced off as included in the first amount. A later bond of £200, with interest, totaled £358 . . 3 . . 0. These were offset by Johnson's account of £5,398 . . 14 . . *JP* 13:36-37. Johnson therefore did not include in his accounting the two accounts last mentioned—Lady Warren's for £966 . . 2 . . 7, or the condolence charge. The condolence ceremony of the Indians for Sir Peter is recorded. *JP* 9:102.
18. *JP* 13:33-35.
19. *JP* 13:38.
20. Pound, *Johnson*, pp. 77-83, dilates on the issues of this case and concludes that "Johnson's position in this controversy leaves vastly much to be desired." He thinks Johnson was quite aware of his debt, that he was playing up his sacrifices and ignoring his obligations. He errs, however, in referring to the arbitration as "long after the event," when Johnson was rich and powerful, implying that then the arbitrators would not dare go against him. The arbitration was in March 1754, which as the settlements of estates go, was contemporary. And Johnson at this time, while his interests were great, was barely solvent in view of all that was due him from the province. The De Lanceys, on the other hand, were riding high, with James De Lancey acting governor.
21. *JP* 13:35. The arbitrators in fact testified in Johnson's favor. "And it Appears to Us that Sir Peter [Warren] himself declared unto Mr. Nichols who wrote or filled up the last Bond that altho he took that Bond from Coll. Johnson it was Chiefly or with a View to make him frugal and Diligent in his Business And that he did not know whether he would ever Demand the payment of it but chose to have it in his Power." *Ibid.*
22. *JP* 1:929-30.
23. *JP* 1:931.
24. *Ibid.* The portrait by John Wollaston is now in the Albany Institute of History and Art. It graced the family halls in Ireland until 1921. Then Warrenstown House, the family house of the Warrens, passed into other hands, and the portrait, with the letter which accompanied it, was purchased and brought to America. Records and correspondence regarding the purchase are in the Albany Institute. For discussion of the portrait see *JP* 2:ix-x; and 13:ix.
25. Oliver De Lancey to William Johnson, February 26, 1769; William Johnson to De Lancey, March 20, 1769, November 9, 1770. *DH* 2:934-37, 979-80. Lady Susan Warren died in London, November 19, 1771.
26. After Sir William's death, Daniel Claus, as one of his executors, reviewed the claim against Warren's estate and stated that the balance in favor of Johnson was "above £900 N. Y. Ccy. Sr. Wm. at the same time considering the Disappointment it would be to his Relations in Ireland, [he] until these Accots. were settled and adjusted which he foresaw would make it appear an imaginary Legacy to them, he made them a present of the Amount of the Sum the 2/3 of that Accot. would have amounted to had there been no Counter Ballance: And thus the Affair stands to this day." *JP* 13:724-25.

CHAPTER 10: WIDENING INFLUENCE

1. *JP* 1:314. For the names of the commissioners see Edgar A. Werner, *Civil List and Constitutional History of the Colony and State of New York* (Albany, 1884), p. 171.
2. *DR* 6:377.
3. *DR* 6:768-69.
4. *WA*, introduction, xcv-xcvi, and p. 3.
5. *Ibid.* This important document, written in 1754 and sent to Lord Halifax, was in England until 1852, when it was brought to New York and sold to the New York State Library. The Abridgement was the basis for an argument, or tract, in behalf of Johnson which Wraxall wrote in 1756: "Some Thoughts Upon the British Indian Interest in North America, more particularly as it relates to the Northern Confederacy Commonly called the Six Nations."*DR* 7:14, 15-29.

6. *JP* 1:332.
7. *JP* 1:220. This unfortunate young man contracted a cold and died in 1750.
8. *JP* 1:228.
9. *JP* 1:296.
10. *JP* 1:295–96, 297.
11. *JP* 1:304–6. September 1750. The canny Swede's gratitude was somewhat chastened by the realization that he had paid the same bill twice—18 shillings to both Printup and Van Wandel—"either Printop or Wandel has plaid a Dutch trick up on me." He could not believe that either was guilty, but after much puzzling correspondence decided "I do leave the 18 shillings to him that has got them; I have got satisfaction [enough] if I can know by whom they are."

Kalm developed a violent distaste for the Dutch of Albany, so that he was greatly relieved to be able to leave. But he grieved for Johnson among such unhappy surroundings: "But a New sorrow did darken my heart, when I remembered that you, Dear Sir, yet did live as a David in the tents of Kedar, & as a child of israel in the middle of the Sons of Enakim, where the most, if not all, which on all sides live round about you, look upon you with a more sowr eye & darker face than a bull can do: I Wonder, Sir, that you dont grow ten times sick in a day in a such place: for me, I have now got my former health, since I came back to the Christian people."

Johnson's contributions to Kalm's scientific observations is treated later.
12. *Daniel Claus' Narrative of his Relations with Sir William Johnson and Experiences in the Lake George Fight* (Society of Colonial Wars, June 1904, n.p.), p. 4.

This printed version was based on two manuscript copies (one in Daniel Claus's hand) in the Claus Papers, Canadian Archives. There are a number of minor errors and misreadings in the printed narrative, which I have corrected from a microfilm of the manuscript, whenever quoted. Claus wrote this autobiography years later, but his usually precise attention to detail indicates it to be a generally accurate firsthand account of the events in which he participated.
13. *Ibid.* See the full story of this journey in P. A. W. Wallace, *Conrad Weiser*, pp. 304–11. Cf. Phyllis Vibbard Parsons, "The Early Life of Daniel Claus," *Pennsylvania History* 39 (1962): 357–72.
14. *Claus Narrative*, pp. 5–6.
15. *Ibid.* Cf. Weiser's journal of the trip, wherein Claus is referred to as Sammy's tutor. P. A. W. Wallace, *Conrad Weiser* pp.323ff.
16. *Claus Narrative*, p. 6.
17. P. A. W. Wallace, *Conrad Weiser*, pp. 323–31.
18. *Claus Narrative* pp. 6–7.
19. P. A. W. Wallace, *Conrad Weiser*, p. 339.
20. *Pennsylvania Archives*, 1st ser. 2:116–19. Hereafter cited as *Pa. Arch.*
21. *WA* p. 151.
22. *DR* 6:964.
23. *JP* 1:6n. *DR* 6:88. Cf. Lydekker, *Faithful Mohawks*, pp. 53–56; Joseph Hooper, *History of Saint Peter's Church in the City of Albany* (Albany, 1900), pp. 72–83.
24. Lydekker, *Faithful Mohawks*, p. 57.
25. *Ibid.*, pp. 57–60.
26. *DR* 6:315. *JP* 1:351.
27. "The Diary of the Reverend John Ogilvie," ed. with introduction by Milton W. Hamilton, *Bulletin of the Fort Ticonderoga Museum*, 10, no. 5 (February 1961): 331–85. (Hereafter referred to as "Ogilvie Diary.")
28. *Ibid.* Introduction, pp. 331–38.
29. March 18, 1756. *DR* 7:43.
30. "Ogilvie Diary," *passim.*
31. *Kalm's Travels*, pp. 455–57.
32. *JP* 1:346, 372–73. It is difficult to figure what was the value of Johnson's shipment of "three hogsheads and a Cask," for the size of the hogshead varied (65 to 140 gallons liquid), and the roots, even when dried and packed, may not have been heavy by bulk.
33. *JP* 1:372.
34. *JP* 1:376. In 1759 he learned of his credit with a London merchant of £144.4.7 sterling for ginseng held there a long time. *JP* 13:126
35. P. A. W. Wallace, *Conrad Weiser*, p. 338, quoting Peters Manuscripts, 3:61, in Historical Society of Pennsylvania.
36. *JP* 1:385. Cf. several letters which were destroyed but listed in *Johnson Calendar*, pp. 108, 205, 213, 254, 256, 333. For later activity also see *JP* 8:276; and *JP* 12:150–51. See David A. Armour, "The Merchants of Albany, New York, 1686–1760" (Ph.D. diss., Northwestern University, 1965).
37. *JP* 1:382.
38. *JP* 1:330–31.
39. *Ibid.*
40. *JP* 1:335.

41. *JP* 1:921. Colonial Land Papers, 14:113.
42. *JP* 1:333, 923–24.
43. *JP* 2:3; 1:391–95.
44. *JP* 1:334n. *DR* 8:188–89. Banyar's first name, variously spelled (Goldsbrough, Goldsborough, etc.), was a puzzle to contemporaries as well as to later writers. Signed "Gw.," it was transcribed in *Pa. Col. Rec.* as "George." A Tory during the Revolution, Banyar remained in seclusion at Rhinebeck. Later he moved to Albany and became a pillar of St. Peter's Episcopal Church, in which he is memorialized by a plaque and a window. Cf. Joseph Hooper, *History of St. Peter's Church.* See also the sketch of him in Gorham A. Worth, *Random Recollections of Albany* (Albany, 1866), pp. 112–19.

CHAPTER 11: IMPERIAL PROBLEMS

1. Weiser's journal of the trip, quoted in P. A. W. Wallace, *Conrad Weiser,* pp. 323–32.
2. P. A. W. Wallace, "Historic Indian Paths of Pennsylvania" (reprinted from *Pennsylvania Magazine of History and Biography,* October 1952), pp. 26–27 and map. See also his *Indians in Pennsylvania,* pp. 42–43.
3. *DR* 6:560, 588. Governor Glen to Clinton, July 7, 1750.
4. P. A. W. Wallace, *Conrad Weiser,* p. 327.
5. *Ibid.* pp. 327–29. See also proceedings of the congress. *DR* 6:717–26.
6. P. A. W. Wallace, *Conrad Weiser,* p. 326.
7. *DR* 6:726.
8. P. A. W. Wallace, *Conrad Weiser,* pp. 326–30. *JP* 1:359–60, 386–88.
9. Severance, *Old Frontier of France.* 1:407–20. Donald H. Kent, *The French Invasion of Western Pennsylvania, 1753* (Harrisburg, 1954), pp. 6–10. *JP* 1:277.
10. *JP* 1:277. Johnson exaggerated, or was misinformed of the size of the expedition, which was of two hundred and fifty men, not five hundred.
11. Kent, *French Invasion,* p. 10. Severance, *Old Frontier of France,* 1:407–20.
12. *JP* 1:277–78.
13. *JP* 1:276.
14. *DR* 6:568, May 31, 1750.
15. *DR* 6:562, June 7, 1750.
16. *DR* 6:604, 608–9. While both Joncaire brothers were with the expedition of Céleron (Severance, *Old Frontier of France,* 1:409–10), the plate appears to have been one which was not planted, but kept in possession of the interpreter. It was not dug up but "by some artifice" was acquired later from Joncaire.
17. *DR* 6:608–11. Translation and publication of a facsimile of this plate, from the London Documents, suggest that it was a surplus plate with an incorrect inscription. All the plates had a similar wording except for the statement as to their location. This inscription mentioned the confluence of the Ohio and the Tchadakoin, the outlet of Chautauqua Lake. Kent, *French Invasion,* p. 7n., points out that these streams do not join, and hence the plate may have been discarded. Four years later, March 12, 1754, Johnson reported that Indians had dug up more of the same sort of plate. *JP* 9:126. Two other plates were dug up years later. One, which was at the mouth of the Great Kanawha, is in the Virginia Historical Society. Another fragment, originally at the mouth of the Muskingun River, is now in the American Antiquarian Society. Severance, *Old Frontier of France,* 1:417–18.
18. *DR* 6:706.
19. *DR* 6:729–30.
20. *DR* 6:730–36.
21. Kent, *French Invasion,* pp. 11–12.
22. *Ibid.* pp. 13–25.
23. *DR* 6:835–37. Deposition of Stephen Coffin. January 10, 1754. Kent has pointed out some inaccuracies in the Coffin deposition.
24. *DR* 6:778–79. Johnson's letter is dated April 20; the first detachment of the French expedition left April 16. Marin's main force left April 26. Kent, *French Invasion,* p. 27.
25. *DR* 6:779–80.
26. Kent, *French Invasion,* pp. 19–52.
27. *Ibid.* pp. 53–80.
28. *JP* 9:104–6.
29. *DR* 6:781–88.
30. *JP* 9:108.
31. *JP* 9:108–9.
32. *JP* 9:109.
33. P. A. W. Wallace, *Conrad Weiser,* pp. 341–42. Weiser's Journal in *DR* 6:795–99.
34. *DR* 6:797.
35. *Ibid.*

36. P. A. W. Wallace, *Conrad Weiser*, pp. 343–44, tells of the reaction to the "indecent repulse" of Weiser upon Thomas Penn, in England, and on secretary Richard Peters.
37. *DR* 6:797.
38. *JP* 9:110–12.
39. *JP* 9:113–15.
40. *JP* 9:115–19.

CHAPTER 12: THE ALBANY CONGRESS

1. *DR* 6:738–45.
2. *DR* 6:799–801.
3. De Lancey to Lords of Trade, October 15, 1753, *DR* 6:803–4; 833.
4. *Ibid.*
5. *DR* 6:801–2. These provinces were supposed to be most concerned with Indian affairs. Others were later invited, and Connecticut and Rhode Island participated.
6. *Pa. Col. Rec.*, 5:717.
7. *DR* 6:817. In 1724 the Six Nations had said: "This town of Albany has been of old a place of Meeting & Treaty between us, & since that time it has been agreed that this should be the place only of Treaty not only between this Govt. & us but with all our Neighbouring Colonies of North America." *WA* p. 153.
8. *DR* 6:817–18. *Pa. Col. Rec.*, 6:15.
9. *DR* 6:827–28, 833.
10. *Pa. Col. Rec.* 5:721, 749; 6:25.
11. See *Papers of Benjamin Franklin*, Leonard W. Labaree, ed. (New Haven, 1959–), 5:357–64.
12. *DR* 6:859. Also noted in the diary of Theodore Atkinson of New Hampshire. Beverly McAnear, "Personal Accounts of the Albany Congress of 1754," *Mississippi Valley Historical Review*, 39 (March 1953): 735. The Reverend John Ogilvie, rector of the English church, also preached to the delegates. His diary recorded a sermon of Peters, on a text from 1 Chron. 19:13: "Be of good courage, and let us behave ourselves valiantly for our people, and for the cities of our God; and let the Lord do that which is good in his sight" ("Ogilvie Diary," p. 344 and note). Apparently Peters's sermon was never printed.
13. *DAB* sketches of Isaac Norris (1701–66) and John Penn (1729–95).
14. Shirley to Hamilton, March 4, 1754. *Pa. Col. Rec.* 6:18–19.
15. See Lawrence Henry Gipson, "The Drafting of the Albany Plan of Union: A Problem in Semantics," *Pennsylvania History*, 26 (October 1959): 291–316, for a discussion of Hutchinson's plan.
16. McAnear, "Personal Accounts," p. 733. See sketch of Elisha Williams (1694–1755) in *DAB*.
17. McAnear, "Personal Accounts," pp. 731. 734. Members of the Council of New York serving were William Johnson, John Chambers, Joseph Murray, and William Smith (1697–1769). The latter is not to be confused with his son, William Smith (1728–93), the historian of the province.
18. See Journal of Mrs. Charlotte Brown, in Isabel M. Calder, *Colonial Captivities, Marches and Journeys* (New York, 1935).
19. "Diary of Journey of Comrs. to Albany 1754," pp. 194–95. *Pa. Arch.*, 1st ser. 2:145. The Pennsylvania delegation were lodged at the home of James Stevenson. Isaac Norris Diary, in Rosenbach Foundation Museum.
20. McAnear, "Personal Accounts," pp. 730–35.
21. *Ibid.* p. 733.
22. *Ibid.* pp. 734–35. Isaac Norris's Diary (manuscript in Rosenbach Museum, Philadelphia) commented on the "Great flood in the River" on the 25th.
23. *DR* 6:853ff. Apparently the Court House, at times erroneously referred to by the Dutch term "Stadt Huis," was built in 1740. In the minutes it is also referred to as the city hall and the council hall.
24. McAnear, "Personal Accounts," p. 731.
25. *Ibid.* pp. 732–35.
26. *Ibid.* p. 731.
27. *Ibid.* Here, as frequently in other places, De Lancey is referred to as "Governor," which for all practical purposes he was. Hence some writers on colonial history regularly use the term when referring to an acting governor.
28. *Ibid.* pp. 732–33. Only the decision is recorded in the minutes. *DR* 6:859.
29. McAnear, "Personal Accounts," pp. 735–36. The two previous meetings, on June 27–28, are reported in the minutes. *DR* 6:865–68; *DH* 2:575–77. These were between smaller groups of Indians and the governor and Council of New York.

The Lower Castle Indians arrived first, June 27; the governor and Council of New York received them and heard an address by Canadaraga, who repeated some of their grievances,

especially in regard to the Kayaderosseras Patent. The next day, June 28, Hendrick and the Indians of the Upper (Canajoharie) Castle arrived; the commissioners were considering the Plan of Union, and so the Indian meeting was deferred until the following day. This was the first formal meeting with the body of Indians in the open, before the governor's house, as described by Atkinson. In the meantime, Hendrick and several other sachems met the governor and Council of New York, and Hendrick reviewed the disagreements of the immediate past. He explained that they had responded to Colonel Johnson's appeal at Onondaga to come down to meet the new governor. He also explained that the Mohawks were in a difficult spot, because the other Nations believed them too much under the influence of Johnson. Thus they had deliberately delayed their coming to forestall criticism, "for if we had come first, the other Nations would have said that we made the Governor's Speech." They had heard rumors of the settlers that they had stayed behind because of pride. The governor answered that they should not listen to rumors; but they should be more punctual for the future. *DH* 2:575–77.
30. McAnear, "Personal Accounts," pp. 731–34. Governor's address in *DR* 6:861–63.
31. The official record shows this meeting in the afternoon (three o'clock) of Tuesday, July 2. Atkinson, however, summarized it under the date of Monday, July 1. But he does say that on Tuesday in the afternoon "the Govr Sot with the Commissionrs when . . . ye Indians speech was read." McAnear, "Personal Accounts," pp. 736–37.
32. *DR* 6:869. *DH* 2:579.
33. *DR* 6:869. *DH* 2:579–80.
34. *DR* 6:870. *DH* 2:580.
35. *DR* 6:870. *DH* 2:580–81.
36. *DR* 6:870-71.*DH* 2:581–82.
37. *DR* 6:871-75.*DH* 2:583–88.
38. *DR* 6:875. *DH* 2:590.
39. *DR* 6:876.*DH* 2:591. In the London Documents the copy of the speech is emphasized in italics.
40. For example, Peter Wraxall, Thomas Pownall, and Goldsbrow Banyar were his later associates. Richard Peters, Thomas Hutchinson, and Benjamin Franklin were correspondents.
41. McAnear, "Personal Accounts," p. 739.
42. *Ibid.* p. 736.
43. *Pa. Col. Rec.* 6:110–14; P. A. W. Wallace, *Conrad Weiser*, pp. 357–58.
44. *DR* 6:877.
45. *Pa. Col. Rec.* 6:14.
46. *DR* 6:878–83.
47. McAnear, "Personal Accounts," pp. 738–39. *DR* 6:884.
48. *DR* 6:804-5. In a letter to the Lords of Trade, October 30, 1753, Pownall had noted reports of Indian factions, one supporting the Albany commissioners, the other Colonel Johnson. McAnear, "Personal Accounts," pp. 740–41.
49. *Ibid.* p. 741.
50. *Ibid.* pp. 741–42.
51. *Ibid.* p. 742.
52. Colden Papers, N. Y. Hist. Soc., *Collections*, (1920) 4:457–58.
53. *DR* 6:859–60.
54. *DR* 6:863–92. McAnear, "Personal Accounts," pp. 735–39. Connecticut's opposition at Albany became more emphatic when presented to her Assembly. Massachusetts Historical Society, *Collections*, (1800), pp. 203–9.
55. *DR* 6:893–99.
56. *Pa. Arch.*, 1st ser. 2:171. Dated September 17, 1754, Stevenson's letter noted "Above 30 Oneydes are now in town" at the invitation of Lydius. Some Mohawks had signed the deed at their castles, others "in Lydius' own house."
57. *Ibid.* 2:174–75.
58. *Ibid.*
59. *JP* 1:405.
60. P. A. W. Wallace, *Conrad Weiser,* pp. 361–62. Claus blamed Hendrick's hesitancy upon a natural reluctance to go among white people to negotiate so far from home.
61. *JP* 9:151–52.
62. *Claus Narrative*, pp. 7–8.
63. For later negotiations see *JP* 1:396–601, 440–41, 485–86; 9:142–45, 148, 150–62, 164–65, 200.

CHAPTER 13: MILITARY CAREER–FROM COLONEL TO GENERAL

1. *DR* 6:852. On October 21, De Lancey reported that £5,000 was appropriated for the Virginia service. From it, however, he deducted £348 which he had expended on victualing the two independent companies sent there. *DR* 6:911.

2. *JP* 2:409–10.

3. *JP* 1:410. Major Washington had been recently raised to the rank of lieutenant colonel. His inexperience and bad judgment in this instant were of course apparent after the event. Criticism by others and the general reaction to the defeat are treated fully in Douglas Southall Freeman, *George Washington* (New York, 1948), 1:415–45; and Appendix I-10, pp. 546–49, on "The Capitulation at Fort Necessity." Johnson's criticism was not concerned with the controversial terms of capitulation, of which he had not learned. There was nothing personal in this criticism in a private letter. It is probable, however, that the next year at Alexandria Johnson met the young Washington, who had come there to give his services to Braddock. His biographer, Freeman, asserts that Washington met the five governors and was impressed by Shirley. It is inconceivable that he should not also have met Johnson, a leading authority on the Indians and the frontier. *Ibid.* 2:23. Johnson became acquainted with Braddock's aides, Captain Orme, Roger Morris, and William Shirley. *JP* 1:523.

4. *DR* 6:909.

5. *DR* 6:911.

6. *DR* 6:915; *JP* 1:434.

7. *DR* 6:920–22.

8. Charles H. McIlwain, introduction to *WA*, xcvii–c, called Wraxall's work "one long argument" for the "withdrawal of authority from men so incompetent and untrustworthy, and its lodgement in the hands of one man, and that man Colonel Johnson." Others have called *WA* "propaganda" for Johnson. John R. Alden, "The Albany Congress and the Creation of the Indian Superintendencies," *Mississippi Valley Historical Review*, 27 (September 1940): 193–210, shows that these claims are not well founded, and that the ministry made its determination largely on the basis of official reports.

9. *JP* 1:415–16.

10. *JP* 1:432–33.

11. Shirley to James De Lancey. February 24, 1755. *JP* 1:445–51. In view of their later disagreement these words of Shirley in nominating Johnson are significant.

12. *JP* 1:456–59.

13. *JP* 1:459–63.

14. "Robert Orme's Journal" in Winthrop Sargent, *The History of an Expedition against Fort Du Quesne in 1755* (Philadelphia, 1856), pp. 300–307.

15. *Ibid.* Minutes of a Council Held at Alexandria. *DH* 2:648–51.

16. See John A. Schutz, *Thomas Pownall, British Defender of American Liberty* (Glendale, Calif., 1951), pp. 59–61. The account here confuses the chronology and seems to be reading back into this time the animosities which developed later. This is true of the source quoted: William Livingston, *A Review of the Military Operations in North America*, pp. 134–35.

17. *DH* 2:648–50; Sargent, *Expedition against Fort Du Quesne*, p. 300.

18. *DH* 2:648–50.

19. Orme, in Sargent, *Expedition against Fort Du Quesne*, p. 300.

20. *Ibid.*

21. Sargent, *Expedition against Fort Du Quesne*, pp. 305–7.

22. Orme, in Sargent, *Expedition against Fort Du Quesne*, pp. 304–5, states that Shirley was to supply £2,000. Shirley's minutes, *DH* 2:648–51, mentioned the sum as £800 sterling—£300 for western Indians at Oswego and £500 for the Five Nations and allies.

23. Commission from Edward Braddock, *JP* 1:465–66. The terms of this are significant in view of the later dispute over his authority.

24. *DH* 2:651–54. It was expected that other governors would also issue commissions and parallel instructions.

25. Writers have frequently referred to Johnson's being an untrained and inexperienced commander. As noted above, however, he had been colonel of militia since 1746, had led a war party against Crown Point, and was more familiar with frontier conditions than were other commanders. Governor Shirley, on the other hand, whose selection as commander of a regiment and second in command to General Braddock occasioned no surprise, was even less qualified. His biographer writes: "He had never led an army, and had no experience in planning a campaign that involved such vast problems of organization and supply as this one. Perhaps he felt it politically unwise to refuse an opportunity that involved considerable honor and patronage." Schutz, *Shirley*, p. 196.

26. Banyar later mentioned the gun carriages "such as we saw at Alexandria." *JP* 1:520.

27. *JP* 1:443-45; 503–4.

28. *JP* 1:479.

29. *JP* 1:479, 482.

30. *JP* 1:476–77.

31. *JP* 1:553.

32. *JP* 1:482–83.

33. *JP* 1:487–88.

34. *JP* 1:478.

35. *JP* 1:518.
36. *JP* 1:536–38.
37. *JP* 1:502–3.
38. *DR* 6:954–55. Shirley to Secretary Robinson, June 20, 1755.
39. *JP* 1:551–55.
40. *JP* 1:534, 577.
41. *JP* 1:514–15.
42. To Robert Orme, May 19, 1755. *JP* 1:522–23; he repeated these forebodings the next day in a letter to Banyar. *JP* 1:525.
43. *JP* 9:171, 1:557, 585, 597.
44. *JP* 1:601–2.
45. Shirley to De Lancey, June 1, 1755. *Correspondence of William Shirley*, C. H. Lincoln, ed. (New York, 1912), 2:182–88. *Pa. Arch.*, 1st ser. 2:338–43. *DR* 6:954.
46. May 19, 1755. *JP* 1:520. Italics are Banyar's.
47. *JP* 1:534. 540–42.
48. Shirley to De Lancey, *Pa. Arch.*, 1st ser. 2:326–28.
49. May 28, 1755. *Ibid.* 2:330–31. Actually the New York Assembly granted ordnance to Shirley over the governor's opposition. *Ibid.* 2:354.
50. *JP* 1:505–6, 513, 598–600; 9:168–69.
51. *JP* 1:501–2.
52. *Shirley Correspondence*, 2:190–92; *JP* 1:487, 611.
53. *JP* 1:615–16.
54. *Ibid.*
55. *JP* 1:500, 504, 604, 611.
56. *JP* 1:543–44, 565, 568, 595–96, 646.
57. *JP* 1:624. Johnson had written Eyre that Shirley's letter to him was "indeed Tart," but advised that he "put it down as the effects of peevishness not as a just Condemnation of your Conduct." *JP* 1:614.

CHAPTER 14: INDIAN AUXILIARIES

1. *JP* 1:430–31.
2. *JP* 1:431.
3. *JP* 1:467, 523.
4. *JP* 1:475–76.
5. Cf. Nicholas B. Wainwright, *George Croghan, Wilderness Diplomat* (Chapel Hill, 1959), Chap. 6, pp. 110–34. This work supersedes Albert T. Volwiler, *George Croghan and the Western Movement, 1741–1782* (Cleveland, 1926).
6. *JP* 1:516.
7. *JP* 1:535–36.
8. *JP* 1:512, 524.
9. *DR* 6:964–89. This is the official record as transmitted by Wraxall. It is compared with the full description in Daniel Claus to Richard Peters, July 10, 1755, *JP* 9:193–203. Claus wrote from his translator's copy of the proceedings. Cf. *JP* 9:189–90.
10. *DR* 6:964–65. *JP* 9:104.
11. *DR* 6:966–67.
12. *DR* 6:973.
13. *DR* 6:975.
14. Thomas Williams, "The Correspondence of Doctor Thomas Williams of Deerfield, Mass.," *Historical Magazine*, 2d ser. 7 (April 1870): 209–16. (Later cited as "Correspondence of Doctor Williams.") These contemporary letters of a participant to his wife are frank and unbiased.
15. *DR* 6:975–79.
16. *DR* 6:980.
17. *DR* 6:980. *JP* 9:198.
18. *DR* 6:981. Cf. Claus's report. *JP* 9:198. "Also, some of You will join General Shirley who is going to Niagara . . ." The later argument was whether Johnson asked the Indians to go all the way from Schenectady to Niagara. At this time it was put in general terms.
19. *DR* 6:982.
20. *DH* 2:665. *DR* 6:961, 982–83. *JP* 9:199, 204, 208. They also were afraid that their presence might bring about trouble between them and the southern Indians.
21. *DR* 6:983. Claus rendered this, "at Niagara there would be a sufficient Number to join General Shirley, as the Place was near their Habitations." *JP* 9:199.
22. *JP* 9:199.
23. *JP* 1:611, 614,
24. *JP* 1:615.

25. In his introductory speech Johnson had said (*DR* 6:965) "With this string of Wampum I make this Council Room clean and free from everything offensive, and I hope that you will take care that no Snake may creep in amongst us or anything which may obstruct our harmony." He evidently was then referring to French agents or spies. Yet it has been asserted that he called Lydius a snake.

26. *DR* 6:984. Daniel Claus in reporting this episode to Richard Peters of Pennsylvania, who would be particularly interested, used slightly different terms (he was transcribing from his notes of the Indian speeches): "That Genl. Johnson promis'd them in his introductory Speech that the Room where the Council Fire was kindled shou'd be kept free from any venomous or base Creatures; But they must see that one crept in Notwithstanding, which was Lidyus (naming him), who like an evil Spirit intended to Steal their Lands at the Sasquehannah by an unfair and Cheating manner, pulling their people slyly by the Blanket, and by the Witchcraft of Dollars got one Nation after the other to sign a Paper which several of them hardly knew what it was for." *JP* 9:199–200. The speaker went on to discuss the Pennsylvania purchase and their grievance regarding it. Johnson later assured them that the purchase by Pennsylvania was right and should be honored.

27. *DR* 6:986–87. Cf. Claus's report, *JP* 9:200.

28. *JP* 1:644. This was the way Wraxall's note first appeared; after Shirley's protest the references to him, shown in brackets, were removed, and so it appeared in the official report. *DR* 6:986.

29. *JP* 1:733–36. From Shirley, July 17, 1755.

30. *DR* 6:987–89.

31. *JP* 9:204. He was at pains to explain to Braddock why the Indians refused to send more men to him. This, on July 15, quite unaware of the disaster of July 9, was on the same day on which he met Shirley.

32. *JP* 1:612.

33. *DH* 2:665–66. See also his letter to De Lancey, July 10, 1755. *JP* 1:706–7.

34. [William Alexander], *Conduct of Major Gen. Shirley Late General and Commander in Chief of His Majesty's Forces in North America* (London, 1758), pp. 20–25. (Hereafter referred to as *Conduct of Shirley*.) *DR* 6:985.

35. *JP* 9:193.

36. *JP* 1:721, 733, 740.

37. *JP* 1:736.

38. *JP* 1:733–36.

39. *JP* 1:740, 803–4.

40. July 29. *JP* 1:789–90.

41. *JP* 1:756–57.

42. To Thomas Pownall. *JP* 1:803–5.

43. Joseph Kellogg had been taken captive at Deerfield, Massachusetts, in 1703 and while living with the Caghnawaga Indians had learned their tongue. He was interpreter for Massachusetts at Albany in 1754 and was considered the ablest in New England. *DH* 3:1037.

44. *JP* 1:737–39, 741.

45. *JP* 1:741.

46. *JP* 1:734–35.

47. *JP* 1:542.

48. *Shirley Correspondence*, 2:177.

49. *JP* 1:732.

50. From Arent Stevens, July 27. *JP* 1:784; 9:214–16.

51. *JP* 9:212–14.

52. Claus Narrative, p. 9: *JP* 1:755. William Alexander (1726–83), better known in American History as Lord Stirling, a general in the Revolution, was the son of Judge James Alexander, who was an opponent of Cosby in the Zenger affair. "Billy," as he was known to his contemporaries, including William Johnson, was talented and well-educated, with many important connections. He was brother-in-law of William Livingston, with whom he became associated in politics. During the Albany Congress of 1754, he acted as go-between in contacts of the Pennsylvania commissioners with the Connecticut speculators, while Lydius was getting his deed to Susquehanna lands. He seemed an ideal choice as Shirley's secretary and agent in New York. He followed Shirley in his campaigns and went to Europe with him, where he published the defense of Shirley, here cited. Returning to America in 1761, he assumed the questionable title "Lord Stirling," for which he was unable to establish a clear claim. His activity in the patriot cause, and military service won him the commendation of General Washington by whom he was highly esteemed. *DAB* 1:175–76. Schutz, *Shirley*, pp. 199–200. *Pa. Col. Rec.* 6:111–12.

53. *JP* 1:786.

54. *JP* 1:794–95.

55. *JP* 1:790. Albany, July 29, 1755, An account of the news enclosed. Draft copy; portion in italics was erased, and therefore probably not sent. Shirley replied rather testily August

4: "You observe to me that my proceedings will have a bad consequence for the common cause; is not the expedition to Niagara part of that cause, or does it wholly Center in the expedition to Crown Point?" Quoted in Schutz, *Shirley*, p. 209n.

56. Schutz, *Shirley*, pp. 208–10.

57. *Claus Narrative*, p. 10. This was written many years afterward, so that Claus referred to "Sir William.," a title not yet received. See also another version in Claus Papers, 21:118.

58. *Claus Narrative*, p. 11.

59. *Ibid.* pp. 11–12. This belt sent among the nations by Claus later came to the attention of Shirley and his friends, who denounced Johnson for it. It was sent without Johnson's knowledge, but became a principal charge against his conduct. See William Livingston, *Review of the Military Operations in North America*, p. 99.

60. *JP* 9:217–18.

61. *JP* 9:219. Alexander, *Conduct of Shirley*, p. 25, states that Shirley "pressed them to send off their Warriors, whom General Johnson had engaged to follow him in the Expedition against Crown Point, giving Sachem Hendrique, who commanded them a Commission for that Purpose"; and this commission was found upon his person at the time of his death.

62. *Shirley Correspondence*, 2:355–56. Shirley to Robinson, December 20, 1755. Alexander, *Conduct of Shirley*, pp. 22, 25–27. These two firsthand accounts are in substantial disagreement with William Livingston, the author of *Review of the Military Operations in North America*, who asserts (p. 99) that no Indians joined General Shirley, due to Johnson's opposition.

63. *JP* 1:771. He wrote to John Watts, July [19?] 1755: "General Shirley forces so much of my time from me that ever since his arrival from New York my Life has been a seene of hurry & altercation & every Person about me as fully engaged by his means. I hope that we have now done & that he will set off from Schenectady tomorrow or Monday morning."

An example of this business was Shirley's demand that Johnson send men to fortify and garrison the Mohawk castles, from his funds for the Crown Point campaign, although they lay in Shirley's line of march. *JP* 1:753–54.

64. *JP* 1:794–95.

65. *JP* 1:795.

66. *JP* 1:796–97.

CHAPTER 15: THE ADVANCE TO LAKE GEORGE

1. *JP* 1:613, 623, 640.

2. *JP* 1:655.

3. *JP* 1:658.

4. Mt. Johnson, June 28. *JP* 1:667–68.

5. *JP* 1:664–65.

6. "Correspondence of Doctor Williams," p. 210. *JP* 1:705, 707, 710, 779. Connecticut had provisions for six months; Rhode Island had enough for four hundred men for twelve weeks, of which four had passed, July 11.

7. *JP* 9:206. "Correspondence of Doctor Williams," p. 210.

8. *JP* 1:539–40. Johnson may have smiled at such ideas as giving watchdogs to sentries, equipping woodsmen with conch shells to be blown when they are lost, and selecting Indians' gifts to please their wives or mistresses.

9. *JP* 1:697. *Journals and Papers of Seth Pomeroy* (Society of Colonial Wars in the State of New York, 1926), pp. 101–2. (Hereafter cited as *Pomeroy's Journals*). Seth Pomeroy (1706–77) was a gunsmith of Northampton, Massachusetts. He was captain of a company in the Louisbourg campaign (1745), major in the 1747 campaign, and in 1755 was made lieutenant colonel for the Crown Point expedition.

10. *Pomeroy's Journals*, p. 102.

11. *Ibid.*

12. "Ogilvie Diary," pp. 357ff. Cf. *Wars and Rumours of War, Heavens Decree over the World. A Sermon, Preached In the Camp of the New England Forces. On Occasion of the Expedition to remove the Encroachments of the French, on his Majesty's Dominions in North-America.* By Theodorus Frelinghuysen, A. M. Pastor of the Reformed Dutch Church in Albany. . . . Printed and sold by Hugh Gaine, [New York] 1755. Listed in P. L. Ford, ed., *Journals of Hugh Gaine*, 2:92.

13. "A Copy of a Journal Kept by James Gilbert of Morton, Mass. in the Year 1755" [hereafter cited as "Gilbert's Journal"], *Magazine of New England History*, 3 (1893): 188–90. "Journal of Chaplain Graham," *Magazine of American History*, 8 (1882): 206–13. *Journals of House of Representatives of Massachuestts*, vol. 32, pt. 2, pp. 437, 459; vol. 33, pt. 1, p. 88, contain instances of the hardships and losses of chaplains for which they sought recompense.

14. Banyar expressed the general opinion. "I believe the chief opposition you will meet with will be before you reach the fort." *JP* 1:792.

15. *JP* 1:518, 670–71.
16. *JP* 1:611.
17. "Correspondence of Doctor Williams," p. 210.
18. *JP* 1:731.
19. *JP* 1:732. The more frequent spelling of his name was "Warraghiyagey." That this instruction might not have been much help is shown by one soldier's report that the Indian name was "Dewoveraygo." "Gilbert's Journal," p. 189.
20. *JP* 9:207.
21. *JP* 1:767–69. The news first reached New York July 24, at 4 P.M. Banyar wrote it to Johnson July 25; he no doubt received the news on the 28th and wrote it to Shirley on the 29th. Ogilvie had a false report the 27th; the truth on the 28th. "Ogilvie Diary," p. 358.
22. *JP* 1:777.
23. *JP* 1:811.
24. *JP* 1:767. Banyar, July 25, 1755. Braddock's death, four days after his defeat, was not then known.
25. *JP* 1:811–12.
26. *JP* 1:287.
27. *JP* 1:824. 882–83.
28. *JP* 1:723. *Pomeroy's Journals*, p. 261.
29. "Gilbert's Journal," pp. 188–91. Gilbert's chronology: July 22, the Flats to Half Moon; 23d, at Schagticoke ("Canty Cook"); 24th, four miles; 29th, Saratoga; 31st, first carry; August 3, the "Chiefe caring Place," Fort Edward, or Lydius's house.
30. *JP* 9:209–10.
31. *JP* 1:782; 9:209.
32. *JP* 1:828–29; 9:209; "Correspondence of Doctor Williams," p. 210.
33. *JP* 1:589, 607, 684, 691–92, 822, 842, 9:206. Theodore Atkinson, delegate and diarist at the Albany congress in 1754, commended Blanchard to him as a "Peculiar friend of Mine." July 25, 1755.
34. *JP* 1:822, 838–39, 844–47, 871–72.
35. "Ogilvie Diary," p. 358–59.
36. *Ibid*. and *JP* 1:782, 838, 842. Ogilvie said that Johnson left August 8, while he wrote on that date to De Lancey that he marched on the morrow. He may have left Albany the 8th, and gone with the troops from the Flats the following day.
37. *JP* 1:838.
38. "Gilbert's Journal," p. 191.
39. To Thomas Pownall, August 25, 1755, *JP* 1:886.
40. *Claus Narrative*, p. 12.
41. *JP* 1:883.
42. *JP* 1:886. August 25.
43. *JP* 1:861, 879, 883; 2:6, 31, 53. A contemporary French map shows a sketch of the "Maison de Lidius," situated on the steep bank of the river. Illustration, *JP* 2:31.
    Colonel Pomeroy was one who was skeptical. On August 20, he mentioned two or three hundred men digging a trench around the storehouse, "but if I was to Judge by ye Present appearance of things an Ill Contry'd Peace of fortification." *Pomeroy's Journals*, p. 109.
44. *DR* 10:333–34.
45. *JP* 2:63, 66. William Cockroft, September 20, 1755—the only instance of this dateline in the *Johnson Papers;* To William Cockroft, September 21, 1755. After this date the new name was used. "Edward" was the Duke of York, grandson of George II and brother of the later George III.
46. *JP* 9:210. July 25, 1755. There is a tacit implication here of the superior moral tone of the New England men!
47. *JP* 1:783.
48. *JP* 1:861. *Pomeroy's Journals*, p. 109.
49. *JP* 2:7. Gilbert's Journal," p. 193.
50. *DH* 2:679–80; *JP* 2:6–7. Soldiers billeted in towns paid their bills and then were reimbursed by the paymaster.
51. *JP* 2:7–8.
52. August 17, 1755, "Correspondence of Doctor Williams," p. 211. *Pomeroy's Journals* pp. 207, 109. Goldsbrow Banyar's letters of July 26 and August 6, 1755, discussed the South Bay route. *JP* 1:773, 834.
53. *JP* 1:860–61.
54. *JP* 9:220–21. On September 4, Johnson noted that the Indians had sent another embassy to the Caghnawagas. *JP* 2:8.
55. *DH* 2:680–81, Wentworth to Secretary Robinson, September 5. 1755. *JP* 2:3–4.
56. *DR* 6:1001.
57. *DR* 6:1000. On August 18, Colonel Pomeroy wrote his wife, "We cant yet Sattisfy our Selves or Fully Determine which way to go Either into Wood creek or to ye South Bay; ye.

Latter is Suppos'd to be ye best If we Can find a way over ye Mountain yt lies a little this Side we sent a Scout yesterday 40 odd white & 6 or 8 Indians to get full Satisfaction in yt affair; and as Soon as they return we Shall Determine." *Pomeroy's Journals*, p. 134.

58. *JP* 1:880–82.
59. *Pomeroy's Journals*, p. 110. *Claus Narrative*, p. 12. *JP* 1:893.
60. *Pomeroy's Journals*, p. 111.
61. *DH* 2:689. *JP* 1:789–90. *Claus Narrative*, p. 12.
62. *JP* 2:9; September 4, 1755. A similar statement was made September 1, *JP* 1:893; and September 3, *DH* 2:689; where in writing to the Board of Trade he used the phrase "undoubted Dominion." Ogilvie mentioned the new name under date September 1, suggesting that it was done earlier. "Ogilvie Diary," p. 366.
63. *DH* 2:689. Cf. also *JP* 2:10.
64. Daniel Claus to Richard Peters, September 11, 1755, in American Philosophical Society. *Pomeroy's Journals*, p. 111.
65. *Pomeroy's Journals*, pp. 111–12. *JP* 2:7.
66. *Pomeroy's Journals* p. 112; *JP* 2:7.
67. *Pomeroy's Journals*, p. 111.
68. Lydekker, *Faithful Mohawks*, p. 83. Quote from papers of the Society for the Propagation of the Gospel.
69. *DR* 10:275–302. These "Paris Documents" contain official reports, commissions, and instructions.
70. Ludwig August von Dieskau, a baron from Saxony, had served under the celebrated Marshal Saxe, and as lieutenant colonel of cavalry. He had a good reputation as a commander of troops.
71. Pierre François de Rigaud, Marquis de Vaudreuil-Cavagnal (1698–1765) was born in Quebec, son of Philippe de Rigaud, Marquis de Vaudreuil, an earlier governor of New France. He remained as governor until the capitulation in 1760.
72. *DR* 10:295.
73. *DR* 10:306–9.
74. *DR* 10:311–12, 340–41. Braddock's papers were sent from Quebec in Bréard's letter to M. de Machault, August 13, 1755.
75. *DR* 10:316, 319. Accounts differ somewhat on the figures for the troops: Dieskau said he took 700 regulars, but others had preceded; Vaudreuil said there were 1,011 of the battalions and detachments of Marine. Figures for the Indians varied.
76. *DR* 10:313. Pierre Pouchot, *Memoir Upon the Late War in North America*, 2 vols. (Roxbury, Mass., 1866), 1:85.
77. Donald H. Kent, *French Invasion*, p. 15. Sylvester K. Stevens and Donald H. Kent, *Wilderness Chronicles of Northwestern Pennsylvania* (Harrisburg, 1941), pp, 76–78.
78. *DR* 10:311–12. Dieskau was told that English militia were "such miserable soldiers that a single Indian would put ten to flight." *DR* 10:341.
79. *DR* 10:316.
80. *DR* 10:316. Account of the Battle of Lake George, by Louis Antoine de Bougainville. New York State Library. (Hereafter cited as Bougainville MS.)
81. *DR* 10:316. For Vaudreuil's censure of Dieskau for his violation of Article 3 of his instructions (not to divide his force), see *DR* 10:319, 328.
82. *DR* 10:319–20.
83. Bougainville MS.
84. *DR* 10:317.
85. *Ibid.*
86. Bougainville MS. See also Dieskau's report. *DR* 10:320–21.
87. *DR* 10:317.
88. *DR* 10:321.

CHAPTER 16: THE BATTLE AT LAKE GEORGE

1. *JP* 2:6, 15–16.
2. *Claus Narrative*, p. 12. Written some years later, this narrative refers to Johnson as "Sir Wm." and the fort at the Carrying Place as "Fort Edward." Although written by a participant and eyewitness, it errs in details and must be checked with other accounts.
3. *JP* 2:16–17.
4. *JP* 2:17.
5. *Claus Narrative*, p. 12. Claus in this may have distorted or embellished at some points. He errs in speaking of Lyman as then commanding at Fort Edward; it was Blanchard to whom the dispatch was sent. Johnson wrote: "I got One Adams a Waggoner, who Voluntarily and Bravely consented to Ride Express with my Orders to Colonel Blanchard." *JP* 9:228.
6. *JP* 9:226, 228.

7. *Claus Narrative* p. 13. Cf. Claus to Richard Peters, September 11, 1755, a contemporary account which agrees on the main points.

The story is told of Hendrick's disapproving the division of the force. Picking up three sticks from the ground, he said, "Put these together and you cannot break them; Take them one by one and you will do it easily." Also, respecting the small force, he was said to have remarked, "If they are to fight they are too few; if they are to be killed they are too many." Stone, *Life and Times*, 1:512-13. There is no evidence that Hendrick disapproved of the force with which he marched.

8. *JP* 9:229.

9. *Pomeroy's Journals*, p. 137.

10. "Gilbert's Journal," pp. 194-95.

11. Peter Wraxall to Henry Fox, camp at Lake George, September 27, 1755. Stanley Pargellis, ed., *Military Affairs in North America, 1748-1765* (New York, 1936), p. 139.

12. *DR* 10:321, 342.

13. *DR* 10:317, 321.

14. *DR* 10:321.

15. *DR* 10:342.

16. Samuel Blodget, *A Prospective-Plan of the Battle Near Lake George, on the Eighth Day of September, 1755* (Boston, 1755). Hereafter referred to as Blodget, *Plan*.

17. *DR* 10:321-22.

18. *DR* 10:317.

19. *Claus Narrative*, pp. 13-14. In his letter to Richard Peters, September 11, 1755, he wrote: "Immediately the French Indians told our Indians to Stand off and not Meddle with the English when they answered Nothing but fired and then the Battle begun."

20. French accounts differ as to the initial effect of the ambush. One wrote "the English were doubled up like a pack of cards and fled, pell-mell, to their entrenchments." *DR* 10:342. Vaudreuil, however, said "The English stood their ground, their Indians being in front. The fight was very brisk; we put the English to flight, but lost M. de St. Pierre who commanded the Indians and Canadians." *DR* 10:321-22.

21. Blodget, *Plan*, pp. 1-2. Charles Chauncy, *Second Letter to a Friend* (Boston, 1755), pp. 3-4. This account, while in the form of a printed letter in a pamphlet, was based on interviews with eyewitnesses. *Claus Narrative*, p. 14.

22. Chauncy, *Second Letter*, pp. 3-4.

23. *Pomeroy's Journals* p. 114. Cf "Gilbert's Journal," pp. 194-95.

24. Chauncy, *Second Letter*, P. 4. His informant was able to time the engagement. "He further gave me to understand, that he took out his watch, when the fire was first heard at the Camp; that he penciled the time; that it was precisely 11 o'clock wanting 5 minutes; and that the retreat was not finished till ½ after 12; So that this retreat, and the fight previous to it continued one hour and 35 minutes." General Lyman, however, wrote: "The fight in the Woods began about one Quarter before Nine and came to us about half an Hour after Ten o'clock." *New York Gazette*, October 6, 1755. Johnson said, however, that the first men came into camp about ten o'clock. *JP* 9:229.

25. Pargellis, *Military Affairs*, p. 139.

26. *JP* 9:229. Chauncy's informant, noting Johnson's statement, asserts that the distance from the camp was only "2 miles and ½ at farthest"; he had this from the survey afterward, measured with a chain. *Second Letter*, p. 4, note.

27. *JP* 9:238.

28. *JP* 9:231.

29. Ephraim Williams (1714-55) achieved immortality in another way. While encamped at Albany July 21, 1755, he made his will. Having neither wife nor child, he left most of his estate to found a free school, which later became Williams College.

30. Thomas Pownall to Lords of Trade, September 20, 1755. *DR* 6:1008.

31. *JP* 9:231.

32. Claus to Peters, September 11, 1755.

33. *Claus Narrative*, p. 14, Pound, *Johnson* pp. 518-19, doubts the story on circumstantial grounds. Yet Claus would have no good reason for concocting such a story of an ignominious end for his hero.

34. *DR* 10:317, 322. *Claus Narrative*, p. 14. Also, Claus Papers.

35. Pargellis, *Military Affairs*, p. 139.

36. Bougainville MS. *DR* 10:322.

37. *DR* 10:317.

38. *Claus Narrative*, p. 15. Blodget, *Plan*.

39. *JP* 9:229; *Pomeroy's Journals*, p. 114. Blodget, *Plan*.

40. Pargellis, *Military Affairs*, p. 139.

41. Johnson said it was at 11:30; Pomeroy and Chauncy stated between 11 and 12; Wraxall said it was 12. *JP* 9:229. Chauncy, *Second Letter*, pp. 6-7. Pargellis, *Military Affairs*, p. 139.

42. *JP* 9:230. Claus Papers. *Pomeroy's Journals*, p. 114. Blodget, *Plan*, says the halt was 140 yards away.
43. *JP* 1:743; 9:230. *DR* 6:1005.
44. *DR* 10:322. "Correspondence of Doctor Williams," p. 212. There was difference of opinion as to how much the guns were used and how effectively. Wraxall wrote, "Our Artillery play'd very briskly in our Front the whole Time"; while Blodget, an eyewitness also, said the heavy cannon "did not do the execution we should have been glad of, while the Regulars were together; and afterwards they were in a manner useless; Nor were they discharged more than 4 or 5 Times." He also said the field piece on the eminence was "not fired more than once or twice." Blodget, *Plan*, p. 2. Certainly, possession of cannon was a great advantage.
45. Warren Johnson's Journal, *JP* 13:197.
46. Lyman's letter. *New York Gazette*, October 6, 1755.
47. Blodget, *Plan*, p. 2.
48. *JP* 9:230.
49. *DR* 6:1005.
50. *DR* 10:322-23. Dieskau later elaborated on his experience with both Indians and whites, who wanted to kill him on the spot. He credited Johnson with saving his life, but asserted that one of the soldiers shot him through the hips when he was already wounded and at their mercy. The Indians would have scalped and tortured him if they had not been restrained by Johnson. *DR* 10:343.
51. Blodget, *Plan*, pp. 3-4. Chauncy, *Second Letter*, p. 7.
52. Pargellis, *Military Affairs*, p. 132. Johnson said, "The Whole Engagement and Pursuit ended about Seven o'Clock." *JP* 9:230.
53. "Correspondence of Doctor Williams," p. 212.
54. Accounts of the wound and of the degree of Johnson's incapacity are contradictory. The assumption that he gave up the command to General Lyman, however, is unsupported by contemporary witness. Cf. Wraxall's letter in *DR* 6:1003-4, and *New York Gazette*, September 18, 1755. *Claus Narrative*, p. 17, *JP* 2:32; 9:230.
55. Letter from the Great Carrying Place, September 9, 1755. *Pennsylvania Gazette*, September 18, 1755. *JP* 9:231.
56. *New York Gazette*, September 18, 1755. *DR* 10:323. *New York Gazette*, October 6, 1755.
57. *JP* 9:231. *DR* 10:323. Chauncy, *Second Letter*, p. 40. Captain Maginnis, who died two days later, is not to be confused with Captain Teady Magin (McGin), the Indian officer who was killed in the first engagement.
58. Pargellis, *Military Affairs*, p. 140.
59. *DR* 10:323. This records the retreat of the French.
60. *Pomeroy's Journals*, p. 138.
61. *New York Gazette*, October 6, 1755.
62. *JP* 9:234-38. *DR* 10:324. Lyman wrote especially of the loss of officers: "Connecticut has not left one Field Officer or Captain, and I think none of the inferior officers," though his company had only nine killed; "We expect we have lost a great many by Death and Captivity in the Woods." *New York Gazette*, October 6, 1755.
63. *DR* 10:324. *New York Gazette*, September 18, 1755.
64. *JP* 2:24-25.
65. *JP* 2:48. *DR* 6:1013.
66. *JP* 2:165. This procedure of Stevenson was, Johnson said, "utterly without My Concurrance & very Contrary to My expectations."
67. *JP* 2:57.
68. Thomas Hutchinson, *History of the Province of Massachusetts Bay* (London, 1828), 3:36-37. He added: "Thus there arose a coldness between the province and the general which seemed to give him no great concern."
69. *JP* 2:172-73. "I am very much out of order with a violent Inflamation in the side of my head, wch. confines me mostly to my bed."
70. To Spencer Phips, October 10, 1755. *JP* 2:165.
71. *JP* 2:172. *DR* 6:1003. Some of the variations in these two versions have been noted.
72. *New York Gazette*, October 6, 1755. William Smith Diary, 2:396-97 (New York Public Library) under date of September 29, 1755, records publication of Johnson's letter in the *New York Mercury*, and Lyman's in the *Connecticut Gazette*, a copy of which is bound in the volume.
73. *DR* 6:1004.
74. *New York Gazette*, October 6, 1755.
75. *JP* 2:31.
76. *JP* 2:39-40.
77. An excellent scholarly study, "The Crown Point Campaign, 1755" by Theodore Burnham Lewis, Jr., *Bulletin of the Fort Ticonderoga Museum*, 12, no. 6 (October 1970): 400-26; 13, no. 1 (December 1970): 19-88. provides an analysis emphasizing the military aspects. Con-

clusions generally are in harmony with those presented here, although somewhat less concerned with the personal side. Appendices give personnel and statistics of the forces involved.

CHAPTER 17: AFTERMATH OF BATTLE

1. Thomas Williams to his wife, October 8, 1755. "Correspondence of Doctor Williams," p. 213.
2. *JP* 13:56.
3. *JP* 2:68.
4. *JP* 2:90.
5. *JP* 2:57-62. Shirley ignored several facts or conditions: (1) that the Indians had gone home, (2) that the English had suffered heavy losses, (3) that his figures for the French force did not include Canadians, and (4) that the fear of another attack was shared by all officers and supported by statements of prisoners.
6. *JP* 2:62.
7. *Ibid.*
8. *Pomeroy's Journals*, p. 139.
9. *JP* 2:40-42, 74. "Ogilvie Diary," p. 362. *DR* 6:1015.
10. *Gentleman's Magazine*, 25 (November 1755): 519-20. Surgeon Williams told the story of several persons whose flesh wounds had resulted in death from poisoning. W. L. Stone, *Life of Sir William Johnson*, 1:517n.
11. *Claus Narrative*, p. 17.
12. *DR* 10:343. This was Dieskau's story. Johnson said the Baron "was brought to my Tent about 6 o Clock, just as a Wound I had received was Dressed." *JP* 9:230.
13. *DR* 10:343-44. *Claus Narrative*, pp. 15-17.
14. *JP* 2:41, 43-47.
15. *JP* 2:184-85. From Albany, September 21, 1755, the aide-de-camp wrote a fulsome letter of thanks for the Baron to General Johnson, with kind references to his "sister and all the ladies of the household"; the "Young captain" (Philip Schuyler) who conducted him to Albany; to "Mr. D'Ayris" (Captain Eyre); and "your aide de camp" (Peter Wraxall) for their "sincere friendship." Bernier, however added a tart postscript about his own treatment. He had given his word of honor for his conduct, "but since I have been here, I have hardly had permission to go to the toilet and when I do so I am escorted at bayonet point and the house is filled with guards." He also protested his inability to visit the city "to see some one who speaks French." As an officer he felt he deserved better treatment. *JP* 13:47-50. Apparently Johnson's orders regarding him were taken literally. According to Dr. Shuckburgh, however, he was ill-favored and disliked.
16. *JP* 2:205, 280, 282, 350. *DR* 10:387, 537, 806.
17. The writer has treated this issue in an article, "Hero of Lake George: Johnson or Lyman?" *New England Quarterly*, 36 (September 1963): 371-82. The evidence shows that while Lyman commanded his Connecticut troops behind the breastworks in the thick of the fighting, he was not recognized as commander of the whole and given no such credit until long after the event.
18. *New York Mercury*, September 18, 1755. *DR* 6:1003.
19. *Claus Narrative*, pp. 16-17.
20. *Pomeroy's Journals*, p. 139.
21. *JP* 9:233.
22. *JP* 2:186.
23. *JP* 2:140-41, 149, 153, 155, 173, 186, 198, 207, 212, 223, 240, 260, 280. Lyman presided at the councils on October 11, 13, 18, 20. He was able to preside again on October 30. *JP* 2:174-79, 250.
24. *DR* 6:1004.
25. *New York Gazette*, October 6, 1755.
26. Claus contended that Hendrick's insistence on not dividing the force of the morning scout saved them from defeat (Claus Papers). Hendrick had denounced Shirley's pleas to him in a speech at Lake George September 4. *DR* 6:998-99; Shirley's commission to Hendrick was found on his body by the French. *DR* 10:323. In 1772 Johnson's account to the crown of his disbursements included £8 . . 13.-"To old Hendricks widow agreeable to my promise to him." *JP* 12:945.
27. *DR* 6:1011-14.
28. *DR* 6:1014. "Ogilvie Diary," p. 361.
29. *JP* 2:52.
30. "Ogilvie Diary," pp. 362-63. *JP* 2:99.
31. *JP* 2:80.
32. *JP* 2:65, 81. An optimistic report, dated Boston, September 17, in the *Gentleman's Magazine*, 25 (November 1755): 520, gave estimates of 3,000, 2,500, and 300, which would bring Johnson's total to "9000 Strong."

33. *Gentleman's Magazine*, 25:520, *JP* 2:105–6; 9:314–15, 318–20.
34. *Gentleman's Magazine*, 25:520. *JP* 2:76, 81.
35. To Shirley, September 22. *JP* 2:74.
36. *JP* 2:49, 50.
37. *JP* 2:38, 56, 66, 275.
38. *JP* 2:284.
39. *JP* 2:107.
40. *JP* 2:64, 76–77, 82, 84. Sir Charles was accompanied to Albany by Councillor Daniel Horsmanden, Lieutenant Colonel John Rutherford, Oliver De Lancey, his secretary, and Goldsbrow Banyar. See "Ogilvie Diary," pp. 361–62.
41. *JP* 2:77, 99.
42. *JP* 2:120–24.
43. *JP* 2:133–34.
44. *JP* 2:136–37, 162, 193. This action of Shirley appears particularly inept in that Wraxall was also an official of the New York government. Sir Charles was also offended by Shirley's attempts to control the Independent Companies of New York and to make military appointments with the authority of General Braddock.
45. *JP* 2:134–37.
46. *JP* 2:163–64.
47. *JP* 2:164.
48. *JP* 2:134.
49. *JP* 2:77.
50. *JP* 2:108.
51. *JP* 2:110. These rumors were to crop up again as ammunition in the factional strife which followed.
52. *JP* 2:108, 110, 129.
53. *JP* 2:147. 186, 189, 210.
54. "Correspondence of Doctor Williams," p. 213.
55. Alexander, *Conduct of Shirley*, pp. 34–38. John Henry Lydius, in charge of Indians for Shirley's campaign, testified in London, September 21, 1756, blaming Shirley's delay and caution for the failure. He asserted that his spies had shown the weak condition of Fort Niagara, that he had asked General Shirley twice for permission to take three hundred men with five days' provision, and that with this small force he could have taken the fort. But Shirley refused. Chatham Papers, Public Record Office.
56. *Shirley Correspondence*, 2:323.
57. *Ibid.* 2:324. Alexander, *Conduct of Shirley*, pp. 52–53.
58. Cf. John A. Schutz, *Thomas Pownall*, pp. 61–62. Gideon Hawley to Andrew Oliver, November 20, 1755. Congregational Christian Historical Society Library, Boston, Mass.
59. Shirley to Robinson, October 5, 1755. *JP* 2:146; Johnson to Hardy, October 10, *JP* 2:161.
60. *JP* 2:305.
61. *JP* 2:313, 319–22. Again Johnson had difficulty with the officers. He gave General Lyman a peremptory order to attend. "The Council of War are met & wait." *JP* 9:320.
62. *JP* 2:288, 301, 307, 324, 326–27; 13:66.
63. *JP* 2:238. To Charles Hardy, October 24, 1755.
64. *DH* 4:259–61. See also John R. Cuneo, *Robert Rogers of the Rangers* (New York, 1959), a popular biography marred by adulation of its hero.
65. To Charles Hardy, October 13, 1755. *JP* 2:189–90.
66. *DH* 4:262–70.
67. *DH* 2:223, 250–52, 256. For Rogers's Scout of October 29–31, see *DH* 4:272–73.
68. November 2–11, 1755. *DH* 4:278.
69. *DH* 4:281–83.
70. *JP* 13:70–71.
71. *JP* 2:318, 326–27; 9:322–23; 13:74–75.
72. *JP* 13:71–73.
73. *JP* 2:335–37.
74. *JP* 2:77. 97, 111.
75. *JP* 2:39–40.
76. *JP* 2:117–18. 130, 144. *DR* 6:1015.
77. *JP* 2:219. The last phrase in this draft may have been "within Battery reach," See also *JP* 2:150, 157–60.
78. *JP* 2:221.
79. *JP* 2:354. To Shirley, November 28, 1755. "There are two Ranges of Barracks at Fort William Henry two Story high, all which want flooring except the upper Story of the North Barrack, the rest would have been finished but for want of Boards, there is no Glass for the Windows. When compleated they will contain about 250 Men. . . ."
80. *JP* 2:332–34.

81. *JP* 9:324–26.
82. *JP* 2:130–31, 240, 281; 9:242.
83. *JP* 2:355; 9:267; 13:74.
84. *JP* 2:355–59.
85. *JP* 2:358.
86. *DR* 6:1021.
87. *JP* 2:341.
88. *JP* 2:361–62.
89. Wraxall was judge advocate as well as aide-de-camp; Eyre served not only as chief engineer but as "Quarter Master General & Director of the Train of Artillery"; and Glazier, arriving just before the engagement, served as adjutant general, with no provision for the post or extra remuneration.
90. *JP* 2:363–64. Dated Albany, December 2, 1755, the draft interpolated the following phrase at the hiatus, which is not in the copy as transmitted to Secretary Robinson: "if I have fallen short of their Expectations & Opinions, it hath been my Misfortune not my Crime, & herein I am very willing to stand the strictest & most impartial Enquiry."

CHAPTER 18: FAME AND CONTROVERSY

1. Some writers have referred to the fall of Fort Beauséjour, on the Acadian isthmus of Nova Scotia, to General Monckton (June 16, 1755) as the only success of that year, since Johnson did not reach Crown Point. Yet it made no such impression as did Johnson's victory over the principal thrust of the French Army. Beauséjour was poorly defended and capitulated to superior force. While strategic as a point of continental defense, it was not as vital to the English settlements. See L. H. Gipson, *The British Empire before the American Revolution,* vol. 6, *The Great War for the Empire, The Years of Defeat,* pp.226–34.
2. *JP* 2:425; 9:386.
3. Cf. *JP* 2:68, 84, 90, 186; 9:309, 471; 13:80–81.
4. William Smith Diary, 2:396. New York Public Library.
5. "Ogilvie Diary," p. 363.
6. *New York Mercury,* November 10, 1755.
7. *JP* 2:65; 13:239.
8. *JP* 9:239. Pownall expected to succeed the ailing Governor Jonathan Belcher of New Jersey on his death.
9. *JP* 2:54, 64–65, 251; 9:239.
10. *JP* 2:384–87.
11. *JP* 2:359–60.
12. *JP* 1:261–62 (Guy Johnson's sketch); 2:269; 13:82–83; see also the French traveller's description of 1757. *DH* 1:532.
13. *JP* 2:267.
14. *JP* 2:338; 9:321.
15. *JP* 2:390. "Attorney general" may have referred to General Shirley, whose earlier career in Massachusetts was in such a legal position.
16. Colden and Kelly, New York, December 3, 1755. *JP* 2:367.
17. Quoted in *New York Gazette,* November, 23, 1755. Another attack appeared in the *Connecticut Gazette.* See William Smith Diary, 2:399.
18. *New York Gazette,* December 15, 1755.
19. *DR* 6:993–97. *DH* 2:684–89.
20. *DR* 6:1024–25. Letter and Instructions. In his letter to Secretary Robinson, December 20, 1755, Shirley explained; "I have revok'd General Braddock's Commission to General Johnson, and sent him one founded upon the intent of his Majesty's Inclosed Instruction without the Words Sole Superintendent . . . " If he would not act under the new commission and instructions, "I shall be under the necessity of appointing another in his stead which will be the Noted Conrad Weiser . . . " *Shirley Correspondence,* 2:362.
21. *DR* 6:1025.
22. *DR* 6:1025–27; *JP* 13:78–79.
23. *DR* 6:1023–24.
24. *DR* 6:1027–28.
25. Schutz, *Shirley,* p. 223, implies that Johnson by this statement put himself in the wrong as having no authority for what he did. Yet Shirley's new commission would have had no more weight than Braddock's; a royal commission, of course, he could not set aside. But Shirley in his letter of January 4, 1756, abandoned his earlier demand and consented to Johnson's acting under his commission from Braddock provided he would acknowledge Shirley's right to give instructions, which Johnson had never denied. Johnson also stipulated that Shirley's agents among the Indians be withdrawn. *DR* 7:13. *JP* 2:403–4.
26. Schutz, *Shirley,* pp. 107–8, 158–67.

27. William Smith Diary, 2:398–400.
28. *Ibid*. William Livingston, *Review of the Military Operations in North America*, pp. 130–36. *Shirley Correspondence*, 2:343–54; James Alexander wrote to Cadwallader Colden, New York, December 11, 1755. Colden Papers, N. Y. Hist. Soc., *Collections*, (1921) 5:50: "Lt. Govr. Pownal represents the Govr. of Jersey."
29. Lawrence H. Gipson, *Lewis Evans* (Philadelphia, 1939), pp. 63–70. In this volume are printed Evans's maps, his description, analysis, and the article from the *New York Mercury*. L. C. Wroth, *An American Bookshelf, 1755* (Philadelphia, 1934), p. 53, favors William Livingston (author of the *Review*) as the writer, but Smith's Diary, 2:400, is explicit: "[William] Alexander desired me to attack the map or rather Pownal to whom it was dedicated and next Morning sent me a sketch of our title to that Garrison [Frontenac] and the Land on the North side of the Lake . . . , Decr. 24 sent a draft . . . . which Wm. Alexander retd. me the next Morning informing me that the General liked it well and it was printed in *New York Mercury* 5 January 1756."
30. Gipson, *Lewis Evans*, pp. 75–76. William Livingston, *Review of the Military Operations in North America*, pp. 136–37n.
31. S. M. Pargellis, *Lord Loudoun in North America* (New Haven, 1933), pp. 54–55. *Shirley Correspondence*, 2:428–29, 368–69.
32. William Smith Diary, 2:400.
33. *New York Mercury*, January 5, 1756.
34. *DR* 7:11, 13–14.
35. *Claus Narrative*, p. 19.
36. *Ibid*. One or two words and phrases here are taken from the Claus Papers, where the printed version omits or is different.
37. *Ibid*. pp. 19–20.
38. The *Claus Narrative*, written in the 1780s in support of Daniel Claus's petition to the Loyalist Claims Commission, some thirty years after these events, suffers from lapses of memory. There are a number of other errors of fact, so that it must be used with caution.
39. *DR* 7:14–31. Wraxall's statement was accompanied by the record of Hendrick's speech at Lake George on September 4 on Shirley's interposition with the Mohawks.
40. *Shirley Correspondence*, 2:368–69.
41. *JP* 13:58–61, 64–65. Pownall wrote: "I know I can be of more Use & benefit to ye. Public Service to Myself [&] to my Freinds, by being in England this Winter than perhaps any other Man."
42. *DH* 2:648.
43. Schutz, *Pownall*, pp. 66–67.
44. *JP* 13:60. See *An Account of Conferences held, and Treaties made, Between Major-general Sir William Johnson, Bart. And The Chief Sachems and Warriours* (London, 1756; reprint ed., Lancaster, Pa., 1930). This contained the record of Johnson's Indian negotiations of December 1755 and February 1756, with a letter of Gideon Hawley; an appendix contains the record of the April 1756 conference in Pennsylvania. The preface, probably by Pownall, is a panegyric to Johnson.
45. S. M. Pargellis, *Lord Loudoun in North America* (New Haven, 1933), pp. 54–55.
46. *Shirley Correspondence*, 2:428. A correspondent of Johnson wrote on July 3, 1756: "States Morris when he was last in England waited on the Duke [of Newcastle], the Duke asked him if he had the returns of the Army he said not, have you brought the returns of the two new raised Regiments, he said not, what do you come for said the Duke, and left him abruptly—the next day States recd. an order to repair to his Regiment." *JP* 2:498. But young Staats had other strings to his bow. "While in England he fell prey to the wiles of the Dowager Duchess of Gordon, became her husband, and through her influence rose to high rank in the British Army." Pargellis, *loc. cit.* Cf. also *JP* 2:516.
47. Pownall sailed February 8, and after a five-week voyage, he would have arrived March 12. Schutz, *Pownall*, p. 67. Schutz assumes that "he successfully completed his work for Johnson, because the superintendency of Indian Affairs was made a regular bureau of the colonial government." *Ibid*. p. 69. But Johnson's commission was dated February 17.
48. *DH* 2:703.
49. *DR* 6:1020.
50. *JP* 2:428, 430, 436.
51. *Gentleman's Magazine*, 25 (November 1755): 519–20.
52. *JP* 2:484. The original patent is now in the possession of a descendant, Mr. James W. Johnson, Spokane, Washington.
53. *JP* 2:343–44. This irrelevant formula had been used since the first baronetcies had been granted in 1612, when the king raised money, through the grant of titles, for the defense of Ireland. Sir William's title therefore fell under the category of "Baronets of Ireland," created in this form until 1801. Francis W. Pixley, *A History of the Baronetage* (London, 1900), pp. 18–24.
54. *JP* 2:346–47. This symbol was also common to all baronets of the period. Johnson some

five years earlier had shown interest in a coat of arms; his brother Warren had the "Ct. of Arms Cut in a very neat manner," but then found they were the O'Neill's. *JP* 1:266. Sir William's original coat of arms, with Indian supporters, and the hand of Ulster, was made for him later. See James Sullivan, "The Johnson Coat of Arms." *JP* 3:vii-xii. I am indebted to R. P. Vivian-Graham, M. V. O., M. C., Windsor Herald, of the College of Arms, London, for information concerning the traditional phrases in the patents of baronets.

55. *JP* 2:346-48. This promise of knighting the male heirs at the age of 21 was omitted from patents after 1827. Pixley, *A History of the Baronetage*, p. 39.

56. Johnson to Board of Trade, July 21, 1755, *DH* 2:671-74. *DR* 6:961-63. September 3, *DH* 2:684-89. *DR* 6:993-97. September 24, *DH* 2:698-700. *DR* 6:1009-10. December 18, *DH* 2:708. *DR* 6:1023-24. Agreement with Johnson's plans for centralized control and development of an independent fund was expressed in Board of Trade to Johnson, October 9, 1755. *DH* 2:702.

57. *JP* 2:419-20. *DR* 7:14-29. Wraxall's "Thoughts" may have been drawn up as a result of the request of the Lords of Trade of October 9. For the "inner cabinet" action, see Pargellis, *Lord Loudoun*, pp. 39-41. They were less sure of the southern superintendent, who was not given "sole" jurisdiction, Cf. J. R. Alden, "The Albany Congress and the Indian Superintendencies," p. 209.

58. *JP* 2:434.

59. *DH* 2:710-11. A letter to the Board of Trade, January 17, 1756, asked for fixed salaries for himself and Secretary Wraxall. *DR* 7:9.

60. Letter of March 13, 1756. *DR* 7:76-77. In his letter of January 14, 1756, which was not sent and was too late to have effect, he again set forth his financial losses. *DH* 2:709.

61. *JP* 2:441, 485.

62. [William Livingston], *Review of the Military Operations in North America*, p. 145. For a fuller account of this tract see below. William Smith Diary, 2:207.

63. *JP* 2:138, 156.

64. November 27, 1755. In Cumberland Papers. Quoted in Pargellis, *Military Affairs*, p. 152. Italics in the original.

65. *JP* 9:385-86. Cf. Schutz, *Shirley*, pp. 225ff. for Shirley's falling fortunes.

66. *JP* 2:450-51.

67. Pargellis, *Lord Loudoun*, pp. 76-77. Loudoun was asked to investigate and discover the author of the intercepted letters. Among those suspected were George Croghan and George Washington—the former because of his knowledge of Indian affairs and the latter because he was a military man in Virginia. Cf. Gipson, *British Empire*, 6:189. Schutz, *Shirley*, pp. 232-33. Schutz suggests that Shirley's diplomatic residence in Paris and marriage to a young French-woman gave color to the suspicion that he was involved. N. B. Wainwright, *George Croghan*, pp. 106-9, explains the suspicion of Croghan, and efforts to discover the author of the letters.

68. Will Eyre to Johnson, February 3, 1756: "No doubt you will hear of or See the Inviteracy of the Boston writers. You and I seem the Butt of their Spleen and Resentment." *JP* 2:428-29.

69. *JP* 2:461. See Shirley to Johnson, August 4, 1755. In Massachusetts Historical Society. In July 1756, Wraxall was ordering "Gorgets with the King's Arms & your Cypher." *JP* 2:523.

70. *DH* 2:718.

71. *A Review of the Military Operations in North-America, from the commencement of the French Hostilities on the Frontiers of Virginia in 1753, to the Surrender of Oswego, on the 14th of August, 1756; in a Letter to a Nobleman. Interspersed with various observations, characters, and anecdotes; necessary to give light into the conduct of American transactions in general, and more especially into the political management of affairs in NEW-YORK.* For later editions and comment see L. C. Wroth, *An American Bookshelf, 1757*, Appendix VII, pp. 167-71. An edition published in Dublin in 1757 had an appendix of letters and documents not included in the English edition. One of these was Johnson's letter of September 9, 1755, to the several governors.

72. Colden Papers, N. Y. Hist. Soc., *Collections*, (1921) 5:157-59. Alexander Colden to Cadwallader Colden, July 12, 1757.

73. William Smith, *History of the Province of New York*, 2:311.

74. London: Printed for R. and J. Dodsley, in Pall Mall; . . . 1758. Introduction, viii.

75. Schutz, *Shirley*, is not uncritical of his subject and supplies material for evaluation of his career. Chap. 12, "Patronage Lost," describes the fall of Shirley, the last section his efforts in London. The author pays little attention to the above-mentioned tracts, and is critical of Johnson and Pownall.

CHAPTER 19: THE FATE OF GENERALS, 1756

1. *JP* 2:400-401. Pargellis, *Military Affairs*, p. 52.

2. *JP* 2:388-89.

3. *DR* 10:326. Vaudreuil wrote September 25, 1755, that Joncaire had gone from village to village meeting the emissaries of Johnson and Shirley in each.

4. *JP* 2:389.

5. *JP* 2:387–89.

6. *JP* 9:328.

7. *JP* 9:329.

8. *JP* 9:334–38. The letter of Gideon Hawley, Missionary at Oquaga, December 27, 1755, telling of the return of the messengers.

9. Cf. Anthony F. C. Wallace, *King of the Delawares, Teedyuscung, 1700–1763* (Philadelphia, 1949).

10. January 3, 1756. *JP* 2:401–3.

11. Cf. Ralph L. Ketcham, "Conscience War and Politics in Pennsylvania, 1755–1757," *William and Mary Quarterly*, 20 (July 1963): 416–39.

12. For biographies of Scaroyady (Monacatootha), and Andrew (sometimes erroneously called "Henry", confusing the French Andre and Henri) Montour, see P. A. W. Wallace, *Indians in Pennsylvania*, pp. 175–76, 178.

13. Narrative of Scaroyady. *Pa. Col. Rec.* 7:65–67.

14. *JP* 2:426–27.

15. *Pa. Col. Rec.* 7:90.

16. *JP* 2:438–39. Richard Peters also tried to enlist Claus to command fifty or sixty Jersey Indians. "I did not give him a conclusive answer but told him I would consult Skaronyade abt. it." *JP* 2:440. The passage of the Indians via New York and Albany is recorded in *JP* 2:461, 465, 521–22.

17. *Pa. Col. Rec.* 7:95.

18. *JP* 9:343–46.

19. *JP* 9:347ff. "Ogilvie Diary," pp. 368–70.

20. "Ogilvie Diary," p. 369.

21. *JP* 9:357. "Ogilvie Diary," p. 370. These prisoners had been taken to New York, but brought up again to satisfy the Indians' demands. Cf. *JP* 2:388.

22. *JP* 9:363.

23. *JP* 9:364.

24. *JP* 9:368.

25. *JP* 9:371.

26. *JP* 9:370–73.

27. *JP* 9:359, 373.

28. *JP* 9:375–82.

29. "Ogilvie Diary," p. 372.

30. *JP* 2:440. *Pa. Col Rec.* 7:74–88.

31. *JP* 2:447.

32. *JP* 2:465, 467–69.

33. To the Board of Trade, May 28, 1756. *DH* 2:721–25. Claus writing from Philadelphia, April 5, 1756, reported "The Govrs. Party and the Quakers, (whose head is Mr. Franklin) are continually in Dispute with one another, and nothing but Confusion reigns here. . . . Mr Peters is Sometimes Most distracted and dreads its Ruin if things go on as they do." *JP* 2:439.

34. *Pa. Col. Rec.* 7:144. Shirley advised Morris that a suspension until after the Onondaga meeting might be prudent. But he sought to place an invidious interpretation upon Johnson's letter. The same protest had been made to him by Sir Charles Hardy "so that Sir William Johnson seems to have taken it from him, otherwise I should be apt to imagine that the Letter was Dictated by the Vanity and Impertinence of Sir William Johnson's conceited Secretary, and I cannot avoid saying that the Treatment of you carries an Assuming Insolent Air in it." *Pa. Col. Rec.* 7:112.

35. *JP* 9:384, 392–93, 407, 416, 435–38. *DR* 7:42.

36. *JP* 9:457–58.

37. *JP* 9:410–11, 416, 425. *DR* 7:42. Forts were also requested by the Schoharie and Oquaga Indians.

38. For French description of the forts, see *DR* 10:403–4. See also the plan and description of the forts at the Carrying Place, *JP* 10:42. Later construction of Fort Wood Creek, with dam and sluice gates, shortened the carry to a little over a mile between that point and Fort Williams.

39. *JP* 9:402–3, 449–50. Warren Johnson wrote in 1760 that Sir William's command of the Albany Regiment reached five thousand men; and was allowed seventy for Fort Johnson. *JP* 13:195.

40. *JP* 403–6, 409, 439, 447.

41. *JP* 9:406, 410, 417.

42. *DR* 10:396–97, 403–4, 529. These French accounts do not agree on details because some had information second hand.

43. *JP* 9:414–15. The French account mentioned firing in the "loop holes," and Shirley could

not understand the absence of portholes and flankers, for he knew the plans for the fort he had seen the previous fall. He praised Johnson's march to the scene, but wondered why he did not follow the enemy; Johnson replied that it was useless, for the enemy had a four-day start on their return. *JP* 9:426, 437.

44. *JP* 9:420, 424.

45. *JP* 9:428-35.

46. *JP* 9:423, 436-38. Alexander, *Conduct of Shirley*, p. 76.

47. *JP* 9:440, 450, 452, 456, 460, 462-70. He also asked the castles to meet him with an escort of warriors.

48. *DR* 7:130-34. *JP* 9:478. For expense accounts of the meeting, see *JP* 2:486-87; 612, 615, 617.

49. *DR* 7:134.

50. *DH* 2:728-29.

51. *DH* 2:729. *DR* 7:145, 148. The overland road to Oswego was not built largely because contractors dared not work in the dangerous country. See *JP* 2:526-27, 533; 9:404-5, 513-14.

52. *DH* 2:729. *DR* 7:149-50.

53. *DR* 7:152-58. *JP* 2:499-500.

54. *DH* 2:730-31. *DR* 7:158-60.

55. *DR* 7:158.

56. *DR* 7:130n., 151; *JP* 2:507n.

57. This is the view of Anthony F. C. Wallace, an anthropologist and student of Indian tribes, in his *King of the Delawares*, pp. 97-100.

58. *DH* 2:731.

59. Pargellis, *Lord Loudoun*, pp. 42-43, 82. *JP* 2:458.

60. *JP* 2:464-65, 471.

61. *JP* 2:514-15.

62 Larabee *et al.*, eds., *Papers of Benjamin Franklin* (New Haven, 1959-) 6:472-77. Later, after the failure of the campaign of 1756-57, Franklin expressed disillusionment.

63. *JP* 2:519.

64. *JP* 2:515-16. Loudoun's elaborate entourage made every earlier general's "family" and "table" look simple and frugal. After returning to New York in August, he rented the house of a wealthy merchant "in Whitehall, a stones throw from Fort George," as his headquarters. "In it he set up a retinue of servants brought from England; in its stables his grooms and his nineteen horses with their housings of black, green and gold, his traveling coach, his chariot, his street coach. Every evening, except when his hospitality was repaid elsewhere, there dined with him at the long table heavily weighted with silver, his own intimate 'family' made up of his aides-de-camp Captain James Cunningham and Lieutenant Gilbert McAdam, his secretary John Appy, Thomas Pownall, and such members of the general staff as Sir John St. Clair, Webb and his aide Captain Roger Morris. Doctor Richard Huck, the gay and learned wit who had been surgeon in Loudoun's Scottish regiment in '45 was often there, as were John Young of the Royal Americans, Loudoun's special protegé, and James Robertson, later governor of New York, upon whose good sense Loudoun came more and more to rely. Governor Sir Charles Hardy and the De Lanceys were regular guests. They drank much wine—nineteen dozen bottles of claret, thirty-one dozen of Madeira, a dozen of Burgundy, four bottles of port and eight of Rhenish in a single week at Christmas of 1757-." Pargellis, *Lord Loudoun*, pp. 167-68.

65. *DH* 2:727.

66. See episode of September 1756. *JP* 9:546-48.

67. *JP* 2:529, 533, 544; 9:496, 499-500; 13:89. *DR* 7:177-78. See also Loudoun's report of the Jerry affair to Cumberland, August 20, 1756. Pargellis, *Military Affairs*, p. 225.

68. Shirley in a letter of April 10, 1756, from Boston expressed great confidence that Bradstreet's armed bateaumen would safeguard Oswego. *JP* 9:426-27. William Smith, reflecting Shirley's partisans' views, April 2, doubted the reports of Oswego's weakness. Diary, 2:405-6.

69. Mackellar's journal, in Pargellis, *Military Affairs*, pp. 187-91.

70. Pargellis, *Lord Loudoun*, pp. 152-55, shows that supplies were unnecessarily held up by merchants and contractors, and bad management was responsible for short rations, discontent, sickness, and even mutiny.

71. Bradstreet's report, as given in the *New York Mercury*, dated in Albany July 13. *DH* 1:482-87. Mackellar's journal at Oswego. Pargellis, *Military Affairs*, p. 200. French reports are found in *DR* 10:471, 483; and Bougainville diary, E. P. Hamilton, ed., *Adventure in the Wilderness* (Norman, Okla., 1964), p. 6.

72. Montcalm's report, *DH* 1:489-95. *DR* 10:440-44. There are many accounts of the fall of Oswego. Other French reports in *DR* 10:459-87. See also Pouchot, *Memoir*, 1:62-67. Pouchot was present as an engineer.

73. *DH* 1:490-94. *DR* 440-44. Brackets indicate variants in the two versions.

74. *DH* 1:494-95. Terms of surrender, *DH* 1:495-97; also given in *DR* 10:474-75.

75. English accounts of the fall of Oswego are widely varied, depending upon the points of view of their authors and their assessment of the blame. Some justify the action of the garrison,

their courage and discretion; others are unsparing in their condemnation and speak of unsoldierly conduct, shameful treachery, and the failure of commanders to heed warnings or to foresee the attack. Sir William was later to say that if Indian intelligence had been trusted Oswego would not have been lost. *DR* 7:170, Johnson to Lords of Trade, November 10, 1756. For firsthand accounts, see *JP* 2:556, 563–64, 653. Pargellis. *Military Affairs*, p. 474.

Loudoun in his reports blamed Shirley for the weakness of the forts, the neglect of the garrison, and for the peculations and intrigues of traders and contractors. Pargellis, *Lord Loudoun*, pp. 152–66, supports these charges and finds Shirley and his secretary, William Alexander, blamable for the shortages of provisions and supply. Shirley was defended by pamphlets, previously cited: Alexander, *Conduct of Shirley,* and William Livingston, *Review of the Military Operations in North America,* pp. 146–63, which was dated September 20, 1756. Gipson, *British Empire*, 6:200–201, strongly supports Shirley against all detractors.

76. *JP* 2:543–47, 549–50, 552, 554. *JP* 9:506–8, 511–14. *DR* 7:187, 193. See Loudoun to Cumberland, in Pargellis, *Military Affairs*, p. 232.

77. *DR* 7:191. The French had no illusions about their influence over the Indians about Oswego. A dispatch dated August 30, 1756, reported: "The Indians of the Upper Countries appear glad that Chouaguen has fallen, but, at the bottom of their hearts, they are not satisfied. It was a place where they found as much Rum as they pleased, goods much cheapers than with us, and I am persuaded that the high prices of our merchandise will drive them to Orange [Albany] to trade their peltries, which is a serious injury to the trade of this Colony." *DR* 10:479.

78. *JP* 9:491–92.

79. *JP* 2:537–38. These instructions may be better understood by referring to Guy Johnson's sketch of Fort Johnson in 1759; this shows the eminence behind the house, the barracks, the flanking blockhouses, and the Indian encampments. See also the description of a French observer of 1757, quoted above.

80. *JP* 9:541.

81. *JP* 9:528–29.

82. Pargellis *Military Affairs*, pp. 170–73, 183.

83. Pargellis, *Lord Loudoun,* pp. 90–91. *JP* 9:543.

84. Pargellis, *Military Affairs*, pp. 239–40.

85. *JP* 9:543.

86. *JP* 9:544.

87. *JP* 9:550.

88. The journals of Louis Antoine de Bougainville cover this period. They reflect his impatience with French officers, graft at the forts, and his dislike of Indians and their ways. E. P. Hamilton, ed., *Adventure in the Wilderness,* pp. 31–64.

89. Gipson, *British Empire*, 6:208.

90. *JP* 2:437–38. *DR* 7:208–10. Pargellis, *Lord Loudoun,* pp. 258–59.

91. *JP* 2:262; 9:537–38.

92. See Anthony F. C. Wallace, *King of the Delawares. JP* 9:522. Johnson to Loudoun, September 8, 1756. See also the full treatment of these conferences in P. A. W. Wallace, *Conrad Weiser,* pp. 439–65.

93. N. B. Wainwright, *George Croghan,* pp. 119–20. P. A. W. Wallace, *Conrad Weiser,* p. 468.

94. N. B. Wainwright, *George Croghan,* pp. 123–25. *JP* 2:658–59, 684.

95. Gipson, *British Empire*, 7:91–107. Pargellis, *Military Affairs*, pp. 391–93, 396. *JP* 2:733.

CHAPTER 20: THE FATE OF GENERALS, 1757–58

1. *Journals of Major Robert Rogers,* F. B. Hough, ed. (Albany, 1883), pp. 66–74. Hereafter cited as *Rogers's Journals.* E. P. Hamilton, ed., *Adventure in the Wilderness,* pp. 80–81.

2. *DR* 10:563–64, 570–72, 646. E. P. Hamilton, ed., *Adventure in the Wilderness,* pp. 95–98.

3. *JP* 9:666–68.

4. *JP* 9:667–68.

5. *DR* 10:591, 594, 647, 734. Bougainville reported the incident with horror for the cruelty of the Indians, who speared the drowning English like fish. "They put in a pot and ate three prisoners." E. P. Hamilton, ed., *Adventure in the Wilderness,* pp. 142–43.

6. Pargellis, *Military Affairs*, pp. 178–80. Letter of Harry Gordon to Robert Napier, June 22, 1756.

7. "An Eyewitness Account by James Furniss of the Surrender of Fort William Henry, August 1757" ed. William S. Ewing, *New York History,* 42 (July 1961): 307–16.

8. *Ibid.* pp. 310–11.

9. E. P. Hamilton, ed., *Adventure in the Wilderness,* pp. 150–51.

10. *Ibid.* pp. 152–53. *DR* 10:606.

11. E. P. Hamilton, ed., *Adventure in the Wilderness,* pp. 154–59.

12. *Ibid.* p. 159. *DR* 10:599. Furniss, "Eyewitness Account," pp. 311–12. See Montcalm's ultimatum and Monro's reply in Loudoun Papers, Huntington Library, no. LO 6660.

13. E. P. Hamilton, ed., *Adventure in the Wilderness*, pp. 159–61. *DR* 10:597–99. Furniss, "Eyewitness Account," pp. 311–12.

14. Pargellis, *Lord Loudoun*, pp. 244–45, analyzed the forces available and the disposition of troops, and the probable strategy. Webb on paper could have mustered six or seven thousand men. Montcalm estimated Webb's strength as six thousand. *DR* 10:597–98. See also *JP* 2:730.

15. *JP* 9:809–10.

16. *JP* 9:810.

17. *Ibid.*

18. *JP* 2:728–29.

19. *JP* 2:729.

20. I am indebted to Colonel Edward P. Hamilton for calling my attention to this letter of Bougainville to Madame Herault, April 21, 1758, printed in French in René de Kerallain, *Jeunesse de Bougainville* (Paris, 1896). He has since translated it and published it in his *Adventure in the Wilderness*, p. 333. Since the romantic story undoubtedly was embroidered and varied in its retelling, one feels justified in a free translation or paraphrase. Perhaps it is only a bit of folklore, but it is a contemporary tale from one who was close to the whole operation.

The translation of the letter poses a number of puzzles. Literally, "Johnson called to witness the Belgian lion" (Johnson alors prend à temoin le Lion Belgique). For *Belgian* we might better read *Celtic* (the Belgae were Celts), for Johnson was an Irishman; and he may well have sworn by the rampant lion on the British arms.

Colonel Hamilton's translation of "son braye" as "a garter" I think is weak; Kerallain interpolated here, pièce de drap qui tient lieu de haute-de-chausse, which can only mean loincloth. And what greater insult could Johnson have given the general, or one which would be better understood by the Indians!

21. Text of the letter written by Bartram, aide-de-camp, in Loudon Papers, no. LO 6660. Letter summarized in *DR* 10:602–3, 612–13, and in Bougainville journal. E. P. Hamilton, ed., *Adventure in the Wilderness*, pp. 162–63.

22. *DR* 10:603, 612–13; E.P. Hamilton, ed., *Adventure in the Wilderness*, pp. 162–63, 166–67 Monro in Loudoun Papers, no. LO 6660.

23. Loudoun Papers, no. LO 6660.

24. *DR* 10:604.

25. *DR* 10:604–5. Bougainville in his official report to Montreal, however, noted 60 killed or wounded. He said the English lost 200 killed, and 150 wounded. *DR* 10:616.

26. *DR* 10:605, 615–16. Loudoun Papers no. LO 6660.

27. Furniss, "An Eyewitness Account," pp. 313–14. The original in the W. L. Clements Library has been consulted on microfilm. Two shorter firsthand accounts of the massacre were printed by Francis Parkman, *Montcalm and Wolfe*, Appendix F (Frontenac edition, Boston, 1907), 3:276–79, by Miles Whitworth, a surgeon, and by one Frye (perhaps Colonel Joseph Fry of the Massachusetts regiment). Bougainville, who had left for Montreal before the massacre, and Pouchot (*Memoir*, 2:89–90) are contemporary French accounts. Gipson (*British Empire*, 7:85–87) relies upon the French historian Waddington, who based his story on French records and who exonerated the French general.

28. *DR* 10:616. Cf. contemporary estimate of numbers in Loudoun Papers, no. LO 6660.

29. E. P. Hamilton, ed., *Adventure in the Wilderness*, pp. 173–74. *DR* 10:616.

30. *DR* 10:598.

31. E. P. Hamilton, ed., *Adventure in the Wilderness*, pp. 172–73.

32. *DR* 7:274. De Lancey to Lords of Trade, August 24, 1757. John Knox, *Historical Journal. . . .* (London, 1769), 1:43–44. *Gentleman's Magazine*, 27 (1757): 475.

33. *DR* 10:615–16.

34. Furniss, "Eyewitness Account," p. 314. E. P. Hamilton, ed., *Adventure in the Wilderness*, p. 174. *DR* 10:616, 640, 650–51.

35. Pouchot, *Memoir*, 1:91–92.

36. *Gentleman's Magazine*, 27 (1757): 475–76.

37. *DR* 7:278. September 28, 1757.

38. Loudoun Papers, LO nos. 5509, 4479, 3994, 4106.

39. Pargellis, *Military Affairs*, pp. 293, 317.

40. Pargellis, *Lord Loudoun*, pp. 337–61; Gipson, *British Empire*, 7:174–75. News of the recall did not reach Albany until late in March. *JP* 2:800.

41. *JP* 2:749, 762, 764–67.

42. *JP* 9:887–88. Dated March 24, 1758. Sir William had taken up these same points with Loudoun, and with Abercromby as his aide. See *JP* 2:762, 767, 772. Loudoun had been a little testy about Wraxall.

43. *JP* 9:890–93. A request by Sir William for favors for "a relative of mine" (Guy Johnson) was turned down.

44. *JP* 9:894–95.

45. *JP* 9:901–6.
46. *JP* 9:912, 924–25, 936.
47. *JP* 9:926–27.
48. *JP* 9:896–97, 917–20.
49. *JP* 2:851–53.
50. *JP* 2:854. See also report of John Appy, secretary to Abercromby, July 2, relating this affair. *JP* 2:869–70.
51. *JP* 2:870–72, 885–86.
52. Biographical sketch. *DR* 10:735. *JP* 2:799–800; 9:858 888, 891. *Pennsylvania Gazette,* December 8, 1757.
53. *Pennsylvania Gazette,* July 6, 1758.
54. *Ibid.*
55. *DR* 10:725–26.
56. *DR* 10:725–26. *Pennsylvania Gazette,* July 27, 1758. Howe's burial in St. Peter's Church, Albany, where today a marble slab in the vestibule commemorates the earlier interment, has been the subject of controversy. Discovery of a rude stone near the battlefield, in 1889, raised the question of whether he was ever taken to Albany. See arguments in *New York State Historical Association Proceedings,* 10 (1910): The weight of evidence, especially the church records, supports the Albany burial. Joseph Hooper, *History of St. Peter's Church,* pp. 167, 519–26.
57. *DR* 10:726. *Pennsylvania Gazette,* July 27, 1758.
58. *DR* 10:723, 726.
59. *DR* 10:726, 735, 763.
60. *DR* 10:726–27, 736. *Pennsylvania Gazette,* July 17, 1758. "Journal of the Rev. John Cleaveland," *Bulletin of the Fort Ticonderoga Museum,* 10, no. 3 (1959): 205.
61. *DR* 10:724, 736, 741.
62. See announcement of his being superseded by General Amherst, Whitehall, September 18, 1758. *DR* 7:345.
63. *DR* 10:725, 739–41, 797–98. After the battle Abercromby commended the Indians for their good behavior and help. *JP* 9:941.
64. *Rogers's Journals,* pp. 121–24.
65. Bradstreet Papers, American Antiquarian Society. Bradstreet to Amherst, March 24, 1758. *JP* 9:930. For this expedition see the contemporary printed account attributed to Bradstreet: *An Impartial Account of Lieut. Col. Bradstreet's Expedition to Fort Frontenac. By a Volunteer on the Expedition* (London, 1759; reprint, Toronto, 1940). Bradstreet [?] related that Lord Howe approved his plan to attack Frontenac but that Abercromby and others raised objections.
66. *JP* 9:933.
67. *JP* 2:882, 886; 9:952–53, 963–64, 967, 969–70; 10:12, 18–19, 51, 54. Parkman, *Montcalm and Wolfe* 2:335–36. stated that "only a few Oneidas joined him (Bradstreet)" and that the colonel had to restrain the Oneidas, who were bent on scalping. Colonel Charles Clinton's Journal, 1758, typed copy now in New York State Library, pp. 13–18. Clinton commanded the New York militia. His journal from June to October 1758 contains a good account of the march to Frontenac, the action and the return journey. The original was burned in the Albany Capitol fire in 1911. Frank H. Severance made a copy before the fire and later deposited it with the State Library.
68. *Boston Gazette,* September 11, 1758. Clinton's Journal, pp. 12–18. *JP* 2:889. *DR* 10:349, 414, 656. Bradstreet's *Impartial Account* differs from other accounts in details; gives the expedition leaving the Carrying Place but 2,737 men, 270 bateaumen, 42 Indians; a writer in the *Boston Gazette* gave the expedition 3,339 men. The Bradstreet account tells of the Indians being recruited by him through the Onondaga chief, Red Head. It makes no mention of Sir William's aid or of the Indian officers, such as the Butlers. In other details it is much fuller.
69. Clinton's Journal, pp. 20–21.
70. *JP* 2:889.
71. Clinton's Journal, pp. 20–21.
72. Clinton's Journal, pp. 21–25. *Boston Gazette,* September 18, 25, 1758. Value of all goods lost by the French, taken or destroyed, was estimated at £700,000. *JP* 2:894–95; 10:7. For French estimates of their loss, see *DR* 10:821, 823, 831.
73. Terms of surrender. *DR* 10:825–26. *Boston Gazette,* September 25, 1758. Clinton Journal, pp. 25–29.
74. "Cleaveland Journal," pp. 217, 219, 221, 225. *JP* 10:1, 5–6.
75. *Boston Gazette,* December 11, 1758.
76. "Cleaveland Journal," pp. 227–29. *JP* 3:12–15.
77. *JP* 10:20, 25, 45. *DR* 10:831.
78. *JP* 3:1.
79. For detailed accounts of the Easton meeting see P. A. W. Wallace, *Conrad Weiser,* pp.

520–52; and N. B. Wainwright, *George Croghan*, pp. 143–51. *JP* 2:873, 890–91; 3:1–2.
80. *JP* 2:770, 826–27.
81. *JP* 3:10–11; 9:951–52.
82. *JP* 2:875–78.
83. *JP* 3:4; 10:43–48, 57; 13:113. See also P. A. W. Wallace, *Conrad Weiser, loc. cit.*
84. *JP* 10:54.

CHAPTER 21: NIAGARA–KEY TO THE CONTINENT, 1759

1. Pitt to Amherst, December 21, 1758. *DR* 10:355–59.
2. *DR* 10:907–11.
3. *JP* 3:14. 16. 18. See also J. C. Long, *Lord Jeffery Amherst, A Soldier of the King* (New York, 1933), pp. 86–90.
4. *JP* 3:19–20. Dated February 16, 1759.
5. *JP* 3:21.
6. *DR* 7:378–90.
7. *DR* 7:391.
8. *DR* 7:391–92.
9. *JP* 3:27–28, 31.
10. *JP* 3:37, 38–39, 40–41.
11. *DH* 2:785. See also *Journal of Jeffery Amherst*, J. Clarence Webster, ed. (Toronto and Chicago, 1931), pp. 107–8. Cited hereafter as *Amherst's Journal.*
12. Quoted in Severance, *Old Frontier of France,* 2:275–76, as in Amherst's journal. The published *Amherst Journal* does not have this entry. Severance, of course, used this material in manuscript, and may have had access to a different source.
13. *JP* 3:42–43. Several entries in his journal show Amherst's fear that the Indians would reveal the plans to the French. *Amherst's Journal* pp. 109, 111, 118.
14. Dated May 17, 1759, and sent with the Indian proceedings at Canajoharie, *DR* 7:376.
15. *JP* 3:43–44; 10:114. *Amherst's Journal*, p. 114.
16. *JP* 3:46, 10:115.
17. *DR* 7:399, biographical note. Severance, *Old Frontier of France,* 2:276, claims there were 2,560 New Yorkers and 700 Rhode Islanders. While the New York Assembly proposed 2,680 men, a study of all the figures for the campaign leads to the conclusion that the militia did not exceed 1,020 active soldiers. Colonel Glen in March said the Albany militia quota was 420. Yates mentions 300 leaving Schenectady with him on June 1; 520 militia were left at Oswego. Another 500 went with the boats from Oswego to Niagara with 1,700 regulars. According to Amherst, some militiamen served as bateaumen. *Amherst's Journal*, pp. 113–14. For the artillery comment, see *JP* 3:112, 139, and *DR* 8:702–3n.
18. Yates Diary. Copy made by Severance in Buffalo Historical Society. *Boston Gazette,* June 25, 1759.
19. *JP* 3:49–54. Prideaux and Johnson Orderly Book, *JP* 3:48–105, covers the period from June 21, at Oneida Lake, until August 19, at Oswego. Original in the New-York Historical Society.
20. Orderly Book, *JP* 3:55–60. Yates Diary.
21. *DR* 7:395. For scouting service see Sir William's accounts of Indian expenses. *JP.* 173–74. *DR* 8:703n.
22. *DR* 7:395; 10:961.
23. *JP* 3:134–35. *New York Mercury,* July 30, 1759. Letter from Camp at Lake Ontario, July 7, 1759. This is the best and most detailed account. A report quoting a courier from Albany in *Boston Gazette,* July 23, 1759, had the dates of the attack wrong and other details at a variance. Amherst, recording the event from a letter from Haldimand written on July 7, implied that there was some warning of the attack and that some scouts had seen a hundred bateaux on the lake; but this seems to have been at the same time as the attack. Amherst also recorded that the one hundred and fifty Indians were led by Abbé Picquet of La Presentation. Chevalier La Corne in the footnote is confused with his brother, La Corne St. Luc. This confusion is also found in Severance, *Old Frontier of France,* 2:288–89, and in Gipson, *British Empire,* 7:357, who rely on the same source. *Amherst's Journal,* pp. 139–40.
24. Prideaux Bay, by a strange orthographical mutation, has now become Braddock's Bay; Johnson Creek remains one of the few place names to his credit. *JP* 3:63.
25. *JP* 3:63–65; 111–12, 174. *DR* 10:977–78. A French journal of the siege was discovered in an embrasure of the fort after its capture. Printed in the *Maryland Gazette,* July 25, 1759, it was later published in Orasmus Turner, *Pioneer History of the Holland Purchase of Western New York* (Buffalo, N. Y., 1849), pp. 206–13, from which present citations are given.
26. Deposition of Stephen Coffen. *DR* 6:837.
27. *DR* 10:325–26, 411, 414, 667–68, and biographical note. See also Severance, *Old Frontier of France,* 2:194, 389. A principal source is Pierre Pouchot, *Memoir upon the Late War in North America between the French and English, 1755–60,* translated and edited by

Franklin B. Hough (Roxbury, Mass., 1866) two volumes. Written after Pouchot's return to France, it was published there in 1781. Another translation of the portion dealing with the siege of Niagara is in Paris Documents, *DR* 10:977–92. Although written by Pouchot, it speaks of him in the third person. For biography of Pouchot, see *DCB* 3:534–37.

28. Pouchot, *Memoir*, 1:52–53. *DR* 10:977.

29. *Ibid.*

30. *Ibid.*

31. *DR* 10:977–78. Severance, *Old Frontier of France*, 2:283, described the terrain as it was in 1917. The shore had eroded considerably since 1759, but its character was substantially the same. See Demler map, discussed below.

32. Complete original map in New-York Historical Society. The left half only, from a copy owned by Peter A. Porter of Niagara Falls, was printed in *JP* 3:81; this was apparently all that was seen by Severance, who made a composite of maps but omitted some of the detail shown on the left half of the map.

33. *DR* 10:978. See also the French journal, Turner, *Holland Purchase*, pp. 209–10.

34. Letter of John Ogilvie, July 14, 1759, quoted in Severance, *Old Frontier of France*, 2:291. Letter of Prideaux, July 13, 1759. *Ibid* 2:288.

35. *DR* 10:979.

36. *Ibid.* A different translation in Pouchot, *Memoir*, 1:166–67. The episode is also mentioned in the Yates Diary, and in the French journal, Turner, *Holland Purchase*, p. 210.

37. Quoted in Severance, *Old Frontier of France*, 2:289.

38. *DR* 10:977–80. These two posts, the fort at Little Niagara above the falls and the Magazin Royal, Chabert Joncaire's trading post below the escarpment (near present-day Lewiston), were the termini of the portage. They were important for the line of communication rather than for defense.

39. *JP* 3:65–76. Orderly book. See also Severance, *Old Frontier of France*, 2:283–85.

40. *DR* 10:980–84, Pouchot's journal.

41. *DR* 10:984.

42. Rutherford to Haldimand, July 14, 1759. Allan Macleane, July 21, was even more caustic: "[Johnson] has nobody can help him for our Engineers god damn them Demler has shown himself a fool & blockhead." Severance, *Old Frontier of France*, 2:289–90.

43. *DR* 10:979–80. Pouchot, *Memoir*, 1:167–71; anonymous French journal in Turner, *Holland Purchase*, p. 211.

44. *DR* 10:979–81. Pouchot, *Memoir*, 1:171–77.

45. *DR* 10:983–84. Pouchot, *Memoir* 1:180–82. The French journal in Turner, *Holland Purchase*, p. 211, says the battery was trying to hit the commandant's house. Pouchot said the battery was on Montreal Point, which is farther north; the battery as shown on the map was directly opposite the fort. Pouchot erred also in placing the death of Prideaux on the 18th.

46. *JP* 3:76–77, 106, 112. Severance, *Old Frontier of France*, 2:290–91, quoting a letter of Allan Macleane.

47. *JP* 3:106. *Amherst's Journal*, p. 147. Amherst, in his general orders at Ticonderoga, July 28, 1759, wrote: "The Gunner inconsiderately firing as the General was passing, the shell burst as it cleared the mouth of the coehorn, and a large piece of it struck him on the side of the head." *Bulletin of the Fort Ticonderoga Museum*, 6 (January, 1942): 104. In both places Amherst incorrectly gave the time of death as the evening of the 19th.

48. *JP* 3:77–78. Another version of this quoted by Severance, *Old Frontier of France*, 2:299, omits the parenthetical "(on me I trust)," which seems to indicate Sir William's uncertainty at the moment.

49. *JP* 3:106–7.

50. Quoted in Severance, *Old Frontier of France*, 2:290–91.

51. *New York Mercury*, August 6, 1759. *Boston Post Boy*, August 6, 1759.

52. *JP* 3:116. In his diary Sir William wrote: "Colonel Haldimand arrived here . . . to claim the command, which I refused giving up, as my commission gave me rank of him. He gave up the point until General Amherst's pleasure was known, which may be soon, as Col. Haldimand, on receipt of my letter, wrote him upon it." *JP* 13:116. A year later Lieutenant Colonel Eyre Massy wrote Pitt, July 11, 1760, that as senior officer of the regulars at Niagara he thought himself entitled to the command, but he made no effort to assert his claim. Gipson, *British Empire*, 7:356n.

53. *Amherst's Journal*, p. 147.

54. *JP* 3:107–8.

55. French journal in Turner, *Holland Purchase*, pp. 211–12. *DR* 10:985. A letter of July 28 in the *Boston Gazette*, August 13, 1759, stated that Sir William had erected a "third battery within 100 yards of the Flag Bastion."

56. *JP* 3:76–77.

57. Pouchot, *Memoir*, 1:184–85. *DR* 10:985–86.

58. *Ibid.*

59. *Ibid.*

60. *DR* 10:950–52.
61. Pouchot, *Memoir*, 1:162–63, 187n. *Boston Gazette*, August 13, 1759, letter from Pittsburgh, July 15, tells of the council at Venango. *DR* 10:986. French journal in Turner, *Holland Purchase*, p. 212.
62. Severance, *Old Frontier of France*, 2:314–15.
63. *DR* 10:986–87; French journal in Turner, *Holland Purchase*, p. 212.
64. *Ibid.*
65. *DR* 7:402.
66. Pouchot, *Memoir*, 1:190–91.
67. *DR* 7:402.
68. *Ibid.* Pouchot, *Memoir*, 1:192.
69. *DR* 7:402–3. Pouchot did report that the "English came out of their abattis almost in file with fixed bayonets and running, but by the little firing we heard, we judged that all the battalion had retired." *Memoir*, 1:192–93.
70. Pouchot, *Memoir*, 1:191–92.
71. *DR* 7:402–3. The anonymous French journal recorded: "Our army was routed and almost all made prisoners, by the treachery of our savages." Turner, *Holland Purchase*, p. 213.
72. Pouchot *Memoir*, 1:193, note by F. B. Hough. *DR* 10:988.
73. Pouchot, *Memoir*, 1:194; *DR* 10:988–89.
74. Pouchot, *Memoir*, 1:194–98.
75. *Ibid.* 1:198–201. *DR* 10:990–92. There is a slight difference in the two translations of the terms. The *Memoir* has a fuller account of the capitulation and its aftermath. The Paris Documents (*DR*:10) version stops rather abruptly at this point.
76. Pouchot, *Memoir*, 1:200–204. *JP* 3:115. *DR* 10:992.
77. Pouchot, *loc. cit. Boston Gazette*, August 13, 1759.
78. Pouchot, *Memoir*, 1:203.
79. *DR* 10:992. Pouchot, *Memoir*, 1:204–7.

CHAPTER 22: VICTORY AND THE WEST

1. *JP* 3:108–11, 114–20.
2. *JP* 10:990, 992.
3. *JP* 13:117.
4. John Knox, *Historical Journal*, 2:135.
5. *JP* 3:115–16.
6. *JP* 13:117. Sir William's diary recorded his intention "to have it printed, or plates made of it for the benefit of the public." Engraved by De Bruls, it bore Sir William's new coat of arms in the lower left corner. It was advertised to be sold by subscription in the *New York Mercury*, June 7, 1762. The original complete engraving in the New-York Historical Society, as indicated above, is a prime source for the siege and battle. See discussion of this map in *New-York Historical Society Quarterly*, 32 (April 1948): 100.
7. *JP* 3:111–13.
8. New-York Historical Society, *Collections*, Lee Papers, 1 (1871): 20-21. Lee, a professional soldier, had been with Abercromby at Ticonderoga. He was with the garrison left at Niagara and on September 24 led fourteen men to Presque Isle to inquire for General Stanwix. *JP* 13:148.
9. *Ibid.*
10. *JP* 3:128–30. *Boston Evening Post*, August 13, 1759. Walpole, quoted in J. C. Long, *Lord Jeffery Amherst*, p. 116.
11. Quoted from a letter in Chatham MSS, Canadian Archives, in Gipson, *British Empire*, 6:354n. Gipson accepts Massy's view, although there is much evidence to support the honorable conduct of the Indians. Severance, *Old Frontier of France*, 2:341, concludes that in the decisive battle of the 24th, by their assistance to Johnson and the troops, "what might have been a victory by force of arms, was turned into a rout and a massacre."
12. *Boston Gazette*, August 13, 1759; same letter, dated August 6, in *Pennsylvania Gazette*, August 23, 1759.
13. Claus Papers, 23:103.
14. *JP* 13:115–17.
15. *JP* 3:115; 13:117.
16. *JP* 13:118.
17. *JP* 13:118–20.
18. *JP* 13:120–21.
19. *JP* 3:114, 120–21. *Boston Gazette*, August 27, 1759. Letter dated at Albany, August 12, at New York August 20. Pouchot, *Memoir*, 1:206–7. Turner, *Holland Purchase*, p. 213, quoting the *Maryland Gazette*. Pouchot was able to command at Fort Lévis the next year.
20. *JP* 13:118–20.

21. *JP* 13:125, 128; *Boston Gazette*, August 27, 1759, quoting a letter from Niagara of August 21.

22. *JP* 3:116-17; 13:113-18. Control of the lake was continually emphasized by Sir William. From Oswego, October 20, 1759, he wrote to William Baker in London: "We are building a Snow at Niagara will carry 10 Six Prs. but for want of Ship Carpenters sufficient I fear she will not be finished timely to be of any Service this year. There is a fine Harbour for building vessels of any Size at Niagara under the Command of the Fort and the greatest Quantity of the best Oaek for that purpose I ever saw in any Part of the World. The Enemy have yet two very pretty vessels carrying 10 Guns each, so that they keep the Dominion of that Lake untill our Snow appears upon it, we must by all Means have & keep the Domn. of this Lake, wch. will not only gain to our Interest with the proper Managmnt. all the Nats. of Indns. living beyond and around them, but secure to us all the Conquests made this Campn. in this Quarter of the Country from whence the Strength and Wealth of Canada have chiefly flowed." *JP* 3:140.

23. *JP* 13:117.

24. *JP* 3:92-94, 120; 13:116-18.

25. *JP* 13:120. See orders for Colonel Farquhar, *JP* 13:157-59.

26. *JP* 3:95-101, 117, 121-23; 13:120-21.

27. *JP* 3:121.

28. *JP* 3:97-99 (Orderly Book), 140; 13:121-25, 150-56. An excellent "Perspective View of Fort Ontario" was drawn by Lieutenant Francis Pfister in 1761, showing the pentagonal design as then completed. See photocopy in Crown Collection, NYSL.

29. *JP* 3:121-22.

30. *JP* 13:122-23. Johnson's diary supplies most of the data for the rest of the year's activities.

31 John Richard Alden, *General Gage in America* (Baton Rouge, La., 1948), pp. 1-48. *JP* 13:123-24.

32. *JP* 3:119, 131, 138; 13:121, 125-40, 44.

33. *JP* 13:122, 129-30, 137-38, 140-49.

34. *JP* 13:123-24.

35. *JP* 13:127, 136-37, 139-41.

36. *JP* 13:143-45.

37. *JP* 13:144-45. Sir William argued for a commando strike by six hundred men, whose small number would be concealed. That this might cause the enemy to abandon Isle Galot, if it was weak; and even if the enemy were too powerful, "I thought we could retreat with care and good conduct."

38. *JP* 3:145-46.

39. *JP* 13:146-47.

40. *JP* 10:126, 13:151.

41. *DR* 7:418. Pitt to Amherst, December 11, 1759.

42. Gipson, *British Empire*, 7:358, concludes that "a much more energetic leader than Gage might have hesitated." The biographer of Gage also justified his decision. Alden, *General Gage in America*, pp. 49-52.

43. *JP* 13:147-49, 154.

44. *JP* 13:153-54.

45. *JP* 3:122-23; 13:125, 186.

46. *JP* 13:135, 147, 150-54.

47. *JP* 3:178; 13:160.

48. *JP* 3:182-83, 185.

49. *Ibid*.

50. *JP* 3:196.

51. *JP* 3:141. He was still reporting to Baker the nonpayment of these services in December 1762. *JP* 3:508-9, 953-54.

52. *JP* 3:201, 278. *DR* 7:433. Dr. Richard Shuckburgh had long been a correspondent and confidant of Sir William. He probably came to this country in the early 1730s. He was an army surgeon to the Independent Companies of New York in 1737. In 1744 Dr. Alexander Hamilton met him in Albany. "Mr. Shakesburrough, surgeon to the fort, came in, who by his conversation seemed to have as little of the quack in him as any half-hewn doctor ever I had met with." *Hamilton's Itinerarium* (Hart, ed.), p. 78; *Gentleman's Progress* (Bridenbaugh, ed.), p. 65. (Neither editor identified him from the spelling of his name.) He served with the troops in 1744-48; was in London, 1754-55; again served with the troops, 1755-56; He attended the wounded Dieskau in New York. Then in 1758 he was with Abercromby's army near Albany, when he was reputed to have written the verses of "Yankee Doodle." Tradition associates this with the well at Fort Crailo, Rensselaer, N. Y. This episode, as well as the authorship, have been much disputed by musicologists. See Lewis A. Maverick, "Yankee Doodle," *American Neptune* (April, 1962). See biographical sketch, *DR* 8:244.

53. *JP* 10:125, 136; 13:136, 149, 151, 154.

54. *JP* 10:131-36. *Amherst's Journal*, p. 189, noted Stanwix's decision of October 10 not to go to the relief of Niagara.

55. *JP* 10:138-39, 148-50. The letter of February 16, 1760, carried by the Indian Andrew Montour, was lost, while Montour was detained in Carlisle by a tavern debt; Johnson's of May 14, 1760, repeated the contents of the earlier letter.

56. *Amherst's Journal*, pp. 182-83, 188, Amherst first learned of Rogers's exploit from the French, November 2; the details came from Rogers on November 7. The hazardous and costly return of the rangers would not be learned of until later.

57. *Amherst's Journal*, pp. 189-98.

58. J. C. Long, *Lord Jeffery Amherst*, pp. 126-27; Gipson, *British Empire*, 7:447.

59. *JP* 3:192-93.

60. *JP* 3:197, 199, 201.

61. *JP* 3:272; 10:137-38, 140-42; 13:167-68.

62. Another breakdown listed 5,300 regulars, 4,300 provincials and 150 of the royal artillery. To these must be added bateaumen and Indians. Gipson, *Britsh Empire*, 7:448-49 and note. *Amherst's Journal*, pp. 198-212 *passim*. A letter from Oneida Lake, July 22, 1760, gave: 6,000 provincials and rangers and 5,000 regulars. *Pennsylvania Gazette*, August 21, 1760.

63. *JP* 10:147. *Amherst's Journal*, p. 199.

64. *JP* 3:238, 250, 260; 10:150. *Amherst's Journal*, p. 213.

65. *JP* 3:218-19, 226.

66. *JP* 3:252-53, 255-56.

67. *Pennsylvania Gazette*, August 21, 1760.

68. *Amherst's Journal*, pp. 217-18, 220-25. Official records once gave the number as 706 warriors. *Pennsylvania Gazette*, August 21, 1760.

69. *Amherst's Journal*, p. 223. Like the brig and schooner, the snow was a square-rigged sailing vessel, but with a trisail mast abaft the main sail.

70. *Ibid*.

71. *JP* 3:261, 272-73; 10:143-44, 152-53, 156.

72. *Amherst's Journal*, p. 227.

73. Fonda's journal. *JP* 13:169-71. *Pennsylvania Gazette*, August 28, 1760. *Amherst's Journal*, pp. 228-30.

74. *Amherst's Journal*, pp. 230-32. *Pennsylvania Gazette*, September 25, 1760.

75. Pouchot, *Memoir*, 2:4-21. Gipson, *British Empire*, 7:450.

76. *Amherst's Journal*, pp. 232-38. A very detailed account of the action involving the boats was written in a letter dated September 22 and printed in the *Pennsylvania Gazette*, September 25, 1760. This told of the hand-to-hand struggle over the *Onondaga*, its surrender to the enemy, and of the retaking of the boat by the English before she sank. This being somewhat to Loring's discredit, a letter of August 25 from Isle Royale (*New York Mercury*, September 29, 1760) gave a fuller account in his defense. According to this account, the crew of the stranded *Onondaga* had mutinied and hoisted the white flag against Loring's will; Loring said he would shoot those who left the boat; succor had not come; Loring had the calf of his leg shot off; and he held on until night, when they abandoned the ship. The episode was very costly in lives.

77. *Amherst's Journal*, p. 239. Pouchot, *Memoir*, 2:34-37.

78. Pouchot, *Memoir*, 2:39-40.

79. *Amherst's Journal*, p. 240. Cf. Parkman, *Montcalm and Wolfe*, 3:215-16, quoting Lévis to Bourlamaque: "We shall be fortunate if the enemy amuse themselves with capturing it. My chief anxiety is that Amherst should reach Montreal so soon that we may not have time to unite our forces and to attack Haviland and Murray."

80. *Amherst's Journal*, pp. 241-43. *JP* 3:273. Warren Johnson, writing the following year, no doubt reflected Sir William's franker view. "The Indians were greatly disgusted at not being admitted into Fort Levi, on Isle Royal, after the Surrender; Some, however got in, & seen the Grenadiers, who took possession of it, plundering, & pillageing, & themsleves, not allowed; but Such as got in, ordered out by the General, they were universally dissatisfied, & many returned home upon that Acct. there were some plundered goods given to them but in all not worth 30£. nor had they Liberty to See the prisonners. Sir Willm had a great Deal of Trouble to Satisfie them." *JP* 13:190.

81. *Amherst's Journal*, pp. 242-43. *Pennsylvania Gazette*, December 25, 1760, Amherst to Pitt.

82. *JP* 3:273.

83. *Amherst's Journal*, pp. 242-44. Amherst to Pitt, September 8, in *Pennsylvania Gazette*, December 25, 1760, Warren Johnson gave the loss as 120 men. *JP* 13:187-88, 202.

84. *Amherst's Journal*, pp. 245-48. *Pennsylvania Gazette*, September 25, 1760. *JP* 13:171. Pouchot, *Memoir*, 2:47.

85. Pouchot, *Memoir*, 2:41. *Pennsylvania Gazette*, September 25, December 25, 1760. General Lévis refused to participate in the conference between Vaudreuil and Amherst, was angry about the pledge not to serve in the war, and turned over no colors—which it was said he burned. Some four thousand French were surrendered. Between five and six hundred soldiers declined to return to France, but stayed to live in Canada. *JP* 13:188. *Amherst's Journal*, pp. 248-50.

86. *Amherst's Journal,* pp. 274–48. Pouchot, *Memoir,* 2:41.
87. *JP* 3:346; 10:189–90.
88. *JP* 3:283–84.
89. *JP* 3:279–82, 308–89, 353–54. For biographical sketch of Pierre Joseph Antoine Roubaud, S. J., see *JP* 3:279.
90. *JP* 3:355; 10:190; 13:297, 330–31. Ogilvie's report to the Society for the Propagation of the Gospel, July 29, 1763, is given in full with the article by A. H. Young, "The Revd. John Ogilvie, D. D., an Army Chaplain at Fort Niagara and Montreal, 1759–1760," *Ontario Historical Society Papers and Records,* 12 (1975): 327–28.
91. *JP* 3:267. *Pennsylvania Gazette,* September 25, 1760.
92. *JP* 3:268, 274, 283, Letter to William Pitt, October 24, 1760, *JP* 3:269–75.
93. Warren Johnson's Journal, a manuscript volume, was acquired by the New York State Library from the family in Ireland. It is a curious document, the daily record of his visit from the time he left England in 1760 until his return in 1761, being erratically interspersed with numerous comments on his personal ailments, the weather, observations of prices, customs, and historical notes which could be repetitions of Sir William's comments. It is a mine of information when carefully studied. A partial transcript by Arthur Pound was published in *The Galleon* (1953). It is given complete and unexpurgated, *JP* 13:180–214.
94. *JP* 13:199–205. He was of course wrong about uniqueness of this honor. Earlier, *JP* 13:200, he had noted: "My Indian Name is Ariwanughne."
95. *JP* 13:194, 198, 205, 301.

CHAPTER 23: DETROIT AND EXPANSION

1. *Amherst's Journal,* p. 251; *Rogers's Journals,* pp. 175–98.
2. *Rogers's Journals,* pp. 175–91. Rogers's narrative, which quite naturally emphasizes his rôle, can be checked after this point with "George Croghan's Journal," 1759–1763, Nicholas B. Wainwright, ed., *Pennsylvania Magazine of History and Biography,* 71, no. 4 (October 1947): 386–95. (Hereafter cited as "Croghan's Journal.")
3. *Rogers's Journals,* pp. 188–96. "Croghan's Journal," pp. 391–94. *JP* 10:198–207.
4. *Rogers's Journals,* p. 198. *JP* 3:301. "Croghan's Journal," pp. 395–98. Rogers's account in his *Journals* is purely factual. In his *Concise Account of North America* (London, 1765), however, he greatly elaborated the story, mentioning Chief Pontiac as playing a great part in welcoming him and assisting on his journey. Howard H. Peckham, *Pontiac and the Indian Uprising* (Princeton, 1947), pp. 58–67, and especially note 3, pp. 59–62, points out this inconsistency which glorified Pontiac and, while accepted by Parkman, was completely contradicted by "Croghan's Journal." The play *Ponteach* (1766), attributed to Rogers, was based on his *Concise Account,* in which the chief was pictured as a kind of emperor over the Indian empire of the west. Robert R. Cuneo in *Robert Rogers of the Rangers* (New York, 1959) tends to accept Rogers's claims and to discount Croghan.
5. *JP* 11:223. See N. B. Wainwright, *George Croghan,* p. 175.
6. *JP* 3:315–18. Letter of February 1, 1761.
7. *JP* 3:330–31. Letter of February 1, 1761.
8. *JP* 3:343–45.
9. "The medals were of silver, representing the City of Montreal with blank Reverse, On Each of which is to be Engraven the Name of One of those Indians," *JP* 3:317–18; 333, 345, 354. A list of 182 Indians who served on the Montreal campaign and who would receive medals was sent to Amherst. *JP* 10:251–54, 258.
10. *JP* 3:302–3; 10:301. "Croghan's Journal," p. 397.
11. *JP* 3:303, 304, 330.
12. *JP* 3:354, 356. Sir William sent word to him in March, but Croghan did not acknowledge his orders until mid-May. He set out May 17 and arrived at Fort Johnson, June 15. "Croghan's Journal," pp. 405–6.
13. Sir William learned of this plan from the Indians and wrote about it to Peters and Governor Hamilton, who denied that he had sent the belts. It did not help Johnson's pique that Peters hoped to reclaim his deputy. *JP* 3:390–92; 10:213–15, 221–22, 231–32, 266–68.
14. *JP* 10:274, 277, 284, 300. *Amherst's Journal,* pp. 266–67.
15. *JP* 10:300–301.
16. *JP* 3:421–22. From Amherst, June 24, 1761.
17. *JP* 10:287.
18. *JP* 10:299–301.
19. *JP* 10:284–85.
20. *JP* 10:286–87.
21. *JP* 3:412–16, 421; 10:291.
22. *JP* 13:216–17. This expedition, one of the most important ever undertaken by Sir William, is fortunately one of the best documented, in spite of the fact that some papers were

lost in the Capitol fire. The Indian Records or proceedings compiled by Guy Johnson as secretary were transmitted to the Board of Trade (*JP* 3:428-501, from the Public Record Office). Sir William's personal record, or diary, here cited, was lost in the Capitol fire, but had been printed in Stone *Life and Times*, 2:429-77, whence it is reprinted, edited and corrected, in *JP* 13:215-17. Stone commented that the diary "was written hastily—in the confusion of camp life—and was, moreover, designed for no eye but the writer's; hence the carelessness of the style. The diary is written in a small leather-covered book, very similar to our modern pocket diaries—exactly suited to the end for which it was designed: viz. to be carried in the pocket, and taken out whenever the writer wishes to jot down a thought." In addition there are many other descriptive letters in the correspondence with Amherst and others, printed in *JP* 3:504-60, and *JP* 10:306-33. "Croghan's Journal" covers his part in the Indian negotiations.

23. *JP* 3:511; 13:216-18. Wood Creek was described by a French writer in 1757 as "full of sinuosities, narrow and sometimes embarrassed with trees fallen from both banks. It is however passable at all times by an ordinary bateau load of 14 to 1500 weight." *DR* 10:675. Sluices had been constructed to increase the water flow in 1757-58; but it was an easy matter in time of war to place obstructions, as General Webb had done in 1758. Another alternative in making passage was to divide the load in half and make two trips.

24. *JP* 3:428-37; 13:218-19. Cf. W. DeLoss Love, *Samson Occom* (Boston, n.d.), p. 89, for Occom's journal, July 3-7, recounting his visit with Sir William for two hours and his reaching the Oneidas.

25. *JP* 3:437-40; 13:217-20. Campbell detailed the plot as follows: "That the Chiefs of the Nations here, should go to a Council at Sandusky, where they would meet with several Chiefs of the Six Nations, Delawares, and Shawanese, who are principally concerned, & that the six Nations had fixed upon a certain time to assemble at the head of french Creek about 25 Leagues from Presqu'Isle, and expected to be joyned by a great many of the Nations who are gone to Niagara by Toronto; and at the same time the Delawares, & Shawanese are to assemble up on the Ohio, & both commence hostilities at the same time by cutting off the communications and endeavouring to surprize the Forts every where and if the Nations here, could be prevailed upon, they were to endeavor to surprize this place; the time fixed upon for beginning is about the end of this Month."

26. *Ibid*.

27. *JP* 3:441-48; 13:219-26.

28. *JP* 3:448; 10:323; 13:221-37. *New York Mercury*, August 31, 1761.

29. *JP* 3:460-68; 10-319; 13:226-29, 230-34, 236-38, 241.

30. *JP* 3:448-60; 10:319-20, 324; 13:230, 233, 236-37.

31. *JP* 3:521; 13:234-42. Letter from Little Niagara, August 19, 1761.

32. *JP* 3:524; 13:242-49.

33. *JP* 13:345.

34. *JP* 13:243, 248-49.

35. Peckham,*Pontiac*, pp. 67-68.

36. *JP* 13:249-50.

37. *Ibid*.

38. Peckham, *Pontiac*, pp. 67-68.

39. Amherst's Instructions to Gladwin, June 22, 1761. *JP* 10:293-96.

40. For biographical sketch of Gladwin, see *DR* 7:961n. *JP* 10:476n.Cf. Peckham, *Pontiac*, pp. 76ff. *passim*.

41. *JP* 3:471-74; 13-250, 252.

42. *JP* 13:251. Rusk was a hard biscuit; shrub was a drink of fruit and spirits.

43. *Ibid*.

44. *Ibid*.

45. For eighteenth century balls and assemblies, see Esther Singleton, *Social New York under the Georges* (New York, 1902) pp. 301-10, and Anne H. Wharton, *Through Colonial Doorways* (Philadelphia, 1893), pp. 197-229.

46. *JP* 13:256.

47. *JP* 13:257. Pound, *Johnson*, pp. 341-42, raises the question of a romantic attachment. Flexner, *Mohawk Baronet*, pp. 242-46, 254-55, taking off from this point fancies an affair, a liaison, which would shock his son John and compromise his position. Without foundation he calls the French girl "no doxie," and suggests that Sir William was contemplating matrimony. He surmised that they could not speak each other's tongue, so that "they flirted in Iroquois, which he spoke with a Mohawk intonation, she with a Huron twang."

48. *JP* 3:759; 4:82. Gladwin's letter has not survived.

49. *Johnson Calendar*, p. 265. The letter from Sterling to Johnson, April 27, 1765, which announced his marriage and sent her compliments, was destroyed by fire. Peckham, *Pontiac*, p. 79, gives a more accurate and reasoned description of Angélique and her social position. "She was 26 years old and lived with her older brother and parents just east of the fort. Her three older sisters were married and at an age Angélique had passed by several years. Why so

popular a girl was still single remains a mystery. Perhaps she was fickle, or felt herself too good for the local swains, or had suffered a disappointment. Certainly her family was respectable. The recent French commandant Captain Bellestre, was her father's half-brother, and through him she was related to Alphonse Tonti, an earlier commandant of Detroit and Cadillac's colleague in founding the post. Her family was more North American than French, as her grandparents were all born in Canada. Her father, a trader, could afford a handsome dowry. Eventually Angélique did marry, and Pontiac unwittingly played cupid."

The evidence for the story that Angélique through her father and husband learned of Pontiac's conspiracy and warned Gladwin is summarized by Peckham, *Pontiac*, pp. 124-25. It is just one of several suppositions of Gladwin's informant.

50. *JP* 3:468-72; 13:249-50.
51. *JP* 13:250-52.
52. *JP* 13:252-53.
53. *JP* 3:474-75. Spelling of Indian names varies; the nations are here given as in the official report. The diary speaks of the attendance of "principal people of the town." Mr. Brehm, Mr. Myers of Pittsburgh, and Mr. Bostwick from Michilimackinac were traders. *JP* 13:253.
54. *JP* 3:475-76.
55. *JP* 3:476.
56. *JP* 3:476-78.
57. *JP* 3:478.
58. *JP* 3:478-80.
59. *JP* 3:480-82; 13:253.
60. *JP* 3:483-87.
61. *JP* 3:484-92; 13:254.
62. *JP* 3:492-93; 13:254-55.
63. *JP* 3:494-95; 13:256-58.
64. *JP* 3:495; 13:256-58.
65. *JP* 13:258.
66. *JP* 3:495-500.
67. *JP* 13:259.
68. *JP* 3:500-503. Croghan was also directed to see to the return of Indian captives. His account included only those monies expended by him, not those of Sir William:

Expenses of Western Indian Meetings

5 Men a hundred Days at 3/ per Day Each	£75:	0:	0
20 thousand Wompum at 60/ per	60:	0:	0
5 hundred Tobaco at £7:10 per hundred—	37:	10:	0
6 Casks powder 400 Weight only for ye.			
Distant posts at 20£;	80:	0:	0
6 Ct Lead at 1/ per Pd	30:	0:	0
1000 flents at 5/ per hundred	02:	10:	0
20 pd. of Vermilian at 20/	20:	0:	0
	£305:	0:	0

Croghan's letter of October 12, 1761, reported the purchase of the hoes and the sending of a gunsmith to Detroit. *JP* 3:549-50.
69. *JP* 13:259-74. His return was noted in the press, *New York Mercury*, December 7, 1761.
70. *JP* 3:559-60. November 5, 1761. Amherst replied approvingly, November 22, and on December 6, Sir William transmitted the proceedings. He even suggested that these might be sent to a printer and published. *JP* 3:570-71, 580-81.
71. *JP* 3:559.

CHAPTER 24: THE MOHAWK SETTLEMENT

1. *JP* 10:324-25.
2. *JP* 3:389; 10:192.
3. *JP* 3:314-15.
4. *JP* 13:203, 228, 235, 248-49.
5. For the history of the Kayaderosseras Patent see: *JP* 3:423-26; 4:360. Sir William gave a summary in a letter to the Lords of Trade. *DR* 7:576-77. A compromise settlement of the issue was finally reached in 1768. A fuller treatment may be found in Georgiana C. Nammack, *Fraud, Politics, and the Dispossession of the Indians* (Norman, Okla., 1969), chap. 4, pp. 53-69.
6. *JP* 3:564, 619-20.
7. *JP* 3:307, 312-13, 328, 338-40; 10:233-34.
8. *JP* 3:292-93, 306-7, 312, January 28, 1761. For this survey he promised to pay Colden

£150 New York currency, and asked that it be done by April 1, 1761.

9. *JP* 3:338-39; 10:233. Colden's letter of June 9, 1736, urged the crown to adopt rules to protect the Indians, and it questioned the Livingston Patent. *DR* 6:68-69.

10. *JP* 13:192.

11. January 2, 1761. *JP* 3:296-97.

12. *JP* 3:296n., 297, 603; 4-90.

13. *JP* 3:313, 319-21, 367-68.

14. *JP* 3:326-27, 366, 368, 399-400; 10:282-83.

15. *JP* 3:397-98, 400, 418-20.

16. *JP* 3:561-63, 572. 583, 595-96, 602-3, 615-16, 646-47, 654, 665. Instructions to the governors, dated December 2, 1761. *DR* 7:478-79.

17. *DR* 7:490-92, 577, 742-45.

18. The Royal Grant, recognizing as its basis the Indians' gift to Sir William, was given by the Kings's Order in Council, May 3, 1769. A survey had been made earlier by order of Colden, and the description was more precise. The total was now about eighty thousand acres. The names of the associates were duly included: there were forty names, each representing two thousand acres. In the interim there had been numerous efforts both in America and in England to acquire this for others, but all had been thwarted. The grant was finally obtained at court through the efforts of Thomas Penn, who was properly grateful to Sir William for assistance in holding up New England claims to Pennsylvania lands. Hence this Canajoharie Patent became a substantial part of the Johnson estate. The King's order, or warrant, and the draft of the grant, dated May 22, 1769, are printed in *JP* 6:735, 770-73.

The draft printed was from the Public Record Office; there was no copy in the Johnson Manuscripts of the New York State Library. The author possesses a contemporary copy, lacking the last few lines, which came down in the Johnson family and was given him by the late Brigadier Guy Ormsby Johnson, Fleet, Hants, England.

19. *JP* 3:286, 289, 400, 561; 4:90.

20. *JP* 3:400.

21. Estimate of the Estate of Sir John Johnson. Manuscript in possession of Sir John Paley Johnson, 6th Baronet. See also Loyalist Claims, Public Record Office.

22. William Augustus, Duke of Cumberland (1721-1765), served as general in the wars against the French. Having defeated the Pretender at Culloden Moor in 1745, he ruthlessly punished the Scots and received the sobriquet "Butcher Cumberland." Sir William was to have a number of Scottish Highlanders as settlers. Cf. *DR* 10:58, 705.

23. The name "Castle Cumberland" appears as a dateline in Johnson's correspondence from April 22, 1760 until May 13, 1762. "Johnson Hall" first appears as a dateline May 19, 1762, after which there is no mention of "Castle Cumberland." *Johnson Calendar*, pp. 102-35 *passim*. *JP* 3:225-742 *passim*.

Stone, *Life and Times*, 2:163-64, confused Castle Cumberland with Sir William's later summer house at Sacandaga, which was not built until 1770. The error was followed by Simms and by Pound, *Johnson*, pp. 384-86. What Simms called "an elegant villa," Pound concluded was what the English termed a "shooting box." Hence these pushed Sir William's sporting activities back a decade. Frequent references to settlement and agricultural improvement show that Kingsborough was not such a resort. It was occupied during the winter, was but seven miles from the river, and is clearly indicated as the later "Johnson Hall." A number of errors and misconceptions regarding the "Summer House" and the reputed "Fish House" will be treated later.

24. *Johnson Calendar*, p. 105; *JP* 3:209. 355, 396; 10:282.

25. W. D. Love, *Samson Occum*, p. 89. *JP* 3:954; 10:227.

26. *JP* 13:243.

27. *JP* 3:355, 591-92, 628, 901, 950; 10:282; 13:243-44.

28. *JP* 13:210-11. Indian corn being unknown to him before, Warren explained its culture: "3 foot Distance, 4 or 5 Grains in a Drill; weed it well, when about 4 Inches high, & put a little Dung or fresh Ground to it; & when about a foot high dung it round in litle hillocks. . . . the Indian Corn ought to be planted in the best Ground."

29. *JP* 3:901.

30. *JP* 3:321; 10:283; 13:186-209 *passim*. Warren Johnson was struck by the indifferent care of horses. They were allowed to run unshod in summer, and were not ridden but turned out to run wild in winter. They were poorly and irregularly fed, tied to a stake often for hours. Horse stealing was common, and Indians caught horses with salt. Virginia horses were the hardiest and best in America.

31. *JP* 4:90-91.

32. *JP* 3:365, 736; 8:413. *Johnson Calendar*, p. 127. Warren Johnson noted on April 16, 1761: "a Lutheran Church was kept in my Brothers Barn which 250 people attended." *JP* 13:210.

33. *Supra*, chap. 5. References and notes. A cryptic letter of Banyar, December 15, 1760, wishes Johnson "all the Comforts of Life of which you can have the fullest measures without

yourself a wife." It appears to be urging him to marry to perpetuate his line or title (?), and deplores his attachment to his "dirty acres." Banyar was apparently not well informed concerning Molly. *JP* 3:287.

34. Stone, *Life and Times*, 1:327–28n.

35. Evidence of Molly Brant's birth date is the statement in a Return of Loyalists on Carleton Island, November 26, 1783, when her age was given—perhaps by herself—to the enumerator as 47. There were a number of Brants in the baptismal records of the Reverend Henry Barclay at Fort Hunter, and they may have been whites. A Joseph and a Mary, children of John Michael Brant, were probably not Indians. Few Indians had surnames as early as 1740. Mrs. Isabel T. Kelsay, who has made the most thorough study of Joseph Brant, thinks that the sachem Brant was only the stepfather of Molly and Joseph. (Letters to the author.)

36. *Claus Narrative*, p. 8.

37. The smallpox carried off a number of Indians, while others were cared for on Johnson's estate. *JP* 9:800, 813, 820–21.

38. *JP* 13:125, 271. Draper MSS, 20 F 68. Petition of John Ferguson gives the date of Peter's birth as September 1759.

39. Items in Robert Adems Accounts. *JP* 13:532–615; Jelles Fonda Accounts, William Fox account, *JP* 7:865.

40. These included a few "trinkets for Molly" which Croghan got abroad; two blankets from Norman McLeod at Niagara; and a "Legg of Vinneson for Madm. Molly" from John Van Eps at Schenectady. *JP* 4:501; 6:604; 7:409.

41. Stone, *Life and Times*, 2:243–44, cites the "letters of Lady Susan" but gives no specific documentation.

42. *JP* 7:379.

43. *JP* 8:16, 974, 1103, 1108. See H. Pearson Gundy, "Molly Brant, Loyalist," *Ontario History*, 55, no. 3 (1953): 63–108. For her earlier career, however, this relies upon such dubious sources as Buell, Max Reid, Lydekker, and Mrs. Grant. For a critical appraisal see my sketch in *Notable American Women*, vol. 1 (1971).

44. Mrs. Isabel T. Kelsay doubts that Joseph, and therefore Mary, his sister, were children of an important chief or sachem. Joseph was never a chief and had to use his natural gifts to influence his people. (Letter to author.) Cf. *Johnson Calendar*, p. 347, reference to Joseph as "ye Indian son to Brant's wife."

45. *Supra*, chap. 5.

46. *Claus Narrative*, pp. 20–21.

47. *Ibid*. p. 21.

48. *Ibid*.

49. *JP* 3:371–72.

50. *JP* 3:379; 10:259–62.

51. *JP* 10:259–61. Draft in Johnson manuscripts, *JP* 3:281–82, varies in some minor details of expression. In rewriting Sir William softened it, especially in speaking of Nancy's "parental regard." The long postscript answering Claus's letter of April 21st was not in the draft.

52. *JP* 10:260–62.

53. *JP* 3:393–94.

54. *JP* 10:281.

55. *JP* 3:74; 10:409, 445, 453. See corrections of Claus chronology, *JP* 19:xi, in *JP* 13:1022.

56. Autograph Album, p. 2. Claus Papers, vol. 21. See also Petition of Ann Claus, in Papers of the Commissioners of Forfeitures. New York State Library.

57. *JP* 10:409, 445; *JP* 4:135. Birth of daughter Catherine: Autograph Album, Claus Papers, vol. 23. The child was baptized February 1, 1763. *JP* 4:32, 40, 92.

58. *JP* 3:625–27.

59. *JP* 4:40, 92. *Johnson Calendar* p. 162.

60. Guy's talent as a draftsman has been insufficiently noted. His sketch plan of Fort Johnson (*Royal Magazine*, 1759) was cited above, chap. 5. His well-known "Map of the Country of the VI Nations, 1771" has been widely copied. *JP* 8:264. *DH* 4:660. Two maps of the western lands are known: that to depict the Fort Stanwix line of 1768 (*JP* 6:450), and a map of the Ohio Country (1763) after a survey by Thomas Hutchins. W. L. Clements Library. Reproduced in Lloyd A. Brown, *Early Maps of the Ohio Valley* (Pittsburgh, 1959), plate no. 38. Many of Guy's maps were lost when his house burned in 1773. *JP* 8:823.

61. *JP* 3:876; 10:438–39, 549.

62. Records of the Academy, Archives of the University of Pennsylvania, courtesy of Dr. Leonidas Dodson, archivist. Accounts give his attendance from October 1757 until July 17, 1760. He missed two quarters in 1758, and one quarter in 1759; he attended two quarters in 1760. In 1760 he was entered by Francis Wade.

63. *DH* 2:785–86.

64. Recalled by sister Nancy as an occasion of his father's tolerance when John wanted to cut short his visit to England in 1766. Claus wrote, "I think he is far from [enforcing any] enfringing upon any Bodys free Agency that has age enough to judge for himself and much less

upon that of his Children for whom his Tenderness is too great to do such a thing." Claus to John Johnson, May 13, 1766. Claus Papers.
65. *JP* 3:551.
66. *JP* 10:400–401; 407–8.
67. For this episode in detail, see the author's "An American Knight in Britain: Sir John Johnson's Tour, 1765-1767." *New York History*, 42, no. 2 (April 1961).
68. *JP* 1:270; 12:1064–65, 1070. Several writers, and early editors of the *Johnson Papers* (*JP* 8:1190n.) erroneously identified "Young Brant" as Joseph and stated that William was the son of the supposed "Caroline." Cf. Pound, *Johnson*, pp. 135–37, 419–20. For "Caroline" see the author's "Sir William Johnson's Wives," *New York History*, 38, no. 1 (January 1957).
69. *JP* 5:343. Later when sent to Philadelphia he showed some promise and received much attention. But he was involved in scrapes, became morose, and was then sent home. His later career in the Revolution was turbulent.
70. *JP* 3:556.

CHAPTER 25: THE BUILDING OF JOHNSON HALL

1. Francis Grant, "Journal from New York to Canada," p. 185. Mereness, *Travels in the American Colonies, 1690-1783*, p. 417.
2. F. W. Halsey, ed., *A Tour of Four Great Rivers*, p. 25.
3. Pound, *Johnson*, p. 365.
4. Jeptha R. Simms, *Trappers of New York* (Albany, 1851), pp. 31–36. This description written in 1850 is pertinent, since the land then was probably not unlike its appearance in the eighteenth century, some ninety years earlier. The Sacandaga Reservoir has since inundated much of the Vlaie. For Kennyetto, see William M. Beauchamp, *Aboriginal Place Names of New York*, New York State Museum Bulletin, 108 (Albany, 1907), p. 81.
5. May 19, 1762.
6. See Anna K. Cunningham, *Schuyler Mansion: A Critical Catalogue of the Furnishings and Decorations* (Albany, 1955), pp. 6–8.
7. Willis T. Hanson, *A History of St. George's Church in the City of Schenectady*, 2 vols. (Schenectady, 1919) 1:41–42; note 25, pp. 46–47.
8. *JP* 13:282.
9. *JP* 13:282–83.
10. *JP* 13:283.
11. *JP* 13:315–17.
12. Warren Johnson in the winter of 1761 wrote of similar work: "My Brother gets Lime Stones carried ten Miles, upon Sleas, at Nine Shillings currency per Load." At the same time, "a good Saw Mill saws, in 24 hours, 16 Logs of 13 Board each at 1 s. per Board." *JP* 13:205, 209.
13. *JP* 4:40.
14. *Johnson Calendar*, p. 166.
15. Journal of Samuel Fuller. "The first part being an a Cont of Woork Done on Capt. Clouse house for Sir Wm. Johnson." *JP* 13:303–7. Work on the Claus house continued even after most of the men were at Johnson Hall.
16. *JP* 10:662.
17. *JP* 10:307–8.
18. *JP* 10:308–14. The Fuller journal is the prime source. For more details on the construction of the Hall, from a careful study of not only the documents but the physical evidence, I am indebted to the excellent master's thesis of Lewis C. Rubenstein, "Johnson Hall," University of Delaware, 1958.
19. *JP* 13:285.
20. See Rubenstein, "Johnson Hall," pp. 62–69. This makes careful analysis of the plans and comparisons with the present restored building. In the nineteenth century the roof was changed and a cupola added, but the first rise remained as before.
21. *Ibid.* pp. 78–85. The old doors have disappeared, but the present restoration is a close copy. Rufus Grider in the 1880s found the old door in storage and made a sketch of it. Rufus Grider Scrapbooks, New York State Library. Cf. Plan of Fort Johnson, *JP* 1:198. Dummy windows with shutters, once thought to be a later addition, were in the original structure.
22. *JP* 4:133.
23. *DH* 3:1039. *JP* 13:307–14.
24. *JP* 10:690–712.
25. *JP* 10:663ff. *passim.*
26. *JP* 10:844–45, 847, 896, 900, 945, 961.
27. *JP* 10:852. Tom Wildman was a Caghnawaga leader who had long been a friend of Sir William.
28. *JP* 10:773.
29. *JP* 13:313.

30. *JP* 10:776.
31. *JP* 4:201. *DR* 7:547-48. The two stone blockhouses which flanked the Hall were probably built several years later. There is no reference to such at this time, and later references call them "wings." or stone houses, rather than forts. One reference by a traveller to Sir William's building of stone is dated 1768. John Lees, *Journal of J. L. of Quebec, Merchant* (Detroit, 1911): "a place of some strength; it was formerly of Wood, but he is at present a rebuilding of stone."
32. For brickmaking, see *Johnson Calendar*, p. 158; Fuller Journal, *JP* 13:309, 312. All of the original fireplaces disappeared with the nineteenth-century remodeling of the house, but structural research by restorers in the 1950s showed their location. The mantels of all are thus a part of the restoration. Cf. Rubenstein, "Johnson Hall," pp. 70–71.
33. Rubenstein, "Johnson Hall," pp. 82–89. The original stairway has engendered romantic legends. Hacks upon the railing were said to have been made by Joseph Brant and his Tory followers during the Revolution as a sign that this was the home of an ally and should not be destroyed. It is more likely that they were the result of rough treatment by the Revolutionary soldiery when the house was sacked. Cf. Benson J. Lossing, *Pictorial Field Book of the Revolution*, 2 vols. (New York, 1851), 1:286. A charming diorama now exhibited at Johnson Hall illustrates the possible social use of the upper hall.
34. *Johnson Calendar*, pp. 191–93. *JP* 13:303. The loss of so many of the Johnson manuscripts of this period in the fire of 1911 accounts for the scanty documentation. Wallpaper on one of the upper rooms, which had not been touched since the Revolution and the days of Sir William, was recorded by two observers, Benson J. Lossing in 1848, and Jeptha R. Simms in 1853. This was a flock paper, which was therefore copied in the restoration. Lossing, *Field Book*, 1:286–87. Simms, *Frontiersmen of New York*, 1:249.
35. *JP* 3:355.
36. *Johnson Calendar*, pp. 182–83, 191. Rubenstein, "Johnson Hall," pp. 112, 228; referring to Joseph Downs, *American Furniture, Queen Anne and Chippendale Period* (New York, 1952).
37. For brickmaking, see account of Daniel Quackenbush. *JP* 7:312–13; also *JP* 8:450, 13:513.
38. Testimony of Guy Johnson, Sir John Johnson, and John Butler: Loyalist Claims, Audit Office, Public Record Office, London. Sir John put the house and buildings at £3,000, with £3,000 for the improved acreage. Reference to courtyard, *JP* 6:178.
39. The historian is unfortunately hampered by certain gaps in the sources for this period. When Sir John Johnson fled to Canada in May 1776, he buried some valuable papers and documents, which were subsequently ruined and lost. These may have contained data for this period. Then the Capitol fire of 1911 destroyed a number of manuscript volumes covering the years 1762–64; manuscript volumes 5, 7, and 9 were totally destroyed; manuscript volumes 8, 10, and 11 survived in fragmentary form.

APPENDIX III. CONTEMPORARY ACCOUNTS OF THE BATTLE OF LAKE GEORGE

1. Copy sent to Shirley. *JP* 9:228–33. *DH* 2:691–95. There was a copy in the Johnson Manuscripts (see *Calendar*, p. 48) which was destroyed by fire. The copy printed in the *Documentary History* was from the *London Magazine*, vol. 24; it was also printed in the *Gentleman's Magazine*, 25:518. Four separate printings, as broadsides or pamphlets, are noted in R. W. G. Vail's bibliography, *Voice of the Old Frontier* (Philadelphia, 1949), pp. 254–55. Cf. Milton W. Hamilton, "Battle Report, General William Johnson's Letter to the Governors, Lake George, September 9–10, 1755," in *Proceedings of the American Antiquarian Society*, 74 (April 1964): 19–36.
2. The contention that Major General Lyman assumed command after Johnson was wounded and removed from the field, and that to him was due the major share of the credit for winning the battle, was first mentioned in William Livingston's *Review of the Military Operations in North America*. This tract in defense of Governor Shirley became a polemic against Johnson, whom it sought to discredit in every way, The contention about Lyman's role was taken up later by Timothy Dwight and Francis Parkman, and hence was widely disseminated.
3. Pargellis, *Military Affairs*, pp. 137–45.
4. In American Philosophical Society, Philadelphia.
5. Claus Papers, Public Archives of Canada. From two copies in these papers is taken the *Narrative*, as published. There are also shorter narratives in Claus's hand: anecdotes of Hendrick and of Joseph Brant.
6. *DR* 10:311–56.
7. The career of Samuel Blodget (1724–1807) is fully described in George Waldo Browne, *Hon. Samuel Blodget, The Pioneer of Progress in the Merrimack Valley* (Manchester, N. H., 1907).
8. The pamphlet and plan were republished in London by Thomas Jeffreys, February 2,

1756. The plan was reengraved—not too accurately—with a rearrangement of its smaller diagrams. On this the cartouche dedication to Governor Shirley was omitted. This version of the engraving appears to have been widely reproduced and is better known than the original, but it was frequently issued without the description and key. Thus it was printed in *DH* 4:169; in Pouchot, *Memoir*, 1:47; *Report of the State Historian of New York*, 3 (1897): 504; and *JP* 9:232. Its value and usefulness without the text and number key, however, are limited. It was reissued with pamphlet text in facsimile in 1911, by Henry Stevens of London.

Something should be said also for the original engraving. It was made by Thomas Johnston (d. 1767), a well-known Boston artist and engraver. After the first issues from his plate, a second was made (indicated by additional trees around the plan of Fort Edward). Careful comparison of this engraving (see Samuel A. Green, *Ten Fac-simile Reproductions Relating to New England*, Boston, 1902, plate V) with the London copy shows a few errors and much carelessness as to detail in the latter. In place of "Mr. Rancelor's House" above Greenbush on the Hudson River plan is given "Mr. Scyler's House," although Schuyler's "The Flats" was on the opposite side of the river. The original clearly distinguishes the kind of trees and terrain described, while the later plan merely symbolizes them without distinction. The action of the figures is better in the original; there is irregularity where the English troops in the first engagement are shown breaking ranks on occasion of the ambush, while in the copy they seem to be in regular formation. One can learn from the original something of the structure of boats, guns, wagons, and buildings, where the copy is careless of detail. Hence as a source the original is greatly preferred.

For library holdings of the original pamphlet and plan, see R. W. G. Vail, *Voice of the Old Frontier*, pp. 250–51.

9. *JP* 2:404–5. Supplementary to the Blodget map is another drawn by Timothy Clement, dated February 10, 1756, and also engraved by Johnston in Boston, April 1756. Entitled a "Plan of Hudson's Rivr. from Albany to Fort Edward, . . ." it had inset maps of Fort Edward, Fort William Henry, and the battlefield of September 8, 1755. It also showed the route of Dieskau's march. Dedicated to Governor Shirley, also commander of all the British forces, it carried legends and keys to the spots where colonels Williams and Titcomb and Captain McGinnis were killed, and where the first and third engagements occurred. The line of battle was much simplified but the English camp was partitioned for each colonel's and the general's "apartments." Notable omissions are any reference to the Indians or to the death of King Hendrick, or to General Johnson as commander or victor in the battle. Hence the engagement was played down. One cannot escape the conclusion that it was a part of the campaign to rehabilitate and defend Shirley's reputation.

The American Antiquarian Society's copy is said to be a proof copy, with colors, owned by Sir William and given to General Monckton. Illustrated and described in *A Society's Chief Joys* (American Antiquarian Society, 1969).

10. . . . Boston, N. E. Printed and sold by Edes and Gill, at their Printing Office, next to the Prison in Queen Street, MDCCLV [1755]. Later in the same year the two letters were combined in one publication, printed n London by T. Jefferys, as *Two Letters to a Friend . . . ; particularly on the vast importance of the victory gained by the New-England Militia under the Command of General Johnston [sic], at Lake George. Being the Most genuine Account of this Action yet published.*

INDEX